La Cucina

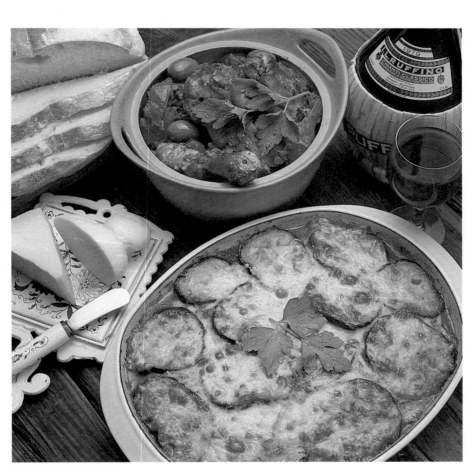

La Cucina

THE COMPLETE BOOK OF ITALIAN COOKING

EDITED AND ADAPTED BY MYRA STREET
WITH SECTIONS ON ITALIAN WINES BY SERENA SUTCLIFFE, MW
AND ITALIAN CHEESES BY AVERIL DOUGLAS

GALLERY BOOKS

This edition first published in the United States of America 1986 by Gallery Books, an imprint of W. H. Smith Publishers Inc, 112 Madison Avenue, New York, NY 10016
Second printing 1987

First published in Great Britain 1986 by Orbis Book Publishing Corporation, London

Printed in Italy by G. Canale & C. SpA

ISBN 0-8317-5408-7

An Imprint of W. H. Smith Publishers Inc.
112 Madison Avenue
New York City 10016

CONTENTS

SYMBOLS

The symbols will enable you to see at a glance how easy a recipe is, and the preparation and cooking times

 easy

 more difficult

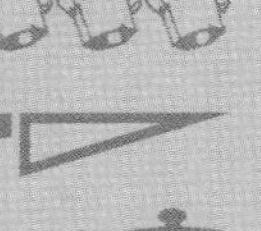 for experienced cooks

 preparation time

cooking time

When using the recipes in this book, remember the following points:

All quantities are for four people, unless otherwise stated.

Use only one set of measurements for the recipes, since American, imperial and metric measurements are not exact equivalents.

In the text of the recipes, American quantities and ingredients are listed first, with the British equivalents in square brackets.

INTRODUCTION

For more than a thousand years, following the disintegration of the Roman Empire, Italy was divided into armed camps and a fragmented assortment of independent states. The terrain contributed to this isolation between states with natural barriers, like the Alps and the Appennines, discouraging travel and the establishment of friendly relations between the natives of the various regions. When unification was finally achieved, in 1861, very great regional differences in cultural and culinary traditions still remained. These traditions have helped to preserve an Italian cuisine which is rich in variety and, at its best, ranks amongst the finest in the world.

French cooking owes much to the refinement of Italian cooking and historians claim this dates from the marriage of Catherine de Medici to Henry II of France. It was said that, until then, French cooking was similar to that of the rest of northern Europe. However, Catherine brought with her a contingent of Italian cooks who introduced many innovations to the cooking of the French court. The Italian cuisine of the sixteenth century, in the upper echelons of society, was superbly elegant. This must be in part attributed to the geographic position of Italy and the wide-ranging mercantile interests congregated around Venice. These brought the spice trade which originated with the Phoenicians and had a lasting influence on the local ingredients and the way in which food was prepared.

In spite of the regional differences which abound throughout Italy there is one common concept, the selection of good-quality, fresh ingredients. This is essential in a cuisine that endeavours to produce food which, while often simple, is always excellent, making it absolutely impossible to disguise inferior produce.

The common idea that Italian food consists of pasta, pizzas and dishes doused in garlic is far from the truth – indeed much of the food in Northern Italy, apart from Piedmont, uses little or no garlic. Italian vegetables are amongst the best in the world and the discerning housewife in Italy expects to buy tender young vegetables. These feature largely in the antipasti, the first course of Italian meals, which is a seemingly endless variety of hors d'oeuvres and snacks.

Just to give you a taste of the flavor of Italian cooking, here are a few notes about the locations and specialities of the various regions:

Piemonte (Piedmont)

This region lies in the extreme north of Italy, bordering on France and Switzerland, with a contrasting terrain ranging from the snow-capped Alps to the rice fields of the Po valley. Here we find the great industrial town of Turin, centre of Italy's car industry, as well as peaceful olive groves and vineyards.

Piedmontése cooking relies heavily on butter and wine, and, although there are some hearty country dishes, there is also a long tradition of sophisticated cuisine, much of it stemming from Turin. Garlic, although not widely used in northern Italy, is popular in this region and great emphasis is laid on fresh ingredients. People from all walks of life have kitchen gardens to ensure fresh produce.

The famous grissini bread sticks, available in Italian restaurants all over the world, were created in Turin. Rice is an important product of the region and truffles grow in the clay soil of certain parts of Piedmont. Truffles flavor many regional dishes from fondue to the game, which abounds here, as well as the more down-to-earth risottos. Bollito Misto is a mixture of beef, tongue, sausage and veal cooked in a cream sauce and is a great regional favorite.

Piedmont produces many well-known cheeses including tome, rabioli and fontina, and familiar wines include the famous Barolo and Barbaresco as well as the sparkling Astis.

Lombardia (Lombardy)

Stretching from the Alps to the river Po, this region has been occupied over the centuries by the Romans, Huns, Goths, Spaniards and Hungarians. Here we find the industrial city of Milan and the beautiful lakes of Maggiore, Lugano, Garda and Como.

Milanese cooking is renowned, especially for the extravagant use of butter as well as laying claim to making the best minestrones in Italy. Polenta is popular in this part of the country and there is also the famous Milanese risotto, cooked in stock with saffron. Excellent veal is raised in Lombardy and, from this, the Ossobuco Milanese served with Milanese risotto has become a world-famous dish.

Liguria

Situated at the top of the Mediterranean side of the boot of Italy on the Ligurian Sea, this region extends east from the French coast along the Mediterranean including the port of Genoa, which once shared with Venice the profitable spice trade from the East. The people of this area, unlike the Venetians, did not incorporate the spices into their food but preferred to flavor it with the wonderful herbs grown locally.

Genoese Pesto, the famous garlic and basil sauce for pasta, suggests that basil is probably the best-loved herb. The Mediterranean produces fish for the fish stews, sometimes known as Burridas, which are more elaborate versions of bouillabaisse. Sage, rosemary, marjoram grow in abundance in this region. Tripe is popular, both honeycomb and blanket, and is transformed into succulent dishes using a variety of pungent herbs.

Emilio-Romagna

Emilio and Romagna stretches almost across the top of the boot of Italy from the Ligurian sea to the Adriatic. The main city is Bologna, one of the most famous homes of Italian cuisine. The sausages of the region are famed throughout the world and it is from here that the baloney, beloved in America, takes its name. Mortadella is a more delicate sausage containing caraway seed.

The province lays claim to some of Italy's most fertile land, producing excellent wheat and fruits such as apples, pears and cherries as well as top quality beef and veal. The pasta is supposed to be the best in Italy, and Bolognese legend attributes the fine mouth-watering tagliatelle to the inspiration of Lucia Borgia's flaxen hair.

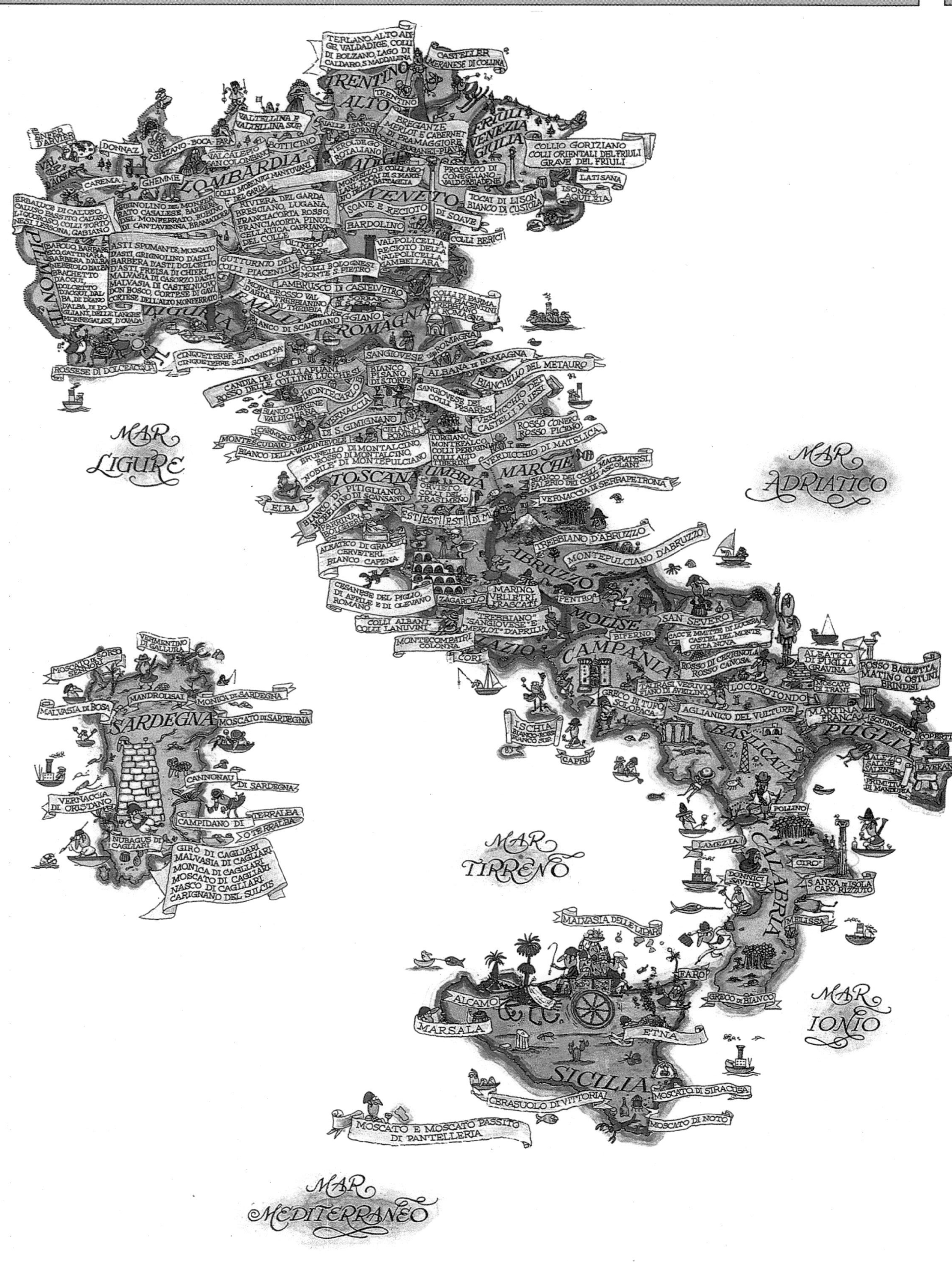

TERLANO, ALTO ADIGE, VALDADIGE, COLLI DI BOLZANO, LAGO DI CALDARO, S.MADDALENA
CASTELLER MERANESE DI COLLINA
TRENTINO
ALTO
ADIGE
BREGANZE MERLOT E CABERNET DI PRAMAGGIORE
FRIULI VENEZIA GIULIA
COLLIO GORIZIANO COLLI ORIENTALI DEL FRIULI GRAVE DEL FRIULI
LATISANA
ISONZO AQUILEIA
VALTELLINA E VALTELLINA SUP.
BOTTICINO
TEROLDEGO ROTALIANO
DONNAZ
CAREMA
GHEMME
LOMBARDIA
PROSECCO DI CONEGLIANO VALDOBBIADENE
VENETO
TOCAI DI LISON BIANCO DI CUSTOZA
RIVIERA DEL GARDA BRESCIANO, LUGANA, FRANCIACORTA ROSSO, FRANCIACORTA PINOT, CELLATICA, CAPRIANO DEL COLLE
SOAVE E RECIOTO
DI SOAVE
BARDOLINO
COLLI BERICI
VALPOLICELLA RECIOTO DELLA VALPOLICELLA AMBELLARA
PIEMONTE
LIGURIA
EMILIA
ASTI SPUMANTE, MOSCATO D'ASTI, GRIGNOLINO D'ASTI, BARBERA D'ASTI, DOLCETTO D'ASTI, FREISA DI CHIERI, MALVASIA DI CASORZO D'ASTI, MALVASIA DI CASTELNUOVO DON BOSCO, CORTESE DI GAVI, CORTESE DELL'ALTO MONFERRATO
GUTTURNIO DEL COLLI PIACENTINI
COLLI BOLOGNESI MONTE S. PIETRO
LAMBRUSCO DI CASTELVETRO
COLLI DI PARMA
BIANCO DI SCANDIANO
ROMAGNA
ROSSESE DI DOLCEACQUA
CINQUETERRE E CINQUETERRE SCIACCHETRA
SANGIOVESE DI ROMAGNA
ALBANA DI ROMAGNA
BIANCHELLO DEL METAURO
CANDIA DEI COLLI APUANI ROSSO DELLE COLLINE LUCCHESI
MONTECARLO
BIANCO VERGINE VALDICHIANA
VERNACCIA DI S. GIMIGNANO
CHIANTI POMINO
SANGIOVESE DEI COLLI PESARESI
VERDICCHIO DEI CASTELLI DI JESI
ROSSO CONERO ROSSO PICENO
MONTESCUDAIO
BIANCO DELLA VALDINIEVOLE
BRUNELLO DI MONTALCINO, ROSSO DI MONTALCINO, "NOBILE" DI MONTEPULCIANO
TORGIANO MONTEFALCO COLLI PERUGINI COLLI ALTO TIBERINI
VERDICCHIO DI MATELICA
MAR LIGURE
TOSCANA
UMBRIA
MARCHE
BIANCO DEI COLLI MACERATESI FALERIO DEI COLLI ASCOLANI
VERNACCIA DI SERRAPETRONA
MAR ADRIATICO
ELBA
BIANCO DI PITIGLIANO, MORELLINO DI SCANSANO
ORVIETO, COLLI DEL TRASIMENO
EST! EST!! EST!!! DI MONTEFIASCONE
TREBBIANO D'ABRUZZO
MONTEPULCIANO D'ABRUZZO
ABRUZZO
ALEATICO DI GRADOLI CERVETERI BIANCO CAPENA
CESANESE DEL PIGLIO, DI AFFILE E DI OLEVANO ROMANO
ZAGAROLO
MARINO VELLETRI FRASCATI
PENTRO
MOLISE
COLLI ALBANI COLLI LANUVINI
"TREBBIANO" "SANGIOVESE" E "MERLOT" D'APRILIA
SAN SEVERO
BIFERNO
MONTECOMPATRI COLONNA
LAZIO
CAMPANIA
CACC'E MMITTE DI LUCERA CASTEL DEL MONTE ORTA NOVA
CORI
ROSSO DI CERIGNOLA ROSSO CANOSA
ALEATICO DI PUGLIA GRAVINA
MOSCATO DI TRANI
ROSSO BARLETTA MATINO OSTUNI BRINDISI
VERMENTINO DI GALLURA
MOSCATO DI SORSO SENNORI
MALVASIA DI BOSA
MANDROLISAI
MONICA DI SARDEGNA
SARDEGNA
MOSCATO DI SARDEGNA
TAURASI VESUVIO FIANO DI AVELLINO
LOCOROTONDO
GRECO DI TUFO SOLOPACA
AGLIANICO DEL VULTURE
MARTINA FRANCA
SQUINZANO
COPERTINO
ISCHIA
CAPRI
BASILICATA
PUGLIA
ALEZIO SALICE SALENTINO
LEVERANO
PRIMITIVO DI MANDURIA
CANNONAU DI SARDEGNA
VERNACCIA DI ORISTANO
CAMPIDANO DI TERRALBA O TERRALBA
NURAGUS DI CAGLIARI
GIRÒ DI CAGLIARI MALVASIA DI CAGLIARI MONICA DI CAGLIARI MOSCATO DI CAGLIARI NASCO DI CAGLIARI CARIGNANO DEL SULCIS
POLLINO
MAR TIRRENO
LAMEZIA
CIRÒ
DONNICI SAVUTO
S.ANNA DI ISOLA CAPO RIZZUTO
CALABRIA
MALVASIA DELLE LIPARI
MELISSA
FARO
GRECO DI BIANCO
MAR IONIO
ALCAMO
MARSALA
ETC.
ETNA
SICILIA
MOSCATO DI SIRACUSA
CERASUOLO DI VITTORIA
MOSCATO DI NOTO
MOSCATO E MOSCATO PASSITO DI PANTELLERIA
MAR MEDITERRANEO

Veneto

The characteristic herb and spice cuisine of Venice, city of canals, gondolas and historic buildings, dates from medieval times. In those days it was one of the wealthiest cities in the world, controlling the import of spices from the orient and then exporting to other countries.

Polenta originated in Venice when maize was imported from America and it is still extensively eaten in this region today.

Rice is usually served with other ingredients such as peas as in Risi e bisi, and meat and shellfish create other interesting combinations.

The region includes the city of Verona with its plentiful supply of trout from Lake Garda.

Toscana (Tuscany)

This is surely one of the most romantic regions of Italy, immortalized by artists and poets over the centuries, as one would expect of an area including both Florence and Pisa with its leaning tower. This region stretches almost two-thirds of the way across the upper leg of the boot of Italy with a coastline running along the Ligurian Sea.

In Tuscany cooking is not only regarded with the same absorbing interest as in other parts of the country, but is considered an art. The essence of the food here is the perfection of raw ingredients, with sauces, spices and herbs playing a very minor role. The famous beefsteak of this region is grilled over charcoal with only salt, pepper and a few drops of olive oil, so the beef must be of prime quality.

Famed for quality beef, pork and poultry, Tuscany is also the home of the best known of all Italian wines, Chianti.

The famous Tuscan olive oil, which is exported to many parts of the world, is liberally used in the cooking of this region, as in the delicious snack, Bruchetta: slices of bread, baked until golden in the oven, rubbed with garlic and eaten with the oil. Another speciality, Fagioli al fiasco, or beans in a flask, was originally cooked over an open fire in a wine flask, and is still done in this way by gourmets today.

Minestrone di fagioli, a bean soup with tomatoes, is also typical. The Tuscans are fond of eating small birds, like quail and snipe, roasted in oil accompanied by fried bread and the cooking juices. The region is known for delicious desserts like Centi, which means tatters. These are bows of fried pastry.

The delicate Panettone cake is used for celebrations in Italian homes and is enjoyed all over the world.

Umbria

This is one of four varied small provinces strung across the middle of Italy with a typically Italian landscape of mountains, valleys, lakes and rivers. Here lie the historic towns of Orvieto, Assisi and, perched on a hill, picturesque Perugia.

Favorite regional dishes are spit-roasted doves and roast suckling pig. Umbria is well served with truffles, ham, sausages and fresh vegetables, as well as an excellent selection of freshwater fish such as dentex (perch), eel and trout.

The well-known Orvieto wine comes from this region, and it is also renowned for spit-roasted foods.

Marche

This mountainous region is to be found in the Appennines. The towns on the coast, including the Adriatic port of Ancona, are famous for many varieties of Brodetto, a fish and rice stew served over toasted bread.

Verdicchio is the well-known wine from the area, which is often enjoyed with fish dishes.

Lazio

This province, dominated by Rome, has an excellent tradition of peasant dishes in which offal is often used. Oxtails, sweetbreads, brains and tripe make up many dishes of country origin and then there is the famous Saltimbocca (veal with prosciutto and sage cooked in butter and white wine).

Roman produce has the reputation of being distinctive because of the sun-drenched volcanic soil, and vegetables found in the local markets are of exceptional quality. A typical dish is Carciofi alla Romagna (artichokes stuffed with anchovies and breadcrumbs and parsley). Both lamb and kid are popular and the well-known pecorino often rounds off the meal.

Abruzzo and Molise

This is a more agricultural region and lies south of the Marche, producing wheat, grapes, potatoes and olives. The coast round the Adriatic abounds with fish for more Brodetti (fish soups). Octopus in oil and tomato is a favorite of this region, along with Maccheroni alla chitarra made with olive oil, red peppers and garlic.

Campania

This southern region still bears traces of the Greeks who settled here in Naples, and this gastronomic centre produces relatively simple, quick, dishes which show great ingenuity in the use of ingredients.

The pizza, which has become so popular all over the world, originated in Naples and is still popular food in the city. The classic Pizza Napoletana is baked freshly for each customer with mozzarella cheese, oil and sometimes anchovies. The much-loved Spaghetti con le vongole (clam sauce) is another Neapolitan speciality.

Peppers are used extensively, and this region has a tradition of really spicy cuisine. Mozzarella is used in many dishes and bread is an important part of the diet.

Neapolitan ice cream is said to be the best in the world and the Baba (rum cake) is sold in every panetteria.

Basilicata, Puglia and Calabria

These southern provinces of Italy are now enjoying a new lease of life with the tourist industry. The Calabrian coast is known for having sunshine almost every day of the year, and huge acreages of citrus fruits have been successfully planted here.

A great variety of vegetables are produced and stuffed: eggplant (aubergine) is a favorite dish. Fish abounds in the Ionian Sea and Cozze alla marinara (mussels with white wine and garlic) is another typical local dish.

Sicilia and Sardegna

These are the largest of the Mediterranean islands and there are rich food legacies from the various invaders through the centuries – Greeks, Romans, Phoenicians, Arabs, Spaniards and even the Normans landed on their shores.

Fish dishes are a great speciality of both islands. The making of ice cream has pride of place on the islands and the Cassata, which was invented in Sicily, consists of contrasting layers of different colored and flavored ice creams, making an ice cream cake.

Marsala, first exported from Sicily by an Englishman called Woodehouse, was a great favorite with Nelson's fleet. It was produced to rival that other famous sweet wine, Madeira.

EQUIPMENT

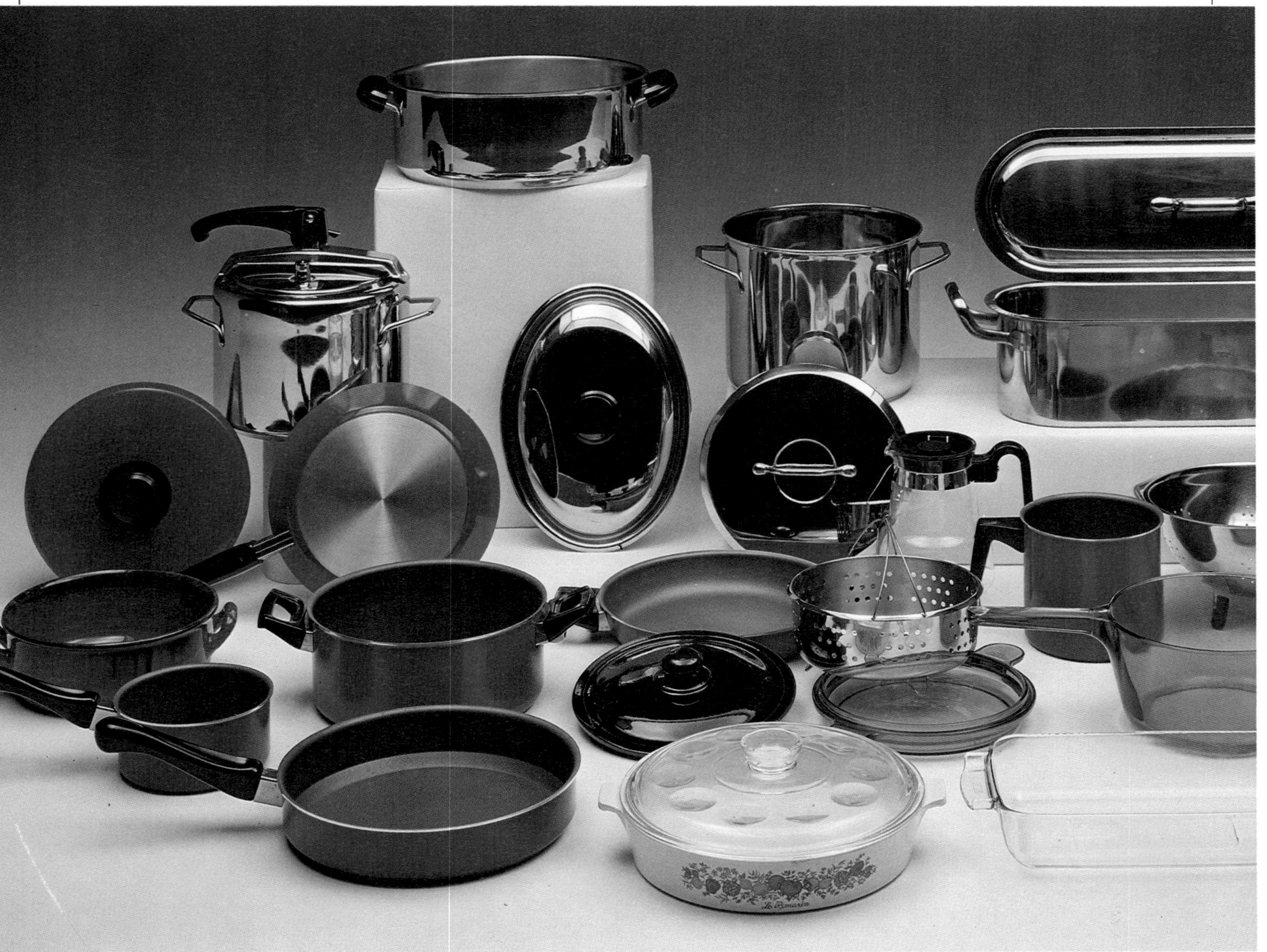

Basic kitchen equipment has not changed greatly over the years. Wooden spoons, rolling pins, sieves, colanders, apple corers, potato peelers and knives are still the main tools needed in the kitchen. A set of sharp knives makes cooking a great deal easier and it is worth investing in good quality ones. A selection of saucepans of different sizes is essential and you can choose from a variety of materials from stainless steel to ceramic glass. Many have non stick linings which last well and are easy to clean.

Useful electrical appliances in the kitchen

There are many different electrical appliances which make the preparation of food quick and easy. The most time consuming and elaborate dishes are brought within the scope of any cook with the careful selection of relatively inexpensive equipment. The difficulty is often in the choice available, as an amazing number of kitchen aids are able to chop, grind, whisk, mix, blend, extract juice etc. Many machines overlap in the tasks they will perform and as most people have limited space in the kitchen it is wise to consider your own needs carefully before selecting a machine. Remember it is not an economy to buy a machine that may only be used several times a month. Generally speaking machines which are hidden in cupboards are seldom used. Therefore there are several factors to remember and consider when purchasing a new piece of equipment.

1. Examine the machine carefully in the shop and make sure it is simple to assemble and wash. Machines which are difficult to clean are the ones which go to the back of the cupboard.

2. Consider the size in relation to your family and the amount you entertain. A machine with a smaller capacity bowl or goblet may be much more useful to households than a larger one which is only used for the occasional dinner party.

3. Decide on a space for the machine in the kitchen which will not inconvenience the cook. Keep sharp blades out of the reach of children. In households with young children it is safer to leave the machines unplugged and without blades until needed.

4. New gadgets need a little practice and it is worth while using the appliance every day until the full potential is realized. This is especially true of the versatile food processor.

5. Read the manufacturer's instructions carefully to make the best use of your machine. It is advisable to clean the equipment according to manufacturer's instructions.

Here are some of the most useful kitchen aids to save labor in the preparation and cooking of food:

Mixers

The cheapest and one of the most versatile labor saving kitchen aids is the small hand-held mixer. Most are stored on wall brackets near the cooker or work surfaces, so they are always ready to use. They are useful for beating eggs, cream or batters, mashing potatoes (in the saucepan), whisking sauces over hot water as well as creaming fat and sugar for cakes. They come with easy-wash, removable beaters, are light to hold, and usually have a choice of 3 speeds.

Large mixers are best for compulsive cooks, who entertain often, and for those who cook for the freezer. They operate on a stand with a bowl and have a number of optional attachments including a blender, shredder, slicer, coffee grinder, grinder (mincer), knife sharpener, pasta making attachment, juice extractor.

Blenders

These can be bought either as a free-standing machine or as an attachment for a big mixer. Either way they are invaluable for making soups, mayonnaise, pâtés, stuffings and some desserts

as well as baby foods, fruit and vegetable purees, milk shakes and fruit drinks. The larger the capacity of the goblet, the more useful the blender.

Add solid food gradually through the hole in the lid for easy operating. It is useless to fill the goblet with solids and expect the machine to blend evenly.

Grinders (mincers)

Very useful machines for those who make their own patés and hamburgers. Food is dropped through a funnel and drawn through a perforated cutting disc. There are a variety of cutting and grating discs and some have attachments, such as citrus juicers and hamburger presses.

Others have a set of rotating blades which cut and chop. Most models have varying grind settings. It is best to have a coffee grinder used solely for that purpose.

Food processors

These are incredibly fast working machines which take but a minute for most tasks. The basic machine is very versatile and can be used for making pastry, rubbing in for cakes and crumble toppings, kneading dough, chopping and blending fruit and vegetables and grinding (mincing) meat. Extra attachments can be bought quite cheaply for coarse or finer slicing and shredding, slicing vegetables, making pasta and other specialized tastes. They are compact and easy to clean.

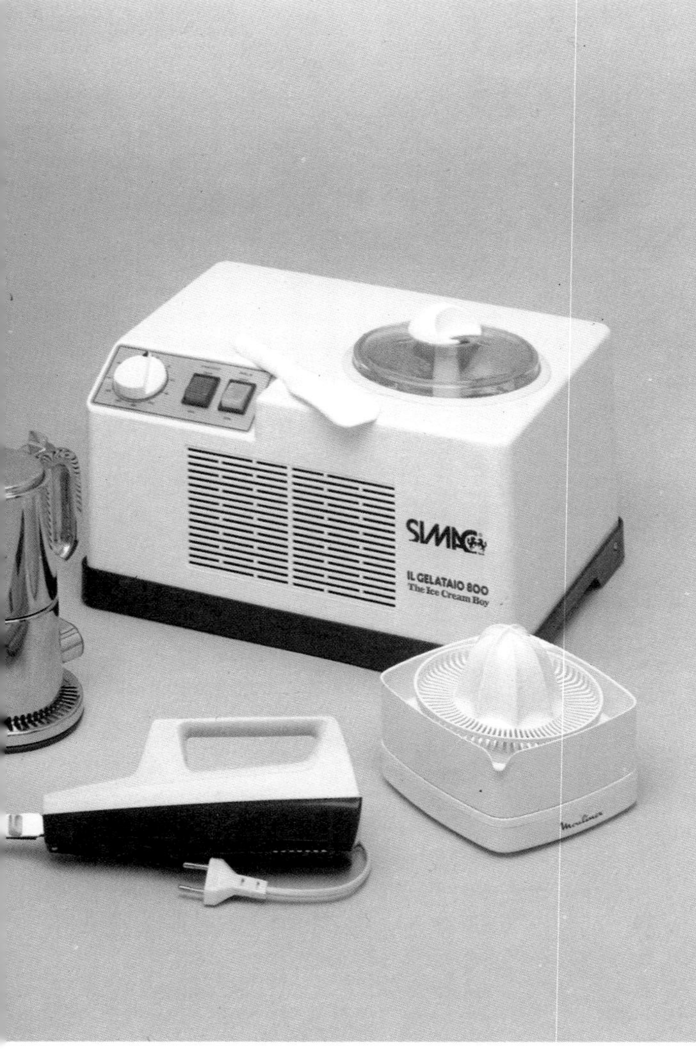

Useful appliances: blender, electric can opener, food processor, electric carving knife, coffee machine and mixer with juice extractor.

Microwave ovens

These are operated on an entirely different principle from a conventional oven. Microwave cooking is fast, efficient, cool and is more economical, as the oven uses less power than a conventional electric oven.

Microwaves produce heat by causing the moisture molecules in the food to vibrate against each other. The microwaves are transmitted through china, glass and paper without heating the containers. It is the heat generated in the food which will eventually make the cooking dish warm. The oven cavity does not become hot. All these factors make the use of microwaves a fast, economic method of cooking. Cooking in a microwave oven often saves washing up as food can be served in the cooking dish.

It is necessary to read the manufacturer's instructions and again some practice is needed to realize the full potential and versatility of this most useful piece of equipment.

Metal containers, foil and china with silver or gold bands must not be used in a microwave oven as microwaves are reflected by metal.

Avoid melamine and soft plastic boxes as the heat in the food can cause these to melt.

Food can be covered with a lid or plastic wrap in the oven to help the heating process and retain moisture.

Although a microwave oven is invaluable for thawing frozen food, heating up food for latecomers and melting foods like chocolate and softening butter, as well as its many other uses, it is best used in conjunction with a conventional oven.

Electric pasta machines

There are now many electric pasta-making machines available in a wide price range as well as the attachments for the equipment already mentioned. Some of the larger machines are probably more practical for small restaurants rather than for the home.

However, if a cook makes pasta often, it is very well worthwhile investigating these machines which do all the hand work of rolling and shaping the pasta. Some of these electric pasta machines actually take much longer to mix the dough than when the process is carried out by hand.

Making an avocado sauce in the blender

1. *Scrape the flesh from half a ripe avocado into the blender, switch on and blend for 10 seconds.*

2. *Add half the lemon juice and the flesh from the other half of the avocado. Switch on and add 1 tablespoon of capers, with the remaining lemon juice, while the machine is blending.*

3. *Add cream if desired, blend and serve with hard-cooked (boiled) eggs or other vegetables.*

ITALIAN WINE

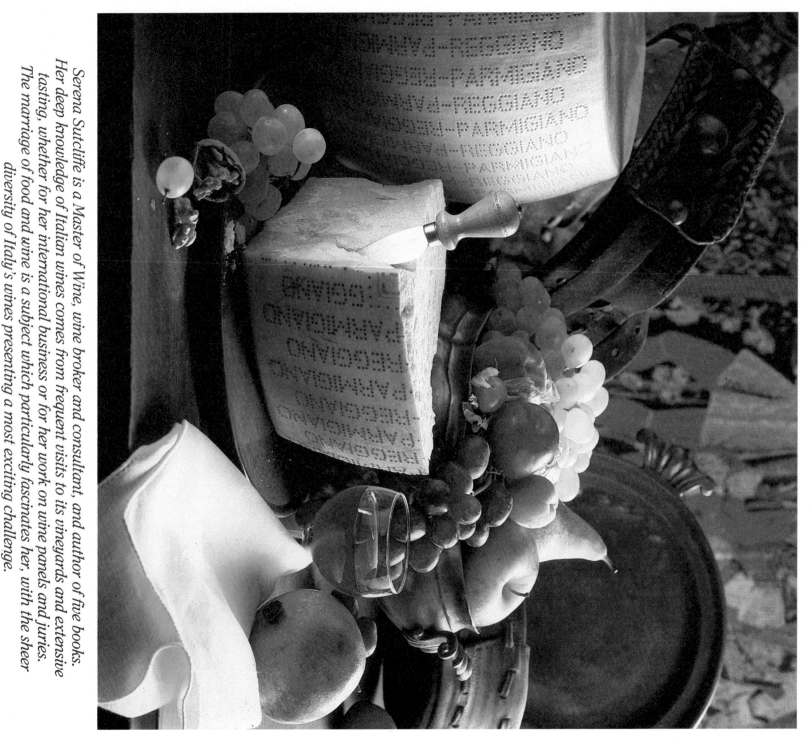

Serena Sutcliffe is a Master of Wine, wine broker and consultant, and author of five books. Her deep knowledge of Italian wines comes from frequent visits to its vineyards and extensive tasting, whether for her international business or for her work on wine panels and juries. The marriage of food and wine is a subject which particularly fascinates her, with the sheer diversity of Italy's wines presenting a most exciting challenge.

Italian wines

Few countries in the world possess such a diversity of wines as Italy. The sheer variety of tastes to be found in Italian wines reflects the ebullience of its volatile, warm-natured people. In every region there are producers striving to make the best wines of the area, each convinced that he has found the key to the whole art of winemaking and produced a wine that will eclipse that of his neighbor. The result is a mosaic of flavors and bouquets, wines with personality and character, and an abundance of bottles to choose from for all who appreciate *la cucina italiana*.

Some Italian wines are produced on mountain slopes, others by the side of one of its many lakes. There are those from the searing heat of the south, while others hail from northerly climes of hard winters and wide temperature fluctuations. Over the centuries, the grape varieties suitable for each area have evolved, giving the wines their 'regional' flavor and identifiable character, even when tasted without looking at the label. Still other producers are blazing a trail and planting grape varieties hitherto unknown in their area, creating new, splendid wines which have surprised everybody.

Then there is the controversy of DOC versus non-DOC. In 1963, when Italy wanted to expand its wine exports (still only about a quarter of annual production is exported), a law was created to control the name and origin of many of its wines—DOC. Today, the 200 DOC zones produce nearly double that number of styles of wine, but only about 10 per cent of production is Denominazione di Origine Controllata. The DOC law is roughly similar to the French Appellation Contrôlée, in that it controls the grape varieties which a producer can use, delimits growing zones, lays down rules for winemaking and ageing, and sets out other parameters a wine must meet in order to be awarded DOC. This encourages quality, but cannot guarantee it – the integrity and knowledge of the producer himself, and his desire to make or keep a reputation for himself, are the best guarantee of quality. There is also a 'super' category of DOC, DOCG or Denominazione di Origine Controllata e Garantita, with some more stringent rules attached to its acquisition. But the name of a good producer is still the best insurance of all. DOCG labels are starting to appear on Barolo, Barbaresco, Brunello di Montalcino, Vino Nobile di Montepulciano and Chianti.

However, the words Vino da Tavola, or Table Wine, still appear on a mass of other wines. This can be because the wine is one which carries a brand name, rather than a regional designation, but some Vino da Tavola labels refer to the color of a wine and its place of origin, or the grape variety and the place from which it comes. There are a number of Italian wines which bear the modest title of Vino da Tavola which are amongst the finest bottles in the land. This may be because the producer has decided to experiment and make wines from

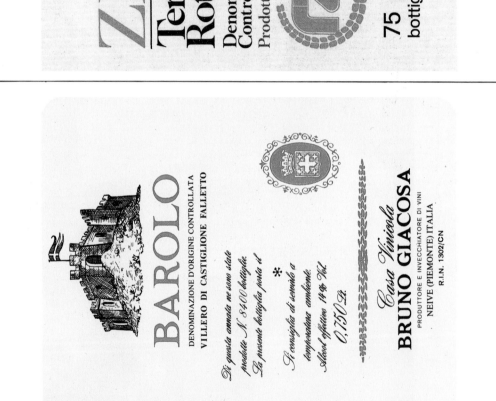

BAROLO
DENOMINAZIONE D'ORIGINE CONTROLLATA
VILLERO DI CASTIGLIONE FALLETTO

Di questa annata ne sono state
prodotte N. 8400 bottiglie.
La presente bottiglia porta il
*
Si consiglia di servirlo a
temperatura ambiente.
Alcool effettivo 14% Vol.
0,750 Lt.

Casa Vinicola
BRUNO GIACOSA
PRODUTTORE E INVECCHIATORE DI VINI
NEIVE (PIEMONTE) ITALIA
R.I.N. 1302/CN

ZENI
Teroldego
Rotaliano
Denominazione d'Origine
Controllata
Prodotto nel vigneto Pini
del Campo Rotaliano
e imbottigliato all'origine
dall'Azienda Agricola
R. Zeni in Grumo
S. Michele a/A-Tn
75 cl. e 12,5 % vol.
bottiglie n. 18360 prodotte nel 1982
PRODUCE OF ITALY

grapes which are not typical of his area, hence foregoing the designation DOC, or because he has voluntarily opted out of the DOC system in order to follow, for instance, his own ideas on ageing his wine (perhaps using small barrels), or to open up some new land not hitherto used for viticulture and therefore outside the DOC zone.

It used to be said that there was an enormous difference, immediately discernible on the nose and the palate, between the wines of the north and the south of Italy. Although this is still true of the reds, where some of the richest, most heady examples come from the sun-drenched south, it is becoming more difficult to tell the difference between whites from the north and those from the south. This is due to modern vinification, or winemaking methods which have tended to produce the fresh clean wines we now like, rather than the slightly heavy, sometimes oxidised examples of yore. If a white wine is fermented at cold temperature, easy to control in large tanks, the result will be youthful flavor, whether the grapes originally came from Sicily or the northern half of the country.

However, as in any winemaking area of the world, the innate quality of the grape variety used will greatly influence the wine which is ultimately made. There are many grape varieties in Italy which are indigenous to the country and which are not found anywhere else. But there are regions in Italy where a number of grape varieties are shared with France and Germany, especially in the north-eastern part of the country. This includes the Cabernet, that famous variety of grape grown with great success in the Bordeaux region of France, California and Australia, and which is now finding favor in the northern vineyards and further south in Tuscany and Umbria.

The best way to consider the wines of Italy, in a limited space, is in relation to Italian food. For this is the context in which Italians themselves see their wines, since they regard wine as an intrinsic part of any meal and expect to marry their regional dishes to their vinous partners. But we need not be so bound by regional distinctions, for we have the whole map of Italy at our disposal. The Italian rarely moves out of his own region when choosing his wine, but with the vast array of Italian wines now in the world's shops, we can be more adventurous. The trick is to see the potential of a dish when married to a wine, to play with contrasting and matching tastes, to understand the nature of the dish being prepared and to know what wine will enhance it.

I have attempted to select some original ideas and to juggle with them, so that there will be some exciting taste combinations and gastronomic experiences. I will deliberately 'name names', so that good producers get the credit they deserve and you can see wines which are among the best examples of their kind. Nothing is definitive in wine, especially not in Italian wine terms where improvement is constant and new discoveries frequent, but if these suggestions send you rushing to a good wine shop, then they will have achieved their purpose. Italian wine and food are for the sensually curious, for those who like the challenge of tastes and flavors, and if some of these wines open up new avenues of gastronomic pleasure, then the liquid research on your behalf will have been worthwhile.

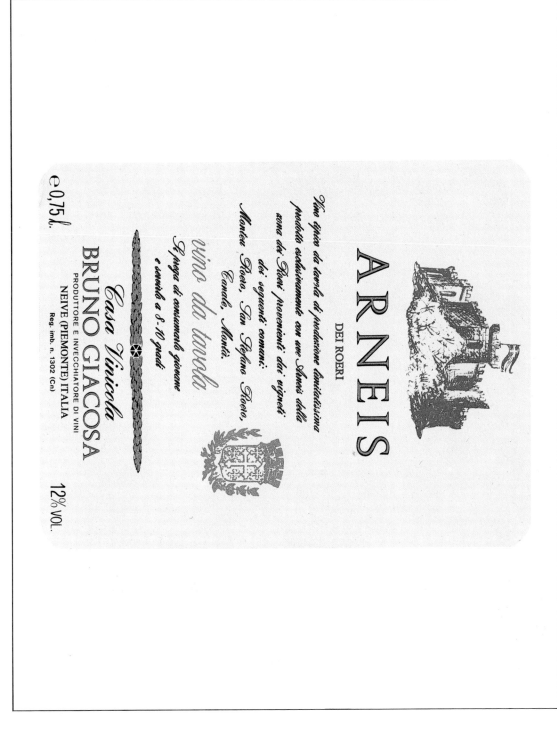

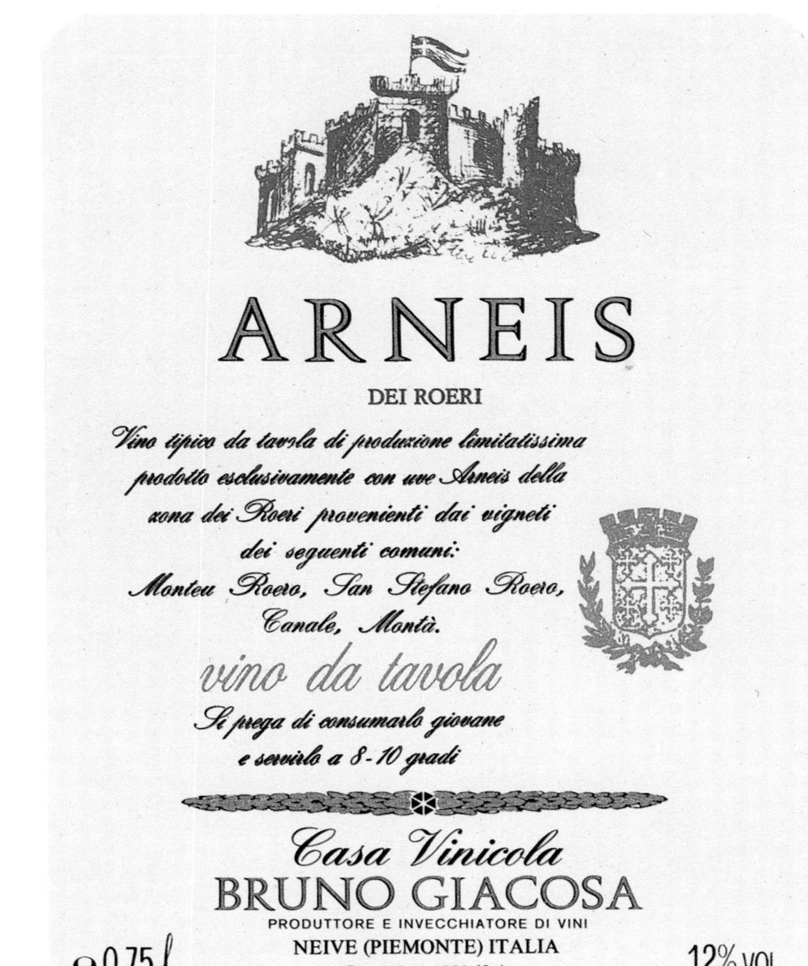

ARNEIS
DEI ROERI
Vino tipico da tavola di produzione limitatissima
prodotto esclusivamente con uve Arneis della
zona dei Roeri provenienti dai vigneti
dei seguenti comuni:
Monteu Roero, San Stefano Roero,
Canale, Montà.
vino da tavola
Si prega di consumarlo giovane
e servirlo a 8-10 gradi
Casa Vinicola
BRUNO GIACOSA
PRODUTTORE E INVECCHIATORE DI VINI
NEIVE (PIEMONTE) ITALIA
Reg. imb. n. 1302 (Cn)
e 0,75 l.
12% VOL.

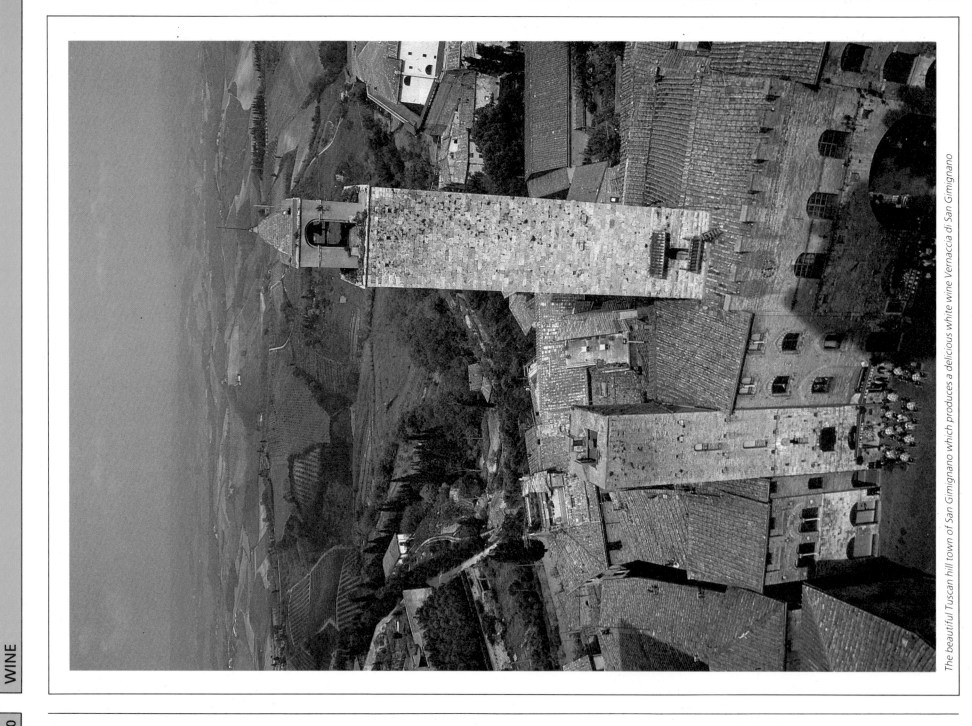

The beautiful Tuscan hill town of San Gimignano which produces a delicious white wine Vernaccia di San Gimignano

Aperitivi and antipasti

The purpose of aperitifs and attractive small eats is to delight the eye and titillate the palate. Of course, it is easy to produce visually effective antipasti, but more difficult to achieve visual impact with the wine. However, the sight of fine bubbles in the glass is unquestionably a temptation, and Italy produces some very high-class sparkling wines. The Italians drink a great deal of sparkling wine, finding an excuse to celebrate on every possible occasion.

The best sparkling wines tend to come from the north-east, especially Trentino. Here there are wines, such as Ferrari and Equipe 5, which are made by the Champagne method (meaning a secondary fermentation in the bottle to achieve the bubble) and with Champagne grapes, Chardonnay and Pinot Nero. There are other good Pinot sparkling wines, such as Berlucchi in Franciacorta, Contratto and Fontanafredda in Piedmont, and Ballabio in Oltrepò Pavese.

A light sparkling wine, of true regional charm, is made near Conegliano (where there is also one of Italy's famous wine schools) and Valdobbiadene in the Veneto. Prosecco is named after the native grape variety which makes it, and this is the only place in the viticultural world where it is grown. You may also see Cartizze, which is a classic area near the town of that name. Prosecco is the aperitif drunk in all the wonderful country restaurants in the hills of Treviso province, and it is also the smart drink in Venetian bars and grand hotels. The famous Bellini is always made with Prosecco, not Champagne, and peach juice, although other exotic fresh fruit juices, such as mango, are exciting alternatives.

Hams, salami and sausages are a vital part of antipasti. Each region has its speciality, whether it is the fennel flavored variety of Tuscany, the luganega from the south, or wild boar salame from Sardinia. Most of these are strong-tasting and so a neutral white wine is swamped by them. In fact, the more peppery sausages take well to the rosato wines of the south, such as Copertino from Barone Bacile di Castiglione, Castel del Monte from Rivera, or Rosato del Salento and Five Roses, both from Leone De Castris. There is also something aesthetically pleasing in the shades of pink between wine and salami.

Paper-thin slices of one of the great hams of Italy, however, are more subtle in taste. Whether it is Parma, San Daniele or Casentino ham, a fruity, rounded, dry white wine usually shows off the flavors to the full. Of course, these hams are often served with melon or figs, which complement the grapiness of the wine. Gewürztraminer from Alto Adige, also known as the Traminer Aromatico (Tramin is the home town of the grape variety), almost chooses itself as an accompaniment to translucent slices of the best ham. The bouquet of the Gewürztraminer is always intriguingly spicy, the texture silky, a recipe for a wine that just slips down. Most firms make very creditable Gewürztraminer, but producers like Hofstätter, Schloss Schwanburg, Kehlburg and Von Elzenbaum excel, as well as Klosterkellerei Muri-Gries, Kettmeir and Tiefenbrunner.

The white wines of Terlano, from a variety of grapes, are also superb with the hams of the north-east, especially the local 'speck' of the South Tyrol. But the greatest taste combination I ever experienced between wine and speck was with the rare Sylvaner made by the Abbazia Novacella, a beautiful abbey between Bolzano and Bressanone (Brixen) in the Isarco Valley. The speck was on wooden plates, the Sylvaner in fine, long-stemmed glasses, and we cracked hard, caraway-flavored flat bread on the table until it shattered into munchable pieces. This was antipasti at its most satisfying.

Tuscany is famous for its Crostini, the little toasts passed around before a meal, often with chopped or puréed chicken livers as a topping. Most Chianti producers serve their white wine with crostini, and very addictive this is too. Villa Antinori, a Vino da Tavola from Tuscan white grapes (50 per cent Trebbiano, 30 per cent Pinot Bianco and 20 per cent Malvasia), is intensely scented and flavored, and quite able to combat the

rich liver mixture. Galestro is a white wine, based on Trebbiano, made by a variety of Chianti producers, light and easy to drink. It is the product of new ways of making white wines at very low fermentation temperatures. Consequently, the wines are always fresh and should be drunk as soon as possible after they are put on the market.

Vernaccia di San Gimignano is another Tuscan white, designed to lead you into a meal or to accompany a sea food salad. Vernaccia is the grape, San Gimignano the ravishing town of many towers. Names to look for include Fattoria di Pietrafitta (a fattoria is an estate or farm), Guicciardini Strozzi, Il Cipressino, Ponte a Rondolino, Il Raccianello and Fratelli Vagnoni.

Bianco di Pitigliano is the 'inside-track' Tuscan white wine, very thirst-quenching and accessible – the Cantina Sociale, or Cooperative, makes it.

The real wine challenge is the Tuscan garlic toast, bruschetta. Personally, I feel that a young, robust Chianti is the answer in this particular case, perhaps poured into an earthenware pitcher to give it air and complete the rustic atmosphere.

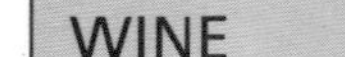

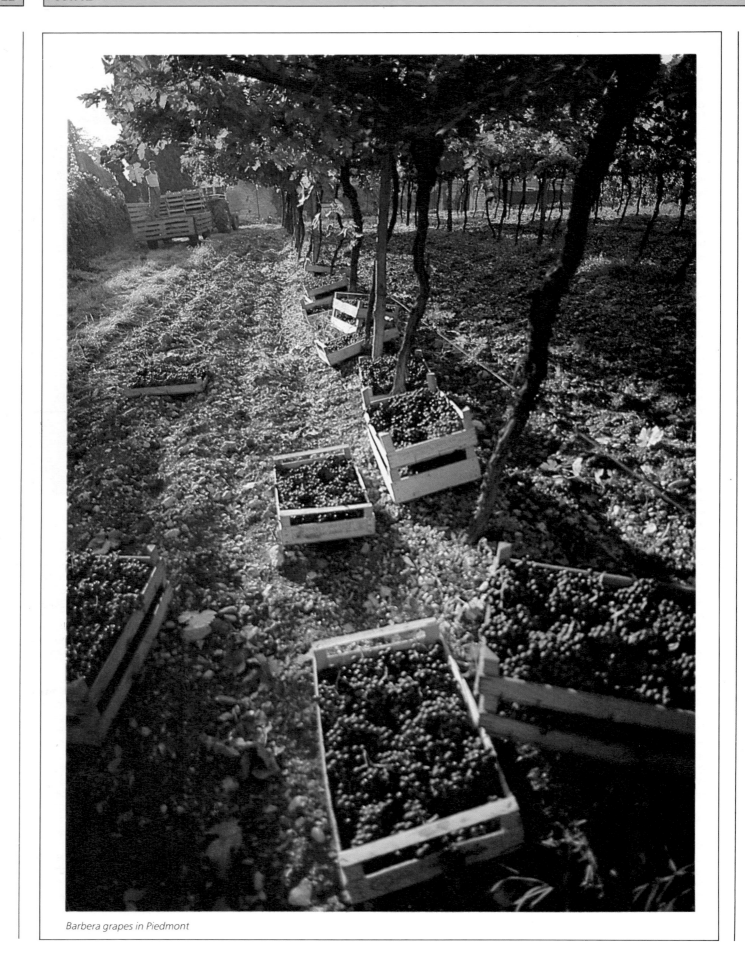

Barbera grapes in Piedmont

Pasta

Of course, it is the sauce of the pasta, rather than the pasta itself, that decides the wine. Classic spaghetti bolognese, or the Roman spaghetti carbonara, with bacon and egg sauce, call for vivid, young, fruity red wines. A vibrant Merlot or Cabernet di Pramaggiore would be ideal. This is the area on the borders of the Veneto and Friuli-Venezia Giulia, and here the wines have a sappy charm which is attractive – try those from Santa Margherita or Tenuta Sant'Anna.

The hot arrabbiata sauce with peppers, beloved by southerners, poses a few problems. Sicilian red can be the answer, whether it is Regaleali, Corvo, or the Etna red from Villagrande. The Romans like their pasta 'all'amatriciana' with tomatoes, bacon and sweet pepper. What better than a young Latium red wine, Velletri, to go with it? The Castelli Romani, or Roman hills, produce more white wine than red, but Velletri rosso is eminently quaffable.

A gorgonzola sauce has become popular with spaghetti, and here the choice of wine may depend on the type of cheese used, the sweet or piquant gorgonzola. The saltiness of the stronger cheese certainly calls for white wine – red wine is always slightly 'emasculated' by salt. Anything labelled Pinot Bianco would be a perfect partner, from Lombardy, Trentino-Alto Adige, the Veneto, or Friuli-Venezia Giulia. With the sweeter gorgonzola, or as an accompaniment to any of the pasta dishes with a cream sauce, try a young white Trebbiano di Romagna from that great gastronomic region, Emilia-Romagna. Producers to rely upon include Ferrucci and Fratelli Vallunga, both of whom also make fine white Albana and red Sangiovese di Romagna.

Pesto, that heavenly basil, garlic and cheese sauce, is another test for the wine buyer. The obvious answer is a Ligurian white, and here the most historic is Cinqueterre. But it is not what it used to be, and a young, fresh Vermentino would probably give much more pleasure. The same grape variety gives a Vermentino di Alghero from Sardinia – the firm of Sella & Mosca are unrivalled in their modern techniques and attention to quality.

Baked lasagne is quite a heavy dish, and a light red usually presents a good contrast – young Valpolicella, or maybe a young Dolcetto d'Alba from Piedmont. Most good producers of Barolo and Barbaresco make a Dolcetto, which could be termed the Beaujolais of Italy, with the Dolcetto grape replacing the Gamay and fulfilling the same role as a soft, fruity wine for youthful drinking. A favourite Dolcetto d'Alba comes from Baracco de Baracho.

Where filled pasta is concerned, whether it be ravioli or tortellini, it all depends on what is in the filling. A tortellini filling of Parma smoked ham, turkey and Bologna mortadella, for instance, would go beautifully with the Romagnan variety of the red grape, Sangiovese. Drink it young, but if you have a filling of stronger meats, you could pair it with a Sangiovese di Romagna Riserva Superiore with more bottle age, perhaps from Spalletti (Rocca di Ribano). Veal is often used to fill ravioli – a young Bardolino would be ideal here. With a ricotta or a spinach filling, my preference would be for a fruity white, maybe a Tocai from Grave del Friuli. Tocai has nothing to do with either the Tokay of Hungary or the Tokay/Pinot Gris of Alsace, but it is a soft, fruity white wine, sometimes quite rich.

Rice, gnocchi, polenta and pizzas

Rice frequently means risotto in Italian. Here it all depends on the flavoring of the risotto and whether fish or meat is used. A sea food risotto, for example, with shrimps and prawns, presents a pleasant dilemma for the wine drinker. Should he or 'she', (as women are increasingly responsible for buying the household's wine) choose a Verdicchio from the Adriatic, or perhaps a Bianco di Custoza from the Veneto? Verdicchio, of course, is one of the best-known Italian wines, perhaps first

discovered on holiday, or in an Italian restaurant in one's home town. Verdicchio dei Castelli di Jesi is the full, poetic title, and producers like Fazi-Battaglia and Garofoli are world-wide ambassadors for the wine – Verdicchio is the grape variety, as well as the name of the wine. Bucci and Brunori are top-flight names – there is also a super-wine, called Villa Bucci (Private Reserve), for a very special occasion.

Bianco di Custoza could be termed the 'thinking man's Soave'. Grown near Lake Garda, it is similar to Soave, but sometimes more flowery and fragrant. Delightful wines are made by Cavalchina, Santa Sofia, Santi and Speri.

Risotto alla milanese, with its pretty saffron colour, is often served with ossobuco milanese, so that is the guideline when choosing a wine for this classic dish. Risotto alla finanziera, with chicken livers, is an immensely satisfying dish – a straightforward Merlot from Grave del Friuli, with all its seductive fruit, would certainly enhance it, especially from Plozner or Duca Badoglio.

Polenta is often served with sausages or game, so look at the suggestions for these robust dishes. Gnocchi can be with spinach and ricotta, so go for either a fruity white or a light red. They can be made of potato and served with butter and cheese, or perhaps with a meat sauce. Use some of the pasta ideas for this kind of gnocchi, matching the wines with the sauces.

One of Italy's greatest treats is to serve pasta, and sometimes gnocchi, with slivers of the precious white truffles of Piedmont. A layer of truffle slices, often grey and not very appetizing in appearance, nevertheless gives off an earthy, root-like smell, quite unlike any other. What wine can match this? I have found Pinot Grigio, that intriguing, slightly aromatic grape variety, excellent in matching the humus-like flavor of truffles, and one

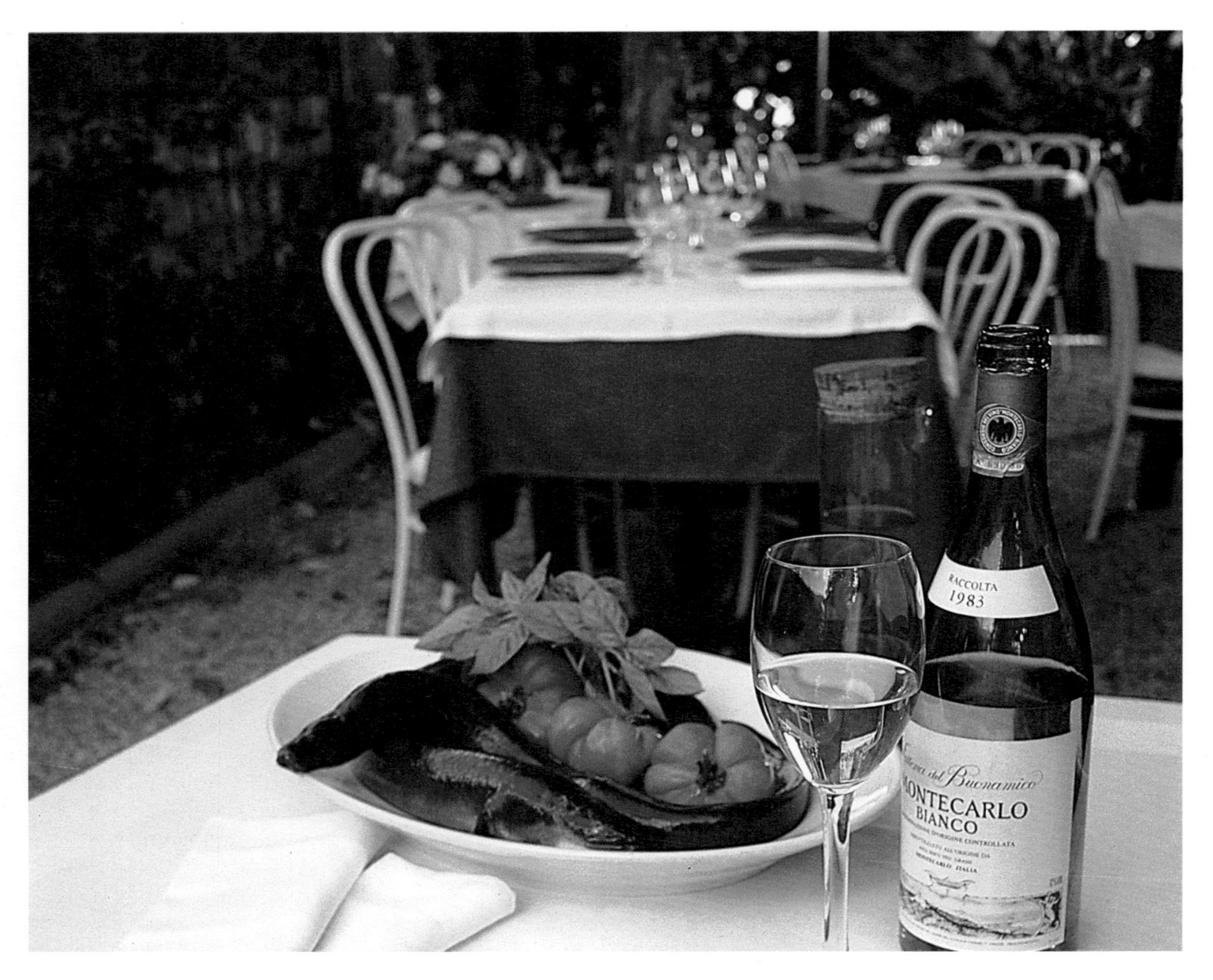

one of the best is that of Jermann in the Collio area of Friuli-Venezia Giulia. It works, also, when truffle slivers are put over Parma ham or the incomparable Bresaola. Other Pinot Grigio wines of class come from Attems, Schiopetto, Gradnik, Villa Russiz, Formentini and the Felluga family. Occasionally a Pinot Grigio will have a pinkish tinge to it, which means that the skins have been left in contact with the fermenting wine, producing extra body, flavor and bouquet. This is an experience not to be missed.

Pizzas are wonderfully warming and somehow sun-filled. Pizza alla napoletana has salty anchovies over the top, so try a rosato from the south with it, or perhaps a light, straw-like Torbato di Alghero from the firm of Sella & Mosca in Sardinia, one of the best value whites in Italy. Pizza quattro stagioni has practically everything in it, including the wine-man's bogey, artichokes. Personally, I find this a delicious vegetable and no block to my enjoyment of wine – a Frascati or Marino would be ideal as an accompaniment. In fact, Romans adore artichokes, and eat them in huge quantity. The Roman hills provide the vinous partner. By far the best-known Frascati, this dry white wine with its almondy taste, is Fontana Candida, which maintains its standards in spite of its sales. But look out also for the names of San Matteo, Gotto d'Oro and De Sanctis. A Superiore version of Frascati is Fontana Candida's Vigneti Santa Teresa. Marino, which used to be for Romans alone, is now almost as well known as Frascati – again look out for Gotto d'Oro.

Fish and shellfish

Italy's elongated coastline ensures that fish is a vital part of the Italian diet. And then there are the lakes, with all the fresh-water fish to please those who are land-locked. A beautifully fresh trout is a wonderful backdrop to any wine, especially if cooked very plainly. A comparatively unknown wine, but one which would arouse much interest around the dinner table, is Clastidio from Lombardy. The white is made from the Riesling and Pinot grapes, and Ballabio is the best wine-maker. It is a refreshing, nutty wine, with an almondy nose. That great Umbrian family wine firm, Lungarotti, produces a delicious white wine, Torre di Giano, from Trebbiano and Grechetto, and this would be perfect with trout. Most people drink it young, but after a few years in bottle it can take on extra richness.

Lake Garda is famous for its small pink trout – mini 'salmon trout'. The ideal wine to drink with these, preferably at lunch 'al fresco', is the local white wine, Lugana. Sometimes the wines have become so modern and technically perfect that they have lost their regional, flowery, straw-like character (a criticism that can also be levelled at some mass-produced wines), but the best Lugana make one instantly relive moments on terraces beside the lake. Fraccaroli, Visconti, Venturelli, Zenegaglia, Ambrosi, Zenato and Dal Cero are all names in which to have confidence.

Of course, all fish cooked 'al cartoccio', or in paper, keep all their moisture and flavor. Something like porgy (bream) is ideally suited to this form of cooking, and the wine can be a classic one. Sole, plain or cooked in white wine, also demands a wine of impeccable quality. The Chardonnay is a grape variety known to all lovers of white Burgundy; the best Chardonnays of Italy still come from the north-east, although experiments are taking place in isolated pockets all over the country. A Chardonnay nearly always gains in splendor with some bottle age (sometimes only a year or two), and it is a pity to drink it as young as many other Italian dry white wines. Pojer & Sandri and Zeni in Trentino-Alto Adige, and Jermann, Berin and Plozner in Friuli-Venezia Giulia, are great exponents of the art of making fine Chardonnay.

The wine school at San Michele in Trentino, the Istituto Agrario Provinciale, also practises what it preaches and makes a fine bottle. If you can find it (and it is well worth making a special effort to do so), Vintage Tunina from Jermann is a fascinating Pinot Bianco, Chardonnay and Sauvignon blend.

The firm, white fish, like John Dory, hake, cod and haddock, are all good with the keen fruit of Riesling Renano, which is the classic Riesling of Germany and much more elegant than the Riesling Italico, a soft, easy wine, for more everyday drinking. Riesling Renano is, again, a grape of the north-east, and there are some superb examples, especially from Alto Adige, like those from Kehlburg, Hofstätter and Castel Rametz.

Scampi and prawns are an essential part of the Italian diet, whether they are just cooked and served with oil and lemon, or grilled, or fried in batter. Antinori will soon be bringing out on to the international markets a fascinating Bianco Speciale from Castello della Sala in Orvieto, made of Sauvignon, Grechetto and Chardonnay, a cocktail of grapes which create a wine simply begging for Gamberi al vino bianco. Of course, an Orvieto Classico is also splendid in this role, maybe from Antinori, Barberani or Cotti.

Another wine with a riveting combination of grapes, and perfect with shellfish, is Montecarlo, intoxicatingly named and as pleasing on the palate. This is a hill village near Lucca and has nothing to do with its namesake on the Côte d'Azur. The base is Trebbiano, but then Semillon, Pinot, Vermentino and Sauvignon are added, all contributing to a wine of fruit and style. Buonamico make a complex, fine example.

Piedmont is not known for its white wines, but it produces two classy examples, ideal with shellfish, or even molluscs. Gavi di Gavi La Scolca from Soldati has a lemons and flowers taste and real character. So has Arneis, a native grape variety, made into a superlative white wine by Bruno Giacosa. Favorita is a

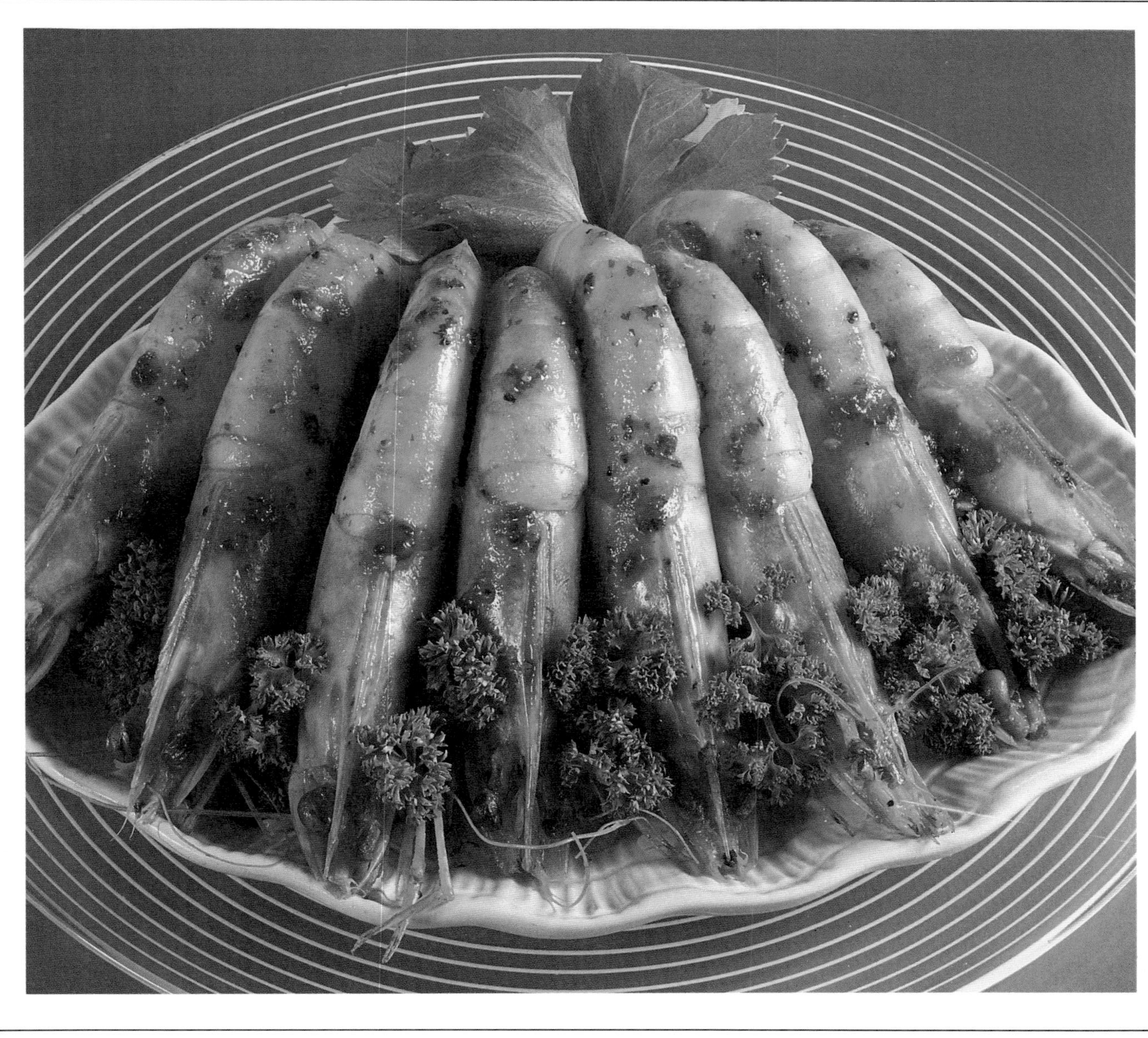

more reasonable alternative, when the pocket does not run to such luxuries as Gavi and Arneis.

Sardines have such a definite flavor that they can swamp some really delicate wines. I love the southern whites with these fish. Two of the most unsung, and interesting, are Fiano di Avellino and Greco di Tufo, both from Campania, and magnificent from the house of Mastroberardino. They can be an acquired taste, but it is one I have taken to with great gusto. There is a volcanic quality about them and the flavor lingers delightfully on the palate.

Sicilian whites also used to have this 'volcanic' quality, but they have now taken on a more flowery character, while retaining a whiff of the south. Libecchio and Rapitalà epitomize these wines, and they are eminently suitable for drinking with sardines and fresh tomato sauce.

Grilled swordfish or tuna give a great deal of scope when choosing a wine, because the solid nature of their flesh makes it possible to drink red wine as an accompaniment. Valpolicella or Sangiovese go well with both these fish, or one of the rosato wines from the south. I would also plump for a rosato with that half-fish, half-meat Italian speciality, vitello tonnato. Red mullet is much appreciated in Italy, and you could stay with a pink wine here too. But a Pinot Grigio from Alto Adige, like that of Santa Margherita, would also be ideal, or a delicious white from Puglia, Locorotondo, with its tangy, flowery character – the Cooperative there makes a good example.

And then there is Soave, which can take you from the aperitivo into the fish, with no trouble at all. Together with Chianti, it is the best-known DOC in Italy and, to some people, ordering a bottle of Soave in a restaurant is almost synonymous with asking for a bottle of dry white wine! Soave Classico can be more than just appealing, especially from houses like Pieropan, Speri and Bolla – look out also for Pasqua (Costalunga), Masi and Santi.

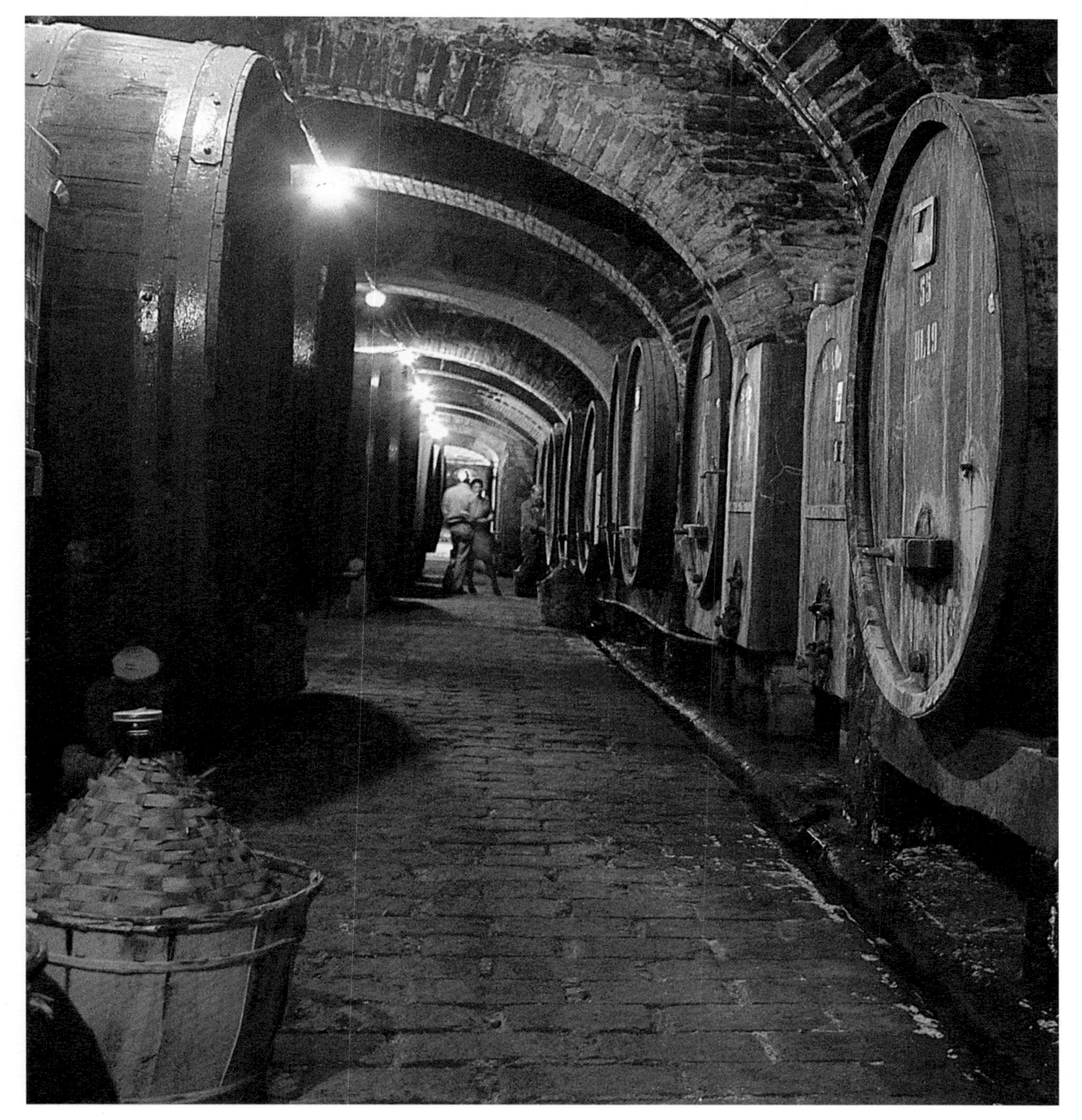

Meat

Here the possibilities are immense, and it is best to adopt a flexible attitude to choosing wines, to spread as wide a net as you can in order not to miss anything good!

Romans, of course, are very fond of baby lamb, especially at Eastertime, and usually cooked with quantities of rosemary. Some of the Cabernet/Merlot blends now made in Italy taste delicious with lamb, a very smooth combination. One of the best is that from Letrari, Maso Lodron, from Trentino. In fact, this is the region from which most of these wines emanate: other splendid examples are Foianeghe from Conti Bossi Fedrigotti, Mori Vecio from Lagariavini, San Leonardo from Guerrieri Gonzaga, Castel San Michele from the wine school of the same name and 4 Vicariati from Càvit.

From the Veneto, comes Venegazzù della Casa of Conte Loredan Gasparini, another Bordeaux-mix wine, with its own Italian touch.

Lombardy contributes the intriguing Franciacorta, which adds Nebbiolo and Barbera to the Cabernet/Merlot mixture. It can have a lovely raspberry smell – try those from Ca' del Bosco or Longhi-De Carli.

Of course, Merlot on its own makes splendid wine, ideal with red meats. The Collio area of Friuli-Venezia Giulia is a happy hunting ground for these wines, and Collavini make an example which has body and tannin. The grape variety of Burgundy, the Pinot Noir, is rare in Italy, but Sandbichler from Lun in the Alto Adige is a fine example of Pinot Nero, marrying beautifully with lamb or kid.

Veal is almost the national dish of Italy, whether roast, or escalopes, or in a stew. Plain veal goes equally well with white or red wine, but the famous ossobuco milanese seems to cry out for a vibrant red. Barbera fits the bill here, a grape grown widely in Piedmont, and most of the top Barolo producers make a good one. To this list, I would add Dessilani at Fara in Piedmont, who is also known for his Caramino Riserva, a predominantly Nebbiolo wine, which would grace the most illustrious of tables.

Beef in all its forms is one of the closest friends of Italian red wine. Tuscany, of course, considers it has the best bistecca, and a char-grilled 'fiorentina' is guaranteed to show off any Chianti Classico at its most alluring. The Classico zone lies between Florence and Siena, and there are some fine wine estates in the hills, most of them historic, some of them successfully resuscitated by newcomers to the area. The Riservas have the capacity to age in bottle, although not many do so to such perfection as the Villa Antinori 1967, drunk on the occasion of the Antinori Seicentenario in 1985. Estates to follow include Badia a Coltibuono, Monte Vertine, Castello di Querceto, Castello di Volpaia, Castello Vicchiomaggio, Castello dei Rampolla, Riecine, Castello di Fonterutoli, Castell'in Villa, and the Fossi selections.

Then there are the 'special' wines of Tuscany, often the inspiration of a man who wants to leave his mark on wine history. These are for anniversaries, birthdays and other celebrations, when there is perhaps some superb roast pork or game, pheasant or even partridge. Antinori's splendid Tignanello, tasting of plums and damsons, is a most exciting wine, made from Sangiovese grown at the Santa Cristina estate, with an addition of about 10 per cent Cabernet Sauvignon. Le Pergole Torte from Monte Vertine is pure Sangiovese, aged in barrels to produce another majestic wine, while La Corte is a single vineyard wine from Castello di Querceto. Sassicaia is a grand Tuscan speciality, a great Cabernet Sauvignon, somewhat Californian in style, made by the Marchesi Incisa della Rocchetta. Carmignano is another beauty, similar to Chianti but with a touch of Cabernet, and Villa di Capezzana is the famous name.

With bollito misto a regional favourite of Piedmont, what could be better than the heady, exotic Teroldego Rotaliano from Trentino, especially the great Maso Scari from Barone de Cles, but also excellent from Zeni and Donati. And then there are the two super-stars from Masi, special variations on the Valpolicella theme: Campo Fiorin, refermented on the skins of Recioto grapes to produce extra richness; and Serègo Alighieri, a Valpolicella Classico Superiore from the estate of Dante's descendants.

When meat dishes are quite 'fatty', such as the zampone of Modena, or sausages, there is nothing better than a slightly sparkling dry red Lambrusco, nothing to do with the sweet, sometimes pink brew that is exported in large quantities. The frizzante aspect of the wine 'cuts' the richness of the cooking and is most exhilerating. Here, look for Lambrusco di Sorbara, Lambrusco Grasparossa di Castelvetro, or Lambrusco Salamino di Santa Croce. An alternative accompaniment to these robust, country dishes is the Trentino red, Marzemino, a wine made famous in Don Giovanni!

Poultry

Chicken and turkey are very adaptable – they are not disturbed particularly by the color of the wine, although a rich sauce usually takes more kindly to a red. Some of the very stylish Cabernet wines of Alto Adige can be uncorked here, or perhaps a Vino Nobile di Montepulciano from Tuscany, with its heady nose of violets and rich taste – Poderi Boscarelli excels, and lovely Riserva comes from the firm of Bigi.

With duck I have enjoyed red Lagrein, or Lagrein Dunkel, from Trentino-Alto Adige (there is also a really perfumed Lagrein Rosato, or Kretzer, delicious with speck), from houses like Conti Martini and the Klosterkellerei Muri-Gries. Guinea

fowl is lovely with a Gattinara from Piedmont (Dessilani and Brugo are recommended), or one of Vallana's imposing Spanna wines. Spanna is the name for the Nebbiolo grape in the Novara-Vercelli hills, and it can be a better buy than the DOC Gattinara.

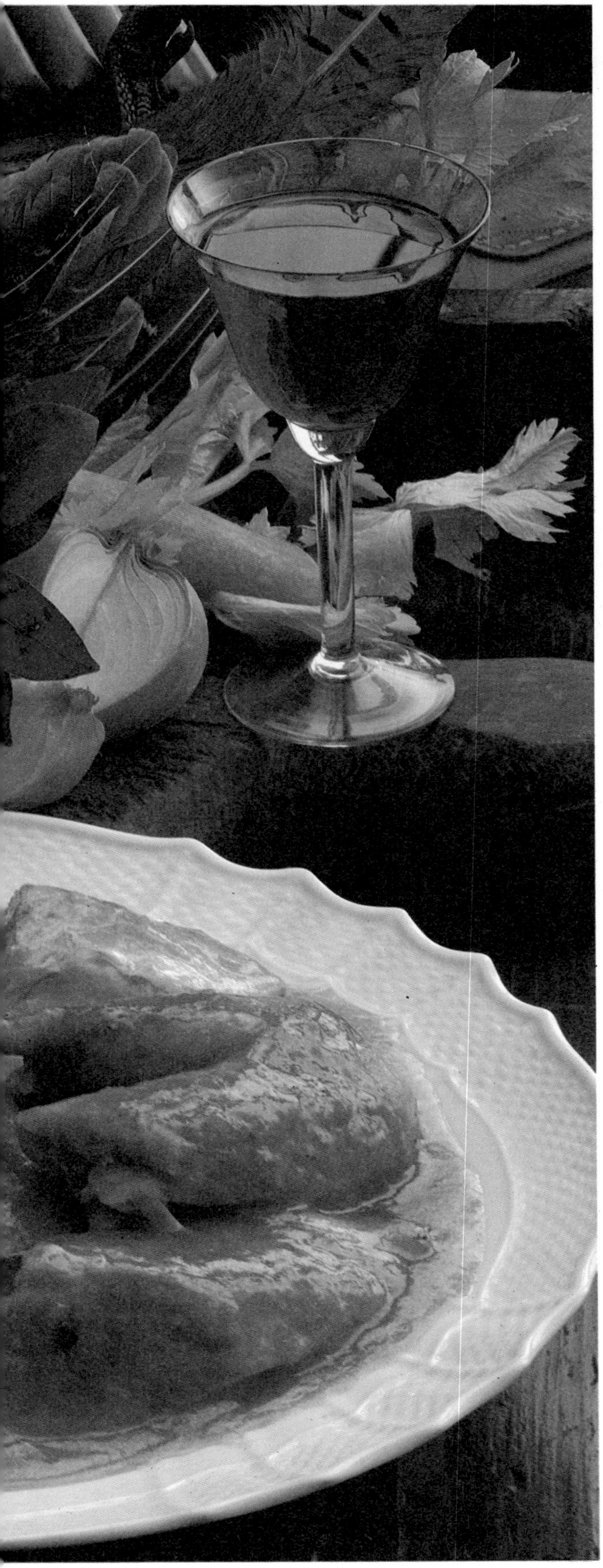

Quail and pigeon are farmed in Italy, but they can often be cooked in salmi, or in a wine sauce, making them into meals of some richness. Barolo or Barbaresco start to come into their own at this point, those great red wines from Piedmont made from the Nebbiolo grape. When young, these wines can be quite astringent, even tarry, so they need some bottle age to soften – I think they also need decanting for their complex bouquet to come out. The great single vineyard Barbarescos of Angelo Gaja, such as Costa Russi, Sorì San Lorenzo and Sorì Tildin, are known wherever wine connoisseurs gather, and usually they live up to their reputation – and their price! Bruno Giacosa makes wonderful Barbaresco and Barolo which contains fruit with power.

Other names to trust (most of whom make the two wines, as well as Nebbiolo, which is sold for younger drinking) include Prunotto, Ratti, Ceretto, Marcarini di Elvio Cogno with the splendid single vineyard wines of La Serra and Brunate, Conterno, and Mascarello with a fascinating single vineyard Barolo called Monprivato. Baracco de Baracho make wines which even the uninitiated can appreciate, and Franco-Fiorina is another less dense style. At their best, these wines are unforgettable, undoubtedly amongst the finest Italy can produce.

The famous Chianti Classico estate of Badia a Coltibuono

Game

While pheasants are not hung as they are in Britain, this is usually compensated for by long, slow cooking and a rich sauce, thus giving the flavor which can support some of Italy's most powerful wines. The great Piedmontese wines described above are all ideal accompaniments, as indeed they are to venison and hare, but some southern reds are also magically good with this kind of game. Perhaps the greatest unsung wine of Italy is Aglianico del Vulture from Basilicata, especially as made by Fratelli d'Angelo. Decant this wine, and watch it unfold to great complexity and an almost bitter-sweet, heathery taste – wine like this ages beautifully. Then there is powerful Copertino from the estate of Barone Bacile di Castiglione in Puglia, with its incredible wine gum, liquorice character; another beautifully made wine. It would also be a pity to miss Mastroberardino's Taurasi from Campania, which combines power with velvet texture. Great Amarone della Valpolicella can also be drunk with game, but some people feel that the immense richness of these wines is better with cheese.

Cheese

It is ironic that many non-Italians only ever eat parmigiano, or parmesan, grated over dishes, when it is such a superb cheese at the end of a meal. The more robust red wines go with it, and all the grana cheeses. Maybe the easiest cheese to match with wine is groviera, which takes all fruity, red wines. Asiago is a true cheese of the north-east, and is good with Cabernet and Merlot. Taleggio is of a creamy type, and I think goes as well with rich whites as with reds, while the central Italian pecorino, made from ewes' milk, is ideal with Chianti, or the great Rubesco Riserva from Lungarotti in Torgiano, Umbria. Sweet gorgonzola is favored by the Italians themselves, and it is easier to put a fruity red wine with it than with the more piccante version often sold abroad, which requires a more tannic wine.

The creamy, mild goat cheeses, caprini, are lovely with north-eastern white wines, while genuine buffalo milk mozzarella seems better, to my taste, eaten in a salad with sun-warmed tomatoes and pungent olive oil, accompanied by beakers of rosato, rather than at the end of a meal.

Maybe the best thing of all is some fresh walnuts and a hunk of parmigiano, with a great Amarone from Quintarelli, Tedeschi, Masi, Speri, or Santi. The strength, richness and intoxicating liquorice scents of these wines will remain on the palate long after the glasses are emptied.

Tuscan Vin Santo is best semi-sweet or nearly dry – again, it is lovely with nuts, probably best late in the evening, with good conversation and perhaps, even better, some music.

Puddings

If Italy has a gap in the national wine cellar, it is a lack of great dessert wines. Picolit from Friuli-Venezia Giulia is really a wine of the past struggling to make a comeback. Much more relevant are some of the Moscato wines which, with their luscious grapiness, make an enticing accompaniment to fruit puddings. The Fontanafredda Moscato d'Asti has a luscious orangey flavor which goes well with orange desserts, while Alto Adige's Moscato Giallo (Goldenmuskateller) is youthful, sweet and aromatic.

To finish, some expresso and a Grappa – but if you put a dash of Grappa *in* your coffee, you have a true caffè corretto.

Marinades

Some meats, notably game like hare and venison, require marinading. Recipes might call for Barolo, dating from the days when this commodity was less expensive, but nowadays a straight Nebbiolo would be more appropriate. Any youthful, robust red wine is suitable, but certainly never use anything you would not like to drink.

RISERVA
1979
San Cosma
ANTI CLASSICO

ITALIAN CHEESE

Italy, land of contrast, of music and of love; of warm, heady evenings filled with romance and of days spent browsing through art galleries and museums; of narrow streets and ancient thoroughfares; of beauty and of awesome history. Rome with its monuments to the past; Milan with its mighty La Scala opera house bearing witness to Italy's great love of music; Verona, setting for one of the most enduring love stores of all time; Florence with its enchanting architecture; and Venice, unique city of water and exquisite craftsmanship.

From its borders with France, Switzerland, Austria and Yugoslavia, to its southern-most points within sight of the isle of Sicily, Italy harbors secrets of a glorious and of a troubled past; from the more wealthy northern and central areas to the quieter, poorer areas of the south.

Throughout all, there is that unmistakable and pervading aroma of Italian cooking; of tomatoes, herbs, pasta and wine not sipped and savored but swallowed appreciatively. And, of course, there is the cheese and even this, in Italy, is steeped in history, myth and anecdote. The greatest of all, Parmesan, is referred to in Boccaccio's Decameron. '...there was a whole mountain of Parmigiano cheese, all finely grated, on top of which stood people who were doing nothing but making macaroni and ravioli', Maso tells Bengodi, adding that all these delicacies were being 'rolled into the cheese after cooking, the better to season them'.

In 1656 Francesco Serra in his *Dictionary of Synonyms* speaks of the excellence of Parmigiano and in a recipe from 1543 the dessert course is said to have included as an accompaniment to pears, grapes, apples, peaches and figs, 'six platefuls of Parmigiano cheese'.

Cheese has always been an integral part of Italian life. The ancient Romans were said to be nauseated by the idea of drinking milk so they ate it instead in an astonishing variety of cheeses. Fresh, smoked or dried cheeses were available; cheeses curdled with fig juice or flavored with nuts or spices and herbs like mint, coriander or marjoram and made with cow's or ewe's milk, even with goat's milk from Liguria. And there was a cheese called Lunar, of the Grana family which includes those aristocrats of Italian cheese, Grana Padano and Parmigiano Reggiano, better known in its grated form as Parmesan.

Today, cheese plays just as important a role in Italy's way of life; the milk and cheese industry occupies a valuable position in the economy, representing about a quarter of the agricultural gross saleable product. Over half the milk produced in Italy is used to make cheese and although small farmers and firms continue their tradition of cheese-making, large companies and cooperatives have grown to meet the demands of home and export markets. The authorities strive to ensure that ancient traditions and accepted quality are maintained in the face of necessary refinements and innovations in production, packing, presentation and marketing techniques.

Italian cheeses are protected by specially appointed consortiums which define and protect from imitation those cheeses with a clearly defined 'name of origin' or 'Zona Tipica'. They ensure that standards are maintained in both production and marketing and the penalties for fraud include prison sentences and fines of up to 50,000 or 100,000 lire.

A cheese with 'zona tipica' is a product of a unique nature which has a specific quality in terms of use and is of known popularity or fame. It also indicates that a cheese comes from a particular area with specific geographical limits and that the product owes a large part of its quality characteristics to the particular environment of that area, taking into consideration human, historical and cultural factors.

It is geographical factors which influence greatly the diversity of Italian cheese. The alpine pastures to the north, just south of the Swiss and French borders, house such prolific cheese-producing regions as Fruili-Venezia Giulia, Trentino and Veneto, and the centre of the Italian cheese industry, Lombardy with Piedmont to the west and Emilia Romagna to the south-east of the lush Po Valley renowned for cow's milk cheeses. Moving further south, the regions of Tuscany, Lazio, Campania and Puglia and the isles of Sardinia and Sicily produce excellent sheep's milk cheeses, sheep being twice as numerous as cattle in Italy, particularly in the South. Goat's milk cheeses, once numerous, are becoming a rarity now and even Caprini, the small and delicate cheeses once made from goat's milk (capra means goat) are now made almost entirely from cow's milk. Individual farmers and concerns produce occasional goat's milk cheese but they are not mass produced.

Indeed the individuality, profusion and variation of Italian cheeses can make their identification and selection most confusing. Practically every corner of Italy can boast a cheese speciality and on a wider scale the same cheese can be sold under different names.

Alternatively, the same name can apply to many cheeses which are totally different in character. So it is the true connoisseur who can confidently find his way round the cheese boards of Italy. Happily, when it comes to exports, the situation is not quite so confusing although the availability of certain cheeses can vary enormously from city to city. All the major cheeses mentioned in this section are available either in supermarkets or specialist shops although some may be difficult to find in remote areas. Many of the lesser-known cheeses may be difficult to buy and are mentioned purely for interest and information.

The best known Italian cheeses, apart from *Grana Padano* and *Parmesan* which have already been mentioned, are: *Gorgonzola,* Italy's principal blue-veined cheese; *Dolcelate,* a milder blue cheese; *Mozzarella,* traditionally made from buffalo milk; *Fior di Latte,* the official name for Mozzarella made with cow's milk; *Taleggio,* a popular mild and aromatic semi-soft cheese; *Pecorino Romano,* a strong-flavored sheep's milk cheese imported mostly by the U.S.A.; *Ricotta* which is not really a cheese but is produced by re-treating the ewe's milk whey after making cheese, often Pecorino, and of which there are many types and flavors; *Mascarponi,* versatile and delicious almost pure whipped cream cheese; *Robiola,* a soft, creamy cheese sometimes likened to Camembert; *Burrini,* specialist cheeses hand molded around a pat of butter; and *Cacetti,* similar to Burrini, without the butter filling.

There are numerous variations to these cheeses produced by individual companies or farms. Gorgonzola, for instance, is produced sometimes with creamy Mascarponi or perhaps with anchovies or caraway seeds or walnuts; Mascarponi itself can be mixed with a variety of other cheeses, maybe Robiola, sometimes with truffles, or herbs, or mixed seasonings; one company produces Mascarponi with cognac while in Tuscany, Ricotta Ubriaca or 'drunken ricotta' is what you get when the cheese is mixed with brandy or rum!

Although cheese is used as a matter of course in cooking and as a seasoning in Italy, it is used mostly as a table cheese eaten before rather than after dessert. Whether in Italy or anywhere else in the world, cheese is one of the most versatile of foods. It can be eaten for breakfast, perhaps with ham; as a mid-morning snack maybe with crackers; for lunch either toasted or in an open sandwich or on its own with celery, salad, fruit or bread. It can be an ideal afternoon snack for children home from school and makes excellent canapés with cocktails. It can be a starter, main course, dessert or the finish of an excellent dinner. And later it might even make an after-dinner savory or midnight snack.

Cheese is a particularly useful food for building up both children and the elderly because of its high nutritional value and because it is easy to prepare and so many varieties are gentle on the digestion. But for the weight and health conscious, it needs, like all other foods, to be enjoyed in moderation. Most cheeses, including those from Italy, can be bought in small portions, so a wide variety can be tasted and enjoyed without excess. And when it comes to including cheese in cookery, there is no need to feel tied to convention; use it whenever and however you like, remembering, of course, that experiment is a vital ingredient of creative cookery.

The Distinguished Cheeses of Italy

The following are a selection of Italy's most popular cheeses.

Bel Paese

This unpressed, cooked and ripened cheese was created by Egidio Galbani in 1906 and made at Melzo in Lombardy. It is one of the most popular cheeses of this century and is creamy white or pale yellow, soft, buttery and elastic, without holes but with a pleasant, tangy flavor. The name, meaning beautiful country, was taken from a book written by Abbot Antonio Stoppani, a friend of the Galbani family, whose portrait, imposed on a map of Italy, appears on the foil wrapping of some of the exported cheeses; others depict a map of the western hemisphere.

The natural rind of Bel Paese is thin and smooth and coated with plastic or paraffin wax and it is produced in a flat, round shape weighing 5½ lb / 2.5 kg with a diameter of 8¼ in / 21 cm and a depth of 2¾-3¼ in / 7-8 cm. It is matured for about fifty days and contains 48-50% fat in dry matter.

It is produced also as a cheese spread, Crema Bel Paese, in round 1 oz / 25 g and 1¼ oz / 28 g portions.

Burrini

This is a speciality cheese from the very south of Italy, the regions of Puglia and Calabria in particular. Small, pear-shaped cheeses of mild and distinctive flavor are carefully molded around a pat of sweet butter which later will be spread on bread and eaten with the rest of the cheese.

These cheeses are ripened for just a few weeks and for export are usually dipped in wax or specially packaged. Sometimes they are called Butirri, Burielli or Provole.

Cacetti

These small cheeses are very similar to Burrini but without the heart of butter. They are spun-curd cheeses, dipped in wax and hung by raffia strands to ripen for about ten days.

Dolcelatte

This is a smooth, creamy blue cheese, milder than Gorgonzola, and a registered trade name meaning 'sweet milk'. It is a semi-soft cheese with 50% fat in dry matter, made from cow's milk and matured for about forty days.

A whole cheese weighs between 2¼-4½ lb / 1-2 kg although smaller cuts of this very popular cheese are usually available.

A selection of Italian cheeses. Top left: Taleggio, Ricotta, Caciocavallo, Caciotta, Fontal. Bottom: Parmigiano Reggiano, Grana Padano, Gorgonzola, Montasio, Provolone and Mozzarella

2. *Marking the cheese.*

3. *The salting process.*

4. *Storage in a cool atmosphere.*

5. *Cheeses being tested for quality.*

1. *Mixing the rennet.*

Gorgonzola – Italy's principal blue-veined cheese.

Gorgonzola

This is another exceptional product from the Po Valley and is said to be even older than Grana cheese.

It is named after the town where it is believed to have originated but is no longer made, not far from Milan. It is produced now at both local and mass production level in the provinces of Bergamo, Brescia, Como, Cremona, Cuneo, Milan, Novara, Pavia, Vercelli and the area of Casale Monferrato. A protected cheese, it is produced all the year round and is Italy's major blue-veined variety. It has a characteristically strong flavor from its compact, creamy texture and is white or straw colored with green flecks. The rind is a natural, rough, reddish-grey color.

Gorgonzola is used for the table as well as in numerous other ways. It is a soft, high fat, unboiled cheese produced from cow's milk with added penicillium glaucum and curdled at 80-90°F / 28-32°C with calf rennet. The cooled curds are salted and layered and turned regularly for about two weeks. Then the cheeses ripen in a cool, humid atmosphere for two to four months, a process which took much longer years ago when the cheeses ripened naturally in the caves of Valsassina.

Gorgonzola should neither have a brown rind nor be hard and it should not smell 'high'. It should have a sharp, clean smell with no hint of sourness. It is sold in foil in various cuts but its production size is usually 10 in-1 ft / 25-30 cm in diameter, 6¼-8 in / 16-20 cm in height and weighing from 13-26 lb / 6-12 kg. It has a protein content of 20-25%; fat/dry matter content, minimum 48%; fats, 25-36%; water, 43% and calories per 4 oz / 100 g, 360.

Grana

Two of Italy's most widely acclaimed cheeses, Parmigiano Reggiano and Grana Padano, belong to the Grana (granular) group of cheeses, those finely-grained hard cheeses which originated in the Po Valley to the north of the country.

Grana cheese can be traced back to the tenth and eleventh centuries and its method of production has not changed that dramatically. It is made from partly skimmed milk and then matured for at least a year in its distinctive drum shape. It is popular for grating although when it is young, it makes an excellent table cheese.

The Grana-producing areas of the Po Valley argued for centuries about who should carry the name 'Grana', and in 1955 the names 'Grana Padano' and 'Parmigiano Reggiano' were given legal protection and the characteristics and areas of production of each were precisely delineated. They are basically very similar cheeses although of the two, Grana Padano matures marginally faster.

Parmigiano Reggiano – its granular texture makes it suitable for grating

Grana Padano

Grana Padano is very similar to Parmigiano Reggiano but ripens more quickly and is left to mature for a year or two, being sold at varying degrees of maturity. Its history is as old as Parmesan and it also is a pressed, cooked cheese from the partly skimmed milk of two milkings.

Unlike Parmesan, Grana Padano, however is made all through the year in the following regions: Cremona, Mantua (on the opposite bank of the Po to Parmesan production), Piacenza, Brescia, Bergamo, Pavia, Alessandria, Asti, Cuneo, Novara, Turin, Vercelli, Como, Milan, Sondrio, Varese, Trento, Padua, Rovigo, Treviso, Venice, Verona, Bologna (on the opposite bank of the river Reno to Parmesan production), Ferrara, Forli and Ravenna.

It has a characteristic fragrance and a delicate flavor, and its appearance is straw white, slightly granular with flaky radial cracks and scarcely visible holes. Its shape and size are similar to Parmesan and its usual weight is between 52-88 lb / 24-40 kg, with a diameter of 14-18 in / 35-45 cm and height of 7-10 in / 18-25 cm.

It has the same uses as Parmesan – as a table cheese in early maturity and later as a dressing or ingredient in cooking. It has a protein content of 35%; fat/dry matter content, minimum 32%; fats, 28%; water; 30% and calories per 4 oz / 100 g, 387.

Parmigiano Reggiano or Parmesan

This undisputed king of Italian cheese is believed to have originated in the province of Reggio Emilia south of the Po Valley. The area was formerly under the rule of the Dukedom of Parma which was the main trading centre, hence its name. It was called the great cheese of seven countries because the ancient formula remained unchanged throughout 700 years of history which altered the face of continents.

Records dating back to AD1200-1300 describe the characteristics of Parmigiano Reggiano as they are today and it is assumed that the real origins of the cheese go back even further to the fine cheeses extolled by early Latin writers.

It is a cheese best known around the world in its grated form, Parmesan, but in early maturity it is a fine table cheese said to have great medicinal properties. The French comic dramatist, Molière, is reputed to have almost lived on the cheese during his declining years.

It is produced only from the first of April to 11 November in large drums weighing anything from 52-97 lb / 224-44 kg, the average being 72-79 lb / 33-36 kg, with a height of 7-9½ in / 18-24 cm and a diameter of 14-18 in / 35-45 cm. It is made with the unpasturized but tested milk of morning and evening milkings in its 'zona tipica' of Bologna, Mantua, Modena, Parma and Reggio Emilia where the soil, climate, vegetation, fodder and cattle-rearing traditions have influenced its flavor and quality over the centuries.

Making the cheese

The two milkings are partly skimmed and poured together into huge copper kettles to which a fermenting whey is added to raise the acid content of the milk and bring about the correct degree of fermentation in the cheese.

The milk is heated gradually to a temperature of 91°F / 33°C at which point kid or calves' rennet is added and coagulation occurs within fifteen minutes. The curds are broken up to particles the size of wheat grains and cooked in increasing heat to 131°F / 55°C. After the heat is switched off, the cheese granules drop to the bottom of the kettles where they form a solid mass. After half an hour, this is raised with a wooden paddle, collected in a hempen cheese-cloth, put in a circular mold and pressed lightly to remove any remaining whey in the cheese.

At this stage, a harmless coloring is used to imprint the name of the cheese all over the sides, so that even the smallest cut will be recognizable as authentic. (Later the cheese will receive a final stamp certifying that it is up to standard and confirming its year of production.)

The cheese is turned regularly but left in its mold for a few days to set when it is immersed in brine for twenty to twenty-five days and then stored on a wooden shelf where it is dusted and turned often. At the end of the year, all the cheeses are transferred to huge store rooms each accommodating from 100,000 to 200,000 cheeses, and here the lengthy maturing process takes place. A cheese is described as new if it was produced in the previous cheese-making season; well-matured or 'vecchio' when eighteen to twenty-four months old; and extra-mature or 'stravecchio' after a period of two or three or more summers.

Storing

Parmigiano Reggiano should ideally be bought in its solid state and either grated at the time of purchase or as required at home although obviously this is not always possible. It is worth double-checking the labelling on grated Parmesan to make sure it is authentic.

As for storing, true Parmesan does not deteriorate rapidly but cuts of cheese can dry out or, if conditions are too humid, become moldy. So, to keep it in the best possible condition, wrap small portions in plastic wrap (cling film) or foil and store them in the refrigerator ideally at 41°F / 5°C or in the fruit and vegetable drawer at the bottom.

Cutting a Parmigiano Reggiano

The cutting of a Parmigiano Reggiano is carried out according to ancient Italian cheese-making tradition.

A special knife is used with a short, almond-shaped, pointed blade. One side is thinner than the other so that as the blade cuts through the cheese, it functions as a wedge separating the severed walls of cheese. In other words, the cheese is split rather than cut and the resulting crack leaves the internal structure and grainy texture of the cheese intact.

To open a new cheese, a line is etched with the knife point along the diameter over top and bottom ends, and down over the convex walls. The rind is then cut along this line to a depth of ¼-¾ in / 1-2 cm when two knives are driven in together and pulled apart until the cheese splits into equal parts.

It needs experience and care because the cheese will only divide properly if its internal structure is in a condition to offer the same resistance on one side as the other. The same technique is used for further splitting of the cheese into quarters and eighths.

Uses and composition

The cheese has a uniform straw hue varying from pale to deep yellow and is soft with a scattering of tiny holes with flaky cracks radiating inwards towards the centre. It has a rich, savory flavor which should never be piquant or bitter. The ¾ in / 6 mm rind should be the color of old gold and is the cheese's natural protective casing which has hardened during maturity. It is edible and should not be thrown away; after a gentle scrape, it can be used in cooking or to flavor soups. The cheese itself is used as a table cheese in Italy and is widely popular as a dressing or ingredient in cooking – for pasta, risotto, antipasti, rice or meat dishes, soups – particularly minestrone, vegetables, soufflés, pies, quiches and, of course, in sauces.

It is considered to be an especially nourishing and digestible cheese often recommended for the elderly and for children and grated on babies' food. 2.2 lb / 1 kg represents 35 US pints [16 litres / 28 imperial pints] of milk, rich in proteins, fats, calcium and phosphorus. Proteins account for 36.14%; the butterfat content is 28.3%; the fat over dry matter content is a minimum 32%; the calcium is 1.30%; phosphorus, 0.70%; water, 28%; and calories per 4 oz / 100 g, about 400.

Parmigiano Reggiano

1. *Collecting the cheese granules in hempen sieve-cloths*
2. *Breaking up the granules.*
3. *The cheeses are salted in brine.*

1

2

3

Mascarpone

Mascarpone is a delicious creamy dessert cheese, almost like pure cream whipped into a light, velvety consistency. It is served either with food or on its own, flavored with cinnamon, powdered chocolate or liqueurs.

Mascarpone was originally made only in Lombardy in the autumn and winter but now it is available all the year round and is usually sold in muslin bags or in tubs.

Mozzarella

Mozzarella is a soft, pliable, porcelain white cheese made since the sixteenth century in southern Italy from the milk of the water buffalo. Now it is often made from a combination of cow's and water buffalo's milk and where it is made entirely from cow's milk, such as in the north, it is called Fior di Latte.

There are various types of Mozzarella. For instance from the hills of Rome in the Abruzzi region, comes a type of cow's milk Mozzarella called Scamorza, sometimes smoked. In the traditional areas of the South, the buffalo milk cheese is sometimes smoked also using wheat straw, leaves or wood, and is called Smoked Mozzarella di Bufala or Smoked Provola di Bufala. Some of the typical areas also produce Ovoli, small balls of Mozzarella, or Trecce, plaits of cheese which have to be eaten immediately.

True Mozzarella has become synonymous with pizza (although less reputable pizza-producers substitute other cheeses) because it becomes wonderfully stringy and tasty when melted and is complemented by the mixture of piquant or spicy flavors. On its own, it has a bland, slightly sour flavor enhanced if eaten, as in Italy, with olive oil, freshly ground black pepper and salt.

Buffalo milk Mozzarella has a stronger flavor and sharper smell than that made with cow's milk which tends to be a little rubbery. All Mozzarella should be eaten fresh although improved refrigeration has increased the availability and popularity of the cheese. It will keep for a few days in the refrigerator and can be moistened with a little fresh milk. It has a protein content of 26%; fat/dry matter content, 50%; fats, 26%; water, 65%; and calories per 4 oz / 100 g, 254.

Mozzarella cheese in a variety of shapes and sizes

Pecorino Romano

Pecorino is the generic term for cheeses made with ewe's milk (pecora means sheep) and this is one of the most important of Italian cheeses associated particularly with central and southern Italy. It is a hard-cooked (boiled), drum-shaped cheese made from fresh, full cream sheep's milk curdled with lamb's rennet and it has a decidedly strong flavor. There are numerous local variations but the most prominent of these, dating back to the first century BC, is Pecorino Romano.

The cheese, made originally as its name suggests in Rome, is mentioned in works by Plinius, Varrone and Columella. Indeed Columella stopped in Rome after arriving in Italy with Hannibal's armies and gave in his work, *De Rustica*, a detailed description of the methods used in making the cheese. He also mentions that because of its qualities it is suitable for shipping overseas, the first reference to Italy's cheese export trade.

It is because of these qualities which allow the cheese to keep so well that its export market has grown consistently. Although it is only made between November and June, production is on a very large scale and the cheese is, of course, protected by law.

The traditional production area is in the Lazio region around Rome but as demand increased, some producers moved to Sardinia where great quantities of the cheese are now produced. The fresh cheese has a whitish, smooth, clean rind while the riper cheese is covered with tallow and olive oil dregs. It is sold after at least eight months ripening, in huge blocks weighing from 35-39 lb / 16-18 kg and 5½-8⅛ in / 14-22 cm deep, and although it is firstly a table cheese, it is used greatly in the cooking of central southern Italy and in those countries with large Italian communities. It was introduced to the United States, for instance, in 1894 and the American market continues to be one of the largest, having imported more than 8,000 tons / 8 million kg of the cheese in 1984, double that for 1983.

It has a protein content of 27%; fat/dry matter content, minimum 36%; fats, 29%; water, 31%, and calories per 4 oz / 100 g, 372.

Ricotta

Ricotta is not really a cheese but is obtained by re-treating whey, although nowadays whole or skimmed milk is sometimes added to produce a richer product. Ricotta cheeses are made from sheep's or cow's milk although the ewe's milk cheeses are considered the best, particularly Ricotta Romana di Pecora, and the cheeses from the regions of Tuscany, Sardinia and Sicily. They are often made from left-over Pecorino whey.

Basically, it is an ivory white cheese with a delicately sour flavor and an after-taste of milk. The fresh cheese is very soft, bland, unripened and unsalted, whereas older cheeses, salted and dried, may be matured for sixty days or more to produce a dry, hard cheese for grating. There are also smoked cheeses and some produced only on special occasions.

Fresh Ricotta is the most popular and is used frequently in Italian cookery, in, for example, gnocchi, ravioli and cannelloni. It is also eaten fresh with fruit or sprinkled with sugar, chocolate or coffee; used as a base for cheesecake or even mixed with brandy or rum.

It is sold usually in weights varying from 18 oz-4½ lb / 500 g-2 kg and has a protein content of 18%; fat/dry matter content, 30%; fats, 8%; water 73%, and calories per 4 oz / 100 g, 136.

Robiola

This is a slightly confusing name which covers a variety of cheese. It is thought to have originated from either the village of Robbio in Lombardy or from the Latin 'rubium' meaning red which is the color of the rind.

Robiola is usually a soft, unpressed cow's milk cheese matured over one to four weeks when it acquires its reddish-brown rind. It resembles Tallegio and becomes stronger with age. There is another type of Robiola which is more like Camembert and ripens for only a few weeks after which it becomes softer and creamier with age.

Taleggio

This is a soft, unboiled cheese of the 'stracchino' type (listed further on) which has been made for centuries in the Bergamo mountain district, north-east of Milan. Again, improved refrigeration transport and storage facilities are increasing its popularity and although its origins were strictly in Lombardy, it is made also in Piedmont to the west, and Veneto to the east.

The cheese is white and supple with a thin, pinkish-grey rind and a mild slightly fruity aromatic flavor. It is ripened for about forty days although a stronger version is matured for twice that period. It is made from full cream cow's milk and is dry salted or salted in brine and has a characteristic brick shape. It usually weighs from 3¾-4¾ lb / 1.7-2.2 kg. It is wrapped in tissue paper and then placed in a carton.

There is also a cheese called Taleggino which is basically four slices from one cheese taken either from fresh cheese in which case it has rind on all four sides, or from the ripe cheese when it has rind on two sides only.

Taleggio is protected by law and has a protein content of 23%; fat/dry matter content, minimum 48%; fats, 26%; water, 50%; and calories per 4 oz / 100 g, 306.

A tempting Italian cheese board, clockwise from left: Taleggio, Parmigiano Reggiano, Ricotta, Crescenza, Stracchino, Gorgonzola, Caciocavallo and Mozzarella plaits, Trecce and titbits, Bocconcini

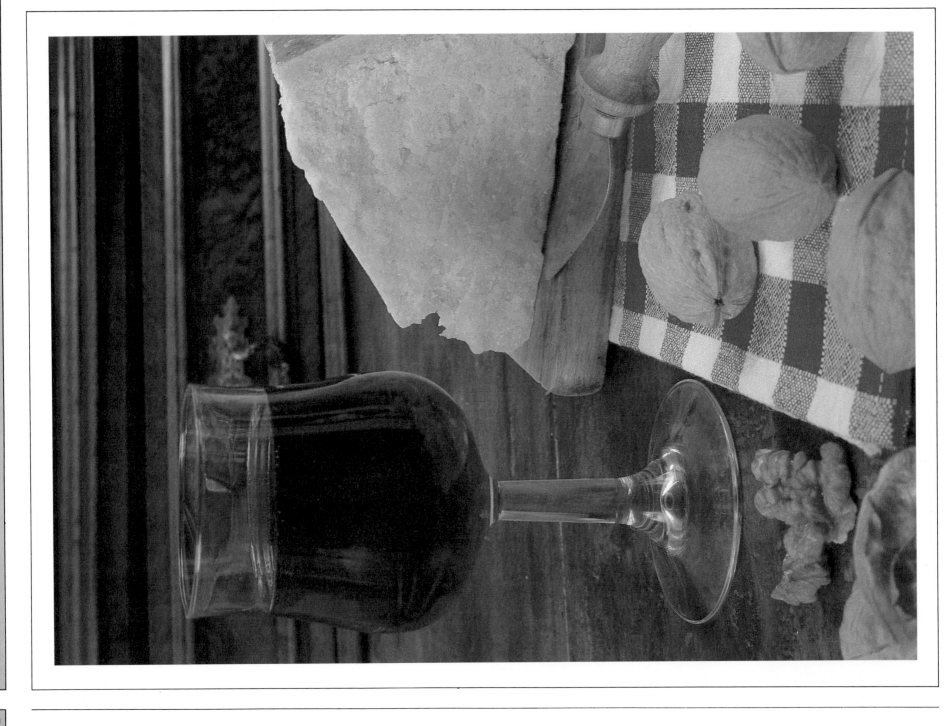

Some lesser known Italian cheeses

Asiago d'Allevo

This was originally a ewe's milk cheese made in the foothills of the Dolomites although now it is made almost entirely from cow's milk in the provinces of Vincenza and Trento and parts of Padua and Treviso.

It is produced from the milk of either twice-milked cows, one milking being skimmed, or from once-milked cows, the milk being partly skimmed, with natural or enzyme-produced acidity, and is dry salted or salted in brine. The curds are scalded and pressed to produce a firm, pleasantly strong table cheese after two to six months. Cheeses ripened for longer are used purely for grating and Asiago d'Allevo is renowned as an extra strong grating cheese.

The name 'Asiago', previously classified as a trade name, was recognized as a name of origin in December 1978.

The cheeses come in weights of from 17-26 lb / 8-12 kg with a diameter of 11¾-14 in / 30-36 cm but are usually cut at the time of purchase in pieces of 2 lb 2 oz / 1 kg or sold in supermarket prepacked portions of 1.1-2.2 lb / ½-1 kg. The protein content is 33%; fat/dry matter content, 34%; fats, 27%; water, 33% and calories per 4 oz / 100 g, 346.

Asiago Pressato is similar to d'Allevo but is a milder cheese ripened for only twenty to forty days and used purely for the table. It is of a white, or light straw color on cutting with marked irregular holes and has a thin, flexible rind.

It is produced only from the milk of once or twice-milked cows and, like d'Allevo, has a natural or enzyme-produced acidity and is salted and pressed. Its usual weight varies from 24-33 lb / 11-15 kg and it has a depth of 4¼-5¾ in / 11-15 cm with a diameter of 11¾-15¾ in / 30-40 cm. Again, it is retailed in portions of around 2.2 lb / 1 kg cut at the time of purchase or in supermarket portions of 1.1-2.2 lb / ½-1 kg. Its protein content is 31%; fat/dry matter content, 44%; fats, 28%; water, 36%; and calories per 4 oz / 100 g, 356.

Baccellone

This is a Ricotta-type cheese made in the spring at Livorno in Tuscany from ewe's milk and eaten usually with fresh broad beans ('baccelli').

Borelli

These are small cheeses made from buffalo milk and sometimes spiced with cumin or caraway seeds.

Bra

This is a strong, white, salty cheese produced occasionally, in Piedmont, from partly skimmed cow's milk. Originally it was made by nomadic herdsmen and its strong flavor is achieved by shredding the curds into tiny pieces, molding and pressing them and then repeating this process numerous times until the texture is particularly firm and compact. The cheese is then double salted, with salt being rubbed into the surface to eventually produce an especially strong cheese in weights of 11 lb / 5 kg with 30% fat.

Caciocavallo

Early references to Caciocavallo date back to 1335 in Southern Italy although since 1874 it has also been made around the Po Plain in the north. There are many theories as to how the cheese got its name, a likely reason being that the cheese – 'cacio' – is placed astride – 'a cavallo' – a pole during fermentation or smoking, usually in pairs. It is a medium-hard stringy cheese produced from full cream cow's milk and curdled by acid fermentation. The cheeses are shaped like skittles and ripened for three months for the table when they are compact, mild and delicate, and for over six months when they are to be grated and need a stronger flavor.

Known under a variety of names, Caciocavallo is used extensively in cooking in much the same way as Grana. It can be roasted, grilled or pan-fried accompanied by olive oil and spices to bring out its rich flavor and fragrance. It can be used also in pies and timbales and goes well with fried vegetables.

In many areas of Southern Italy, no distinction is made between Provola and Caciocavallo as a table cheese although the name of the latter is protected by law. The unusually shaped cheeses weigh around 4½ lb / 2 kg and have a smooth, thin rind ranging in color from straw or golden yellow to light brown. It is composed as follows: protein content, 30%; fat/dry matter content, minimum 44%; water, 30%; fats, 30% and calories per 4 oz / 100 g, 387.

Caciotta

There are innumerable types of Caciotta produced throughout Italy, the best known coming from Tuscany, Urbino, Assisi, Norcia, Cascia and Rome. The name is thought to have originated from the word, 'cacio', meaning cheese, which gives an idea of how widely distributed the cheese has always been.

Caciotta, Cacio, Caciotella – there are so many names relating to this type of cheese and the one described here refers to the medium-hard Caciotta of Tuscany and Urbino. It is usually produced from a mixture of cow's and ewe's milk and has a round, flattened shape. It is easy to keep and is made in such a way that it is soft and springy with various flavors, and is particularly good to eat although it is also used in cooking.

It is usually ripened for ten to twenty days but some are ripened for two months and have a more pronounced flavor. Its depth varies from 1¾-3½ in / 3-9 cm and its diameter is from 4¼-8¾ in / 11-22 cm and it retails at 1¾ lb / 800 g for the smallest cheeses to from 2½-3¼ lb / 1.2-1.5 kg for the medium and large ones. Its protein content is 23%; fat/dry matter content, 45%; fats, 29%; water, 40% and calories per 4 oz / 100 g, 365.

Canestrato or Pecorino Siciliano

This is a ewe's milk cheese from Sicily which is stored and ripened in a wicker basket ('canestro') which leaves its imprint on the cheese. It is made between October and June from full cream sheep's milk, curdled with lamb's rennet and ripened for at least four months. It is mostly a grating cheese and is white or slightly yellowish with a strong flavor.

Its shape is cylindrical with flat or slightly concave surfaces although sometimes the cheese is made with the addition of a special kind of pepper in which case it has a truncated cone shape. They vary greatly in size with a depth of 4-7 in / 10-18 cm and weights of from 8¾-26 lb / 4-12 kg, the smaller ones of 8¾-11 lb / 4-5 kg being used in the area of production and the larger ones being marketed elsewhere. Once again, its name is protected by law. It is composed as follows: protein content, 26%; fat/dry matter content, minimum 40%; fats, 25%; water, 42% and calories per 4 oz / 100 g, 332.

Crescenza

Crescenza is a typical product of the Italian dairy industry and the name embraces a wide variety of cheeses. Usually it is a soft, unboiled high fat cheese produced from full cream cow's milk, dry salted and without a rind. It is ripened for eight to ten days and is deliciously creamy. It is produced in Lombardy and Piedmont with the best known varieties of cheese coming from Milan and Pavia.

It is compact with few holes and of a white or light straw color. A flat cheese, it has a depth of about 1½ in / 4 cm with sides about 7 in / 18 cm long and an average weight of 4 lb / 1.8 kg. Crescenza is sold wrapped in greaseproof paper and then double-wrapped in special paper usually bearing the producer's trademark. Its protein content is 15%; fat over dry matter content, minimum 48% for summer cheese and 50% for winter cheese; fats, 21%; water, 60% and calories per 4 oz / 100 g, 270.

Emiliano

This is a flavorsome pale straw colored cheese from Emilia, just south of the Po river. It is a Grana type of cheese and it is ripened for one or two years and has a dark brown or black oiled rind.

Fiore Sardo

This is a hard, unboiled cheese produced in Sardinia with full cream ewe's milk either fresh or curdled with kid or lamb rennet. Its rind ranges from dark yellow to hazel while the cheese itself is white or a yellow straw color depending on the stage of ripening. From one to three months the cheese is used for eating after which it can be grated. It has a mild flavor, the after-taste of which remains even when the ripened cheese becomes stronger tasting. Fiore Sardo is said by connoisseurs to combine all the best qualities of the Sardinian cheese-making tradition, although there has been a reduction in the number and size of its production centres since the rapid development of the Pecorino Romano industry in Sardinia.

The cheese is composed of two very flattened truncated cones joined together at the wide base and weighing usually from 3-8¾ lb / 1.5 -4 kg in each shape. The cheese on commercial sale has an average diameter of 7½-7¾ in / 19-20 cm, a depth of 5-5½ in / 13-14 cm and an average weight of 4½-6 lb / 2-3 kg. Its name is protected by law and it was recently up-graded to a name of origin. It is composed as follows: protein content, 25%; fat/dry matter content, minimum 40%; fats, 29%; water, 41% and calories per 4 oz / 100 g, 382.

Fontal

Fontal is produced on an industrial scale throughout Piedmont and Lombardy and used to be called Fontina until 1951 when the name was given exclusively to those cheeses made in the Valle d'Aosta.

Fontal is similar in a number of ways and, like Fontina, derived its name from 'fondere' to melt and, as such, is ideal in recipes requiring a cheese which melts uniformly. It is delicious as a table cheese, in salads and with potatoes, tomatoes, carrots and other raw vegetables.

It is produced from full cream and/or pasturized half cream cow's milk and is ripened for thirty to fifty days. The dark brown rind is sometimes coated with paraffin and the cheese itself is straw-colored, well pressed with a few uniformly distributed holes and a mild and delicate flavor. Its diameter is from 15¾-17¾ in / 40-45 cm and its depth varies between 3-4 in / 8-10 cm. It weighs on average between 22-35 lb / 10-16 kg and for marketing, the whole cheeses or slices are usually given a protective coating of paraffin or wrapped in special plastic film. The cheese is comprised of: protein, 25%; fat/dry matter, 45%; fats, 30%; water, 45% and calories per 4 oz / 100 g, 343.

Fontina

A very popular Italian cheese, genuine Fontina comes from the Valle d'Aosta in the north-west and plays an important part in the cuisine of that area. It is made from the full cream milk of once-milked cows with acidity produced by natural fermentation.

The cheese is medium-hard although its flesh is soft and melts easily. It is straw colored with a mild and delicate flavor while its rind is soft and pliable either light brown or slightly orange. It is ripened for about three months and each cheese is marked with a circle containing an outline of the Matterhorn (which majestically marks the borders of Italy and Switzerland) with 'Fontina' written in the centre. The cheese has been likened to Swiss Gruyère but it is sweeter and softer.

It is produced in weights of 17-39 lb / 8-18 kg with a diameter of 11¾-17¾ in / 30-45 cm and depth of 2¾-4 in / 7-10 cm and is comprised of: protein, 25%; fat/dry matter content, minimum 45%; fats, 30%; water, 39% and calories per 4 oz / 100 g, 374.

Italico

This was the name given in 1941 to a range of semi-soft delicately flavored high fat cheeses, sometimes likened to Bel Paese, and made in the Lombardy region. Their characteristics vary according to each producer and only recently have achieved some stability of quality. It is believed that the cheeses originated from the very soft and creamy Robiola and similarly must be eaten immediately.

The Italico range of cheeses are produced from full cream cow's milk and are ripened for twenty to forty days after which they need to be kept on the dairy shelf of the refrigerator either wrapped in foil or in a plastic container.

The rind of Italico cheeses is light and smooth while the texture inside is soft, slightly pliable with scarcely any holes and ranging in color from pale straw to ivory. The protein content is 21%; fat over dry matter, 50%; fats, 26%; water; 50% and calories per 4 oz / 100 g, 318.

Lodigiano

This is another Grana type cheese of note produced near Milan. It is matured even longer than Parmesan, sometimes up to five years, and is a very strong cheese with a greenish tinge and is quite expensive.

Logudoro

This is a factory made cheese from Lombardy and is used as a table cheese after ripening for three to four weeks. It is made from a mixture of ewe's and cow's milk and has a mild, delicate and slightly acid flavor. It is a flat, round cheese with a protected trade name, and has a diameter of 6¼ in / 16 cm, a depth of 3-4 in / 8-10 cm, and weighs around 4½ lb / 2 kg. The rind of Logudoro is thin and straw colored while the cheese itself is crumbly with small holes and contains about 48-50% fat in dry matter.

Montasio or Carnia

This high fat, boiled and pressed cheese was originally made by monks in their monastery at Moggio in the northern Lombardy region in the thirteenth century. Its production is now centred mostly at Véneto and, further east, at Udine in the region of Friuli-Venezia Giulia.

It is made purely from cow's milk, partly skimmed, and is soft and springy when young and hard and brittle when older with a quite strong taste. Its rind is smooth and ranges in color from golden to dark yellow and it is matured for from two to five months for the table and for grating, from six months to a year.

Its average weight is from 11-20 lb / 5-9 kg, with a more usual marketing weight of between 13 and 17 lb / 6-8 kg, while its diameter is from 11¾-15¾ in / 30-40 cm and its depth is from 2¼-4 in / 6-10 cm. Its protein content is 30%; fat/dry matter content, 40%; fats, 32%; water, 32% and calories per 4 oz / 100 g, 411

Provolone

Provolone, which is similar to Caciocavallo, is recognizable by its various shapes and its thin, smooth and shiny brownish or golden yellow rind. It is a protected trade name and originally was of a truncated cone shape. It is more commonly produced now in pear, melon or sausage shapes and bears imprints of the cords or reeds used while it hangs to mature over a medium ripening period of two to three months.

Again, this is a cheese sold under various names but the best comes from the regions of Campania and Puglia in the south. It is a medium-hard stringy cheese made from full cream cow's milk. The curds are spun before acid is produced by fermentation and it is because the curd can be molded at the moment of spinning that so many shapes can be made. Mild Provolone is made by using calf rennet and a stronger variety by using kid rennet. Many of the larger cheeses are smoked. Because of the different shapes and sizes, it is difficult to give a typical size, however the cheeses are usually between 2.2-13 lb / 1-6 kg in weight with a depth of 14-17¾ in / 36-45 cm.

Provolone is a protected trade name and is comprised as follows: protein, 28%; fat/dry matter, minimum 44%; fats, 30%; water, 38% and calories per 4 oz / 100 g, 406.

Ragusano

Another Sicilian cheese, this is hard and stringy and produced from full cream cow's milk. It is shaped in a special way and then salted in brine and hung in pairs to ripen. The table cheese is ripened within six months and has a thin, golden yellow rind while the grating cheese, matured for longer, has a dark brown rind. The cheese itself is white or straw yellow, compact and uniform with a few holes and it has a mild taste until ripened for grating when it becomes strong and flavorsome.

It is sold in its characteristic square parallel piped shape weighing between 13-26 lb / 6-12 kg although bigger cheeses weighing 30 lb / 14 kg are available. Again, the smaller cheeses are kept for home consumption while the bigger ones are marketed elsewhere. It is composed of: protein, 27%; fat/dry matter content, minimum 44%; fats, 29%; water, 31% and calories per 4 oz / 100 g, 382.

Stracchino

Stracchino is very similar to Crescenza and originally owed its soft texture to the use of milk from cows which had just come down from the mountains in search of new pastures and so had arrived tired, or 'stracche', hence the name.

The cheeses are often sold under brand names, such as Certosa and Certosina.

It is made from full cream milk and dry salted and is also of a white or light straw color and ripened for about ten days after which it should be eaten as soon as possible. It has a mild, slightly bitter taste, and is used in sandwiches and as a filling, as well as a table cheese. Its protein content is 15%; fat over dry matter content, minimum 48% for summer cheese and 50% for winter cheese; fats, 21%; water, 60% and calories per 4 oz / 100 g, 270.

Toscanello

This is a piquant yet delicately flavored cheese from Tuscany. It is made with either ewe's milk or a mixture of ewe's and cow's milk which produces a small, firm, pale yellow cheese. The hard brown rind is coated with paraffin. It is used as a table cheese up to ten to twelve months maturity after which it is grated.

PRESERVING

Most people preserve food today, whether it is stocking the freezer or making jams and bottling fruit. It is always useful to revise the basic rules of food preservation to make sure that the end results are the best that can be achieved.

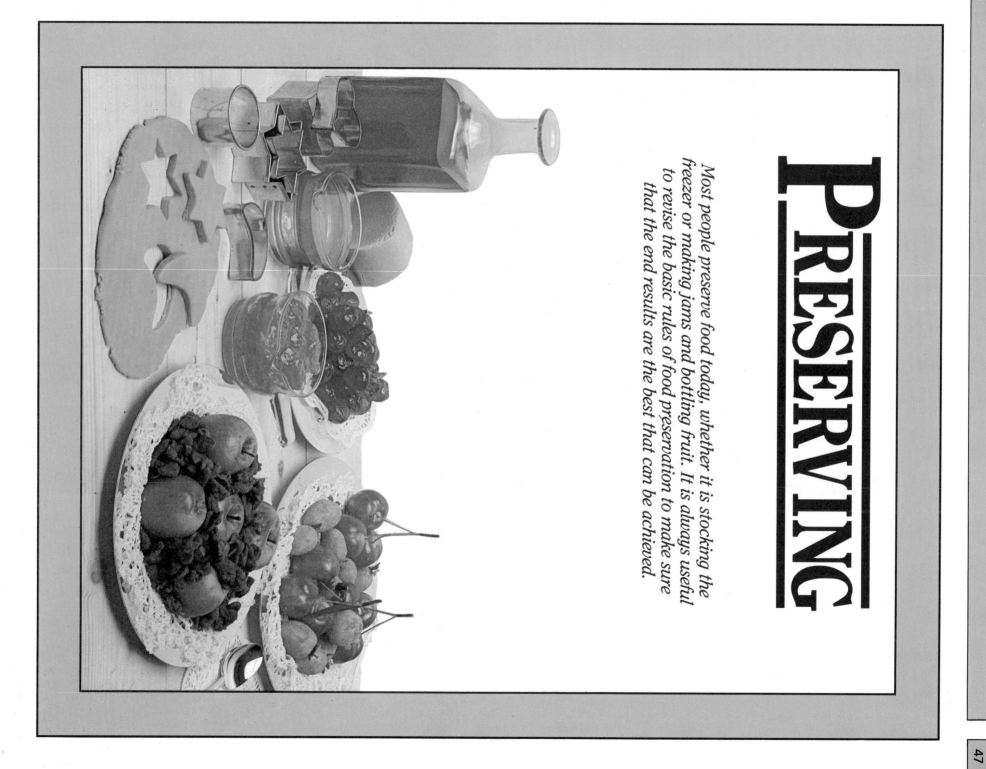

Freezing

The home freezer is an excellent way to preserve and store food in good condition. Rapid freezing lowers the temperature of food and stops the growth of micro-organisms such as bacteria and molds. The low temperature deprives them of suitable growth conditions and also stops the activity of enzymes in the food. However, it must always be remembered that these 'spoiling agents' are brought back to life when the food is thawed, and conditions are once again congenial for them.

The domestic freezer will store food safely at a temperature of 0°C / −18°F and to ensure the quality of the frozen food, this should be checked from time to time.

It is not wise to overload the freezer and it is essential that the door is always closed properly. Do not add more than 3 lb / 1.5 kg extra food for each cubic foot of freezer space during a 24 hour period as this will cause the temperature to rise and the quality of the food already stored will be affected. Before adding food in any quantity, turn the switch to the coldest setting or switch to the fast freeze. After a time the temperature in the freezer will then drop below the 0°C / −18°F. This will prevent the temperature rising above 0°C / −18°F when a quantity of unfrozen food is introduced.

If freezing a large amount of food make sure that the temperature control is turned down several hours before the new food is put in the freezer.

A guide to home freezing

- Freezing does not kill micro-organisms but only arrests the development, therefore it is essential that all food is handled with care and under hygienic conditions before it is frozen and when it is thawed.
- Do not refreeze thawed food.
- The food you put into the freezer is the food you will take out, therefore it is essential to freeze only produce which is fresh and of prime quality.
- Packaging in the freezer is important to keep food in good condition. Any exposure to air will result in a loss of quality and nutriments in the food.
- Label and date the food in the freezer to ensure that it is used in rotation. It is difficult to distinguish the contents of packages of goods when frozen unless they are labelled.
- Return the switch to a normal setting 24 hours after adding a quantity of home frozen produce.
- Try to store commercially frozen food as soon as possible after purchase. If the packets of vegetables or fruit which should be freeflowing are stuck together, do not buy them as this indicates the product has been badly stored. This happens from time to time to food at the top of supermarket cabinets.
- Pack solids as tightly as possible so that all the air is expelled. Do not leave rigid containers half empty as the vacant space will expose the food surface to air which will affect the food, it is also a waste of freezer space. Use crumpled foil to fill spaces in rigid containers.
- To pack liquids, the opposite applies as at least ½ in / 1 cm headspace to each 2½ cups [600 ml / 1 pint] packet of liquid must be left at the container top. Because water expands when frozen, a box of liquid food without a headspace will expand and, when frozen, push off the container's lid.
- In the case of the food combining both solid and liquid like stews or fruit salad, try to cover the surface with liquid and leave a headspace.
- To seal packs, expel the air and use a coated wire fastener. Make sure plastic lids are sealed properly on rigid boxes.

Cooked food packed for freezing in foil containers

To freeze cooked food

- Use shallow dishes rather than deep ones for faster freezing. The contents of these can be turned out after the food is frozen and stored in suitable bags or foil.
- Do not add all the seasonings to a savory dish. Herbs and seasoning are better added when the dish is reheated.
- Cool as quickly as possible, place in the refrigerator for some time and then freeze as fast as is practical.
- Cooked dishes from the freezer are better thawed and consumed within 2 months for best flavor.

Packaging

The freezing process makes the water in the cell structure of the food turn into ice and this must be protected by the packaging. Bad packaging allows air to flow around the food; this draws moisture from the food and the freezer inside. This can result in some dehydration of the food with a subsequent loss of flavor. Meat, poultry or other food which has lost its packaging in the freezer becomes freezer 'burned' which means outside tissues have been attacked by moisture and become tough and spongy thus destroying the texture of the food. Well packaged food will not pick up flavors or smells from another type of food. Pack the food in quantities which are suitable for the household needs, in portions of 2, 4 or 6 according to the size of the family.

Packaging materials

- Heavy duty foil is ideal for freezing packages of food as it will mold round uneven shapes.
- Polyethlene (polythene) bags are suitable for many products as they are flexible and vapour-proof.
- Foil containers are suitable for freezing cooked food and can be used from the freezer direct to the oven. If they have cardboard-type lids, remove these before cooking or heating.
- Cling wrap is ideal for separating chops, steaks, fish etc before packaging.
- Rigid plastic boxes are best for fragile fruits and vegetables but these tend to take up a great deal of space in the freezer. This problem can be overcome by lining the boxes with cling wrap and tipping the contents out when frozen. The package can then be wrapped and stacked leaving the box free for future use.
- Microwave containers are also suitable for use in the freezer.
- Pies and puddings are best frozen in the dishes in which they will be cooked and served, as they will not transfer well when thawed.

Open freezing

This is a method of freezing individual pieces of food separately. It is particularly useful for raspberries, strawberries and other berries. Line baking sheets with foil, arrange food on the trays separately and freeze until solid, do not leave for long periods before packing; it should be done as soon as the food is firm. When the food is firm pack as usual. Hamburgers, steaks and fish fillets can also be done this way but to avoid freezer burn package the meat or fish as soon as it is firm.

Decorated cream cakes or puddings can be open frozen before packing to avoid spoiling the decoration. Pack immediately they are firm.

1. Dry pack freezing. *Arrange the raspberries in a tray and freeze.*

2. *When the berries (or other fruit) are firm, pack into containers.*

3. *Cover and seal. Pack carefully in freezer to avoid bruising fruit.*

Dry sugar pack freezing.
4. *This method is suitable for red and black currants, blackberries, blueberries, strawberries, raspberries, loganberries, gooseberries and cherries. It is also useful to pack stems and leaves for decoration later.*

5. *After the fruit is frozen it is then packed in sugar. Use ½-¾ cup [100-175 g / 4-6 oz] sugar to 1 lb / 450 g of fruit. Arrange the fruit in suitable containers which should not be too shallow because several layers of fruit may be made.*

6. *Cover one layer of fruit with sugar, arrange another layer of fruit on top, sprinkle with more sugar. Continue layering in this way until the container is filled. Finish with a sprinkling of sugar on the top layer, cover and seal.*

Thawing

- Many households now have microwave ovens which thaw frozen food safely and quickly. However, it is essential to remove the food from foil or foil boxes before putting into the microwave.
- Food may be thawed in the refrigerator and it is most important to leave poultry for at least 24 hours to thaw as it should not be cooked while still frozen.
- Delicate foods such as game, shellfish, cheese and soft fruits should thaw gently in the refrigerator.
- Baked goods such as bread, rolls, plain cakes and pastries will thaw at room temperature, cover while thawing.
- Quiches, pizzas, tarts and other cooked pastry-based dishes can be heated straight from the freezer.
- Frozen vegetables can be thawed and cooked by plunging into boiling water.
- Cooked dishes must be brought up to boiling point to make sure that they are safe to eat.
- Fish fillets, ground (minced) beef, croquettes, hamburgers can be cooked in the frying pan from the frozen state.
- Frozen potatoes, coated fritters or croquettes can also be deep fried in oil directly from the freezer.
- It is better to thaw meat joints and it is essential to thaw poultry and game before cooking in the oven.

Foods which are unsuitable for freezing

- Vegetables with a high water content such as lettuce, tomatoes, celery, cucumber, scallions (spring onions), do not freeze. Tomatoes can be frozen but can then only be used in soups and stews.
- Bananas and avocados do not freeze well unless pureéd with lemon juice.
- Mayonnaise and hollandaise sauces do not freeze.
- Desserts set with gelatin are not satisfactory if left in the freezer for any length of time.
- Frosting and royal icing tends to crumble on cakes if frozen.
- Hard-cooked (boiled) eggs do not freeze well.
- Yogurt and cream cheese can only be frozen if mixed with other ingredients.
- Only freeze cream with a high fat content.

Blanching and freezing vegetables

Vegetables for the freezer must be fresh, in prime condition, and frozen just as they are coming to maturity. Blanching is essential for vegetables which are to be frozen. The process is carried out by plunging the vegetables into boiling water to destroy the enzymes, reduce the micro-organisms present, retain color, texture and some vitamin content. The water is brought back to the boil within 1 minute and the vegetables blanched in it for a short while (individual times are given on pages 52-53). The vegetables are then plunged into cold water with ice cubes added.

1. Firm white heads of cauliflower are prepared by removing the green stalks.
2. The cauliflower heads are then carefully washed under cold running water.
3/4. The thick stalk is cut away and the cauliflower broken into florets.
5. The cauliflower florets are placed in a wire basket, and lowered into the boiling water. Cauliflower is blanched for 3 minutes after the water returns to the boil.
6. The vegetables are then plunged into ice cold water, dried and packed into suitable containers.

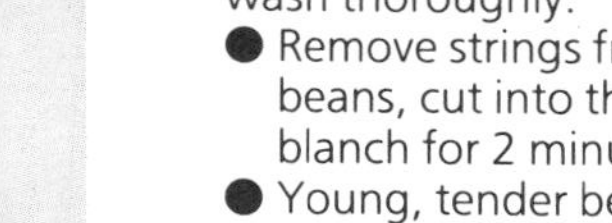

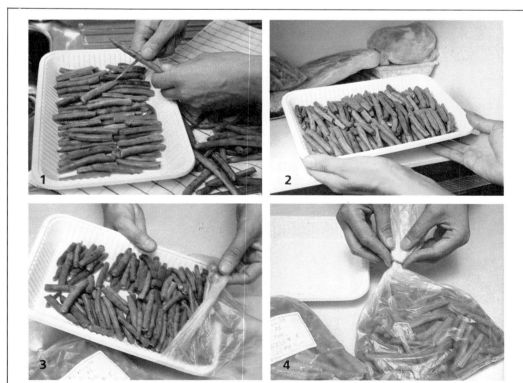

Open freezing beans

Select young, tender beans and wash thoroughly.

- Remove strings from green beans, cut into thick slices and blanch for 2 minutes.
- Young, tender beans should be trimmed at both ends and blanched for 2 minutes.
- Broad beans should be shelled and blanched for 3 minutes.

1. Arrange the blanched beans on a tray lined with foil or cling wrap. Do not put too many on the tray if they are to be free-flowing.
2. Place in the freezer, without covering, until firm.
3. Separate the beans by moving around with a spoon. Pack into plastic bags or suitable containers.
4. Remove the air by squashing the bag or suck the air out using a drinking straw. Seal by twisting a plastic covered tie. If using boxes do not leave air spaces at the top, fill the spaces with pieces of crumpled foil.

Preserving Vegetables

Vegetable	Preparation	Freezing	Other forms of preserving
Beans in shells	**1.** Shell the beans. **2.** Blanch for 5 minutes in unsalted boiling water so as not to harden them. **3.** Rinse under cold water.	**1.** Put in bags. Seal tight and label. **2. To use:** do not thaw. Boil for 1 hour in water without soaking. Add salt after 20 minutes cooking to avoid hardening.	Drying: **1.** Pull up the plants and hang in a dry, airy place. **2.** As soon as the shells begin to open, place the beans in a large plastic bag and shake vigorously to separate the shells from the beans. **3.** Sort and keep only the soundest beans, putting them into a canvas or paper bag. **To use:** soak for 12 hours. Do not use the soaking water for cooking. Will keep 1 year.
Brussels sprouts	**1.** Cut off the stalks and remove damaged leaves. **2.** Place in acidulated water. **3.** Blanch in boiling salted water for 2 minutes, rinse in cold water and drain.	**1.** Put in plastic bags or boxes. **2.** Seal tight and label. **To use:** do not thaw. Cook in boiling water. Will keep 8–10 months.	
Carrots	**1.** Scrub and peel. **2.** Blanch in boiling salted water for 3 minutes if sliced and 5 minutes if left whole. **3.** Drain and rinse in cold water.	**1.** Put in boxes or bags. **2.** Seal tight and label. **To use:** do not thaw. Cook for 15 minutes in boiling salted water or 1 hour in a stew. Will keep 12 months.	In the cellar: raw as soon as they are picked. **1.** Cut off the stalks, leaving ½ in / 1 cm. **2.** Place the carrots in heaps and cover with dry sand. Will keep 4–6 months.
Cauliflower	**1.** Remove the florets and leave ¾ in / 2 cm of stalk. Wash in acidulated water. **2.** Blanch for 2–3 minutes in boiling salted acidulated water. Dry in a thick cloth.	Place in bags and label. **To use:** without thawing, cook in boiling water for 15 minutes. Will keep 6 months.	In vinegar: **1.** Place in jars, adding small white onions. **2.** Cover with vinegar that has been boiled for 5 minutes and cooled. **3.** Seal and leave to marinate for 2 weeks before using as a relish.
Eggplant [Aubergines]	**1.** Peel and dice or cut into ¾ in / 2 cm slices. **2.** Brown for 6 minutes in 6 tbsp [75 g / 3 oz] butter or 3 tbsp oil over a low heat.	**1.** Pack in bags or boxes. **2.** Seal tight and label. **To use:** do not thaw for a slowly stewed dish. Thaw for 12 hours in the refrigerator for a dish cooked *au gratin* or fritters. Will keep 5 months.	
Globe artichokes	**1.** Break off the artichoke stalks by hand. **2.** Remove the hard outside leaves and cut the other leaves level with the heart. Put them into water containing vinegar or lemon as you go along to avoid blackening. **3.** Blanch for 10 minutes in salted acidulated water. **4.** Free the hearts from their leaves, discard the chokes and rinse in cold water. **5.** Leave to cool.	**1.** Place the very cold hearts in freezer bags and then in plastic containers. **2.** Seal tight and label. **To use:** do not thaw. Put directly into boiling water and cook for 12–15 minutes (in a stew: 25 minutes). Will keep 6–9 months.	In oil: (small artichokes) **1.** Wash the artichokes and cook whole for 20 minutes in boiling salted water. **2.** Drain them and remove the leaves and choke, keeping only the hearts. **3.** Place in jars together with black peppercorns, coriander seeds and bay leaves. **4.** Cover with oil. Seal the jars. Leave to marinate for 1 month before eating. Will last indefinitely.
Green beans	**1.** Remove strings and wash. **2.** Blanch in boiling salted water for 3 minutes. **3.** Rinse for 2 minutes under cold running water.	**1.** Pack in plastic bags. **2.** Seal tight and label. **To use:** without thawing, cook uncovered, in boiling water for 15–20 minutes depending on size.	

Preserving Vegetables

Vegetable	Preparation	Freezing	Other forms of preserving
Mushrooms	**1.** Sort the mushrooms, keeping only those which are fresh and perfectly sound. **2.** Trim stems. **3.** Clean in fresh water and drain. **4.** Wipe with a clean cloth.	Raw mushrooms are not suitable for freezing because they contain too much water and blacken easily.	Drying: **1.** Thread the mushrooms on strings, piercing the stem under the head. **2.** Hang for 10–15 days in the dry air, in the sun if possible. **3.** Put into cool oven, with the door open, and dry for 2 hours, turning occasionally. **4.** Place in jars. **To use:** put them dry into a sauce that is simmered or soak first for 1–3 hours.
Peas	**1.** Shell the peas and sort out the soundest. **2.** Blanch for 5 minutes in boiling salted water (1 tbsp salt to 1 quart [1 l / 1¾ pints] water). **3.** Rinse under cold water and drain.	Place in plastic sachets. Seal tight and label. **To use:** without thawing, cook in boiling water for 15 minutes. Will keep 10 months.	
Potatoes *(croquettes)*	Make croquettes according to the recipe chosen.	Freeze raw or cooked, spread out on a tray, until hard. Then put into plastic bags. **To use:** if the potatoes are raw, do not thaw but cook gently in butter in a frying pan for about 15 minutes. If they are cooked, warm up in the frying pan for 3-5 minutes.	
Spinach	**1.** Wash carefully and remove stalks. **2.** Blanch in boiling salted water for 3 minutes. **3.** Drain and dry.	Place whole leaves or chopped spinach in plastic bags. Seal tight and label. **To use:** do not thaw. Cook in boiling water for 10–15 minutes. Will keep 12 months.	

Preserving fruit

Fruit	Preparation	Freezing	Canning [bottling]	Other ways of preserving
Apples and pears	**1.** Peel and remove the core and seeds.	In slices: **1.** Cut into slices ½ in / 1 cm thick. Sprinkle with lemon juice (1 lemon per 2 lb / 1 kg fruit). **2.** Roll in sugar (1 cup [250 g / 8 oz] per 2 lb / 1 kg fruit). In compote: **1.** Boil for 20 minutes together with 1 cup [250 g / 8 oz] sugar per 2 lb / 1 kg fruit. Place in plastic containers and seal tight. **To use:** thaw in the refrigerator for 8 hours. Will keep 8 months.	Natural: **1.** Cut in half. Place in jars, sprinkling with sugar (2 cups [500 g / 1 lb] per 2 lb / 1 kg fruit). Leave to stand for 3 hours in a cool place. **2.** Seal and process. In syrup: **1.** As you peel them, sprinkle with lemon juice to prevent them turning brown. **2.** Plunge for 30 seconds in boiling water and drain. **3.** Place in jars to the ⅔ mark. Cover with a syrup made from 1 cup [250 ml / 8 fl oz] water boiled with 1 cup [250 g / 8 oz] sugar and a vanilla pod [bean]. **4.** Seal and process. **To use:** as they are. Will keep 1 year.	In sugar: Pear jam. Pear conserve. In alcohol: Pears in brandy. Apple conserve. Apple jelly.

Preserving fruit

Fruit	Preparation	Freezing	Canning [bottling]	Other ways of preserving
Apricots	**1.** Wash and cut in half. **2.** Remove pits [stones].	**1.** Place in plastic containers **2.** Seal and label. **To use:** do not thaw for cooked dishes. Thaw in the refrigerator to eat cold. Will keep 6–8 months.	**1.** Put the halved fruit into a jar. **2.** Sprinkle with 1 tbsp sugar, or cover with a sugar syrup made from 2 cups [500 g / 1 lb] sugar dissolved in 1 quart [1 l / 1¾ pints] water and boiled for 1 minute. **To use:** as they are with the juice. Will keep 12 months.	In sugar: Apricot jam. Apricot conserve. In alcohol: Apricots in brandy. Drying: **1.** Choose apricots which are very ripe but in good condition. **2.** Place them whole in a very low electric oven and dry for 6 hours. **3.** Leave to cool. Cut in half and remove pits [stones]. **4.** Return to the cool oven and dry for a further 6 hours. Leave to cool. **5.** Place in the cool oven again for 6 hours. Store in sealed jars. Will keep 8 months.
Blackcurrants	**1.** Wash and dry on a clean cloth. **2.** Destalk with a fork.	**1.** Place in plastic containers, alternating the layers with sugar (½ cup [100 g / 4 oz] for 2 lb / 1 kg fruit). **2.** Seal and label. **To use:** do not thaw for cooked dishes. Thaw to eat cold. Will keep 8 months.	Not suitable for blackcurrants because they break down in the heat.	In sugar: Blackcurrant jam.
Cherries	**1.** Wash and dry. Remove stalks. **2.** Leave the fruit whole with their pits [stones].	**1.** Place in plastic containers. **2.** Cover with a cold syrup made from 1 cup [250 g / 8 oz] sugar dissolved in 1 quart [1 l / 1¾ pints] water. **3.** Seal and label. **To use:** do not thaw for cooked dishes. Thaw to eat cold.	Natural: **1.** Place in jars sprinkling with sugar (1 cup [250 g / 8 oz] per 1¼ lb / 750 g fruit.) **2.** Leave to stand for 3 hours and seal. In syrup: **1.** Cover with a cold syrup made from 2 cups [500 g / 1 lb] sugar per 1 quart [1 l / 1¾ pints] water. **2.** Seal and process. **To use:** as they are in their juice. Will keep 1 year.	In sugar: Cherry jam. In alcohol: Cherries in brandy.

Preserving fruit

Fruit	Preparation	Freezing	Canning [bottling]	Other ways of preserving
Peaches	**1.** Plunge for 30 seconds in boiling water. Peel. **2.** Cut in half and remove pits [stones].	**1.** Place in plastic containers. **2.** Cover with a cold syrup prepared from 1 cup [250 g / 8 oz] sugar dissolved in 1 quart [1 l / 1¾ pints] water and boiled for 2 minutes. **3.** Seal and label. **To use:** thaw in the refrigerator for 8 hours. Will keep 8 months.	Natural or in syrup: **1.** Place the halved peaches in jars (with the cavity downwards). Natural: Sprinkle with 1 tbsp sugar per quart [1 l / 2 pint] jar. In syrup: **1.** Cover with a syrup made from 3 cups [750 g / 1½ lb] sugar dissolved in 1 quart [1 l / 1¾ pints] water. **2.** Seal and process. **To use:** as they are. Will keep 12 months.	In sugar: Peach jam.
Plums	**1.** Wash and dry. **2.** According to your preference, leave the fruit whole with their pits [stones] or cut in half and pit.	**1.** Place in plastic containers. **2.** Seal and label. **To use:** do not thaw for cooked dishes. Thaw for fruit salad. Will keep 8–10 months.	Place in jars: Natural: add 1 tbsp sugar and the juice of 1 lemon per 1 quart [1 l / 2 pint] jar. Seal. In syrup: **1.** Cover with a syrup made from 2 cups [500 g / 1 lb] sugar and 1 quart [1 l / 1¾ pints] water and some lemon juice. **2.** Seal and process. **To use:** as they are in the juice.	In sugar: Plum jam. Plum marmalade. In alcohol: Plums in brandy. Prunes in brandy.
Raspberries	**1.** Remove stalks. **2.** Wipe without washing.	**1.** Place in plastic containers. **2.** Sprinkle with sugar (1 cup [250 g / 8 oz] per 2 lb / 1 kg fruit). **3.** Sprinkle with the juice of a lemon. Seal tightly. **To use:** do not thaw for hot dishes. Thaw to eat cold. Will keep 10 months.	Place in jars: Natural: add sugar (1 cup [250 g / 8 oz] per 2 lb / 1 kg fruit). Leave to stand for 3 hours in a cool place. Seal and process. **To use:** as they are. Will keep 10 months.	In sugar: Raspberry jam. In alcohol: Raspberries in brandy.
Red currants	**1.** Wash and dry on a clean cloth. **2.** Destalk with a fork.	**1.** Place in plastic containers. **2.** Sprinkle with sugar (⅔ cup [150 g / 5 oz] sugar per 2 lb / 1 kg fruit). **3.** Sprinkle with the juice of 1 lemon. Seal tightly. **To use:** do not thaw for hot dishes. Thaw to eat cold. Will keep 8 months.	Place in jars: Natural: add sugar (1½ cups [350 g / 12 oz] per 2 lb / 1 kg fruit). Cover and process. **To use:** as they are, in the syrup. Will keep 1 year.	In sugar: Red currant jam, conserve and jelly.
Strawberries	**1.** Wash and dry on a clean cloth. **2.** Remove stalks.	**1.** Place in plastic containers. **2.** Sprinkle with sugar (½ cup [100 g / 4 oz] per 2 lb / 1 kg fruit). **3.** Sprinkle with lemon juice. Seal tightly. **To use:** do not thaw for hot dishes. Thaw to eat cold. Will keep 10 months.	Place in jars: Natural: add 1 tbsp sugar per jar. Seal and process.	In sugar: Strawberry jam. Strawberry conserve.
Tomatoes	Pulp: Peel the tomatoes (first plunging them in boiling water for 10 seconds), remove stalks and quarter. Juice: Peel (as above) and purée in a blender or food processor. Strain to remove seeds.	Whole tomatoes do not stand up very well to freezing. Pulp: Fill a plastic container to the ¾ mark. Cover and label. **To use:** without thawing, heat according to chosen recipe. Juice: Fill containers to the ¾ mark. Seal and label. **To use:** thaw and serve cold. Will keep 6 months.	**1.** Place the peeled tomatoes (whole or in pieces) in jars. **2.** Cover with salted water (2 tsp salt to 1 quart [1 l / 1¾ pints] water). **3.** Seal and process. **To use:** drain and use according to the recipe chosen. Will keep 8–10 months.	In oil: (whole tomatoes) **1.** Heat some salted water (3 tbsp salt to 1 quart [1 l / 1¾ pints] water). As soon as it boils, leave to cool. **2.** Wipe the tomatoes. Place in jars. Cover with the cold salted water up to 1½ in / 3 cm of the rim. Fill up to the top with olive oil. **3.** Seal and keep cool. **To use:** in salads. Will keep 6 months.

Preserving

Jam making

Making jams, jellies and marmalades is probably the most popular way of preserving fruit today apart from home freezing. The flavor of good home-made jam is hard to equal even with the best commercial brands. Although it takes some time and effort it is a satisfying and rewarding task and the appreciation of family and friends often outweighs the work involved.

Ingredients

Fruit sets when combined with sugar and then boiled. This is because of a substance in the cells known as pectin. Different methods can be used to make jams and jellies but the rules are common to all methods.

The fruit should be fresh and firm but not over ripe as fruit which is over ripe will not set well.

Fruits which have a high pectin content are oranges, lemons, grapefruits, limes, cooking apples, gooseberries, damsons, quinces, cranberries.

Fruits which have slightly less pectin are raspberries, plums, greengages, apricots, peaches, loganberries, black and red currants.

Fruits which are low in pectin are strawberries, blackberries, cherries, pears, melon, rhubarb, marrow, figs, pineapple, grapes, pears.

Equipment for making jam

There are a few utensils used for jam making which, although, not absolutely essential, do make the process easier.

Sieve

If using a sieve make sure that it is made of nylon and not metal as metal tends to discolor the fruit.

Preserving pan

This pan can be a heavy saucepan made of aluminium or a preserving pan which is made of aluminium or tin-lined copper. It is essential for the pan to have a thick base as the high sugar content in jam will burn if the saucepan is too thin. The wide shape of the preserving pan is to allow a rapid evaporation of water and the depth also gives enough space for the jam to come to a rolling boil without splashing over the cook and the stove.

It is better to use ingredients for jam which only come half way up the pan, this will give enough space for the jam to boil. If a normal heavy based saucepan is used for jam making, remember that the jam will take longer to make and boil because most saucepans are not as wide as a preserving pan and evaporation is much slower.

A slotted spoon or ladle

This can be most useful for skimming jam and can be used to remove stones as they rise to the surface.

A funnel

A wide funnel with a large tube is most useful and much safer for filling jam jars.

Jam jars

Make sure the jars are free from cracks and flaws. It is easy to collect jars from groceries bought over a period of time.

Wash the jars thoroughly in soapy water and rinse well in several bowls of clean hot water. Heat gently in a very low oven and use the jars while still warm to prevent cracking from the hot jam.

Jam pot covers

These can be bought in packets and usually have labels, wax and cellophane discs and elastic bands for sealing the jam.

Sugar thermometer

This is a useful piece of equipment for those who make jam often. These thermometers are marked 312°F – 350°F / 160°C – 180°C, and the higher temperatures can be used for making toffee and sweets.

Before using the thermometer, dip into hot water then place in the boiling jam. A good set has probably been reached when the thermometer reads 220°F / 110°C but it is wise to allow the thermometer to reach 222°F / 111°C to be sure.

The pectin test

If you are unsure of the fruit and the setting qualities try the following test before making the jam. Cook the fruit until the stage before adding the sugar, remove 1 teaspoon of fruit and liquid, add 3 teaspoons methylated spirits and mix in a glass. If there is enough pectin present in the fruit, the juice will clot. If there is not enough pectin and it does not form a real clot, the pectin in the fruit is poor and some other form of pectin will be needed to set the jam. Lemon juice is most widely used for adding pectin as it not only helps the setting of the jam but brings out the flavor of the fruit.

You will need the juice of 2 small lemons to 4 lb / 2 kg / 4 lb fruit with a poor response to a pectin test.

Commercial pectin can also be used to set jam and jellies. If using this always follow the manufacturer's instructions.

To make jam

1. Prepare the fruit by picking off stalks according to type, wash if necessary. Drain as quickly as possible without damaging the fruit.
2. Place the fruit in a preserving pan, add the water given in the recipe and simmer until tender. The timing will depend on the type of fruit; tough skinned fruits such as gooseberries and plums will take at least 30 minutes.
3. Take the pan off the heat, add the sugar and stir until it is dissolved.
4. Return the pan to the heat, bring to the boil over a low heat, skimming off the froth that rises to the surface. Cook quickly until a rolling boil, stirring until the jam sets when tested.

To test for a set

The most accurate method to test for setting is to use a sugar thermometer. Place the thermometer in the jam and when it reaches 222°F / 111°C a good set should result. Some jams and jellies vary slightly therefore it is wise to double check with the following old-fashioned jam making tests.

Flake test

Stir the jam with a spoon and turn to allow to cool. If the jam has set the flakes will run together and drop as one large flake. If the jam has not reached setting time the jam will drop in several droplets.

Plate test

Drop a teaspoon of jam on to a cold plate. Allow to cool for a few minutes, push the finger across the jam. The surface should wrinkle if the jam is ready.

Bottling

This form of preserving is still popular in Italy and other European countries. Bottling is heat sterilizing for varying lengths of time in order to kill bacteria in the fruit. Sealing air from the jar protects the fruit from bacteria.

Fruit
There are two important factors to remember when preserving fruit:

Perfectly sealed jars
Thoroughly sterilized fruit

A guide to preserving in syrup

- Check all your jars and tops. All purpose preserving jars with wide mouths are best and the new ones have easy seal discs with rubber bands. For old jars make sure they are not chipped or damaged and it is safer to buy new rubber rings for each new batch of fruit. Scald jars and lids in boiling water. Leave to drain but do not dry with a tea towel. If liked place in a low oven to dry.
- Fruit should be unblemished, just ripe but still firm, apart from goosberries which are usually bottled when green and underripe. Arrange fruit in sizes to make sure that it cooks evenly in the jars. Fruit can be bottled in water if you do not want to add sugar but it is generally more useful if flavored with a light sugar syrup. A suitable syrup can be made with ½-¾ cup [100-175 g / 4-6 oz] sugar to 2½ cups [600 ml / 1 pint] water. More sugar can be added to taste but a very heavy syrup can cause the fruit to rise in the bottles.
- Pack the prepared fruit into the jars. Tap them several times on a folded cloth to settle the contents, then add more fruit until it reaches a level of ¾ in / 2 cm from the rim.
- Cover the fruit with sugar syrup or brine, leaving a space of ½ in / 1 cm under the lid to allow room for the steam to expand without bursting the jar. With a clean cloth, carefully wipe the top of the jar.
- Seal the filled jars, following the manufacturer's directions. Arrange them in the pan on a rack, making sure they do not touch each other or the sides of the pan.
- Fill the hot-water canner (bottling pan) with enough hot water to cover the jars by at least 1 in / 2.5 cm, then bring it to a boil. Do not start the timing process until the water has boiled.
- When the process is completed, carefully remove the jars using tongs and place them on a wooden board or several layers of cloth or newspaper to cool. Complete the seals according to the manufacturer's instructions.
- Leave the jars upright and undisturbed for 12 hours, then test the seals in the way recommended for the type of jar and lid you have used.
- Label the jars with their contents and the date and store them in a cool, dark place.

All these operations must be carried out with the utmost care to avoid the danger of contamination.

Preserving in vinegar, salt and oil

Pickled vegetables, chutneys and relishes
In Italy many vegetables are preserved and used as *antipasti*. It is a useful method of storing vegetables ready for use when the freezer is already full. Making pickles and chutneys is another rewarding task as they are expensive to buy and not always to one's own taste, sometimes they are either too highly spiced or the taste of vinegar is too strong.

Equipment for pickling

- Use earthenware or pyrex bowls for mixing
- Cook the pickles in heavy aluminium or enamel pans, never use brass, copper or tin.
- Use wooden not metal spoons for mixing and stirring.
- Use glass preserving jars which do not have metal rings as these will discolor if the metal is allowed to contact the pickle. Jam jars can be covered with waxed (greaseproof) paper discs and then cling wrap. Jars with clip on lids which are plastic lined can be used as long as the metal clip does not contact the pickle.

Vinegar
Malt and spirit vinegars are the most suitable for preserving as wine vinegars have a delicate flavor which is lost in this type of preserving unless the recipes call for it. Vinegar is produced by fermentation when alcohol is turned into vinegar by the action of acetic acid. This acetic acid penetrates into the food and inhibits the growth of the bacteria found in most vegetables thus prolonging the life.

Oil
This is a short term method of preserving and any product kept in oil can usually be kept in the refrigerator but does not have a long shelf life.

Salt
Coarse salt will draw moisture from food and will therefore inhibit the growth of micro-organisms. Do not use table salt as this contains additives. Sea salt crystals or coarse block salt is best for this type of preserving.

Dry salt can also be used for preserving by layering the vegetables with coarse salt.

Wet salt
To make a brine for preserving you will need ½ lb [225 g / 8 oz] coarse salt to 1½ quarts [1.5 litres / 3 pints] water. Bring to the boil and allow to cool before use. Allow 2½ cups [600 ml / 1 pint] brine solution to 1 lb [450 g / 1 lb] vegetables.

Spiced Vinegar

00:15 00:10

American	Ingredients	Metric/Imperial
1 quart	*Malt vinegar*	*1 litre / 1¾ pints*
10	*Cloves*	*10*
8	*Peppercorns, slighlty crushed*	*8*
1	*Blade of mace*	*1*
4	*Bay leaves*	*4*
1 × ½ in	*Piece of root ginger*	*1 × 1 cm / ½ in*
2 tsp	*Mustard seeds*	*2 tsp*
1 tsp	*Whole allspice*	*1 tsp*
1	*Stick of cinnamon*	*1*
2	*Chilli peppers, deseeded*	*2*
	Salt	

1. Bring half the vinegar to the boil with all the spices for 4 minutes, add remaining vinegar. Bring to the boil again and allow to cook briskly for another 4 minutes.
2. Allow to cool, strain and use as required either over raw prepared vegetables or vegetables which have been blanched for a few seconds, depending on the degree of crispness required.

Cook's tip: Do not attempt to pickle with unboiled vinegar as it goes sour in a fairly short time.

Jelly making
Top: *wash fruit, drain and mash to obtain juice.*
Middle: *strain through muslin or a nylon sieve. Add 3 cups [750 g / 1½ lb] sugar to 1 quart [1 litre / 1¾ pints] juice. Bring to boil on low heat, stirring to dissolve sugar.*
Bottom: *Skim and boil until setting point (220°F / 104°C) is reached. Test for setting, pot in sterilized jars, seal.*

Marmellata di fragoline di bosco

Wild Strawberry Jam

00:05
Plus 3 days
Yield: about 4½ lb / 2 kg

00:20

American	Ingredients	Metric/Imperial
2 lb	*Wild strawberries*	*1 kg / 2 lb*
3¼ cups	*Sugar*	*700 g / 1½ lb*

1. Put strawberries in a basin with layers of sugar and leave for 24 hours. Place in a preserving pan and boil for 5 minutes.
2. Return to the basin and leave for 48 hours, then replace in preserving pan and boil for 10 to 15 minutes until set.
3. Cool slightly, stir and pour into clean warmed jars. Cover with waxed paper and wetted cellophane tops. Secure with elastic bands. Label and store in a cool dry place.

Marmellata di pesche

Peach Jam

00:10
Marinating time 48:00
Yield: about 4½ lb / 2 kg

00:20

American	Ingredients	Metric/Imperial
2 lb	*Peaches*	*1 kg / 2 lb*
¼	*Lemon*	*¼*
6	*Peach leaves*	*6*
2¾ cups	*Sugar*	*600 g / 1¼ lb*

1. Wash the peaches carefully, peel and remove the stones then cut into large chunks. Put them in a large bowl, add the lemon peel and peach leaves and cover with sugar. Cover with a clean tea towel and leave to marinate in a cool place for 48 hours, stirring from time to time.
2. After 2 days, transfer the contents of the dish to a large saucepan, remove peach leaves and boil over a high heat for 20 minutes until setting point is reached. Take the pan off the heat.
3. Cool slightly, then pour into clean warmed jars. Cover with waxed discs and wetted cellophane tops. Secure with elastic bands, label and store in a cool dry place.

To make peach jam

1. *Peel the fruit and cut into slices.*
2. *Weigh the fruit and put into a bowl.*
3. *Add the sugar to the fruit and leave in a cool place to steep.*
4. *Add ½ cup [125 ml / 4 fl oz] water to the fruit and sugar in a preserving pan. (It is not necessary to add water if using the recipe opposite which has a long marinating time.) Stir on a low heat until the sugar is completely dissolved. Skim off the froth that rises to the surface.*
5. *Bring to a rolling boil. Test for setting with a sugar thermometer. It should reach 220°F / 111°C and double check by using the plate test. Drop a teaspoon of jam onto a cold plate. Allow to cool for a few minutes, push your finger across the jam. The surface should wrinkle if the jam is ready.*
6. *Ladle into sterilized jars or use a wide funnel.*
7. *Seal the jam, cover and label with variety and the date.*

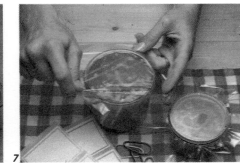

Marmellata di mele

Apple Jam

Preparation: 01:00 · Cooking: 01:20
Yield: about 4 lb / 2 kg

American	Ingredients	Metric/Imperial
2 lb	*Canadian or cox apples*	*1 kg / 2 lb*
1¼ cups	*Water*	*300 ml / ½ pint*
	Sugar (see recipe)	

1. Wash apples, remove stalks and core, removing all pips, but do not peel. Place in a large heavy based pan, cover with water and simmer for about 1 hour until soft. Rub through a sieve then measure pulp allowing 3¾ cups [800 g / 1¾ lb] sugar per 2 lb / 1 kg pulp.
2. Return pulp to pan, add sugar and stir until dissolved. Bring to the boil and boil rapidly until setting point is reached. To test for setting point, drop a teaspoon of jam onto a plate and leave to cool. If it sets, the jam is ready but if not boil for another 5-10 minutes and test again.
3. Allow jam to cool slightly, then pour into clean, warmed jars. Cover with waxed discs and wetted cellophane, secure with elastic bands, label and store in a cool dry place.

Marmellata di lamponi

Raspberry Jam

Preparation: 00:05 · Cooking: 00:20
Marinating time 12:00
Yield: about 4½ lb / 2 kg

American	Ingredients	Metric/Imperial
2 lb	*Raspberries*	*1 kg / 2 lb*
4¼ cups	*Sugar*	*900 g / 2 lb*
1 tbsp	*Lemon juice*	*1 tbsp*
1 tbsp	*Butter*	*15 g / ½ oz*

1. Wash the raspberries very rapidly under running water and drain. Leave them to marinate in the sugar overnight. Then transfer to a heavy based saucepan with lemon juice.
2. Add a knob of butter to remove scum, cool slightly, then pour into clean, warmed jars. Cover with waxed discs and wetted cellophane, secure with elastic bands, label and store in a cool dry place.

Marmellata di mirtilli

Bilberry Jam

Preparation: 00:10 · Cooking: 00:50
Yield: about 4½ lb / 2 kg

American	Ingredients	Metric/Imperial
2 lb	*Bilberries*	*1 kg / 2 lb*
4 cups	*Water*	*900 ml / 1½ pints*
3¼ cups	*Sugar*	*700 g / 1½ lb*
1 tbsp	*Honey*	*1 tbsp*
1 tbsp	*Butter*	*15 g / ½ oz*

1. Rinse bilberries in water, drain thoroughly and put in a large heavy based pan or preserving pan. Cover with water and simmer gently until tender and the contents of pan are reduced considerably.
2. Add sugar and honey, stir until dissolved, bring to boiling point and boil hard until setting point is reached. Remove from the heat.
3. Add a knob of butter to pan to remove scum, then cover with waxed paper and wetted cellophane. Secure with elastic bands, label and store in a cool dry place.

Marmellata di frutta secca

Dried Fruit Jam

Preparation: 00:15 · Cooking: 00:50
Soaking time 24:00
Yield 10 lb / 4½ kg

American	Ingredients	Metric/Imperial
½ lb	*Dried apricots*	*225 g / 8 oz*
½ lb	*Prunes*	*225 g / 8 oz*
½ lb	*Dates*	*225 g / 8 oz*
½ lb	*Dried figs*	*225 g / 8 oz*
	Weak tea to cover	
6 lb	*Sugar*	*2.8 kg / 6 lb*
1	*Lemon or orange*	*1*
3 tbsp	*Brandy*	*2 tbsp*

1. Wash the various types of fruit, soak them for 24 hours in the tea. Drain, place fruit in a preserving pan, add water and cook over a very low heat for 30 minutes.
2. Put the fruit through a sieve or food processor, return to the pan, add the sugar, rind of the lemon or orange and the brandy. Stir until sugar has dissolved, then boil rapidly until setting point is reached.
3. Allow to cool slightly before pouring into clean, warmed jars. Cover with waxed discs and wetted cellophane tops and secure with elastic bands. Label and store in a cool dry place.

Cotognata

Quince Jelly or Quince Candies

Preparation: 00:20 · Cooking: 01:30
12:00 for straining pulp
Yield: about 10 lb / 4½ kg

American	Ingredients	Metric/Imperial
4½ lb	*Quince*	*2 kg / 4½ lb*
1 lb	*Canadian or cox apples*	*500 g / 1 lb*
3½ quarts	*Water*	*3½ litres / 6 pints*
3 tbsp	*Lemon juice*	*2 tbsp*
	Sugar (see recipe)	

1. Wash quinces and apples, cut or grind (mince) fruits, put in a preserving pan, cover with the water and lemon juice and simmer for about 1 hour until tender.
2. Strain through a jelly bag overnight, measure extract and allow 2 cups [500 g / 1 lb] sugar per 2½ cups [600 ml / 1 pint] extract. Replace extract in preserving pan, add sugar, stir until dissolved then boil rapidly until setting point is reached.
3. For jelly, cool then pour into clean warmed jars. Label and store in a cool dry place.
4. For candies, pour jam into a large pyrex bowl. When set, cut into diamond shapes, dip each one in sugar and arrange in paper patty shells (pastry cases) and store in a well sealed box.

Cherry jam

Marmellata di ciliegie

Cherry Jam

00:20 Yield: about 5½ lb / 2½ kg — 00:50

American	Ingredients	Metric/Imperial
5½ lb	*Cherries with the pits (stones) removed but retained*	*2½ kg / 5½ lb*
2	*Lemons*	*2*
1	*Small stick of cinnamon*	*1*
7½ cups	*Sugar*	*1.7 kg / 3½ lb*
¼ cup	*Cherry brandy*	*50 ml / 2 fl oz*

1. Remove stalks from cherries, place in a sieve and rinse under cold water. Tie stones in a muslin bag and put in a preserving pan with the cherries. Add lemon juice and the cinnamon stick.
2. Cook over a low heat for 30 minutes stirring with a wooden spoon occasionally. Remove muslin bag of stones and cinnamon stick and discard. Add sugar, stir until dissolved, then boil rapidly until setting point is reached. (See recipe for apple jam opposite). Stir in cherry brandy.
3. Cool slightly, then pour into clean warmed jars. Cover with waxed discs and wetted cellophane. Secure with elastic bands, label and store in a cool dry place.

Marmellata di arance

Orange Marmalade

00:40 Yield: about 5 lb / 2.5 kg — 02:20

American	Ingredients	Metric/Imperial
2¼ lb	*Oranges*	*1 kg / 2¼ lb*
2½ quarts	*Water*	*2.5 litres / 4½ pints*
1	*Lemon*	*1*
4¼ cups	*Sugar*	*900 g / 2 lb*
1 tbsp	*Butter*	*15 g / ½ oz*
¼ cup	*Kirsch*	*50 ml / 2 fl oz*

1. Scrub fruit, cut in half, squeeze out the juice and pips and slice the peel without removing the pith.
2. Put sliced peel, soft pulp and juice in a pan with the water and the pips tied in a muslin bag. Add lemon juice and cook gently for 2 hours until peel is soft.
3. Remove muslin bag after squeezing. Measure the yield left in the pan allowing 1 lb / 500 g sugar per 2½ cups [1 pint / 600 ml] pulp. Stir in sugar until dissolved then boil rapidly until setting point is reached.
4. Add a knob of butter to pan to remove scum, then stir in the kirsch or other liqueur. Allow to cool slightly before pouring into clean warmed jars.
5. Cover with waxed discs and wetted cellophane and secure with elastic bands. Label and store in a cool dry place.

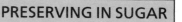

Beetroot in oil

Scorzette candite

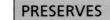

Candied Peel

00:40 Soaking time 3 days | 00:00

American	Ingredients	Metric/Imperial
	Oranges with thick skin	
	Sugar	

1. Peel the oranges (or tangerines, lemons, citrons, grapefruit) and soak the peel for 3 days, repeatedly changing the water. Drain well.
2. Carefully remove the pith, cut the rind into matchsticks and weigh. Dissolve the same weight of sugar in a pan on a very low flame and dip the peel in it. When the peel has completely absorbed the sugar, spread on a marble slab or an enamelled baking tray and leave to dry, uncovered, until the sugar has crystallized.

Cook's tip: it keeps well in an airtight sealed plastic box or glass jar. It is used in cassata, puddings, cakes and pastries.

Barbabietole in vasetto

Beetroot in Oil

00:20 Serilizing time 00:30 — 00:00

American	Ingredients	Metric/Imperial
2 or 3	*Large cooked beetroot*	*2 or 3*
6	*Salted anchovies*	*6*
	Oil to fill jars	
Scant ¼ cup	*Vinegar*	*3 tbsp*
	Salt and pepper	
1 tbsp	*Finely chopped parsley*	*1 tbsp*
2	*Garlic cloves*	*2*

1. Peel beetroot, cut into quarters and remove the stringy centres. Slice and put in a dish.
2. Wash and fillet anchovies.
3. Season beetroot with oil, vinegar, salt and pepper, add chopped anchovies, the finely chopped parsley and garlic. Mix well and put into small jars, then pour in oil so that no air is left in the jars.
4. Check the jars on the following day and add more oil if necessary, then hermetically seal the jars (see page 57). Store in cool dark place.
5. Once opened, store in refrigerator and consume within 7-10 days.

Alici piccanti

Spicy Anchovies

00:30 — 00:35

American	Ingredients	Metric/Imperial
2 lb	*Salted anchovies*	*1 kg / 2 lb*
1 tbsp	*Vinegar*	*1 tbsp*
1	*Sprig parsley*	*1*
1	*Sprig of thyme*	*1*
2	*Bay leaves*	*2*
1	*Celery stalk*	*1*
1	*Small carrot*	*1*
1	*Small onion*	*1*
1	*Piece of red chilli pepper*	*1*
1	*Small jar of capers in oil*	*1*
½ cup	*Dry white wine*	*125 ml / 4 fl oz*
1½ cups	*Olive oil*	*350 ml / 12 fl oz*

1. Wash anchovies quickly in water and vinegar and lay out to dry on a tea towel or kitchen paper and pat dry.
2. Chop together all herbs and vegetables and a few capers until they are reduced to a pulp and transfer to a frying pan.
3. Add the wine and oil and cook over a very low heat for 30 minutes. (If the mixture becomes dry, add a little more white wine.) Then remove pan from the heat and set on one side to cool for a while.
4. Meanwhile, roll up anchovies and place a caper in the centre of each one. Arrange anchovies in a jar, pouring a little sauce over each layer.
5. Store for a few days in the refrigerator before using and consume entire contents within 7-10 days.

Alcolato di fragole

Strawberries in Alcohol

00:20 Marination time 2 weeks — 00:00

American	Ingredients	Metric/Imperial
7 or 8 cups	*Ripe and very fragrant strawberries*	*1 kg / 2 lb*
1 quart	*90° proof alcohol*	*1 litre / 1¾ pints*

1. Remove stalks from strawberries and place in an earthenware bowl. Pour over alcohol and leave to marinate for 2 weeks, stirring frequently.
2. Rub fruit through a sieve and strain. Pour into small jars and seal with jam pot covers. Once opened, consume all contents as the flavor is soon lost.
3. Use for flavoring ice creams, liqueurs, sauces, flan cases and fruit salads.

Mousse al prezzemolo

Parsley Butter

00:15 — 00:00

American	Ingredients	Metric/Imperial
1	*Bunch of parsley*	*1*
¼ cup	*Cognac*	*50 ml / 2 fl oz*
2	*Garlic cloves*	*2*
⅔ cup	*Butter*	*150 g / 5 oz*

1. Chop the parsley in a blender or food processor, add the cognac and the garlic cloves, crushed. Switch on again for 10 seconds.
2. Remove the chopped mixture to a bowl and with a small wooden spoon cream the butter with it thoroughly, working to have a smooth mixture which is well marbled with green.
3. Arrange in a small earthenware dish and store in the refrigerator until needed. Serve on hot toast, fried bread or on baked vegetables such as potatoes. Also useful for adding to broiled (grilled) meat or fish just before serving.

Noci in salsa

Walnuts in Sauce

00:30 Marinate for 01:00 — 00:00

American	Ingredients	Metric/Imperial
1 cup	*Skinned walnuts*	*100 g / 4 oz*
¼ cup	*Water*	*50 ml / 2 fl oz*
¼ cup	*Vinegar*	*50 ml / 2 fl oz*
	Salt and pepper	
¼ tsp	*Nutmeg*	*¼ tsp*
1 lb	*Sour grapes*	*450 g / 1 lb*

1. Peel the walnuts and put them to marinate for about 1 hour in water, vinegar, salt, pepper and nutmeg.
2. Remove the juice from a bunch of tart grapes, retaining 20 for garnish, by sieving or using juice extractor. Leave to stand for a few minutes, then add a sprinkling of vinegar and filter through a fine sieve. Drain the walnuts from the marinade and serve them with the grape dressing and stoned grapes as part of a cold buffet.

Anguilla marinata

Marinated Eel

00:30 00:25

American	Ingredients	Metric/Imperial
2 lb	Eel	1 kg / 2 lb
4-6	Bay leaves	4-6
	Salt	
2 tbsp	Oil	1½ tbsp
1	Garlic clove	1
2	Cloves	2
3	Peppercorns	3
1	Sprig of rosemary	1
1 tbsp	Parsley	1 tbsp
2¼ cups	White vinegar	500 ml / 18 fl oz

1. Preheat oven to 325°F / 160°C, Gas Mark 3.
2. Gut the eel, remove head and tail, wash and dry without removing the skin and cut into pieces of about 2½ in / 6 cm. Arrange in a glass dish, alternating with bay leaves. Salt and pour over a trickle of oil, cover then place the dish in the oven for 20 minutes. Remove eel dish and lay the pieces on kitchen paper to absorb excess oil.
3. Meanwhile peel clove of garlic and add to pan with the other herbs and spices, pour over vinegar and boil for 5 minutes. Place the eel pieces in a jar, strain vinegar before pouring it over the eel, while still hot. After a few days, check vinegar still covers the eel, and if necessary boil up some more and add.
4. Store for up to 2 weeks in the refrigerator.

Carciofini sott'olio

Baby Artichokes in Oil

00:35 (including sterilizing) 00:50

American	Ingredients	Metric/Imperial
4	Lemons	4
2½ cups	Vinegar	600 ml / 1 pint
2 lb	Baby artichokes	1 kg / 2 lb
1 tbsp	Salt	1 tbsp
A few	Mint leaves	A few
1	Piece of red chilli pepper	1
½ tsp	Oregano	1 tsp
1	Garlic clove	1
	Good quality olive oil to cover	

1. Fill a large bowl with water and add juice of 2 lemons and ½ cup [125 ml / 4 fl oz] vinegar. Remove hard leaves and bristles from artichokes. Cut stalks leaving only ½ in / 1 cm and immerse in the water. (If artichokes are on the large side, make a cross-shaped incision on bases.)
2. Boil 2 quarts [2 litres / 3½ pints] water with remaining vinegar in a large saucepan with salt and juice of 2 remaining lemons. Add artichokes and cook for 8-10 minutes depending on size. Stir with a wooden spoon to ensure even cooking.
3. Remove, drain thoroughly and place in glass jars. Add mint leaves, red chilli, oregano and a few thin slices of garlic then cover with olive oil. Seal hermetically (see page 57) and store in a cool, dark place. Consume within 3 months.

Antipasto piemontese

Piedmontese Antipasto

00:25 Sterilizing time 00:30 00:45

American	Ingredients	Metric/Imperial
4½ lb	Ripe tomatoes	2 kg / 4½ lb
¾ lb	Small onions	350 g / 12 oz
¾ lb	Carrots	350 g / 12 oz
¾ lb	Celery	350 g / 12 oz
¾ lb	Sweet yellow peppers	350 g / 12 oz
¾ lb	French beans	350 g / 12 oz
½ cup	Olive oil	125 ml / 4 fl oz
1 tbsp	Coarse salt	1 tbsp
1 tbsp	Sugar	1 tbsp
1 cup	Red vinegar	225 ml / 8 fl oz
	Grated nutmeg	

1. Wash tomatoes thoroughly, halve and parboil to remove the liquid. Drain and purée then put mixture into a large steel saucepan.
2. Peel and chop onions, dice carrots, chop celery, deseed and chop yellow peppers, top and tail beans.
3. Add oil, salt, sugar, vinegar to the tomato purée in the pan and slowly bring to the boil. Then add carrots and celery and cook for 15 minutes. Stir in beans and cook a further 10 minutes. Add onions and simmer for 10 minutes, then finally add sweet yellow peppers and nutmeg and simmer for 2-3 minutes.
4. Pour into good quality, clean jars whilst still hot. Cool and cover with a film of olive oil. Cover bottles with tops and screw bands, loosened by a quarter turn to allow air to escape.
5. Pour sufficient water into a pressure cooker to reach a depth of 2 in / 5 cm. Stand bottles on rack in cooker ensuring they do not touch. Carefully replace cooker lid. Bring up to 10 lb / 4.5 kg pressure and maintain for 30 minutes.
6. Allow cooker to cool completely, then remove lid. Screw lids tightly on bottles, when removed from cooker. When bottles are cold, test lids to check they are properly sealed. Discard contents of unsealed bottles.
7. Store for up to 6 months in a cool dry place.

Aglio in vasetto

Garlic in Oil

00:20 Sterilizing time 00:30 00:00

American	Ingredients	Metric/Imperial
4 or 5	Heads of fresh garlic with large, fat cloves	4 or 5
1 cup	Vinegar	225 ml / 8 fl oz
1 cup	Water	225 ml / 8 fl oz
1 tbsp	Salt	1 tbsp
	Good quality olive oil to fill jar	

1. Divide garlic into cloves and peel carefully. Heat vinegar and water in a saucepan with the salt and bring to the boil. Put in garlic and parboil for about 10 minutes. Drain and leave garlic to cool on a plate keeping cloves well apart.
2. When cooled, place in a glass jar, cover with oil and seal the jars hermetically (see page 57).

Piedmontese antipasto

ANTIPASTI

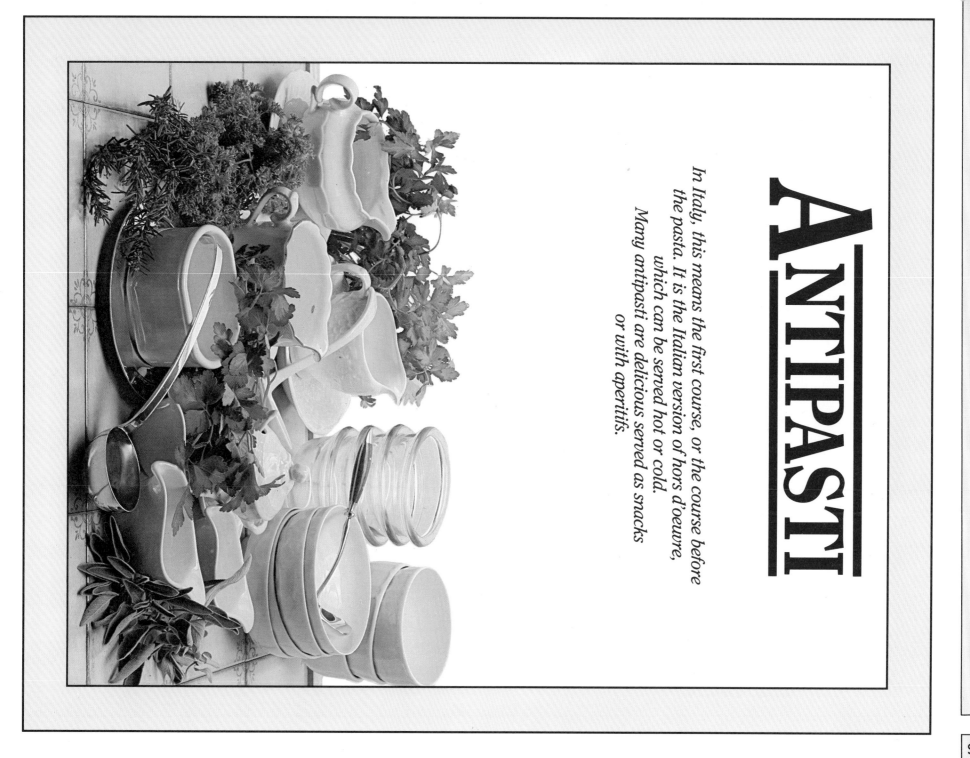

In Italy, this means the first course, or the course before the pasta. It is the Italian version of hors d'oeuvre, which can be served hot or cold. Many antipasti are delicious served as snacks or with aperitifs.

Flagship-style anchovies

Acciughe in salamoia

Anchovies in Brine

00:60 | 00:00

American	Ingredients	Metric/Imperial
2 lb	*Anchovies*	*1 kg / 2 lb*
	Fine salt	

1. Remove the heads from the anchovies and wash in salted water and allow to drain thoroughly.
2. In the bottom of a wide-necked glass vessel put a layer of salt, place on the salt a layer of anchovies with the tails radiating from the centre, cover with a layer of salt and continue until the ingredients are used up. The last layer must be of salt.
3. Place a glass disc on the layered anchovies with a weight on top. Close the mouth of the vessel and return it to a cold store-room. After several months if the anchovies are too dry, pour over some salted water. To prepare the salted water, put as much cold water as you need, together with some salt and dissolve it very thoroughly. Immerse a small raw potato in the water; if the potato comes to the surface it means that the water is salted to the right degree.

Acciughe alla piemontese 

Piedmont-Style Anchovies

00:25 | 00:00

American	Ingredients	Metric/Imperial
½ lb	*Fresh anchovies*	*225 g / 8 oz*
3 tbsp	*Vinegar*	*2 tbsp*
Scant ¼ cup	*Olive oil*	*3 tbsp*
1	*Truffle*	*1*
	Parsley sprigs	

1. Wash the anchovies, bone and divide them into fillets. Soak in vinegar for 10 minutes.
2. Drain and arrange the anchovies in a serving dish. Cover with olive oil.
3. Slice a truffle very finely and sprinkle over the anchovies. Keep in a cool place, but not in the refrigerator. Serve the dish garnished with sprigs of parsley.

Acciughe alla ammiraglia

Flagship-Style Anchovies

00:20 plus 12 hours standing
Serves 4–6 | 00:00

American	Ingredients	Metric/Imperial
1 lb	*Fresh anchovies*	*450 g / 1 lb*
2	*Lemons*	*2*
3 tbsp	*Oil*	*2 tbsp*
	Salt and pepper	
	Oregano or chopped parsley	

1. Thoroughly clean the fresh anchovies, remove bones, head and tail them and divide into fillets. Wash the fillets in cold water and then drain well. Arrange on a serving dish.
2. Completely cover the anchovies with plenty of well-strained lemon juice and leave to stand for 12 hours. Just before serving beat oil with a little salt and pepper in a cup and sprinkle over anchovies before serving. The lemon causes the anchovies to have a cooked effect and they appear very white. According to taste, complete the dish with a sprinkling of fresh oregano or chopped parsley.

Acciughe con peperoni gialli

Anchovies with Yellow Peppers

00:15
Serves 6–8 | 00:05

American	Ingredients	Metric/Imperial
1 lb	*Anchovy fillets*	*450 g / 1 lb*
3	*Yellow peppers*	*3*
½ cup	*Oil*	*6 tbsp*
¼ lb	*Capers*	*100 g / 4 oz*
2	*Eggs*	*2*
1	*Lemon*	*1*
	Black pepper	
1 tbsp	*Chopped parsley*	*1 tbsp*

1. Arrange rows of anchovy fillets on a serving dish.
2. Deseed peppers and cut into thin strips. Heat 3 tablespoons oil in a frying pan and cook the strips of pepper over a medium heat for 5 minutes.
3. Arrange the anchovies and peppers in alternate rows. Sprinkle with chopped capers and decorate with rounds of hard-cooked (boiled) eggs.
4. Mix the strained juice of the lemon with 3 tablespoons oil, freshly ground black pepper and chopped parsley. Pour over the anchovies and peppers.

Scodelline di granchi cinesi

Little Bowls of Chinese Crabs

00:25 | 00:15

American	Ingredients	Metric/Imperial
1 lb	*Canned crab flesh*	*450 g / 1 lb*
1	*Small onion*	*1*
1 tbsp	*Butter*	*1 tbsp*
1¼ cups	*Béchamel sauce (see page 162)*	*300 ml / ½ pint*
1 tbsp	*Cognac*	*1 tbsp*
3 tbsp	*Cream*	*2 tbsp*
1 tbsp	*Tomato purée*	*1 tbsp*
	Salt and pepper	

1. Drain the canned crab.
2. Peel and finely chop a small onion. Heat the butter and cook over a low heat until transparent.
3. Make the béchamel sauce, add onion, cognac, cream and tomato purée, season with salt and pepper. Add the crab flesh, turn off the heat. Arrange in small dishes and decorate with basil leaves and triangles of hot toast.

Conchiglie al cartoccio

Clams in Parcels

00:20 | 00:12

American	Ingredients	Metric/Imperial
4	*Clams*	*4*
1	*Bunch of parsley*	*1*
2	*Lemons*	*2*
	Salt and pepper	
3 tbsp	*Cognac*	*2 tbsp*
4	*Egg yolks*	*4*
1 tbsp	*Grated parmesan cheese*	*1 tbsp*

1. Preheat the oven to 350°F / 180°C / Gas Mark 4.
2. Wash the clams thoroughly without detaching the mollusc from the valve. Chop the parsley finely, mix with the strained lemon juice, a little salt, pepper and cognac.
3. Arrange 4 ovenproof saucers or china dishes, such as ramekins, each on a large square of foil. Place a clam in each dish and divide the lemon juice and parsley mixture equally amongst the clams.
4. Break an egg into a cup to ensure the yolk remains whole, slip the egg yolk into the centre of each clam, sprinkle with the parmesan cheese.
5. Wrap each clam in a square of foil leaving a little crown of foil at the top of the dish where the square has been gathered together. Place on a baking sheet and cook in the oven for 12 minutes.
6. Remove the foil and serve hot.

Ostriche vellutate

Velvet Oysters

00:10 | 00:50

American	Ingredients	Metric/Imperial
24	*Oysters*	*24*
½ cup	*Red wine*	*125 ml / 4 fl oz*
6 tbsp	*All-purpose (plain) flour*	*40 g / 1½ oz*
3 tbsp	*Butter*	*40 g / 1½ oz*
1 cup	*Fish stock (see page 212)*	*300 ml / ½ pint*
	Salt and pepper	
	Lemon rind	
3 tbsp	*Cream*	*2 tbsp*
1 tbsp	*Chopped parsley*	*1 tbsp*

1. Place the shelled oysters with the liquid from the shells in a saucepan, add red wine, bring to the boil and simmer for 10 minutes. Strain the liquid through a sieve lined with muslin into another pan and reduce by half. Arrange the oysters in a serving dish.
2. Prepare a savory white sauce with flour, butter and stock (see page 164), blend with the oyster juice, add salt and pepper, a little grated lemon rind and cook slowly for 10 minutes. Add the cream.
3. Pour the sauce over the oysters, garnish with chopped parsley. Place in the refrigerator to chill before serving.

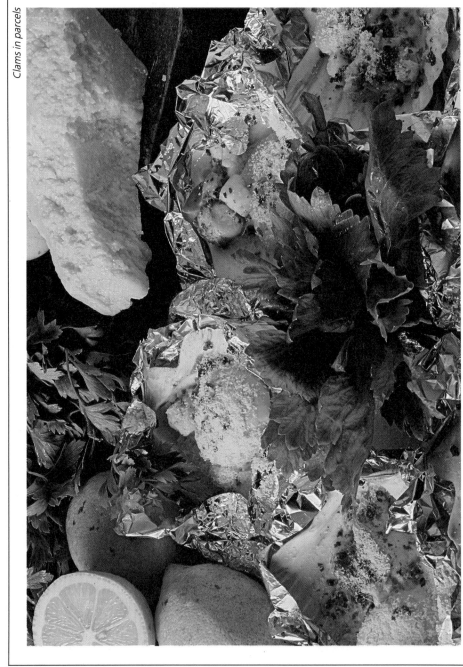

Clams in parcels

Ostriche charenteises

Charente Oysters

00:20 00:08

American	Ingredients	Metric/Imperial
24	*Oysters*	*24*
12	*Small sausages*	*12*
1 tbsp	*Oil*	*1 tbsp*
8	*Sprigs of parsley*	*8*

1. Remove oysters from the shells, scald in boiling water for a few minutes, then keep on one side.
2. Place the sausage in boiling water for 1 minute, pat dry with kitchen paper.
3. Heat the oil in a frying pan and fry sausages until golden brown.
4. Arrange the sausages and the oysters on a heated serving dish and garnish with parsley sprigs.

Ostriche alla Napoleone

Napoleon-Style Oysters

00:15 00:00

American	Ingredients	Metric/Imperial
24	*Oysters*	*24*
	Ice	
	Lettuce leaves	
	Freshly ground white pepper	
1	*Lemon*	*1*
Scant ¼ cup	*Cognac*	*3 tbsp*
	Salt	
Scant ¼ cup	*Olive oil*	*3 tbsp*

1. Arrange the oysters on a serving dish covered by a bed of finely chopped ice. Cover with well washed and drained lettuce leaves.
2. In a small bowl beat some freshly ground white pepper, the juice of a lemon, good quality cognac and a little salt. Beat until you have a smooth mixture, then add a drop at a time of fine olive oil. Pour the seasoning over the oysters and serve them immediately at table.

Canapés con le ostriche

Canapés with Oysters

00:60 00:00

American	Ingredients	Metric/Imperial
½ cup	*Butter, softened*	*100 g / 4 oz*
4 tbsp	*Mild mustard*	*3 tbsp*
12	*Slices of bread*	*12*
12	*Oysters*	*12*
3 tbsp	*White wine*	*2 tbsp*
1 cup	*Mayonnaise (see page 175)*	*225 ml / 8 fl oz*

1. Beat the butter until it becomes creamy. Add half the mustard and mix well.
2. Place the slices of bread without crusts in the oven for a few minutes, then spread with the butter.
3. Wash and brush the oyster shells thoroughly, then open the oysters, add a sprinkling of white wine, put in an earthenware dish with some mayonnaise flavored with the remaining mustard.
4. Place an oyster on each slice of bread, arrange on a large serving dish and decorate all around with the best shells containing a little finely chopped ice.

Coppe di gamberoni

Crayfish Cups

00:25 00:08

American	Ingredients	Metric/Imperial
2 lb	*Crayfish*	*1 kg*
1¼ cups	*Mayonnaise (see page 175)*	*300 ml / ½ pint*
2 tsp	*Tomato purée*	*2 tsp*
¼ tsp	*Tabasco sauce*	*¼ tsp*
1 tbsp	*Cognac*	*1 tbsp*
	Lettuce	

1. Cook the crayfish in boiling water for 5 minutes, then drain and shell.
2. Prepare the mayonnaise and flavor it with tomato purée, Tabasco sauce and a little cognac. Mix the crayfish with the pink sauce.
3. Arrange leaves of well washed and drained fresh lettuce in 4 cups. Place a few crayfish all around the rim of the cup. Serve cold.

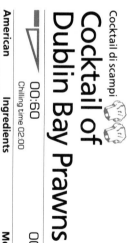

Cocktail di scampi

Cocktail of Dublin Bay Prawns

00:60 00:10
Chilling time 02:00

American	Ingredients	Metric/Imperial
1	*Leek*	*1*
1	*Lemon*	*1*
1	*Head of lettuce*	*1*
3 tbsp	*Vinegar*	*2 tbsp*
1 lb	*Dublin Bay prawns*	*450 g / 1 lb*
1 cup	*Coffee (single) cream*	*225 ml / 8 fl oz*
3 tbsp	*Rum*	*2 tbsp*

1. Wash the leek and remove any discolored leaves. Chop into thin slices and blanch in boiling water for 4 minutes, drain well and allow to cool. Sprinkle with lemon juice.
2. Place a few washed lettuce leaves in an earthenware dish and add the leek.
3. Place some water with vinegar in a saucepan, bring to the boil and drop in the prawns, bring back to the boil and cook for 5 minutes, drain and allow to cool, then remove shells.
4. Put the prawns in the dish, mix thoroughly with the cream and rum.
5. Divide the mixture between 4 glasses, and garnish with some more lettuce leaves torn or cut into strips. Place in the refrigerator for 2 hours, then serve.

Cocktail di gamberetti all'americana

American-Style Prawn Cocktail

00:30 Chilling time 01:00 — 00:10

American	Ingredients	Metric/Imperial
¾ lb	*Prawns*	350 g / 12 oz
5 tbsp	*Mayonnaise*	4 tbsp
Scant ¼ cup	*Tomato purée*	3 tbsp
1 tsp	*Worcester sauce*	1 tsp
½ tsp	*Tabasco sauce*	½ tsp
¼ cup	*Brandy*	50 ml / 2 fl oz
	Salt	
½	*Lemon*	½
	Lettuce leaves as required	
1 tsp	*Curry powder*	1 tsp
1 cup	*Whipped (double) cream*	225 ml / 8 fl oz
	Basil and radishes for garnish	

1. Toss the prawns into salted boiling water and drain them after 5 minutes. Allow to cool, remove shells.
2. Mix the mayonnaise, tomato purée, Worcester sauce, Tabasco sauce, brandy, salt and a little lemon juice carefully, then coat the prawns well.
3. Cover the bottom of a glass hors d'oeuvre dish with well-washed and dried lettuce leaves and arrange the prawns.
4. Mix the curry powder with the cream so that the result is an evenly colored sauce. Pour this sauce over the prawns arranged in the salad bowl.
5. Place in the refrigerator for 1 hour in the less cold zone. Just before serving, decorate the tops with fresh basil leaves and a few rosettes made from radishes.

Coppe di gamberetti alla marinara

Marine-Style Prawn Cups

00:50 — 00:40

American	Ingredients	Metric/Imperial
6	*Eggs*	6
1 lb	*Prawns*	450 g / 1 lb
1	*Carrot*	1
1	*Onion*	1
1	*Celery stalk*	1
1	*Bay leaf*	1
	Ground pepper	
½ tsp	*Vegetable extract*	½ tsp
	Salt	
6	*Medium-sized tomatoes*	6
2 tsp	*Basil*	2 tsp
1¼ cups	*Mayonnaise (see page 175)*	300 ml / ½ pint
1 tsp	*Worcester sauce*	1 tsp
2 tsp	*Tomato purée*	2 tsp
1 tsp	*Lemon juice*	1 tsp

1. Hard-cook (boil) the eggs, run cold water over the eggs before removing shells.
2. Cook the Dublin Bay prawns, placing them in the boiling water for 4 minutes and then drain. Put a carrot, an onion, a stalk of celery, a bay leaf, ground pepper in a saucepan, boil for about 30 minutes then strain the stock and let it cool. Return to a saucepan, add the vegetable extract and a pinch of salt, then the prawns and cook them for 3 minutes, before draining and placing on one side.
3. Prepare the tomatoes, cut them in half and turn them upside down in such a way that they lose the natural juice and a part of the seeds, slice them thickly.
4. Prepare some large cups, arrange the slices of tomato on the bottom and all around. Sprinkle with some finely-chopped basil.
5. Put the prawns in the centre and cover with chopped hard-cooked (boiled) eggs.
6. Make a mayonnaise, putting all the ingredients in the blender, add the Worcester sauce, blend a little more, then add the tomato purée and lemon juice, blend again. Pour the sauce over the prawns and put in the refrigerator for 30 minutes without chilling too much.

Gran misto

Spicy Grapefruit Seafood

00:30 Chilling time 02:00 — 00:03

American	Ingredients	Metric/Imperial
2	*Grapefruits*	2
1	*Slice of onion*	1
1	*Celery stalk*	1
1	*Bay leaf*	1
14 oz	*Fresh prawns*	400 g / 14 oz
	Salt and pepper	
1 cup	*Mayonnaise (see page 175)*	225 ml / 8 fl oz
1 tsp	*Mustard*	1 tsp
1	*Lemon*	1
4 tsp	*Caviar*	4 tsp
1 tbsp	*Butter*	1 tbsp
¼ lb	*Fresh cheese*	100 g / 4 oz
1 tsp	*Curry powder*	1 tsp
1	*Grated coconut*	1

1. Cut the grapefruit in half and with a sharp knife extract the pulp. Free the half segments from the white fibres and cut into cubes, taking care that the juice is not lost.
2. In a saucepan of cold water immerse the onion, the celery and the bay leaf, bring to boil, throw in the prawns and cook for 3 minutes. This step can be omitted if using cooked prawns. Drain and shell prawns.
3. Mix the mayonnaise with the mustard and dilute with lemon and grapefruit juice. Season with salt and pepper.
4. Add the prawns to the sauce with the cubes of grapefruit. Then fill halved grapefruit skins with mixture. Sprinkle each portion with 1 teaspoon of caviar.
5. To make coconut balls, place the butter in a bowl kept at room temperature with the fresh cheese. Mix well with a fork and then blend in the curry powder. When the mixture is thoroughly mixed, shape into little balls and roll them in freshly grated coconut. Place in the refrigerator for 2 hours before serving.
6. Arrange the halved grapefruit shells on 4 plates surrounded by coconut balls.

Insalata russa classica

Traditional Russian Salad

00:30 Cooling time 01:00 — 00:30

American	Ingredients	Metric/Imperial
2	*Carrots*	2
3 tbsp	*Frozen peas*	2 tbsp
2	*Potatoes*	2
1	*Celery stalk*	1
1	*Cooked beetroot*	1
1 cup	*Mayonnaise (see page 175)*	225 ml / 8 fl oz
¼ tsp	*Tabasco sauce*	¼ tsp
1 tbsp	*Tomato purée*	1 tbsp
8	*Prawns* or	8
4	*Artichokes (cooked or canned)*	4

1. Scrape the carrots and cut into small dice, put in cold salted water and bring to boil. When almost tender add the peas for the last 5 minutes.
2. Wash the potatoes in cold salted water and bring to the boil, simmer until cooked, drain. When cooled, remove the skins and cut into dice.
3. Remove the strings from the celery and cut into thin slices. Peel the skin from the cooked beetroot and cut into small dice. Place all the vegetables in a bowl and mix well.
4. Mix the mayonnaise with the tomato purée and Tabasco sauce and fold carefully into the vegetables to avoid breaking them down.
5. Decorate with cooked prawns or artichoke hearts and chill for 1 hour before serving.

Avocado ripieni

Stuffed Avocado Pears

00:20 — 00:00

American	Ingredients	Metric/Imperial
½ lb	*Dublin Bay prawns*	225 g / 8 oz
2	*Avocado pears*	2
1¼ cups	*Mayonnaise (see page 175)*	300 ml / ½ pint
1 tbsp	*Chopped parsley*	1 tbsp
3 tbsp	*Cognac*	2 tbsp
2	*Carrots*	2
2	*Eggs*	2
1 tbsp	*Capers*	1 tbsp

1. Cook the Dublin Bay prawns, allow to cool, remove shells. Alternatively use cooked prawns.
2. Wash the avocado pears, cut them lengthwise and remove stones. Scoop out some of the flesh from the fruit, mash and mix it with mayonnaise. Add chopped parsley and the cognac.
3. Pour the sauce into a sauceboat which is not made of metal.
4. Scrape and finely grate the carrots, fill the cavities of the avocados and arrange on a serving dish, surrounded with the Dublin Bay prawns.
5. On each halved avocado place half a hard-cooked (boiled) egg sliced lengthwise, brush with a little mayonnaise and sprinkle with a few chopped capers.
6. Serve with mayonnaise handed separately.

Avocado pears with prawns and mayonnaise

Sandwiches esotici

Whole Meal Avocado

00:15 00:00

American	Ingredients	Metric/Imperial
1 or 2	Avocado pears	1 or 2
5 tbsp	Mayonnaise	4 tbsp
1 tbsp	Lemon juice	1 tbsp
Scant ¼ cup	Soy (soya) sauce	3 tbsp
	Salt and pepper	
1 tbsp	Chopped parsley	1 tbsp
8 slices	Slices whole wheat (wholemeal) bread	8 slices

1. Cut avocado pear in half, take out the stone and remove the flesh with a spoon. Put the flesh in a bowl and add the mayonnaise, lemon, soy sauce and season with a pinch of salt, pepper and chopped parsley.
2. Beat ingredients thoroughly and spread the smooth mixture on slices of whole wheat bread, plain or toasted. Cut into strips.

Avocado saporito

Savory Avocado

00:20 00:00
Cooling time 00:10

American	Ingredients	Metric/Imperial
2	Ripe avocado pears	2
1	Lemon	1
2	Onions	2
1 tbsp	Vinegar	1 tbsp
½ lb	Goat's milk cheese	225 g / 8 oz
1 tbsp	Oil	1 tbsp
	Salt and pepper	

1. Cut the avocado in two lengthwise, remove the stones and sprinkle them with lemon juice to prevent them turning black.
2. Cut the peeled onions into very thin slices and put to soak in a little vinegar and water to allow them to become less pungent.
3. Mix the goat's milk cheese in bowl with oil, salt, pepper and the drained onions. Blend into a cream.
4. Fill the avocados with goat's milk cheese. Leave in the refrigerator for 10 minutes and serve.

Avocado in coppa

Avocado Pear in a Cup

00:30 00:00
Cooling time 02:00

American	Ingredients	Metric/Imperial
2	Ripe avocado pears	2
¼ lb	Gruyère cheese	100 g / 4 oz
¼ lb	Cooked ham in a single slice	100 g / 4 oz
2 oz	Smoked salmon	50 g / 2 oz
⅔ cup	Mayonnaise (see page 175)	150 ml / ¼ pint
3 tbsp	Coffee (single) cream	2 tbsp
¼ tsp	Paprika	¼ tsp
1	Small lettuce	1

1. Peel and cut the avocado pears, the cheese and cooked ham into very small dice. Cut the salmon into little pieces.
2. Place everything in a bowl and add the mayonnaise softened with the cream and flavored with the paprika. Mix gently.
3. Line 4 small dishes or wine glasses with choice washed and drained lettuce leaves and divide the mixture into each dish. Put in the refrigerator for 2 hours before serving.

Avocado in insalata

Avocado Pear in Salad

00:30 00:00

American	Ingredients	Metric/Imperial
4	Celery stalks	4
1	Lemon	1
2	Ripe avocado pears	2
2 oz	Fresh almonds, shelled	50 g / 2 oz
1	Lettuce	1
2	Hard-cooked (boiled) eggs	2
Scant ¼ cup	Oil	3 tbsp
1 tbsp	Wine vinegar	1 tbsp
	Salt and pepper	
3 tbsp	Coffee (single) cream	2 tbsp
	A small piece of horseradish root	
½ tsp	Tomato ketchup	½ tsp

1. Trim the celery and cut the stalks into matchstick slices. Peel the avocado pear and cut the flesh into small dice. Sprinkle with lemon juice.
2. Skin the almonds and halve them. Line 4 small plates with the leaves from the heart of the lettuce, arrange on them the celery, avocado and almonds and surround with segments of hard-cooked (boiled) eggs.
3. Mix oil, vinegar, salt and pepper and cream in a bowl, add the freshly grated horseradish, a dash of tomato ketchup and pour the well mixed sauce over the prepared salad.

Coppe di cozze

Mussel Cups

00:40 00:20
Cooling time 01:00

American	Ingredients	Metric/Imperial
3 lb	Mussels	1.5 kg / 3 lb
2	Small onions	2
1 oz	Parsley	1 oz / 25 g
⅔ cup	White wine	150 ml / ¼ pint
	Freshly ground black pepper	
1	Aspic cube	1
⅔ cup	Mayonnaise (see page 175)	150 ml / ¼ pint
1 tbsp	Cream	1 tbsp
½ tsp	Strong mustard	½ tsp
1	Lemon	1

Mussel cups

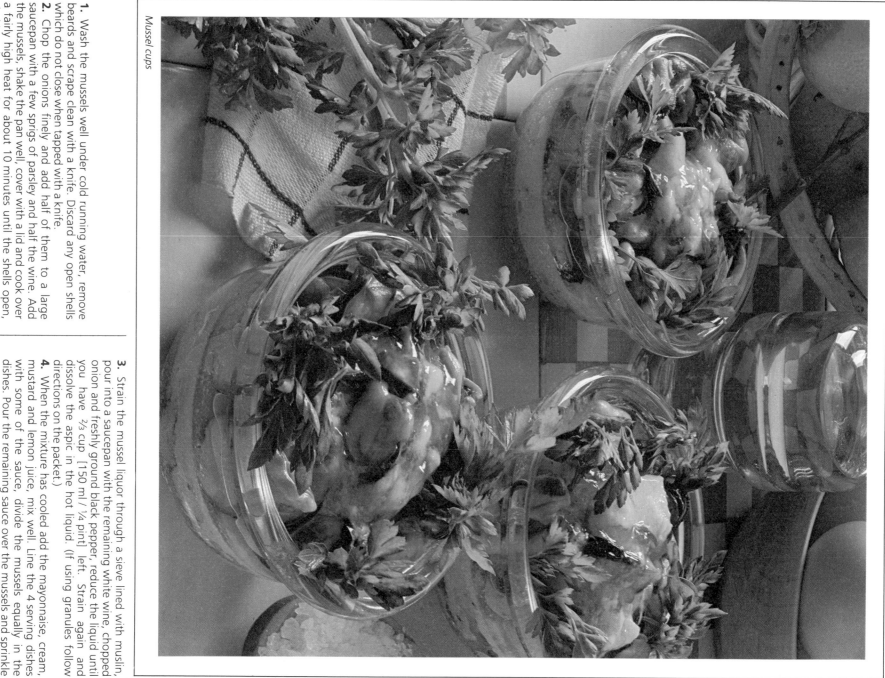

1. Wash the mussels well under cold running water, remove beards and scrape clean with a knife. Discard any open shells which do not close when tapped with a knife.
2. Chop the onions finely and add half of them to a large saucepan with a few sprigs of parsley and half the wine. Add the mussels, shake the pan well, cover with a lid and cook over a fairly high heat for about 10 minutes until the shells open, shaking the pan from time to time. Cool and remove the mussels from the shells.
3. Strain the mussel liquor through a sieve lined with muslin, pour into a saucepan with the remaining white wine, chopped onion and freshly ground black pepper, reduce the liquid until you have ⅔ cup [150 ml / ¼ pint] left. Strain again and dissolve the aspic in the hot liquid. (If using granules follow directions on the packet.)
4. When the mixture has cooled add the mayonnaise, cream, mustard and lemon juice, mix well. Line the 4 serving dishes with some of the sauce, divide the mussels equally in the dishes. Pour the remaining sauce over the mussels and sprinkle with chopped parsley. Refrigerate for at least 1 hour or until the sauce is set before serving.

Farfalline al salmone

Salmon Butterflies

00:30 00:25

American	Ingredients	Metric/Imperial
¼ cup	Butter	50 g / 2 oz
2 oz	Smoked salmon	50 g / 2 oz
1 cup	Single cream	225 ml / 8 fl oz
1 lb	Pasta butterflies	450 g / 1 lb

1. Melt the butter in a small saucepan, add the salmon, cut into very small pieces, leave to cook over a low heat until it absorbs the flavour and does not colour the butter.
2. Turn off the heat and add the cream.
3. Put the pasta to cook in boiling salted water, cook 'al dente', drain well, season with the salmon sauce. (Grated cheese should not be served with this dish.)

Tartine al salmone

Salmon Canapés

00:25 00:00

American	Ingredients	Metric/Imperial
1 cup	Mayonnaise (see page 175)	225 ml / 8 fl oz
8	Slices of bread	8
¼ cup	Butter	50 g / 2 oz
	Milk	
½ lb	Smoked salmon	225 g / 8 oz
1	Lemon	1

1. Prepare the mayonnaise and put on one side. Toast the bread, remove crusts and cut them into small rectangles. In the meantime soften all the butter with a little milk.
2. Slice the smoked salmon very thinly. Spread canapés with butter and arrange the slices of salmon on each canapé and place on the serving dish.
3. Garnish the canapés with the mayonnaise. Serve with lemon cut into wedges.

Insalata di bianchetti crudi

Salad of Whitebait

00:10 00:00
Standing time 02:00

American	Ingredients	Metric/Imperial
¾ lb	Whitebait (anchovy fry)	350 g / 12 oz
5 tbsp	Oil	4 tbsp
1	Lemon	1
	Salt and pepper	

1. Place the whitebait in a sieve with a very fine mesh and pass under cold running water. Drain very thoroughly, pat dry with kitchen paper, then tip into a glass or crockery bowl.
2. Beat oil with lemon juice, pepper and salt in a jug. Pour the seasoning over the raw whitebait and mix thoroughly with a wooden spoon.
3. Allow to stand for 2 hours in a cool place, then serve. Red sea-bream may be treated in the same way.

Antipasto di uova e salmone

Hors D'Oeuvre of Eggs and Salmon

00:40 00:10

American	Ingredients	Metric/Imperial
2 oz	Pickled gherkins	50 g / 2 oz
8	Eggs	8
¼ lb	Smoked salmon	100 g / 4 oz
	Salt and pepper	
	Paprika	
Few drops	Worcester sauce	Few drops
1	Fresh cucumber	1
3 tbsp	Oil	2 tbsp
1	Lemon	1
1 tbsp	Chopped parsley	1 tbsp

1. Wash the gherkins, cut them into fine slices.
2. Cook the eggs till hard-cooked (boiled), cool under running cold water. Shell the eggs, cut in half and extract the yolks, taking care not to break the whites.
3. Place the yolks in a mortar or food processor, add the pickled gherkins and 2 oz [50 g] of salmon. Pound well with seasoning. Add a pinch of paprika and a few drops of Worcester sauce and blend thoroughly.
4. Fill the hole in the centre of the egg whites with this mixture.
5. Slice the cucumber thinly and arrange in an earthenware bowl, add the remaining salmon. Season with oil and lemon juice mixed with salt and pepper.
6. Arrange the halved eggs on the cucumber and salmon, sprinkle with chopped parsley.

Aringhe alla canadese

Canadian-Style Herrings

00:20 00:07

American	Ingredients	Metric/Imperial
4	Medium-sized herrings, filleted	4
1 tbsp	Vinegar	1 tbsp
2	Large potatoes	2
2	Large apples	2
3 tbsp	Chopped parsley	2 tbsp
1 tbsp	Chives	1 tbsp
¼ tsp	Fennel seeds	¼ tsp
⅔ cup	Vinaigrette dressing (see page 179)	150 ml / ¼ pint

1. Put the filleted herrings in a large frying pan, cover the fish with water and 1 tablespoon vinegar, bring to the boil and simmer over a low heat for 5 minutes. Drain and remove the flesh from the skin and cut into squares.
2. Boil the potatoes in the skins in cold salted water, drain when cooked and remove the skins and cut into dice.
3. Peel the apples or leave skin as liked and cut into dice, the same size as the potatoes.
4. Mix the herrings, potatoes and apples in a bowl with parsley, chives and fennel seeds. Pour over the vinaigrette dressing, mix well and serve slightly chilled.

Little pastry triangles

Triangolini pasticciati

Little Pastry Triangles

00:15 00:10

American	Ingredients	Metric/Imperial
¾ lb	*Frozen puff pastry*	350 g / 12 oz
2 oz	*Black olives*	50 g / 2 oz
2 oz	*Anchovies*	50 g / 2 oz
2 oz	*Smoked salmon*	50 g / 2 oz
2 oz	*Cooked ham*	50 g / 2 oz
2 oz	*Fontina cheese*	50 g / 2 oz

1. Preheat the oven to 425°F / 210°C / Gas Mark 7.
2. Roll out the puff pastry to a thickness of ¼ in / 5 mm and cut out from it several pieces about 3¼ in / 8 cm square.
3. Divide the squares into two batches, place a little chopped black olives and half an anchovy fillet on one half. On the other half place a small slice of salmon. Top half the squares with a slice of cooked ham and the other half with fontina cheese. Fold the squares over diagonally so that they form triangles.
4. Wet a baking sheet, arrange the little triangles on it and cook for about 10 minutes. Serve hot.

Tortini di riso e tonno

Rice and Tuna Pies

00:30 00:50

American	Ingredients	Metric/Imperial
1¾ cups	*All purpose (plain) flour*	200 g / 7 oz
	Salt	
½ cup	*Milk*	125 ml / 4 fl oz
3 tbsp	*Oil*	2 tbsp
2 tbsp	*Butter*	25 g / 1 oz
1⅓ cups	*Rice*	250 g / 9 oz
7 oz	*Tuna in oil*	200 g / 7 oz
⅔ cup	*Stoned green olives*	100 g / 4 oz
1 oz	*Capers*	25 g / 1 oz
½	*Lemon*	½
1	*Egg*	1
⅓ cup	*Coffee (single) cream*	65 ml / 2½ fl oz

1. Preheat the oven to 400°F / 200°C / Gas Mark 6.
2. Sieve the flour with the salt. Make a well in the centre and add the milk, oil and butter. Prepare a smooth and even dough, allow to rest in the refrigerator for a few minutes.
3. Boil the rice until firm to the bite, drain it and cool.
4. Roll out the dough, stretch it until it is ⅛ in / 2½ mm thick. Butter the sides of 4 little molds and line them with the paste. Line with wax (greaseproof) paper. Place some dry baking beans on the bottom to prevent the paste swelling and losing shape during cooking.
5. Cook in the oven at a moderately high heat for 20 minutes.
6. Chop up the tuna fish and mix it with the rice, olives and capers, add lemon juice, beaten egg and cream.
7. Remove the baking beans from the molds and fill with rice and tuna mixture. Cook until golden at 325°F / 170°C / Gas Mark 3. Serve the pies hot or cold.

Fantasia alla recchelina

Recchelina Fancy

00:60
Standing time 02:00
Serves 6–8
00:30

American	Ingredients	Metric/Imperial
¾ lb	*Squid*	350 g / 12 oz
1	*Onion*	1
1	*Carrot*	1
1	*Bay leaf*	1
2	*Cloves*	2
4	*Peppercorns*	4
⅓ cup	*Dry white wine or vinegar*	4 tbsp
1½ lb	*Clams*	700 g / 1½ lb
1½ lb	*Mussels*	700 g / 1½ lb
2 cups	*Peeled prawns*	350 g / 12 oz
1	*Garlic clove*	1
3 tbsp	*Chopped parsley*	2 tsbp
½	*Red sweet pepper*	½
½	*Yellow sweet pepper*	½
Scant ¼ cup	*Oil*	3 tbsp
¼ tsp	*Cayenne pepper*	¼ tsp
1	*Lemon*	1

1. Rinse and drain the squid several times, cut into thin strips and place in an ovenproof casserole together with the peeled onion. Cut the carrot into four strips, add to the casserole with the bay leaf, cloves and peppercorns and cover with the vinegar or white wine. Leave to simmer over a moderate heat until the squid are cooked and the liquid reduced. Allow to cool in the liquid.
2. Clean the clams and the mussels, by running under cold water then remove beards and scrape shells.
3. Heat a little wine with a crushed clove of garlic and 1 tbsp chopped parsley. Add the clams and mussels and shake over a moderate heat until shells open. When the shells open, cool slightly then take out the molluscs one by one and put them in a glass salad-bowl.
4. Add the cooked squid, the peeled prawns, the red sweet pepper and yellow sweet pepper cut into dice to the salad bowl. Add 2 tablespoons of cooking liquid from the squid and from the clams and mussels. Season the fish salad with the chopped parsley, and the oil, a pinch of cayenne pepper and juice of lemon mixed together. Leave to stand in a cool place for 2 hours before serving.

Antipasto alla contadina

Peasant-Style Hors D'Oeuvre

00:60 Cooling time 02:30 — 00:00

American	Ingredients	Metric/Imperial
3 oz	Cooked tongue, thickly sliced	75 g / 3 oz
3 oz	Cooked ham, thickly sliced	75 g / 3 oz
3 oz	Cooked breast of chicken	75 g / 3 oz
1	Head of celery	1
1	Artichoke, cooked	1
1 cup	Mayonnaise (see page 175)	225 ml / 8 fl oz
	Lettuce leaves	
1 tbsp	Aspic	1 tbsp
2	Eggs	2
4	Gherkins	4
8	Black olives,	8

1. Slice the tongue and ham into matchstick pieces. Chop the chicken meat into very small pieces.
2. Chop the inner part of a head of celery finely and the artichoke with the hard leaves removed.
3. Mix the mayonnaise and put everything in a bowl. Place in the refrigerator for 2 hours.
4. Line an oval serving dish with washed and drained lettuce leaves, tip the chilled ingredients over the lettuce leaves, then coat everything with a light covering of cooled aspic.
5. Return to the refrigerator. Just before serving, hard-cook (boil) two eggs, cool and cut them into slices. Before serving, decorate the top of the salad with the eggs, olives and gherkins as desired.

Antipasto di riso 'pallino'

Rice Balls Hors D'Oeuvre

00:20 Chilling time 00:30 — 00:30

American	Ingredients	Metric/Imperial
⅔ cup	Risotto rice	100 g / 4 oz
1 cup	Ground (minced) beef	225 g / 8 oz
½ cup	Grated cheese	50 g / 2 oz
	Salt and pepper	
2	Eggs	2
1	Small onion	1
1 tbsp	Oil	1 tbsp
2½ cups	Tomato sauce (see page 171)	600 ml / 1 pint

1. Cook the rice for half the usual cooking time, drain and rinse with cold water.
2. Tip the rice into a bowl and mix with the beef, cheese and seasoning. Chop the onion finely and sauté in the oil until transparent. Add to the rice mixture.
3. Blend together with beaten egg. Chill the mixture for 30 minutes then form into egg-shaped balls.
4. Place the rice balls in a pan with the tomato sauce and simmer for 20 minutes. This dish can be served hot or cold.

Antipasto di lesso marinato

Hors D'Oeuvre of Marinated Boiled Meat

00:40 Standing time 04:00 — 00:00

American	Ingredients	Metric/Imperial
1 lb	Cold left-over boiled or roast meat	450 g / 1 lb
1 oz	Parsley	25 g / 1 oz
2	Garlic cloves	2
1	Small onion	1
1 tbsp	Capers	1 tbsp
⅓ cup	Oil	4 tbsp
	Salt and pepper	
2	Pickled gherkins	2
⅓ cup	Green olives	50 g / 2 oz
1	Egg yolk	1
2 tbsp	Wine vinegar	1½ tbsp
2	Anchovies	2

1. Prepare the left-over meat by removing all the fat, cut into small cubes. Place in an earthenware dish.
2. Chop the parsley and crush cloves of garlic, mix with the meat. Cut a small onion into rings, arrange over the meat.
3. Wash and chop the capers and add to the meat. Season well, add a little oil and mix thoroughly. Allow to stand in the refrigerator for 4 hours. Just before serving, mix finely chopped pickled gherkins, olives, the vinegar and egg yolk with the chopped anchovies and add to the meat. Serve slightly chilled.

Pâté di fegato 

Liver Pâté

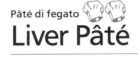

00:30 Chilling time 02:00 — 00:10

American	Ingredients	Metric/Imperial
⅔ cup	Butter	150 g / 5 oz
1	Medium onion	1
5 oz	Calf's liver or chicken liver	150 g / 5 oz
¼ tsp	Thyme	¼ tsp
	Salt and pepper	
3 tsp	Brandy	2 tsp
½ cup	Bread crumbs	25 g / 1 oz
3 tbsp	Marsala	2 tbsp

1. Use butter at room temperature, cream in a bowl until soft.
2. Peel and finely chop the onion. Heat half the butter in a pan, add the onion and cook for 4 minutes over a low heat.
3. Slice the liver into strips, add to the onion with the thyme and continue cooking over low heat for a few minutes until liver is cooked, then add seasoning and brandy.
4. Make fresh bread crumbs in a blender or food processor and moisten with the marsala.
5. Blend the liver mixture and bread crumbs in a blender or food processor. Turn into the bowl with the creamed butter and mix well until smooth. Scrape into a dish and smooth the top, chill in the refrigerator for 2 hours. Garnish with a sprig of thyme or parsley.
6. Serve with hot toast.

Crocchette di pollo

Chicken Croquettes

00:30 00:20

American	Ingredients	Metric/Imperial
1 lb	*Cooked chicken*	*450 g / 1 lb*
1½ cups	*Mushrooms*	*150 g / 5 oz*
1	*Lemon*	*1*
¼ cup	*Butter*	*50 g / 2 oz*
½ cup	*Flour*	*50 g / 2 oz*
1 cup	*Milk*	*225 ml / 8 fl oz*
	Salt and pepper	
2	*Yolks*	*2*
1	*Whole egg*	*1*
2 tsp	*Olive oil*	*2 tsp*
½ cup	*Bread crumbs*	*50 g / 2 oz*
1 cup	*Oil for frying*	*225 ml / 8 fl oz*

1. Remove bones and skin from the chicken and mince the flesh finely.
2. Clean the mushrooms and cut into very fine slices and sprinkle with lemon juice.
3. In a saucepan melt the butter, add the flour, mix to a roux with a wooden spoon and moisten with the milk; sprinkle with salt and pepper according to taste and tip in the minced chicken and mushrooms.
4. Cook until the mixture is thick, stirring to avoid sticking. Remove from the heat and bind with the 2 egg yolks before cooling. (The sauce will be very thick.)
5. Using floured hands prepare medium-sized croquettes. Beat the egg with the olive oil and immerse the croquettes in the egg and oil, then in the bread crumbs. Put 4 croquettes in a pan of hot oil, browning them on both sides. Drain on a sheet of absorbent paper. Fry next batch when oil has reheated. Serve crisp and hot.

Antipasto alla greca

Greek-Style Hors D'Oeuvre

00:20 00:22
Serves 4–6

American	Ingredients	Metric/Imperial
2 lb	*Small leeks*	*1 kg / 2 lb*
¼ cup	*Butter*	*50 g / 2 oz*
	Salt and pepper	
2	*Eggs*	*2*
2	*Lemons*	*2*

1. Preheat the oven to 300°F / 150°C / Gas Mark 2.
2. Trim and wash the leeks, cut in half. Melt the butter in a large frying pan and cook the leeks over a low heat to prevent browning for 6 minutes.
3. Place a sheet of foil in an ovenproof dish and arrange the leeks on top. Season with salt and pepper.
4. Beat the eggs with the lemon juice and pour over the leeks. Close the foil parcel and cook in the oven for 15 minutes.

Cook's tip: if using large old leeks, it is better to blanch in boiling water for 5 minutes and drain well before cooking in the butter.

Pâté casalingo

Country Pâté

00:30 00:12
Chilling time 04:00

American	Ingredients	Metric/Imperial
1	*Onion*	*1*
1	*Garlic clove*	*1*
½ lb	*Calf's liver*	*225 g / 8 oz*
¼ lb	*Raw ham*	*100 g / 4 oz*
⅔ cup	*Butter*	*150 g / 5 oz*
3 tbsp	*Sherry or marsala*	*2 tbsp*
1	*Slice of bread*	*1*
3 tbsp	*Milk*	*2 tbsp*
	Salt and pepper	
1	*Truffle (optional)*	*1*

1. Peel and chop the onion and crush the garlic clove.
2. Wash and chop the liver and ham into strips.
3. Melt 4 tbsp [50 g / 2 oz] butter in a frying pan and cook the onion and garlic for 4 minutes, add the liver and ham and continue cooking over a low heat for about 8 minutes. Add the sherry or marsala for the last 2 minutes of cooking. Allow to cool.
4. Pass the liver and onion mixture through a blender, food processor or mincer little by little with bread which has been soaked in the milk and squeezed.
5. Cream the remaining butter in a bowl and mix with the liver, seasoning well.
6. Place half the mixture in a china or earthenware dish and spread with sliced truffle, top with the other half of the mixture. Chill for about 4 hours before serving with toast or crusty bread.

Tartellette al foie gras

Foie Gras Tartlets

00:60 00:00

American	Ingredients	Metric/Imperial
½ lb	*Goose liver pâté*	*225 g / 8 oz*
4 tbsp	*Butter*	*50 g / 2 oz*
1 tbsp	*Cognac*	*1 tbsp*
8	*Slices of bread*	*8*
¼ lb	*Cooked ham cut into 2 slices*	*100 g / 4 oz*
	Radishes and mushrooms in oil, as desired	
1 cup	*Aspic*	*225 ml / 8 fl oz*

1. Cream the goose liver pâté in a bowl with the butter and cognac until smooth. Spread the creamed pâté over the slices of crustless bread, cut into 2 or 4 pieces depending on the size of the bread.
2. With a small cutter cut flower-shapes from the ham, one per savory. Place a flower of ham in the centre of each piece of bread. On the 'petals' of the ham flowers arrange slices of radish, alternated with slices of mushroom in oil.
3. Put the remaining pâté cream in a forcing bag and pipe around savories to form a border around the edge.
4. Arrange the pâté savories on a serving dish. They may be coated with aspic for special occasions. Allow aspic to cool and start thickening. Brush lightly over piping and run a little aspic inside each border.

Uova capricciose

Tomato Egg Toadstools

00:30 00:10

American	Ingredients	Metric/Imperial
6	*Eggs*	6
1 cup	*Mayonnaise (see page 175)*	225 ml / 8 fl oz
3	*Red pear-shaped tomatoes*	3
10	*Sprigs of parsley*	10
	Small pieces of pickled red and yellow pepper	
	Pickles as desired	

1. Prick the eggs and place in the cold water, bring to the boil and simmer for 10 minutes until hard-cooked (boiled). Place the eggs in the saucepan under running cold water and then remove shells, removing a slice from the bottom of each one to make them stand up.
2. Pour the mayonnaise onto the bottom of the serving dish and stand the eggs in it, at a distance from each other. Slice the pear-shaped tomatoes in half, remove their pips and place a halved tomato as a 'little cap' on each standing egg.
3. Chop the parsley roughly and place sprigs on the bed of mayonnaise, then beside each sprig place a small piece of yellow or red pepper to look like flowers.
4. Pipe some dot of mayonnaise on the tomato caps to simulate the spots on toadstools. Decorate according to taste with pickles and keep in a cool place until ready to serve.

Mousse ai funghi

Mushroom Cream

00:20 00:25
Cooling time 01:00

American	Ingredients	Metric/Imperial
3 cups	*Mushrooms*	300 g / 11 oz
1	*Small bunch of parsley*	1
2	*Garlic cloves*	2
1 ½ cups	*Butter*	275 g / 10 oz
¼ cup	*Brandy*	50 ml / 2 fl oz
½ cup	*Grated cheese*	50 g / 2 oz
	Nutmeg	

1. Wash and dry mushrooms thoroughly then slice thinly. Finely chop the parsley, crush the garlic and mix together.
2. Melt ½ cup [100 g / 4 oz] butter in a large frying pan on a low heat taking care not to let it brown. As soon as the butter is melted, add the mushrooms and the chopped parsley, mixing with a wooden spoon.
3. Cook for 5 minutes, then pour in the brandy, stir until the liquid has evaporated. Remove from the heat. Add the cheese working it in carefully to obtain a smooth mixture. Leave to cool.
4. Put the remaining in a bowl and using a wooden spoon, beat vigorously until it becomes a smooth cream. Add a pinch of nutmeg and then gradually add the mushroom mixture stirring all the time. Mix until smooth and put into an earthenware dish and refrigerate. Serve with hot toast.

Teste di funghi farcite

Stuffed Mushrooms

00:30 00:35

American	Ingredients	Metric/Imperial
8	*Medium-sized mushrooms*	8
5 tbsp	*Olive oil*	4 tbsp
2	*Garlic cloves*	2
1 tbsp	*Chopped parsley*	1 tbsp
	Salt and pepper	
¼ tsp	*Oregano*	¼ tsp

1. Preheat the oven to 375°F / 190°C / Gas Mark 5. Remove the mushroom stalks and wipe the caps with a damp cloth. Pour half the oil into a frying pan and arrange the mushrooms in it, the underside facing up. Cook lightly.
2. Scrape the stalks, chop and add to the crushed garlic and chopped parsley. Season with salt and pepper and mix the ingredients together thoroughly. Add a trickle of olive oil if necessary.
3. Stuff the mushroom caps with this mixture, pour over a little oil, sprinkle with oregano and put in a moderately hot oven for 30 minutes.

Tortiera di patate e funghi

Potato and Mushroom Pie

00:60 01:00

American	Ingredients	Metric/Imperial
2 lb	*Potatoes*	1 kg / 2 lb
3 tbsp	*Oil*	2 tbsp
2	*Garlic cloves*	2
3 ½ cups	*Mushrooms*	400 g / 14 oz
6 tbsp	*Butter*	75 g / 3 oz
1	*Large chicken breast*	1
	Salt and pepper	
¼ tsp	*Chopped fresh rosemary*	¼ tsp
¼ tsp	*Sage*	¼ tsp
5 tbsp	*Dry white wine*	4 tbsp
½ cup	*Stock*	125 ml / 4 fl oz
3 tbsp	*Milk*	2 tbsp
2	*Egg yolks*	2
1 tbsp	*Bread crumbs*	1 tbsp

1. Preheat the oven to 350°F / 180°C / Gas Mark 4.
2. Peel and boil the potatoes in salted water. Meanwhile prepare the filling. Pour the oil into a large pan and cook 1 crushed clove of garlic for 2 minutes.
3. Wash, dry and cut the mushrooms into thin slices. Add these to the oil with the garlic. Cook the mushrooms for a while without covering the pan, adding 5 tablespoons boiling water if necessary.
4. In a small pan melt the butter and brown the chicken breast, add salt and pepper, the rosemary and sage and pour in a little white wine. Add the stock and continue simmering.
5. When the potatoes are cooked, mash them in a vegetable mill or ricer (do not use a food processor). Put the purée in another saucepan and add a knob of butter, a little milk and 2 egg yolks. Mix thoroughly and adjust the seasoning.

6. Butter a pie dish and sprinkle with dried bread crumbs before lining it with the potato. Cut up the chicken and mix with the mushrooms and place the mixture in the centre of the pie. Lightly season with salt and pepper and put in a hot oven for 30 minutes. Serve piping hot, cut into slices.

Verdure e funghi saltati in padella

Sautéed Vegetables and Mushrooms

00:30 Serves 6 — 00:25

American	Ingredients	Metric/Imperial
1 lb	*New potatoes*	*500 g / 1 lb*
¼ lb	*Tender young carrots*	*100 g / 4 oz*
2	*Onions*	*2*
6 cups	*Fresh mushrooms*	*650 g / 1½ lb*
5 tbsp	*Butter*	*65 g / 2½ oz*
	Salt	
	Cayenne pepper	

1. Peel the potatoes and dice them into pieces the thickness of an olive. Boil the potatoes and carrots.
2. Finely chop the onions. Wash, dry and slice mushrooms.
3. Heat half the butter in a frying pan and sauté the onions and mushrooms for a few minutes over a low heat, taking care not to brown the onions.
4. Remove the mushrooms and onions from the pan to a plate.
5. Add the remaining butter to the pan and sauté the potatoes and carrots for 5-6 minutes on a medium heat. Add the onions and mushrooms, season with salt and cayenne pepper. Cook on a low heat for another 10 minutes and serve with crusty bread.

Puré di champignons

Mushroom Purée

00:20 — 00:20

American	Ingredients	Metric/Imperial
2 lb	*Fresh mushrooms*	*1 kg / 2 lb*
½ cup	*Butter or margarine*	*100 g / 4 oz*
1¼ cups	*Béchamel sauce (see page 162)*	*300 ml / ½ pint*
½ cup	*Coffee (single) cream*	*125 ml / 4 fl oz*
	Salt and pepper	
1 tsp	*Nutmeg*	*1 tsp*

1. Remove the mushroom stalks (these can be used for a sauce), wash the caps and dry with kitchen paper. Only peel if using wild mushrooms.
2. Chop the mushrooms finely or make into fine slivers by passing through a food mill or food processor.
3. Heat ¼ cup [50 g / 2 oz] butter in a saucepan, raise the heat, add the mushrooms and brown, stirring all the time until most of the moisture has evaporated. Take care that they do not stick to the pan.
4. Mix the béchamel sauce and the cream together, add to the mushrooms, lower the heat, allow to reduce for a further 5 minutes. Season with salt, pepper and nutmeg. Remove from the heat, cut remaining butter into small pieces and stir vigorously into the purée with a wooden spoon until it is frothy. Serve with toast or cold as part of an hors d'oeuvre.

Spuntino alla turca 

Turkish Cucumber

00:15 — 00:00

American	Ingredients	Metric/Imperial
2	*Small cucumbers*	*2*
1¼ cups	*Natural yogurt*	*300 ml / ½ pint*
	Salt and pepper	
2 tsp	*Fresh mint*	*2 tsp*

1. Remove the peel in alternate strips from the cucumbers and cut into ⅛ in / 3 mm thick slices (the slices must be crunchy to bite).
2. Dress the cucumber with natural yogurt, mixing well, add salt and pepper. Freshly chopped mint can be added for extra flavor.

Porcini in gratella

Broiled [Grilled] Mushrooms

00:15 — 00:11

American	Ingredients	Metric/Imperial
8	*Large open capped mushrooms*	*8*
1 tbsp	*Oil*	*1 tbsp*
2 tbsp	*Butter*	*25 g / 1 oz*
1	*Garlic clove*	*1*
1 tbsp	*Chopped parsley*	*1 tbsp*

1. It is most important to use very fresh whole mushrooms for this recipe. Choose largish open mushrooms with good-sized caps. Wash and dry with kitchen paper, remove the stalks (these can used for a bolognese sauce or risotto).
2. Brush with oil and arrange under hot broiler (grill). Cook for 5 minutes each side.
3. When cooked, arrange on an oval serving dish with the underside facing up. Mix the butter with the crushed clove of garlic and chopped parsley, spread on the mushrooms, flash under the hot broiler for 1 minute.

Quadratini di spinaci

Little Squares of Spinach

00:45 — 00:15

American	Ingredients	Metric/Imperial
1 lb	*Spinach*	*500 g / 1 lb*
3 tbsp	*Olive oil*	*2 tbsp*
	Salt and pepper	
2 cups	*All purpose (plain) flour*	*225 g / ½ lb*
2	*Eggs*	*2*
1 ¼ cups	*Oil for frying*	*300 ml / ½ pint*

1. Wash and cook the spinach in a little water, drain well, arrange on a plate and cover it with the oil, and a sprinkling of salt and freshly ground pepper.
2. In a bowl sieve the flour with a little salt, add two beaten eggs, work into the flour gradually, add some lukewarm water until you obtain a mixture which is smooth and not sticky.
3. Roll out the paste into a layer which is not too thin, cut out some pieces about 2 in / 5 cm square.
4. Fill each square with the seasoned spinach and damp the edges with water or egg, fold over the edges of the paste. Heat the oil and fry the little pastries until well browned. Serve hot.

Pere e peperoni

Pears and Peppers

00:10 — 00:00

American	Ingredients	Metric/Imperial
3	*Sweet peppers of different colors*	*3*
2	*Ripe Williams pears*	*2*
5 tbsp	*Oil*	*4 tbsp*
1	*Lemon*	*1*
	Salt and pepper	

1. Deseed the peppers and cut into thin strips.
2. Peel the pears, cut in half and remove cores. Cut into matchstick pieces.
3. Arrange the peppers and pears in a dish in layers.
4. Put the oil, juice of one lemon, salt and pepper in a screw-top jar and shake well to blend.
5. Pour over the salad and serve immediately.

Mousse dei Balcani

Balkan Mousse

00:25 Cooling time 01:00 — 00:00

American	Ingredients	Metric/Imperial
1 cup	*Mayonnaise (see page 175)*	*225 ml / 8 fl oz*
2	*Scallion (spring onions)*	*2*
3 tbsp	*Caviar or lump fish*	*2 tbsp*
1 ¼ cups	*Cream*	*300 ml / ½ pint*
¼ tsp	*Paprika*	*¼ tsp*
2 tsp	*Gelatin*	*2 tsp*
Scant ¼ cup	*Boiling water*	*3 tbsp*
1	*Lemon*	*1*

1. Make up a well flavored mayonnaise, add scallions, finely chopped, with caviar or lump fish.
2. Whip the cream and fold it very carefully into the mixture of mayonnaise, along with the paprika.
3. Prepare gelatin by sprinkling on to the boiling water. Make sure that it is dissolved by standing the cup in boiling water. Allow to cool slightly.
4. Fold gelatin into mixture and pour into a 2½ cup [600 ml / 1 pint] mold.
5. Place the mold in the coldest part of the refrigerator. This is a very delicate hors d'oeuvre which you must prepare in advance. Serve with wedges of lemon.

Strisce colorate

Hot Rainbow Vegetables

00:30 — 01:00

American	Ingredients	Metric/Imperial
1	*Sweet yellow pepper*	*1*
1	*Sweet green pepper*	*1*
2	*Onions*	*2*
1	*Eggplant (aubergine)*	*1*
2	*Gourds*	*2*
4	*Tomatoes*	*4*
	Salt and pepper	
5 tbsp	*Oil*	*4 tbsp*

1. Preheat the oven to 325°F / 170°C / Gas Mark 3.
2. Deseed the peppers and cut into thin strips, keeping the colors separate.
3. Peel the onions and cut into thin rings. Wash and cut the eggplant and gourds into thin strips. Skin the tomatoes, cut in half, remove seeds and then divide into thin segments.
4. Fill an oven-to-table dish using the strips of vegetables, one for each kind, alternating the colors. For example the first strip of onion, the second of sweet green pepper, the third of gourd, then one of tomato, the fifth of eggplant, and finally, one of sweet yellow pepper.
5. Sprinkle with salt and pepper, pour the oil over the vegetables, cover with foil and cook for 1 hour until vegetables are fairly dry.
6. Serve the vegetables hot or cold.

Panini ripieni al formaggio

Hot Cheese Rolls

00:10 — 00:08

American	Ingredients	Metric/Imperial
8	*Bread rolls*	*8*
1	*Large mozzarella cheese*	*1*
3 oz	*Cooked ham*	*75 g / 3 oz*
	Butter	

1. Preheat the oven to 350°F / 180°C / Gas Mark 4.
2. Make a hole on the top of the rolls and remove the soft crumb part, without breaking the crust.
3. Cut the mozzarella into cubes and chop the ham into small cubes. Fill each roll with the mozzarella, ham and a little butter. Place the rolls on a buttered baking sheet in the oven for 8 minutes. Take out of the oven when the mozzarella begins to become stringy, serve at once.

Rainbow vegetables

Pizzette al basilico

Little Pizzas with Basil

00:05 00:07

American	Ingredients	Metric/Imperial
1 tbsp	*Milk*	1 tbsp
Scant ¼ cup	*Tomato purée*	3 tbsp
	A few sprigs of basil	
8	*Slices of bread*	8
4	*Small processed cheeses*	4
	Freshly ground pepper	

1. Preheat the oven to 400°F / 200°C / Gas Mark 6.
2. Mix a little milk with tomato purée and half the chopped basil.
3. Remove crusts from bread and spread with cheese, put on a baking sheet in a moderately hot oven for 5-7 minutes. Serve sprinkled with chopped basil and freshly ground black pepper.

Pizzette rapide

Quick Pizzas

00:10 00:15

American	Ingredients	Metric/Imperial
8	*Slices of bread*	8
3 tbsp	*Oil*	2 tbsp
8	*Slices large tomato*	8
	Salt and pepper	
1 tsp	*Oregano*	1 tsp
8	*Slices of cheese*	8
8	*Anchovy fillets (optional)*	8

1. Preheat the oven to 425°F / 210°C / Gas Mark 7.
2. Cut the crust from the slices of bread, sprinkle with a few drops of oil, and on each slice place a slice of tomato, a pinch of salt and pepper, sprinkle with oregano and top with a slice of cheese which will melt easily.
3. Arrange the little pizzas on a baking sheet greased with oil and put in a very hot oven for a quarter of an hour. If liked add 2 halved anchovy fillets to each slice.

Little pizzas with basil

Pizzette di San Gennaro

Little Pizzas from San Gennaro

01:30 00:10

American	Ingredients	Metric/Imperial
½ lb	*Pizza dough (see page 156)*	225 g / 8 oz
3 tbsp	*Oil*	2 tbsp
3	*Tomatoes*	3
4	*Anchovies*	4
¼ cup	*Green olives*	40 g / 1½ oz
	Freshly ground pepper	
1 tsp	*Oregano*	1 tsp

1. Prepare a dough bread and allow to rise. Roll it out thinly and once it has risen, cut out some rounds with a 3 in / 7.5 cm cutter or glass.
2. Preheat the oven to 450°F / 220°C / Gas Mark 8.
3. Brush each round with oil and place on an oiled baking sheet.
4. Slice the tomatoes and arrange on the round with anchovy fillets and green olives. Sprinkle with fresh oregano, if possible, and brush over with oil.
5. Cook in a hot oven for 8-10 minutes. Serve hot.

Toast con germogli e salsa di soia

Toasted Sandwiches with Bean Sprouts and Soya

00:10 00:15

American	Ingredients	Metric/Imperial
2	*Eggs*	2
¼ cup	*Flour*	25 g / 1 oz
8-12	*Slices of bread*	8-12
½ cup	*Oil*	125 ml / 4 fl oz
1	*Garlic clove*	1
	Paprika	
4 cups	*Bean sprouts*	225 g / 8 oz
¼ lb	*Fontina cheese*	100 g / 4 oz
¼ lb	*Lean cooked ham*	100 g / 4 oz
	Soy sauce	

1. Beat the eggs in a plate and sieve the flour on to another plate.
2. Dip each slice of bread in egg and flour, coating each side. Heat three-quarters of the oil in a frying pan and fry the bread over a good medium heat until golden brown both sides. Remove the bread, arrange on the serving dish and season.
3. In another frying pan heat the rest of the oil and sauté a clove of garlic with the paprika and bean sprouts.
4. Make toasted sandwiches with the slices arranged on the plate, placing on top of each other and filling them with a slice of fontina, a slice of ham, the bean sprouts and a sprinkle of soy sauce.
5. Before serving reheat for 1 minute in the oven.

Tramezzini al gorgonzola e noci

Sandwiches with Gorgonzola and Walnuts

00:10 00:00

American	Ingredients	Metric/Imperial
8	*Slices of bread*	8
5 tbsp	*Butter*	65 g / 2½ oz
	Salt	
7 oz	*Gorgonzola cheese*	200 g / 7 oz
10	*Walnuts*	10
¼ lb	*Cooked ham*	100 g / 4 oz

1. Cut some triangles of medium sliced bread, spread them with butter worked with a pinch of salt and some gorgonzola, then sprinkle on a few chopped walnuts.
2. Top with a slice of cooked ham, a little more gorgonzola, and another of chopped walnuts. Two triangles may be sandwiched together or leave them single.

Pane ripieno

Baked Filled Bread

00:20 00:15

American	Ingredients	Metric/Imperial
8	*Slices of bread*	8
¼ lb	*Cooked ham*	100 g / 4 oz
¼ lb	*Fresh mozzarella cheese*	100 g / 4 oz
2	*Eggs*	2
3 tbsp	*Milk*	2 tbsp
	Salt and pepper	
2 tbsp	*Butter*	25 g / 1 oz

1. Preheat the oven to 400°F / 200°C / Gas Mark 6.
2. Slice a sandwich loaf, discarding the crusts. Cut the cooked ham into thin strips and slice the mozzarella finely.
3. Separately, beat eggs with milk, salt and pepper. Then butter a baking tin with sides. Arrange in it a layer of bread dipped in egg, one of ham and mozzarella, another of bread and so on until the ingredients are used up. Pour over the remaining egg, finish with dabs of butter and cook in the oven for about 15 minutes.

Piadine al pomodoro

Tomato Rolls

These 'piadine' rolls are found near the Adriatic and are popular seaside fare.

00:10 | 00:00

American	Ingredients	Metric/Imperial
4	*Piadine (type of roll)*	*4*
1 lb	*Creamy soft cheese*	*225 g / 8 oz*
1 tbsp	*Chopped parsley*	*1 tbsp*
¼ lb	*Chopped cooked ham*	*100 g / 4 oz*
2 or 3	*Tomatoes*	*2 or 3*
	Salt	
2 *4*	*Gherkins or* *Fresh scallion (spring onion)*	*2* *4*

1. Use some long rolls, cut in half and fill with a mixture of cream cheese blended with chopped parsley and chopped ham. Top with slices of tomato, a little salt and a few rounds of gherkin or, if preferred, fresh scallions.

Tartine rustiche

Rustic Canapés

00:15 Standing time 01:00 | 00:00

American	Ingredients	Metric/Imperial
1 tbsp	*Parsley*	*1 tbsp*
1 tsp	*Basil*	*1 tsp*
½ tsp	*Bay leaf*	*½ tsp*
5 oz	*Fresh ricotta cheese*	*150 g / 5 oz*
4	*Slices of whole wheat (wholemeal) bread*	*4*
2 tbsp	*Butter*	*25 g / 1 oz*
	Freshly ground pepper	

1. Finely chop the parsley, basil and bay leaf. Use a wooden spoon to work the ricotta and the chopped herbs together until it is a soft cream, then put it in the refrigerator and allow to stand for at least 1 hour.

2. Toast four thick slices of whole wheat or sandwich bread. Serve the bread very hot, spread with butter and then ricotta mixture with freshly ground pepper.

Tartine di pollo

Chicken Canapés

00:45 | 00:00

American	Ingredients	Metric/Imperial
¾ lb	*Left over boiled or roasted chicken*	*350 g / 12 oz*
1 cup	*Mayonnaise (see page 175)*	*225 ml / 8 fl oz*
1 tsp	*Pale mustard*	*1 tsp*
	Salt	
8	*Slices of bread*	*8*
8 oz	*Can of asparagus*	*225g / 8 oz*
	Small crisp lettuce leaves	

1. Bone the chicken and remove the skin. Prepare mayonnaise and mix with 1 teaspoonful of pale mustard and salt.
2. Cut the chicken into small pieces and season it with the sauce.
3. Lightly toast the slices of bread, remove crusts, then place on each slice some heaped chicken with plenty of sauce.
4. To garnish, use some well drained canned asparagus. Place the chicken canapés on a large serving dish, decorate around them with asparagus alternated with small crisp lettuce leaves.

Tartine fantasia

Fancy Canapés

00:15 plus 01:00 starting time | 00:10

American	Ingredients	Metric/Imperial
3	*Eggs*	*3*
6 tbsp	*Butter*	*75 g / 3 oz*
¾ cup	*Grated parmesan cheese*	*75 g / 3 oz*
4 tsp	*Mustard*	*3 tsp*
	Salt and pepper	
¼ lb	*Cooked or raw ham*	*100 g / 4 oz*
1 tbsp	*Chopped parsley*	*1 tbsp*
1 tbsp	*Capers*	*1 tbsp*
1 small	*Cucumber*	*1 small*
8	*Slices of bread*	*8*
	Pickles	

1. Hard-cook (boil) 2 eggs and rinse in cold water before removing shells.
2. Cream the butter in a bowl until it becomes foamy, then add the grated parmesan, 1 raw egg yolk, a little mustard, salt, pepper and some ham chopped together with parsley, capers and cucumbers. Thoroughly blend the ingredients then spread on the slices of bread, which can be cut into squares, rectangles or triangles.
3. Garnish each slice with a little piece of hard-cooked egg and pickles. Before serving, refrigerate for at least 1 hour.

Goufietti

Puffs

00:30 00:05

American	Ingredients	Metric/Imperial
2 cups	*All purpose (plain) white flour*	225 g / 8 oz
	Salt	
⅓ cup	*Milk*	4 tbsp
½ cup	*Butter*	100 g / 4 oz
½ lb	*Fontina cheese*	225 g / 8 oz
	Cayenne pepper	

1. Sieve the flour and salt onto a clean pastry board or work surface. Make a well in the centre, add the warmed milk and the butter, cut into dice.
2. Work into a dough and knead the pastry on a floured board. Roll out with a floured rolling pin until a sheet the thickness of a coin is obtained.
3. Cut the fontina into cubes. Cut the pastry into rounds using a 2 in / 5 cm cutter.
4. In each round, place the cubes of cheese and fold over, sealing the edges well. Allow to rest for 20 minutes in refrigerator. Sprinkle pastry rounds with cayenne pepper.
5. Heat the oil until hot (350°F / 180°C) and fry the half moon shapes until golden brown on each side. Serve hot.

Polenta e chiodini

Polenta and Chiodini Mushrooms

Chiodini are mushrooms which appear around November. They grow in clusters and in Italy are often called famigliole, little families.

00:60 Serves 8 00:60

American	Ingredients	Metric/Imperial
2 lb	*Mushrooms*	1 kg / 2 lb
	Butter	25 g / 1 oz
3 tbsp	*Oil*	2 tbsp
2	*Garlic cloves*	2
1¼ cups	*Meat extract or stock cube*	300 ml / ½ pint
	Salt and pepper	
1 tbsp	*Chopped parsley*	1 tbsp
1¼ lb	*Diced cooked veal or cooked veal or sausages*	600 g / 1¼ lb
	Polenta (see page 154)	

1. Separate the mushrooms from each other, scrape and soak them. Leave them for a while until any earth is deposited at the bottom of the bowl.
2. Drain then place on a tea towel, dab to remove excess moisture but take care not to crush them. If they are very small, cook them whole, but if they are large, remove the hard, woody stalks and boil the rest for about 30 minutes in salted water.
3. Heat the butter and oil in a frying pan and add the garlic. Fry slowly until the garlic begins to brown. Then put in the mushrooms and sauté over a very gentle heat for a few minutes. Dissolve a little meat extract or stock cube in boiling water and from time to time splash over the mushrooms. Season with salt and pepper. Sprinkle with chopped parsley.
4. This can be served as a dish on its own, or, to make it a main meal, add diced veal, chicken pieces or sausage. Serve as an accompaniment to a dish of steaming polenta.

Crespelle

Fritters

00:40 00:35

American	Ingredients	Metric/Imperial
½ cup	*All purpose (plain) White flour*	50 g / 2 oz
2	*Eggs*	2
1 cup	*Milk*	225 ml / 8 fl oz
	Salt and pepper	
¼ cup	*Butter*	50 g / 2 oz
1	*Small onion*	1
3 tbsp	*Oil*	2 tbsp
1 lb	*Peeled tomatoes*	500 g / 1 lb
2	*Mozzarella cheeses*	2
1 tbsp	*Grated parmesan cheese*	1 tbsp
1 tsp	*Oregano*	1 tsp

1. Sieve the flour in a bowl, make a well in the centre of the flour, add two eggs and beat with a whisk, taking care that lumps do not form.
2. Pour into the beaten mixture, a little at a time, the milk with a little salt added to it. Heat a little butter in a frying pan, tip in enough batter to cover the bottom and form a small fritter. Lightly brown it on both sides. Remove from the frying pan and make other fritters in the same way.
3. Prepare the sauce separately. Chop the onion and brown it in the heated oil. Add the tomatoes, salt and pepper, cook for about 20 minutes.
4. Preheat the oven to 350°F / 180°C / Gas Mark 4.
5. Cut the mozzarella into cubes. Place the fritters on a surface and fill them with the cheese, roll them up and cut them into points to make small diamonds.
6. Pour a little sauce into a fireproof dish. Arrange the fritters in the dish and cover with the sauce. Sprinkle with the cheese and oregano. Put in a moderate oven for about 15 minutes.

Fagottini

Cheese Puff Turnovers

00:15 Serves 6 00:15

American	Ingredients	Metric/Imperial
½ lb	*Frozen puff pastry*	225 g / 8 oz
7 oz	*Fontina cheese*	200 g / 7 oz
	Butter	
1	*Egg*	1

1. Preheat oven to 425°F / 210°C / Gas Mark 7.
2. Roll out the thawed pastry into a fairly thin layer. Cut out 6 medium-sized shapes from the pastry with a round saucer.
3. Cut all the cheese into dice. Place on each round of pastry the same quantity of cheese and a knob of butter. Fold over the dough, damp the edges and form 6 turnovers. Glaze with beaten egg. Place in the oven for 15 minutes or until golden brown.

Panini nonno Ati

Grandfather Ati's Rolls

00:10 00:10

American	Ingredients	Metric/Imperial
1	*Egg*	*1*
8	*Small milk rolls*	*8*
3-4	*Pieces of mozzarella cheese*	*3-4*
3 oz	*Tuna fish in oil*	*75 g / 3 oz*
3 tbsp	*Oil*	*2 tbsp*
1 tsp	*Chopped oregano, basil and sage*	*1 tsp*

1. Hard-cook the egg and then rinse in cold running water. Remove shell.
2. Open the rolls and divide in half. Fill with a slice of mozzarella, a teaspoonful of tuna fish in oil, a round slice of hard-cooked egg, a drop of oil, and finally the chopped oregano, basil and sage. Close and serve.

Panini alla frutta

Fruit Sandwiches

00:15 00:05

American	Ingredients	Metric/Imperial
8	*Slices of bread*	*8*
¼ lb	*Fontina cheese, cut thinly*	*100 g / 4 oz*
¼ lb	*Smoked ham*	*100 g / 4 oz*
2	*Orange segments*	*2*
2	*Slices of apple*	*2*
2	*Bananas*	*2*
3 tbsp	*Cognac*	*2 tbsp*

1. Toast the slices of bread under the grill, place on 4 slices the fontina, the ham, the orange segments (without peel and without pips), the slices of apple and banana, or any other fruit in season.
2. Sprinkle with cognac and cover with the other slices of bread.
3. Alternatively preheat the oven to 350°F / 180°C / Gas Mark 4 and heat the sandwiches for 5 minutes.

Panini dorati

Golden Rolls

00:20 00:10

American	Ingredients	Metric/Imperial
16	*Bread Rolls*	*16*
2 tbsp	*Butter*	*25 g / 1 oz*
¼ lb	*Liver sausage*	*100 g / 4 oz*
2 or 3	*Tomatoes*	*2 or 3*
¼ lb	*Cooked ham*	*100 g / 4 oz*
1 tbsp	*Oil*	*1 tbsp*
1 tsp	*Oregano*	*1 tsp*
	Salt	

1. Preheat the oven to 350°F / 180°C / Gas Mark 4.
2. Cut the rolls in half, leaving them joined on one side.
3. In a bowl, mix the butter with the sausage. Remember, when buying the sausage, that it must be fine paste. When a very smooth mixture has been obtained, spread it on the rolls.
4. Wash the tomatoes and having sliced and salted them, leave to drain for 5 minutes.
5. Cover the rolls with slices of tomato, a slice of ham, oil, oregano and top with more tomato and a pinch of salt. Close the rolls and, when they are all prepared arrange on an ovenproof dish. Just before serving, place in the oven for 10 minutes.

Stuzzichini al gruyère

Gruyère Titbits

00:45 00:10

American	Ingredients	Metric/Imperial
2 cups	*White flour*	*225 g / 8 oz*
1 cup	*Butter*	*225 g / 8 oz*
2	*Eggs*	*2*
2 cups	*Gruyère cheese, grated*	*225 g / 8 oz*

1. Preheat the oven to 400°F / 200°C / Gas Mark 6.
2. Tip the flour onto a pastry-board and make a hollow in it. Add the butter and eggs to the flour, then work into dough.
3. Grate the gruyère and blend with the dough. Wrap the mixture in a clean cloth or plastic bag and leave it to stand in a cool place for about 30 minutes.
4. Roll out the paste into a layer about ⅛ in / 3 mm thick and cut out little crescent shapes from it with a cutter or the rim of a glass. Butter and flour a large baking tray, then arrange the crescents on it. Place in a hot oven until the surface is quite golden. Serve hot or cold.

Crostini al gorgonzola

Gorgonzola Toasts

00:30 00:40

American	Ingredients	Metric/Imperial
12	*Slices of cold polenta (see page 154)*	*12 slices*
½ cup	*Oil or lard for frying*	*125 ml / 4 fl oz*
½ lb	*Strong gorgonzola cheese*	*225 g / 8 oz*
½ cup	*Butter*	*100 g / 4 oz*

1. Preheat the oven to 350°F / 180°C / Gas Mark 4, if using oven method.
2. Cut the cold polenta into 1 in / 2½ cm thick slices.
3. Heat oil or lard in a very large frying pan. Fry the slices of polenta on both sides, they must be really crisp, then take them out of the frying pan, drain on absorbent kitchen paper.
4. Prepare a cheese mixture by creaming the strong gorgonzola and softened butter until smooth.
5. Spread fried polenta with the cheese mixture. Remove the cooking fat from the frying pan, arrange the slices in the pan, cover with a lid and heat over a very low heat until the cheese has completely melted. Serve really hot. Alternatively arrange slices on a baking sheet and put into a preheated oven.

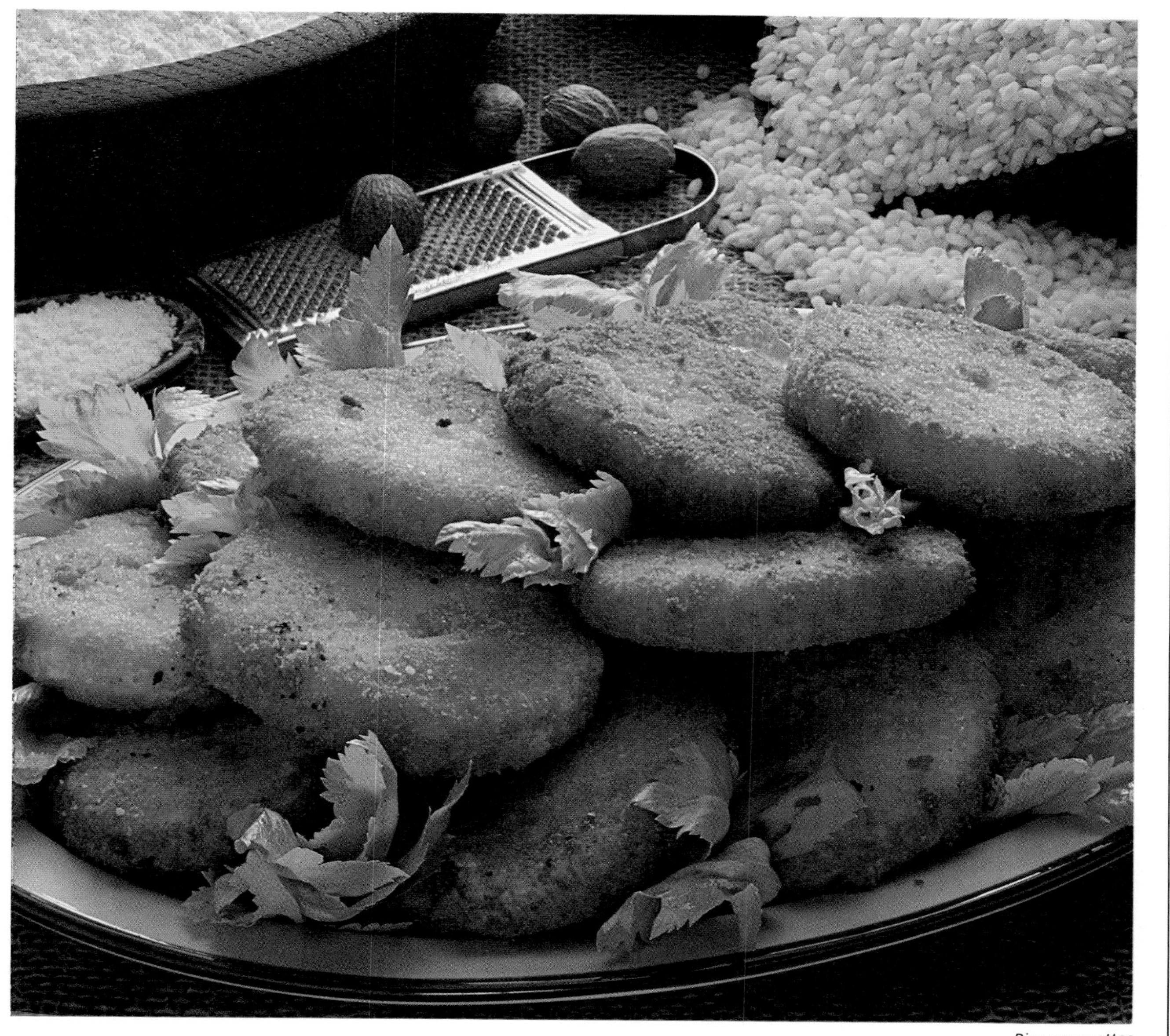

Rice croquettes

Suppli di riso

Rice Croquettes

00:60 each batch · Serves 6–8 · 00:25

American	Ingredients	Metric/Imperial
1	*Onion*	1
¾ cup	*Butter*	175 g / 6 oz
1½ cups	*Rice*	300 g / 11 oz
1½ quarts	*Meat stock*	1.5 litres / 2½ pints
4	*Eggs*	4
¼ tsp	*Nutmeg*	¼ tsp
1 cup	*Grated parmesan cheese*	100 g / 4 oz
	Salt	
4 tbsp	*All purpose (plain) flour*	3 tbsp
	Bread crumbs	
1¼ cups	*Oil*	300 ml / ½ pint

1. Chop the onion finely and cook in ½ cup (100 g / 4 oz) heated butter in a pan until golden. Add the rice to the lightly fried onion and baste from time to time with hot stock stirring all the time.

2. When cooking is completed add the rest of the butter, mix briskly and leave to cool slightly.

3. Add 2 eggs to the rice and mix thoroughly, sprinkle with nutmeg and grated parmesan.

4. Butter a baking sheet and pour the mixture onto it, roll it out and flatten thoroughly with a spoon. Wait until it is cold and compact, and then with a round cutter or with a glass, cut out several small discs.

5. Beat the other eggs and add salt to them. Dip the discs (which will be about ¾ inch / 2 cm thick) on both sides first in the flour, next in the beaten eggs, then in the bread crumbs.

6. Heat the oil in a frying pan. When it is hot (190°F / 90°C), fry the croquettes until golden. Drain well and serve hot.

Cook's tip: this dish can be prepared in advance and finished just before serving.

Uova alla boscaiola

Woodland Eggs

00:25 00:20

American	Ingredients	Metric/Imperial
1 lb	*Potatoes, not starchy*	*500 g / 1 lb*
5 cups	*Fresh mushrooms ceps, or others*	*500 g / 1 lb*
⅓ cup	*Butter or margarine*	*65 g / 2½ oz*
1	*Garlic clove*	*1*
¼ cup	*Stock*	*3 tbsp*
	Salt and pepper	
⅔ cup	*Grated parmesan cheese or grated gruyère cheese*	*65 g / 2½ oz*
4	*Eggs*	*4*
1 cup	*Cream*	*225 ml / 8 fl oz*

1. Preheat oven to 400°F / 200°C / Gas Mark 6.
2. Wash and slice the potatoes and cook them in boiling salted water. Clean and slice the mushrooms.
3. Heat the butter with the crushed garlic and then remove the garlic and sauté the mushrooms for about 10 minutes. Pour in a little stock if they need more liquid. Season with salt and pepper.
4. Butter an oven dish and cover the bottom with slices of potato. Sprinkle over half the grated cheese and finish with a layer of mushrooms. Make four small hollows, sprinkle the remaining cheese into these and break an egg into each one, trying to keep the yolk intact. Season with salt and peper and pour the cream over the dish. Put the dish into a moderately hot oven for about 10 minutes until the eggs are done. Serve in the same dish.

Ricotta alle erbe

Ricotta with Herbs

00:20 Standing time 01:00 00:00

American	Ingredients	Metric/Imperial
1 tbsp	*Basil*	*1 tbsp*
3 tbsp	*Parsley*	*2 tbsp*
1⅓ cups	*Ricotta cheese*	*300 g / 11 oz*
	Salt and pepper	
½ tsp	*Fennel seeds*	*½ tsp*

1. Chop the fresh basil and parsley then add to the ricotta with seasoning and fennel. Mix well. Leave the cheese in a cool place for 1 hour.
2. Serve with triangles of toast or small crackers.

Antipasto di lumache alla ponentina

Western-Style Hors D'Oeuvre of Snails

00:20 01:10

American	Ingredients	Metric/Imperial
24	*Snails, fresh or canned*	*24*
Scant ¼ cup	*Vinegar*	*3 tbsp*
3 tbsp	*Oil*	*2 tbsp*
2	*Garlic cloves*	*2*
½ cup	*Dry white wine*	*125 ml / 4 fl oz*
10 oz	*Peeled tomatoes*	*275 g / 10 oz*
2	*Anchovies*	*2*
	Salt and pepper	
1	*Bunch of parsley*	*1*
½ cup	*Butter*	*100 g / 4 oz*

1. If using fresh snails wash under cold running water and then toss them into boiling water, simmer for 15 minutes. Drain and pass the snails once again under cold water. Remove the natural white cap which is formed at the aperture and then use a small wire to take the snails from the shells. Thoroughly rinse the shelled snails with water and vinegar, bring to the boil in water and vinegar and simmer for a further 15 minutes, then drain thoroughly.
2. Fry the snails (fresh or canned) on a low heat in the oil with added crushed garlic. When they have browned, add a glass of dry white wine a little at a time. The wine will evaporate gradually then add the peeled tomatoes, the chopped anchovies and salt and pepper to taste. Leave to cook for a further 30 minutes.
3. In the meantime, prepare the shells, washing and draining them well.
4. Chop the parsley, blend with the butter, and finally add a little salt and pepper. Fill each shell with a snail and a little cooking juice, close with a ball of butter.
5. Preheat the oven to 450°F / 220°C / Gas Mark 8.
6. Arrange the snails in an ovenproof dish, with the aperture upwards. Place in a very hot oven for 10 minutes or until all the butter has melted and the snails are piping hot.
7. Serve at once with crusty bread.

Mozzarella fritta

Fried Mozzarella

00:15 each batch 00:03

American	Ingredients	Metric/Imperial
½ lb	*Mozzarella cheese*	*225 g / 8 oz*
1 tbsp	*Flour*	*1 tbsp*
1	*Egg*	*1*
½ cup	*Bread crumbs*	*50 g / 2 oz*
	Oil for frying	

1. Cut the mozzarella into large slices and coat them with flour.
2. Beat the egg in a bowl and dip the mozzarella slices in the egg, then into the bread crumbs.
3. Fry in plenty of very hot oil, drain on a sheet of absorbent paper and serve very hot.

Tortini della Clara

Clara's Little Pies

00:30 00:20

American	Ingredients	Metric/Imperial
2 cups	*All purpose (plain) flour*	*225 g / 8 oz*
	Salt	
½ cup	*Butter*	*100 g / 4 oz*
½ lb	*Gruyère cheese*	*225 g / ½ lb*
2	*Eggs*	*2*
1¼ cups	*Milk*	*300 ml / ½ pint*
	Freshly ground pepper	
	Powdered cinnamon	

1. Preheat the oven to 400°F / 200°C / Gas Mark 6.
2. Sieve the flour and salt on to the pastry board. Cut the butter into very small cubes, leave it to soften then add it to the flour and knead roughly until the ingredients are blended. The less you work the dough the lighter the result. Make the dough into a ball, wrap it in a clean cloth or polythene bag and put in the refrigerator for 20 minutes.
3. Cut the gruyère into small pieces. Use a fork to beat the eggs without whipping into a foam. Season lightly, add the milk and allow to stand.
4. Take the dough out of the refrigerator and roll it out into a rectangle about ½ in / 1 cm thick. Butter and flour 8 little round molds or small quiche pans, then line them with the dough. Use your fingers to lift and build up the pastry round the edges.
5. Place pieces of gruyère in each mold or quiche pan then cover with the beaten egg and milk. Sprinkle with freshly ground pepper and cinnamon.
6. Arrange the little molds on a baking sheet. Place in the oven and reduce the temperature to 350°F / 180°C / Gas Mark 4 and bake for 20 minutes. Remove from the oven, allow to cool slightly and remove from the molds.

Clara's little pies

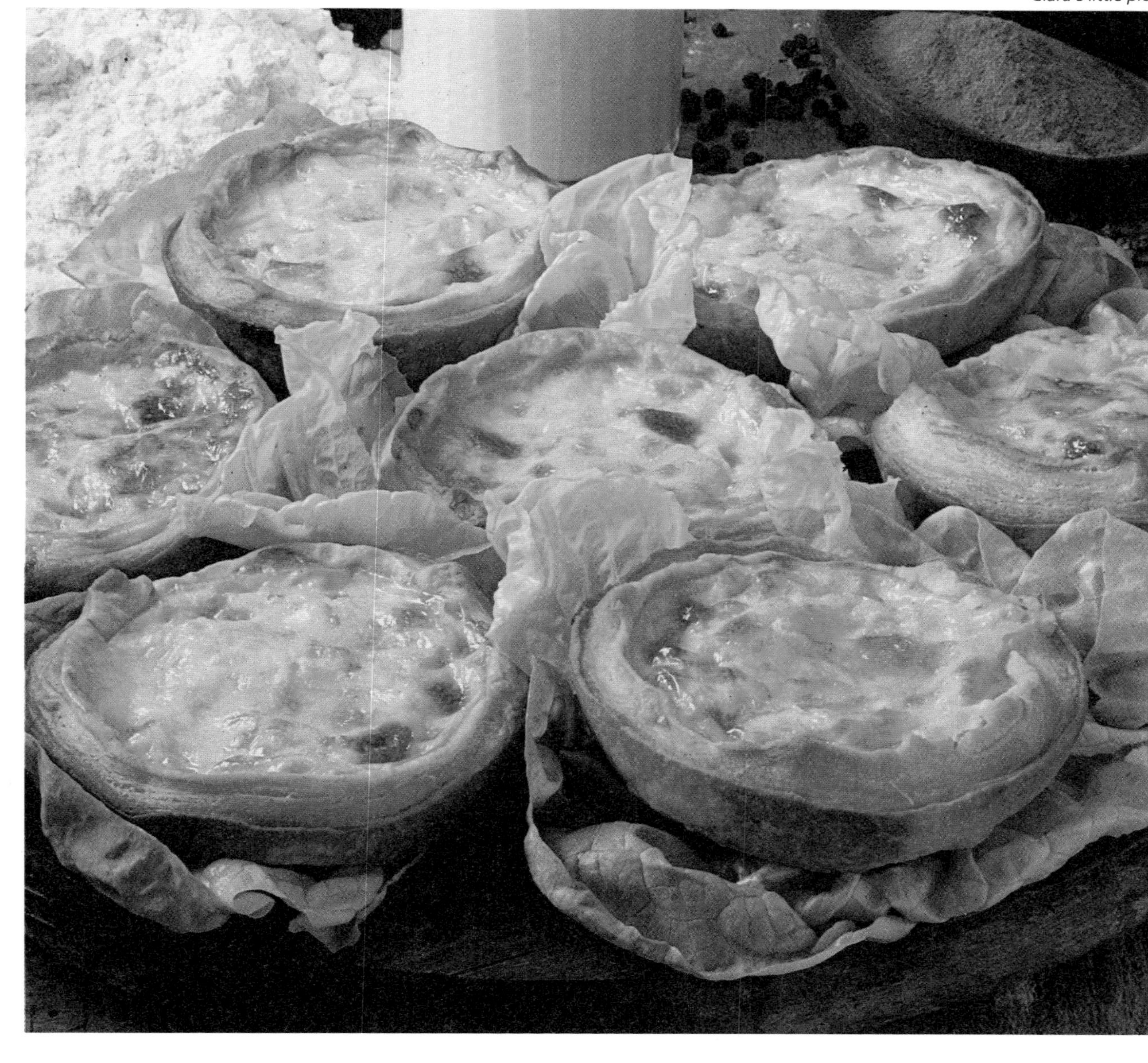

PASTA

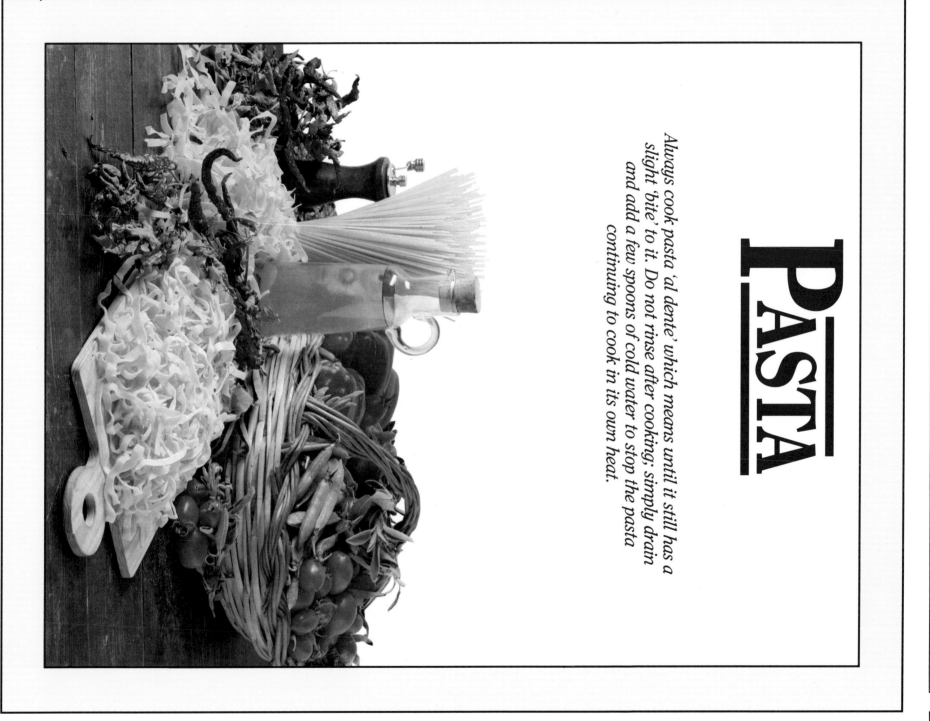

Always cook pasta 'al dente' which means until it still has a slight 'bite' to it. Do not rinse after cooking; simply drain and add a few spoons of cold water to stop the pasta continuing to cook in its own heat.

To make pasta
1. Sift the flour onto the board, mix with some beaten egg and salt (add any other ingredients such as sieved spinach or grated cheese). Knead with floured hands.

2. Add more beaten egg and knead again until the dough is smooth. Continue in this way until all the eggs are added. Divide into several pieces, knead each piece well and then re-shape all together to form a ball.

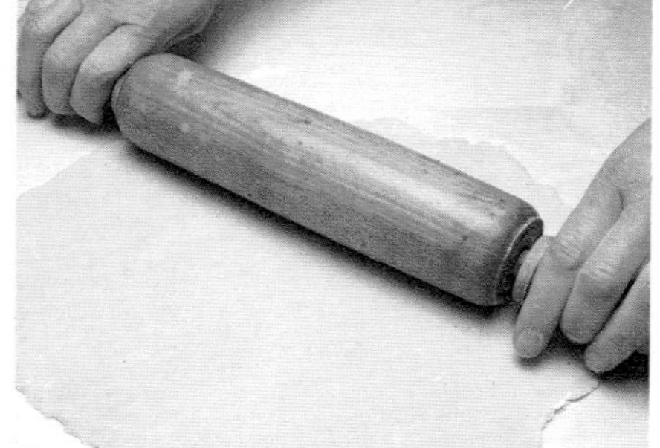

3. Leave in a cool place to rest for 30 minutes to 1 hour. Roll out thinly and cut into noodles, lasagne or use for filled pasta shapes such as agnolotti, ravioli or cappelleti.

Pasta con semolino

Pasta with Semolina

01:00 plus 00:30 in refrigerator — 00:05

American	Ingredients	Metric/Imperial
1 lb	*Semolina, finely ground or all purpose (strong white) flour*	*450 g / 1 lb*
5	*Eggs*	*5*
1 tbsp	*Salt*	*1 tbsp*
	Flour	

1. Put semolina in a heap on the pastry board, make a hole in the centre and put in eggs beaten with salt. Begin to knead with your hands, forming a ball-shaped mixture. Work until dough is smooth and even. Continue kneading dough firmly until bubbles form on the surface. Wrap ball of dough in foil and put in the bottom of the refrigerator for 30 minutes.
2. Remove and knead again for about 10 minutes. Flour pastry board and roll out dough, not too thinly. Leave dough to dry, turn over and dry on the other side, then cut into shape.
3. Cook in plenty of boiling salted water with a few drops of oil until 'al dente', cooking time according to shape.

Cook's tip: unless you can get very finely ground semolina it is better to use plain white flour. Allow 3-4 oz / 75-125 g of pasta per person.

Pasta al formaggio

Pasta with Cheese

01:30 — 00:03 to 00:08

American	Ingredients	Metric/Imperial
2 cups	*Reggiano or parmesan cheese*	*225 g / 8 oz*
2 cups	*Flour*	*225 g / 8 oz*
5	*Eggs*	*5*
1 tsp	*Salt*	*1 tsp*

1. Finely grate cheese and mix with the flour, then tip onto a pastry board. Make a well in the centre. In a bowl beat one of the eggs with salt and pour into the well.
2. Flour hands, begin to knead mixture, add another beaten egg, knead again and continue this process until all eggs are added, to produce a smooth even dough.
3. Break dough into several pieces kneading each piece well, then reshape all pieces together to form a smooth ball. Wrap in transparent film or seal in a plastic bag and leave in a cool place (not the refrigerator) for 1 hour.
4. Flour pastry board, put dough in centre, flatten with a rolling pin and turning over the dough frequently, roll into a thickish rectangle. Cut into required shape and cook immediately in plenty of boiling salted water. Cooking time will depend on shape and thickness of the pasta.

Pizzoccheri

Pizzoccheri

A typical dish from the mountain pastures of Valtellina.

01:00 — 00:20

American	Ingredients	Metric/Imperial
3 cups	*Buckwheat flour*	*350 g / 12 oz*
1½ cups	*White flour*	*175 g / 6 oz*
4	*Eggs*	*4*
½ cup	*Milk*	*125 ml / 4 fl oz*
	Salt	
½ lb	*Potatoes*	*225 g / 8 oz*
½ lb	*French beans*	*225 g / 8 oz*
½ cup	*Butter*	*100 g / 4 oz*
1 tsp	*Sage*	*1 tsp*
5 oz	*Bitto or any fresh dairy cheese*	*150 g / 5 oz*
1 tbsp	*Grated parmesan cheese*	*1 tbsp*
	Pepper	

1. Combine flours together and tip onto a pastry board. Make a well in the centre, break eggs into the middle with the milk, salt and a few drops of tepid water.
2. Knead ingredients well together to form a smooth dough, shape into a ball then wrap in transparent film or put in to a plastic bag and seal. Leave in a cool place for 30 minutes.
3. Roll the dough into a thickish rectangle, cut into strips ½ in / 1 cm wide by 1 in / 2.5 cm long.
4. Peel and dice potatoes. Bring a pan of salted water to the boil, add potatoes and beans to the pan and cook for about 10 minutes, then add the pizzoccheri pasta and cook a further 5 minutes. Drain vegetables and pasta, add butter, sage, chunks of bitto, parmesan and pepper.
5. Spoon onto a hot serving dish and put under a medium grill to melt cheese. Serve immediately.

If you enjoy making pasta it is well worth investing in a machine that will cut your pasta into interesting different shapes

Pasta alla toscana

Tuscan-Style Pasta

00:10 01:10

American	Ingredients	Metric/Imperial
1	*Onion*	*1*
1	*Sweet yellow pepper*	*1*
1	*Carrot*	*1*
1	*Celery stalk*	*1*
2 oz	*Bacon*	*50 g / 2 oz*
	Oil	
2	*Garlic cloves*	*2*
¾ lb	*Tomato purée*	*350 g / 12 oz*
1	*Bunch of basil*	*1*
½ cup	*Dry white wine*	*125 ml / 4 fl oz*
1 oz	*Capers*	*25 g / 1 oz*
	Pepper	
¼ tsp	*Oregano*	*¼ tsp*
14 oz	*Spaghetti*	*400 g / 14 oz*
¼ cup	*Grated pecorino cheese*	*25 g / 1 oz*

1. Peel and chop onion, sweet yellow pepper, carrot and celery. Dice bacon. Heat oil in a saucepan and cook prepared vegetables, bacon, garlic, tomato purée and basil for 5 minutes. Pour over the wine and simmer over a low heat for about 1 hour. Add capers, pepper and oregano 5 minutes before the end of cooking time.
2. Cook spaghetti in plenty of boiling salted water until 'al dente', drain and mix pasta into vegetable mixture.
3. Spoon onto a serving dish and sprinkle over the grated cheese. Serve immediately.

Pasta alla sbirraglia

Policeman's Pasta

00:05 00:50

American	Ingredients	Metric/Imperial
14 oz	*Fresh lasagne*	*400 g / 14 oz*
1 tsp	*Cornstarch (cornflour)*	*1 tsp*
½ cup	*Whipping (double) cream*	*125 ml / 4 fl oz*
½ cup	*Cognac*	*125 ml / 4 fl oz*
	Nutmeg	
	Salt and pepper	
1	*Truffle*	*1*
2 tbsp	*Butter*	*25 g / 1 oz*
1 tbsp	*Grated cheese*	*1 tbsp*

1. Preheat oven to 350°F / 180°C / Gas Mark 4. Grease an oblong ovenproof serving dish.
2. Cook lasagne a few pieces at a time in boiling salted water until 'al dente'. Drain and leave to dry on a clean tea towel or kitchen paper.
3. Meanwhile blend cornstarch with a little of the cream. Pour remaining cream into a saucepan, add blended cornstarch, cognac, nutmeg, pepper, salt and thinly sliced truffle, and bring to the boil stirring all the time. Simmer for 2 minutes.
4. Layer cooked lasagne in serving dish, add butter and pour over sauce. Sprinkle over grated cheese and bake in the oven for 25 minutes. Serve piping hot.

Pappardelle del cacciatore

Huntsman's Noodles

00:10 00:30

American	Ingredients	Metric/Imperial
½ lb	*Mushrooms or dried mushrooms, softened*	*225 g / 8 oz*
Scant ¼ cup	*Olive oil*	*3 tbsp*
1	*Garlic clove*	*1*
	Salt and pepper	
14 oz	*Pappardelle*	*400 g / 14 oz*
1 cup	*Coffee (single) cream*	*225 ml / 8 fl oz*
1 tbsp	*Tomato sauce*	*1 tbsp*
1 tbsp	*Grated parmesan cheese*	*1 tbsp*

1. Rinse fresh mushrooms under hot water then slice thinly. (Reconstitute dried mushrooms in water).
2. Heat oil in a pan, fry garlic for 1-2 minutes then remove. Add mushrooms to the pan and sauté for 2 minutes, then allow to simmer for about 20 minutes. Season with salt and pepper.
3. Meanwhile cook the pappardelle in boiling salted water until 'al dente', drain and put on a hot serving dish.
4. Add cream and tomato sauce to mushroom sauce, stir well then pour over pasta, sprinkle with the parmesan cheese.

Pappardelle con la lepre

Noodles with Hare

00:20 02:10

American	Ingredients	Metric/Imperial
	Legs and back of a hare with liver and lights	
1	*Onion*	*1*
1	*Garlic clove*	*1*
Scant ¼ cup	*Oil*	*3 tbsp*
¼ tsp	*Thyme*	*¼ tsp*
¼ tsp	*Sweet marjoram*	*¼ tsp*
¼ tsp	*Rosemary*	*¼ tsp*
½ cup	*Red wine (or more as required)*	*125 ml / 4 fl oz*
1 cup	*Meat stock*	*225 ml / 8 fl oz*
¼ tsp	*Nutmeg*	*¼ tsp*
	Pepper	
14 oz	*Pappardelle*	*400 g / 14 oz*

1. Remove meat from the hare and cut into small pieces. Chop liver and lights and reserve.
2. Peel and chop onion, peel garlic. Heat half the oil in a large pan, fry onion, garlic, thyme, marjoram and rosemary together for 2-3 minutes.
3. Add hare meat to the pan and brown quickly. Pour over the wine and stock, bring to the boil, then reduce heat. Cover and simmer for about 2 hours.
4. Pour hare sauce into a blender and purée. Heat remaining oil in a pan and fry the prepared liver and lights together for 3-4 minutes. Pour hare purée into pan and mix ingredients together. Add nutmeg and pepper.
5. Cook pappardelle in boiling salted water until 'al dente', drain and stir into hare sauce.
6. Spoon on to a heated serving dish and serve.

Maccheroni Trinacria al forno

Sicilian Baked Macaroni

00:45 01:00

American	Ingredients	Metric/Imperial
2	*Large eggplant (aubergines)*	2
	Salt and pepper	
2	*Garlic cloves*	2
14 oz can	*Tomatoes*	400 g / 14 oz can
⅔ cup	*Oil*	150 ml / ¼ pint
14 oz	*Pilchards*	400 g / 14 oz
¾ lb	*Macaroni*	350 g / 12 oz
	Oregano	
½ cup	*Grated cheese*	50 g / 2 oz
1 tbsp	*Butter*	1 tbsp

1. Preheat oven to 350°F / 180°C / Gas Mark 4. Grease an ovenproof serving dish.
2. Slice eggplant thinly, place in a colander and sprinkle with salt. Leave for 30 minutes, then rinse under cold water and dry well.
3. Peel garlic and chop finely. Heat 1 tablespoon of the oil in a large saucepan and add garlic and fry gently until golden. Add tomatoes and juice from can. Season with salt and pepper and simmer for 15 minutes.
4. Meanwhile clean pilchards. Slit to open but leave halves joined, wash under cold running water and add to sauce. Cover and leave to cook a further 10 minutes.
5. Heat remaining oil in a large pan and fry slices of eggplant until lightly browned, then drain on kitchen paper.
6. Cook macaroni in boiling salted water until 'al dente', drain and add a dash of oil to prevent it sticking together. Arrange pasta on the base of the dish, top with pilchard sauce, then the eggplant.
7. Add freshly ground pepper and oregano to grated cheese and scatter dabs of butter over surface. Bake for about 30 minutes until lightly browned. Serve piping hot.

Pasta alla livornese

Leghorn-Style Pasta

00:15 00:20

American	Ingredients	Metric/Imperial
¼ lb	*Lean raw ham*	100 g / 4 oz
¼ lb	*Neck of pork*	100 g / 4 oz
1	*Onion*	1
Scant ¼ cup	*Oil*	3 tbsp
2	*Garlic cloves*	2
1	*Bunch of basil*	1
	Salt and pepper	
¼ tsp	*Thyme*	¼ tsp
¼ tsp	*Paprika*	¼ tsp
¼ cup	*Best quality cognac*	50 ml / 2 fl oz
14 oz	*Semolina pasta (see page 94)*	400 g / 14 oz

1. Chop ham and pork into small pieces. Peel and chop onion. Heat oil and fry meat and onion together with the crushed garlic, basil, thyme, paprika and cognac for 10 minutes, stirring from time to time. Add salt and freshly ground pepper.
2. Meanwhile cook pasta in boiling salted water until 'al dente', drain and stir into the meat sauce, mixing well.
3. Spoon on to a hot serving dish and serve immediately.

Pasta alla potentina

Potentina Pasta

00:10 00:50

American	Ingredients	Metric/Imperial
6	*Eggs*	6
	Salt and pepper	
3 tbsp	*Flour*	2 tbsp
3 tbsp	*White wine*	2 tbsp
14 oz	*Cooked fine macaroni*	400 g / 14 oz
Scant ¼ cup	*Oil*	3 tbsp
1 tbsp	*Butter*	1 tbsp
1 tbsp	*Bread crumbs*	1 tbsp
¾ lb	*Mozzarella cheese*	350 g / 12 oz

1. Preheat oven to 400°F / 200°C / Gas Mark 6. Grease a large ovenproof serving dish.
2. Beat eggs with salt and pepper, add the flour, whisk well, and then the white wine. Mix in the macaroni.
3. Heat remaining oil in an iron frying pan. When just beginning to smoke, slide mixture into it, as for making normal omelette, cook for about 10 minutes, turn and cook the other side for 5 minutes. Place cooked omelette in dish, dot with butter, sprinkle with bread crumbs and cover with thin slices of mozzarella. Bake for about 25 minutes. Serve hot.

Pasta alla panna e funghi

Pasta with Cream Mushrooms

00:15 00:15

American	Ingredients	Metric/Imperial
½ lb	*Mushrooms*	225 g / 8 oz
	Salt and pepper	
1 tsp	*Oil*	1 tsp
14 oz	*Pasta*	400 g / 14 oz
1 cup	*Whipping (double) cream*	225 ml / 8 fl oz
1 tsp	*Powdered truffle*	1 tsp
	Nutmeg	
1 oz	*Fontina or melting cheese*	25 g / 1 oz
1	*White truffle*	1

1. Rinse mushrooms under hot water then remove stalks, slice tops and put into a bowl. Add salt, pepper and oil to mushrooms and leave to stand.
2. Put pasta to cook in boiling salted water until 'al dente'.
3. Meanwhile pour cream into a saucepan, add the truffle, the nutmeg and the mushrooms and leave to simmer for about 10 minutes. Slice cheese and white truffle thinly.
4. Drain pasta, mix in the cheese and spoon on to a serving dish. Cover with the mushroom sauce and garnish with slices of white truffle.

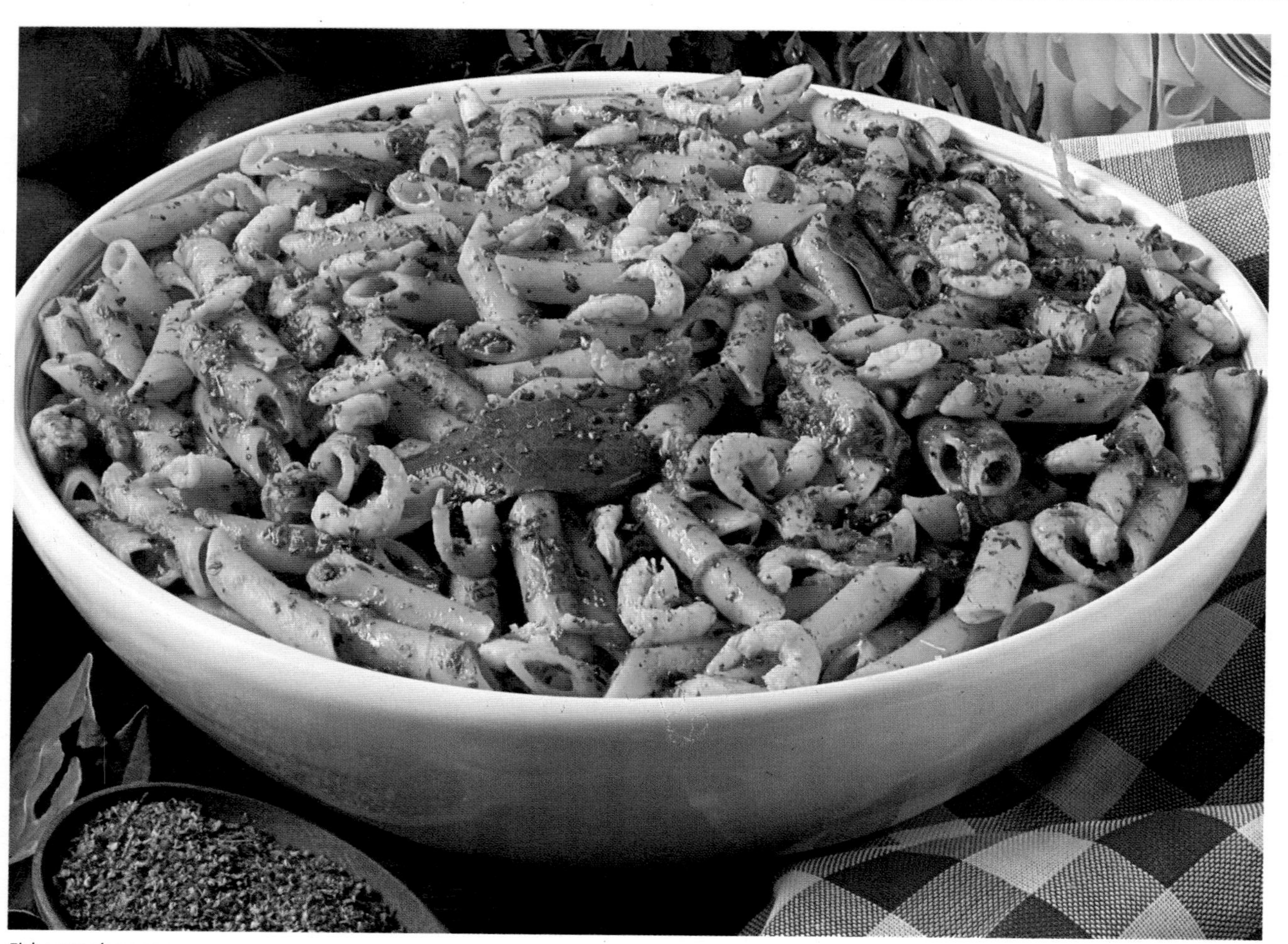

Fisherman's penne

Penne del pescatore

Fisherman's Penne

Preparation 00:10 — Cooking 00:25

American	Ingredients	Metric/Imperial
1¾ lb	*Fresh prawns*	800 g / 1¾ lb
5 or 14 oz can	*Tomatoes*	5 or 400 g / 14 oz can
3 tbsp	*Oil*	2 tbsp
2 or 3	*Bay leaves*	2 or 3
	Salt and black pepper	
¾ lb	*Penne pasta (smooth, short-cut pasta tubes)*	350 g / 12 oz
1 tbsp	*Chopped parsley*	1 tbsp

1. Plunge prawns into a pan of boiling salted water, cover, remove from the heat and leave to cool, then shell.
2. Peel and quarter tomatoes and remove seeds; if using canned tomatoes, use juice and fruit.
3. Heat oil in a large pan, add bay leaves, tomatoes and cook for 5-10 minutes, until mixture is reduced to a pulp.
4. Stir prawns gently into tomato sauce and season with salt and freshly ground black pepper. Leave to simmer over a low heat for 5 minutes.
5. Meanwhile cook penne pasta in plenty of boiling salted water until 'al dente'. Drain well.
6. Add the pasta to the prawn sauce over a medium heat and discard the bay leaves.
7. Spoon onto a hot serving dish, season with black pepper and garnish with chopped parsley.

Pasta alla cipolla

Onion Pasta

Preparation 00:10 — Cooking 00:25

American	Ingredients	Metric/Imperial
2	*Large onions*	2
¼ cup	*Butter*	50 g / 2 oz
	Salt	
2	*Eggs*	2
14 oz	*Bavette (thin noodles)*	400 g / 14 oz
1 tbsp	*Grated parmesan cheese*	1 tbsp

1. Peel and thinly slice onions. Melt butter and cook onions slowly for about 10 minutes until soft without browning, then remove from the heat.
2. Add salt and beaten eggs to the pan and mix ingredients thoroughly.
3. Cook bavette in boiling salted water until 'al dente', drain, add the onion sauce and top with grated cheese. Serve immediately.

Corzetti alla rivierasca

Coastal-Style Corzetti

This dish is famous throughout the Riviera.

00:30 00:45

American	Ingredients	Metric/Imperial
1 (½ lb)	*Fresh salmon slice*	*1 (225 g / 8 oz)*
Scant ¼ cup	*Oil*	*3 tbsp*
1	*Onion*	*1*
½ cup	*Dry white wine*	*125 ml / 4 fl oz*
½ cup	*Stock*	*125 ml / 4 fl oz*
5 tbsp	*Tomato purée*	*4 tbsp*
1 tsp	*Fresh, chopped basil*	*1 tsp*
2	*Walnuts*	*2*
14 oz	*Corzetti (spiral pasta shapes)*	*400 g / 14 oz*
	Salt	

1. Cut the fresh salmon into thin strips.
2. Heat the oil, add the chopped onion, cook for 4 minutes then add the salmon strips. Cook for about 10 minutes, add the white wine, the stock and the tomato purée, allow to simmer over a very low heat, so that the sauce remains very thick.
3. Pass through the blender. Chop the fresh basil and walnuts finely, retain a quarter for the garnish and mix the rest with the sauce.
4. Heat a saucepan with plenty of salted water and when it boils cook the corzetti. Drain, season at once with the fish sauce and serve hot. Add extra chopped basil and walnuts sprinkled on top.

Maccheroni di primavera

Springtime Macaroni

00:15 00:50

American	Ingredients	Metric/Imperial
2 lb	*Asparagus or frozen packets of asparagus*	*1 kg / 2 lb*
½ cup	*Butter*	*100 g / 4 oz*
¾ lb	*Roman ricotta or piedmontese cheese*	*350 g / 12 oz*
¼ cup	*Milk*	*50 ml / 2 fl oz*
	Salt and pepper	
14 oz	*Macaroni*	*400 g / 14 oz*
¼ cup	*Grated parmesan cheese*	*25 g / 1 oz*
2	*Eggs*	*2*
¼ tsp	*Nutmeg*	*¼ tsp*
3 tbsp	*Grated cheese*	*2 tbsp*

1. Preheat oven to 375°F / 190°C / Gas Mark 5. Grease an ovenproof serving dish.
2. Clean asparagus and cook for 5 minutes in boiling salted water, drain well. Cut into small pieces discarding hard stems.
3. In a large pan, melt a quarter of the butter add asparagus and cook until golden.
4. In a bowl beat ricotta with the milk, salt and pepper to obtain a smooth cream.
5. Cook macaroni until 'al dente', then drain. Add the rest of the butter and parmesan to the pasta, and spoon over the base of the dish.
6. Top with the asparagus and half the ricotta. Continue layering in this way finishing with a layer of macaroni.
7. Beat eggs with salt, pepper, nutmeg and grated cheese and pour over macaroni. Bake for 30 minutes until golden. Serve piping hot.

Maccheroni con la piovra

Macaroni with Octopus

00:10 00:40

American	Ingredients	Metric/Imperial
1¼ lb	*Octopus*	*600 g / 1¼ lb*
2	*Bay leaves*	*2*
Scant ¼ cup	*Oil*	*3 tbsp*
3	*Garlic cloves*	*3*
3 tbsp	*Chopped parsley*	*2 tbsp*
14 oz	*Macaroni*	*400 g / 14 oz*
	Salt	

1. Clean octopus thoroughly, beat and put in a saucepan, with plenty of water; do not add salt. Add bay leaves, bring to the boil and cook until the octopus becomes red, drain and cool.
2. In a frying pan heat oil, peel and crush 2 cloves of garlic, add to the pan with most of the chopped parsley.
3. Cut octopus into small pieces, add to the pan, stirring for about 10 minutes.
4. Meanwhile boil macaroni until 'al dente' in plenty of lightly salted water, drain well and stir into the octopus and its cooking juices, until thoroughly mixed.
5. Spoon onto a hot serving dish and garnish with chopped parsley and crushed garlic.

Maccheroni alla vodka

Macaroni with Vodka

00:05 00:30

American	Ingredients	Metric/Imperial
1	*Large onion*	*1*
1 oz	*Sausage*	*25 g / 1 oz*
3 tbsp	*Butter*	*2 tbsp*
½ cup	*Vodka*	*125 ml / 4 fl oz*
2 cups	*Whipping (double) cream*	*450 ml / 16 fl oz*
	Salt and pepper	
14 oz	*Macaroni*	*400 g / 14 oz*

1. Peel and chop onion, skin sausage and slice into small pieces.
2. Melt butter and cook the onion and sausage for about 5 minutes over a medium heat. Pour over three-quarters of vodka and bring to the boil. Reduce heat and simmer for 8-10 minutes. Finally stir in all but 2 tablespoons [25 ml / 1 fl oz] of the cream, simmer for a further 3-5 minutes, then season.
3. Boil macaroni in salted water until 'al dente', drain and stir into the vodka cream sauce.
4. Spoon onto a large serving plate, pour over the remaining vodka and cream and serve immediately.

Maccheroni alla siciliana

Sicilian-Style Macaroni

00:10 00:25

American	Ingredients	Metric/Imperial
1	*Small onion*	1
½	*Sweet pepper*	½
1	*Garlic clove*	1
Scant ¼ cup	*Oil*	3 tbsp
1	*Bay leaf*	1
Scant ¼ cup	*Tomato purée*	3 tbsp
8	*Black olives*	8
½ tsp	*Anchovy paste*	½ tsp
¼ tsp	*Oregano*	¼ tsp
¼ tsp	*Basil*	¼ tsp
	Salt and pepper	
½ lb	*Fine macaroni*	225 g / 8 oz
¼ cup	*Grated pecorino cheese*	25 g / 1 oz

1. Chop onion and sweet pepper, peel garlic. Heat oil in a pan and sauté these with a bay leaf for 3 minutes.
2. Add tomato purée, black olives, anchovy paste, oregano and basil. Season with salt and pepper, cover and cook over a low heat for 8-10 minutes.
3. Cook macaroni in boiling salted water until 'al dente', drain and add to the sauce, stirring both ingredients carefully until thoroughly mixed. Sprinkle with fresh pepper and grated pecorino and serve immediately.

Maccheroni alla chitarra 

Guitar Macaroni

00:35 00:25

American	Ingredients	Metric/Imperial
¼ lb	*Bacon*	100 g / 4 oz
Scant ¼ cup	*Oil*	3 tbsp
1	*Sweet red pepper*	1
6	*Tomatoes, peeled*	6
3 cups	*Flour*	350 g / 12 oz
4	*Eggs*	4
	Salt and pepper	

1. Cube the bacon, heat oil in a pan and cook bacon for 2 minutes. Add chopped sweet pepper and tomatoes, stir with a wooden spoon and cook over a low heat until of a thickish consistency.
2. Sift flour onto a pastry board, make a well in the centre and tip in beaten eggs to obtain a firm dough and draw out with a rolling-pin over a guitar (a frame on which wires are stretched) to obtain thin strips of pasta, or cut into thin strips.
3. Cook these in plenty of boiling salted water until 'al dente'. Drain, season with hot sauce and serve.

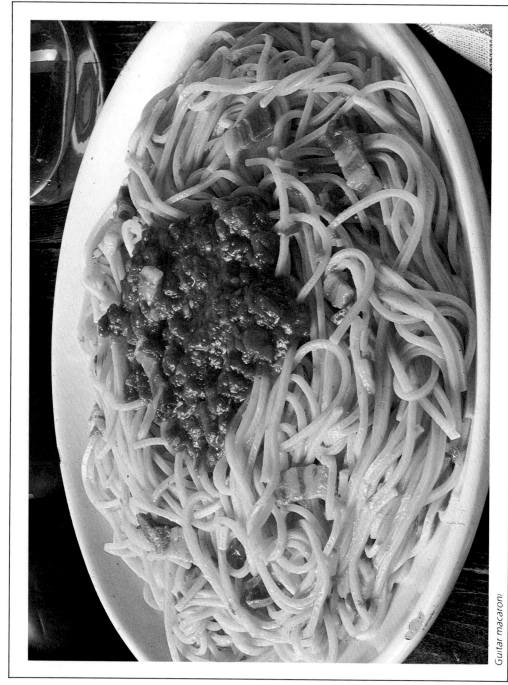

Guitar macaroni

Pasta e bisi

Pasta and Peas

Preparation 00:10 — Cooking 00:25

American	Ingredients	Metric/Imperial
2¼ cups	*Small new peas, or frozen peas*	350 g / 12 oz
½ cup	*Butter*	100 g / 4 oz
½ lb	*Chicken livers*	225 g / 8 oz
2	*Sage leaves*	2
14 oz	*Pasta*	400 g / 14 oz
1 tbsp	*Grated parmesan cheese*	1 tbsp
	Cognac (optional)	

1. Boil peas for 10 minutes then drain. Melt butter in a frying pan, add peas and washed chopped chicken livers and brown slightly, stirring frequently. Add sage leaves, and continue cooking a further 5 minutes.
2. Bring a large saucepan of salted water to the boil, add chosen pasta and cook until 'al dente'.
3. Drain and sprinkle with grated parmesan, then stir in the chicken liver sauce. Add a little cognac if desired and serve.

Maccheroni gratinati

Macaroni au Gratin

Preparation 00:15 — Cooking 01:05

American	Ingredients	Metric/Imperial
5 oz	*Thick slice of cooked ham*	150 g / 5 oz
7 oz	*Mushrooms*	200 g / 7 oz
14 oz can	*Peeled tomatoes*	400 g / 14 oz can
2	*Garlic cloves*	2
Scant ¼ cup	*Oil*	3 tbsp
	Salt and pepper	
14 oz	*Macaroni*	400 g / 14 oz
3 tbsp	*Cornstarch (cornflour)*	2 tbsp
1¼ cups	*Milk*	300 ml / ½ pint
3 tbsp	*Butter*	2 tbsp
¼ tsp	*Nutmeg*	¼ tsp
1 tbsp	*Grated cheese*	1 tbsp

1. Preheat oven to 350°F / 180°C / Gas Mark 4. Grease an oblong serving dish.
2. Dice ham, wash mushrooms and slice, peel tomatoes and roughly chop. Peel garlic.
3. In a large frying pan, heat oil and cook mushrooms and crushed garlic for 1-2 minutes, stirring all the time. Add ham, season with salt and pepper and cook for a few minutes.
4. Add tomatoes to the pan, cover and simmer for 10 minutes.
5. Meanwhile cook macaroni in plenty of boiling salted water until 'al dente', drain and rinse under cold water, then stir into the tomato sauce.
6. Make a sauce by blending cornstarch with a little milk, add remainder of milk and heat in a pan until boiling, stirring all the time. Add half the butter, salt, pepper and nutmeg.
7. Spoon the macaroni and tomato sauce over the base of the serving dish, cover with the white sauce, sprinkle with grated cheese and scatter remaining butter in knobs over the top.
8. Bake for 35-40 minutes until golden and serve hot.

Pasta and peas

Bigoli con sardelle

Bigoli with Sardines

This is a typical Lombard recipe.

Preparation 00:20 — Cooking 00:20

American	Ingredients	Metric/Imperial
¼ lb	*Sardines*	100 g / 4 oz
14 oz	*Bigoli pasta*	400 g / 14 oz
	Salt	
3 tbsp	*Olive oil*	2 tbsp
2	*Garlic cloves*	2

1. Clean, bone and wash the fish and place them on a board.
2. Cook the bigoli pasta in a large saucepan with plenty of salted water.
3. Heat the oil, add the garlic, and when the garlic turns golden, put in the sardines. While they are cooking squash them with a wooden fork without frying them.
4. Drain the bigoli when firm to the bite and put them in an earthenware dish, pour over the fish sauce and serve very hot.

Spaghetti in foil

Spaghetti al cartoccio

Spaghetti in Foil

00:15 | 00:15

American	Ingredients	Metric/Imperial
1 ¼ lb	*Shellfish (mussels, clams, limpets) weighed with the shell*	*600 g / 1 ¼ lb*
⅓ cup	*Vegetable oil*	*5 tbsp*
2	*Garlic cloves*	*2*
1	*Bunch of parsley*	*1*
Scant ¼ cup	*Chopped tomatoes*	*3 tbsp*
14 oz	*Spaghetti*	*400 g / 14 oz*
	Salt and pepper	
	Aluminium foil	

1. Preheat oven to 400°F / 200°C / Gas Mark 6.
2. Clean shell fish thoroughly. Heat oil in a frying pan, and when very hot, add shellfish, garlic, chopped parsley, and chopped tomatoes. Cook for 5 minutes, stirring all the time, then leave sauce to thicken over a low heat.
3. Half cook spaghetti in boiling salted water, then drain and pass under running cold water. Stir into shellfish sauce, mixing well.
4. Spread a big sheet of aluminum foil over a baking sheet. In the centre place the seasoned spaghetti, sprinkle the top with a thin trickle of oil, add pepper and close up the foil, leaving a fairly large space above, so that the steam may circulate inside.
5. Bake in the oven for 10 minutes, then serve parcel of spaghetti at the table.

Note: the shellfish may be cooked with or without valves.

Spaghetti all'arrabbiata

Arrabbiata-Style Spaghetti

00:30 | 00:20

American	Ingredients	Metric/Imperial
14 oz	*Chitterlings mixed with pork*	*400 g / 14 oz*
10	*Shelled walnuts*	*10*
½ cup	*Vegetable oil*	*125 ml / 4 fl oz*
4	*Garlic cloves*	*4*
¼ tsp	*Red paprika*	*¼ tsp*
	Salt and pepper	
⅓ cup	*Raisins*	*50 g / 2 oz*
14 oz	*Spaghetti*	*400 g / 14 oz*
1 tbsp	*Grated pecorino cheese*	*1 tbsp*

1. Clean chitterlings and chop, blend walnuts to a purée with a little of the oil. Heat remaining oil in a frying pan and when very hot fry chopped chitterlings with pork, crushed garlic, red paprika and pepper for 5 minutes.
2. Blanch raisins, drain and add to pan with walnut purée and wine. Stir well then purée sauce in a food processor or blender, return to pan and leave over a very low heat.
3. Meanwhile cook spaghetti in plenty of boiling salted water until 'al dente' and drain.
4. Stir grated pecorino into spaghetti and then mix pasta and cheese into sauce in frying pan and continue to cook over a low heat for 5 minutes.
5. Spoon onto a hot serving dish, sprinkle over fresh pepper and serve hot.

Spaghetti alle vongole

Spaghetti with Clams

00:20 | 00:20

American	Ingredients	Metric/Imperial
1 ¼ lb	*Clams*	*600 g / 1 ¼ lb*
Scant ¼ cup	*Vegetable oil*	*3 tbsp*
6	*Sprigs of parsley*	*6*
14 oz can	*Peeled tomatoes*	*400 g / 14 oz can*
	Salt and pepper	
1 ¼ lb	*Spaghetti*	*600 g / 1 ¼ lb*

1. Wash clams in several changes of water until water remains clear, then wipe dry. Heat oil in a pan, add clams, cover and cook for 5 - 8 minutes until shells open, discarding any that remain closed.
2. Add the parsley and the tomatoes to the pan and cook for a further 7 minutes. Taste and adjust seasoning.
3. Cook spaghetti in plenty of boiling salted water until 'al dente', drain and spoon onto a hot serving dish. Pour over clam sauce and serve immediately.

Spaghetti with clams

Spaghetti ai frutti di mare

Seafood Spaghetti

00:05 00:20

American	Ingredients	Metric/Imperial
½ lb	*Frozen shellfish, without shells*	225 g / 8 oz
2	*Plum tomatoes, ripe or pulped*	2
2	*Garlic cloves*	2
Scant ¼ cup	*Vegetable oil*	3 tbsp
1	*Bunch of basil*	1
	Salt and pepper	
14 oz	*Fine spaghetti*	400 g / 14 oz
1 tbsp	*Grated pecorino cheese*	1 tbsp

1. Put shellfish in a pan with tomato, garlic, half of the oil, basil, salt and plenty of pepper. Cover and simmer for 20 minutes.
2. Meanwhile cook pasta in boiling salted water with the rest of the oil, until 'al dente'. Drain and put in a serving bowl, sprinkle over the pecorino and pour over shellfish sauce. Serve immediately.

Seafood spaghetti

Spaghetti alla creola

Creole-Style Spaghetti

00:15 00:45

American	Ingredients	Metric/Imperial
1 lb	*Fresh or frozen scampi and shrimps, without shells*	500 g / 1 lb
3 tbsp	*Vegetable oil*	2 tbsp
7 oz	*Tomato pulp*	200 g / 7 oz
1 tsp	*Pepper*	1 tsp
2 tsp	*Curry powder*	2 tsp
½ cup	*Bourbon*	125 ml / 4 fl oz
14 oz	*Spaghetti*	400 g / 14 oz
	Salt	
1 cup	*Coffee (single) cream*	225 ml / 8 fl oz
1 tbsp	*Grated cheese*	1 tbsp

1. Thoroughly clean fresh shrimps and scampi and remove shells. Heat oil and when very hot quickly fry prepared fish with tomato pulp for 5 minutes, stirring all the time. Season, add curry powder and pour over the bourbon. Cover and simmer for about 30 minutes.
2. Cook spaghetti in boiling salted water until 'al dente', drain and stir in cream and cheese, then pour over fish sauce and serve.

Variations: lobster, sea crab or abalone may be substituted for shrimps and scampi in this recipe.

Conchiglie ai cavolini di Bruxelles

Pasta Shells with Brussels Sprouts

00:20 00:30

American	Ingredients	Metric/Imperial
¼ cup	*Butter*	50 g / 2 oz
2 oz	*Bacon*	50 g / 2 oz
1	*Garlic clove*	1
1 lb	*Brussels sprouts*	500 g / 1 lb
½ lb	*Peeled tomatoes*	225 g / 8 oz
1 tsp	*Chopped basil*	1 tsp
	Salt	
1 lb	*Shell-shaped pasta*	450 g / 1 lb
1 tbsp	*Grated parmesan cheese*	1 tbsp

1. In a large pan, heat the butter, add the bacon chopped into cubes. Add a clove of crushed garlic.
2. Wash and dry the brussels sprouts, mix with the bacon and garlic and allow to absorb the flavor for about 15 minutes, then add the chopped peeled tomatoes, some chopped basil and stir. Continue cooking for a further 15 minutes.
3. Heat plenty of salted water, boil the pasta shells until firm to the bite. Drain, keep a little of the cooking liquid and add the sprouts immediately.
4. Mix in two or three spoonfuls of cooking liquid, sprinkle with plenty of grated cheese and serve piping hot.

Cook's tip: If there should be any left over, this pasta is also excellent heated in the oven with half a cup of béchamel sauce mixed with it. Place the pasta and béchamel in an ovenproof dish and reheat in a moderate oven.

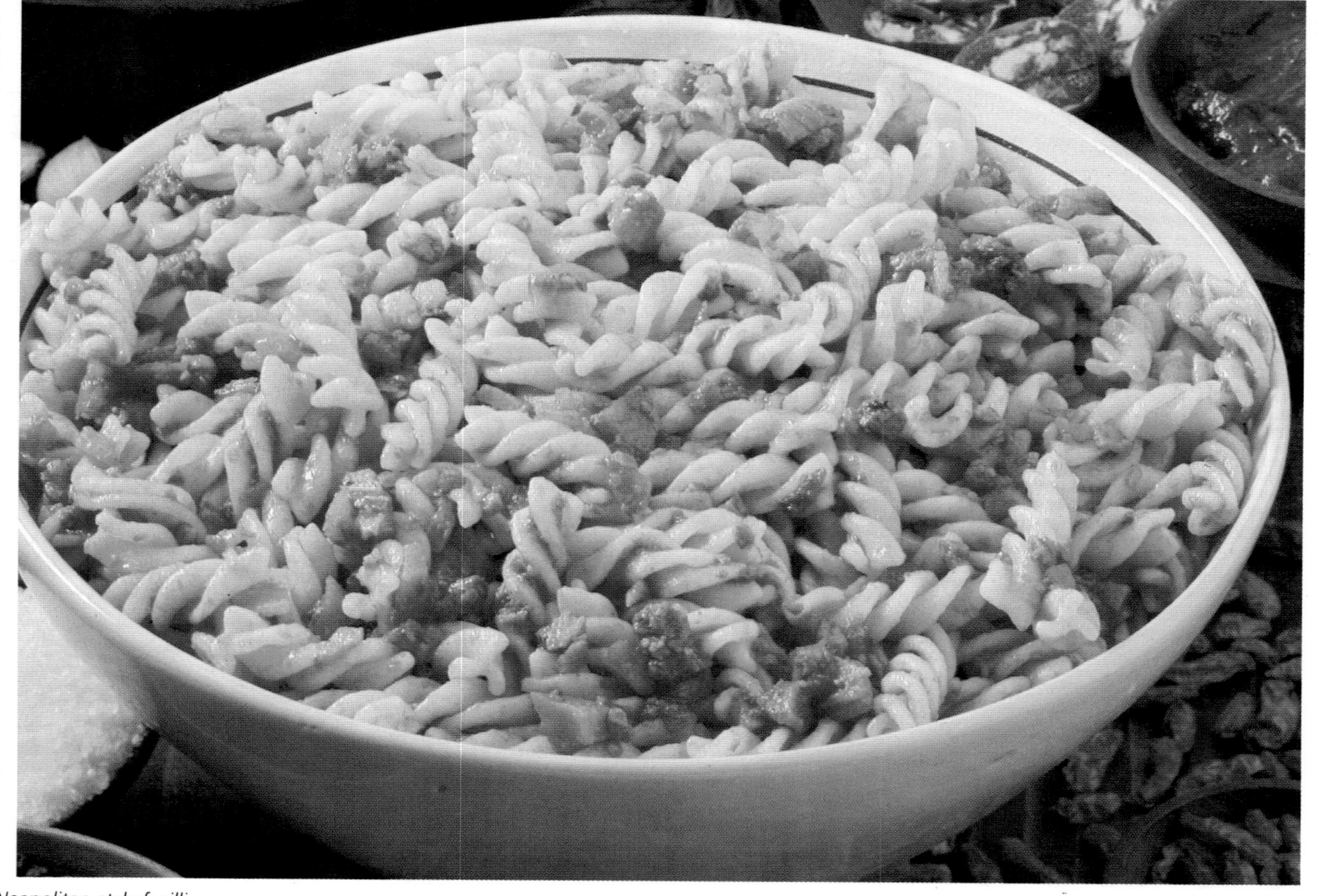

Neapolitan-style fusilli

Fusilli alla napoletana

Neapolitan-Style Fusilli

This recipe is very ancient and famous throughout Campania.

00:30 01:25

American	Ingredients	Metric/Imperial
½ cup	Oil	125 ml / 4 fl oz
1	Onion	1
1	Celery stalk	1
1	Carrot	1
2	Garlic cloves	2
¼ lb	Neapolitan spicy salami	100 g / 4 oz
¾ lb	Ground (minced) lamb or pork	350 g / 12 oz
½ cup	Dry white wine	125 ml / 4 fl oz
½ lb	Ricotta cheese	225 g / 8 oz
	Salt and freshly ground black pepper	
½ tsp	Hot paprika	½ tsp
5 tbsp	Tomato purée or sauce	4 tbsp
14 oz	Fusilli (spiral-shaped pasta)	400 g / 14 oz

1. Heat the oil in a frying pan over a low heat. Prepare the vegetables. Chop the onion, slice celery, dice the carrot and crush the cloves of garlic.
2. Chop bacon and chop salami. Add to pan with vegetables and ground (minced) meat. Mix well and brown over a medium heat moistening a little at a time with dry white wine.
3. Crumble the ricotta into the sauce, mix and season with salt, pepper and hot paprika.
4. Add tomato purée to the meat sauce and continue cooking for 1 hour.
5. Heat a saucepan containing plenty of salted water and, when boiling, toss in the fusilli. Cook until 'al dente' and drain. Season at once with the sauce.

Spaghetti alla barese

Bari-Style Spaghetti

00:10 00:10

American	Ingredients	Metric/Imperial
2 lb	Turnip tops	1 kg / 2 lb
1 lb	Large spaghetti	450 g / 1 lb
3 tbsp	Vegetable oil	2 tbsp
2	Garlic cloves	2
½ lb	Tomato purée	225 g / 8 oz
1	Bunch of basil	1

1. Trim turnip tops, retaining tip and using remainder of green part for minestrone.
2. Cook turnip tops and spaghetti in a large pan of boiling salted water for 8-10 minutes, until pasta is 'al dente'.
3. Meanwhile heat oil in a pan, and when very hot fry the garlic for 1-2 minutes. Add tomato purée and chopped basil, stir well and remove from heat.
4. Drain pasta and turnip tops, stir in tomato sauce and spoon onto a hot serving dish. Serve immediately.

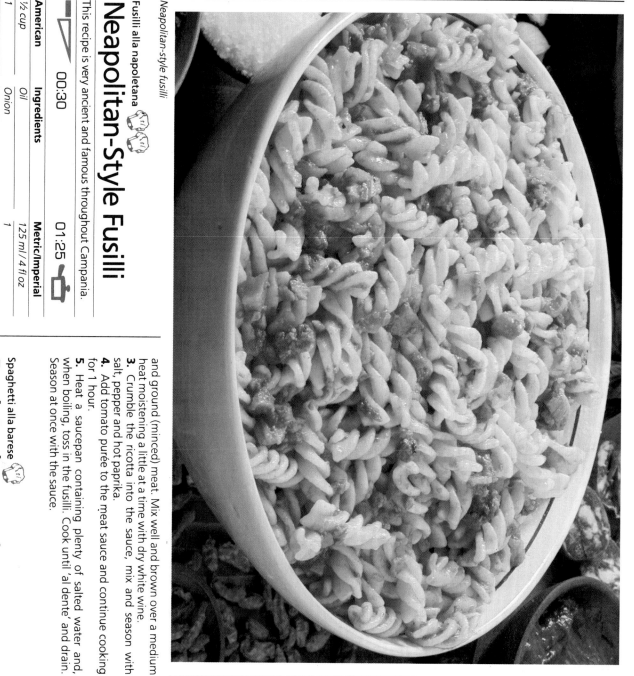

Fusilli grande estate

High Summer Fusilli

00:25 plus 00:30 in refrigerator — 00:25

American	Ingredients	Metric/Imperial
½ lb	*Frozen or shelled fresh peas*	*225 g / 8 oz*
1⅓ cups	*Shelled, cooked prawns*	*225 g / 8 oz*
2	*Ripe but firm pear-shaped tomatoes*	*2*
3 tbsp	*Pickled capers*	*2 tbsp*
7 oz can	*Tuna*	*200 g / 7 oz can*
Scant ¼ cup	*Oil*	*3 tbsp*
1	*Lemon*	*1*
½ lb	*Fusilli pasta*	*225 g / 8 oz*
	Salt and pepper	
¼ tsp	*Oregano*	*¼ tsp*

1. Cook the frozen or fresh peas, drain and place into an earthenware dish.
2. Cut the prawns in half and add them to the peas.
3. Plunge the tomatoes into boiling water, skin them, remove their seeds and cut into small pieces. Add the tomatoes to the other ingredients with pickled capers.
4. Drain the oil from a small can of tuna fish, break it up with a fork and then add it to the dish, mixing gently. Season with oil and the juice of a lemon.
5. Cook the fusilli in plenty of boiling salted water, drain and pass under cold water. Drain well and season with a small amount of oil. Allow to cool.
6. Mix the pasta with the other ingredients, add pepper, salt and sprinkle with oregano. Cover and chill in the refrigerator for about 30 minutes before serving.

Bucatini alla gaetana

Gaeta-Style Bucatini

This is a typical recipe of Gaeta and dates back to the time of wild boar hunting in southern Italy.

00:20 — 00:20

American	Ingredients	Metric/Imperial
14 oz	*Young wild pig meat or pork*	*400 g / 14 oz*
Scant ¼ cup	*Oil*	*3 tbsp*
1	*Onion*	*1*
2 or 3	*Mint leaves*	*2 or 3*
1	*Garlic clove*	*1*
½ lb	*Green olives*	*225 g / 8 oz*
½ cup	*Dry white wine*	*125 ml / 4 fl oz*
¼ lb	*Wild boar or calf's liver*	*100 g / 4 oz*
Scant ¼ cup	*Stock*	*3 tbsp*
14 oz	*Bucatini pasta*	*400 g / 14 oz*
	Salt	
1 tbsp	*Pecorino (ewe's milk cheese)*	*1 tbsp*
¼ tsp	*Oregano*	*¼ tsp*

1. Finely chop the pork. Heat the oil in a frying pan, and brown the meat. Lower the heat and add the finely chopped onion, mint leaves and crushed garlic. Cook for 5 minutes.
2. Mix well, add the green olives and white wine.
3. Chop the liver into small pieces and add to the sauce with the stock. Allow to simmer for 10 minutes.
4. Cook the pasta in boiling salted water until 'al dente', drain and toss it with the pecorino and oregano. Mix with the sauce and serve.

Pasta con ragù al tonno

Pasta with Tuna Sauce

00:10 — 00:40

American	Ingredients	Metric/Imperial
1	*Onion*	*1*
1	*Garlic clove*	*1*
3	*Anchovies in oil*	*3*
¼ lb	*Tuna fish in oil*	*100 g / 4 oz*
3 tbsp	*Olive oil*	*2 tbsp*
¼ cup	*Butter*	*50 g / 2 oz*
½ lb	*Peeled tomatoes*	*225 g / 8 oz*
2 or 3	*Basil leaves*	*2 or 3*
	Salt and pepper	
¾ lb	*Pasta (sedani rigati)*	*350 g / 12 oz*

1. Peel and finely chop onion and garlic. Pound anchovies to a pulp and break up tuna fish and stir into anchovies with half of the oil.
2. Heat oil and butter together in a pan and when foaming sauté onion and garlic for 2-3 minutes. Add peeled tomatoes, basil, salt and pepper and pounded fish. Cook for 2-3 minutes, stirring all the time, cover and allow to simmer over a low heat for 30 minutes.
3. Cook pasta in boiling salted water until 'al dente', drain and stir into tuna sauce.
4. Spoon onto a hot serving dish and serve immediately.

Pasta con le verdure piccanti

Pasta with Spicy Vegetables

00:10 — 00:25

American	Ingredients	Metric/Imperial
2	*Sweet yellow peppers*	*2*
1	*Onion*	*1*
Scant ¼ cup	*Vegetable oil*	*3 tbsp*
1½ cups	*Spinach, boiled and squeezed*	*350 g / 12 oz*
2	*Garlic cloves*	*2*
1	*Bunch of basil*	*1*
½ tsp	*Red paprika*	*½ tsp*
	Pepper	
1 cup	*Dry white wine*	*225 ml / 8 fl oz*
¾ lb	*Pasta*	*350 g / 12 oz*
	Grated pecorino cheese	

1. Deseed and slice peppers, peel and chop onion.
2. Heat oil and add the cooked spinach and garlic and sauté for 5 minutes stirring all the time. Add peppers, onion and basil to pan and cook for a further 2 minutes.
3. Finally stir in paprika, pepper and white wine. Cover and simmer for 10 minutes.

4. Meanwhile cook pasta in boiling salted water until 'al dente'. Drain and stir into vegetable sauce.
5. Spoon onto a hot serving dish, sprinkle a little oil over surface and grated pecorino and serve at once.

Pasta e ricotta sprint

Pasta with Two Cheeses

00:05 00:15

American	Ingredients	Metric/Imperial
½ lb	*Very fresh ricotta cheese*	25 g / 8 oz
½ cup	*Coffee (single) cream*	100 ml / 3½ fl oz
4 tbsp	*Butter*	50 g / 2 oz
	Pepper	
3 tbsp	*Grated parmesan cheese*	2 tbsp
14 oz	*Pasta*	400 g / 14 oz
1 tsp	*Grated parmesan cheese*	1 tsp
1 tsp	*Grated pecorino cheese*	1 tsp

1. Sieve ricotta into a saucepan. Stir in cream with butter, season with pepper and add parmesan. Heat gently over a low heat. Do not allow to boil.
2. Cook pasta in boiling salted water until 'al dente', drain and tip into the ricotta sauce.
3. Spoon onto a heated serving dish, mix together the teaspoon of parmesan and pecorino cheeses and sprinkle over the top.

Pasta con le sarde

Pasta with Sardines

00:30 00:45

American	Ingredients	Metric/Imperial
1	*Head of wild fennel*	1
2	*Onions*	2
14 oz	*Sardines*	400 g / 14 oz
4	*Anchovies*	4
Scant ¼ cup	*Vegetable oil*	3 tbsp
2 oz	*Pine kernels*	50 g / 2 oz
⅓ cup	*Sultanas*	50 g / 2oz
	Salt	
1 lb	*Macaroni*	450 g / 1 lb

1. Preheat oven to 350°F / 180°C / Gas Mark 4. Grease an oblong ovenproof serving dish.
2. Trim and thinly slice the fennel, cook in boiling salted water for 10 minutes, drain. Peel and chop onions, clean and pound sardines, clean and bone anchovies.
3. Heat the oil in a large pan, add the onions and cook for 2-3 minutes. Add fennel, half the sardines and anchovies to pan. Cook for 3 minutes stirring all the time, add pine nuts, sultanas and ⅔ cup [150 ml / ¼ pint] of vegetable water to the pan, cover and simmer over a low heat for 10 minutes.
4. Put the remaining sardines in a bowl and add salt and oil. Leave to stand. Cook macaroni in boiling salted water until 'al dente'.
5. Drain and spoon half the cooked pasta over the base of the serving dish. Mix the remaining macaroni with half the fennel sauce. Spoon the sardines over the pasta then top with the mixed pasta and sauce.
6. Bake for 20 minutes and serve with a crunchy salad.

Conchiglie alla spagnola

Spanish-Style Shells

00:30 01:15

American	Ingredients	Metric/Imperial
4 tbsp	*Butter*	50 g / 2 oz
Scant ¼ cup	*Oil*	3 tbsp
2	*Onions*	2
2	*Carrots*	2
1	*Celery stalk*	1
1 lb	*Lean veal pieces*	500 g / 1 lb
3 tbsp	*Flour*	2 tbsp
¼ cup	*White wine*	50 ml / 2 fl oz
1 cup	*Stock*	225 ml / 8 fl oz
½ lb	*Peeled tomatoes*	225 g / 8 oz
2	*Large sweet peppers*	2
1 tsp	*Oregano*	1 tsp
	Salt and pepper	
¾ lb	*Durum wheat shells*	350 g / 12 oz
½ lb	*Mozzarella cheese*	225 g / 8 oz

1. Preheat the oven to 400°F / 200°C /Gas Mark 6.
2. Heat half the butter and oil in a frying pan, add thinly sliced onions, carrots and celery, cook over a medium heat.
3. Push the vegetables to one side after 5 minutes.
4. Cut the veal into small pieces, toss in flour and add to the pan and fry on both sides until brown.
5. Sprinkle with white wine and when it has evaporated, continue the cooking moistening with stock, with the lid on the pan. Stir occasionally and after 10 minutes add 2 peeled and squashed tomatoes.
6. In a separate pan, heat remaining oil and butter and lightly fry a large diced onion. When the onion becomes transparent, add the deseeded sweet peppers which have been cut into fairly small slices, and the peeled tomatoes, season with salt and pepper, sprinkle with oregano and leave to cook. After 20 minutes add the onion and sweet pepper sauce to the meat mixture, mix well and adjust seasoning. Continue cooking until pasta is ready.
7. Cook the shells in plenty of salted and boiling water. Drain the pasta, mix with meat mixture, and sauce. Turn into an ovenproof dish, sprinkle the surface with oregano and mozzarella cut into small pieces. Place in hot oven for 15 minutes and serve immediately.

Dashing bucatini

Bucatini alla brava

Dashing Bucatini

00:20 | 00:30

American	Ingredients	Metric/Imperial
¼ cup	*Butter*	50 g / 2 oz
1	*Onion*	1
1 cup	*Cooked prawns*	175 g / 6 oz
½ cup	*Whipping (double) cream*	125 ml / 4 fl oz
¼ tsp	*Chopped thyme*	¼ tsp
¼ tsp	*Chopped sweet marjoram*	¼ tsp
1 tsp	*Curry powder*	1 tsp
1 tsp	*Fine-grain semolina*	1 tsp
	Salt	
14 oz	*Bucatini pasta*	400 g / 14 oz

1. In a small saucepan, melt the butter, add the finely chopped onion, the peeled prawns, cream, thyme, marjoram and the curry powder, mix well over a low heat.
2. Sprinkle on the semolina, keeping the heat low and mixing carefully.
3. Heat plenty of salted water in a large saucepan, when it boils toss in the bucatini pasta stirring frequently. When cooking is completed, drain and season at once with the sauce. Cheese is not necessary. You may use other types of pasta, from macaroni to spaghetti, according to taste.

Pasticcio alla Bambi

Bambi-Style Pie

00:15 | 00:55

American	Ingredients	Metric/Imperial
3 cups	*Béchamel sauce (see page 162)*	700 ml / 1¼ pints
3 tbsp	*Grated parmesan cheese*	2 tbsp
⅓ cup	*Butter*	75 g / 3 oz
1½ oz	*Dried mushrooms*	40 g / 1½ oz
14 oz	*Canned peas*	400 g / 14 oz
7 oz	*Fontina cheese*	200 g / 7 oz
2 oz	*Slice of cooked ham*	50 g / 2 oz
1 lb	*Conchiglioni (large shell-shaped pasta)*	450 g / 1 lb
¼ cup	*Butter*	50 g / 2 oz

1. Preheat oven to 350°F / 180°C / Gas Mark 4. Grease an oblong ovenproof serving dish.
2. Make béchamel sauce and stir in half the grated parmesan.
3. Heat the butter, sauté the mushrooms and the drained peas for 3 minutes. Cut the fontina and the ham into small pieces and put in a bowl. Add the cooked mushrooms and the peas and mix well.
4. Cook conchiglioni in plenty of boiling salted water until 'al dente', drain and spoon half the pasta over base of dish. Top with half the mushroom sauce then a layer of béchamel. Continue to layer remaining pasta sauce and béchamel. Sprinkle over remaining parmesan, add dabs of butter and bake for 30 minutes until golden brown.

Pasta con la ricotta

Pasta with Ricotta

00:10 | 00:10

American	Ingredients	Metric/Imperial
7 oz	*Ricotta cheese*	200 g / 7 oz
1 cup	*Whipping (double) cream*	225 ml / 8 fl oz
	Salt and pepper	
¼ tsp	*Paprika*	¼ tsp
1 tbsp	*Sugar*	1 tbsp
1 tbsp	*Cinnamon*	1 tbsp
14 oz	*Hard-grain semolina pasta, e.g. spaghetti, macaroni, zite, or rigatoni*	400 g / 14 oz

1. In a bowl mix the ricotta with cream, pepper, salt, paprika, sugar and cinnamon.
2. In a large saucepan cook the pasta till 'al dente', in plenty of salted water. Drain well and stir in the ricotta sauce over a low heat, then serve.

Variations: other cheeses may be used such as romand or piedmont ricotta, ligurian curd cheese or strong apulian ricotta.

Penne con le zucchine crude

Penne with Raw Gourds

00:15 | 00:15

American	Ingredients	Metric/Imperial
4	*Coastal gourds*	4
¼ cup	*Refined lard*	50 g / 2 oz
2	*Garlic cloves*	2
⅔ cup	*Ripe black olives*	100 g / 4 oz
1 lb	*Penne pasta*	450 g / 1 lb
	Salt and pepper	

1. Wash gourds carefully and slice finely.
2. Heat lard until hot, add the crushed cloves of garlic and cook for 1-2 minutes, then add black olives and cook for a further 2 minutes, stirring all the time.
3. Cook pasta in boiling salted water until 'al dente', then drain and add olive sauce to pasta and stir in the gourds. Season with pepper and serve immediately.

Pasticcio di fegatini e maccheroni

Chicken Livers and Macaroni Pie

00:30 00:40

American	Ingredients	Metric/Imperial
1	*Onion*	*1*
1	*Celery*	*1*
2	*Leeks*	*2*
2	*Carrots*	*2*
⅓ cup	*Butter*	*65 g / 2½ oz*
	Salt and pepper	
1¼ cups	*Tomato sauce (see page 171)*	*300 ml / ½ pint*
8	*Chicken livers*	*8*
2 cups	*Béchamel sauce (see page 162)*	*450 ml / ¾ pint*
1 lb	*Macaroni*	*450 g / 1 lb*
¼ cup	*Grated parmesan cheese*	*25 g / 1 oz*

1. Preheat oven to 375°F / 190°C / Gas Mark 5. Grease an overproof serving dish.
2. Peel and chop onion, slice celery, leeks and carrots. Heat most of the butter and, when foaming, sauté the vegetables for 5 minutes, season and stir in tomato sauce.
3. Chop trimmed chicken livers into small pieces and add to the pan. Cook for 5 minutes stirring from time to time. Remove pan from heat.
4. Make a béchamel sauce. Cook macaroni in boiling salted water until 'al dente', drain and spoon half over the base of dish. Top with half the liver and vegetable mixture. Continue layering pasta and liver sauce, then cover with béchamel.
5. Sprinkle with parmesan, dot with dabs of remaining butter and bake for 30 minutes until golden brown. Serve hot.

Spaghetti al dolce

Sweet-Style Spaghetti

00:15 00:10

American	Ingredients	Metric/Imperial
14 oz	*Thin spaghetti (fidelini)*	*400 g / 14 oz*
Scant ¼ cup	*Vegetable oil*	*3 tbsp*
2 tbsp	*Vinegar*	*1½ tbsp*
	Salt and pepper	
1	*Red beetroot, cooked*	*1*
3	*Medium-sized carrots*	*3*
2	*White celery stalks*	*2*
1 cup	*Mayonnaise (see page 175)*	*225 ml / 8 fl oz*

1. Cook spaghetti in boiling salted water until 'al dente'. Beat the oil, vinegar, salt and pepper together. Drain pasta and toss in some of the dressing.
2. Peel beetroot, dice into small cubes and put in a bowl. Scrape carrots, grate finely and add to the beetroot; slice celery thinly and add to bowl. Toss vegetables in prepared dressing and mayonnaise and stir into spaghetti. Mix carefully and serve cold.

Variation: canned white tuna fish may be added with the vegetables.

Pasta con coniglio alla sarda

Sardinian-Style Rabbit with Pasta

00:25 00:30

American	Ingredients	Metric/Imperial
¾ lb	*Rabbit meat, raw or cooked*	*350 g / 12 oz*
2 tbsp	*Oil*	*1½ tbsp*
1	*Sprig of sage*	*1*
1	*Sprig of myrtle*	*1*
½ cup	*White wine*	*125 ml / 4 fl oz*
½ cup	*Stock*	*125 ml / 4 fl oz*
	Salt and pepper	
14 oz	*Pasta*	*400 g / 14 oz*
1 cup	*Coffee (single) cream*	*225 ml / 8 fl oz*

1. Grind (mince) rabbit meat finely. Heat oil and quickly brown meat with sage and myrtle. Pour over wine and stock, season, cover and simmer for 20 minutes.
2. Meanwhile cook pasta in boiling salted water until 'al dente', then drain.
3. Purée rabbit sauce in a blender or food processor, stir in cream, add drained pasta, and mix well. Serve immediately.

Pasta alla veneziana

Venetian-Style Pasta

00:15 00:50

American	Ingredients	Metric/Imperial
1¼ lb	*Well-filleted fish in a slice or whole*	*600 g / 1¼ lb*
1	*Onion*	*1*
⅓ cup	*Butter*	*65 g / 2½ oz*
3 tbsp	*White wine*	*2 tbsp*
5 tbsp	*Tomato concentrate*	*4 tbsp*
¼ lb	*Pine kernels*	*100 g / 4 oz*
1 cup	*Béchamel sauce (see page 162)*	*225 ml / 8 fl oz*
1 tbsp	*Grated parmesan cheese*	*1 tbsp*
14 oz	*Spaghetti*	*400 g / 14 oz*
	Bread crumbs as required	
	Salt	

1. Preheat the oven to 400°F / 200°C / Gas Mark 6. Grease an ovenproof dish.
2. Poach fish in simmering water for about 10 minutes, then drain, and chop up flesh into bite-size pieces. Peel and finely chop onion.
3. Melt half the butter in a pan and when foaming add onion and fish and sauté for 2 minutes. Add white wine, tomato concentrate, pine kernels. Simmer for 5 minutes, uncovered.
4. Prepare a béchamel sauce with the rest of the butter, ¼ cup [25 g / 1 oz] flour and 1 cup [225 ml / 8 fl oz] milk. Stir in the parmesan.
5. Cook spaghetti in boiling salt water until 'al dente' then drain and add to the fish sauce mixing gently.
6. Sprinkle bread crumbs over base of serving dish, spoon a layer of spaghetti sauce over base, top with some béchamel. Continue layering in this way finishing with béchamel.
7. Bake in the oven for 15 minutes until golden. Serve at once.

Penne e beccacce

Penne Pasta and Woodcocks

00:20 00:50

American	Ingredients	Metric/Imperial
2	*Oven-ready woodcocks*	2
1	*Onion*	1
¼ cup	*Vegetable oil*	50 ml / 2 fl oz
½ cup	*Butter*	100 g / 4 oz
¼ tsp	*Sage*	¼ tsp
¼ tsp	*Thyme*	¼ tsp
¼ tsp	*Sweet marjoram*	¼ tsp
¼ tsp	*Rosemary*	¼ tsp
¼ tsp	*Chervil*	¼ tsp
2	*Garlic cloves*	2
	Salt and pepper	
¼ cup	*Cognac*	50 ml / 2 fl oz
½ lb	*Strained tomato pulp*	225 g / 8 oz
14 oz	*Penne pasta*	400 g / 14 oz
6 oz	*Fresh fontina cheese*	175 g / 6 oz
	Truffle	

1. Cut all flesh from woodcocks into small pieces. Peel and chop onion.
2. Heat oil and butter together and, when foaming, brown meat, stirring all the time. Add onion, herbs, garlic, salt, pepper and cognac to the pan with the tomato pulp. Cook for a further 45 minutes until woodcock is done.
3. Cook pasta in boiling salted water until 'al dente', then drain. Cut fontina into thin slices and mix into the pasta with the woodcock sauce.
4. Serve on a hot serving dish garnished with grated truffle.

Pizzoccheri ai colombacci

Pizzoccheri with Wood Pigeons

00:15 00:50

American	Ingredients	Metric/Imperial
2	*Oven-ready wood pigeons*	2
1	*Onion*	1
¼ cup	*Lard*	50 g / 2 oz
½ cup	*Red wine*	125 ml / 4 fl oz
2 or 3	*Sage leaves*	2 or 3
1 cup	*Coffee (single) cream*	225 ml / 8 fl oz
14 oz	*Pizzoccheri*	400 g / 14 oz
10 oz	*Bitto cheese*	275 g / 10 oz

1. Remove all flesh from the bones of the pigeons, and cut into even-sized pieces. Peel and chop onion, heat lard and when hot brown pigeon flesh lightly, stirring from time to time.
2. Pour the red wine into the pan, add onion and sage leaves, cover and simmer a further 45 minutes. Cool slightly, then stir in cream and keep warm over a low heat.
3. Cook pizzoccheri in boiling unsalted water until 'al dente'. Drain, stir in the bitto cheese, and cream sauce. Serve immediately.

Sformato di maccheroncelli

Small Macaroni Mold

00:20 01:00

American	Ingredients	Metric/Imperial
1	*Bread roll*	1
	Milk as required	
1¾ cups	*Ground (minced) meat*	400g / 14 oz
2	*Eggs*	2
3 tbsp	*Grated cheese*	2 tbsp
	White flour, as required	
½ cup	*Vegetable oil*	125 ml / 4 fl oz
1	*Large onion*	1
6 - 7	*Plum tomatoes (fresh or canned)*	6 - 7
2	*Garlic cloves*	2
½ tsp	*Oregano*	½ tsp
½ tsp	*Basil*	½ tsp
	Salt and pepper	
¾ lb	*Small macaroni*	350 g / 12 oz
1	*Scamorza cheese*	1

1. Preheat oven to 375°F / 190°C / Gas Mark 5.
2. Soak inside of roll in milk, then squeeze out excess liquid. Mix ground meat with beaten eggs, the soaked bread crumbs and grated cheese. Mix all ingredients well, divide mixture into even-sized small balls and toss in flour.
3. Heat all but 2 tablespoons of the oil in a frying pan and, when very hot, fry meat balls until evenly browned – about 5-8 minutes, then drain on absorbent paper.
4. Peel and slice onion, sieve tomatoes. Heat remaining oil in another pan and cook onion and crushed garlic for 5 minutes until golden brown. Add tomatoes, oregano, basil and pepper, then the meat balls. Cover and simmer for about 20 minutes.
5. Meanwhile cook small macaroni until 'al dente' in boiling salted water, drain then add meat balls and sauce. Skin and dice scamorza cheese and stir into pasta mixture.
6. Spoon pasta and sauce into an ovenproof serving dish. Bake for 25 minutes until a golden brown crust forms. Serve with grated cheese.

Pennette alla contadina

Peasant Quills

00:10 00:20

American	Ingredients	Metric/Imperial
8	*Tomatoes*	8
3 tbsp	*Olive oil*	2 tbsp
1	*Garlic clove*	1
1 tbsp	*Oregano*	1 tbsp
	Salt and pepper	
14 oz	*Pennette pasta*	400 g / 14 oz
	Grated cheese as required	

1. Skin tomatoes and quarter. Heat oil in a pan and when hot fry crushed garlic, tomatoes and oregano for 5 minutes. Season and simmer for 10 minutes.
2. Cook pennette in boiling salted water until 'al dente', drain and stir into tomato sauce.
3. Spoon onto a serving dish, sprinkle with black pepper and grated cheese. Serve very hot.

Pasta del pirata Barbanera

Pirate Barbanera's Pasta

00:10 01:15

American	Ingredients	Metric/Imperial
1	*Onion*	1
4	*Garlic cloves*	4
3 tbsp	*Olive oil*	2 tbsp
¼ tsp	*Rosemary*	¼ tsp
1	*Chilli pepper*	1
¾ lb	*Ripe plum tomatoes*	350 g / 12 oz
	White wine as required	
14 oz	*Spaghetti or trenette (long narrow noodles)*	400 g / 14 oz
4	*Garlic cloves (optional)*	4

1. Peel and finely chop onion and garlic. Heat oil in a pan and when hot add onion, garlic, rosemary and deseeded, chopped chilli and cook for 3 minutes.
2. Purée tomatoes and add to pan. Cover and simmer over a very low heat for 1 hour, adding white wine if sauce becomes too thick.
3. Cook spaghetti or trenette in boiling salted water until 'al dente', drain and put in a serving bowl. If liked add a further 4 cloves of crushed garlic to sauce, pour tomato sauce over pasta, stir well and serve.

Bucatini al garganello

Bucatini with Teal

00:35 00:60

American	Ingredients	Metric/Imperial
1	*Small teal (wild duck)*	1
2	*Lemons*	2
4	*Anchovies*	4
1 oz	*Capers*	25 g / 1 oz
½ cup	*Butter*	100 g / 4 oz
3 tbsp	*Flour*	2 tbsp
½ cup	*Concentrated clear soup*	125 ml / 4 fl oz
½ cup	*Strong red wine*	125 ml / 4 fl oz
	Salt and pepper	
¼ tsp	*Nutmeg*	¼ tsp
14 oz	*Bucatini pasta*	400 g / 14 oz

1. Clean the teal with water and rub over with a slice of lemon, then cut into pieces.
2. Chop anchovies and capers, sprinkle with lemon juice.
3. Melt 2 tablespoons [25 g / 1 oz] butter in a saucepan, add the white flour, mix well and add the mixture of soup and red wine. Add the chopped anchovies and capers, mix well and then add pieces of teal. Cook over a moderate heat until tender.
4. Remove the teal and take off all the flesh. Chop finely or blend the meat in an electric food blender or processor, add the sauce, season, mix well and warm again.
5. Cook the bucatini pasta in boiling salted water, drain when 'al dente' and dress the pasta with the teal sauce.

Spaghetti with a selection of sauces

Tagiatelle alle cozze

Noodles with Mussels

Preparation 00:25 | Cooking 00:25

American	Ingredients	Metric/Imperial
2 lb	*Mussels*	*1 kg /2 lb*
2	*Garlic cloves*	*2*
1 tbsp	*Chopped parsley*	*1 tbsp*
Scant ¼ cup	*Vegetable oil*	*3 tbsp*
½ cup	*Whipping (double) cream*	*100 ml / 3½ fl oz*
	Salt and pepper	
14 oz	*Noodles*	*400 g / 14 oz*
¼ cup	*Butter*	*50 g / 2 oz*
2	*Egg yolks*	*2*

1. Preheat oven to 325°F / 160°C / Gas Mark 3. Butter a large piece of foil and place on a heatproof serving dish.
2. Wash and scrub mussels individually in three changes of water and remove beards. Put in a large pan of water, bring to the boil and cook for 8-10 minutes until all the mussel shells have opened. Discard any closed mussel shells. Remove the moluscs carefully from the shells and leave on one side. Retain the cooking liquid.
3. Finely chop garlic and parsley. Heat oil in a pan and when very hot add garlic and parsley and cook for 1 minute then add mussels, seasoning and half the cooking water used for the mussels. Boil until liquid has reduced by half, then stir in cream and simmer for 3 minutes.
4. Cook noodles in boiling salted water until 'al dente', drain and put in a serving bowl. Add mussel sauce and butter and stir in well with the beaten egg yolks.
5. Spoon noodle mixture over foil in dish, close up foil to form a parcel. Bake for 10 minutes and serve 'parcel' in the dish at the table.

Tagliatelle alle cipolle e porro

Noodles with Onions and Leek

Preparation 00:05 | Cooking 00:15

American	Ingredients	Metric/Imperial
2	*Onions*	*2*
1	*Leek*	*1*
1	*Bunch of chives*	*1*
1	*Bunch of parsley*	*1*
½ cup	*Vegetable oil*	*125 ml / 4 fl oz*
14 oz	*Noodles*	*400 g / 14 oz*
	Salt	
1 tbsp	*Grated pecorino cheese*	*1 tbsp*

1. Finely chop onions and leek with chives and parsley. Heat oil and cook half the vegetable and herb mixture for 3-5 minutes, stirring all the time.
2. Cook the noodles in the boiling salted water until 'al dente', drain and stir in the grated pecorino cheese and the hot vegetable mixture.
3. Finally stir in remaining raw chopped vegetables.
4. Spoon onto a hot serving dish and serve immediately.

Rigatoni con le zucchine

Rigatoni with Gourds

Preparation 00:10 | Cooking 00:40

American	Ingredients	Metric/Imperial
14 oz	*Gourds*	*400 g / 14 oz*
Scant ¼ cup	*Vegetable oil*	*3 tbsp*
1	*Garlic clove*	*1*
	Salt and pepper	
1 tbsp	*Chopped parsley*	*1 tbsp*
14 oz	*Rigatoni*	*400 g / 14 oz*
¼ cup	*Grated parmesan cheese*	*25 g / 1 oz*

1. Wash gourds and slice thinly.
2. Heat oil and, when hot, add crushed garlic and cook for 1 minute. Put prepared gourds in pan, season, add chopped parsley, cover and cook for 40 minutes over a low heat, stirring from time to time.
3. Cook rigatoni in plenty of boiling salted water until 'al dente', drain and put in a serving bowl. Stir in the cooked gourds and sprinkle over parmesan cheese, just before serving.

Bavette e pesce

Noodles and Fish

This delicious pasta dish is eaten throughout Versilia, but even more in the south. It is essential to use fresh fish or left-over boiled fish, sieved carefully. A typical seaside dish which has several names and is often enjoyed near the Mediterranean.

Preparation 00:40 | Cooking 00:60

American	Ingredients	Metric/Imperial
1½ lb	*Fish*	*600 g / 1½ lb*
1	*Piece of skate*	*1*
1	*Piece of octopus*	*1*
¼ cup	*Oil*	*3 tbsp*
2	*Onions*	*2*
1	*Red chilli pepper*	*1*
1 tbsp	*Parsley*	*1 tbsp*
¼ tsp	*Basil*	*¼ tsp*
2	*Garlic cloves*	*2*
1 cup	*Strained tomato pulp*	*225 ml / 8 fl oz*
1	*Sweet yellow pepper*	*1*
⅔ cup	*Shelled, cooked prawns*	*100 g / 4 oz*
	Salt and pepper	
14 oz	*Noodles*	*400 g / 14 oz*

1. Boil the fish in salted water, drain when firm, cool and remove the bones.
2. Pass the fish flesh through the blender, then tip it into a large saucepan with oil and peeled chopped onions.
3. Add chopped chilli pepper already deseeded, some chopped parsley and basil and 2 crushed cloves of garlic. Cook for about 10 minutes, mixing thoroughly, add the strained tomato pulp and a sweet yellow pepper cut into thin strips. Continue to cook the sauce, stirring from time to time. Add prawns and season well.
4. Cook the noodles in plenty of salted water. Drain them well while still firm and add to the sauce, stir for a few moments, increasing the heat, then serve, if possible in the cooking pot.

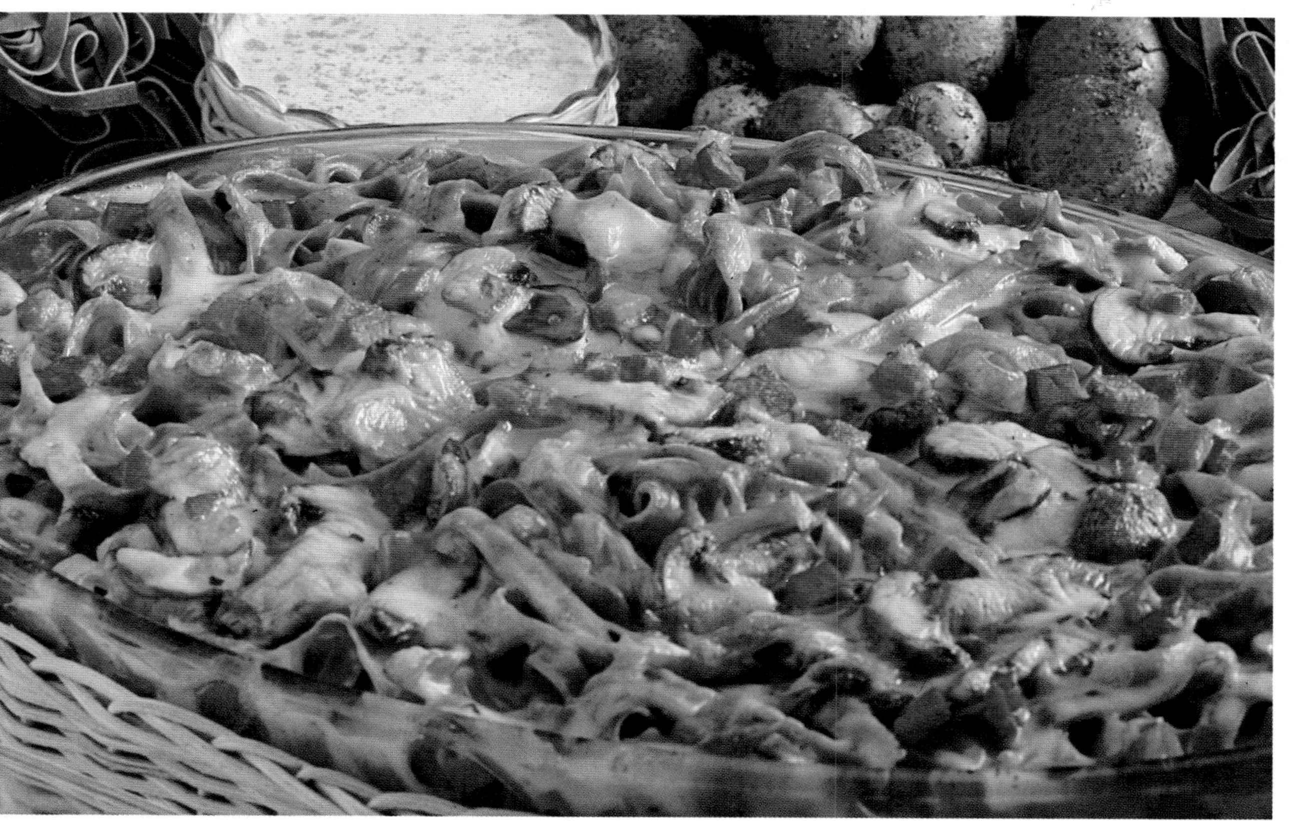

Gratinated green noodles

Tagliatelle verdi gratinate

Gratinated Green Noodles

00:10 | 00:45

American	Ingredients	Metric/Imperial
¾ lb	*Noodles*	*350 g / 12 oz*
1 cup	*Béchamel sauce (see page 162)*	*225 ml / 8 fl oz*
5 oz	*Mushrooms*	*150 g / 5 oz*
½ lb	*Ham cut into dice*	*225 g / 8 oz*
	Butter as required	
1 tbsp	*Bread crumbs*	*1 tbsp*
2	*Eggs*	*2*
	Salt and pepper	
1 tbsp	*Grated parmesan cheese*	*1 tbsp*
1 cup	*Cream*	*225 ml / 8 fl oz*
2 tsp	*Curry powder*	*2 tsp*
	Black or powdered truffle (optional)	

1. Heat oven to 350°F / 180°C / Gas Mark 4.
2. Parboil noodles for 5 minutes, then drain and rinse under cold water. Prepare a cup of béchamel.
3. Add mushrooms and ham to the béchamel, blend with the noodles, mixing carefully.
4. Butter an ovenproof dish, scatter with bread crumbs and slip mixture into it. Beat eggs with salt, pepper and parmesan and pour over the noodle mixture.
5. Place dish in centre of the oven and bake for 20-25 minutes until a golden crust forms.
6. Meanwhile beat cream with the curry powder. Add grated black truffle (or powdered form) to sauce. Pour into a sauceboat and serve cold as an accompaniment to the dish of hot gratinated noodles.

Tagliatelle al caviale e panna

Noodles with Caviar and Cream

00:05 | 00:15

American	Ingredients	Metric/Imperial
1 cup	*Coffee (single) cream*	*225 ml / 8 fl oz*
1	*Small jar of caviar or substitute*	*1*
1 tbsp	*Butter*	*1 tbsp*
2 or 3	*Sage leaves*	*2 or 3*
¼ cup	*Cognac (optional)*	*50 ml / 2 fl oz*
14 oz	*Egg noodles*	*400 g / 14 oz*
3 tbsp	*Grated parmesan cheese*	*2 tbsp*

1. Pour cream into a saucepan, add caviar and simmer over a low heat for 10 minutes, stirring all the time, but do not allow to boil. Add butter, sage and cognac and cook for a further 2 minutes.
2. Cook noodles in plenty of boiling salted water until 'al dente', drain and stir into caviar sauce with grated parmesan.
3. Spoon onto a hot serving dish and serve immediately.

Tagliatelle al mascarpone

Mascarpone Noodles

00:15 00:10

American	Ingredients	Metric/Imperial
7 oz	*Mascarpone cheese*	*200 g / 7 oz*
2	*Egg yolks*	*2*
½ cup	*Grated parmesan cheese*	*50g / 2 oz*
14 oz	*Noodles*	*400 g / 14 oz*
	Salt and pepper	

1. Put mascarpone in a bowl and beat with a wooden spoon. Add egg yolks and grated parmesan. Continue to mix until ingredients are well blended to a soft cream consistency.
2. Boil noodles in boiling salted water until 'al dente'. Drain and stir in the mascarpone cream. Sprinkle with freshly-ground pepper and serve piping hot.

Tagliatelle alla russa

Russian-Style Noodles

00:05 00:10

American	Ingredients	Metric/Imperial
1 tbsp	*Butter*	*1 tbsp*
1 cup	*Coffee (single) cream*	*225 ml / 8 fl oz*
	Salt and pepper	
7 oz can	*Russian crab*	*200 g / 7 oz can*
1 tsp	*Vodka*	*1 tsp*
½ lb	*Noodles*	*225 g / 8 oz*

1. Melt butter in a pan, add cream, salt, pepper, flaked crab and vodka. Simmer gently for 5 minutes. Do not allow to boil.
2. Cook noodles in boiling salted water until 'al dente', drain and stir into crab sauce. Spoon onto a hot serving dish and serve immediately.

Pizzoccheri valtellinesi

Valtellina Noodles

00:45 00:15

American	Ingredients	Metric/Imperial
¾ lb	*Mixed valtellina cheeses*	*350 g / 12 oz*
3	*Potatoes*	*3*
¾ lb	*Green vegetables (spinach, beet, savoy cabbage)*	*350 g / 12 oz*
2	*Garlic cloves*	*2*
1	*Large onion*	*1*
14 oz	*Pizzoccheri (see page 94)*	*400 g / 14 oz*
1 tbsp	*Butter*	*1 tbsp*

1. Cut valtellina cheeses – a mixture of bitto, magnuca and toma – into small cubes. Dice peeled potatoes, trim green vegetables and shred. Chop garlic and onion.
2. Make pasta according to recipe for pizzoccheri pasta. Boil potatoes and vegetables separately in salted water.
3. In a small pan heat butter and fry chopped garlic and onion for 3 minutes. When vegetables are almost cooked, add pizzoccheri to saucepan. When pasta is 'al dente', drain with the vegetables. Stir in garlic and onion mixture, then mix in the pieces of cheese.
4. Spoon into an ovenproof serving dish and place under a hot broiler [grill] to brown. Serve at once.

Tagliatelle alla veneta

Venetian-Style Noodles

00:40 00:40

American	Ingredients	Metric/Imperial
14 oz	*Mixed veal meat skinned and chopped*	*400 g / 14 oz*
5 oz	*Sausage*	*150 g / 5 oz*
1	*Onion*	*1*
¼ cup	*Butter*	*50 g / 2 oz*
	Salt and pepper	
¼ tsp	*Nutmeg*	*¼ tsp*
½ cup	*Strong red wine*	*125 ml / 4 fl oz*
1 cup	*Cream*	*225 ml / 8 fl oz*
14 oz	*Noodles*	*400 g / 14 oz*
	Plenty of grated parmesan cheese	

1. Chop veal and sausage into small pieces. Peel and chop onion. Heat butter in a pan and when foaming fry veal and sausage for 5 minutes, stirring all the time, until lightly browned. Add salt, pepper, nutmeg and wine to pan with onion and cream. Leave to simmer for about 30 minutes over a very low heat.
2. Cook pasta in boiling salted water until 'al dente', drain, stir in grated parmesan and hot meat sauce. Serve immediately.

Tagliatelle al capriolo

Roebuck Noodles

00:20 00:40

American	Ingredients	Metric/Imperial
14 oz	*Roebuck (venison) meat*	*400 g / 14 oz*
1 cup	*Whipping (double) cream*	*225 ml / 8 fl oz*
1 cup	*Milk*	*225 ml / 8 fl oz*
½ cup	*Cognac*	*125 ml / 4 fl oz*
1	*Onion*	*1*
1	*Bunch of chervil*	*1*
	Salt and pepper	
14 oz	*Fresh noodles*	*400 g / 14 oz*
	Black truffle (optional)	

1. Cut roebuck meat into small pieces and put in a pan with cream, milk and three quarters of the cognac. Peel and chop onion, chop chervil and add to pan and cook over a very low heat for 40 minutes, stirring from time to time. Season with salt and pepper.
2. When meat is cooked, add remaining cognac, keep sauce warm over a very low heat.
3. Meanwhile cook tagliatelle in boiling salted water until 'al dente', drain and stir in prepared sauce.
4. Spoon onto a hot serving dish and garnish with a sprinkling of truffle if wished.

Russian-style noodles

Fettuccine dorate

Golden Noodles

00:10 | 00:20

American	Ingredients	Metric/Imperial
	Salt	
14 oz	*Noodles*	*400 g / 14 oz*
4 tbsp	*Margarine*	*50 g / 2 oz*
3 tbsp	*Bread crumbs*	*2 tbsp*
1 tsp	*Chopped basil*	*1 tsp*
	Pepper	
	Pecorino cheese as desired	

1. Bring to the boil a large saucepan of salted water, drop in the egg noodles, drain when cooked 'al dente'.
2. Heat the margarine in a frying pan, lightly brown the bread crumbs and the very finely chopped basil in the fat, add the drained noodles and cook till golden over a brisk heat. Season and sprinkle with grated strong pecorino.

Bavette alla livornese

Leghorn-Style Noodles

00:25 | 00:35

American	Ingredients	Metric/Imperial
3 tbsp	*Oil*	*2 tbsp*
4	*Red rock mullet*	*4*
1	*Onion*	*1*
1	*Garlic clove*	*1*
½ lb	*Peeled tomatoes*	*225 g / 8 oz*
	Salt and pepper	
1½ tsp	*Chopped basil*	*1½ tsp*
14 oz	*Noodles, fresh or dried*	*400 g / 14 oz*

1. Heat the oil in a frying pan, add the well-cleaned mullet, a chopped onion, crushed garlic, peeled tomatoes, salt, pepper, and 1 teaspoon of basil and cook gently; turn the fish over only once. (The fish will be cooked when the eyes appear white.)
2. Remove the fish without breaking, open and bone carefully.
3. Beat the fish flesh with the cooking liquid, then return to a small saucepan to thicken well.
4. Heat plenty of salted water in a large saucepan, add the noodles when the water is boiling and cook until firm. Drain and season at once with the mullet sauce. Sprinkle with basil.

Agnolotti alla parmense

Parmesan Ravioli

00:60 | 00:12 to 00:18 depending on size

American	Ingredients	Metric/Imperial
½ cup	*Grated stale bread*	*50 g / 2 oz*
1 cup	*Grated parmesan cheese*	*100 g / 4 oz*
	Salt and pepper	
½ tsp	*Nutmeg*	*½ tsp*
1 lb	*Pasta dough (see page 94)*	*450 g / 1 lb*

1. Mix the bread, grated parmesan, salt and pepper with the nutmeg, blending together well.
2. Prepare the pasta by halving the dough, rolling 2 pieces out thinly on the table.
3. Place little heaps of filling on one half, cover with the remaining half of the dough and shape some perfectly round agnolotti with a small glass or cutter.
4. Heat plenty of salted water in a saucepan and when the water comes to the boil, toss in ravioli and serve them with meat sauce or in clear soup.
5. Serve grated parmesan separately with this delicately flavored dish.

Agnolotti

Small Ravioli

00:30 The pasta dough 01:00 | 00:08 to 00:10

American	Ingredients	Metric/Imperial
¼ cup	*Butter*	*50 g / 2 oz*
¼ lb	*Veal*	*100 g / 4 oz*
5 oz	*Lean pork*	*150 g / 5 oz*
	Salt and pepper	
5 oz	*Chopped raw ham*	*150 g / 5 oz*
1	*Truffle (optional)*	*1*
1	*Egg, beaten*	*1*
¼ cup	*Grated parmesan cheese*	*25 g / 1 oz*
	A little dry white wine (if required)	
	A sheet of fresh pasta dough (see page 94)	
	Grated parmesan cheese	
2 tbsp	*Butter for seasoning*	*25 g / 1 oz*

1. Melt butter in a saucepan, add the ground (minced) veal, pork, salt, pepper, chopped ham, half the truffle cut in fine slices, cook over a low heat.
2. Add the beaten egg and the grated cheese, mix all the ingredients thoroughly, cooking and moistening only if necessary with a little dry white wine. Allow to cool.
3. Make the pasta according to the basic recipe for fresh pasta (see page 94). Roll out the dough in two equal pieces, on one half place spoonfuls of prepared filling in little heaps. Fold over and cut with the ravioli cutter to give the desired shape.
4. Continue with remaining dough and mixture. Leave the filled ravioli for 30 minutes.
5. Boil plenty of salted water in a large saucepan and as soon as it reaches boiling point, toss the pasta in.
6. The ravioli will be ready when they rise to the surface. Take out of the water with a slotted spoon, arrange on a hot serving dish. Toss in butter and sprinkle with grated parmesan cheese. Finally, scatter with fine slices of the remaining truffle and serve.

Preparing small ravioli
1. When you have cooked the filling of veal, pork, seasoning ham and truffle over low heat, transfer it to a bowl and add the egg and grated parmesan cheese. Mix thoroughly, moistening if necessary with a little dry wine. Cool.
2. Roll the pasta dough out into two equal pieces. On one half place teaspoonfuls of prepared filling.
3. Fold the rest of the dough over and press down between the rows of filling. Cut out with the ravioli cutter.
4. Cook the pasta in a saucepan of boiling salted water.
5. Serve tossed in butter and sprinkled with grated parmesan.

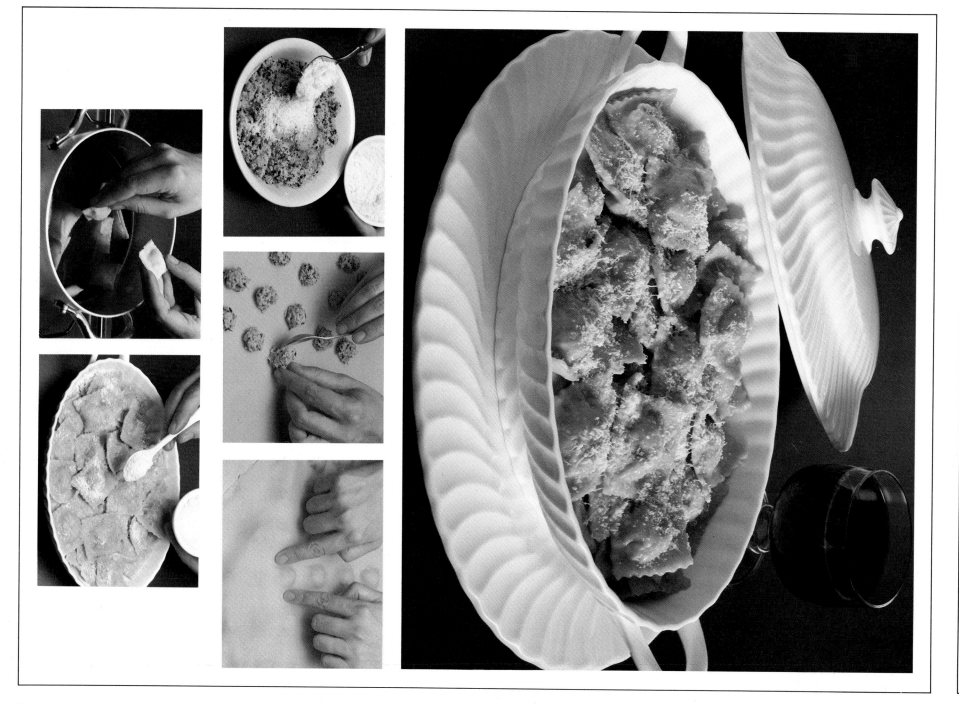

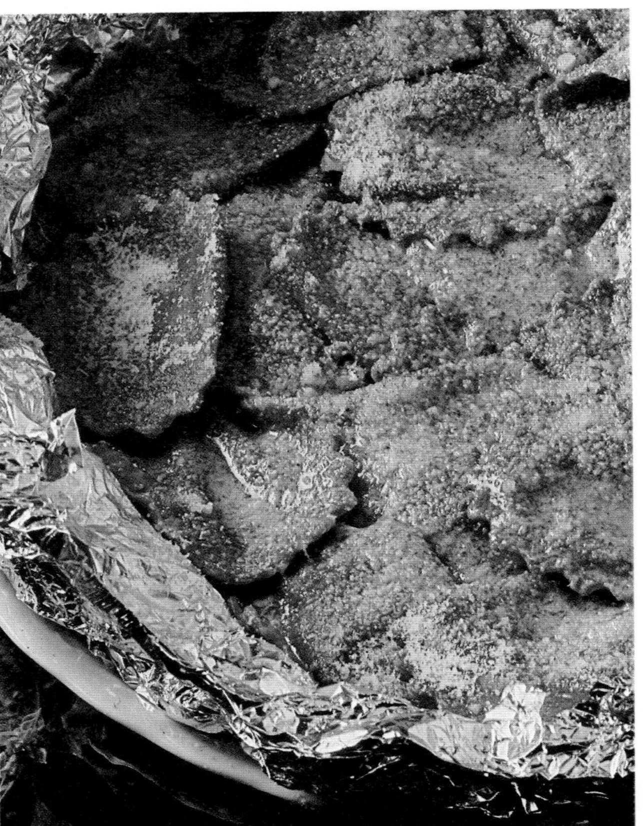

Green ravioli with ricotta

Ravioli verdi alla ricotta

Green Ravioli with Ricotta

Preparation 01:15 — Cooking 00:12

American	Ingredients	Metric/Imperial
3½ cups	*Flour*	400 g / 14 oz
4	*Eggs*	4
	Salt	
7	*Sprigs of parsley*	7
2 or 3	*Basil leaves*	2 or 3
¾ lb	*Ricotta cheese*	350 g / 12 oz
½ cup	*Grated parmesan cheese*	50 g / 2 oz
¼ tsp	*Nutmeg*	¼ tsp
	Butter and nutmeg for seasoning	

1. Prepare pasta dough according to basic recipe using flour, eggs, a few drops green colouring and salt (see page 94) and leave to stand, wrapped in foil.
2. Finely chop parsley, basil and ricotta and put in a bowl with remaining egg, parmesan, salt and nutmeg. Stir to mix well, then beat to a smooth mixture.
3. Roll out pasta dough into 4 equal thin oblongs. On one sheet drop tiny mounds of filling 1½ in / 4 cm apart. Brush water between mounds and place a sheet of dough evenly over the top. Press dough firmly down between mounds of filling to form 2 in / 5 cm squares. Cut into squares using pastry wheel or cutter. Repeat with remaining dough and filling.
4. Bring a pan of salted water to the boil and drop in ravioli. Boil 5-6 minutes. Remove carefully with a slotted spoon, place on a hot serving dish and dot with butter and nutmeg.

Raviolini al gratin

Little Ravioli au Gratin

Preparation 00:15 — Cooking 01:00

American	Ingredients	Metric/Imperial
1	*Small onion*	1
3 tbsp	*Butter*	2 tbsp
5 oz	*Ham cooked in a single slice*	150 g / 5 oz
1 cup	*Frozen peas*	150 g / 5 oz
	Salt and pepper	
3	*Peeled tomatoes*	3
14 oz	*Ravioli*	400 g / 14 oz
¼ lb	*Sliced fontina*	100 g / 4 oz
1 tbsp	*Grated cheese*	1 tbsp

1. Preheat oven to 400°F / 200°C / Gas Mark 6. Grease an ovenproof dish.
2. Peel and slice onion. Melt half the butter and fry the onion for 2 - 3 minutes. Dice ham, add to pan and cook a further minute, then add the peas, salt, pepper and crushed tomatoes. Cook for 10 minutes.
3. Meanwhile cook the ravioli in the boiling salted water for 6-8 minutes. Remove with a slotted spoon. Put half ravioli over the base of the dish, top with slices of fontina cheese and pour over half the tomato sauce. Continue layering in this way with ravioli and sauce, then sprinkle top with grated cheese and add dabs of butter.
4. Bake for 30 minutes until golden and crusty. Serve piping hot.

Ravioli alla Val Passiria

Passer Valley Ravioli

Preparation 01:00 — Cooking 00:15

American	Ingredients	Metric/Imperial
1 lb	*Pasta dough (see page 94)*	450 g / 1 lb
2	*Potatoes*	2
2	*Eggs*	2
1	*Bunch of mint*	1
¼ lb	*Ricotta cheese*	100 g / 4 oz
	Salt and pepper	
¼ tsp	*Nutmeg*	¼ tsp
1 tsp	*Bread crumbs*	1 tsp
1¼ lb	*Tender green beans*	600 g / 1¼ lb
1 tbsp	*Butter*	1 tbsp
1 tbsp	*Grated parmesan cheese*	1 tbsp

1. Prepare pasta dough using basic recipe.
2. Peel the potatoes and boil until tender, drain and mash. Add 2 beaten eggs, mint, ricotta, salt, pepper, nutmeg and bread crumbs and mix to form a firm mixture.
3. Prepare ravioli using potato and ricotta filling following procedure opposite for 'Port Maurice little ravioli'.
4. Put on a large wide pan of salted water and bring to the boil, then cook beans until just tender, drain and keep warm. Drop in ravioli, simmer for 6-8 minutes until tender when ravioli will rise to surface.
5. Remove carefully using a slotted spoon and put on a hot serving dish. Mix in beans, dot with butter, sprinkle with parmesan and serve immediately.

Ravioli alla mantovana

Mantuan-Style Ravioli

00:40 00:20

American	Ingredients	Metric/Imperial
¾ lb	*Mixed herbs*	350 g / 12 oz
1 cup	*Grated parmesan cheese*	100 g / 4 oz
¾ lb	*Ricotta cheese*	350 g / 12 oz
1	*Egg*	1
	Salt and pepper	
	Meat sauce (see page 168)	
	Grated parmesan cheese	
14 oz	*Pasta dough (see page 94)*	400 g / 14 oz

1. Wash and boil herbs in salted water for 5 minutes, drain and squeeze out well, then chop finely. Mix herbs with parmesan, ricotta and egg to obtain a smooth mixture. Season with salt and pepper.
2. Roll out the dough very finely and make ricotta filled ravioli, following procedure for 'Port Maurice little ravioli'.
3. Prepare a large wide pan with a plenty of boiling salted water and drop in ravioli. Simmer until tender for 6-8 minutes when ravioli will rise to surface.
4. Remove carefully with a slotted spoon and place on a hot serving dish. Serve with a meat sauce and parmesan.

Raviolini alla Porto Maurizio

Port Maurice Little Ravioli

00:30 00:45

American	Ingredients	Metric/Imperial
Scant ¼ cup	*Vegetable oil*	3 tbsp
1½ cups	*Ground (minced) meat or left-over roast or boiled meat*	350 g / 12 oz
½ tsp	*Sage*	½ tsp
½ tsp	*Rosemary*	½ tsp
½ tsp	*Thyme*	½ tsp
½ tsp	*Sweet marjoram*	½ tsp
½ tsp	*Basil*	½ tsp
2	*Bay leaves*	2
	Salt and pepper	
1	*Egg*	1
1 tbsp	*Grated cheese*	1 tbsp
¼ tsp	*Nutmeg*	¼ tsp
For the pasta		
3½ cups	*White flour*	400 g / 14 oz
4	*Eggs*	4
1 tsp	*Fine salt*	1 tsp

1. Heat oil until very hot, fry meat until lightly browned all over. Add sage, rosemary, thyme, sweet marjoram, basil, bay, salt and pepper. Allow to simmer for 30 minutes stirring from time to time, then remove from heat and leave to cool.
2. Grind meat and herb mixture in a food processor until very fine. Add beaten egg, cheese, nutmeg and seasoning to forcemeat and mix thoroughly to obtain a smooth mixture.
3. Prepare pasta according to basic recipe (see page 94).
4. Roll out pasta on a floured board into 4 equal thin oblongs. On one sheet drop tiny mounds of filling 1½ in / 4 cm apart in straight lines. Brush water in straight lines between mounds. Place a sheet of dough evenly over the top. Working quickly press down between each mound of filling along wetted line to form 2 in / 5 cm squares. Cut pasta into squares using a pastry cutter or wheel. Separate squares and put on a floured tea towel. Repeat with remaining pasta and filling.
5. Prepare a large wide pan with plenty of boiling salted water and drop in ravioli. Simmer for 6-8 minutes, when ravioli will rise to surface. Remove with a slotted spoon and place on a hot serving dish.
6. Serve with a tomato sauce (see page 171), poured over ravioli.

Ravioli alle noci

Ravioli with Walnuts

00:20 00:10

American	Ingredients	Metric/Imperial
½	*Bread roll*	½
	Milk	
20	*Shelled walnuts*	20
½	*Garlic clove*	½
Scant ¼ cup	*Vegetable oil*	3 tbsp
¼ cup	*Grated cheese*	25 g / 1 oz
¼ tsp	*Marjoram*	¼ tsp
	Salt and pepper	
¼ cup	*Coffee (single) cream*	50 ml / 2 fl oz
1¼ lb	*Ravioli (without meat)*	600 g / 1¼ lb
1 tbsp	*Butter*	1 tbsp

1. Soak bread crumbs from roll in milk, then squeeze and put in blender with walnuts, garlic, oil, cheese, marjoram, salt, pepper and cream. Blend until a thick purée is formed, then put in a pan over a low heat to heat through whilst ravioli cooks.
2. Cook ravioli in boiling salted water for 6 - 8 minutes then carefully remove with a slotted spoon and place on a hot serving dish.
3. Pour walnut sauce over pasta, add a few dabs of butter and serve immediately.

Gnocchi fritti senza ripieno

Fried Gnocchi without Filling

00:20 00:05

American	Ingredients	Metric/Imperial
2 cups	*White flour or finely ground semolina*	225 g / 8 oz
½ tsp	*Salt*	½ tsp
2 tbsp	*Lard*	25 g / 1 oz
	Oil for deep frying	

1. Knead flour with a little water, salt, and the lard and roll out paste to a very thin layer. Cut into squares and prick with a fork.
2. Heat oil in a large heavy based pan, fitted with a basket and fry squares for 2 minutes, then drain on absorbent paper.
3. Fried gnocchi can be served as an hors d'oeuvre with cold dishes such as cooked pressed pork, mortadella, ham or various kinds of sausages.

Gnocchi verdi

Green Gnocchi

Preparation 00:25 · Cooking 00:25

American	Ingredients	Metric/Imperial
1 lb	*Spinach*	*500 g / 1 lb*
	Salt and pepper	
14 oz	*Very fresh ricotta cheese*	*400 g / 14 oz*
2	*Egg yolks*	*2*
	All purpose (plain) flour	
2 tbsp	*Butter*	*25 g / 1 oz*
1 tbsp	*Grated parmesan cheese*	*1 tbsp*

1. Cook the spinach in boiling, salted water, for a few minutes.
2. Work the ricotta in an earthenware dish, mixing continuously with a wooden spoon.
3. Drain the spinach, chop and pass through a food processor or vegetable mill. Add the purée obtained to the ricotta and blend. Mix in the two egg yolks. Allow the mixture to stand for a few minutes then make it into many little gnocchi, with the aid of a spoon.
4. Flour a large pastry-board and, for convenience, lay the little gnocchi on it as you make them.
5. Heat a large saucepan of salted water, when it is boiling tip the gnocchi into it a few at a time. Leave them to cook for about 2 minutes. Drain them, without breaking.
6. Melt the butter and when it turns golden, remove from the heat and pour it over the gnocchi. Sprinkle with grated cheese, freshly-ground pepper, and serve. If there should be any left over, remember that they are also excellent browned in butter.

Gnocchi gialli

Yellow Gnocchi

Preparation 00:60 · Cooking 00:20

American	Ingredients	Metric/Imperial
1¾ lb	*Pumpkin pulp*	*800 g / 1¾ lb*
¾ cup	*Butter*	*175 g / 6 oz*
	Salt and pepper	
¼ lb	*Emmental cheese*	*100 g / 4 oz*
¼ lb	*Gouda cheese*	*100 g / 4 oz*
¼ lb	*Bergkase cheese*	*100 g / 4 oz*
2	*Eggs*	*2*
1 cup	*White flour*	*100 g / 4 oz*
3	*Sage leaves*	*3*

1. Cut the pumpkin into small pieces. In a large saucepan melt about ½ cup [100 g / 4 oz] of butter, thin with a little water and add the pieces of pumpkin. Season with salt and sprinkle with freshly-ground pepper, allow to cook until, by stirring briskly, you succeed in obtaining a thick and smooth cream from the pumpkin. Remove from the heat and allow to stand.
2. Chop up all the cheeses and mix them together. Then add them to the pumpkin. Add the eggs and the flour and work until you obtain a fairly stiff mixture. Make many little gnocchi from the mixture.
3. Bring a large saucepan of salted water to the boil. Tip the gnocchetti in the water, in batches, for about 3 minutes and when they begin to float, take them out on a slotted spoon.
4. In a frying pan melt the rest of butter and flavour by adding sage leaves. Season the gnochetti with melted butter.

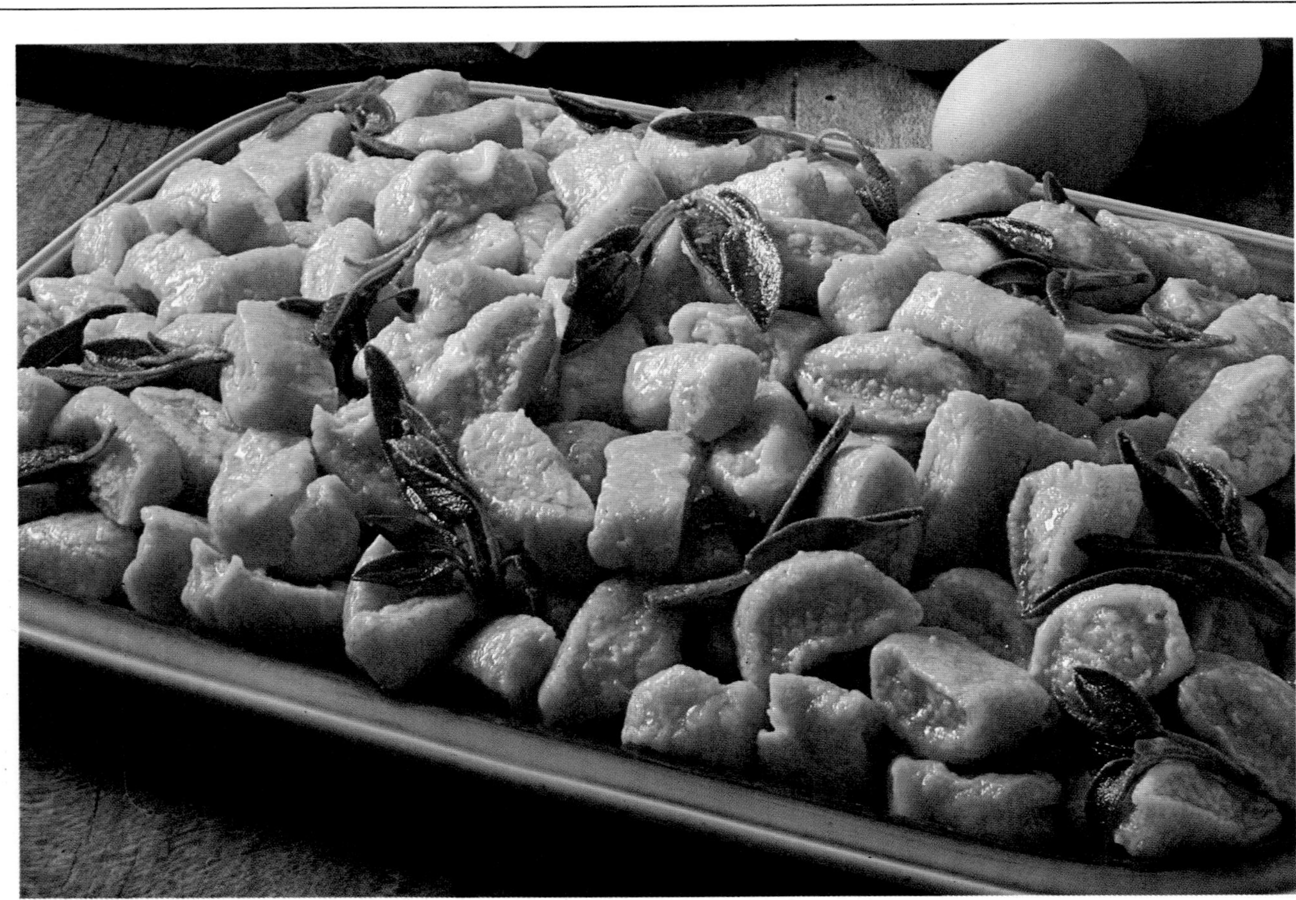

Yellow gnocchi

Veronese-style gnocchi

Gnocchi alla veronese 

Veronese-Style Gnocchi

01:20 01:10

American	Ingredients	Metric/Imperial
2 oz	*Dried mushrooms*	50 g / 2 oz
5 oz	*Brains*	150 g / 5 oz
3 tbsp	*Vinegar*	2 tbsp
½ cup	*Butter*	100 g / 4 oz
1	*Onion*	1
¼ cup	*Brandy*	50 ml / 2 fl oz
	Salt and pepper	
½ cup	*Stock*	125 ml / 4 fl oz
1 lb	*Gnocchi (see page 119) or pasta*	450 g / 1 lb
2½ cups	*Béchamel sauce (see page 162)*	600 ml / 1 pint
¼ cup	*Grated parmesan cheese*	25 g / 1 oz
¼ cup	*Bread crumbs*	25 g / 1 oz

1. Preheat the oven to 400°F / 200°C / Gas Mark 6.
2. Steep the mushrooms in hot water for 1 hour, drain well.
3. Soak the brains in vinegar and water.
4. Heat the butter in a pan over a low heat, add the chopped onion and the mushrooms.
5. Drain the brains, pat dry with absorbent kitchen paper. Cut into small pieces, add to the mixture in the frying pan with the brandy, season with salt and pepper, mix in the stock and cook for about 45 minutes, pouring in additional stock if necessary.
6. Cook the gnocchi in a saucepan with plenty of salted water, drain them and place them in a buttered ovenproof dish. Cover with the béchamel sauce and sprinkle them with a generous amount of grated parmesan and bread crumbs. Place in the oven for about 20 minutes and serve immediately.

Gnocchi filanti

Stringy Gnocchi

00:15 00:30

American	Ingredients	Metric/Imperial
	Salt	
7 oz	*Fontina cheese*	200 g / 7 oz
1 cup	*Coffee (single) cream*	225 ml / 8 fl oz
½	*Vegetable stock cube*	½
	Pepper	
2 lb	*Potato gnocchi (see page 122)*	1 kg / 2 lb
4 tbsp	*Grated parmesan cheese*	3 tbsp

1. Bring to the boil a large saucepan of salted water.
2. Cut the fontina into small cubes. Heat the cream in a little pan and flavour it with half a stock cube and freshly-ground pepper. Add the fontina and remove it immediately after from the heat. Pour into a soup tureen.
3. Cook the gnocchi in the boiling water. When they begin to float to the surface, drain with a slotted spoon. Tip into the soup tureen, stir and serve sprinkled with plenty of grated parmesan.

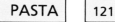

1

2

3

4

5

6

Potato gnocchi
Sieving the potatoes, adding the egg and sausage mixture and the flour.
Bottom from left to right: Shaping the gnocchi, arranging the cheese and sage in an ovenproof dish and adding the cooked gnocchi.

Gnocchetti di semola alle zucchine

Little Semolina Gnocchi with Gourds

00:35 | 00:30

American	Ingredients	Metric/Imperial
4	*Gourds*	*4*
1 cup	*Cream*	*225 ml / 8 fl oz*
½ cup	*Butter*	*100 g / 4 oz*
¼ tsp	*Nutmeg*	*¼ tsp*
	Salt and pepper	
½ tsp	*Cornstarch (cornflour)*	*½ tsp*
14 oz	*Pasta gnocchi (see page 119)*	*400 g / 14 oz*
1 tbsp	*Grated parmesan cheese*	*1 tbsp*
1	*Bunch of mint, chopped*	*1*

1. Boil 2 gourds until they are 'al dente', then pass through the vegetable mill or blender.
2. Add the cream and put in a small saucepan with the butter (retaining a little for the pasta), nutmeg, salt and pepper. Gradually thicken this sauce, adding the cornstarch mixed with a few drops of water.
3. Boil the little gnocchi in salted water until 'al dente'. Drain and season them with cheese and a little butter.
4. Wash separately two raw tender gourds, and slice finely, if possible with a slicing machine. Slightly heat the sauce made with the sieved gourds and mix with the gnocchetti, complete with the slices of raw gourds, sprinkle with mint and serve.

Gnocchi di patate

Potato Gnocchi with Cheese

00:40 | 00:45

American	Ingredients	Metric/Imperial
2 lb	*Potatoes*	*1 kg / 2 lb*
3 cups	*All purpose (plain) flour*	*350 g / 12 oz*
1	*Egg*	*1*
¼ lb	*Mortadella sausage*	*100 g / 4 oz*
¼ tsp	*Nutmeg*	*¼ tsp*
	Salt	
¼ lb	*Mozzarella cheese*	*100 g / 4 oz*
24	*Sage leaves*	*24*
1 tbsp	*Butter*	*15 g / ½ oz*
½ cup	*Grated cheese*	*100 g / 4 oz*

1. Preheat the oven to 400°F / 200°C / Gas Mark 6.
2. Boil the potatoes in cold salted water. When they are tender, drain and remove the skins and put through a ricer or food mill or coarse sieve.
3. Sprinkle some of the sifted flour on to the board, place the heap of potatoes in the centre and make a well in the centre. Add the egg, mixed with the finely chopped mortadella, nutmeg and salt, sprinkle in a little flour and mix together to be a fairly firm dough.
4. Roll the strips into thin sausage shapes and then cut off pieces 1½ in / 4 cm long. Mark on the rough side of a grater.
5. Cook in boiling salted water or stock for about 5 minutes until they start floating to the surface.
6. Arrange some slices of mozzarella on the bottom of a buttered ovenproof dish, sprinkle with grated cheese and arrange some leaves of sage on top.
7. Drain the gnocchi onto the cheese and sprinkle with the remaining cheese, bake in the oven for 20 minutes. Serve piping hot with a tomato sauce (see page 171).

Pizzicotti dei romani

Romans' Pinches

00:30 | 00:20

American	Ingredients	Metric/Imperial
1½ lb	*Spinach*	700 g / 1½ lb
	Salt and pepper	
¾ lb	*Ricotta cheese*	350 g / 12 oz
3	*Eggs*	3
Scant ¼ cup	*Grated parmesan cheese*	3 tbsp
¼ tsp	*Nutmeg*	¼ tsp
	Flour as required	
4 tbsp	*Butter*	50 g / 2 oz
Scant ¼ cup	*Whipping (double) cream*	3 tbsp
¼ tsp	*Sage*	¼ tsp
¼ tsp	*Basil*	¼ tsp
Scant ¼ cup	*Grand Marnier*	3 tbsp
3 tbsp	*Grated cheese*	2 tbsp

1. Clean spinach in several changes of water, put in a pan and cook for about 5 minutes over a medium heat. Season with salt and then press spinach well to remove all excess water.
2. Sieve spinach and ricotta cheese together into a bowl or blend in a food processor.
3. Add beaten eggs, parmesan cheese, salt, pepper and nutmeg and blend all ingredients well together with the hands adding sufficient flour to form a smooth paste.
4. Grease hands and divide paste into small pieces the size of a cherry and roll each into a ball.
5. To make sauce, melt butter in a pan, add salt, pepper and cream and boil for 5 minutes. Stir in sage, basil and Grand Marnier, then the grated cheese.
6. Bring a pan of salted water to the boil and drop in balls of gnocci, poach until they rise and float on the water. Carefully remove with a slotted spoon.
7. Put the gnocchi in a serving bowl, top with the cream sauce and serve at once.

Gnocchetti alla Maddalena

Magdalene's Little Gnocchi

00:30 | 01:10

American	Ingredients	Metric/Imperial
3	*Artichokes*	3
1	*Lemon*	1
⅓ cup	*Butter*	75 g / 3 oz
½ cup	*Oil*	125 ml / 4 fl oz
	Salt and pepper	
2	*Large chicken breasts*	2
2	*Garlic cloves*	2
¼ tsp	*Rosemary*	¼ tsp
¼ tsp	*Sage*	¼ tsp
1	*Stock cube*	1
¾ lb	*Little gnocchi made with hard-grain wheat (see page 119) or other pasta*	350 g / 12 oz
¼ cup	*Grated cheese*	25 g / 1 oz

1. Preheat oven to 400°F / 200°C / Gas Mark 6.
2. Carefully clean the artichokes, removing the hardest leaves, chokes and the spines, cut into thin slices and place them in water and lemon juice.
3. Melt half the butter in a large frying pan, add 3 tablespoons of oil and, when it begins to brown, add the well-drained artichokes, season with salt and pepper and cover with a lid. Cook on a very low heat, check from time to time and if the pan should become too dry, add a little hot water.
4. Clean the chicken breasts, cut them in small pieces. Heat the oil, garlic, rosemary and sage. When they are nicely browned, add salt and pepper and continue cooking, moistening with a little water and stock cube. Cook the chicken and the artichokes for about 45 minutes.
5. Heat a saucepan with plenty of salted water, bring it to the boil and cook the little gnocchi till 'al dente'. Drain the pasta well and season it with the artichokes and the chicken, mix and tip into an ovenproof dish. Sprinkle the surface with small dabs of the remaining butter and grated cheese. Place in the moderately hot oven and cook for about 15 minutes, until the surface is golden.

Lasagne piccanti

Spicy Lasagne

00:15 | 01:45

American	Ingredients	Metric/Imperial
1	*Onion*	1
1	*Garlic clove*	1
¼ lb	*Sausage*	100 g / 4 oz
1 oz	*Dried mushrooms*	25 g / 1 oz
Scant ¼ cup	*Oil*	3 tbsp
½ cup	*Ground (minced) beef*	100 g / 4 oz
1	*Chilli pepper*	1
½ cup	*Red wine*	125 ml / 4 fl oz
½ lb	*Peeled tomatoes*	225 g / 8 oz
	Salt and pepper	
6 tbsp	*Flour*	65 g / 1½ oz
3 tbsp	*Butter*	65 g / 1½ oz
2½ cups	*Milk*	600 ml / 1 pint
½ cup	*Grated parmesan cheese*	50 g / 2 oz
7 oz	*Lasagne*	200 g / 7 oz
7 oz	*Noodles*	200 g / 7 oz

1. Peel and chop onion, crush garlic clove, chop sausage and soften mushrooms in warm water for 10 minutes.
2. Heat half the oil in a pan, sauté the onions and the garlic for 2 minutes, add meat, sausage and drained mushrooms.
Cook a further 2-3 minutes. Add chopped deseeded chilli.
3. Pour in red wine, add tomatoes, season with salt and pepper and cook over a low heat for about 1 hour in an uncovered pan.
4. Preheat the oven to 350°F / 180°C / Gas Mark 4.
5. Meanwhile make béchamel sauce with the flour, butter and milk (see page 162). Finally stir in parmesan cheese.
6. Cook lasagne, a few sheets at a time, in boiling salted water with a dash of oil added until 'al dente'. Remove and rinse with cold water then dry on a tea towel.
7. Cook noodles in boiling salted water with a dash of oil added until 'al dente', drain and stir in the tomato sauce. Spoon mixture onto an oblong ovenproof serving dish.
8. Top with a layer of lasagne and finally pour over the béchamel sauce.
9. Bake in the oven for 30 minutes, then serve with a salad.

Lasagne primavera

Springtime Lasagne

00:30 00:45

American	Ingredients	Metric/Imperial
3½ cups	*Flour*	*400 g / 14 oz*
4	*Eggs*	*4*
	Salt	
1 lb	*Asparagus*	*500 g / 1 lb*
½ tsp	*Basil*	*½ tsp*
1 cup	*Coffee (single) cream*	*225 ml / 8 fl oz*
2 tbsp	*Butter*	*25 g / 1 oz*
	Pepper	
1 cup	*Béchamel (see page 162)*	*225 ml / 8 fl oz*

1. Preheat the oven to 350°F / 180°C / Gas Mark 4.
2. Prepare pasta dough using flour, egg and salt (see page 94), and cut out lasagne, then cook in boiling salted water until 'al dente'. Rinse under cold water and dry. Put half the lasagne into a rectangular ovenproof serving dish.
3. Cook asparagus until just softened, then drain. Meanwhile add chopped basil, half the cream, half the butter, salt and pepper to the béchamel sauce. Stir in asparagus and spoon over lasagne in serving dish.
4. Top with remaining lasagne, pour over remaining cream and dab with butter.
5. Bake for 25-30 minutes and serve immediately.

Lasagnette e lumache

Small Lasagne and Snails

00:10 00:45

American	Ingredients	Metric/Imperial
2 lb	*Snails with the shell*	*1 kg / 2 lb*
Scant ¼ cup	*Oil*	*3 tbsp*
1	*Bunch of parsley*	*1*
2	*Garlic cloves*	*2*
½ cup	*White wine*	*125 ml / 4 fl oz*
14 oz	*Small lasagne*	*400 g / 14 oz*
	Salt and pepper	

1. Preheat oven to 325°F / 170°C / Gas Mark 3.
2. Toss snails in boiling salted water for 10 minutes, drain and carefully remove snails from shells using a sharp-pronged fork.
3. Heat half of the oil in a pan, chop parsley and add to pan with crushed garlic. Cook for 1 minute, then add snails and cook a further 2-3 minutes to brown.
4. Pour in the wine and cook for 10 minutes. Cook lasagne in boiling salted water until 'al dente', drain, then add snail sauce to pasta with remaining oil.
5. Spoon into 4 individual ovenproof serving dishes, reheat in the oven for 15 minutes and serve.

Lasagne verdi alla ligure

Ligurian-Style Green Lasagne

00:40 00:40

American	Ingredients	Metric/Imperial
1 lb	*Basic mixture for fresh pasta (see page 94)*	*500 g / 1 lb*
1 lb	*Nettles or beet*	*500 g / 1 lb*
1	*Egg*	*1*
1 lb	*Meat sauce (see page 168)*	*500 g / 1 lb*
2½ cups	*Béchamel (see page 162)*	*600 ml / 1 pint*

1. Preheat oven to 350°F / 180°C / Gas Mark 4.
2. Make pasta.
3. Finely chop nettles or beet, boil in a little water then squeeze thoroughly to remove all water.
4. Blend the pressed vegetables with the pasta, adding a beaten egg. Roll out pasta dough thinly, cut out lasagne in desired shape.
5. Cook lasagne in boiling salted water, a few pieces at a time until 'al dente'. Lay pasta on a clean teatowel to dry thoroughly.
6. Grease an oblong ovenproof serving dish, place a layer of lasagne over base, top with a layer of meat sauce. Cover with more lasagne then sauce, ending with a layer of pasta.
7. Pour over béchamel and bake for 25 minutes. Serve hot.

Variation: lasagne can be cooked and served at once with garlic and basil sauce, fresh tomato or meat sauce, without baking.

Ligurian-style green lasagne

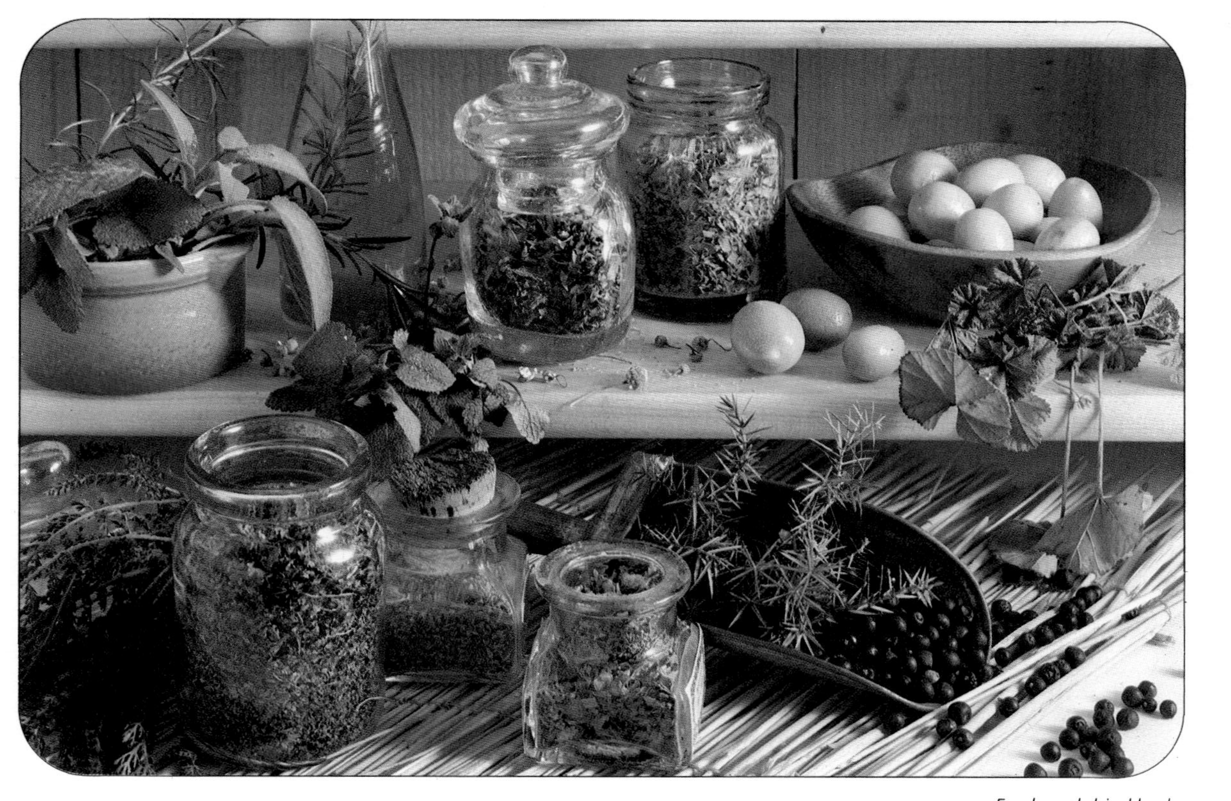

Fresh and dried herbs

Cannelloni alla siciliana

Sicilian-Style Cannelloni

00:30 | 00:40

American	Ingredients	Metric/Imperial
2 cups	*Coffee (single) cream*	*450 ml / 16 fl oz*
¾ lb	*Ricotta cheese*	*350 g / 12 oz*
2 oz	*Softened pine nuts*	*50 g / 2 oz*
⅓ cup	*Raisins*	*50 g / 2 oz*
1	*Onion*	*1*
	Salt and pepper	
½ tsp	*Red paprika*	*½ tsp*
½ lb	*Cooked ham*	*225 g / 8 oz*
½ cup	*Dry marsala*	*125 ml / 4 fl oz*
1 lb	*Cannelloni*	*500 g / 1 lb*
	Butter	
½ cup	*Grated pecorino cheese*	*50 g / 2 oz*
½ tsp	*Cumin seeds*	*½ tsp*

Preheat oven to 400°F / 200°C / Gas Mark 6.

1. Prepare the sauce by heating the cream over a low heat. Add the crumbled ricotta, pine nuts, raisins, finely chopped onion, salt, pepper, red paprika, the cooked ham, diced, and dry marsala. Allow the sauce to simmer over a very low heat.

2. Boil the cannelloni in salted water till firm to the bite, drain.

3. In a well-buttered ovenproof dish arrange a layer of cannelloni, cover with a little sauce, then sprinkle with grated pecorino. Continue with a layer of cannelloni, one of sauce and one of pecorino. Finish with a layer of sauce, sprinkle with plenty of pecorino and finally scatter with cumin seeds. Put in oven to cook for 25 minutes.

Cannelloni della nonna 

Granny's Cannelloni

00:40 | 00:40

American	Ingredients	Metric/Imperial
¾ lb	*Spinach*	*350 g / 12 oz*
¾ lb	*Braised meat*	*350 g / 12 oz*
2	*Eggs*	*2*
7 tbsp	*Grated cheese*	*5½ tbsp*
	Salt and pepper	
¼ tsp	*Nutmeg*	*¼ tsp*
2½ cups	*Béchamel (see page 162)*	*600 ml / 1 pint*
12	*Cannelloni or squares of fresh pasta*	*12*
2 tbsp	*Butter*	*25 g / 1 oz*

1. Preheat the oven to 375°F / 190°C / Gas Mark 5.

2. Cook the spinach in very little salted water, drain and squeeze well, then pass through a vegetable mill, collecting the purée in an earthenware dish.

3. Chop the braised meat, removing any fat from it and add to the spinach, mix and blend with two egg yolks and most of the grated cheese. Season the filling with salt and pepper and a little grated nutmeg.

4. Cook the cannelloni in boiling salted water, drain on a table napkin or on absorbent kitchen paper.

5. Use a spoon to fill the cannelloni with the mixture of meat and spinach and arrange them in an ovenproof dish.

6. Prepare separately the béchamel sauce and pour over the cannelloni. Scatter with little dabs of butter, sprinkle with grated cheese and place in the oven for 30 minutes.

RICE

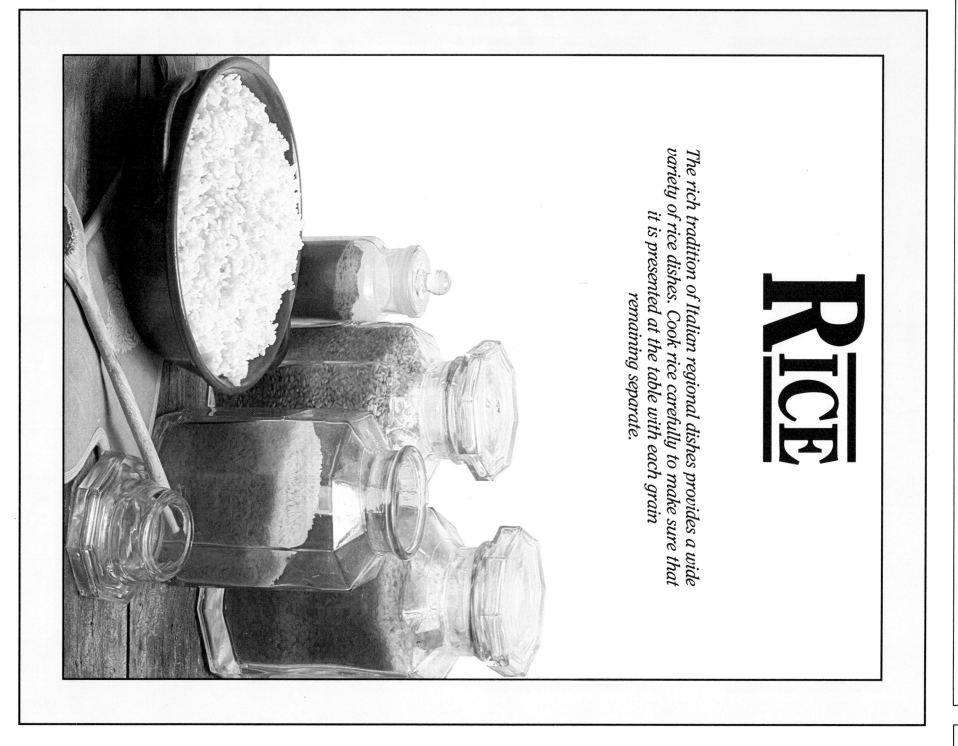

The rich tradition of Italian regional dishes provides a wide variety of rice dishes. Cook rice carefully to make sure that it is presented at the table with each grain remaining separate.

To make a risotto in a pressure cooker

1. Heat 1 tbsp oil with 2 tbsp [25 g / 1 oz] butter. Add onion and cook for 4 minutes.

2. Gradually add the risotto rice and continue frying over a medium heat for 3 minutes.

3. Make sure all the rice is well coated in oil and butter, by stirring well.

4. Stir in the saffron, mixing it well with the grains of rice.

5. Ladle in the measured quantity of vegetable or chicken stock and mix well.

6. Cook until tender following manufacturers directions for your pressure cooker.

Long grain brown rice

This is a long grain rice which has been milled to remove only the inedible husk. This type of rice is much less refined, contains fibre and B vitamins as well as a small amount of protein. It has a distinctly nutty flavor and has a slightly chewy texture when cooked. A slightly strange smell when cooking is normal and the cooking time is much longer than other rice. You will need to cook 1 lb / 450 g for 45 minutes to 1 hour. However, there are now several types of pre-fluffed brown rice available and the cooking times are very little more than white rice. Read the manufacturers instructions. Long grain rice is normally used with savory dishes and, unless processed, should be washed in cold running water before using. This can be used in risottos.

Italian risotto rice

This short grain rice is perfect for dishes which are expected to absorb all the flavors of the liquid in the recipe. Risottos take more careful cooking than other rice dishes as the liquid is usually added gradually as the dish is being cooked on the top of the stove. Risottos are generally named after the town in Italy where the special recipe originated.

Italian rice has a larger grain than the short grained carolina (pudding) rice and the two should not be confused when buying. Risotto rice should be cooked until 'al dente' and this takes longer than the long grain rice. It is served slightly moist. It should never be sticky, each grain should remain separate at the end of the cooking period.

Wild rice

Wild rice which grows in Northern Italy, Canada, the USA and the Far East is not a true rice, but the seed of a wild grass. Because of the difficulty experienced in harvesting it, it is expensive and for economy can be combined with cooked white or brown rice. Its nutty flavor goes well with roast meat, poultry or game. It contains more protein and vitamins than regular rice. Wash 2 cups [400 g / 14 oz] wild rice well in several changes of water before adding to 1½ quarts [1.5 litres / 2½ pints] boiling water. Lower the heat and cook for about 45 minutes or until the grains have absorbed all the water and are tender. Toss in 3 tbsp [40 g / 1½ oz] butter and serve.

To boil rice

The pre-washed and pre-fluffed rice are the long grain varieties of rice which have been specially treated to give a fluffy texture when cooked by the easy absorbtion method.

For 1 cup, whatever the size, of rice you will need 2 cups of boiling water (same size cup), ½-1 teaspoon salt. Alternatively 1 cup [125 g / 8 oz] can be cooked with 2½ cups [600 ml / 1 pint] water.

Sprinkle the long grain rice into the measured boiling salted water, stir round with a fork, bring to the boil. Cover with a lid and allow to cook on a very low simmering heat for 12-15 minutes. At the end of this time the rice can be stirred through and should have absorbed all the water and the grains should be separate and fluffy.

Preparing rice

There are many varieties of rice available now and it is essential for the inexperienced cook to read the manufacturer's instructions to find out if it is plain rice or one of the pre-cooked varieties. If you have bought easy-cook rice follow the instructions for best results.

- Only wash non-processed rice before cooking or when using a microwave oven.
- To boil rice, use the correct amount of water or stock and add boiling liquid to the rice.
- Take care not to over salt as the rice absorbs the liquid.
- Stir a risotto from time to time while it is cooking.
- To keep rice white when cooking in hard water, add 1 teaspoon lemon juice or 1 tablespoon vinegar.
- Only stir boiled rice when it goes into the saucepan but not during the cooking process.
- Cover the rice tightly with a lid and do not remove until the cooking time is nearly finished.
- It is not wise to leave the cooked rice in a saucepan for more than 10 minutes as it will continue to cook and form a solid mass. It is best to fork it into a heated serving dish.
- A wooden fork is useful for fluffing cooked rice, try not to use a spoon.
- Browning rice in a pan – with or without fat – prior to cooking with moisture, helps to keep the grains separate and gives the rice a good flavor.

Rice Navarre

Riso al Marquis de Navarra

Rice Navarre

00:15 | 00:20

American	Ingredients	Metric/Imperial
1	*Sweet red pepper*	1
1	*Garlic clove*	1
½ lb	*Mushrooms*	225 g / 8 oz
¾ lb	*Scampi*	350 g / 12 oz
¼ cup	*Vegetable oil*	50 ml / 2 fl oz
1⅔ cups	*Rice*	350 g / 12 oz
3 cups	*Stock*	750 ml / 1¼ pints
½ envelope	*Saffron*	½ sachet
	Pepper	
	Lemon wedges	

1. Preheat oven to 400°F / 200°C / Gas Mark 6. Grease a large piece of foil and place on a baking sheet.
2. Deseed and chop pepper with garlic, rinse mushrooms in hot water then slice, wash scampi.
3. Heat oil and, when very hot, cook pepper and garlic for 2 minutes. Add rice to pan, cook a further minute stirring briskly. Pour over the stock, cover and simmer for 10 minutes.
4. Add scampi, mushrooms and saffron to rice, season with pepper. Spoon onto foil, parcel up rice in foil and bake for 10 minutes.
5. Place rice parcel on serving dish, open foil, garnish with lemon wedges and serve hot.

Insalata preziosa 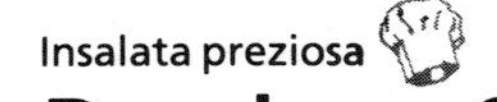

Precious Salad

00:35 | 00:15

American	Ingredients	Metric/Imperial
⅔ cup	*Vegetable oil*	150 ml / ¼ pint
½	*Onion*	½
1½ cups	*Rice*	300 g / 11 oz
½ cup	*Dry white wine*	125 ml / 4 fl oz
2¼ cups	*Meat stock*	500 ml / 18 fl oz
3 oz	*Smoked cooked ham*	75 g / 3 oz
3 oz	*Smoked salmon*	75 g / 3 oz
3 oz	*Cooked tongue*	75 g / 3 oz
3 oz	*Prawns, cooked and shelled*	75 g / 3 oz
½	*Lemon*	½
Scant ¼ cup	*Vinegar*	3 tbsp
1 tbsp	*Vodka*	1 tbsp
	White pepper	
1 tbsp	*Caviar*	1 tbsp

1. Heat 4 tablespoons [50 ml / 2 fl oz] of the oil in a large pan and cook the onion until it is golden brown, tip the rice into it and sprinkle it with the wine and stir. Cook for 3 minutes.
2. Prepare about 2¼ cups [500 ml / 18 fl oz] of boiling stock. Pour it over the rice and cook over a low heat for 10 minutes, when 'al dente' cool and drain.
3. Cut the ham, smoked salmon and the tongue into cubes. Add the prawns to the other ingredients in a large bowl.
4. Add the rice and stir. Sprinkle the mixture with the juice of half a lemon. Season with remainder of oil, vinegar, vodka and white pepper. Mix and finally top with the caviar.

Precious salad

Risi e bisati

Rice and Little Eels

Preparation 00:10 · Cooking 00:20

American	Ingredients	Metric/Imperial
1 lb	*Small eels*	*500 g / 1 lb*
2	*Garlic cloves*	*2*
Scant ¼ cup	*Vegetable oil*	*3 tbsp*
1 tbsp	*Parsley*	*1 tbsp*
3	*Bay leaves*	*2*
1	*Lemon*	*1*
2 cups	*Rice*	*400 g / 14 oz*
3¾ cups	*Stock*	*900 ml / 1½ pints*
½ cup	*Grated parmesan cheese*	*50 g / 2 oz*

1. Cut eels into small pieces and crush the garlic. Heat the oil in a pan and, when very hot, brown pieces of eel quickly with garlic, parsley and bay leaves.
2. Sprinkle over with lemon juice, add rice and stir into mixture. Pour over stock, cover and cook for about 15 minutes, until all stock is absorbed.
3. Remove pan from heat, stir in parmesan cheese, spoon onto a hot serving dish, and serve hot.

Riso alla Sandokan

Sandokan Rice

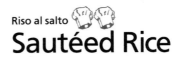

Preparation 00:05 · Cooking 00:15

American	Ingredients	Metric/Imperial
3¾ cups	*Water or stock*	*900 ml / 1½ pints*
2 cups	*Rice*	*400 g / 14 oz*
1 tsp	*Curry powder*	*1 tsp*
	Salt and pepper	
1½ oz	*Prawns*	*40 g / 1½ oz*
3 tbsp	*Butter*	*40 g / 1½ oz*
½ cup	*Grated parmesan cheese*	*50 g / 2 oz*

1. Pour the measured quantity of boiling water or stock over rice in pan. Add curry powder, bring to boil. Reduce heat, cover and simmer for 10 minutes. Season well.
2. Add well washed prawns to the rice and cook a further 5 minutes. Tip rice and prawn mixture into individual bowls. Add knobs of butter to each bowl, and sprinkle with cheese.

Riso alla salsiccia

Rice with Sausage

Preparation 00:10 · Cooking 00:25

American	Ingredients	Metric/Imperial
1⅔ cups	*Rice*	*350 g / 12 oz*
1	*Large onion*	*1*
½ lb	*Sausage*	*225 g / 8 oz*
4	*Pear-shaped tomatoes*	*4*
3 tbsp	*Butter*	*40 g / 1½ oz*
3	*Sprigs of rosemary*	*3*
¼ cup	*Dry white wine*	*50 ml / 2 fl oz*
	Salt and pepper	

1. Cook rice in boiling salted water for 15 minutes. Meanwhile peel and chop onion, chop sausage. Skin and quarter tomatoes.
2. Heat butter and when foaming sauté onion for 2-3 minutes to soften. Add sausage to the pan with rosemary and cook a further 2-3 minutes. Pour over the wine, add tomatoes, season and simmer for 10 minutes.
3. Stir sausage and tomato mixture into cooked rice. Spoon onto a hot serving dish and serve at once.

Riso al salto

Sautéed Rice

Preparation 00:10 · Cooking 00:30

American	Ingredients	Metric/Imperial
1	*Onion*	*1*
1 envelope	*Saffron*	*1 sachet*
3 cups	*Stock*	*750 ml / 1¼ pints*
¾ cup	*Butter*	*175 g / 6 oz*
2 cups	*Rice*	*400 g / 14 oz*
½ cup	*Red wine*	*125 ml / 4 fl oz*
	Salt and pepper	
¼ cup	*Grated parmesan cheese*	*25 g / 1 oz*

1. Chop onion finely, dissolve saffron in a tablespoon of boiling stock. Heat a third of the butter in a pan and when hot sauté the onion for 2 minutes. Add rice to pan and cook a further minute, stirring briskly.
2. Pour over the red wine and stock, stir in saffron and season. Cover and simmer for 15 minutes until rice is cooked. Remove from heat, add a knob of butter and stir in parmesan and leave to cool.
3. Heat another third of butter in a frying pan, spread rice over the base of pan to form a flat cake and cook for 5 minutes over a medium heat. Invert onto a plate placed over pan. Heat remaining butter in frying pan, slip rice cake back in pan to brown the other side. Cook a further 5 minutes.
4. Turn the rice cake onto a hot serving dish and serve immediately.

Riso al caviale

Rice with Caviar

Preparation 00:15 · Cooking 00:25

American	Ingredients	Metric/Imperial
1	*Onion*	*1*
¼ cup	*Butter*	*50 g / 2 oz*
1⅔ cups	*Rice*	*350 g / 12 oz*
1 cup	*Dry white wine*	*225 ml / 8 fl oz*
2½ cups	*Stock*	*600 ml / 1 pint*
2 oz	*Jar caviar*	*50 g / 2 oz*
	or	
⅓ cup	*Lumpfish cream*	*60 ml / 2½ fl oz*

1. Chop the onion. Heat butter and when hot sauté onion for 2 minutes to brown lightly. Add rice to the pan and cook briskly for 1 minute all the time.
2. Pour over the wine and stock. Bring to the boil, then reduce heat, cover and simmer for about 15-20 minutes, until rice is cooked.
3. Remove pan from heat, stir in caviar and spoon into a hot serving dish and serve immediately.

Cantonese-style rice

Riso alla cantonese

Cantonese-Style Rice

00:10 00:40

American	Ingredients	Metric/Imperial
3 oz	*Dried mushrooms*	*75 g / 3 oz*
16	*Large prawns*	*16*
3 oz	*Boiled chicken*	*75 g / 3 oz*
3 oz	*Cooked ham*	*75 g / 3 oz*
1 ⅓ cups	*Rice*	*250 g / 9 oz*
3 tbsp	*Vegetable oil*	*2 tbsp*
½ lb	*Peeled tomatoes*	*225 g / 8 oz*
2	*Eggs*	*2*
	Salt	
2 tbsp	*Butter*	*25 g / 1 oz*

1. Preheat oven to 350°F / 180°C / Gas Mark 4. Oil an ovenproof serving dish.
2. Soak mushrooms in a little tepid water for 15 minutes, then drain and chop. Shell prawns, wash thoroughly and break into small pieces. Slice chicken and ham into thin strips.
3. Cook rice in boiling salted water for 15 minutes then drain and cool under running water. Spoon into the ovenproof dish and spread over base.
4. Heat the oil and when very hot sauté the mushrooms for 2 minutes, then add tomatoes and cook a further minute. Add prawns, chicken and ham to pan and simmer for 10 minutes.
5. Spread mushroom mixture over rice in dish. Cover with foil and bake for 35 minutes.
6. Meanwhile make an omelette. Beat eggs with salt. Heat the butter and when very hot add egg to pan and cook until set. Roll up and slice thinly to form strips.
7. Remove cooked rice dish from oven, garnish with omelette strips and serve piping hot.

Riso 'cuscus'

Couscous Rice

00:10 Soaking time 12:00 — 01:30

American	Ingredients	Metric/Imperial
1 cup	*Chickpeas*	*200 g / 7 oz*
1	*Large onion*	*1*
¼ cup	*Butter*	*50 g / 2 oz*
2 cups	*Rice*	*400 g / 14 oz*
3¾ cups	*Stock*	*900 ml / 1½ pints*

1. Cover chickpeas with water and leave to soak overnight, then drain. Boil chickpeas for 10 minutes, reduce heat, cover and simmer for about 50 minutes until tender.
2. Chop the onion. Heat the butter and when foaming sauté the onion for 2-3 minutes to brown lightly. Add chickpeas to pan and sauté for another 2 minutes. Next, add the rice and sauté for 2-3 minutes. Pour over the stock, cover and simmer for 15 minutes.
3. Spoon couscous rice onto a hot serving dish and serve immediately.

Timballo di riso giallo

Yellow Rice Timbale

00:20 — 00:45

American	Ingredients	Metric/Imperial
1	*Onion*	*1*
½ cup	*Butter*	*100 g / 4 oz*
1 cup	*Risotto rice*	*200 g / 7 oz*
¼ cup	*White wine*	*50 ml / 2 fl oz*
1	*Stock cube*	*1*
Several strands	*Saffron*	*Several strands*
2	*Sprigs of sage*	*2*
7 oz	*Chicken livers*	*200 g / 7 oz*
2 tbsp	*Brandy*	*1½ tbsp*
	Salt and pepper	
½ lb	*Petit pois*	*225 g / 8 oz*
½ cup	*Grated cheese*	*50 g / 2 oz*
¼ lb	*Gruyère cheese*	*100 g / 4 oz*

1. Chop the onion very finely and sweat it in half the butter. Add the rice and flavor it well in the butter and onion, moisten with the white wine, raise the heat to medium. Make up 2½ cups [600 ml / 1 pint] stock with a cube. Add 2¼ cups [550 ml / scant 1 pint] stock gradually to the rice. Add the saffron. Continue cooking the rice for 15 minutes.
2. In a separate frying pan, heat half the remaining butter, add the sage. Clean the chicken livers, chop into pieces and brown in the butter. Add the remaining stock, brandy, a pinch of salt and a little pepper, and cook on a slow heat for 10 minutes.
3. Preheat the oven to 350°F / 180°C / Gas Mark 4.
4. Add the peas and flavor them in the cooking juices from the livers.
5. Before removing the risotto from the heat, adjust the seasoning, add half the grated cheese, stirring until it melts.
6. Butter an ovenproof dish and spread in half the risotto, put in the peas and the chicken livers, the gruyère cut into cubes, and cover with more risotto. Sprinkle remaining grated cheese on the surface and dot with butter. Place in the oven and cook for 25 to 30 minutes until a golden crust forms on the surface.

Riso alla cubana

Cuban-Style Rice

A Cuban dish to serve in the spring to boost the morale after the dreary winter months.

00:40 — 00:30

American	Ingredients	Metric/Imperial
2	*Boned chicken breasts*	*2*
4	*Sweet green peppers*	*4*
2	*Onions*	*2*
Scant ¼ cup	*Vegetable oil*	*3 tbsp*
¼ cup	*Lard*	*50 g / 2 oz*
1	*Garlic clove*	*1*
½ envelope	*Saffron*	*½ sachet*
1 quart	*Dry white wine*	*1 litre / 1¾ pints*
2 cups	*Rice*	*400 g / 14 oz*
½ cup	*Meat stock, strained*	*125 ml / 4 fl oz*
¼ cup	*White rum*	*50 ml / 2 fl oz*
	Pepper	
¼ tsp	*Paprika*	*¼ tsp*
	Grated cheese (best if strong)	

1. Slice chicken into thin pieces, chop peppers and onions.
2. Heat oil and lard together in a pan and when very hot brown chicken pieces all over, then add peppers, onion and garlic to pan and cook a further 2-3 minutes. Sprinkle in saffron and pour over the wine. Cover and cook for 10 minutes.
3. Add the rice to the pan, pour in the stock, cover and cook a further 15 minutes. Stir in white rum.
4. Spoon rice mixture onto a hot serving dish, season with black pepper and paprika. Serve immediately, accompanied with a bowl of grated cheese.

Risotto alle fragole

Strawberry Risotto

00:10 — 00:20

American	Ingredients	Metric/Imperial
1	*Small onion*	*1*
20	*Very ripe fresh strawberries*	*20*
2 tbsp	*Butter*	*25 g / 1 oz*
2 cups	*Rice*	*400 g / 14 oz*
½ cup	*Dry white wine*	*125 ml / 4 fl oz*
3 cups	*Stock*	*750 ml / 1¼ pints*
	Salt	
3 tbsp	*Coffee (single) cream*	*2 tbsp*

1. Peel and finely chop onion, hull and wash strawberries. Heat butter and, when foaming, sauté onion for 2-3 minutes, then add all but 6 strawberries and cook a few more minutes until fruit becomes mushy.
2. Add rice to pan, cook for 2 minutes then pour over white wine and stock. Bring to the boil, cover, reduce heat and allow to simmer for 10 minutes. Taste and add salt if needed then allow to cook a further 5 minutes until rice is tender.
3. Off the heat, stir in cream, spoon strawberry risotto onto a hot serving dish and decorate with remaining strawberries.

Strawberry risotto

Fiocchetti di riso e noci

Rice and Walnut Balls

00:30 — 00:04 per batch

American	Ingredients	Metric/Imperial
1 ⅓ cups	*Rice*	*250 g / 9 oz*
	Salt	
2 oz	*Cooked ham*	*50 g / 2 oz*
¼ lb	*Fontina cheese*	*100 g / 4 oz*
1 cup	*Walnuts*	*100 g / 4 oz*
½ cup	*Flour*	*50 g / 2 oz*
2	*Eggs*	*2*
1 cup	*Bread crumbs*	*100 g / 4 oz*
	Oil for frying	

1. Boil the rice till 'al dente' in salted water and then allow to cool.
2. Cut up the ham, the fontina, the chopped shelled walnuts and add them to the rice, together with a beaten egg.
3. Season well and form the mixture into small balls. Roll the balls in the flour. Beat the remaining egg with ¼ teaspoon salt and the milk. Dip the balls in beaten egg.
4. Heat the oil until hot 350°F / 180°C. Coat the rice balls in bread crumbs and fry until golden brown.
5. Remove from the oil and drain on absorbent kitchen towels. Serve with a savory sauce, such as tomato (see page 171) or chilli (see page 180).

Fettine saporite

Tasty Slices

00:15 — 00:30

American	Ingredients	Metric/Imperial
6	*Eggs*	*6*
	Salt and pepper	
⅔ cup	*Rice*	*150 g / 5 oz*
¼ lb	*Mushrooms*	*100 g / 4 oz*
¼ cup	*Butter*	*50 g / 2 oz*
2 oz	*Fontina cheese*	*50 g / 2 oz*
2 oz	*Mozzarella cheese*	*50 g / 2 oz*

1. Break the eggs into a bowl, season with salt and beat them until the yolks and whites are properly blended.

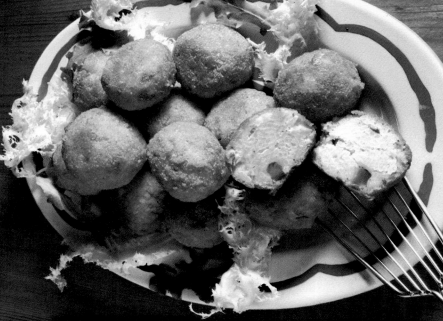

1

2

3

4

Rice and walnut balls
1. *Mix the cooked rice with the ham, cheese and walnuts, beaten egg and seasoning and form into small balls. Roll the rice balls in flour which has been seasoned with salt and (freshly ground black) pepper.*
2. *Dip the floured balls into the well-beaten egg.*
3. *Coat in bread crumbs.*
4. *Deep fry in hot fat until golden, then drain on paper kitchen towels to absorb the fat.*
Serve the rice and walnut balls with a savory sauce, such as tomato (see page 171) and a green salad.

2. Cook the rice in boiling salted water and drain.
3. Wash the mushrooms, slice and sauté in half the butter in a pan for 5 minutes.
4. Dice the fontina and mozzarella. Add the mushrooms, rice, fontina and mozzarella to the eggs.
5. Heat the remaining butter in a thick pan. When the butter has browned, pour in the mixture. When the eggs begin to thicken, remove the omelette, shaking the pan. Put the omelette on a plate, cover with another plate and turn upside down.
6. Put back in the frying pan and add a knob of butter. Leave to cook for 2 minutes. When the omelette is cooked, cut it into slices and serve with a green salad.

Riso con le lattughe

Rice with Lettuces

00:10 | 00:18

American	Ingredients	Metric/Imperial
11 oz	*Fresh lettuce*	*300 g / 11 oz*
6	*Walnuts*	*6*
½ cup	*Pine kernels*	*50 g / 2 oz*
1	*Small onion*	*1*
2 tbsp	*Vegetable oil*	*1½ tbsp*
3 tbsp	*Butter*	*40 g / 1½ oz*
2 cups	*Rice*	*400 g / 14 oz*
3 cups	*Meat stock*	*750 ml / 1¼ pints*
¼ cup	*Dry white wine*	*50 ml / 2 fl oz*
	Salt and pepper	
½ cup	*Grated cheese*	*50 g / 2 oz*

1. Wash lettuce thoroughly, then drain. Chop lettuces, walnuts, pine kernels and onion.
2. Heat oil and butter together, and when foaming, cook onion for 2 minutes, then add rice and cook a further 1-2 minutes, stirring all the time.
3. Pour over the stock and bring to the boil. Cover and simmer for 8 minutes. Stir lettuces and nuts into rice, pour over wine, cover and continue to cook for a further 8 minutes.
4. Season rice with salt and pepper. Stir in grated cheese, spoon onto a hot serving dish and serve immediately.

Riso con salsa di soia e asparagi

Rice with Soy Sauce and Asparagus

00:10 | 00:25

American	Ingredients	Metric/Imperial
2 cups	*Rice*	*400 g / 14 oz*
	Salt and pepper	
1	*Onion*	*1*
½ cup	*Butter*	*100 g / 4 oz*
¼ lb	*Asparagus tips*	*100 g / 4 oz*
Scant ¼ cup	*Soy sauce*	*3 tbsp*

1. Cook rice in boiling salted water for 15 minutes. Peel and chop the onion. Heat butter and when foaming, sauté the onion for 2-3 minutes.
2. Add rice to the pan and cook for 10 minutes over a moderate heat stirring from time to time until tender.
3. Cook asparagus tips in boiling salted water for 5 minutes, then drain well.
4. Add soy sauce to rice and stir in asparagus tips. Continue to cook over a gentle heat for a further 3-5 minutes until the mixture is golden brown.
5. Season with salt and pepper, spoon onto a hot serving dish and serve.

Riso alla boscaiola

Rice of the Forests

00:10 | 00:20

American	Ingredients	Metric/Imperial
1 oz	*Sachet of dried mushrooms*	*25 g / 1 oz*
1	*Small onion*	*1*
5 or 6	*Peeled tomatoes*	*5 or 6*
1⅔ cups	*Rice*	*350 g / 12 oz*
	Salt and pepper	
Scant ¼ cup	*Vegetable oil*	*3 tbsp*
1	*Garlic clove*	*1*
	Grated cheese	

1. Soak the mushrooms in warm water for 10 minutes. Drain and finely chop mushrooms and onion. Roughly chop the tomatoes.
2. Cook rice in boiling salted water for 15 minutes until it is 'al dente' and drain.
3. Heat the oil in a pan and when very hot sauté onion for 2-3 minutes with garlic, then remove garlic. Add mushrooms to pan and cook a further 2 minutes on a lower heat. Stir in tomatoes and season well. Simmer for 2-3 minutes.
4. Stir the rice into the mushroom mixture and spoon onto a hot serving dish. Season with freshly-ground pepper and sprinkle cheese over the top.
5. Serve as an accompaniment to a main dish.

Riso alla polpa di cocco

Rice with Coconut Pulp

00:10 | 00:20

American	Ingredients	Metric/Imperial
1	*Coconut*	*1*
½	*Onion*	*½*
1 cup	*Milk*	*225 ml / 8 fl oz*
2 cups	*Water*	*450 ml / ¾ pint*
¼ cup	*Butter*	*50 g / 2 oz*
1½ cups	*Rice*	*300 g / 11 oz*
	Salt	

1. Grate coconut pulp, chop onion. Bring milk and water to boil in a large pan. Add all but 1 tablespoon of coconut pulp, return to pan. Remove from heat, leave to infuse for 5 minutes, then drain, retaining cooking liquid.
2. Heat butter in a thick pan and when hot, cook onion for 2-3 minutes to brown lightly. Add rice to the pan and cook a further 1 minute. Pour over coconut milk, add salt, cover and cook for 15 minutes until rice is 'al dente'.
3. Divide coconut rice between 4 serving bowls, sprinkle with remaining coconut and serve.

Imperial-style rice and crayfish

Riso e gamberi all'imperiale

Imperial-Style Rice and Crayfish

00:10 00:30

American	Ingredients	Metric/Imperial
	Oil	
1	*Medium onion*	*1*
1 lb	*Crayfish or prawn tails*	*500 g / 1 lb*
¼ cup	*Butter*	*50 g / 2 oz*
¼ cup	*Dry white wine*	*50 ml / 2 fl oz*
Scant ¼ cup	*Curry powder*	*3 tbsp*
½ cup	*Water*	*125 ml / 4 fl oz*
⅓ cup	*Whipping (double) cream*	*65 ml / 2½ fl oz*
	Salt and pepper	
1⅓ cups	*Rice*	*250 g / 9 oz*

1. Preheat oven to 325°F / 170°C / Gas Mark 3. Grease a baking pan. Peel and finely chop onion.
2. Bring a pan of salted water to the boil, immerse crayfish, turn off the heat, cover and leave for 5 minutes.
3. Heat butter and when hot sauté the onion for 2-3 minutes without browning. Drain and shell crayfish and add to onion in pan. Pour over white wine and simmer for 5 minutes.
4. Add curry powder, water and cream and stir in well. Season with salt and pepper. Cover and leave to simmer on a low heat for 10 minutes.
5. Meanwhile cook rice in boiling salted water for 15 minutes, drain and spread over a baking sheet. Place in oven for 5 minutes to separate grains.
6. Make a border of rice around a hot serving dish, pour curried fish sauce in centre and serve immediately.

Riso al salmone Principe di Savoia

Prince of Savoy Salmon Rice

00:10 00:40

American	Ingredients	Metric/Imperial
¼ cup	*Butter*	*50 g / 2 oz*
¾ lb	*Fresh salmon*	*300 g / 12 oz*
1	*Onion*	*1*
1⅔ cups	*Pre-fluffed rice*	*350 g / 12 oz*
½ cup	*Dry white wine*	*125 ml / 4 fl oz*
½ cup	*Dry champagne or sparkling wine*	*125 ml / 4 fl oz*
	Salt and pepper	
½ cup	*Grated parmesan cheese*	*50 g / 2 oz*
2	*Egg yolks*	*2*
1 tsp	*Cognac*	*1 tsp*
	Lemon wedges	

1. Preheat oven to 400°F / 200°C / Gas Mark 6. Grease a large piece of foil with butter and place on a baking sheet.
2. Poach the salmon in 2 cups [450 ml / ¾ pint] water for 5 minutes. Cool in liquid then remove fish and flake into bite-size chunks. Retain cooking liquid.
3. Chop onion, heat butter in a pan and when foaming sauté onion for 2-3 minutes. Add rice to the pan and cook for 1 minute stirring briskly.
4. Pour over fish cooking liquid, wine and champagne, season and stir in salmon, then cover and simmer for 10 minutes.
5. Remove from heat, gently stir in parmesan cheese, egg yolks and cognac. Spoon mixture onto foil, close up loosely to form a parcel and bake for 15 minutes.
6. Place foil parcel on a large serving dish, open foil, garnish with lemon wedges and serve hot.

Riso con castrato

Rice with Mutton

00:10 00:45

American	Ingredients	Metric/Imperial
1	Onion	1
¾ lb	Peeled tomatoes	350 g / 12 oz
1 lb	Lean lamb	500 g / 1 lb
½ cup	Butter	100 g / 4 oz
1 tsp	Cinnamon	1 tsp
3 cups	Stock	750 ml / 1¼ pints
1½ cups	Rice	300 g / 11 oz
	Oil	
	Parsley sprigs	

1. Chop onion and tomatoes, cut lamb into small pieces. Heat butter and when hot, brown meat all over, then add onion to pan and cook a further minute. Stir in tomatoes and cinnamon and pour over the stock. Cover and simmer for about 30 minutes.
2. Add rice to the pan, add more stock if needed, cover and cook for 15 minutes, until rice is tender.
3. Lightly oil a 3 cup [750 ml / 1¼ pint] ring mold, spoon rice mixture into mold, pressing down well. Leave for 5 minutes, then turn out onto a serving plate and garnish with sprigs of parsley.

Cook's tip: if you wish, the mold may also be served cold.

Pizza di riso 

Rice Pizza

00:15 00:35

American	Ingredients	Metric/Imperial
½	Small onion	½
1	Sweet yellow pepper	1
2	Tomatoes	2
⅓ cup	Vegetable oil	4 tbsp
¼ cup	Butter	50 g / 2 oz
1⅓ cups	Rice	250 g / 9 oz
2½ cups	Stock	600 ml / 1 pint
	Salt	
½ cup	Grated parmesan cheese	50 g / 2 oz
1	Egg yolk, beaten	1

1. Preheat oven to 425°F / 220°C / Gas Mark 7. Grease a baking sheet.
2. Chop the onion, clean and deseed pepper and cut into thin strips. Slice the skinned tomatoes.
3. Heat half the oil and half the butter in a pan, sauté the onion for 2 minutes and add rice to pan, cook for 1-2 minutes, stirring briskly.
4. Pour over stock, add salt, cover and cook for 15 minutes.
5. Remove pan from the heat, stir in grated cheese, egg yolk and remaining butter. Mix together well then divide mixture into 4.
6. Smooth each portion into rounds to form pizzas and place on baking sheet. Heat remaining oil and fry pepper strips for 5 minutes.
7. Arrange tomatoes and peppers on pizza bases to form wheel shapes. Bake for 10 minutes and serve immediately.

Rice with mutton

Nido di riso giallo

Yellow Rice Nest

00:10 01:00

American	Ingredients	Metric/Imperial
1	Onion	1
½ lb	Chicken livers	225 g / 8 oz
½ cup	Butter	100 g / 4 oz
1 cup	Risotto rice	200 g / 7 oz
¼ cup	White wine	50 ml / 2 fl oz
2 cups	Stock	450 ml / ¾ pint
1 envelope	Saffron	1 sachet
1 tsp	Dried sage	1 tsp
2 tbsp	Brandy	1½ tbsp
½ cup	Water	125 ml / 4 fl oz
	Salt and pepper	
½ lb	Frozen peas	225 g / 8 oz
1 cup	Grated cheese	100 g / 4 oz
2 oz	Gruyère cheese	50 g / 2 oz

1. Slice onion, chop chicken livers into small pieces. Heat half the butter and, when foaming, sauté onion for 1 minute then add rice and sauté for a further minute. Pour over the wine, increase heat and cook for 5 minutes to allow the wine to evaporate.
2. Add stock to the rice, then cover and simmer for about 15 minutes. Soak saffron in a little water in a cup.
3. Preheat oven to 375°F / 190°C / Gas Mark 5.
4. Meanwhile melt butter in another pan, add livers and sage, cook for a few minutes to brown all over. Pour in the brandy, water, salt and pepper, cover and simmer over a low heat for about 10 minutes, then add peas.
5. Remove risotto from heat, taste and adjust seasoning, add saffron and half the grated cheese and stir well. Grease an ovenproof serving dish, spoon half the risotto over the base, pour over the peas and chicken livers, sprinkle over diced gruyère and cover with remaining risotto.
6. Sprinkle surface with grated cheese and dab with knobs of butter. Bake for 25-30 minutes until golden brown, and serve very hot.

Risotto with asparagus tips

Risotto con punte di asparagi

Risotto with Asparagus Tips

00:10 | 00:30

American	Ingredients	Metric/Imperial
1	Small onion	1
2 tbsp	Oil	1½ tbsp
¼ cup	Butter	50 g / 2 oz
½ lb	Fresh or frozen asparagus tips	225 g / 8 oz
2⅓ cups	Rice	450 g / 1 lb
1 quart	Stock	1 litre / 1¾ pints
3 tbsp	Cream	2 tbsp
3 tbsp	Grated parmesan cheese	2 tbsp

1. Peel and chop the onion. Heat the oil and half the butter in a pan and, when foaming, sauté onion for 2-3 minutes but do not brown. Remove with a slotted spoon and put on one side.
2. Add asparagus tips to pan and sauté for 10 minutes over a low heat. Add rice to pan, cook for 2 minutes stirring all the time, then stir in onion. Pour over stock, cover and simmer for 15 minutes.
3. Remove from heat, stir in cream, add butter and parmesan, spoon onto a hot serving dish and serve.

Riso e patate al pesto

Garlic and Basil Rice with Potatoes

00:10 | 00:30

American	Ingredients	Metric/Imperial
2	Medium-sized potatoes	2
Scant ¼ cup	Vegetable oil	3 tbsp
1 quart	Water	1 litre / 1¾ pints
1	Stock cube	1
1 cup	Rice	200 g / 7 oz
3 tbsp	Garlic and basil sauce (see page 180)	2 tbsp
¼ cup	Grated parmesan cheese	25 g / 1 oz

1. Peel and dice potatoes into ¾ in / 1½ cm cubes. Heat oil and, when very hot, add potatoes and cook over a brisk heat until lightly golden.
2. Bring water to boil in a large pan, add stock cube then rice, cover and simmer for 15 minutes.
3. Stir in potatoes and garlic and basil sauce, simmer for 5 minutes and spoon onto a deep serving dish. Sprinkle over parmesan and serve immediately.

Riso alla mantovana

Mantuan-Style Rice

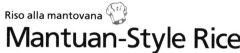

00:15 | 00:55

American	Ingredients	Metric/Imperial
2	Rounds of topside beef	2
7 oz	Sausage	200 g / 7 oz
1	Onion	1
¼ cup	Butter	50 g / 2 oz
1 cup	Rice	200 g / 7 oz
	Salt and pepper	
1 tbsp	Chopped parsley	1 tbsp

1. Simmer rounds of beef in water for about 40 minutes, then drain and retain stock.
2. Boil sausage for 10 minutes, drain and coarsely chop beef and sausage together in a food processor or grinder (mincer). Peel and chop onion.
3. Heat the butter and when foaming, sauté onion for 2-3 minutes. Add rice to pan and cook a further minute, stirring briskly. Pour over 2 cups [450 ml / ¾ pint] beef stock, cover and simmer for 15 minutes.
4. Stir chopped meats into rice and cook a further 5 minutes. Season well, spoon rice mixture onto a hot serving dish, sprinkle with chopped parsley and serve.

Riso e pollo alla normanna

Normandy-Style Rice and Chicken

00:30 | 00:15

American	Ingredients	Metric/Imperial
1⅔ cups	Rice	350 g / 12 oz
	Salt	
1	Herring fillet	1
2¼ cups	Milk	500 ml / 18 fl oz
11 oz	Cooked chicken	300 g / 11 oz
2	Pickled cucumbers	2
1 tbsp	Butter	1 tbsp
2	Egg yolks	2

1. Cook rice in boiling salted water for 15 minutes until soft, drain and leave to cool in a serving bowl. Cover herring fillet with milk and leave to soak for 20 minutes, drain, chop and add to rice. Retain milk.
2. Cut chicken into bite-size pieces, slice cucumbers thinly and stir these into rice.
3. Heat milk used for soaking fish, add butter and beat in egg yolks. Pour over rice on a low heat and stir well, season and serve at once.

Riso e noci al cartoccio

Rice and Walnuts in Foil

00:10 00:35

American	Ingredients	Metric/Imperial
¼ cup	*Butter*	50 g / 2 oz
2 oz	*Raw ham, chopped fine*	50 g / 2 oz
1⅔ cups	*Carnaroli rice*	350 g / 12 oz
2 cups	*Stock*	450 ml / ¾ pint
½ cup	*Dry white wine*	125 ml / 4 fl oz
⅓ cup	*Whipping (double) cream*	65 ml / 2½ fl oz
½ lb	*Walnuts*	225 g / 8 oz
1 tbsp	*Parsley*	1 tbsp
½ cup	*Grated parmesan cheese*	50 g / 2 oz
	Salt and pepper	
	Watercress	

1. Preheat the oven to 400°F / 200°C / Gas Mark 6. Grease a large piece of foil and place on a baking sheet.
2. Melt butter and, when foaming, add ham and rice and stir-fry for 2 minutes.
3. Pour over the stock, wine and cream, cover and simmer for 15 minutes.
4. Shell walnuts, chop parsley and add to rice with grated cheese. Season, then spoon rice onto foil, close up like a parcel and bake for 15 minutes.
5. Place foil parcel on a serving plate. Open, garnish with watercress and serve hot.

Crêpes al riso e funghi

Rice and Mushroom Pancakes

00:50 00:30

American	Ingredients	Metric/Imperial
1 cup	*Rice*	200 g / 7 oz
	Salt and pepper	
2 oz	*Fontina cheese*	50 g / 2 oz
¼ cup	*Coffee (single) cream*	50 ml / 2 fl oz
½ cup	*Butter*	100 g / 4 oz
2 oz	*Mushrooms*	50 g / 2 oz
1½ cups	*Milk*	350 ml / 12 fl oz
1 cup	*All purpose (plain) flour*	100 g / 4 oz
1	*Egg*	1
¼ cup	*Vegetable oil*	50 ml / 2 fl oz

1. Boil the rice in lightly salted water, halfway through cooking remove it from the heat and drain.
2. Chop up the fontina into small cubes and melt it in a small pan with the cream and the butter.
3. Wash and chop the mushrooms, add to the cream mixture. Pour the mixture into a large pan together with the rice, stirring well. Continue cooking over a very low heat, adding ½ cup [125 ml / 4 fl oz] milk to keep the mixture creamy.
4. Prepare a thin batter by sifting the flour and salt into a bowl, make a well in the centre and drop in the egg. Add some of the milk and whisk well, then add remaining milk. Season with pepper.
5. Pour some oil into a small iron omelette pan and when it is really hot, put 1 tablespoon of batter into it. The pancake will curl up at the edges: turn it with a fork or slice and take it off the heat almost at once. Drain on kitchen towels. Make the other pancakes.
6. Cover each pancake with 2 tablespoons of rice mixture and roll them up. Brown a little butter and pour it over the rolls. Put the pancakes in a hot oven for 5 minutes before serving them.

Risi e bisi alla veneta

Venetian-Style Rice and Peas

00:10 00:25

American	Ingredients	Metric/Imperial
½	*Onion*	½
1	*Rasher of bacon fat*	1
3 tbsp	*Parsley*	2 tbsp
1 tbsp	*Vegetable oil*	1 tbsp
2 tbsp	*Butter*	25 g / 1 oz
¾ lb	*Peas*	350 g / 12 oz
1 quart	*Stock*	1 litre / 1¾ pints
2 cups	*Rice*	400 g / 14 oz
½ cup	*Grated parmesan cheese*	50 g / 2 oz

1. Chop onion, bacon fat and parsley. Heat oil and butter in a large pan and sauté onion and bacon for 2-3 minutes. Add peas and cook a further 5 minutes. Pour over the stock and bring to the boil, then add rice. Cover and simmer for about 20 minutes.
2. Remove pan from the heat, stir in parmesan and parsley. Spoon rice mixture onto a hot serving dish and serve.

Riso Foresta Nera

Black Forest Rice

00:10 00:20

American	Ingredients	Metric/Imperial
1⅔ cups	*Rice*	350 g / 12 oz
	Salt and pepper	
1	*Onion*	1
2 pairs	*Würsteln sausage*	2 pairs
1 tbsp	*Vegetable oil*	1½ tbsp
2 tbsp	*Butter*	25 g / 1 oz
½ cup	*Dry white wine*	125 ml / 4 fl oz
½ cup	*Grated pecorino cheese*	50 g / 2 oz

1. Cook rice in boiling salted water for 15 minutes.
2. Meanwhile chop onion finely, cut Würsteln into chunks and prick skins.
3. Heat the oil and the butter together and, when hot, sauté onion for 2-3 minutes, add Würsteln chunks to pan and cook for 5 minutes to brown all over. Pour over wine and cook a further 5 minutes.
4. Drain rice and stir into sausage and onion in pan. Season with freshly-ground black pepper, spoon onto a hot serving dish, sprinkle with pecorino cheese and serve.

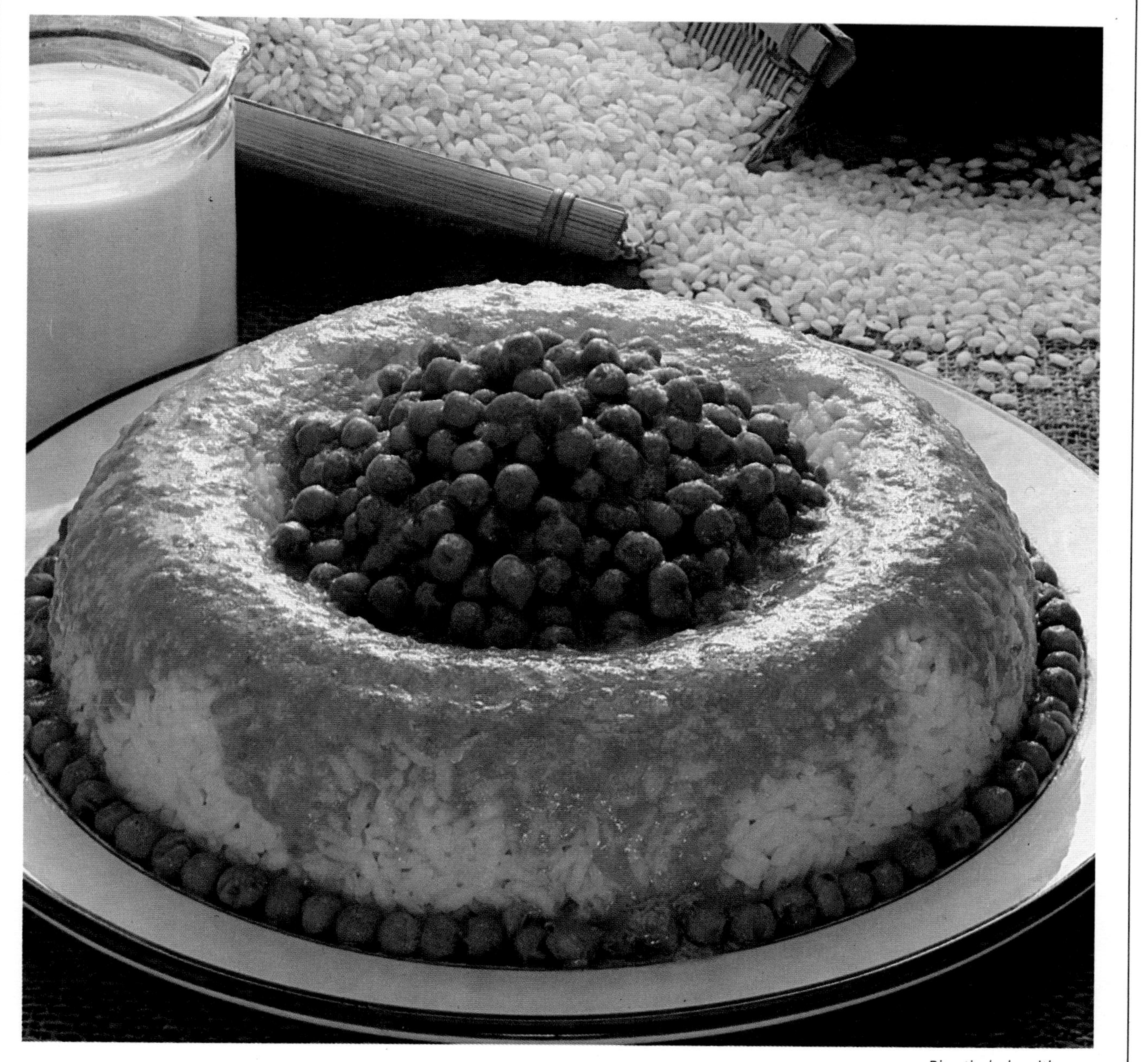

Rice timbale with peas

Timballo di riso

Rice Timbale with Peas

00:15 01:00

American	Ingredients	Metric/Imperial
1	*Carrot*	*1*
1	*Onion*	*1*
1	*Celery heart*	*1*
½ cup	*Butter*	*100 g / 4 oz*
¾ lb	*Tomatoes*	*350 g / 12 oz*
	Salt and pepper	
¾ lb	*Canned peas*	*350 g / 12 oz*
¼ cup	*Milk*	*50 ml / 2 oz*
2 cups	*Rice*	*400 g / 14 oz*
½ cup	*Grated parmesan cheese*	*50 g / 2 oz*

1. Peel carrot and onion, then chop with celery. Heat a quarter of the butter and, when foaming, cook vegetables for 10 minutes over a medium heat.
2. Chop the tomatoes and add to pan, season and simmer for 25 minutes over a low heat, then purée vegetables and liquidize in a blender.
3. Heat another quarter of butter and add drained peas to pan with salt and pour over milk. Cover and simmer for 15 minutes, then drain and keep warm. Preheat oven to 400°F / 200°C / Gas Mark 6.
4. Boil rice for 10-15 minutes, then drain and stir in remaining butter with parmesan cheese.
5. Butter a 1 quart [1 litre / 1¾ pint] ring mold, press rice into mold, place mold in a bain-marie and bake for 8 minutes.
6. Reheat vegetable sauce. Remove mold from oven, invert onto a hot serving dish, fill centre with peas, pour sauce over whole mold and serve hot.

Riso all'indiana

Indian-Style Rice

Preparation 00:00 — Cooking 00:00

American	Ingredients	Metric/Imperial
1 ⅓ cups	Rice	250 g / 9 oz
	Salt and pepper	
⅓ cup	Butter	75 g / 3 oz
1 ¼ lb	Fillet of veal	600 g / 1 ¼ lb
	Flour	
1	Large onion	1
½ cup	Dry white wine	125 ml / 4 fl oz
1	Stock cube	1
3 tsp	Curry powder	3 tsp
1 cup	Cream	225 ml / 8 fl oz

1. Cook the rice in plenty of salted water. Drain and rinse well, then spread it out on a lightly buttered oven tray so that the grains are well separated.
2. Prepare the veal by cutting into strips and dipping in seasoned flour.
3. Gently cook a finely chopped onion in the butter; when it is transparent add the floured meat and fry it golden without allowing the onion to brown.
4. Moisten with the dry white wine and allow to evaporate; season with pepper and dilute with 1 cup [225 ml / 8 fl oz] boiling water with a stock cube dissolved in it. Add curry powder, stirring all the time.
5. Cover and cook slowly for 20 minutes. At the end of cooking quickly stir in the cream and heat for a few minutes.
6. Serve with the rice heated in the oven arranged in a ring around the meat, or served in a separate bowl.

Indivie belghe con riso

Belgian Endive with Rice

Preparation 00:20 — Cooking 01:00

American	Ingredients	Metric/Imperial
2 lb	Belgian endive (chicory)	1 kg / 2 lb
½ lb	Mushrooms	225 g / 8 oz
⅓ cup	Butter	75 g / 3 oz
⅔ cup	Long grain rice	150 g / 5 oz
	Salt and pepper	
½ cup	Coffee (single) cream	100 ml / 3 ½ fl oz
1 tbsp	Chopped parsley	1 tbsp

1. Preheat the oven to 325°F / 180°C / Gas Mark 3.
2. Remove any withered outside leaves from the endive and using a small sharp knife take out the inside part of the core which is usually bitter.
3. Wash the mushrooms, drain and cut into thin slices.
4. In a well-buttered deep ovenproof dish, arrange the endive, continue with the mushrooms, little dabs of butter and sprinkle everything with the rice. Add salt, pepper and approximately 3 cups [725 ml / 1 ¼ pints] of water or stock. Cover the container firstly with a sheet of foil, then with the lid (it must be very well sealed).
5. Place in the oven for 45 minutes, remove, test the rice and season well.
6. Pour in the cream, then return the dish to the oven for a further 10 minutes, remove and sprinkle the top with chopped parsley before serving.
7. Serve at table, piping hot, in the cooking vessel.

Insalata di riso alla boscaiola

Rice Salad of the Forests

Preparation 00:30 — Cooking 00:15

American	Ingredients	Metric/Imperial
¾ lb	Mushrooms	325 g / 12 oz
3 oz	Piece of parmesan cheese	75 g / 3 oz
4	Sprigs parsley	4
2	Celery stalks	2
1 cup	Rice	200 g / 7 oz
⅔ cup	Vegetable oil	150 ml / ¼ pint
	Salt and pepper	
1	Lemon	1

1. Wash the mushrooms and cut into very thin slices.
2. Crumble the parmesan and chop it very finely with the washed celery and the parsley. Put the ingredients in a salad bowl.
3. Boil the rice till 'al dente', drain, cool under running water, drain again and mix with the mushrooms mixture. Season with oil, salt, pepper and lemon juice.

Insalata di riso all'ananas

Rice Salad with Pineapple

Preparation 00:30 — Cooking 00:15

American	Ingredients	Metric/Imperial
2	Pineapples	2
5 oz	Emmental cheese	150 g / 5 oz
1 ½ cups	Parboiled rice	300 g / 11 oz
1	Orange	1
12	Glacé cherries	12
	Salt and pepper	
1	Lemon	1
⅔ cup	Vegetable oil	150 ml / ¼ pint

1. Cut the pineapples in half lengthwise without removing the tuft of leaves from them. Hollow out inside and cut the pulp into cubes.
2. Cut the cheese into dice.
3. Put the rice to cook in boiling salted water and after about 15 minutes (the rice must remain fairly firm to the bite) drain, rinse it under running cold water and drain again. This will stop the cooking and at the same time free the rice from starch.
4. Mix the rice, once it is quite cold, with the pineapple and cubed cheese.
5. Fill the half shells with this mixture, decorate with orange slices cut thinly and with the cherries.
6. Sprinkle with some freshly-ground black pepper. Serve with a sauce prepared by dissolving the salt in the juice of the lemon and then blending in the oil.

Riso al forno alla siciliana

Sicilian Baked Rice

00:35 01:00

American	Ingredients	Metric/Imperial
5	*Sweet peppers*	5
5	*Large onions*	5
Scant ¼ cup	*Vegetable oil*	3 tbsp
2 tbsp	*Butter*	25 g / 1 oz
1	*Garlic clove*	1
½ lb	*Canned tomatoes*	225 g / 8 oz
	Salt and pepper	
2	*Medium cans tuna in oil*	2
⅔ cup	*Black olives*	100 g / 4 oz
3 tbsp	*Capers*	2 tbsp
4	*Anchovies*	4
1⅔ cups	*Rice*	350 g / 12 oz
2	*Mozzarella cheeses*	2
½ tsp	*Chopped basil*	½ tsp
2 tbsp	*Grated parmesan cheese*	1½ tbsp
¼ tsp	*Chopped oregano*	¼ tsp

1. Wash the deseeded peppers and cut them into large pieces. Peel the onions and cut them into thin slices.
2. Heat the oil and butter in a pan and gently fry the crushed garlic, add the onion and when it is golden brown, the peppers. Cover and cook for 10 minutes.
3. Add the tomatoes and break them with a fork; add salt, pepper and 1 cup [225 ml / 8 fl oz] water. Cover, lower the heat and cook on a moderate heat for 30 minutes.
4. Add the drained tuna, the olives, capers and chopped anchovies. Cook for a further 10 minutes.
5. Cook the rice in boiling salted water until firm but tender. Drain and quickly mix in a knob of butter.
6. Preheat the oven to 350°F / 180°C / Gas Mark 4.
7. Spread a layer of rice in an ovenproof dish, cover with the pepper and tuna mixture. Add more rice and some slices of mozzarella and basil.
8. Continue alternating rice, pepper and tuna mixture and mozzarella. Finish with a layer of rice. Sprinkle with grated parmesan cheese and oregano and season with pepper.
9. Place in the preheated oven for 20 minutes until the surface is golden. Serve piping hot, or cold as a salad.

Riso freddo alla hawaiana

Hawaiian-Style Cold Rice

00:30 00:15

American	Ingredients	Metric/Imperial
1 cup	*Parboiled rice*	200 g / 7 oz
2	*Small Spanish melons*	2
⅔ cup	*Olive oil*	150 ml / ¼ pint
	Salt and pepper	
½ cup	*Dry port*	125 ml / 4 fl oz
8	*Black olives*	8
2 oz	*Pistachio nuts*	50 g / 2 oz

1. Wash the rice and cook in plenty of boiling salted water. When cooked, drain and rinse it under cold running water, drain well.
2. Cut the melons in half and remove the seeds, retain skins. Make little balls from the flesh.
3. Collect the melon balls, season them with oil, salt and pepper and mix them in a bowl with the cold boiled rice.
4. Pour the dry port wine over everything and stir in the black olives and shelled pistachio nuts. Mix together thoroughly.
5. Wash the melon skins and dry them. Fill them with the well-seasoned rice and melon. Keep in a cool place (or refrigerator) for about 20 minutes before serving.

Sicilian baked rice

Timballo di riso

Rice Mold

00:25 | 01:30

American	Ingredients	Metric/Imperial
¼ lb	Dried mushrooms	100 g / 4 oz
½ lb	Chicken livers	225 g / 8 oz
½ lb	Sweetbreads	225 g / 8 oz
1⅔ cups	Rice	300 g / 12 oz
¼ cup	Butter	50 g / 2 oz
2	Beaten egg yolks	2
½ cup	Grated cheese	50 g / 2 oz
8	Sage leaves	8
	Salt and pepper	
¼ cup	White wine	50 ml / 2 fl oz
Scant ¼ cup	Oil	3 tbsp
2	Garlic cloves	2
¼ lb	Sausages	100 g / 4 oz
¼ cup	Brandy	50 ml / 2 fl oz
2 tbsp	Butter	25 g / 1 oz

1. Soak mushrooms in hot water for 30 minutes, drain and chop. Clean chicken livers, slice sweetbreads.
2. Cook rice in plenty of boiling salted water for 15 minutes, drain and rinse under cold water, stir in half the butter, beaten egg yolks and 1 tablespoon grated cheese.
3. Preheat oven to 425°F / 220°C / Gas Mark 7. Grease an ovenproof dish.
4. Melt the remaining butter and, when foaming, add chicken livers and sage leaves, season with salt and pepper, sauté for 2-3 minutes, then pour over wine. Cover and cook over a low heat for 10 minutes.
5. In another pan, heat oil and, when very hot, sauté garlic and mushrooms for 5 minutes, reduce the heat and simmer for 10 minutes, then add to chicken livers in pan.
6. Lightly fry sausages until evenly browned, pour over brandy and simmer for 10 minutes. Pour juices into chicken liver mixture, taste and adjust seasoning.
7. Cover base of ovenproof dish with a layer of rice, top with half the chicken liver filling, then the sausages and half the cheese. Continue layering ingredients in this way, finishing with a rice layer.
8. Sprinkle remaining cheese over surface, add knobs of butter and bake for 30 minutes until golden brown. Serve hot accompanied by a tomato sauce (see page 171) if wished.

Riso in 'cagnun'

'Cagnun' Rice

A true Milanese recipe.

00:10 | 00:15

American	Ingredients	Metric/Imperial
1⅔ cups	Rice	350 g / 12 oz
¼ lb	Back bacon	100 g / 4 oz
2	Garlic cloves	2
3 tbsp	Butter	40 g / 1½ oz
3	Plum tomatoes, peeled	3
	Salt and pepper	
	Grated cheese	

1. Cook rice in boiling salted water for 15 minutes. Remove rind from bacon and dice. Chop garlic.
2. Melt the butter, lightly fry the bacon, add the tomatoes, sieved to a purée, and a pinch of pepper. Cook for 5 minutes, then remove garlic.
3. Drain rice, and stir tomato sauce into rice. Spoon onto a hot serving dish and serve grated cheese separately.

Riso e ossibuchi

Rice and Marrow Bones

00:10 | 01:10

American	Ingredients	Metric/Imperial
1	Celery stalk	1
1	Carrot	1
1	Garlic clove	1
3 tbsp	Olive oil	2 tbsp
½ cup	Butter	100 g / 4 oz
¾ lb	Peeled tomatoes	350 g / 12 oz
4	Large marrow bones	4
3 tbsp	White flour	2 tbsp
½ cup	Dry white wine	125 ml / 4 fl oz
	Salt and pepper	
4	Sprigs of parsley	4
1½ cups	Rice	300 g / 11 oz

1. Clean and finely chop celery, carrot and garlic. Heat oil and butter and, when foaming, fry the prepared vegetables for 3-4 minutes, stirring from time to time.
2. Add tomatoes to pan and cook for a further 2 minutes. Dip marrow bones in flour and add to pan. Pour over the wine, add seasoning and parsley, cover and cook for about 1 hour.
3. Cook rice in boiling salted water for 15 minutes, then drain. Border a large hot serving dish with rice, place the marrow bones in centre, pour over sauce and serve hot.

Risotto con gli scampi

Risotto with Prawns

00:10 | 00:22

American	Ingredients	Metric/Imperial
1 lb	Cooked prawns, shelled	450 g / 1 lb
½	Onion	½
2	Small sage leaves	2
½ cup	Butter	100 g / 4 oz
½ lb	Canned peas	225 g / 8 oz
1⅔ cups	Rice	350 g / 12 oz
3 cups	Stock	750 ml / 1¼ pints
	Grated cheese	

1. Wash and rinse prawns well, then dry on a kitchen towel. Chop onion and sage leaves.
2. Heat half the butter and, when foaming, sauté onion and sage for 3 minutes to lightly brown. Add drained peas to pan with prawns and cook for a further 5 minutes, stirring all the time until prawns are lightly browned.
3. Tip rice into pan, sauté for 1 minute, pour over stock, cover and cook for 15 minutes. Off the heat stir in remaining butter and spoon onto a hot serving dish. Serve grated cheese separately.

Riso verde freddo

Cold Green Rice

00:10 | 00:15

American	Ingredients	Metric/Imperial
1⅔ cups	Rice	350 g / 12 oz
12	Basil leaves	12
1 tbsp	Grated pecorino cheese	1 tbsp
1 tbsp	Pine kernels	1 tbsp
	Salt	
½ cup	Olive oil	125 ml / 4 fl oz
1	Medium-sized can tuna	1
6	Pickled gherkins	6

1. Cook rice in boiling salted water for 15 minutes then drain and leave to cool in a large serving bowl.
2. Put all but 4 basil leaves, the pecorino, pine nuts, salt and all but 1 tablespoon of olive oil into a blender goblet. Blend to a purée, adding water if mixture is too thick.
3. Drain the tuna and flake. Quarter and slice the gherkins. Mix with the rice and add remaining oil. Spoon into a serving dish, pour over the sauce and garnish with basil leaves.

Riso tricolore

Three-colored Rice

00:10 | 00:20

American	Ingredients	Metric/Imperial
1⅔ cups	Rice	350 g / 12 oz
1	Small onion	1
15	Basil leaves	15
¼ cup	Butter	50 g / 2 oz
5 tbsp	Tomato purée	4 tbsp
	Salt and pepper	
1¼ cups	Grated hard cheese	150 g / 5 oz

1. Cook rice in plenty of boiling salted water for 15 minutes. Finely slice onion, chop 10 basil leaves.
2. Heat butter and, when foaming, sauté onion for 2 minutes, stir in tomato purée, add chopped basil and seasoning and cook for 5 minutes. Add remaining whole basil leaves, and simmer a further 5 minutes.
3. Drain rice and add to basil sauce in pan. Stir well and cook over a low heat for 2-3 minutes.
4. Spoon onto a hot serving dish, sprinkle over grated cheese and serve.

Risotto con le lumache

Risotto with Snails

00:15 | 03:15

American	Ingredients	Metric/Imperial
1 tbsp	Cornmeal	1 tbsp
Scant ¼ cup	Vinegar	3 tbsp
48	Fresh snails	48
1	Onion	1
1	Celery stalk	1
2	Garlic cloves	2
¼ cup	Dry white wine	50 ml / 2 fl oz
2 cups	Rice	400 g / 14 oz
3 cups	Stock	750 ml / 1¼ pints
1	Bunch of parsley	1
1 cup	Grated cheese	100 g / 4 oz

1. Prepare a saucepan of salted water, add cornmeal and vinegar, put snails in and leave to boil for 3 hours. Drain and shell, then wash under a jet of hot running water.
2. Chop onion, celery and garlic. Heat oil and lightly fry onion, celery and garlic, then add snails and cook until brown. Pour over white wine, leave to evaporate, then add rice and pour over stock. Cover and cook for 15 minutes.
3. Spoon rice onto a hot serving dish, garnish with parsley and serve grated cheese separately.

Cold green rice

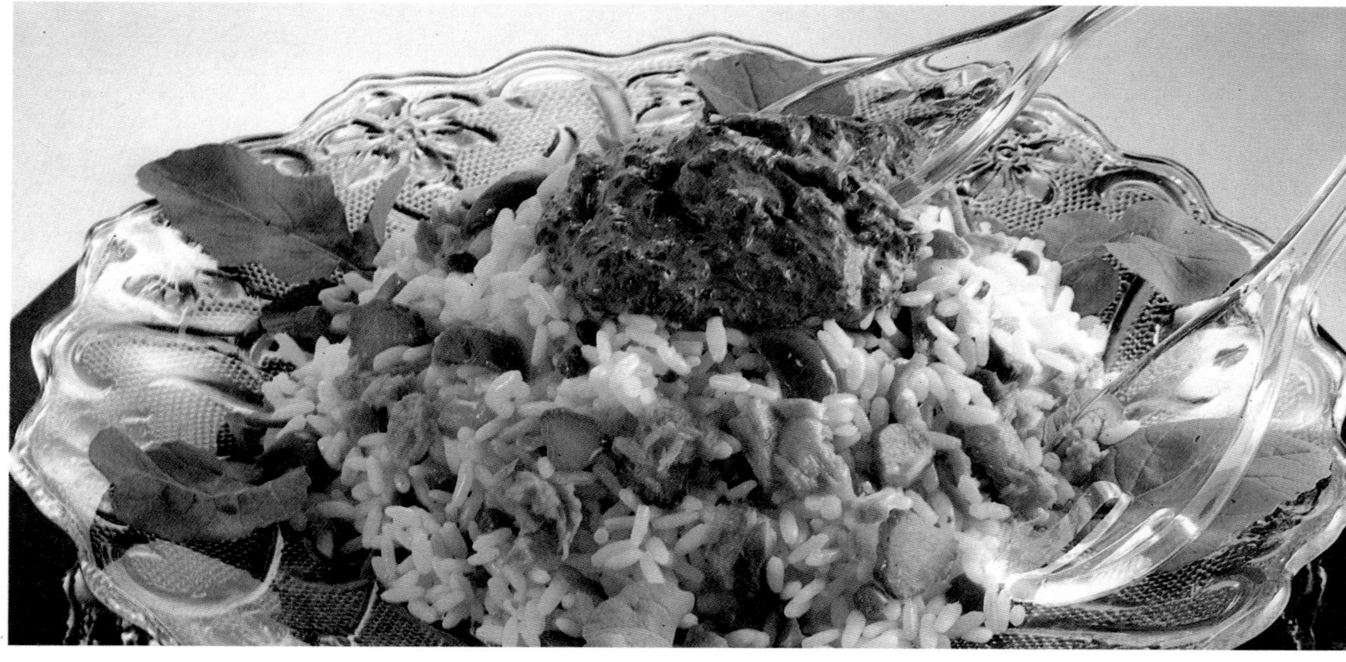

Venetian-style risotto

Risotto con carciofi

Risotto with Artichokes

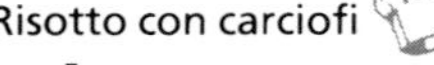

00:10 | 00:30

American	Ingredients	Metric/Imperial
4	*Globe artichokes*	4
1 tbsp	*Lemon juice*	1 tbsp
2	*Slices of raw ham*	2
⅓ cup	*Butter*	65 g / 2½ oz
1 tbsp	*Chopped parsley*	1 tbsp
1	*Garlic clove*	1
2 cups	*Rice*	400 g / 14 oz
¼ cup	*White wine*	50 ml / 2 fl oz
3 cups	*Stock*	750 ml / 1¼ pints
	Salt and pepper	
½ cup	*Grated cheese*	50 g / 2 oz

1. Trim artichokes, cut each one into 8 and cover with water and lemon juice. Chop ham.
2. Heat ¼ cup [50 g / 2 oz] butter and when foaming add ham, parsley and garlic and cook for 2 minutes. Stir artichokes into mixture in pan and cook gently for 10 minutes.
3. Tip rice into pan, cook for 1 minute to brown lightly. Pour over wine and stock and cook covered for 15 minutes.
4. Just before serving, taste and adjust seasoning. Stir in remaining butter and grated cheese, spoon onto a hot serving dish and serve immediately.

Risotto delicato alla veneta

Venetian-Style Risotto

00:15 | 00:45

American	Ingredients	Metric/Imperial
2	*Fennel bulbs*	2
1	*Chicken breast*	1
1	*Onion*	1
2 tbsp	*Butter*	25 g / 1 oz
¼ cup	*Dry white wine*	50 ml / 2 fl oz
1 quart	*Stock*	1 litre / 1¾ pints
	Salt and pepper	
1⅔ cups	*Rice*	350 g / 12 oz
½ cup	*Grated parmesan cheese*	50 g / 2 oz

1. Clean fennel, removing outer leaves, wash thoroughly and cut into thin segments. Trim chicken of skin and bone, chop coarsely. Thinly slice onion.
2. Heat butter and, when foaming, sauté onion for 3-4 minutes to brown lightly. Add fennel and chicken, cover and cook over a low heat for 5 minutes. Pour over wine, add stock. Season with salt and pepper, cover and cook for about 30 minutes until fennel is almost falling apart.
3. Add rice to pan, cover and simmer a further 15 minutes. Before taking off the heat, stir butter into risotto with grated parmesan cheese, then spoon onto a hot serving dish and serve piping hot.

Risotto del vagone

Wagon Risotto

00:10 00:50

American	Ingredients	Metric/Imperial
1 tbsp	*Vinegar*	*1 tbsp*
1	*Sage leaf*	*1*
8	*Sausages*	*8*
	Salt and pepper	
14 oz	*Brussels sprouts*	*400 g / 14 oz*
½ cup	*Butter*	*100 g / 4 oz*
2 cups	*Coffee (single) cream*	*450 ml / ¾ pint*
1	*Stock cube*	*1*
¼ cup	*Brandy*	*50 ml / 2 fl oz*
½ lb	*Peeled tomatoes*	*225 g / 8 oz*
1 tsp	*Chopped basil*	*1 tsp*
1⅔ cups	*Rice*	*300 g / 12 oz*
½ cup	*Dry white wine*	*125 ml / 4 fl oz*
1 quart	*Stock*	*1 litre / 1¾ pints*
½ cup	*Grated parmesan*	*50 g / 2 oz*

1. Heat a saucepan with a little water, vinegar and a sage leaf. Prick sausages and cook in the water for about 20 minutes.
2. Trim and wash the sprouts. Boil in lightly salted water for 8 minutes then drain. Melt half the butter in a pan and when foaming lightly brown sprouts. Remove from heat, pour over cream, sprinkle in stock cube and stir.
3. Drain sausages, return to heat, pour over brandy and cook a further 15 minutes.
4. Prepare sauce. Break down tomatoes to form thick purée. Melt butter in a pan, add tomato pulp and chopped basil. Cook for 5 minutes. Tip in rice, pour over wine and stock, cover and simmer for 15 minutes. Reheat sprouts in sauce but do not boil.
5. Remove rice from heat, add pepper and stir in parmesan cheese. Spoon onto the centre of a hot serving dish, arrange sausages around border of plate with the brussels sprouts and sauce. Serve hot.

Wagon risotto

Risotto alla Radetzky

Radetzky-Style Risotto

A recipe dedicated to Marshal Radetzky as he particularly liked this Milanese dish.

00:10 00:40

American	Ingredients	Metric/Imperial
1	*Small onion*	*1*
1 oz	*Beef marrow*	*25 g / 1 oz*
¼ lb	*Chicken giblets*	*100 g / 4 oz*
½ lb	*Small peas*	*225 g / 8 oz*
2 oz	*Hard cheese*	*50 g / 2 oz*
¼ lb	*Gorgonzola*	*100 g / 4 oz*
2 oz	*Dried mushrooms*	*50 g / 2 oz*
⅓ cup	*Butter*	*65 g / 2½ oz*
1⅔ cups	*Rice*	*350 g / 12 oz*
2¼ cups	*Stock*	*500 ml / 18 fl oz*
	Salt and pepper	
2 cups	*Barolo wine*	*450 ml / ¾ pint*
1¼ cups	*Béchamel sauce*	*300 ml / ½ pint*

1. Preheat the oven to 400°F / 200°C / Gas Mark 6. Butter an ovenproof serving dish.
2. Chop onion, beef marrow and chicken giblets. Shell or defrost peas. Slice hard cheese and dice gorgonzola. Clean dried mushrooms.
3. Heat butter and, when foaming, sauté onion for 3-5 minutes to brown lightly. Add rice to pan and cook a further minute stirring all the time, then add beef marrow pieces. Pour over stock, cover and simmer for about 8 minutes.
4. Add peas, three quarters of the mushrooms, and chicken giblets to pan, season with salt and pepper, pour over wine, cover and cook a further 8 minutes until rice is just cooked.
5. Spoon rice mixture into ovenproof dish, cover with cheese slices and dabs of butter. Bake for 20 minutes until golden.
6. Meanwhile prepare sauce. Stir the rest of the mushrooms into prepared béchamel sauce with gorgonzola chunks. Stir and cook in a double saucepan until sauce is smooth and thickened. Serve with the baked risotto.

Port risotto

Risotto del porto

Port Risotto

00:20 | 00:30

American	Ingredients	Metric/Imperial
1 lb	*Mussels*	*500 g / 1 lb*
7 oz	*Squid*	*200 g / 7 oz*
½ lb	*Tomatoes*	*225 g / 8 oz*
1	*Small bunch of parsley*	*1*
1	*Garlic clove*	*1*
1	*Green pepper*	*1*
½ cup	*Vegetable oil*	*125 ml / 4 fl oz*
2 tbsp	*Butter*	*25 g / 1 oz*
1½ cups	*Rice*	*300 g / 11 oz*
2½ cups	*Water*	*600 ml / 1 pint*
	Salt and pepper	

1. Wash mussels in several changes of water to remove all grit. Remove beards. Put mussels in a saucepan of boiling water, cover and cook for 8-10 minutes until mussels are fully opened. Discard any that have not opened. Drain mussels and shell.
2. Clean squid and slice lengthwise into thin strips. Chop tomatoes, parsley, garlic and pepper. Heat oil and butter and when foaming add squid, parsley, garlic and mussels and brown lightly. Add tomatoes to pan and leave to cook over a brisk heat for 5 minutes. Tip in rice, pour over water, cover and cook for 15 minutes until rice is tender.
3. Season risotto, spoon onto a hot serving dish and serve.

Paella peruviana

Peruvian Paella

00:30 | 01:00

American	Ingredients	Metric/Imperial
1½ cups	*Rice*	*300 g / 11 oz*
7 oz	*Chicken, cooked*	*200 g / 7 oz*
7 oz	*Stewed pork*	*200 g / 7 oz*
7 oz	*Duck, cooked*	*200 g / 7 oz*
14 oz	*Canned tomatoes*	*400 g / 14 oz*
4	*Garlic cloves*	*4*
¼ tsp	*Paprika*	*¼ tsp*
2 tsp	*Chilli sauce*	*2 tsp*
½ cup	*White rum*	*125 ml / 4 fl oz*
	Salt and pepper	
7 oz	*Crab or lobster meat*	*200 g / 7 oz*
1 tbsp	*Chopped parsley*	*1 tbsp*

1. Cook the rice until tender but still quite firm.
2. Put the chicken, cut into pieces, the pork and the duck in a pot with the tomatoes and crushed garlic, season with a generous pinch of paprika, mix in the chilli sauce and cook over a low heat, stirring. Mix in a glass of white rum during cooking. Taste and adjust seasoning during cooking.
3. Add the crab or the lobster meat and stir. Cook for a further 10 minutes.
4. Mix the cooked rice into the pan with the meat, stir well and serve hot, sprinkle with chopped parsley.

Paella alla castigliana

Castilian Paella

Paella lends itself to endless variations according to the region of origin: In Asturia saffron is used; in the Basque version they use shallots in place of onions and pork rather than chicken.

00:30 01:00

American	Ingredients	Metric/Imperial
7 oz	Left-over chicken	200 g / 7 oz
1	Sweet yellow pepper	1
1	Sweet red pepper	1
3	Onions	3
1½ cups	Parboiled rice	300 g / 11 oz
14 oz	Fish pieces	400 g / 14 oz
	Salt and pepper	
14 oz	Plum tomatoes	400 g / 14 oz
4	Garlic cloves	4
1 tsp	Chopped basil	1 tsp
7 oz	Diced cooked ham	200 g / 7 oz
2 cups	Red wine	450 ml / ¾ pint
½ lb	Peas	225 g / 8 oz
3 tbsp	Spanish brandy	2 tbsp

1. Remove chicken bones and cut meat into small pieces.
2. Clean and deseed the peppers. Chop the onions.
3. Boil the rice in 3 cups [750 ml / 1¼ pints] water and drain.
4. Clean the fish and remove all the bones.
5. Heat the oil in a large pan and brown the onions, season with salt and pepper; mix in the tomatoes chopped in pieces, the peppers, crushed garlic, basil and fish. Cook, stirring often.
6. When the fish is half cooked, add the chicken pieces and the diced ham. Add the red wine, then taste and adjust the seasoning. Stir in the rice, continue stirring and, when the fish is cooked, add boiled and drained peas, rice and brandy.

Paella alla valenzana

Valencian Paella

01:20 01:00

American	Ingredients	Metric/Imperial
1	Small chicken	1
½ lb	Filleted pork	225 g / 8 oz
½ lb	Squid	225 g / 8 oz
2	Garlic cloves	2
⅔ cup	Vegetable oil	150 ml / ¼ pint
1 cup	Rice	200 g / 7 oz
½ lb	Peas	225 g / 8 oz
2 oz	Salami	50 g / 2 oz
4 – 5	Artichokes	4 – 5
1 envelope	Saffron	1 sachet
	Paprika	
1	Stock cube	1
	Salt and pepper	
20	Mussels	20
5 oz	Shrimps	150 g / 5 oz
2 or 3	Tomatoes	2 or 3
2 or 3	Sweet peppers	2 or 3

1. Clean the chicken and cut into small pieces (see jointing page 312). Chop the pork into cubes, wash the squid and cut it into small rounds.
2. Fry a clove of garlic gently in a large frying pan with half the oil and cook one ingredient at a time: first the chicken, then the pork and finally the squid. Keep the individual ingredients warm.
3. Preheat the oven to 350°F / 180°C / Gas Mark 4.
4. Brown a clove of garlic in remaining oil in an oven pan, add the rice and add the cooked meats, the squid, peas, sliced salami, artichokes, saffron, a pinch of paprika, 2 cups [450 ml / ¾ pint] stock made up with the cube. Bring to the boil, season, cover and place in a hot oven.
5. After 10 minutes check the moisture of the rice and if it is too dry add a little boiling water and stir this unusual 'risotto'. Return the pan to the oven and continue cooking for a further 6-10 minutes.
6. Cook the mussels (see page 218) and the shrimps (in a separate pan). Deseed the tomatoes and cut into strips. Deseed the peppers, blanch in boiling water, peel and cut into thin strips.
7. Serve the paella in the cooking pan, decorated with mussels, shrimps, tomato and pepper strips.

Paella all'aragonese

Aragon Paella

01:00 01:15

American	Ingredients	Metric/Imperial
1	Skinned rabbit	1
½ cup	Oil	125 ml / 4 fl oz
¾ lb	Veal	350 g / 12 oz
1	Onion	1
1	Celery stalk	1
3	Sweet peppers	3
½ lb	Peas	225 g / 8 oz
¼ lb	White beans, cooked	100 g / 4 oz
2 b	Fish for soup	1 kg / 2 lb
3	Artichokes	3
12	Asparagus spears	12
2	Garlic cloves	2
Several strands	Saffron	Several strands
6	Plum tomatoes	6
2 cups	Rice	400 g/ 14 oz
¼ lb	Italian sausage	100 g / 4 oz
1 quart	Stock	1 litre / 1¾ pints
	Salt and pepper	
12	Prawns	12

1. Clean the rabbit, wash it, cut it into pieces, heat the oil and cook the rabbit joints.
2. In the same oil, add the veal with the chopped onion, and the diced celery. Add the deseeded peppers cut into strips, the peas and at the last moment the cooked beans and fish.
3. Cook the artichokes and the asparagus. Crush the garlic in a mortar with the saffron and the tomato pulp.
4. Preheat the oven to 375°F / 190°C / Gas Mark 4.
5. Mix the rice in the cooking pan with all the prepared ingredients. Add the peeled and chopped sausage. Add the stock, season well and boil for 5 minutes, then put the covered pan in the oven and leave for 15 minutes or until rice is cooked.
6. Cut the asparagus and artichoke into wedges and dip in oil.
7. Remove the paella from the oven and decorate with the prawns, artichoke and asparagus tips. Put in the oven for a further 5 minutes before serving.

Polenta, Pizzas and Soufflés

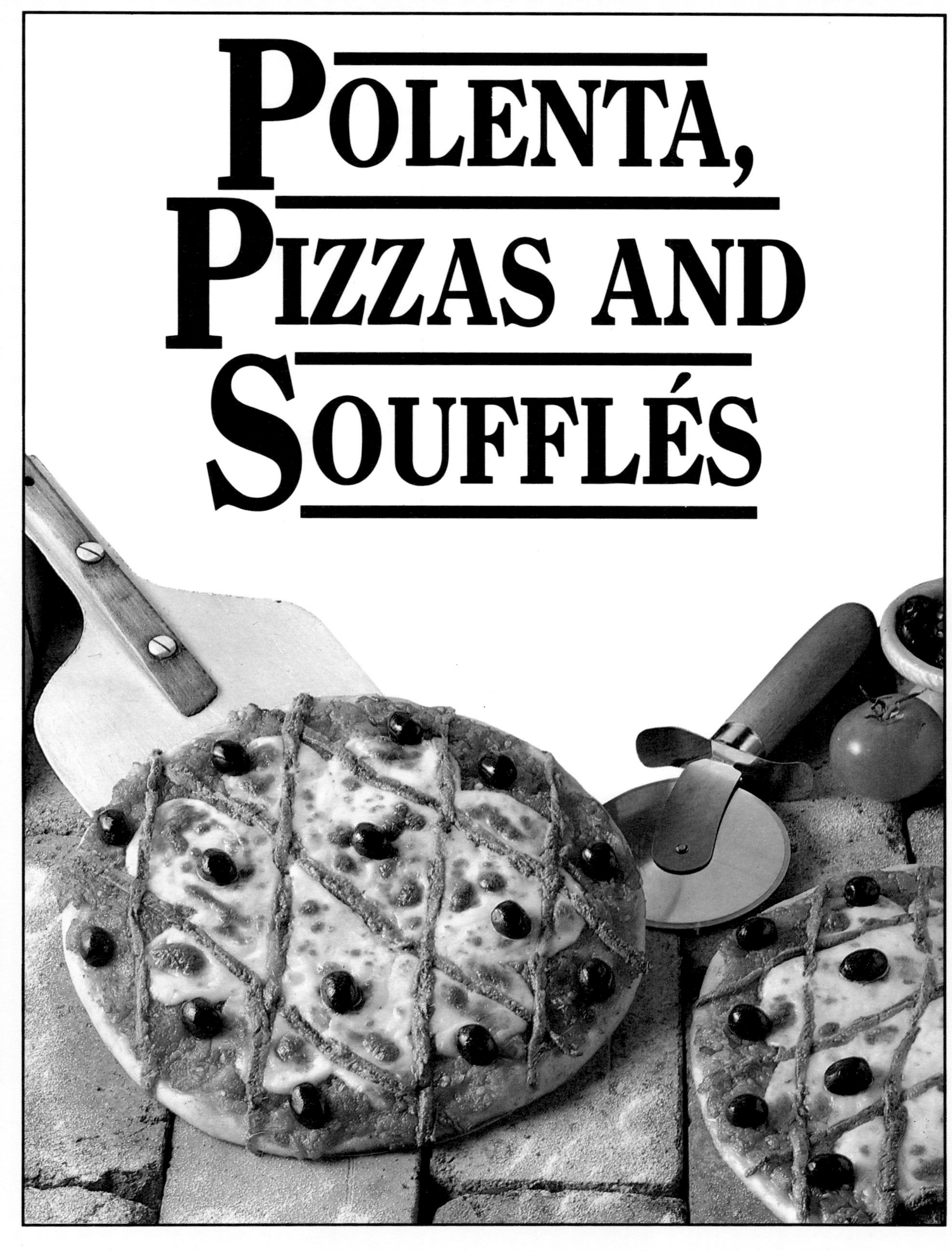

Polenta

To make this traditional dish Italian cooks use a 'paiolo' which is rather like a copper cauldron with a rounded bottom. This pan is not lined with tin. It is better to cook polenta in a copper pan but it can be made in any heavy saucepan.

There is now available in Italy an automatic polenta cooker with an electric beater. It is a very good purchase for a dish which requires such a long time to cook and a lot of attention from the person cooking it.

Polenta is made from maize flour which is not unlike American cornmeal. The consistency varies from region to region. In Bergamo, the home of polenta, a coarse grain cornmeal is used; in Verona it is less coarse whereas in Padua and Venice finely ground meal is much favoured. Polenta Taragna is made from equal quantities of cornmeal and wheat flour.

There are a few basic rules that you should remember when you are preparing polenta:

1. The meal should be added to the water as soon as it reaches boiling point in a steady flow.

2. Stirring is always done in a clockwise direction with a wooden spoon. A special polenta spoon is used for this and is a slightly different shape from the usual wooden spoon.

3. The polenta must be cooked for at least 50 minutes in an ordinary saucepan. It will take at least 1½ hours in a double boiler and must be stirred constantly.

Polenta 

Polenta

00:05 00:50

American	Ingredients	Metric/Imperial
2 quarts	*Boiling water*	*2 litres / 3½ pints*
2 tsp	*Salt*	*2 tsp*
3 cups	*Coarsely ground cornmeal (maize)*	*450 g / 1 lb*

1. Bring the water up to the boil with the salt in a large saucepan. Bring a kettle of water to the boil for later, if needed.

2. When the water has just boiled, sprinkle in half the cornmeal stirring always in a clockwise direction with a wooden spoon. Reduce the heat and as the mixture thickens, add a little more boiling water.

3. When the mixture is smooth, sprinkle in remaining meal continuing to stir in a clockwise direction. Add a little boiling water when the mixture becomes too thick.

4. Cook for about 45-50 minutes when the mixture should leave the sides of the pan clean. Turn onto a marble slab or clean board and form the polenta into a dome shape.

5. Serve the polenta hot or allow to cool and use as required.

Cook's tip: polenta can be eaten when it is just cooked and still hot with many of the sauces that are given in the sauce section. Alternatively, it can be allowed to cool and harden, arranged in a dish with butter and cheese with or without a savory sauce and baked in the oven. Sliced cold polenta can be served in place of bread with stews or dishes which have a rich gravy.

Polenta falcadina 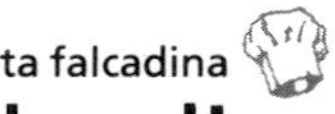

Falcadina Polenta

This is a quick and very tasty method of using left-over polenta and scraps of cheese thought up by the mountain-dwellers of Falcade.

00:20 00:20

American	Ingredients	Metric/Imperial
½ lb	*Left-over cheese*	*225 g / 8 oz*
¼ cup	*Butter*	*50 g / 2 oz*
¼ cup	*Cream*	*50 ml / 2 fl oz*
1	*Basic quantity of cold polenta*	*1*
	Salt and pepper	

1. Cut the cheese (use more if it is available) in small pieces or grate if possible.

2. Heat the butter in a pan over a low heat in a double boiler, add the cheese and allow to melt into the butter to form a cream. Add a little cream if liked.

3. Cut the polenta into little cubes slightly larger than a walnut and toss them in salted boiling water. After a few minutes, just enough time to heat the polenta, drain and season with salt and pepper.

4. Arrange the polenta in a heated serving dish and pour the creamy cheese over it.

1

2

3

4

5

Polenta

***1.** Pour the cornmeal into boiling salted water and stir clockwise with a wooden spoon.*

***2.** When too thick to be stirred, gradually add more boiling water.*

***3.** After about 50 minutes turn the polenta out onto a clean board.*

***4.** Serve the hot polenta cut in slices to accompany a main meal.*

***5.** When the polenta is cold, it can be easily cut with a cheese wire.*

Polenta fritta con erbe e funghi

Fried Polenta with Herbs and Mushrooms

00:25 01:00

American	Ingredients	Metric/Imperial
1	*Onion*	*1*
Scant ¼ cup	*Oil*	*3 tbsp*
½ lb	*Mushrooms*	*225 g / 8 oz*
1 tsp	*Chopped tarragon*	*1 tsp*
	Salt	
¼ tsp	*Red paprika*	*¼ tsp*
12	*Slices of polenta (see recipe opposite)*	*12*
3 tbsp	*Flour*	*40 g / 1½ oz*
	Vegetable oil for frying	
1	*Sprig of rosemary*	*1*

1. In a frying pan lightly brown the sliced onion with a little oil, add the washed, sliced mushrooms and cook for 5 minutes over a low heat. Add chopped tarragon, salt and red paprika.
2. Prepare the polenta and halfway through cooking tip in the fried mixture.
3. When the polenta is cooked, turn out onto a suitable chopping-board and leave to cool, flattened as much as possible.
4. Cut the polenta into slices, dip it in the flour.
5. Heat the oil until hot with a little rosemary. Fry the floured slices until golden on each side. Drain and serve hot.

Polenta in bianco al forno

Baked Polenta in White Sauce

00:25 01:30

American	Ingredients	Metric/Imperial
1 lb	*Cornmeal (maize)*	*500 g / 1 lb*
¼ cup	*Butter*	*50 g / 2 oz*
¼ lb	*Fontina cheese*	*100 g / 4 oz*
	Salt and pepper	
1	*Mozzarella cheese*	*1*
1 tsp	*Oregano*	*1 tsp*
1 cup	*Grated parmesan cheese*	*100 g / 4 oz*
¼ lb	*Taleggio cheese*	*100 g / 4 oz*
1 cup	*Cream*	*225 ml / 8 fl oz*

1. Prepare a polenta, following the basic recipe for polenta (see opposite), let it cool and cut it into slices.
2. Preheat the oven to 375°F / 190°C / Gas Mark 5.
3. Butter an ovenproof dish and arrange in it a layer of polenta slices and add the finely chopped fontina. Sprinkle with freshly milled pepper and add a few knobs of butter.
4. Cover with more slices of polenta, then the thinly sliced mozzarella and sprinkle with oregano and salt. Cover with more slices of polenta, sprinkle with grated parmesan, pepper and a few knobs of butter. Cover the final layer of polenta with slices of taleggio cheese.
5. Pour the cream over the dish, moistening the surface thoroughly, place in the oven and cook for at least 30 minutes.

Pizza

It has been said that the pizza was the invention of bakers in the back streets of Naples. The poverty in this city was so great that it was a way of making a very little food stretch a long way and fill hungry stomachs.

On the other hand historians record that it was served at the palace of Casenta. King Ferdinand IV had it specially cooked in the ovens of the famous porcelaine works at Capodimarte.

Whatever historians say about pizza it has now travelled world wide and is one of the most popular 'fast foods'. It is available on most high streets all over the USA, Australia, Great Britain and many other European countries. Home-made pizzas have a slightly different texture from those cooked in a special pizza oven but are delicious because of the innumerable amount of fillings or toppings which can be used to suit the individual diner.

Pizza

Pizza Dough

00:00 Make 4 × 8 in / 20 cm pizza bases Rising time 01:00 — 00:00

American	Ingredients	Metric/Imperial
1½ lb	*All purpose (plain) flour*	*650 g / 1½ lb*
	Salt	
1 tbsp	*Dry active yeast*	*15 g / ½ oz*
1 cup	*Water*	*225 ml / 8 fl oz*
1 tsp	*Sugar*	*1 tsp*
2 tsp	*Oil*	*2 tsp*
½ cup	*Milk*	*125 ml / 4 fl oz*

1. Sieve the flour into a large bowl with the salt, leave covered in a warm atmosphere, e.g. in the airing cupboard or above the cooker but do not allow to become hot.
2. Activate the yeast by mixing half the water with dissolved sugar at hand-hot temperature, 140°F / 43°C, and allow to ferment. Packet yeast, which can be mixed directly with the flour, requires no reconstituting. Read directions on dried yeast packets carefully.
3. Make a well in the centre of the slightly warmed flour and pour in the liquid with yeast and 1 teaspoon oil. Mix the milk with the water (tepid temperature), add gradually, mixing well to ensure the dough becomes soft and pliable, but not sticky because too much liquid has been added.
4. Knead the dough for 10 minutes, place in a bowl covered with a clean cloth or in an oiled plastic bag. Leave in a warm place to double in size (never near direct heat). This means warm room temperature rather than warm cooking temperature. The yeast cells will be killed if the temperature is too hot.
5. Knock back the dough and use as pizza bases.
6. This quantity will make 4 to 6 8 in / 20 cm pizza bases, depending on thickness or 3 larger thin bases.

Pizza alla napoletana

Neapolitan Pizza

01:20 — 00:20

American	Ingredients	Metric/Imperial
¼	*Pizza dough recipe*	*¼*
1 tbsp	*Olive oil*	*1 tbsp*
6	*Ripe tomatoes*	*6*
1	*Garlic clove*	*1*
	Salt and pepper	
2	*Sprigs of oregano*	*2*
	or	
1 tsp	*Dried oregano*	*1 tsp*
6	*Basil leaves*	*6*

1. Preheat the oven to 450°F / 220°C / Gas Mark 7.
2. Knock back the risen dough, roll it into the shape of a pizza pan or 8 in / 20 cm tart pan or even a flan ring on an oiled baking sheet. Brush pan well with olive oil.
3. Work the dough until the pan is lined and if liked make a round edge.
4. Skin the tomatoes by plunging into boiling water, blend or sieve the tomatoes to make a purée, mix with crushed garlic. Use canned plum tomatoes if fresh are unavailable or expensive. Season well.
5. Brush the dough with olive oil, spread with tomato and garlic purée. Sprinkle with chopped oregano and basil and brush with oil.
6. Bake in a very hot oven for 15-20 minutes until cooked. Serve hot.

Variations

Pizza bases can be filled with toppings to suit the individual taste. Use the basic tomato base with the following toppings:

Anchovies, olives and parmesan cheese
Anchovies and mozzarella cheese
Mushrooms, fried onion and parmesan cheese
Blanched green sweet peppers and salami with cheese
Chopped chilli with cheese
Tuna fish, capers and anchovies
Ham, mortadella or any spicy sausage or salami
Use a béchamel sauce (see page 162) in place of the tomato filling
Top with ham and various cheeses (mozzarella is the most suitable)
Mushrooms and chopped parsley
Lightly fried onions with herbs
Sliced tomatoes and sweet peppers
Bacon with cheese
Prawns with cheese

1

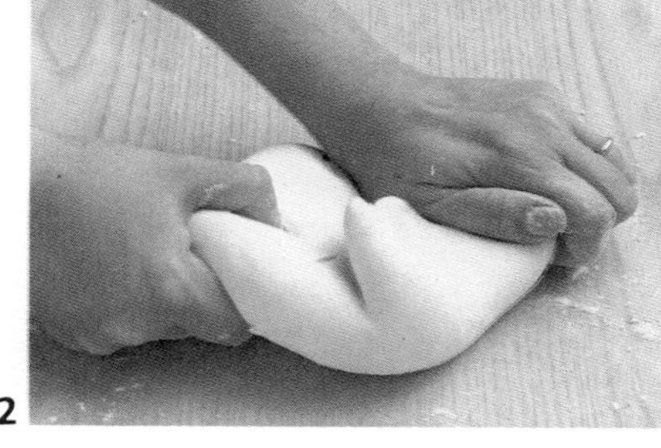

2

3

4

5

Pizza

__1.__ Make a well in the centre of the flour, add sugar, water, yeast, oil and milk.

__2.__ Knead dough for 10 minutes and leave to double in size.

__3.__ Roll out the dough to fit the pizza pan or spread it out with your knuckles.

__4.__ Spoon tomato purée over the base and sprinkle with herbs.

__5.__ Add diced cheese and a light covering of olive oil.

Bake in a hot oven for 15-20 minutes until cooked.

Soufflé Royal Laforêt

Royal Laforêt Soufflé

00:30 01:05

American	Ingredients	Metric/Imperial
3	*Eggs*	3
2 cups	*Grated cheese*	225 g / 8 oz
	Salt and pepper	
¼ tsp	*Nutmeg*	¼ tsp
3 tbsp	*Cornstarch (cornflour)*	40 g / 1½ oz
1 lb	*Asparagus tips*	450 g / 1 lb
⅓ cup	*Butter*	75 g / 3 oz
¼ cup	*Bread crumbs*	25 g / 1 oz
½ lb	*Mushrooms*	225 g / 8 oz
2 tbsp	*Chopped parsley*	1½ tbsp
2	*Garlic cloves*	2
½ cup	*Cream*	125 ml / 4 fl oz
½ lb	*Sweetbreads and brains*	225 g / 8 oz
2 tbsp	*Cognac*	1½ tbsp

1. Preheat the oven to 400°F / 200°C / Gas Mark 6.
2. Beat the egg yolks with the finely grated cheese, salt and pepper, a pinch of nutmeg and the cornstarch. Add the asparagus tips, boiled and drained, then fold in the egg whites, whisked to a stiff froth.
3. Butter a charlotte mold, sprinkle with bread crumbs and tip in the egg mixture and cook for 30 minutes in the middle of the oven.
4. Prepare the sauce by washing the mushrooms, cut into dice and brown in a pan in a little heated butter. Then mix in the chopped parsley, crushed garlic and a little cream, over a very low heat so that it all simmers gently. No stock need be added unless it is strictly necessary.
5. Trim the sweetbreads and brains, chop them finely and add to the mushroom sauce, together with a little cream and the cognac. Stir and continue to cook over a very low heat for about 35 minutes.
6. Remove the soufflé from the oven.
7. Turn the soufflé out of the mold as soon as the cooking is finished and, if desired, pour the sauce, well reduced, into the centre. Serve at once!

Soufflé al formaggio

Cheese Soufflé

00:15 00:25

American	Ingredients	Metric/Imperial
¼ cup	*Butter*	50 g / 2 oz
½ cup	*Flour*	50 g / 2 oz
1¼ cups	*Milk*	300 ml / ½ pint
1½ cups	*Grated cheese*	175 g / 6 oz
6	*Eggs*	6
	Salt and pepper	
¼ tsp	*Nutmeg*	¼ tsp
1	*Lemon*	1

1. Melt the butter in a large saucepan on a medium heat, mix the flour with it and add, a little at a time, the milk and the cheese, working until a smooth cream is formed.
2. Remove from the heat, add 1 egg yolk at a time, working it well, then season with salt and pepper, flavor with the nutmeg and the finely grated rind of the lemon.
3. Preheat the oven to 400°F / 200°C / Gas Mark 6.
4. Beat the whites in stiff peaks and fold in sauce delicately.
5. Butter an 8 in / 20 cm soufflé dish and scatter it with bread crumbs. Slide the mixture into the soufflé dish and put it in the middle of the oven for 35 minutes, without opening the oven further.

Cook's tip: other flavorings may be used in place of cheese, e.g. ¼ lb [100 g / 4 oz] chopped ham, prawns, cooked spinach. Never use too much filling or the soufflé will be heavy.

Cheese soufflé

Making a soufflé

1. *Melt the butter in a saucepan, add the flour to make a roux. Gradually stir in the milk. Cook the sauce until thick and heated just to a boil.*

2. *Remove from the heat and add the egg yolks, one by one.*

3. *Mix well with lemon rind and season with salt and pepper. Add some of the grated cheese gradually, stirring all the time. Do all this with the pan off the heat.*

4. *Sprinkle in a little grated nutmeg with the remaining cheese. Taste for seasoning.*

5. *Whisk up the egg whites until they are soft and peaky. Do not overbeat or they will be difficult to mix. Begin folding the egg whites gently into the mixture with a spoon.*

6. *Continue folding the egg whites until the mixture is smooth and contains no pockets of egg white.*

7. *Pour the mixture into the prepared soufflé dish and cook immediately in a preheated oven.*

To prepare a soufflé dish for baking, grease the bottom and sides well with butter and then coat the buttered surfaces thoroughly with bread crumbs. This will help the soufflé rise up the sides of the dish and make it easier to serve.

If you want to give the soufflé a crown, just before putting it in the oven make a groove with a spoon about 1½ in / 4 cm deep all around the top about 1¼ in / 3 cm from the edge of the dish.

7

SAUCES

A sauce is served as an accompaniment to a main dish and therefore the flavors of the sauce should never swamp the food. Season delicately to make sure that the flavors of the sauce and the food mingle well.

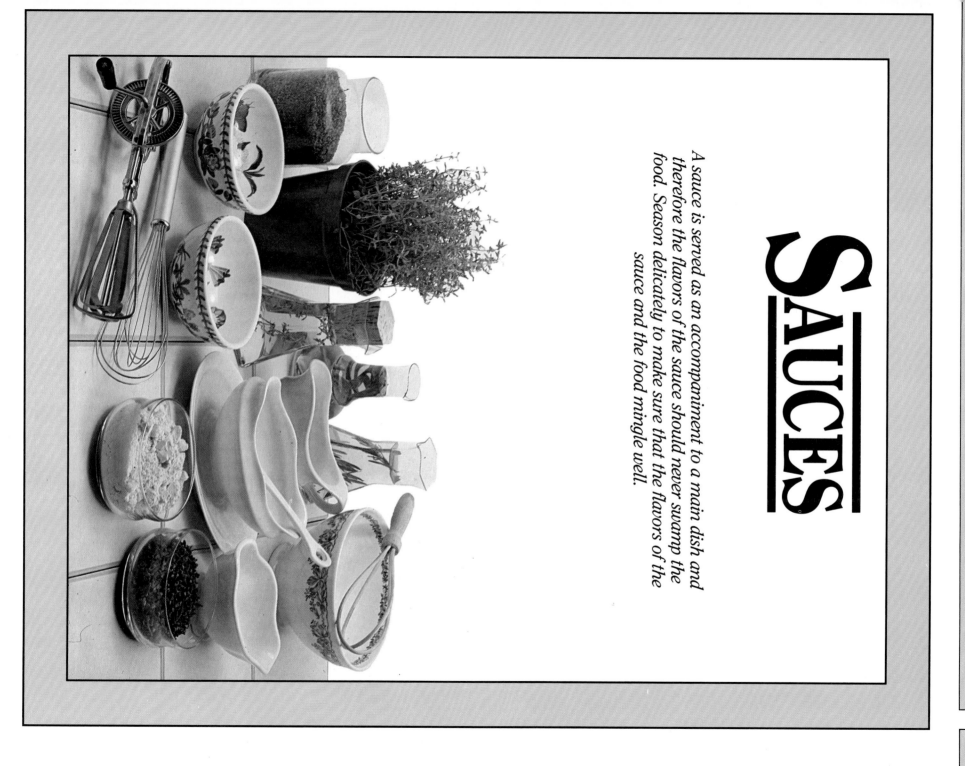

Salsa besciamella

Béchamel Sauce

00:20 00:20

American	Ingredients	Metric/Imperial
2½ cups	*Milk*	*600 ml / 1 pint*
1	*Medium-sized onion*	*1*
1	*Small carrot*	*1*
1	*Bay leaf*	*1*
1	*Bouquet garni*	*1*
8	*Peppercorns*	*8*
3 tbsp	*Butter*	*40 g / 1½ oz*
6 tbsp	*Flour*	*40 g / 1½ oz*
	Salt and pepper	
3 tbsp	*Coffee (single) cream (optional)*	*2 tbsp*

1. Pour the milk into a saucepan, add the peeled and quartered onion, a scraped and roughly chopped carrot, bay leaf, bouquet garni and peppercorns. Heat gently over a very low heat. When the milk looks as if it is about to boil turn off the heat, cover and leave to infuse for 15 minutes.
2. Heat the butter in a saucepan over a low heat, do not allow to brown. Tip in the sieved flour and mix well to make a roux, cook for at least 1 minute then strain in the infused milk whisking or stirring briskly with a wooden spoon.
3. Continue cooking, stirring all the time to prevent lumps forming, until a thick pouring sauce is made. Taste and season, add cream for a rich sauce. Use for vegetables, fish, eggs and pasta dishes.

Besciamella classica

Quick Béchamel Sauce

Apparently, this sauce, which is a delicious accompaniment to so many dishes, was invented by the Marquis of Béchamel who, unable to stand the complicated sauces of French cuisine, set about resolving his own gastronomical problems. But a sauce similar to béchamel was already well-known in Renaissance time and was served with every type of dish.

00:05 00:15

American	Ingredients	Metric/Imperial
¼ cup	*Butter*	*50 g / 2 oz*
½ cup	*Flour or cornstarch*	*50 g / 2 oz*
2½ cups	*Milk*	*600 ml / 1 pint*
	Salt and pepper	

1. Heat the butter in a small pan over a low heat, do not allow to brown. As soon as the butter has melted, stir in the flour and blend it vigorously with the butter to form a smooth mixture known as a roux, which should take on a pinkish colour.
2. Immediately add the milk, whisking or stirring briskly with a wooden spoon. Season with salt and white pepper to taste and cook until you have a thick pouring consistency. Do not leave a white sauce on the stove unattended. It will burn on the bottom of the pan and spoil the sauce.

Cook's tip: it is essential to season this sauce well or the vegetable, fish or poultry served with it will be bland.
For a thick sauce add a further 2 tablespoons [15 g / ½ oz] butter and flour to the recipe.

Besciamella verde

Green Béchamel Sauce

00:10 00:12

American	Ingredients	Metric/Imperial
⅓ cup	*Butter*	*75 g / 3 oz*
¾ cup	*Flour*	*75 g / 3 oz*
2¼ cups	*Milk*	*500 ml / 18 fl oz*
1	*Small bunch of parsley*	*1*
2 or 3	*Mint leaves*	*2 or 3*
	Salt and pepper	
1 tbsp	*Brandy*	*1 tbsp*

1. Melt butter, add flour and cook for 1-2 minutes. Allow to cool slightly, then add the milk and bring to the boil stirring all the time. Continue cooking for 2 minutes then remove from the heat.
2. Finely chop the parsley and mint and stir into the béchamel until thoroughly blended, season, then add the brandy.
3. Reheat and serve with poached fish, white vegetables such as fennel, cardoons, leeks and celery.

Cook's tip: béchamel sauce keeps very well in the refrigerator. Cover it with a sheet of film to prevent a skin forming.

Besciamella al prosciutto e tartufi

Béchamel with Ham and Truffles

00:30 00:00

American	Ingredients	Metric/Imperial
1 cup	*Béchamel sauce*	*225 ml / 8 fl oz*
1 cup	*Consommé (see page 185)*	*225 ml / 8 fl oz*
2 oz	*Onion*	*50 g / 2 oz*
2 oz	*Cooked ham*	*50 g / 2 oz*
2 tbsp	*Butter*	*25 g / 1 oz*
¼ cup	*Flour*	*25 g / 1 oz*
5 tbsp	*Marsala*	*4 tbsp*
1 cup	*Stock*	*225 ml / 8 fl oz*
	Salt and pepper	
	Truffle, sliced	

1. Prepare the thick béchamel sauce and keep warm in a bain-marie or bowl over warm water until it is needed.
2. Add consommé to the béchamel.
3. Wash and chop the onion and cut the ham into strips. Heat the butter, add the onion and ham, cook over a low heat stirring with a wooden spoon for 4 minutes. When the onion is transparent, raise the heat, add the flour, stirring well to avoid the formation of lumps. Lightly brown the flour for 2-3 minutes.
4. Pour in the marsala and stir until smooth. Gradually pour in the hot stock to dilute the juices in the pan. Stir well, season with salt and pepper and simmer for 20 minutes over a low heat, stirring constantly.
5. Add the ham sauce to the béchamel sauce and mix the two sauces thoroughly. Add the truffle slices and pour into a sauceboat. Serve warm with any roast white meat.

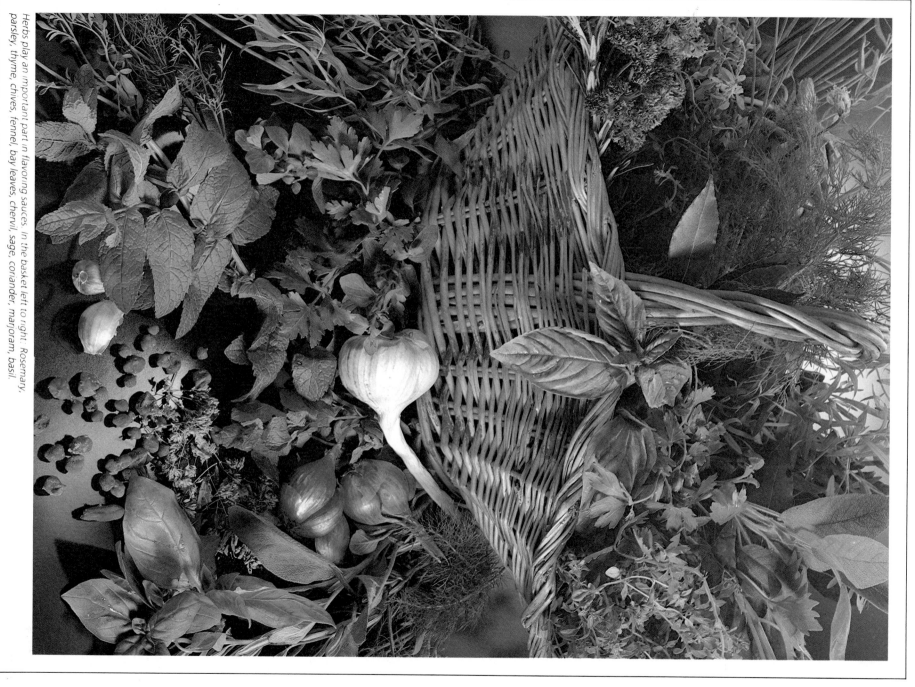

Herbs play an important part in flavoring sauces. In the basket left to right: Rosemary, parsley, thyme, chives, fennel, bay leaves, chervil, sage, coriander, marjoram, basil.

Besciamella al curry

Curry Béchamel

00:10 00:10

American	Ingredients	Metric/Imperial
⅓ cup	Butter	75 g / 3 oz
⅔ cup	Rice flour or rice cream	8 tbsp
2¼ cups	Whipping (double) cream	500 ml / 18 fl oz
2 tsp	Curry powder	2 tsp

1. Melt the butter in a saucepan, stir in the rice flour and cook for 1-2 minutes, then cool slightly. Gradually stir in most of cream, mixing thoroughly until smooth. Bring to the boil stirring all the time, until sauce thickens.
2. Dissolve the curry in a little cream to obtain an evenly colored mixture. Combine this with the creamy béchamel, mixing until they are perfectly blended and then simmer for 2 minutes.
3. Serve in a sauceboat as an accompaniment for baked or poached fish. Can also be served over thickly sliced smoked ham, cooked in a moderate oven for 10 minutes.

Besciamella allo scalogno

Shallot Béchamel

00:10 00:10

American	Ingredients	Metric/Imperial
⅓ cup	Butter	75 g / 3 oz
¾ cup	Cornstarch (cornflour)	75 g / 3 oz
5 cups	Milk	1.2 litres / 2 pints
¼ lb	Shallots or small onion	100 g / 4 oz

1. Melt butter, add cornstarch, and cook for 2 minutes. Cool slightly, then pour in the milk and bring to the boil stirring all the time. Finely chop shallots and add to the sauce. Simmer for another 3-4 minutes.
2. Serve sauce with crunchy cooked vegetables or with left-over pasta and rice.

Variation
1. Substitute a finely chopped onion for the shallots.
2. 1 tablespoon vodka can be added to the sauce.

Cook's tip: cover sauce with film whilst cooling to prevent a skin forming.

Besciamella alla vodka

Béchamel with Vodka

00:10 00:30

American	Ingredients	Metric/Imperial
½ cup	Shellfish stock	125 ml / 4 fl oz
2 tbsp	Butter	25 g / 1 oz
¼ cup	Flour	25 g / 1 oz
½ cup	Milk	125 ml / 4 fl oz
	Salt and pepper	
1 tbsp	Vodka	1 tbsp

1. Boil the shellfish of your choice for 20 minutes, then strain and retain stock for the sauce.
2. Melt the butter in a saucepan, stir in the flour, and cook for 1-2 minutes, then cool slightly.
3. Gradually add the shellfish stock and milk to the roux over heat, stirring all the time. Bring to the boil and cook for 1-2 minutes constantly stirring with a wooden spoon. Taste and adjust the seasoning, add the vodka and cook for a further 2 minutes.
4. Pour sauce into a sauceboat and serve with shellfish.

Salsa bianca piccante

Savory White Sauce

00:15 00:10

American	Ingredients	Metric/Imperial
2 tbsp	Butter	25 g / 1 oz
¼ cup	Flour	25 g / 1 oz
1 cup	Stock	225 ml / 8 fl oz
1	Anchovy fillet	1
3 tbsp	Capers	2 tbsp
½	Lemon	½

1. Melt the butter in a saucepan over a low heat and blend in the flour, stirring vigorously to obtain a smooth mixture.
2. Cook for 1 minute, remove from heat and allow to cool slightly.
3. Gradually add the stock to the roux over heat, stirring all the time, while bringing to the boil.
4. Meanwhile clean the anchovy and finely chop together with the capers. Place in a bowl, pour over lemon juice and crush with a fork.
5. Add the caper and anchovy mixture to the thickened sauce, stirring thoroughly.
6. Serve in a sauceboat as an accompaniment for roast or boiled veal or chicken.

Salsa con le noci

Walnut Béchamel Sauce

00:10 00:10

American	Ingredients	Metric/Imperial
1 cup	Shelled walnuts	100 g / 4 oz
1 cup	Béchamel sauce (see page 162)	225 ml / 8 fl oz
1	Egg yolk	1
3 tbsp	Grated parmesan cheese	2 tbsp

1. Shell the walnuts and blanch them for a few minutes to facilitate peeling. Remove as much of the membrane as possible and finely chop.
2. Pour the béchamel sauce into a saucepan and add the chopped walnuts and egg yolk.
3. Stir the béchamel sauce vigorously with a wooden spoon to obtain a smooth creamy sauce.
4. Place the saucepan over a low heat and then cook the sauce for 10 minutes stirring constantly, but do not allow to boil. Finally, mix in the grated parmesan.
5. Serve with spaghetti or to accompany pansotti.

Salsa al cognac

Brandy Sauce

00:05 00:10

American	Ingredients	Metric/Imperial
2 tbsp	*Butter*	*25 g / 1 oz*
¼ cup	*Flour*	*25 g / 1 oz*
1 cup	*Milk*	*225 ml / 8 fl oz*
	Salt and pepper	
3 tbsp	*Brandy*	*2 tbsp*

1. Melt butter in a saucepan and stir in flour. Cook for 1-2 minutes then allow to cool before adding the milk very gradually, stirring constantly with a wooden spoon. Bring to the boil, then simmer for 2-3 minutes. Season with salt and pepper, add brandy and mix well.
2. Serve sauce hot with roast pigeon, quail or pheasant.

Salsa champagne per pesci e uova

Champagne Sauce for Fish and Eggs

00:05 00:10

American	Ingredients	Metric/Imperial
2 tbsp	*Butter*	*25 g / 1 oz*
¼ cup	*Flour*	*25 g / 1 oz*
1 cup	*Champagne or dry white wine*	*225 ml / 8 fl oz*
	Salt	
1 heaped tsp	*Radish, grated*	*1 heaped tsp*

1. Heat the butter in a saucepan, add the flour and then cook for 1-2 minutes stirring well. Allow to cool, gradually pour in the champagne. Bring to the boil stirring all the time, allow to simmer for 5 minutes. Season with salt, then remove from the heat and stir in the freshly grated radish.

Salsa di cipolle 

Onion Sauce

00:20 00:10

American	Ingredients	Metric/Imperial
1	*Large onion*	*1*
4 tbsp	*Butter*	*50 g / 2 oz*
½ cup	*Flour*	*50 g / 2 oz*
1 cup	*Whipping (double) cream*	*225 ml / 8 fl oz*
	Salt	

1. Peel onion and soak for about 15 minutes in a cup of cold water, to soften the acid flavour. Drain and finely chop.
2. Melt butter and cook the onion until it becomes transparent. Add the flour, stirring vigorously with a wooden spoon and cook for 1-2 minutes, then allow to cool before adding the cream. Bring to the boil stirring continuously to obtain a smooth cream sauce free of lumps. Sprinkle in a little salt and cook over a very low heat for 2-3 minutes, stirring constantly.
3. Serve with poached or boiled eggs (hard or soft).

Salsa per coniglio

Anchovy and Caper Sauce for Rabbit

00:20 00:15

American	Ingredients	Metric/Imperial
½	*Onion*	*½*
½	*Sweet pepper*	*½*
1 tbsp	*Capers*	*1 tbsp*
2	*Anchovies*	*2*
1	*Small bunch of parsley*	*1*
	Rabbit or chicken giblets	
3 tbsp	*Butter*	*40 g / 1½ oz*
1 cup	*Stock*	*225 ml / 8 fl oz*
1 tbsp	*Flour*	*1 tbsp*
1	*Lemon*	*1*
	Salt and pepper (optional)	
1 tbsp	*Water*	*1 tbsp*

1. Peel, wash and finely chop the onion, sweet pepper, capers, anchovies and parsley. Roughly chop giblets. Sauté vegetables and giblets in half the heated butter and cook over a low heat for about 10 minutes.
2. Add stock to the pan and bring to the boil, then sieve and pour liquid back into pan.
3. Beat the rest of the butter and flour together to form a paste with lemon juice. Add this in small pieces to the contents of the pan, off the heat. Return pan to the heat, season with salt and pepper, add the water and bring to the boil, stirring all the time. Cook for 2 minutes.
4. Serve hot as an accompaniment to roast rabbit.

Salsa alle vongole

Clam Sauce

00:20 00:20

American	Ingredients	Metric/Imperial
20	*Clams*	*20*
1 cup	*White wine*	*225 ml / 8 fl oz*
½	*Onion*	*½*
1	*Celery stalk*	*1*
2 tbsp	*Butter*	*25 g / 1 oz*
¼ cup	*Flour*	*25 g / 1 oz*
¼ cup	*Brandy*	*50 ml / 2 fl oz*

1. Clean the clams thoroughly then put in a pan with the white wine. Cover and boil for a few minutes until the clams have opened.
2. Remove pan from the heat and remove the clams from their shells. Leave to cool and then chop finely and reserve. Strain the stock and keep it warm over a low heat.
3. Finely chop the onion and celery and sauté in butter in a saucepan, until onion is golden.
4. Stir in the flour mixing vigorously to obtain a roux. Cool slightly then gradually pour in the hot stock, stirring vigorously to stop the sauce becoming lumpy. Cook for at least 3-4 minutes until the sauce is thick and creamy. Mix in the chopped clams and the brandy. Stir and continue cooking over a low heat for another 5 minutes.
5. Serve the sauce with other shellfish or with any kind of fish.

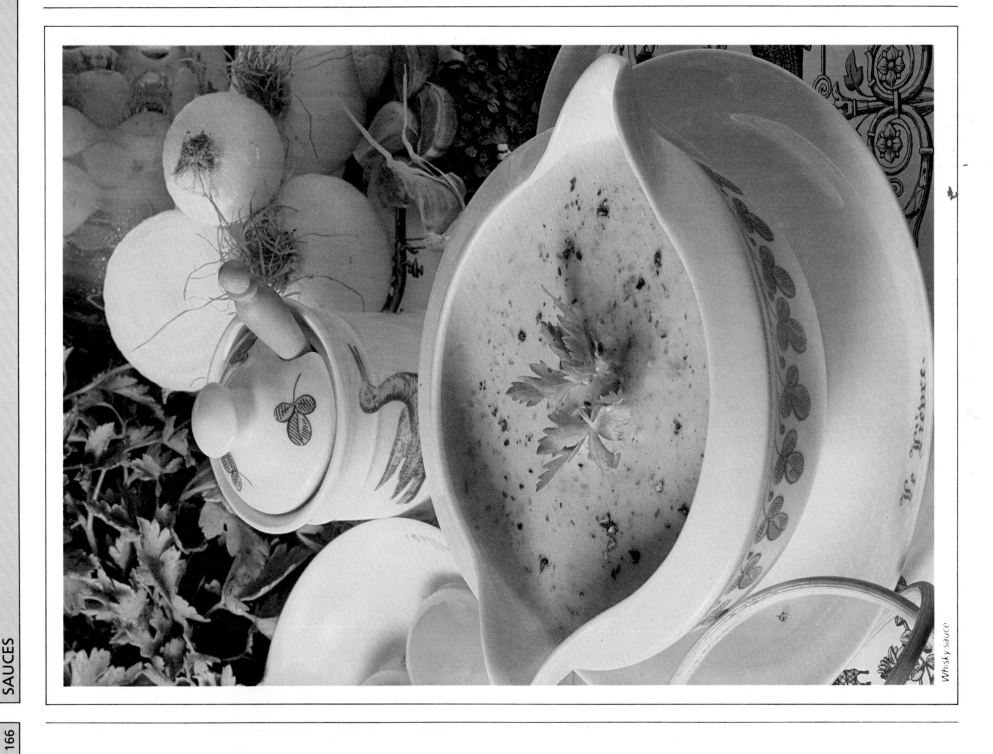

Whisky sauce

Salsa al whisky

Whisky Sauce

00:10 00:20

American	Ingredients	Metric/Imperial
1	*Small bunch parsley*	1
2	*Garlic cloves*	2
1	*Small onion*	1
¼ tsp	*Tarragon*	¼ tsp
1 tbsp	*Butter*	15 g / ½ oz
3 tbsp	*Flour*	2 tbsp
	A little milk	
¼ cup	*Coffee (single) cream*	50 ml / 2 fl oz
2	*Egg yolks*	2
	Salt and pepper	
¼ cup	*Whisky*	50 ml / 2 fl oz
2 tsp	*Dijon mustard*	2 tsp

1. Finely chop the parsley together with the garlic. Chop the onion into fine dice and add this to the parsley and garlic with the tarragon.
2. Heat butter and sauté onion and herbs for a few minutes. Blend the flour in a little milk and stir this into the ingredients in the pan to obtain a smooth mixture. Now stir in the cream and continue mixing over a very low heat, then remove from the heat.
3. Whisk with a hand or electric whisk and add the egg yolks one at a time, then add salt and pepper to taste. Place over a bain-marie and continue heating, stirring constantly until sauce thickens, but do not allow to boil.
4. Pour in the whisky a little at a time and lastly add the mustard. Remove from the heat and serve warm in a sauceboat with game, roast or grilled meats.

Salsa per anatra

Game Sauce

00:15 00:20

American	Ingredients	Metric/Imperial
4 tbsp	*Butter*	50 g / 2 oz
¼ cup	*Flour*	25 g / 1 oz
1 cup	*Whipping (double) cream*	225 ml / 8 fl oz
1	*Rind of orange, chopped*	1
¼ cup	*Curaçao liqueur*	50 ml / 2 fl oz
	Salt and pepper	
¼ tsp	*Cinnamon or nutmeg*	¼ tsp
1	*Egg yolk*	1
3 tbsp	*Red currant jelly*	2 tbsp

1. Melt the butter, add the flour, stirring well, and cook for 1-2 minutes. Cool, add the cream, stirring constantly to prevent lumps forming. (If lumps appear, remove from the heat and beat with an electric whisk.) Bring to the boil and then cook for 1-2 minutes. Reduce heat and add orange peel, free of pith.
2. Pour in the curaçao, season with salt, pepper, and cinnamon or nutmeg and simmer for a few minutes, stirring from time to time. Remove from the heat and beat in the egg yolk. Finally, add red currant jelly.
3. Serve sauce warm, with pheasant, partridge or duck.

Salsa ai gamberetti

Shrimp Sauce

00:15 00:20

American	Ingredients	Metric/Imperial
¾ lb	*Shrimps*	350 g / 12 oz
5 tbsp	*Butter*	65 g / 2½ oz
3 tbsp	*Flour*	2 tbsp
Scant ¼ cup	*Tomato sauce*	3 tbsp
¼ cup	*White wine*	50 ml / 2fl oz
	Salt and pepper	

1. Wash but do not peel the shrimps. Put them into a saucepan, cover with cold water and bring to the boil. Simmer for 5 minutes to obtain a little fish stock to use later. Drain and peel the shrimps taking care not to break them, and reserve.
2. Heat half the butter in a saucepan and, when it has melted, stir in the flour. Cook over a moderate heat for 2 minutes. Cool slightly then gradually pour in the hot fish stock and continue stirring while adding the tomato sauce. Bring to the boil, then continue cooking over a very low heat for about 3 minutes, stirring continuously. Finally, taste and adjust seasoning and remove from the heat.
3. In another saucepan, melt the remaining butter and add the shrimps. Sauté over a low heat and pour in the wine. Allow the wine to evaporate over a moderate heat then pour the tomato sauce over the shrimps, add a little freshly milled pepper and continue cooking for another 10 minutes stirring frequently with a wooden spoon.
4. Serve with boiled rice or risotto.

Salsa di cozze

Mussel Sauce

00:20 00:20

American	Ingredients	Metric/Imperial
10	*Mussels*	10
1	*Medium-sized onion*	1
1	*Small bunch of parsley*	1
2 tbsp	*Butter*	25 g / 1 oz
¼ cup	*Flour*	25 g / 1 oz
	Salt and pepper	

1. Clean the mussels thoroughly and finely chop the onion. Put these in a frying pan together with a few sprigs of parsley. Cover with water and heat. After about 5 minutes, the mussels should have opened indicating that they are cooked. Strain the stock, and make up 2 cups [225 ml / 8 fl oz] with water.
2. Remove the mussel shells and finely chop the mussels into an earthenware bowl.
3. Melt the butter in a saucepan and as soon as it begins to sizzle, stir in the flour. Mix vigorously with a wooden spoon, allow to cool then gradually stir in the hot stock using a ladle to measure it out. Stir constantly to prevent lumps forming and bring to the boil. Reduce heat and simmer for 2-3 minutes. Taste and adjust seasoning, add a little chopped parsley and the chopped mussels. Cook for another 5 minutes. Finally, taste and adjust the seasoning.
4. Serve piping hot to accompany baked or boiled fish. As a variation, the mussels can be replaced by other shellfish, such as clams.

Ragu alla cacciatora

Beef Sauce for Pasta and Gnocchi

00:10 01:40

American	Ingredients	Metric/Imperial
1	*Onion*	1
1	*Carrot*	1
1	*Celery stalk*	1
¼ cup	*Butter*	50 g / 2 oz
⅓ cup	*Oil*	5 tbsp
1 oz	*Dried mushrooms*	25 g / 1 oz
1	*Garlic clove*	1
1 cup	*Ground (minced) beef*	225 g / 8 oz
	Salt and pepper	
½ cup	*Red wine*	125 ml / 4 fl oz
1 lb	*Peeled tomatoes*	450 g / 1 lb
1	*Bay leaf*	1

1. Finely chop onion, carrot and celery. Melt butter and oil and sauté vegetables for 2 minutes. Soak mushrooms in hot water and when soft, chop coarsely and add to the pan with a peeled crushed clove of garlic.
2. Cook these ingredients together for about 5 minutes then add the meat, salt and pepper and brown thoroughly.
3. Pour in the wine, then add the tomatoes. Crush a bay leaf and add to the sauce. Cover and simmer over a low heat for about 1½ hours.

Cook's tip: this sauce can be frozen for up to 6 months.

To freeze: cool, quickly pour into small containers, cover, seal and label.

To reheat: from frozen put in a moderate oven for 45 minutes or reheat in a saucepan over a very low heat.
In a microwave, select thaw or defrost setting and stir from time to time. Cook on 'High' for 3-4 minutes.

Carbonara

Egg and Bacon Sauce

00:10 00:15

American	Ingredients	Metric/Imperial
5 oz	*Streaky bacon*	150 g / 5 oz
2	*Eggs*	2
2	*Egg yolks*	2
¾ cup	*Grated pecorino cheese*	75 g / 3 oz
	Pepper	
1 lb	*Spaghetti*	450 g / 1 lb

1. Cut bacon into thin strips and brown gently over a low heat. Break eggs into a bowl with the egg yolks and whisk lightly. Grate the pecorino and add to the eggs. Continue whisking with a fork to ensure the mixture is smooth.
2. Put spaghetti on to cook in boiling salted water with a dash of oil added. When pasta is 'al dente', drain and put straight into the pan with the bacon.
3. Pour the egg and cheese mixture on top of the spaghetti and mix quickly, keeping the pan over the heat to keep the pasta hot.
4. Season generously with pepper and serve.

Variations
1. Fry a clove of crushed garlic in a tablespoon of oil, and then add the bacon.
2. Add 2 tablespoons cream to the eggs for a creamier sauce.

Sughi per bollito misto

Green and Red Sauces for Mixed Meat Dishes

00:35
Standing time 02:00 to 03:00
00:00

American	Ingredients	Metric/Imperial
Green sauce		
1	*Large bunch of parsley*	1
1	*Hard-cooked (boiled) egg*	1
	The inside of a bread roll	
3 tbsp	*Vinegar*	2 tbsp
½	*Sweet red pepper*	½
½	*Sweet yellow pepper*	½
4	*Anchovies in salt*	4
	Salt	
½ cup	*Virgin olive oil*	125 ml / 4 fl oz
1	*Garlic clove*	1
Red sauce		
1 lb	*Tomatoes*	500 g / 1 lb
1	*Onion*	1
1	*Sweet green pepper*	1
1	*Carrot*	1
1	*Celery stalk*	1
1 tbsp	*Basil*	1 tbsp
	Salt	
1	*Chilli pepper*	1
1 tsp	*Olive oil*	1 tsp

Green Sauce
1. Clean parsley, remove stalks, rinse thoroughly and dry. Shell the egg, soak bread in vinegar and when the vinegar has been absorbed, squeeze it out by hand. Wash and cut sweet peppers into thin strips, and remove filaments and seeds. Wash and fillet anchovies, then chop all the ingredients together on a board.
2. Transfer to a bowl, add salt, stir in the olive oil to obtain the right consistency and then add the halved garlic. Leave for a few hours and then remove garlic. Chop garlic finely with the other ingredients if it is to be retained in sauce.

Red Sauce
1. Clean, wash and coarsely chop the tomatoes, onion, sweet pepper, carrot, celery and basil.
2. Heat all these ingredients together in a covered pan over a low heat, adding a little water if there is not enough liquid from the tomatoes.
3. When cooked, rub through a sieve, return to pan and continue cooking, stirring frequently. Season with salt. Just before serving, remove from heat, crumble in the chilli and stir in a trickle of oil.
4. Serve thickened sauce either hot or cold.

Cook's tip: if you wish, the ingredients for the green sauce can be finely chopped in a blender or food processor before adding the olive oil.

Green and red sauces

Ragu

Bologness Sauce

00:15 01:15

American	Ingredients	Metric/Imperial
1	*Carrot*	1
1	*Medium-sized onion*	1
1	*Celery stalk*	1
2½ oz	*Bacon*	65 g / 2½ oz
2 tbsp	*Butter*	25 g / 1 oz
Scant ¼ cup	*Olive oil*	3 tbsp
5 oz	*Sausage meat*	150 g / 5 oz
1 cup	*Ground (minced) beef*	225 g / 8 oz
½ cup	*Red wine*	125 ml / 4 fl oz
1 cup	*Tomato sauce (see page 171)*	225 ml / 8 fl oz
½ cup	*Stock*	125 ml / 4 fl oz
	Salt and pepper	

1. Finely chop the carrot, onion, celery and bacon. Heat the butter and oil in a saucepan over a low heat, and sauté prepared vegetables until golden brown.
2. Break the sausage meat up with a fork and add to the beef and stir thoroughly. After a few minutes, pour in red wine and allow to evaporate, keeping the heat turned low.
3. When all the wine has evaporated, pour in the tomato sauce and the hot stock. Stir in and leave to simmer for at least 1 hour over a low heat, stirring from time to time with a wooden spoon. If the sauce becomes too dry, add more stock.
4. Finally taste and adjust seasoning, adding salt if necessary and freshly milled pepper and cook for a further 5 minutes.
5. Serve with tagliatelle (made with eggs), spaghetti and other pasta. Coarsely chopped mushrooms may be added to the chopped vegetables if wished.

Salsa al vino rosso

Red Wine Sauce

00:10 00:30

American	Ingredients	Metric/Imperial
1 cup	*Stock*	225 ml / 8 fl oz
½ cup	*Red wine*	125 ml / 4 fl oz
1	*Bay leaf*	1
1 tbsp	*Chopped onion*	1 tbsp
1 tbsp	*Chopped parsley*	1 tbsp
	Salt and pepper	
4 tbsp	*Butter*	50 g / 2 oz
½ cup	*Flour*	50 g / 2 oz

1. Bring the stock to the boil together with the wine. Simmer very gently for a few minutes, add the bay leaf, chopped onion and parsley. Season with salt and freshly milled pepper.
2. Melt the butter in another saucepan and as soon as it begins to sizzle, blend in the flour, stirring vigorously to obtain a smooth mixture.
3. Add the boiling stock to the butter and flour, pouring in gradually. Continue stirring and simmer for a further 20 minutes until the sauce has thickened. Red wine sauce should be served hot. Serve with steak, chops or poached eggs.

Salsa per pasta

Hot Sauce for Pasta

00:20 00:20

American	Ingredients	Metric/Imperial
1	*Large onion*	1
¼ cup	*Butter*	50 g / 2 oz
	Pinch of salt	
1 tsp	*Flour*	1 tsp
1 cup	*Whipping (double) cream*	225 ml / 8 fl oz
¼ cup	*Brandy*	50 ml / 2 fl oz
1	*Red chilli pepper*	1
2 lb	*Ripe tomatoes*	1 kg / 2 lb
1 lb	*Shell pasta*	450 g / 1 lb
½ cup	*Grated parmesan cheese*	50 g / 2 oz
	Few fresh basil leaves	

1. Finely chop the onion, heat butter and sauté the onion until soft but not brown. Sprinkle with salt, add the flour and cook for 2 minutes, stirring with a wooden spoon.
2. Allow to cool slightly then mix in the cream and bring to the boil, stirring with a wooden spoon until the sauce thickens, then add the brandy and deseeded chopped chilli.
3. Peel and sieve all but 6 of the tomatoes, adding the sieved mixture to the sauce.
4. Meanwhile, cook the pasta in boiling salted water. When the pasta is 'al dente', drain and pour into the pan containing the sauce, add parmesan, cut the remaining tomatoes into strips and add these with the chopped basil leaves to the sauce. Allow the pasta to absorb the sauce for a few minutes over a low heat, then serve.

Salsa di pomodoro con fegatini

Tomato and Chicken Liver Sauce

00:20 00:35

American	Ingredients	Metric/Imperial
½	*Onion*	½
2 oz	*Raw ham*	50 g / 2 oz
2 tbsp	*Butter*	25 g / 1 oz
1 cup	*Fresh mushrooms*	100 g / 4 oz
2 oz	*Chicken livers*	50 g / 2 oz
1 cup	*Tomato sauce (page 171)*	225 ml / 8 fl oz
	Salt and pepper	
1	*Small bunch of parsley*	1
½ cup	*Dry red wine*	125 ml / 4 fl oz

1. Finely chop the onion and cut the ham into thin strips. Heat these in the butter in a saucepan and cook over a very low heat for about 10 minutes.
2. Thickly slice the mushrooms, add to the pan and cook for a few minutes stirring with a wooden spoon.
3. Coarsely chop the chicken livers and add to the other ingredients together with the tomato sauce and a little pepper. Stir and bring to the boil. Boil for a few seconds then turn down the heat again and simmer for 15 minutes, stirring constantly.
4. Chop the parsley. Heat the wine in another saucepan and reduce by a half. Add this to the sauce with the parsley.
5. Serve with cooked tagliatelle or any other pasta.

Al tonno e ai piselli

Tuna and Pea Sauce

00:20 00:20

American	Ingredients	Metric/Imperial
1	*Medium-sized onion*	*1*
Scant ¼ cup	*Olive oil*	*3 tbsp*
1 cup	*Tomato juice*	*225 ml / 8 fl oz*
14 oz	*Fresh peas, unshelled*	*400 g / 14 oz*
¼ lb	*Tuna*	*100 g / 4 oz*
1 cup	*Stock*	*225 ml / 8 fl oz*
	Salt and pepper	

1. Peel and finely chop the onion. Heat oil and sauté onion until it begins to turn golden. Add the tomato juice and simmer for a few minutes.
2. Shell the peas, add to the pan and continue to simmer for 15 minutes, adding a little stock if tomato juice has reduced too much. Stir from time to time.
3. When the peas are cooked, break up drained tuna fish with a fork and add to the pan. Cook for 5 minutes then taste and adjust seasoning.
4. Serve with boiled rice.

Salsa per beccaccia e tordi

Sauce for Woodcock

00:20 00:10

American	Ingredients	Metric/Imperial
2	*Anchovy fillets*	*2*
1	*Small onion*	*1*
1	*Shallot*	*1*
1	*Small bunch of parsley*	*1*
¼ tsp	*Basil*	*¼ tsp*
¼ tsp	*Sage*	*¼ tsp*
¼ tsp	*Rosemary*	*¼ tsp*
¼ tsp	*Thyme*	*¼ tsp*
½ lb	*Spinach*	*225 g / 8 oz*
½ lb	*Endive*	*225 g / 8 oz*
4 tbsp	*Butter*	*50 g / 2 oz*
3 tbsp	*Oil*	*2 tbsp*
⅔ cup	*Reduced meat stock or diluted stock cube*	*150 ml / ¼ pint*
1	*Egg yolk*	*1*
1 oz	*Capers*	*25 g / 1 oz*
1	*Lemon*	*1*

1. Clean and finely chop anchovy fillets. Chop onion, shallot, parsley, basil, sage, rosemary and thyme. Wash and chop spinach and endive and add these to the other chopped ingredients.
2. Heat butter and oil together, then sauté prepared ingredients for a few minutes, and stir in a little reduced stock. Remove from heat, stir in the egg yolk, rinsed and dried capers and lemon juice. Mix again and heat over a bain-marie before serving in a sauceboat.

Cook's tip: woodcock should be hung for up to a week before plucking and cooking. They are considered to be a special delicacy when cooked with all their innards (apart from the gizzard but including the brain). They are roasted undrawn.

Salsa al pomodoro

Tomato Sauce

00:30 00:50

American	Ingredients	Metric/Imperial
2 lb	*Tomatoes*	*1 kg / 2 lb*
1 tbsp	*Oil*	*1 tbsp*
2 tbsp	*Butter*	*25 g / 1 oz*
1	*Onion*	*1*
2	*Garlic cloves*	*2*
1	*Carrot*	*1*
1 tbsp	*Flour*	*1 tbsp*
2 lb	*Tomatoes*	*1 kg / 2 lb*
½ tsp	*Basil*	*½ tsp*
1	*Bay leaf*	*1*
½ tsp	*Thyme*	*½ tsp*
½ tsp	*Sugar*	*½ tsp*
	Salt and pepper	
1 tbsp	*Tomato purée*	*1 tbsp*
½ cup	*White wine (optional)*	*125 ml / 4 fl oz*

1. Plunge the tomatoes into boiling water, remove the skins and drain.
2. Heat the oil and butter in a pan over a low heat, add the peeled and finely chopped onion and the crushed garlic. Allow to cook for 5 minutes, stirring from time to time. Add the grated carrot, stir for 1 minute then add the flour and stir well until the vegetables have absorbed it.
3. Add the remaining ingredients with 1 cup [225 ml / 8 fl oz] water and the wine, allow to simmer for 45 minutes on a low heat. Remove bay leaf and sprigs of herbs before serving or using in other dishes.

Cook's tip: for a smooth tomato sauce, pass through a sieve, blender or food processor.

Salsa di prugne

Prune Sauce

00:10 00:35

American	Ingredients	Metric/Imperial
½	*Onion*	*½*
1 oz	*Raw ham*	*25 g / 1 oz*
2 tbsp	*Butter*	*25 g / 1 oz*
¼ cup	*Vinegar*	*50 ml / 2 fl oz*
10	*Prunes*	*10*
	Salt	
1	*Bay leaf*	*1*
4	*Sprigs of thyme*	*4*

1. Chop the onion and ham, heat the butter and sauté onion and ham over a moderate heat until onion is transparent. Pour over the vinegar and boil until half of it has evaporated.
2. Meanwhile stone the prunes, and add to the onions and ham. Pour in enough water to cover, add salt, bay leaf and thyme. Cover the pan and cook over a low heat until the prunes have softened, about 20 minutes.
3. Rub the prunes through a sieve and mix thoroughly with the juices from the pan. Reheat and serve as an accompaniment to loin of pork.

Salsa peverada

Savory Sauce for Game

00:15 | 00:30

American	Ingredients	Metric/Imperial
	Giblets	
1	*Small onion*	*1*
5 tbsp	*Olive oil*	*4 tbsp*
2	*Anchovy fillets*	*2*
4	*Sage leaves*	*4*
1	*Sprig of rosemary*	*1*
3 tbsp	*Vinegar*	*2 tbsp*
¼ cup	*Full bodied red wine*	*50 ml / 2 fl oz*
Scant ¼ cup	*Brandy*	*3 tbsp*
	Juices from roasting pan	
	Salt and pepper	

1. Wash and chop giblets and if using gizzard, boil for a few minutes to soften. Reserve the chopped giblets and finely chop the onion.
2. Heat the oil and fry giblets and onion together with the crushed anchovy fillets.
3. Chop the sage and rosemary and add when onion begins to soften. Sauté over a low heat for a few minutes and then pour in the vinegar and red wine.
4. Boil until the liquid has reduced slightly, add the chopped giblets and cool for a minute. Pour in the brandy and stir with a wooden spoon. Cover and then simmer over a low heat for about 15 minutes, then pass through a sieve. Remove the giblets and discard.
5. Add juices from the roast, diluted with a little water if necessary. Reheat and add salt and freshly milled black pepper, then pour into a sauceboat.
6. Serve with roast game and poultry.

Salsa diablotin

Devilled Sauce

00:10 | 00:10

American	Ingredients	Metric/Imperial
2	*Shallots*	*2*
½ cup	*Full-bodied red wine*	*125 ml / 4 fl oz*
3 tbsp	*Vinegar*	*2 tbsp*
Scant ¼ cup	*Flour*	*25 g / 1 oz*
2	*Egg yolks*	*2*
	Red chilli powder	
¼ cup	*Brandy*	*50 ml / 2 fl oz*

1. Finely chop the shallots and put in a saucepan with the wine and the vinegar over a high heat and boil uncovered until half the liquid has evaporated.
2. Liquidize in a blender and stir in the flour before pouring back into the saucepan. Bring to the boil, stirring continuously to obtain a smooth sauce.
3. Remove the sauce from the heat and continue stirring with a wooden spoon.
4. Beat in the egg yolks, pinch of chilli powder and the brandy until well mixed.
5. Pour the warm sauce into a sauceboat and serve.

Salsa di mare

Seafood Sauce

00:20 | 01:05

American	Ingredients	Metric/Imperial
½ lb	*Scorpion fish*	*225 g / 8 oz*
¼ lb	*Prawns*	*100 g / 4 oz*
5 oz	*Squid*	*150 g / 5 oz*
5	*Peppercorns*	*5*
1	*Garlic clove*	*1*
1	*Small bunch of parsley*	*1*
Scant ¼ cup	*Olive oil*	*3 tbsp*
1 cup	*Tomato sauce (page 171)*	*225 ml / 8 fl oz*
	Red chilli pepper powder	
	Salt and pepper	

1. Carefully wash and clean all the fish, leaving the head on the scorpion fish, and the prawns unpeeled. Cut the squid into pieces. Fill a saucepan with 1 quart [1 litre / 1¾ pints] water add the peppercorns and bring to the boil. First put in the squid and then after 10 minutes, add the scorpion fish and prawns. Boil for another 10 minutes.
2. When the fish is cooked, remove from the water. Strain the fish stock and reserve for the risotto. Peel the prawns and remove the head, the tail and the backbone from the scorpion fish. Then finely chop the prawns, scorpion fish and squid together. Put in a bowl and crush with a fork to form a smooth paste.
3. Finely chop the garlic and parsley and heat in the oil in a saucepan. Add fish mixture, tomato sauce, and pinch of chilli powder. Simmer over a low heat for about 30 minutes, stirring from time to time with a wooden spoon. Taste and adjust seasoning.
4. While the sauce is simmering, prepare a white risotto in a separate saucepan using the fish stock. When the rice is cooked, pour over the fish sauce, mix and serve immediately. The sauce can also be served with pasta.

Salsa alle nocciole

Hazelnut Sauce

00:10 | 00:15

American	Ingredients	Metric/Imperial
1	*Garlic clove*	*1*
3 tbsp	*Oil*	*2 tbsp*
1	*Anchovy*	*1*
1 cup	*Hazelnuts*	*100 g / 4 oz*
3 tbsp	*Grated parmesan cheese*	*2 tbsp*
1 lb	*Spaghetti*	*450 g / 1 lb*

1. Crush garlic, heat oil and cook garlic over a low heat. Remove garlic from pan when it begins to brown.
2. Clean anchovy and chop into small pieces, add to the oil and cook for 1 minute stirring with a wooden spoon. Remove from heat.
3. Grate or blend hazelnuts with the parmesan, mixing well and put directly into a serving dish.
4. Cook spaghetti until 'al dente' (8-10 minutes), drain, and put in serving dish. Mix in the nuts and parmesan, then pour over the oil and serve hot.

Tomato sauce (see page 171)

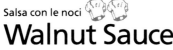

Salsa al gorgonzola 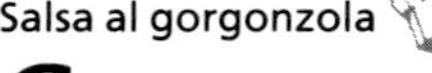

Gorgonzola Sauce

00:10 00:10

American	Ingredients	Metric/Imperial
2 oz	*Mild gorgonzola cheese*	*50 g / 2 oz*
3 oz	*Mature gorgonzola cheese*	*75 g / 3 oz*
⅔ cup	*Butter*	*125 g / 5 oz*
5 tbsp	*Coffee (single) cream*	*4 tbsp*
3 tbsp	*Brandy*	*2 tbsp*

1. Finely dice both gorgonzolas, put into a bowl and crush with a fork to blend together. Add half the butter and continue beating with a wooden spoon to obtain a smooth paste.
2. Melt remaining butter in a saucepan and add gorgonzola mixture. Mix and warm over a low heat for a few minutes. Remove from the heat, add cream and brandy.
3. Serve with plain risotto by pouring over and mixing in well just before serving. This sauce can also be served with gnocchi.

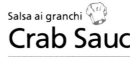

Salsa con le noci 

Walnut Sauce

01:15 00:10

American	Ingredients	Metric/Imperial
3½ cups	*Shelled walnuts*	*400 g / 14 oz*
1 cup	*Stock*	*225 ml / 8 fl oz*
	Salt	
1 cup	*Coffee (single) cream*	*225 ml / 8 fl oz*

1. Shell walnuts and keep kernels as whole as possible. Blanch in boiling water, then peel and remove membranes.

2. Place in a food processor, add half the stock and process to a creamy pulp. (A pestle and mortar can be used instead.)
3. Transfer to a saucepan and stir in the remaining stock. Season with salt and cook over a low heat, until the mixture has thickened, then strain. Collect purée in the saucepan, stir in cream and place over a low heat to warm the cream. Serve immediately with pasta.

Salsa ai granchi 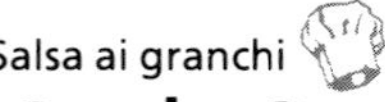

Crab Sauce

00:15 00:35 to 00:40 using fresh crab
00:20 using canned crab

American	Ingredients	Metric/Imperial
3 oz	*Crab*	*75 g / 3 oz*
1	*Garlic clove*	*1*
2 tbsp	*Butter*	*25 g / 1 oz*
1 tbsp	*Olive oil*	*1 tbsp*
1 tsp	*Anchovy paste*	*1 tsp*
1 cup	*Tomato sauce (see page 171)*	*225 ml / 8 fl oz*
1	*Bunch of parsley*	*1*

1. If using canned crab, drain off liquid. If fresh, boil crab allowing 15 minutes per 1 lb / 450 g, then finely dice and set aside.
2. Crush the garlic. Heat butter and oil in a pan over a low heat, and add garlic. When it begins to brown, remove from the pan and add anchovy paste, dissolved in the tomato sauce.
3. Simmer for 15 minutes, add crab and chopped parsley, then remove from the heat after a few minutes.
4. Serve with spaghetti or tagliatelle.

Salsa verde

Green Sauce

00:30 00:00

American	Ingredients	Metric/Imperial
2	*Anchovies*	*2*
½	*Garlic clove*	*½*
1	*Large bunch of parsley*	*1*
1 tbsp	*Capers*	*1 tbsp*
4 drops	*Soy sauce*	*4 drops*
1	*Slice soft bread*	*1*
	Vinegar) Oil) as required Salt)	

1. Crush and chop together the anchovies, garlic and parsley and a few capers. Mix in the meat extract and soak the bread in vinegar before squeezing it out and adding to the mixture.
2. Chop all the ingredients together again and put in a bowl, adding a little vinegar, oil and salt until the sauce reaches the required consistency.
3. Serve in a sauceboat as an accompaniment to boiled fish or meat.

Variations
1. Omit the anchovies, capers and garlic and the meat extract.
2. Instead of soaking the bread in vinegar, add a sieved hard-cooked (boiled) egg yolk or mashed boiled potato.

Salsa Colbert 

Colbert Sauce

00:25 00:15

American	Ingredients	Metric/Imperial
1 cup	*Butter*	*225 g / 8 oz*
1 oz	*Parsley*	*25 g / 1 oz*
1	*Lemon*	*1*
A pinch	*Nutmeg*	*A pinch*
1 tbsp	*Meat extract*	*1 tbsp*
⅓ cup	*Water*	*5 tbsp*
1 tsp	*Iced water*	*1 tsp*

1. Put the butter in a bowl and beat with a wooden spoon until softened. Then add the chopped parsley, lemon juice and a little grated nutmeg.
2. Place meat extract in a saucepan, add boiling water and dissolve over a medium heat. Place saucepan in a bain-marie and beat in butter mixture, stirring vigorously and taking care not to allow sauce to boil. Just before serving, add iced water.

Salsa col mascarpone

Mascarpone Sauce

00:15 00:00

American	Ingredients	Metric/Imperial
3 oz	*Mascarpone cheese*	*75 g / 3 oz*
1	*Egg yolk*	*1*
2 oz	*Raw ham*	*50 g / 2 oz*
3 tbsp	*Grated parmesan cheese*	*2 tbsp*
	Salt and pepper	

1. Whisk together the mascarpone cheese and the egg yolk in a bowl. Cut the ham into thin strips and add this to the mixture together with the parmesan, salt and pepper.
2. Stir ingredients well together and add 1 tablespoon boiling water (for convenience use the water from the pasta). Then beat thoroughly with a wooden spoon until the mixture becomes soft and light.
3. Serve with pasta such as fettucine.

Salsa al curry 

Curry Sauce

00:10 00:10

American	Ingredients	Metric/Imperial
1	*Ripe pear*	*1*
1	*Ripe banana*	*1*
1 tbsp	*Butter*	*15 g / ½ oz*
1 tbsp	*Curry powder*	*1 tbsp*
Scant ¼ cup	*Coffee (single) cream*	*3 tbsp*
1 tsp	*Gin*	*1 tsp*
	Salt	

1. Peel and slice pear and banana. Melt butter in a saucepan and add prepared fruits. Place over a low heat and stir to obtain a purée.
2. Dissolve curry powder in the cream and stir into the purée. Add gin, season with salt, and after a few minutes, remove from the heat.
3. Serve sauce hot or cold.

Cook's tip: this sauce can be served to accompany crudités, meat fondue, finely sliced raw fish, or pilau rice.

Salsa Villeroy 

Villeroy Sauce

00:10 00:30

American	Ingredients	Metric/Imperial
2 oz	*Dried mushrooms*	*50 g / 2 oz*
1	*Onion*	*1*
3 tbsp	*Butter*	*40 g / 1½ oz*
1 cup	*Stock*	*225 ml / 8 fl oz*
	Salt	
	Pepper	
1 cup	*Béchamel sauce (see page 162)*	*225 ml / 8 fl oz*

1. Soak mushrooms in warm water.
2. Meanwhile, peel and finely chop the onion. Heat butter and sauté the onion over a very low heat. Dissolve stock cube in boiling water. Drain mushrooms and cut into pieces. Add to the onion and, after a few minutes, add a little stock. Season with salt and pepper, cover and simmer for at least 15 minutes, adding more stock if mushrooms become too dry.
3. When cooked, put in the blender with the juices, liquidize and reserve the purée.
4. Pour the hot béchamel sauce into another saucepan and stir in the mushroom purée until thoroughly mixed.
5. Serve hot with lamb cutlets or chicken breasts dipped in egg and bread crumbs and fried in butter with a dash of marsala.

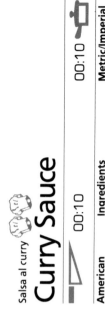

Mayonnaise

Maionese 

Mayonnaise

00:20 | 00:00

American	Ingredients	Metric/Imperial
2	*Egg yolks*	2
	Salt	
1 cup	*Vegetable or olive oil*	225 ml / 8 fl oz
1	*Lemon*	1

1. Using eggs stored at room temperature, separate yolks carefully and place in a bowl. Add a pinch of salt and start whisking gently with a fork, metal whisk or electric hand beater.
2. As soon as yolks are combined, start adding the oil, drop by drop, continuing to whisk until yolks gradually absorb all the oil. To ensure success, do not add more oil until the previous oil has been absorbed. Finally, mix in lemon juice and add salt if necessary.
3. Serve mayonnaise with poached fish, salads or as a decoration.

Cook's tip: if the mayonnaise should curdle, beat another egg yolk and gradually add the curdled mayonnaise to this, whisking regularly. Store in the least cold part of the refrigerator for up to 1 month.

Salsa tonné

Tuna Sauce

00:20 | 00:00

American	Ingredients	Metric/Imperial
1 cup	*Mayonnaise*	*225 ml / 8 fl oz*
3	*Anchovies*	*2*
¼ lb	*Tuna*	*100 g / 4 oz*
1 tsp	*Capers*	*1 tsp*
½	*Lemon*	*½*
1 tbsp	*Oil*	*1 tbsp*
1 pinch	*Salt*	*1 pinch*
⅓ cup	*Stock*	*5 tbsp*

Method I
1. Put the mayonnaise into a bowl. Wash and fillet the anchovies and chop them very finely with the tuna and the capers. Purée these in a vegetable mill, then stir into the mayonnaise with lemon juice, oil, salt and stock. Mix until thoroughly blended.
2. Serve as an accompaniment to cold boiled veal.

Method II – using a blender
1. Clean and fillet the anchovies, break up the tuna with a fork and add the capers, lemon juice, oil and salt and put all the ingredients in the blender. Add stock and purée until thoroughly blended. Can be stored in the refrigerator for 3-4 days.

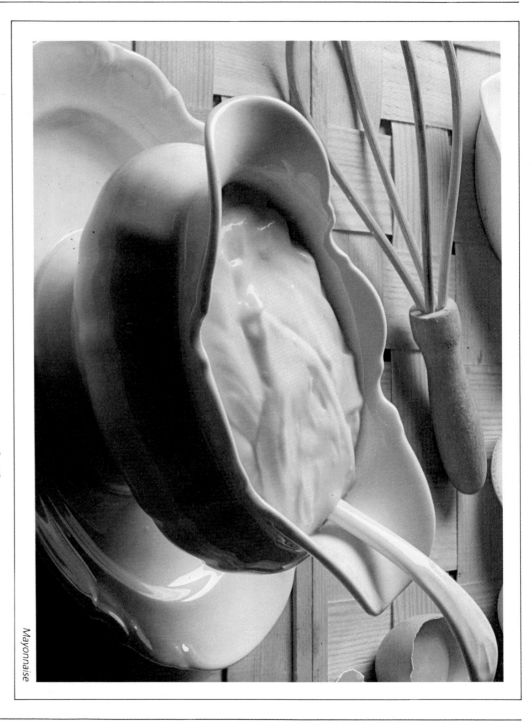

Maionese ai gamberetti

Shrimp Mayonnaise

00:25 00:10

American	Ingredients	Metric/Imperial
1 cup	*Chopped shrimps*	*150 g / 5 oz*
	Salt	
½ tsp	*Paprika*	*½ tsp*
1 cup	*Mayonnaise (see page 175)*	*225 ml / 8 fl oz*

1. Wash shrimps thoroughly and boil for 10 minutes only. Drain, shell and leave to cool, then chop in a food processor with a pinch of salt and paprika. Make mayonnaise and combine with the shrimp purée, stirring carefully.
2. Serve with all types of boiled fish.

Variations: Substitute prawns, crab or lobster for shrimps.

Maionese gelatinata

Jellied Mayonnaise

00:40 00:05

American	Ingredients	Metric/Imperial
1 envelope	*Gelatin*	*15 g / ½ oz*
3 tbsp	*Water*	*2 tbsp*
1 cup	*Mayonnaise*	*225 ml / 8 fl oz*

1. Soak gelatin in the cold water in a bowl. Leave to soften for about 5-10 minutes, put it over a saucepan of water and allow to simmer until gelatin has dissolved. Put mayonnaise into a bowl. Add the dissolved gelatin, stirring continuously to make a smooth sauce, and leave in a cool place to set.
2. Serve with salads. If required to decorate fish and cold meats, use when it is just beginning to set.

Maionese con noci e mandorle

Mayonnaise with Walnuts and Almonds

00:30 00:00

American	Ingredients	Metric/Imperial
1 cup	*Mayonnaise (see page 175)*	*225 ml / 8 fl oz*
¼ cup	*Walnuts*	*25 g / 1 oz*
¼ cup	*Ground almonds*	*25 g / 1 oz*

1. Prepare mayonnaise then peel walnuts and almonds and crush with a pestle and mortar or chop them finely. Stir the nuts into the mayonnaise, mixing carefully to blend the ingredients to a smooth paste.
2. Serve with grilled or poached fish.

Salsa aioli

Garlic Mayonnaise

00:30 00:00

American	Ingredients	Metric/Imperial
4	*Garlic cloves*	*4*
	Salt	
1	*Egg yolk*	*1*
½ cup	*Vegetable or olive oil*	*125 ml / 4 fl oz*

1. Peel garlic and crush with a little salt using a pestle and mortar, or herb chopper and reduce to a pulp. Place in a bowl and add the egg yolk, at room temperature.
2. Whisk egg yolk and garlic and begin to pour in the oil very slowly, continuing to whisk all the time. Incorporate oil drop by drop at first, then trickle in oil when it begins to thicken.
3. Serve with poached or baked fish.

Crema di avocado

Avocado Sauce

00:20 00:00

American	Ingredients	Metric/Imperial
1	*Ripe avocado*	*1*
½	*Small onion*	*½*
2 tsp	*Lemon juice*	*2 tsp*
	Worcestershire sauce	
1 tbsp	*Mayonnaise*	*1 tbsp*
	Salt	

1. Cut the avocado in half and remove stone. Using a stainless steel spoon, scrape out the flesh and crush with a stainless steel fork. Finely chop onion and add to the avocado together with lemon juice, a few drops of Worcestershire sauce, mayonnaise. Season with salt.
2. Use to fill four avocado halves and serve as a starter, or serve in a sauceboat to accompany boiled fish.

Salsa rosa

Rosy Sauce

00:10 00:00

American	Ingredients	Metric/Imperial
Scant ¼ cup	*Mayonnaise*	*3 tbsp*
Scant ¼ cup	*Coffee (single) cream*	*3 tbsp*
½	*Lemon*	*½*
2 oz	*Condensed tomato purée*	*50 g / 2 oz*
	Salt and pepper	

1. Stir the mayonnaise, cream, lemon juice and tomato purée into a bowl.
2. When the ingredients are well blended, add a little salt and a pinch of pepper.
3. Serve as an accompaniment for boiled vegetables such as asparagus, cauliflower, or brussels sprouts.

Sauces – from left to right. Garlic and basil, tomato, mustard, curry, mayonnaise, rosy, herb, lemon and tartare.

Salsa alla senape

Mustard Sauce

00:10 00:30

American	Ingredients	Metric/Imperial
2 tbsp	Dijon mustard	1½ tbsp
½ cup	White wine	125 ml / 4 fl oz
3	Egg yolks	3
½	Lemon	½
	Salt and pepper	
¾ cup	Butter	175 g / 6 oz
½ tsp	Flour or cornstarch	½ tsp

1. Stir mustard and wine together and set aside. Whisk egg yolks in a bowl and add lemon juice. Season with salt and pepper, stir in the mustard, wine, about one third of the butter cut into knobs and the flour.
2. Place bowl over a pan of boiling water and whisk mixture all the time. When butter has been completely absorbed, add another third of the butter, cut into small knobs, and beat, taking care not to let the sauce boil.
3. When the butter is absorbed, add remainder of the butter in the same way and continue stirring until sauce has consistency of mayonnaise.
4. Serve sauce with poached fish and hard-cooked (boiled) eggs.

Variation: soak a teaspoon freshly chopped thyme in the wine instead of using mustard.

Cook's tip: if sauce curdles, remove from heat and add 1 tablespoon of iced water then continue whisking.

Tartara

Tartare Sauce

00:30 00:00

American	Ingredients	Metric/Imperial
3	Hard-cooked (boiled) eggs	3
1 tbsp	Chopped onion	1 tbsp
2 tsp	Mustard	2 tsp
	Salt and pepper	
1 tbsp	Chopped parsley	1 tbsp
½ cup	Oil	125 ml / 4 fl oz
3 tbsp	White vinegar	2 tbsp

1. Shell eggs and separate yolks from the whites. Chop yolks and transfer to a bowl, then mash with a fork.
2. Add the finely chopped onion, the mustard, salt, pepper and the parsley. Mix thoroughly until the ingredients are perfectly blended.
3. Slowly trickle in the oil, as for mayonnaise, (see page 175). Continue mixing as you pour the oil, preferably with a whisk until the sauce is light and frothy. Lastly, add the vinegar and when mixed, chop egg whites and add to the sauce. Mix again, taste and correct the seasoning if necessary.
4. Serve in a sauceboat as an accompaniment to either hot or cold boiled meats.

Variation: add a tablespoon of chopped cucumber and capers to the sauce.

Salsa mousseline

Mousseline Sauce

00:10 00:20

American	Ingredients	Metric/Imperial
5 tbsp	White vinegar	4 tbsp
3	Egg yolks	3
½ cup	Butter	100 g / 4 oz
	Salt and pepper	
	Grated nutmeg	
½	Lemon	½
½ cup	Whipped (double) cream	100 ml / 3½ fl oz

1. Pour vinegar into a saucepan and reduce by half over a low heat, then dilute with 2 tablespoons water and remove from the heat. Mix in egg yolks, blending thoroughly.
2. Place saucepan in a bain-marie and ensure there is enough water in the bain-marie to keep sauce hot but do not allow water to boil over into the sauce.
3. Whisk eggs over a low heat adding butter, a knob at a time. (The sauce must remain smooth and velvety.) When butter has been incorporated, season with salt, pepper and a sprinkle of nutmeg.
4. Add the juice of the lemon to the sauce, stirring constantly, and remove from the heat.
5. Keep the sauce in the bain-marie and whisk in the whipped cream. The sauce will rise and become frothier.
6. Serve in a sauceboat to accompany vegetables, particularly asparagus or fish.

Salsetta gustosa per pesci e uova

Savory Sauce for Fish and Eggs

00:20 00:15

American	Ingredients	Metric/Imperial
1	Small piece of onion	1
2 oz	Capers	50 g / 2 oz
⅓ cup	Green olives	50 g / 2 oz
3 tbsp	Oil	2 tbsp
2½ oz	Tuna	65 g / 2½ oz
3	Hard-cooked (boiled) egg yolks	3
3	Anchovies	3
1	Small bunch parsley	1
	Salt and pepper	
1 tbsp	Vinegar	1 tbsp

1. Peel onion and wash capers to eliminate the taste of brine, remove stones from the olives and finely chop all these ingredients together.
2. Heat oil and cook the onions, capers and olives over a low heat, then remove from heat.
3. Mash tuna, egg yolks and anchovies and chop parsley. Add these to the ingredients in the pan. Season with salt and pepper and a splash of vinegar and cook over a low heat until thoroughly heated, stirring with a wooden spoon.
4. Serve sauce with fish or eggs.

Salsa Chantilly

Chantilly Sauce

00:05 | 00:00

American	Ingredients	Metric/Imperial
½ cup	*Mayonnaise (see page 175)*	125 ml / 4 fl oz
3 tbsp	*Whipped cream*	2 tbsp

1. Spoon the mayonnaise into a bowl and gradually stir in the whipped cream very carefully.
2. Serve as an accompaniment to a dish of cooked vegetables, such as cauliflower, carrots or asparagus.

Salsa di magro

Tuna, Caper and Anchovy Sauce

00:10 | 00:12

American	Ingredients	Metric/Imperial
1	*Egg*	1
2	*Fresh anchovies*	2
¼ lb	*Tuna*	100 g / 4 oz
1 oz	*Capers*	25 g / 1 oz
¼ cup	*Olive oil*	50 ml / 2 fl oz
1	*Lemon*	1

1. Hard-cook (boil) the egg and shell. Separate the yolk from the white. Clean and fillet the anchovies and put in a vegetable chopper together with the tuna and the rinsed and drained capers.
2. Add the egg yolk and crush all the ingredients together to combine. Trickle the olive oil and lemon juice into the mixture and mix thoroughly.
3. Serve sauce with hard-cooked (boiled) eggs or a rice salad. Use for stuffing raw and cooked tomatoes, or as an accompaniment with boiled vegetables. Vary the flavor using canned or fresh salmon instead of tuna.

Salsa francese per volatili

French Sauce for Poultry

00:15 | 00:00

American	Ingredients	Metric/Imperial
3	*Egg yolks*	3
3 tbsp	*Light mustard*	2 tbsp
3	*Anchovies*	3
Scant ¼ cup	*Oil*	3 tbsp
1	*Lemon*	1
	Salt and pepper	
1	*Garlic clove*	1
1 tsp	*Dark mustard*	1 tsp

1. Put the egg yolks in a bowl with the light mustard and the crushed anchovies and begin to beat as if to make mayonnaise. Add the oil a little at a time and then strained lemon juice. Adjust the seasoning with salt and pepper and add the crushed garlic with the dark mustard.
2. Serve the sauce cold, on fried croûtons as an accompaniment to game.

Salsa ai carciofi

Artichoke Sauce

00:15 | 00:45

American	Ingredients	Metric/Imperial
2	*Artichokes*	2
1	*Lemon*	1
4	*Egg yolks*	4
⅔ cup	*Oil*	150 ml / ¼ pint
½ cup	*Mushrooms in oil*	50 g / 2 oz
1 tbsp	*Capers*	1 tbsp
5	*Sprigs of parsley*	5
1	*Garlic clove*	1
⅓ cup	*Green olives, stoned*	50 g / 2 oz
½ tsp	*Brandy (optional)*	½ tsp
	Salt and pepper	

1. Clean artichokes thoroughly, remove hard outer leaves and boil in a little water with lemon juice for about 45 minutes, then drain and finely chop. Put in a blender to obtain a smooth purée, then transfer to a bowl.
2. Beat in egg yolks one by one and add oil drop by drop, beating as for mayonnaise.
3. Drain and chop the mushrooms, capers and parsley, crush the garlic, chop the olives and add to the artichoke mixture. Beat to obtain a smooth mixture, using an electric whisk. (If sauce is too thick, dilute with a little brandy.) Taste and adjust the seasoning and serve in a sauceboat. Store in a cool place until ready to serve.

Cook's tip: 4 canned artichoke hearts may be used in place of fresh artichokes.

Olio e aceto 

Vinaigrette Dressing

00:07 | 00:00
Makes 8 tablespoons

American	Ingredients	Metric/Imperial
	Salt and pepper	
¼ cup	*Vinegar*	50 ml / 2 fl oz
2 tsp	*Prepared mustard*	2 tsp
½ cup	*Oil*	125 ml / 4 fl oz
	Chopped mixed fresh herbs (parsley, tarragon, chervil chives) to taste	

1. Dissolve a pinch of salt in the vinegar. Mix the mustard with the vinegar. Add pepper to taste.
2. Add the oil and chopped herbs. Mix thoroughly.

Cook's tip: this dressing is easily made. Keep it stored in a screw-top jar when it can be shaken before use.

Paté di tonno

Tuna Butter

00:20 00:00

American	Ingredients	Metric/Imperial
¼ lb	*Tuna*	*100 g / 4 oz*
⅔ cup	*Softened butter*	*150 g / 5 oz*
3 tbsp	*Brandy*	*2 tbsp*

1. Drain can of tuna and break up fish with a fork or vegetable chopper to produce a smooth paste.
2. Beat butter until creamy, then beat in the tuna until the ingredients are well mixed. Finally pour in brandy and mix again.
3. Use for canapés or on grilled fish.

Salsa esotica Pili Pili

Exotic Chilli Sauce

00:10 00:00
Standing time 5-6 days

American	Ingredients	Metric/Imperial
20	*Small red dried chilli peppers*	*20*
3 tbsp	*Coarse salt*	*2 tbsp*
1 tbsp	*Unrefined sugar*	*1 tbsp*
	White vinegar	
	Oil	

1. Put the chillies in a glass jar. Sprinkle with salt and sugar. Pour over the white vinegar until the chillies are completely covered and then pour on a layer of oil about ¼ in / 1 cm deep to keep the air out. Cover and leave to marinate for at least 5 or 6 days. The longer you leave it to marinate, the hotter the chilli sauce will be.
2. Serve with Creole rice, couscous or with raw fish.

Pesto alla genovese

Garlic and Basil Sauce

00:30 00:00

American	Ingredients	Metric/Imperial
¼ lb	*Fresh basil*	*100 g / 4 oz*
1 oz	*Marjoram*	*25 g / 1 oz*
1 oz	*Parsley*	*25 g / 1 oz*
1	*Garlic clove*	*1*
¼ cup	*Mixed grated pecorino and parmesan cheeses*	*25 g / 1 oz*
6 tbsp	*Olive oil*	*5 tbsp*

1. Crush basil, marjoram, parsley and garlic using a pestle and mortar, blender or food processor. Add pecorino and parmesan. Continue to crush and add oil in a thin trickle. Taste and adjust seasoning.

Variation: the marjoram can be omitted, and parsley reduced to half the quantity.

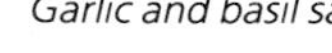

Garlic and basil sauce

Salsa con acciughe

Anchovy Sauce

00:20 00:00

American	Ingredients	Metric/Imperial
2	*Fresh anchovies*	2
1 tbsp	*Vinegar*	1 tbsp
10	*Black olives*	10
	Pepper	
6 tbsp	*Olive oil*	5 tbsp

1. Thoroughly wash and fillet the anchovies then finely chop them and put them in a bowl. Pour over the vinegar and crush with a fork (the vinegar will gradually soften the anchovy).
2. Stone the olives and finely chop, then add to the anchovy. Mix in a little freshly grated pepper and finally pour over the olive oil, a little at a time, combining it with the other ingredients.
3. Continue stirring the mixture to obtain a thick, tasty sauce and serve as an accompaniment for veal, and grilled chicken breast.

Salsa menta

Mint Sauce

00:15 00:00

American	Ingredients	Metric/Imperial
2 oz	*Mint leaves*	50 g / 2 oz
	The inside of a bread roll	
½ cup	*White vinegar*	125 ml / 4 fl oz
½ cup	*Confectioner's (icing) sugar*	50 g / 2 oz
	Salt	

1. Finely chop the mint leaves. Soak the bread in the vinegar in a bowl. Strain and reserve the vinegar. Squeeze the bread and rub it through a sieve.
2. Add sugar, a pinch of salt and vinegar to the bread crumbs in a bowl and stir in the mint. Mix thoroughly to obtain a smooth creamy sauce.
3. Pour into a sauceboat and serve with spit roast lamb.

Crema al limone

Lemon Sauce

00:15 00:00

American	Ingredients	Metric/Imperial
¼ cup	*Softened butter*	50 g / 2 oz
¼ cup	*Cream cheese*	50 g / 2 oz
1	*Lemon*	1
	Salt	

1. Beat butter to a soft paste, then beat in the cream cheese. Grate the lemon, squeeze juice and add rind and juice to cheese mixture with salt.
2. Use to stuff celery stalks or to accompany crudités.

Salsa di ciliege

Cherry Sauce

00:05 00:15

American	Ingredients	Metric/Imperial
1	*Orange*	1
½ cup	*Marsala wine*	125 ml / 4 oz
¼ tsp	*Cinnamon powder*	¼ tsp
⅓ cup	*Redcurrant jelly*	100 g / 4 oz
1½ cups	*Cherries in syrup*	350 g / 12 oz

1. Cut the orange peel into matchsticks, then squeeze to obtain the juice. Heat peel and juice in a saucepan with the marsala. Cook over a low heat until half the liquid has evaporated. Add cinnamon and the redcurrant jelly.
2. When the jelly has dissolved, drain the cherries and add to the pan. As soon as the sauce begins to boil pour it into a sauceboat.
3. Serve with venison or fillet of pork.

Salsa di mirtilli

Cranberry Sauce

00:20 00:10

American	Ingredients	Metric/Imperial
2 cups	*Cranberries*	225 g / 8 oz
	Sugar to taste	

1. Wash the cranberries well. Remove leaves and stalks and put the berries in a saucepan. Cover with water and boil for a few minutes.
2. Remove the cranberries with a slotted spoon, retaining the liquid, strain and rub them through a fine sieve, a few at a time. Pour the purée back into the pan and dilute with the cooking water, adding 1 tablespoon at a time, until the sauce has the desired consistency. Add sugar to taste.
3. Serve with roast turkey.

Salsa alla mela

Apple Sauce

00:15 00:00

American	Ingredients	Metric/Imperial
1	*Large apple*	1
¼ lb	*Fontina cheese*	100 g / 4 oz
2 oz	*Cooked ham*	50 g / 2 oz
¼ cup	*Walnuts*	25 g / 1 oz
5 tbsp	*Olive oil*	4 tbsp
	Salt and pepper	
½	*Lemon*	½

1. Peel and dice apple. Put into a bowl and add diced fontina, strips of ham, and peeled and coarsely chopped walnuts.
2. Season with oil, salt, pepper and lemon juice, mix and pour over boiled, well-drained rice. Serve cold.

SOUPS

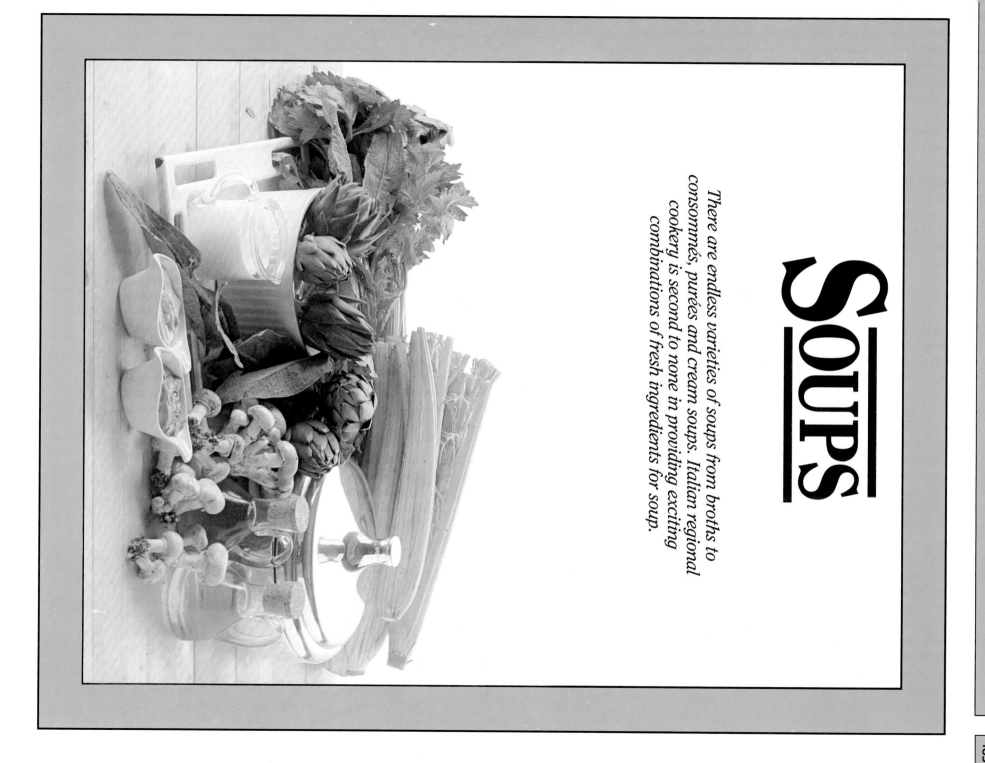

There are endless varieties of soups from broths to consommés, purées and cream soups. Italian regional cookery is second to none in providing exciting combinations of fresh ingredients for soup.

1

2

3

4

5

Beef broth
1. *Put the beef and seasoning in a large pan. Add the cold water.*
2. *Bring up to the boil and ladle off any froth.*
3. *Skim off any fat on the surface.*
4. *Add the vegetables, bring back to the boil, then simmer for 3 hours.*
5. *Strain the broth into a soup tureen.*

Vegetable Stock

00:15 02:00

American	Ingredients	Metric/Imperial
2	*Onions*	*2*
1	*Carrot*	*1*
2 oz	*Turnip*	*50 g / 2 oz*
2	*Celery stalks*	*2*
1	*Leek*	*1*
3 quarts	*Water*	*3 litres / 5 pints*
2	*Parsley sprigs*	*2*
1	*Bouquet garni*	*1*
	Salt and pepper	
1 tsp	*Vegetable extract*	*1 tsp*

1. Wash and peel all the vegetables, chop into slices or dice.
2. Pour the measured water into a large saucepan, add the vegetables with the parsley sprigs, bouquet garni and seasoning. Bring to the boil and simmer partly covered for 2 hours.
3. Add the vegetable extract, mix well and allow to cool. Strain through a fine sieve and use as required. This stock is suitable for vegetarian dishes.

Beef Broth

00:25 03:30
Makes about
2 quarts [2 litres / 3½ pints]

American	Ingredients	Metric/Imperial
2 lb	*Beef for stew with bones*	*1 kg / 2 lb*
2 tsp	*Salt*	*2 tsp*
6	*Black peppercorns*	*6*
3 quarts	*Water*	*3 litres / 5 pints*
3	*Carrots*	*3*
3	*Turnips*	*3*
2	*Leeks*	*2*
1	*Celery stalk*	*1*
	Slices of bread	

1. Put the beef and bones, salt and peppercorns into a large pan and cover with the cold water. Bring to the boil, skimming off the scum that rises to the surface.
2. Meanwhile, peel the carrots and turnips. Trim the leeks and celery.
3. Add the vegetables to the pan. Bring back to the boil, then lower the heat and leave to simmer for 3 hours.
4. A few minutes before serving, toast a few slices of bread and place them in a warmed soup tureen.
5. Skim off any fat from the surface of the broth and strain the broth into the tureen. The meat can be chopped and added if you wish.

Cook's tip: if you leave the broth to cool, so much the better. The fat will set on the surface and can be removed easily.

Chicken Stock

00:25 Makes about 2 quarts [2 litres / 3½ pints] 03:00

American	Ingredients	Metric/Imperial
1 lb	*Shin knuckle of veal*	500 g / 1 lb
2 lb	*Veal bones*	1 kg / 2 lb
1	*Chicken giblet*	1
1	*Chicken carcass*	1
3 quarts	*Water*	3 litres / 5 pints
2	*Onions*	2
1	*Carrot*	1
1	*Leek*	1
2	*Celery stalks*	2
1	*Bay leaf*	1
2	*Parsley sprigs*	2
1	*Bouquet garni*	1
	Salt and pepper	

1. Wash the veal bones and place the chicken giblets and the carcass with the bones in the water. Bring to the boil and simmer for 30 minutes.
2. Wash, peel and chop the vegetables into even-sized pieces.
3. Skim the bone stock and then add the vegetables, herbs and seasoning. Simmer for 3 hours, allow to cool and remove fat from the surface.
4. Strain through a fine sieve or through muslin. Allow the strained stock to cool completely and remove any fat from the surface again.

Consommé 

Consommé

This is a beef or chicken broth from which the impurities have been removed, making it perfectly clear.

00:10 01:40

American	Ingredients	Metric/Imperial
2 quarts	*Beef or chicken stock*	2 litres / 3½ pints
1	*Carrot*	1
1	*Leek*	1
1	*Celery stalk*	1
2-3	*Fresh chervil or parsley sprigs*	2-3
1	*Fresh tarragon sprig*	1
4	*Very ripe tomatoes, peeled*	4
1 lb	*Lean beef*	500 g / 1 lb
1	*Egg white*	1
	Pepper	

1. Cool the broth in the saucepan until the fat has set on the surface. Remove this fat using a skimming spoon.
2. Peel the carrot, trim the leek and celery and slice them all finely. Chop the chervil, tarragon and tomatoes.
3. Mix together the vegetables, herbs and egg white. Add a little pepper and then a little water.
4. Put the meat into the saucepan containing the broth, add the vegetables and warm over a very gentle heat, scraping the bottom of the saucepan so that the egg white does not stick. Leave to cook gently for 1½ hours without stirring.
5. When the mixture froths and rises in the pan, skim off the fat and froth with a ladle, and leave to continue cooking.
6. Strain the consommé through a fine sieve or through muslin. Season in various ways.

Consommé with finely sliced vegetables.

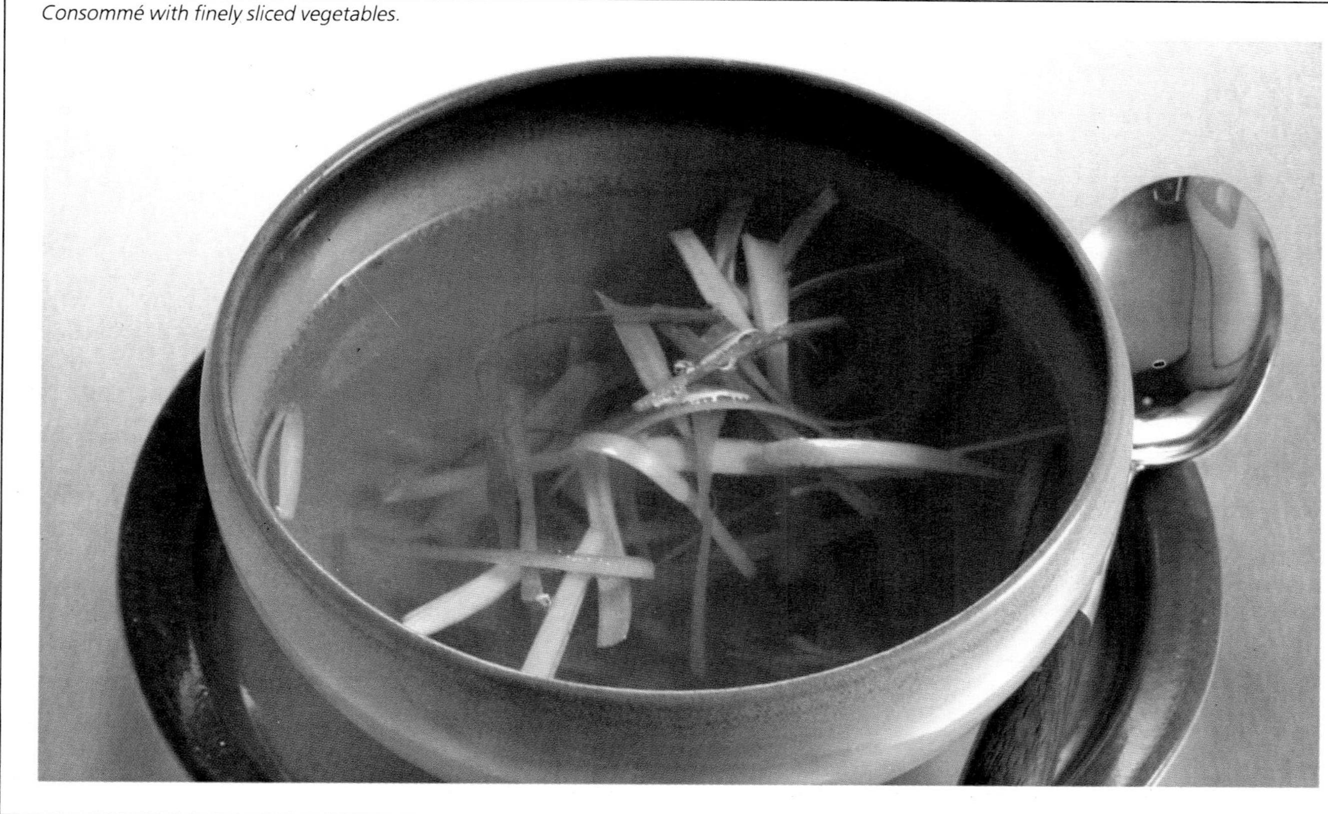

Ribollita con il pesce

Fish Soup

This soup is typical of the region around Leghorn and the Tuscany coast of the Ligurian sea.

00:30 01:00

American	Ingredients	Metric/Imperial
1 lb	*Cooked fish*	*500 g / 1 lb*
1 quart	*Stock*	*1 litre / 1¾ pints*
½ cup	*Red wine*	*125 ml / 4 fl oz*
2	*Garlic cloves*	*2*
¾ lb	*Puréed tomatoes*	*350 g / 12 oz*
4	*Slices of brown bread*	*4*
3 tbsp	*Vegetable oil*	*2 tbsp*
3 tbsp	*Chopped parsley*	*2 tbsp*

1. Carefully remove the bones and sieve all the leftover fish, whether it is baked, boiled or fried, then put the fish into a pot.
2. Add vegetable stock, red wine, cloves of garlic and the puréed tomatoes.
3. Begin cooking over a very low heat and continue until the stock is reduced by one third.
4. Prepare croûtons of homemade brown bread fried in the oil and put them in the bottom of a soup tureen. Pour over the boiling soup and serve with plenty of freshly ground black pepper and chopped parsley.

Zuppa ai frutti di mare

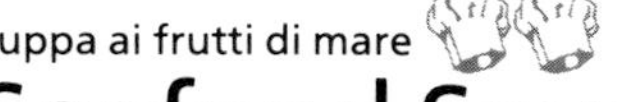

Seafood Soup

00:20 00:50

American	Ingredients	Metric/Imperial
2 lb	*Mixed mussels and clams*	*1 kg / 2 lb*
6 tbsp	*Vegetable oil*	*5 tbsp*
1	*Onion*	*1*
3	*Garlic cloves*	*3*
¾ lb	*Tomatoes*	*350 g / 12 oz*
	Salt and pepper	
½ lb	*Scampi, cooked*	*225 g / 8 oz*
½ lb	*Prawns, cooked*	*225 g / 8 oz*
1	*Small red chilli pepper*	*1*
¼ cup	*White wine*	*50 ml / 2 fl oz*
4	*Slices homemade bread*	*4*

1. Carefully clean and scrub the mussels and clams, drain and put into a large frying pan with a little heated oil. Shake the pan over a medium heat until they open. Throw away closed shells, and collect those with fish in them in a bowl.
2. In a large frying pan heat the remaining oil, sweat finely chopped onion and 2 cloves crushed garlic. Peel the tomatoes, remove the seeds and, after chopping or sieving them, add to the fried onion and garlic. Season with salt and pepper and cook on a low heat for 20 minutes.
3. Clean the scampi and prawns, shelling them carefully. Add the piece of red chilli pepper, the scampi, prawns, mussels and clams and wine to the tomato sauce and allow the flavors to mingle for 5 minutes.
4. Toast the slices of homemade bread in the oven, rub over with a clove of garlic and lay a slice of bread in each bowl; then pour over the soup.

Bouillabaisse alla marsigliese

Marseilles Bouillabaisse

This is a typical Marseilles recipe, very spicy but delicious. If you do not like a too spicy soup, leave out the pepper and the red chilli pepper, but remember that the saffron and the garlic are essential.

00:20 00:45

American	Ingredients	Metric/Imperial
2 lb	*Fresh mixed fish for soup, cleaned*	*1 kg / 2 lb*
2	*Onions*	*2*
½ lb	*Plum tomatoes*	*225 g / 8 oz*
	Salt and pepper	
1 envelope (a few strands)	*Saffron*	*1 sachet (a few strands)*
1 tsp	*Basil*	*1 tsp*
4	*Garlic cloves*	*4*
1 quart	*Wine*	*1 litre / 1¾ pint*
3 tbsp	*Whisky*	*2 tbsp*
1	*Chopped sweet red chilli pepper*	*1*
4	*Slices of brown bread*	*4*
Scant ¼ cup	*Oil*	*3 tbsp*

1. Wash the fish well and place in a large pot with the chopped onions, tomatoes, salt, pepper, saffron, chopped basil, crushed garlic, wine and whisky.
2. Start cooking over a low heat, moving the fish round with a fish-slice, without breaking it.
3. Continue cooking for 40 minutes. Add the chopped red pepper and keep hot.
4. Fry the brown bread in heated oil until golden brown. Place the bread in the bottom of soup plates or bowls, then pour the fish over the slices of fried bread.

Minestra alla còrsa

Corsican Soup

00:20 01:30

American	Ingredients	Metric/Imperial
2 lb	*Fish for soup*	*1 kg / 2 lb*
1½ quarts	*Fish stock (see page 212-5)*	*1.5 litres / 2½ pints*
14 oz	*Peeled plum tomatoes*	*400 g / 14 oz*
4	*Garlic cloves*	*4*
3 tbsp	*Chopped parsley*	*2 tbsp*
	Salt and pepper	
	Croûtons	
1 cup	*Grated pecorino cheese*	*100 g / 4 oz*

1. Use heads and bones of fish to make a fish stock (see page 212-5). Cook for 30 minutes and drain.
2. Crush the peeled tomatoes in the fish stock, add the garlic, chopped parsley and all the fish, cleaned and boned. Simmer gently for 1 hour, then season to taste and whisk with a hand or electric whisk.
3. Prepare and fry croûtons in oil. Sprinkle grated pecorino cheese onto the soup, stir, add the croûtons and serve very hot.

Marseilles bouillabaisse

Zuppa di cozze

Mussel Soup

00:20 01:00

American	Ingredients	Metric/Imperial
2 lb	*Mussels*	*1 kg / 2 lb*
2 tbsp	*Butter*	*25 g / 1 oz*
1	*Leek*	*1*
1	*Potato*	*1*
2¼ cups	*Milk*	*500 ml / 18 fl oz*
1 cup	*Fresh bread crumbs*	*50 g / 2 oz*
	Salt and pepper	

1. Scrape the mussels and wash them twice under running water. Put in a large pan on the heat, without adding water, and as they open, remove from the shells and keep on one side.
2. Strain the juice from the mussels through a muslin cloth, and retain.
3. Melt the butter in a pan, slice the white part of the leek and the peeled potato, and add to the pan on a low heat; allow them to soften, and stir.
4. Heat the milk and moisten the vegetables with half the milk, add half the mussel liquid. Stir the bread crumbs into the mixture and cook everything for 30 minutes over a low heat. Blend or put the mixture through a food processor, return the purée to the cooking stock, season with salt and pepper, add remaining milk, the mussels, and a little finely chopped parsley. Heat gently and serve.

Finta zuppa di pesce

Mock Fish Soup

This soup is commonly, and with Neapolitan irony, called fish soup 'a mare' (at sea). It is a soup which has only the flavor of fish – the real fish have remained 'at sea', and are not used at all in the preparation.

00:20 00:45

American	Ingredients	Metric/Imperial
2	*Garlic cloves*	*2*
3 tbsp	*Vegetable oil*	*2 tbsp*
¼ lb	*Anchovies*	*100 g / 4 oz*
3 tbsp	*Chopped parsley*	*2 tbsp*
3 tbsp	*Tomato purée*	*2 tbsp*
	Salt and pepper	
3	*Long rolls*	*3*

1. Put the crushed garlic in the oil and brown it over a very slight heat. When the garlic is browned, but not blackened, discard and add the rinsed, boned and chopped anchovies to the oil, together with most of the parsley.
2. Add the tomato purée, 1 quart [1 litre / 1¾ pints] of water and simmer until all the ingredients are well mixed, then season with salt and plenty of pepper.
3. In the meantime soak one of the rolls in water, drain and squeeze it out by hand as much as possible, chop finely, then add a few tablespoons of cooking juices to the pulp, mixing well with a wooden spoon. Pour the bread mixture into the pan, a little at a time, stirring all the time to avoid lumps forming. Allow to boil for a few minutes more until the sauce has thickened. Slice the other rolls, rub with garlic, and toast them. Arrange in the 4 soup plates and pour over the boiling soup. Garnish each plate with remaining parsley.

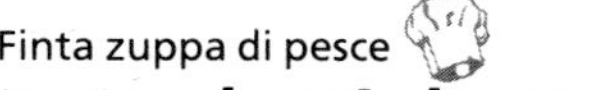

Mussel soup

Zuppa di merluzzo

Cod Soup

00:35 00:40

American	Ingredients	Metric/Imperial
2	*Leeks*	*2*
	Olive oil	
2	*Garlic cloves*	*2*
5 oz	*Peeled tomatoes*	*150 g / 5 oz*
1 lb	*Cod, boned*	*500 g / 1 lb*
5	*Sprigs of parsley*	*5*
1	*Bay leaf*	*1*
2	*Sprigs of thyme*	*2*
¼ tsp	*Fennel seeds*	*1 tsp*
1	*Red chilli pepper*	*1*
1 envelope (a few strands)	*Saffron*	*1 sachet (a few strands)*
2	*Slices of bread*	*2*
1	*Lemon*	*1*

1. Cut the white part of the washed leeks in two, lengthwise, and then into slices. Heat the olive oil in a pan then sweat the white part of the leeks together with the crushed cloves of garlic.
2. When the mixture starts to brown, add the peeled tomatoes and crush them slightly with a fork.
3. Add the cod, which has been previously cut into fairly large pieces, with a few sprigs of parsley, bay leaf, thyme, fennel seeds and the red chilli pepper, deseeded and cut into small pieces. Cook on a very low heat for about 5 minutes.
4. Dissolve the saffron in ½ cup [125 ml / 4 fl oz] warm water, and stir it into the mixture.
5. Continue cooking the fish for 20 minutes, then remove the garlic and the bay leaf.
6. Toast the bread, which can be stale, and keep warm.
7. Serve the soup with the slices of toast and garnish with parsley and lemon segments.

Zuppa di vongole

Clam Soup

00:20 00:25

American	Ingredients	Metric/Imperial
1	*Garlic clove*	1
3 tbsp	*Vegetable oil*	4 tbsp
6	*Tomatoes*	6
¼ cup	*Dry white wine*	50 ml / 2 fl oz
	Salt and pepper	
6½ lb	*Clams*	3 kg / 6½ lb
	French or homemade bread	
5	*Sprigs of parsley*	5

1. Gently fry a clove of garlic in half the oil. As soon as the garlic is well browned, remove it and add the tomatoes, peeled and with the seeds removed, dry white wine, and the salt and pepper. Cook, covered, on a low heat.
2. Wash, scrub and rinse the clams in cold running water to remove any remaining sand, add to the sauce, stir and cover, raising the heat. In 5 minutes the clams should open. Discard shells which remain closed.
3. Preheat the oven to 400°F / 200°C / Gas Mark 6.
4. Prepare the slices of bread by dipping in the hot oil then place in the oven to crisp for 10 minutes.
5. Put one or two slices of bread in each plate and cover with the clam soup sprinkled with chopped parsley. Serve with freshly ground pepper.

Lattughe ripiene in brodo

Consommé with Stuffed Lettuce

00:30 00:30

American	Ingredients	Metric/Imperial
¾ lb	*Beef, boiled, roast or stewed*	350 g / 12 oz
16	*Large lettuce leaves*	16
3	*Eggs*	3
3 tbsp	*Breadcrumbs*	2 tbsp
1 tbsp	*Milk*	1 tbsp
	Salt and pepper	
¼ tsp	*Nutmeg*	¼ tsp
1 quart	*Stock or consommé*	1 litre / 1¾ pints
3 tbsp	*Garlic and basil sauce (see page 180)*	2 tbsp

1. Grind (mince) the cooked beef finely, including the fat.
2. Wash the lettuce and divide it into leaves, retaining the smallest ones to make a salad.
3. Mix the eggs, breadcrumbs and milk with the minced meat, season with salt, pepper and nutmeg, to form a smooth mixture.
4. Put the stock into a pan and bring up to the boil.
5. Place 2 tablespoons of the mixture in the centre of each lettuce leaf, securing firmly with two toothpicks. When the stock is boiling, lower the stuffed lettuce leaves gently into the pot and cook for about 10 minutes. Carefully lift out with a slotted spoon, place on a serving dish and dress with the sauce. Serve the remaining broth as an accompaniment.

Gnocchetti di riso in brodo

Consommé with Rice Dumplings

01:00 01:00

American	Ingredients	Metric/Imperial
1 quart	*Stock (see page 184)*	1 litre / 1¾ pints
1 cup	*Milk*	225 ml / 8 fl oz
	Salt	
½ cup	*Rice*	100 g / 4 oz
2 tbsp	*Butter*	25 g / 1 oz
1	*Egg*	1
¼ cup	*Grated cheese*	25 g / 1 oz
2 tbsp	*Flour*	15 g / ½ oz
3 tbsp	*Vegetable oil*	2 tbsp

1. Prepare the stock and let it simmer over a low heat.
2. Put into a large saucepan the milk and 1 cup [225 ml / 8 fl oz] of water, with a little salt.
3. Add the rice and cook gently until it has absorbed all the milk liquid.
4. When the rice is cooked, remove from the heat and mix in the butter, the whole egg and the grated cheese. Leave it to cool.
5. Shape rice into small balls and roll in flour. Heat the oil in a pan over a high heat, put in the rice balls and fry until golden. Remove from the oil, drain and arrange in soup plates. Pour the boiling broth over the dumplings and serve.

Gnocchetti di semolino in brodo

Consommé with Semolina Dumplings

00:20 00:45

American	Ingredients	Metric/Imperial
6 tbsp	*Butter*	75 g / 3 oz
3	*Eggs*	3
¾ cup	*Semolina*	150 g / 5 oz
	Salt and pepper	
2 quarts	*Best stock*	2 litres / 3½ pints
1 tbsp	*Chopped parsley*	1 tbsp
3 tbsp	*Grated parmesan cheese*	2 tbsp

1. Cream the butter until soft. Separate the eggs and add yolks to the butter and mix well. Add the semolina, salt and mix well.
2. Whisk the egg whites until stiff, fold the egg whites into the mixture.
3. Heat the stock until boiling, drop in 1 tablespoon of the mixture to check whether it remains like a dumpling or breaks up. If the mixture breaks up, add a little more semolina to the dough, then drop in the dumplings, one tablespoon at a time into the broth.
4. Allow to boil for 15 minutes, add parsley and then leave in the covered pan for another 5 minutes with the heat turned off. Serve very hot with grated parmesan.

Cook's tip: these dumplings can be used in other vegetable soups. The size of the dumplings can be varied to suit the vegetables in the soup.

Zucchini soup

Minestra di zucchine

Zucchini [Courgette] Soup

00:15 | 00:35

American	Ingredients	Metric/Imperial
3 tbsp	Vegetable oil	2 tbsp
1	Sliced onion	1
6	Zucchini (courgettes)	6
2	Potatoes	2
12	Peeled tomatoes	12
2 quarts	Stock	2 litres / 3½ pints
¾ lb	Pasta	350 g / 12 oz
¼ tsp	Nutmeg	¼ tsp
3	Sprigs of parsley	3

1. Heat the oil in a large saucepan, add the chopped onion and cook for 3 minutes.
2. Wash and dice the zucchini, peel and dice the potatoes.
3. Add the tomatoes to the onion and then stir in the zucchini and the potatoes, allow to brown over a medium heat for a few minutes.
4. Add the stock and cook for 10 minutes, throw in the pasta and cook until it is 'al dente'.
5. Serve the soup sprinkled with a little grated nutmeg and finely chopped parsley.

Minestrone al pesto 

Minestrone with Garlic and Basil Sauce

00:40 Soaking time 12:00 | 00:60

American	Ingredients	Metric/Imperial
5 oz	Haricot beans	150 g / 5 oz
1 oz	Dried mushrooms	25 g / 1 oz
2	Eggplant (aubergines)	2
¼ lb	Green beans	100 g / 4 oz
3	Potatoes	3
1	Red cabbage	1
¼ lb	Zucchini (courgettes)	100 g / 4 oz
2 oz	Pumpkin	50 g / 2 oz
4	Peeled tomatoes	4
3 tbsp	Vegetable oil	2 tbsp
2 oz	Pasta or rice	50 g / 2 oz
	Garlic and basil sauce (see page 180)	

1. Allow beans to soak overnight and soak dried mushrooms.
2. Bring 2 quarts [2 litres / 3½ pints] water to the boil and put in the beans and cook for 40 minutes. Dice the eggplant and green beans. Peel and dice the potatoes, and slice and chop the red cabbage. Slice the zucchini and dice the pumpkin. Add the vegetables, the peeled tomatoes, oil and dried mushrooms to the beans. Season well. When the ingredients are almost cooked, put in the pasta or rice, according to choice.
3. Before serving the soup, add a good helping of the garlic and basil sauce to the pan. Serve very hot.

Cook's tip: this also makes an excellent cold dish, which will keep for several days.

Minestrone toscano

Tuscan Minestrone

00:30 | 01:40

American	Ingredients	Metric/Imperial
11 oz	Shelled white beans	300 g / 11 oz
2 oz	Parsley	50 g / 2 oz
1	Small onion	1
1	Celery stalk	1
2	Small carrots	2
1	Sprig of rosemary	1
2	Basil leaves	2
1	Garlic clove	1
2 oz	Bacon	50 g / 2 oz
½ cup	Olive oil	125 ml / 4 fl oz
4	Tomatoes	4
½	Savoy cabbage	½
2 or 3	Thyme leaves	2 or 3
	Salt and pepper	
5 oz	Pasta	150 g / 5 oz

1. Boil the beans in plenty of water and add salt towards the end of the cooking time. When they are cooked, drain, reserving the cooking water, and sieve or blend half of them.
2. While the beans are cooking, prepare the other ingredients. Chop the parsley, onion, celery, peeled carrots, sprig of rosemary and the basil together with the garlic clove and the bacon.
3. Heat the oil in a large pan, add the vegetable and herb mixture, cook gently over a low heat for 5 minutes, then add the peeled and chopped tomatoes, shredded cabbage, thyme, the sieved and whole beans.
4. Add 2 quarts [2 litres / 3¼ pints] cooking water from the beans made up with water or stock. Season lightly with salt and pepper. Cook on a slow heat for 40 minutes, then add the cabbage and the pasta. Serve without cheese when the pasta is cooked.

Cook's tip: if using dried haricot beans, soak overnight before cooking.

Garlic and basil sauce

Minestra di bue

Beef Stew

00:10 | 01:30

American	Ingredients	Metric/Imperial
1 lb	*Spinach*	*500 g / 1 lb*
1 lb	*Stewing beef*	*500 g / 1 lb*
2 quarts	*Stock*	*2 litres / 3½ pints*
1	*Egg*	*1*
1 tbsp	*Grated parmesan cheese*	*1 tbsp*
⅔ cup	*Rice*	*150 g / 5 oz*
	Salt and pepper	
¼ tsp	*Nutmeg*	*¼ tsp*

1. Wash and cook the spinach for 4 minutes, drain well then chop finely.
2. Slice the beef and bring to the boil in the stock or water, then simmer until well cooked.
3. Add the spinach, the egg and the parmesan to the stock and continue cooking until the meat is very well cooked. Break up the larger pieces of meat with a fork or whisk, place on the heat again and bring the stock to the boil.
4. Add the rice and continue cooking until the rice is tender and the stock reduced.
5. Season with salt and add a pinch of nutmeg. Pour into a soup tureen and serve piping hot.

Minestrone alla milanese

Milanese-Style Minestrone

01:00 | 02:00
Soaking time for beans 12:00

American	Ingredients	Metric/Imperial
2	*Carrots*	*2*
2	*Celery stalks*	*2*
3	*Leeks*	*3*
2	*Potatoes*	*2*
1	*Small zucchini (courgette)*	*1*
½	*Cabbage*	*½*
2 oz	*French beans*	*50 g / 2 oz*
4	*Ripe plum tomatoes*	*4*
¼ lb	*Spinach*	*100 g / 4 oz*
1	*Onion*	*1*
1	*Bunch of basil leaves*	*1*
1	*Small bunch of parsley*	*1*
¼ lb	*Bacon*	*100 g / 4 oz*
5 tbsp	*Butter*	*65 g / 2½ oz*
6 tbsp	*Vegetable oil*	*5 tbsp*
2 oz	*Haricot beans (soaked)*	*50 g / 2 oz*
2 quarts	*Stock*	*2 litres / 3½ pints*
1 cup	*Rice*	*200 g / 7 oz*
	Salt and pepper	
⅓ cup	*Frozen peas*	*50 g / 2 oz*
	Parmesan cheese	

1. Scrape and dice the carrots. Slice the celery and the leeks. Peel, wash and dice the potatoes. Halve the zucchini and cut it first into slices, then into small cubes. Strip the leaves from the cabbage and cut into strips. Trim the beans and cut into two or three pieces. Wash the tomatoes and cut into pieces. Wash the spinach well and cut it into strips. Peel the onion and chop it finely together with the basil and parsley.
2. Cut the bacon into very small strips or cubes and fry it with the onion and herbs in a large saucepan in the heated butter and oil for 5 minutes. Add the tomatoes. After a few minutes, put all the prepared vegetables in the pot together with the soaked haricot beans.
3. Stir and allow the flavors to mingle; then moisten with the hot stock, season with salt and pepper and cook gently for 1½ hours, covered.
4. At the end of this time, pour in the rice and cook for 15 minutes; it should still be quite firm. Then add the peas, cook for 10 minutes, switch off the heat, cover and allow to rest for 5 minutes. Serve with grated parmesan.

Minestrone alla genovese

Genoese Minestrone

01:00 | 01:00
Soaking time for dried beans 12:00

American	Ingredients	Metric/Imperial
¼ lb	*Dried beans*	*100 g / 4 oz*
4 tbsp	*Olive oil*	*3 tbsp*
1	*Onion*	*1*
1	*Celery stalk*	*1*
1	*Slice of raw ham*	*1*
1	*Small savoy cabbage*	*1*
2	*Carrots*	*2*
6	*Swiss chard leaves*	*6*
6	*Lettuce leaves*	*6*
1 tbsp	*Tomatoe purée*	*1 tbsp*
2 quarts	*Stock*	*2 litres / 1¾ pints*
2	*Garlic cloves*	*2*
5	*Sprigs of parsley*	*5*
3	*Basil leaves*	*3*
3	*Rosemary leaves*	*3*
½ cup	*Grated parmesan cheese*	*50 g / 2 oz*
1	*Chilli pepper*	*1*
½ lb	*Pasta*	*225 g / 8 oz*

1. Boil the beans in lightly salted water; if using dried beans, leave them soaking in warm water for 12 hours.
2. Pour half the oil into a soup pan over a low heat and put in the chopped onion, celery and the ham cut into thin strips and allow to cook until golden.
3. Add cabbage, chopped carrots, chard and the washed lettuce cut into thin strips, the boiled beans and finally 1 tablespoon of tomato purée. Pour the stock into the pan, bring to the boil and simmer.
4. Meanwhile chop some garlic with the parsley and a few leaves of basil and rosemary, then add grated parmesan, chilli pepper and remaining oil. Reduce these ingredients to a pulp by crushing vigorously and then sieve them. (This can be done in a blender or food processor.)
5. As soon as the vegetables are ready, add the pasta, also mixing in the 'pulp'. Stir, and when the pasta is still rather firm, sprinkle with parmesan. Serve after a few minutes.

Crema del pellegrino

Pilgrims' Soup

00:30 00:45

American	Ingredients	Metric/Imperial
4	*Carrots*	4
⅓ cup	*Butter*	75 g / 3 oz
	Salt and pepper	
4	*Chicken livers*	4
1 tbsp	*Port*	1 tbsp
1 quart	*Chicken stock*	1 litre / 1¾ pints
3 tbsp	*Semolina*	2 tbsp
½ cup	*Grated parmesan cheese*	50 g / 2 oz

1. Scrape the carrots and cut into even slices. Melt half the butter in a saucepan, stir in the carrots, adding salt and pepper to taste. Cover with water and cook for 30 minutes. Drain and pass through a sieve or food processor, collecting the purée in a bowl.
2. Clean the chicken livers and dice. Melt the remaining butter in a frying pan and brown the livers over a brisk heat. Season with a pinch of salt, moisten with the port and allow to evaporate.
3. Bring the chicken stock to the boil and sprinkle over the semolina, stirring continuously. After 10 minutes cooking, add the carrot purée and continue cooking for a further 5 minutes, stirring all the time. Finally mix in the chicken livers and the grated parmesan.

Zuppa di cipolle

Onion Soup

This is a more sophisticated version of the popular 'soupe a l'oignon'.

00:45 01:10

American	Ingredients	Metric/Imperial
4	*Onions*	4
⅓ cup	*Butter*	75 g / 3 oz
5 tbsp	*Flour*	4 tbsp
2 quarts	*Stock*	2 litres / 3½ cups
2	*Egg yolks*	2
	Salt	
4	*Slices of bread*	4
½ cup	*Grated parmesan cheese*	50 g / 2 oz
½ cup	*Emmental cheese*	50 g / 2 oz

1. Peel and wash the onions, slice thinly. Heat some of the butter, add onion and allow to fry gently in a saucepan. Cook the onions slowly until they are transparent, stirring very frequently.
2. Add the white flour, mix well and dissolve it by pouring in the stock, a little at a time to avoid lumps forming. Bring to the boil and simmer for about 1 hour.
3. Sieve, and use just the cooking water if you like a delicately flavored soup. If, on the other hand, you prefer a stronger taste, sieve the onions and put them back in the stock.
4. Put the egg yolks in a bowl, break them with a fork, add salt, stirring all the time, then add the soup a little at a time.
5. Preheat the oven to 400°F / 200°C / Gas Mark 6.
6. Slice a homemade loaf, or use a sliced loaf, and brown the slices in butter in a frying pan; drain and use them to line the bottom of four small pottery ovenproof dishes, preferably with a handle.
7. Sprinkle grated parmesan cheese over the bread, pour over some soup, then sprinkle over with more cheese, but this time it should be emmental cut into flakes.
8. Dust with a generous twist of pepper and then place the dishes in a hot oven until the cheese has melted.

Zuppa all'aglio

Garlic Soup

00:25 00:60

American	Ingredients	Metric/Imperial
16	*Garlic cloves*	16
1	*Clove*	1
1	*Sprig of thyme*	1
1	*Sprig of sage*	1
16	*Bread*	16
½ cup	*Grated cheese*	50 g / 2 oz
	Salt and pepper	
	Slices of bread	

1. Put the peeled garlic, clove, thyme and sage in 1 quart [1 litre / 1¾ pints] of water, season with salt and pepper and bring to the boil. Simmer briskly for 30 minutes.
2. Preheat the oven to 400°F / 200°C / Gas Mark 6.
3. Butter an oven tray and place on it the slices of bread sprinkled with grated cheese; brown them in the oven.
4. Soak 8 of the crisp slices until they are thoroughly saturated in the soup, after it has been taken from the heat, then purée the mixture in a blender or food processor.
5. Arrange the remaining 8 slices of bread in individual bowls, cover with the purée and serve.

Zuppa della Valsesia

Valsesia Soup

This is a well-loved soup eaten by the shepherds of Valsesia; many of the ingredients grown and produced in the valleys are used in this dish.

00:35 01:00

American	Ingredients	Metric/Imperial
2	*Potatoes*	2
1	*Onion*	1
1	*Leek*	1
2	*Celery stalks*	2
1	*Garlic clove*	1
1	*Stock cube*	1
2 slices	*Rye bread*	2 slices
¼ lb	*Toma or fontina cheese*	100 g / 4 oz

1. Peel the potatoes and cut them into small pieces; chop the onion, the washed leek, celery and a clove of garlic.
2. Put all the ingredients into a pot, season well. Pour over 1 quart [1 litre / 1¾ pints] of water, with a crumbled stock cube. Cover the pot and cook for 1 hour.
3. When the soup is ready to serve, add some cubes of rye bread and cheese.

Minestra di fagioli

Bean Soup

00:40 Soaking time 12:00 Serves 8 — 04:30

American	Ingredients	Metric/Imperial
1¾ lb	*Haricot beans, soaked*	*800 g / 1¾ lb*
2 oz	*Raw ham*	*50 g / 2 oz*
1	*Onion*	*1*
2	*Garlic cloves*	*2*
1	*Small carrot*	*1*
1	*Celery stalk*	*1*
3 tbsp	*Parsley*	*2 tbsp*
1 tsp	*Basil*	*1 tsp*
3 tbsp	*Olive oil*	*2 tbsp*
10	*Swiss chard leaves*	*10*
2	*Potatoes*	*2*
3 tbsp	*Tomato purée*	*2 tbsp*
	Salt and pepper	

1. Cook the beans, covered with water for 2-3 hours until tender, add salt at the end of the cooking time.
2. In the meantime, chop or put through a food processor the raw fat, lean ham, peeled onion, garlic, carrot, celery, and parsley and basil.
3. Heat the oil in a frying pan and cook the chopped vegetables for 5 minutes.
4. Put the cooked beans through the blender or food processor with the fried ingredients, add 1 quart [1 litre / 1¾ pints] of water and simmer for 1 hour.
5. Add leaves of Swiss chard, coarsely chopped, and 2 potatoes cut into small pieces; also add a little tomato purée, season with salt and pepper and continue cooking for 30 minutes. Remove the soup from the heat and leave until cold.
6. Serve the soup cold (but not chilled) with slices of toast placed on the bottom of the plate. Rice or pasta can be added to taste. It is even better eaten the next day.

Minestra St Germain

Potage St Germain

00:15 — 01:00

American	Ingredients	Metric/Imperial
2¼ cups	*Peas, shelled or frozen*	*350 g / 12 oz*
1½ oz	*Sorrel*	*40 g / 1½ oz*
1	*Stock cube*	*1*
	Salt and pepper	
	Croûtons	
¼ cup	*Grated parmesan cheese*	*25 g / 1 oz*

1. Wash the sorrel carefully in cold water, drain and chop. Cook the peas with the sorrel in 1 quart [1 litre / 1¾ pints] water. Add 1 crumbled stock cube, reduce the heat and cook very gently, stirring often.
2. Add salt and pepper when the soup is half cooked, then finish cooking. Sieve or blend the soup.
3. Arrange the fried croûtons in the bottom of a tureen and pour the soup over them. Finish by sprinkling with grated parmesan.

Zuppa povera

Pauper's Soup

00:20 — 01:00

American	Ingredients	Metric/Imperial
2 oz	*Bacon or fat ham*	*50 g / 2 oz*
3 tbsp	*Vegetable oil*	*2 tbsp*
1 lb	*Lima (broad) beans, shelled*	*500 g / 1 lb*
2	*Lettuce heads*	*2*
2	*Large onions*	*2*
	Salt and pepper	
¼ tsp	*Chopped basil*	*¼ tsp*
¼ tsp	*Chopped parsley*	*¼ tsp*
¼ tsp	*Chopped marjoram*	*¼ tsp*
1 tbsp	*Tomato purée*	*1 tbsp*

1. Grind (mince) or chop bacon and put it in a pan with oil over a medium heat. Add the shelled beans, the cleaned and shredded lettuce, and the peeled and sliced onions.
2. Season with salt and pepper and chopped basil, parsley and marjoram, and allow to soften in the uncovered pan. When all the vegetable juices have evaporated, moisten with the tomato purée, mixed with 2½ cups [600 ml / 1 pint] boiling water.
3. If the soup becomes dry again, cover with more boiling water or stock to finish cooking.
4. Serve with slices of crusty bread.

Zuppa alla Casal Bosco

Casal Bosco Soup

00:20 — 00:50

American	Ingredients	Metric/Imperial
¾ lb	*Dried mushrooms or fresh mushrooms*	*350 g / 12 oz*
3 tbsp	*Vegetable oil*	*2 tbsp*
3	*Garlic cloves*	*3*
2½ quarts	*Meat stock*	*2.5 litres / 4½ pints*
4 cups	*Spinach, cooked and chopped*	*1 kg / 2 lb*
1 tbsp	*Chopped parsley*	*1 tbsp*
	Salt and pepper	
4	*Slices of toasted stale bread*	*4*
1 tbsp	*Olive oil*	*1 tbsp*
	Grated parmesan cheese	

1. Soak and clean the dried mushrooms, or wash the fresh ones thoroughly. Heat the vegetable oil in a large pan, chop the mushrooms and sweat them with 2 cloves of garlic in the vegetable oil, without browning.
2. Add the stock, a little at a time to finish cooking the mushrooms, and the chopped spinach.
3. Chop the other clove of garlic and add to the spinach mixture with the parsley and all the remaining stock. Season with salt and pepper.
4. Whisk the soup so that it is quite smooth, then place the slices of toast in bowls, pour over the olive oil, grated parmesan and then the soup. Serve very hot.

Minestra di gianchetti

Anchovy Soup

00:15 | 00:45

American	Ingredients	Metric/Imperial
14 oz	*Anchovy fry (whitebait)*	*400 g / 14oz*
1 quart	*Vegetable stock*	*1 litre / 1¾ pints*
2	*Garlic cloves*	*2*
1	*Bunch of fragrant minestrone herbs*	*1*
½ lb	*Spinach*	*225 g / 8 oz*
	Salt and pepper	
⅔ cup	*Fresh cream*	*150 ml / 5 fl oz*
4 tsp	*Cornstarch (cornflour)*	*4 tsp*
3 tbsp	*Milk*	*2 tbsp*
	Croûtons	

1. Put the anchovy fry in a thin mesh sieve and wash under running cold water until the water runs clean.
2. Heat a pot with 1 quart [1 litre / 1¾ pints] of vegetable stock, put in the anchovy, 2 finely chopped cloves of garlic, a bunch of fragrant herbs, chopped, and a handful of raw chopped spinach.
3. Bring to a slow boil, seasoning with salt and pepper during cooking. Simmer for 30 minutes.
4. Pour a quarter of the cream into the soup, together with 4 teaspoons of cornstarch mixed in a little milk. Thicken over a low heat until it has a creamy consistency.
5. Correct the seasoning, then pour into soup bowls and serve with a garnish of croûtons.

Different garnishes for soup

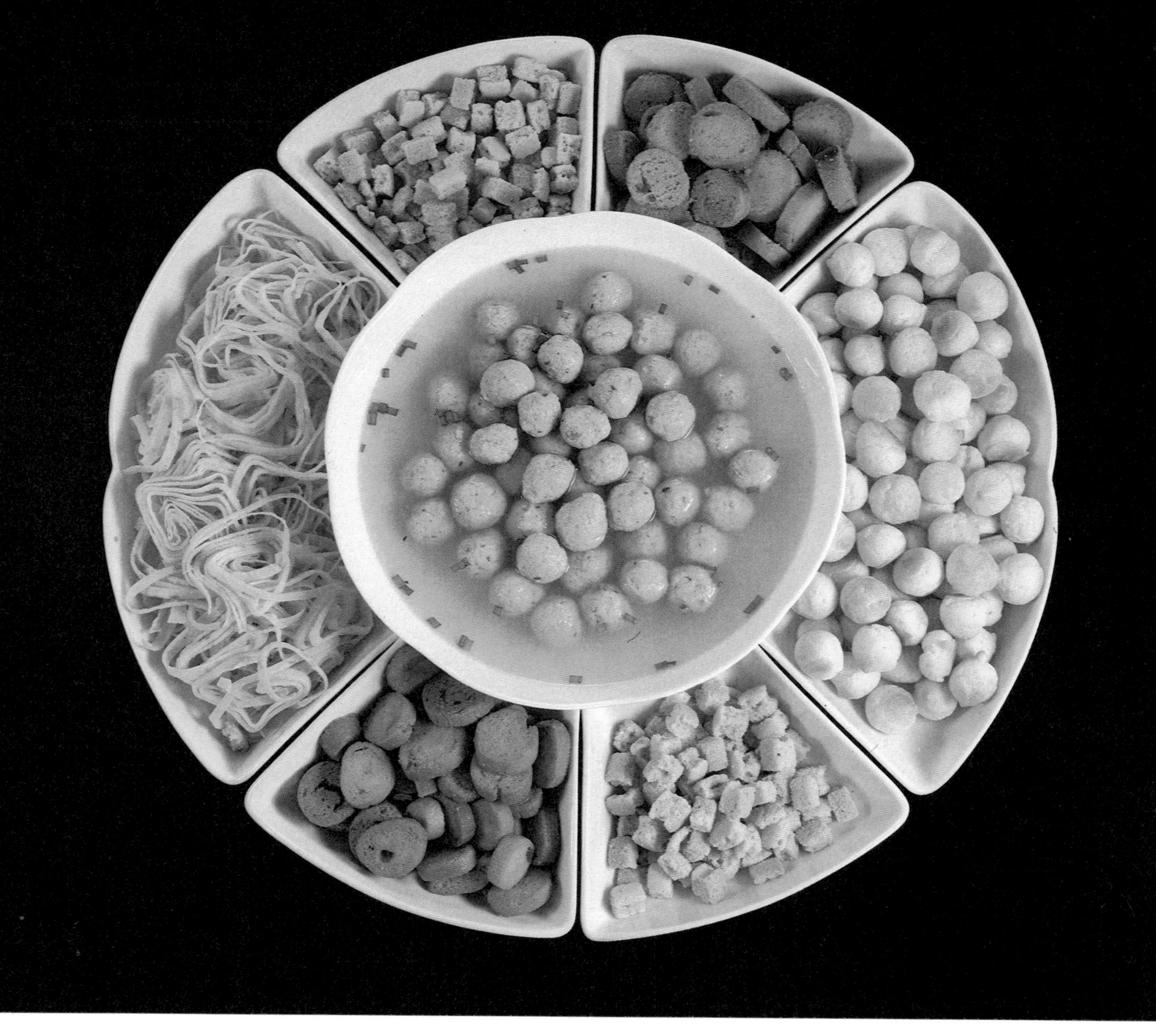

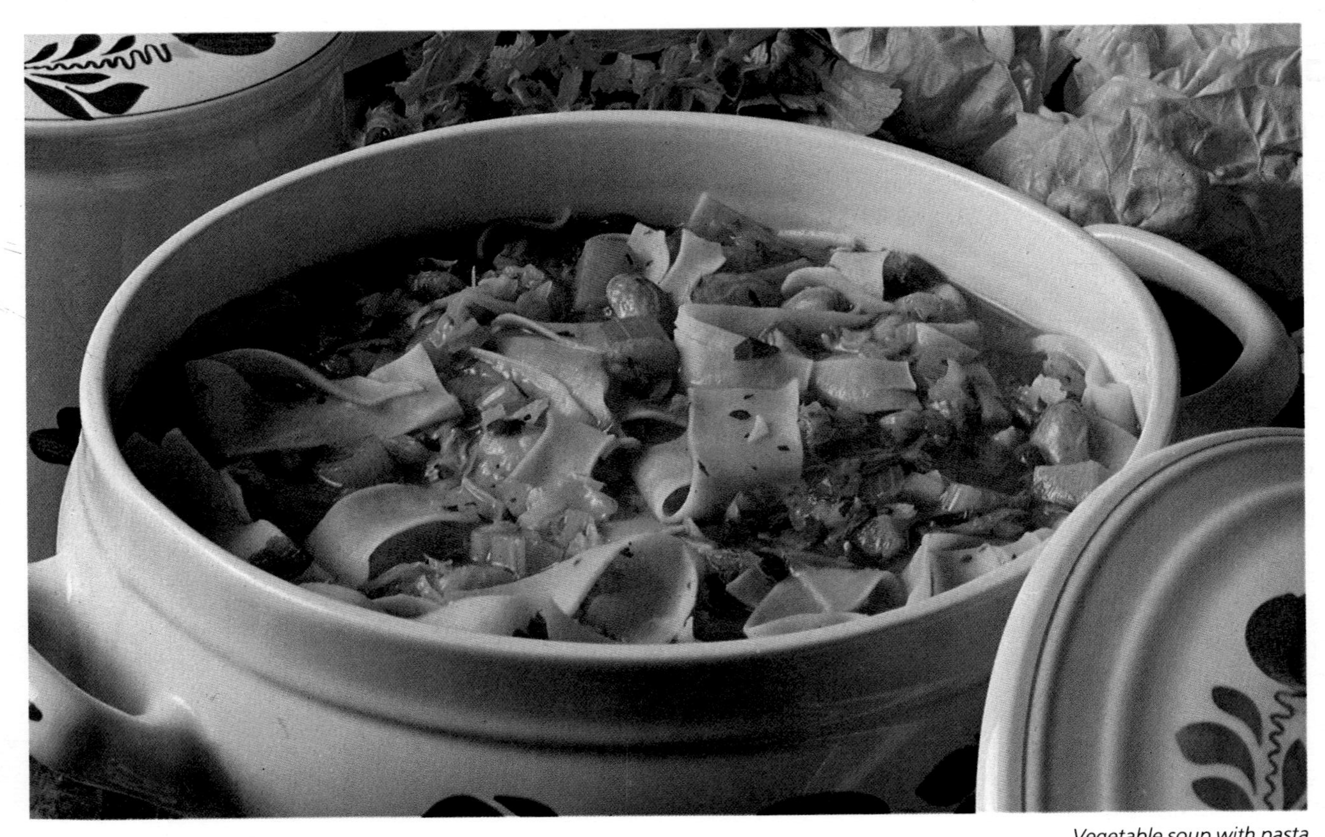
Vegetable soup with pasta

Zuppa alla genovese

Genoese Soup

Preparation 00:30 — Cooking 00:30

American	Ingredients	Metric/Imperial
1	*Lettuce head*	1
1	*Bunch of borage*	1
1	*Small onion*	1
5	*Sprigs of parsley*	5
3	*Basil leaves*	3
¼ cup	*Butter*	50 g / 2 oz
4	*Eggs*	4
½ cup	*Grated parmesan cheese*	50 g / 2 oz
1 quart	*Stock or consommé*	1 litre / 1¾ pints
	Salt and pepper	

1. Wash the vegetables and herbs, peel the onion. Chop the onion, lettuce, borage, parsley and basil leaves.
2. Heat a little of the butter in a frying pan over a low heat, add the onion and cook for 3 minutes. Add the remaining chopped ingredients and cook for a further 4 minutes stirring all the time; season well.
3. Beat the eggs in a bowl with the grated cheese. Remove the frying pan from the heat and mix in the egg and cheese. Butter a mold and empty the vegetable and cheese mixture into the mold, a ring mold is suitable or a sandwich cake tin. Place some water in a large frying pan and the mold in the pan, water should come half way up the side, and cook until firm. Turn out and allow to cool.
4. Bring the stock or consommé to the boil and drop in the cold mixture cut into slices. Add salt and pepper. Serve very hot, accompanied by croûtons.

Zuppa alla toscana

Tuscany Soup

Preparation 00:25 — Soaking time 12:00 — Cooking 02:30

American	Ingredients	Metric/Imperial
¼ lb	*Lentils*	100 g / 4 oz
¼ lb	*Dried beans*	100 g / 4 oz
1	*Garlic clove*	1
1	*Onion*	1
3	*Sage leaves*	3
1	*Sprig of rosemary*	1
2 oz	*Bacon*	50 g / 2 oz
¼ cup	*Butter*	50 g / 2 oz
3 tbsp	*Vegetable oil*	2 tbsp
2 quarts	*Stock*	2 litres / 3½ pints
	Pasta	

1. Put the lentils and beans in water and leave to soak overnight; throw away those which float to the surface.
2. Finely chop the garlic, peeled onion, sage leaves, rosemary and the bacon. Mix together.
3. Sweat all these ingredients in the butter and oil in a large pan on a very low heat; they should be softened, but not fried. Add the drained lentils and beans, allow the flavors to mingle and cover with the stock, cooking for 2 hours.
4. Put the mixture through a blender or food processor. Dilute with more stock, if necessary. Throw in the pasta and cook until 'al dente'. Add a tablespoon of cold oil as the finishing touch to this robust but truly delicious dish.

Minestra della nonna

Grandmother's Soup

00:15 00:40

American	Ingredients	Metric/Imperial
1	*Leek*	1
3 tbsp	*Butter*	40 g / 1½ oz
5 oz	*Greens or spinach*	150 g / 5 oz
1 quart	*Stock*	1 litre
½ cup	*Rice*	100 g / 4 oz
1	*Potato*	1
2	*Peeled tomatoes*	2
	Grated cheese	

1. Wash and slice a leek, heat the butter in a pan and cook the leek for 4 minutes.
2. Wash the greens, cut into strips, add them to the leek and braise for a few minutes; moisten with stock prepared with 2 stock cubes and 1 quart [1 litre / 1¾ pints] of boiling water.
3. Bring back to the boil and drop in the rice, potato, peeled and cut into small pieces and the peeled tomatoes. Cook half-covered for about 30 minutes. Serve with plenty of grated cheese.

Minestra del giovedì

Thursday Soup

00:20 01:00

American	Ingredients	Metric/Imperial
14 oz	*Peeled tomatoes*	400 g / 14 oz
1	*Garlic clove*	1
4	*Basil leaves*	4
2	*Egg yolks*	2
2	*Onions*	2
3 tbsp	*Vegetable oil*	2 tbsp
11 oz	*Small zucchini (courgettes)*	300 g / 11 oz
2	*Small potatoes*	2
⅔ cup	*Rice*	100 g / 4 oz
	Salt and pepper	
½ cup	*Grated parmesan cheese*	50 g / 2 oz

1. Prepare a sauce as follows: put into the blender 2 peeled tomatoes, clove of garlic, a few basil leaves and the egg yolks. Switch on and mix well. Keep on one side until you have cooked the soup.
2. Chop the onions, put the oil in a saucepan, heat and cook the chopped onions over a low heat for 5 minutes.
3. Moisten with a little water and allow to evaporate, raise the heat and brown the onions.
4. Trim the zucchini, wash, cut them lengthwise into 4 parts and then into small pieces. When the onions are well browned, add the zucchini and sauté them.
5. Wash and dice all the other vegetables, add them to the fried onions, allow the flavors to mingle, then cover with 1 quart [1 litre / 1¾ pints] of warm water. Bring to the boil, lower the heat again and cook for about 15 minutes, then pour in the rice.
6. When the rice is cooked, remove the soup from the heat. Now mix the sauce into the soup adding a ladleful at a time and stirring carefully so that the eggs do not set. When all the sauce has been mixed, put back on the heat and warm the soup, add salt and pepper to taste.
7. Remove the soup from the heat, pour into a tureen, sprinkle with grated parmesan and serve.

Minestra di Oliena

Oliena Soup

00:15 01:15

American	Ingredients	Metric/Imperial
1 lb	*Fresh peas*	500 g / 1 lb
1 quart	*Chicken stock*	1 litre / 1¾ pints
¼ lb	*Cooked chicken or veal*	100 g / 4 oz
3	*Eggs*	3
	Salt and pepper	
¼ tsp	*Nutmeg*	¼ tsp
5 tbsp	*Grated pecorino cheese*	4 tbsp
1 tbsp	*Vegetable oil*	1 tbsp

1. Shell the peas or use frozen, put into the stock and cook on a moderate heat.
2. Chop the chicken or veal very finely. Break the eggs into a bowl, add salt and pepper and if you like, a pinch of nutmeg. Beat well with a fork and add the minced meat and 2 tablespoons of grated pecorino.
3. Heat the oil and make an omelette with the egg and meat mixture then cut into ½ in / 1 cm cubes and place in soup tureen. When the peas are cooked, pour them together with the stock into the tureen, stir and serve accompanied by the remaining grated pecorino.

Zuppa alla fiamminga

Flemish Soup

00:15 00:30

American	Ingredients	Metric/Imperial
14 oz	*Potatoes*	400 g / 14 oz
½ lb	*Turnips*	225 g / 8 oz
2	*Leeks*	2
1	*Stock cube*	1
7 oz	*Stale bread*	200 g / 7 oz
	Salt and pepper	
1	*Egg yolk*	1
2 tbsp	*Butter*	25 g / 1 oz
2 tbsp	*Olive oil*	1½ tbsp
	Chopped parsley	

1. Wash and peel the potatoes and the turnips. Wash the leeks, running the water between the leaves. Dice these vegetables and put in a pan with 2 quarts [2 litres / 3½ pints] boiling water together with a crumbled stock cube and the stale bread. Season with salt and pepper, cover and simmer over a low heat.
2. Shortly before serving, place the egg yolk into a bowl and mix in little by little a ladleful of hot soup. Stir the mixture into the soup remaining in the pan.
3. Add a knob of butter or a few tablespoons of olive oil, according to taste, sprinkle with chopped parsley and serve immediately without further cooking.

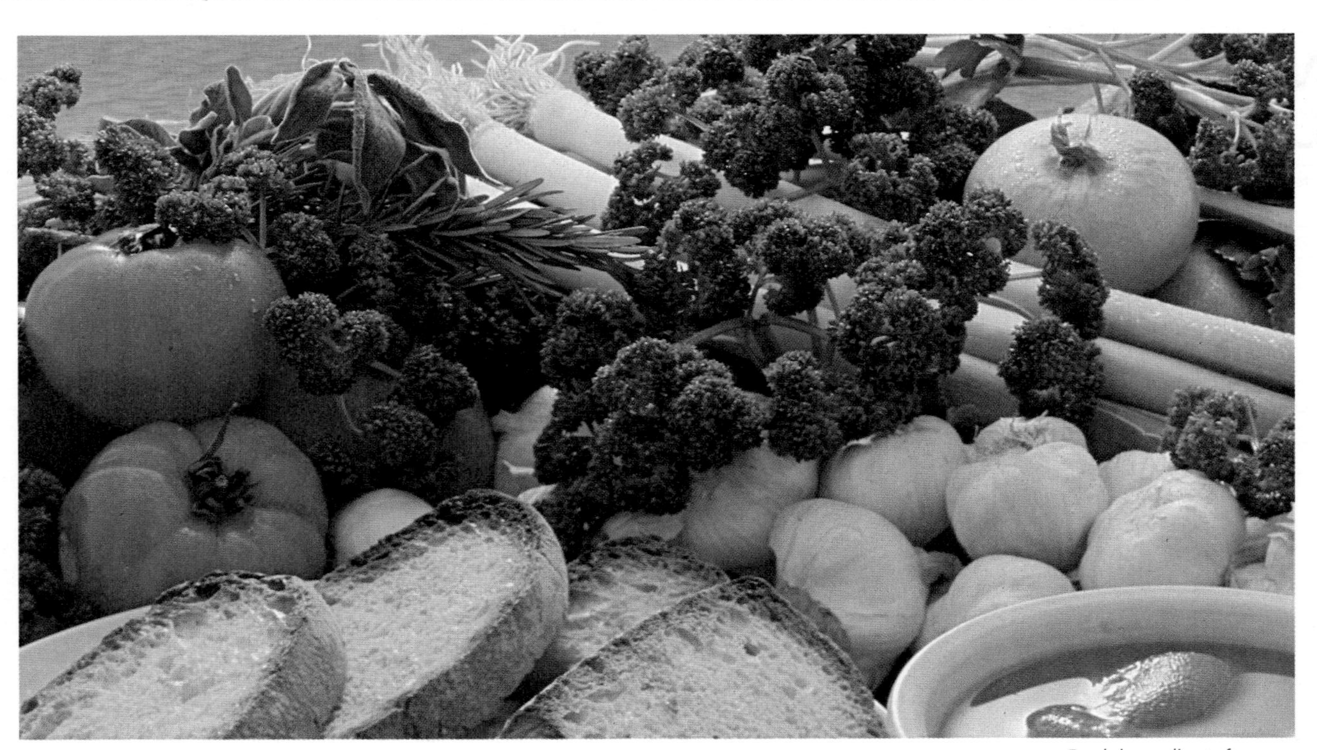

Fresh ingredients for soup

Minestra di fagioli alla bolognese

Bolognaise Bean Soup

02:00 Soaking time 12:00 — 01:30

American	Ingredients	Metric/Imperial
7 oz	*Dried beans*	*200 g / 7 oz*
	Salt and pepper	
2 or 3	*Garlic cloves*	*2 or 3*
3 tbsp	*Olive oil*	*2 tbsp*
1	*Small bunch of parsley*	*1*
¾ lb	*Very ripe tomatoes, puréed*	*350 g / 12 oz*
	or	
1 ¼ cups	*Tomato sauce (see page 171)*	*300 ml / ½ pint*
¾ lb	*Pasta*	*350 g / 12 oz*
½ cup	*Grated grana cheese*	*50 g / 2 oz*

1. Soak the dried beans overnight in cold water. The following day put them in 2 quarts [2 litres / 3½ pints] of cold water and boil, adding salt at the end of cooking. When beans are quite tender, drain and reserve the water.
2. Fry garlic in a pan with heated olive oil. As soon as the garlic is browned, add a little chopped parsley, the tomato purée and the boiled beans. Cook for 15 minutes, then add the cooking water from the beans.
3. At this point you can proceed in different ways, either sieve or blend (liquidize) everything, or leave the beans whole. Alternatively, sieve only half of them; this is a matter of personal taste.
4. When the soup begins to boil, throw in the pasta. Allow to cook, pour into a soup tureen and accompany it with a generous portion of grated cheese, chopped parsley and pepper to taste.

Zuppa del diavolo

Devil's Soup

00:45 — 01:00

American	Ingredients	Metric/Imperial
2 quarts	*Stock*	*2 litres / 3½ pints*
¾ lb	*Cooked ham*	*350 g / 12 oz*
¾ lb	*Mortadella*	*350 g / 12 oz*
2	*Garlic cloves*	*2*
1	*Onion*	*1*
5	*Sprigs of parsley*	*5*
2 or 3	*Basil leaves*	*2 or 3*
1 ¼ cups	*Spinach*	*250 g / 9 oz*
¾ lb	*Noodles*	*350 g / 12 oz*
1 cup	*Cream*	*225 ml / 8 fl oz*
½ cup	*Cognac*	*125 ml / 4 fl oz*
¼ lb	*Peas*	*100 g / 4 oz*
½ cup	*Butter*	*100 g / 4 oz*
	Grated cheese	

1. Prepare the stock and put in the diced ham and mortadella, the whole garlic cloves, the peeled onion, chopped with the parsley and basil.
2. Add the well washed spinach to the soup, and simmer for 10 minutes or so.
3. Throw in the pasta, add the cream and the cognac and the peas; for a fairly thick soup, it is best to use small peas, which will break down.
4. When cooking is almost finished, remove garlic cloves, add butter, stir well, and remove from the heat as soon as the butter is dissolved but not cooked.
5. Pour into bowls, garnish with plenty of grated cheese.

Minestrone alla coda di bue

Minestrone with Oxtail

Preparation 00:45 — Cooking 04:15

American	Ingredients	Metric/Imperial
1	*Oxtail*	1
1	*Calf's knuckle*	1
1	*Calf's foot*	1
¼ cup	*Butter*	50 g / 2 oz
2	*Onions*	2
2	*Carrots*	2
2	*Leeks*	2
2	*Celery stalks*	2
2	*Cloves*	2
3	*Sprigs of parsley*	3
1	*Sprig of thyme*	1
2	*Bay leaves*	2
3 tbsp	*Tomato purée*	2 tbsp
	Salt and pepper	
1 tbsp	*Potato flour*	1 tbsp
3 tbsp	*Madeira wine*	2 tbsp
	Grated cheese	

1. Cut the washed oxtail into eight pieces. Bone and cut up the calf's knuckle and foot. Melt the butter in a large pan and fry the meat with 2 peeled chopped onions for 7 minutes.
2. Wash and cut all the vegetables into medium-sized pieces, add to meat and on a low heat cook for a further 5 minutes, stirring all the time.
3. Add 2 quarts [2 litres / 3½ pints] of water, the cloves, herbs and the tomato purée. Add salt and pepper and cook on a low heat for about 4 hours.
4. Remove meat and cut it up into smaller pieces. Strain the stock, return it to the pan on the heat and bring to the boil. Blend in 1 tablespoon of potato flour dissolved in the madeira and mixed with a little hot stock. Add the meat, season well and pour into the tureen. Accompany with grated cheese.

Cook's tip: the butcher will usually cut up the oxtail, knuckle and foot for you.

Zuppa alla monzese

Monza-Style Soup

Preparation 00:15 — Cooking 00:20

American	Ingredients	Metric/Imperial
1	*Garlic clove*	1
1 tbsp	*Dripping (roast beef fat)*	1 tbsp
	Sliced homemade bread	
1 cup	*Grated parmesan cheese*	100 g / 4 oz
2 quarts	*Stock*	2 litres / 3½ pints

1. Rub the sides and bottom of a soup tureen thoroughly with the clove of garlic, put the dripping in the bottom, alternating with slices of homemade bread, and sprinkle over the grated parmesan.
2. Cover with plenty of very hot meat stock, or stock made from a cube, and keep hot for 10 minutes. If necessary you can add more stock, but it must be hot. Stir just before serving, and ladle into bowls. Sprinkle with more grated parmesan.

Minestra di riso e verze

Rice and Cabbage Soup

Preparation 00:15 — Cooking 00:30

American	Ingredients	Metric/Imperial
2	*Stock cubes*	2
1 lb	*Cabbage*	500 g / 1 lb
1	*Onion*	1
1 tbsp	*Vegetable oil*	1 tbsp
1 cup	*Rice*	200 g / 7 oz
1 cup	*Grated parmesan cheese*	100 g / 4 oz

1. Heat 1½ quarts [1.5 litres / 2½ pints] of water in a pan, add stock cubes. Wash the cabbage and trim it, removing the tougher leaves. Removing the remaining leaves one by one, lay them one on top of another and cut them into thin strips.
2. Chop the onion. Put the oil in a frying pan on a medium heat, fry the onions until golden. Add 4 tablespoons of hot stock, then the cabbage, braise for 5 minutes. Tip into the stock. Bring to the boil and simmer for 10 minutes.
3. Pour the rice into the cabbage stock and leave on the heat until cooked.
4. When cooking is finished pour the soup into plates and sprinkle generously with the grated parmesan.

Minestra di pasta e carciofi

Pasta and Artichoke Soup

Preparation 01:00 — Cooking 00:25

American	Ingredients	Metric/Imperial
6	*Jerusalem artichokes*	6
½	*Lemon*	½
2 tbsp	*Butter*	25 g / 1 oz
1	*Small onion*	1
1	*Slice of lean bacon*	1
2	*Peeled tomatoes*	2
	Salt and pepper	
5 oz	*Fresh pasta*	150 g / 5 oz
1 tbsp	*Chopped parsley*	1 tbsp
½ cup	*Grated parmesan cheese or pecorino*	50 g / 2 oz

1. Peel the artichokes and cut in half vertically and then into slices about 1 in / 2½ cm, then throw them into water made acid with lemon juice.
2. In a saucepan heat the butter, fry the chopped onion and bacon in the butter over a gentle heat. When they are transparent and only lightly colored, add the slices of artichoke, well drained. Fry on a moderate heat.
3. Add well crushed peeled tomatoes, allow the flavors to mingle for a couple of minutes and moisten with 1 quart [1 litre / 1¾ pints] of water, adding salt.
4. Bring to the bcil, drop in the fresh pasta, and complete cooking over a fairly even heat, adding a little water if necessary. Remove from the heat, season, add chopped parsley. Serve parmesan separately.

Minestra campagnola

Country Soup

Preparation 00:15 — Cooking 00:45

American	Ingredients	Metric/Imperial
3	*Plum tomatoes, fresh or canned*	3
1	*Onion*	1
Scant ¼ cup	*Vegetable oil*	3 tbsp
	Salt and pepper	
2½ cups	*Stock*	600 ml / 1 pint
14 oz	*Fresh pasta*	400 g / 14 oz
2	*Eggs*	2
½ cup	*Grated parmesan cheese*	50 g / 2 oz
1 tbsp	*Chopped parsley*	1 tbsp

1. Scald the tomatoes in boiling water, drain them, peel and cut into strips, removing the seeds. Peel and finely chop the onion.
2. Heat the oil in a large pan, sweat the onion until transparent over a low heat, add tomatoes, seasoning, 1 cup [225 ml / 8 fl oz] water and continue cooking gently for 20 minutes.
3. Add the stock to the pan, bring to the boil and throw in the pasta. Cook for 8 minutes, lower heat.
4. Whisk the eggs, flavor with a pinch of seasoning, the parmesan and the chopped parsley. Add some hot soup to the egg then mix together and pour into the pan with the pasta a few moments before removing from the heat. Stir, allow the eggs to thicken the soup, then transfer to a heated tureen.

Minestra della massaia

Housewife's Soup

Preparation 00:20 — Cooking 00:40

American	Ingredients	Metric/Imperial
2 oz	*Smoked bacon*	50 g / 2 oz
1	*Garlic clove*	1
1	*Onion*	1
5	*Sprigs of parsley*	5
3 tbsp	*Lard*	40 g / 1½ oz
14 oz	*Fresh or canned plum tomatoes*	400 g / 14 oz
	Salt and pepper	
1 quart	*Stock*	1 litre / 1¾ pints
3	*Potatoes*	3
1 cup	*Rice*	200 g / 7 oz
1 cup	*Grated emmental cheese*	100 g / 4 oz

1. Finely chop or mince the smoked bacon together with the garlic, onion and parsley. Alternatively all the ingredients may be chopped in a food processor. Heat the lard and cook the bacon mixture over a low heat.
2. Scald the tomatoes in boiling water (if using fresh), drain, peel and cut them into strips, removing the seeds, add to the bacon. Stir, season with salt and pepper and after a few minutes cover with stock or water. Bring to the boil.
3. Peel and wash the potatoes, dice and throw into the boiling soup; after 5 minutes also add the rice. Cook over a low heat for a further 20 minutes, stirring gently with a wooden spoon. Transfer the soup to heated serving bowls and sprinkle with grated emmental. Serve hot.

Minestra di asparagi

Rice and Asparagus Soup

Preparation 00:30 — Cooking 00:40

American	Ingredients	Metric/Imperial
¼ cup	*Butter*	50 g / 2 oz
1	*Onion*	1
1	*Garlic clove*	1
1 tbsp	*Tomato purée*	1 tbsp
14 oz	*Asparagus, green and slender*	400 g / 14 oz
1 quart	*Meat stock*	1 litre / 1¾ pints
1 cup	*Rice*	200 g / 7 oz
	Salt and pepper	
½ cup	*Grated parmesan cheese*	50 g / 2 oz

1. Heat the butter in a saucepan, cook the peeled, diced onion and garlic over a medium heat until onion is golden brown. Add 1 cup [225 ml / 8 fl oz] of water mixed with tomato purée and put in the asparagus tips. Cover and cook on a moderate heat for 10 minutes.
2. Heat the stock in a large pot and when it comes to the boil, throw in the rice and cook until tender. Add the fried onion and asparagus mixture, season well. Stir on the heat for a few minutes longer. Serve the soup accompanied with the grated parmesan cheese.

Minestra di broccoli alla romana

Roman-Style Broccoli Soup

Preparation 00:30 — Cooking 01:00

American	Ingredients	Metric/Imperial
14 oz	*Broccoli*	400 g / 14 oz
2 oz	*Bacon*	50 g / 2 oz
1	*Garlic clove*	1
1 tsp	*Lard*	1 tsp
1 tbsp	*Tomato purée*	1 tbsp
2 cups	*Stock*	450 ml / 16 fl oz
	Salt and pepper	
¼ lb	*Pork rind*	100 g / 4 oz
7 oz	*Spaghetti*	200 g / 7 oz
	Grated parmesan cheese	

1. Divide the broccoli into small pieces, wash well and drain.
2. Mince or finely chop the bacon with a clove of garlic. Heat the lard in a saucepan, add the bacon and garlic and brown for a few minutes. Add tomato purée, the broccoli pieces, 2 cups [450 ml / 16 fl oz] of stock or water, salt and pepper, and cook on a low heat.
3. Meanwhile scrape the pork rind thoroughly, cover with water and heat in a saucepan, boil for 1 minute, drain and cut the rind into thin strips. Return to the heat, add 1 cup [225 ml / 8 fl oz] of water and boil until soft.
4. When the pieces of broccoli are still firm, add the rind together with its cooking juices and continue cooking for another 10 minutes. Taste and add salt and pepper if necessary. When the soup comes to the boil, add the spaghetti broken into small pieces. Serve with parmesan.

Riso in brodo alla paesana

Country Broth with Rice

00:20 — 01:00

American	Ingredients	Metric/Imperial
1 lb	Small onions	500 g / 1 lb
1 quart	Stock	1 litre / 1¾ pints
	Salt and pepper	
3 tbsp	Vegetable oil	2 tbsp
3 tbsp	Tomato purée	2 tbsp
1 cup	Rice	200 g / 7 oz

1. Peel the onions, put them in a saucepan with the stock, a sprinkling of salt and pepper, oil and the tomato purée. Stir, cover the pan and bring to the boil; then lower the heat to minimum and cook the onions until tender.
2. Throw the rice into the saucepan and add a ladleful of boiling water. Cook on a low heat, adding more hot water if necessary and stirring often; the rice soup should turn fairly thick. Check seasoning and, when cooked, transfer to a tureen and serve piping hot.

Cipollata 

Pork Ribs with Onions

00:35 — 01:45

American	Ingredients	Metric/Imperial
14 oz	Pork ribs	400 g / 14 oz
1	Carrot	1
1	Celery stalk	1
2 lb	White onions	1 kg / 2 lb
	Salt and pepper	
5 tbsp	Olive oil	4 tbsp
2 oz	Fat bacon	50 g / 2 oz
2 oz	Salami	50 g / 2 oz
7 oz	Stale homemade bread	200 g / 7 oz
1	Garlic clove	1

1. Put the pork in a large pot with a scraped carrot cut in half, the washed and sliced celery and a piece of onion; cover with 1 quart [1 litre / 1¾ pints] of salted water. Bring to the boil and simmer until the meat begins to separate from the ribs.
2. Strain the stock, strip off the meat and place on one side.
3. Slice all the onions and put them under running water for a few minutes.
4. Pour the oil into a separate saucepan, add the chopped bacon, the peeled and diced salami, brown for a few minutes and then add the onions. Cook for 3 minutes.
5. Pour over 2½ cups [600 ml / 1 pint] stock, cover and cook over a moderate heat; add more stock from time to time. After about 1 hour add the meat cut into strips and the remaining stock to the onions. Return to the heat for a further 10 minutes. Season to taste.
6. Toast the bread under the grill or in a hot oven, rub the slices over with a clove of garlic, place in soup bowls or in a heated tureen. Pour the soup over the bread. Wait a few minutes before serving so that the bread soaks into the soup.

Pasta e fagioli

Pasta and Beans

00:35 — 01:15

American	Ingredients	Metric/Imperial
1	Onion	1
1	Celery stalk	1
1	Carrot	1
2 tbsp	Butter	25 g / 1 oz
1 tbsp	Oil	1 tbsp
1	Garlic clove	1
3	Rosemary leaves	3
1	Stock cube	1
1 lb	Fresh beans, shelled	500 g / 1 lb
3	Tomatoes	3
	Salt and pepper	
1 tbsp	Olive oil	1 tbsp

1. Finely chop the peeled onion, celery and scraped carrot and sweat them in heated butter and oil with a clove of garlic in a large pan with a few chopped rosemary leaves.
2. When the vegetables are browned, add hot water, crumbled stock cube and the shelled beans. Bring back to the boil, add the peeled tomatoes, broken up with a fork, salt, pepper and a sprig of rosemary tied with white thread so that it does not dissolve into the soup.
3. Cook the beans slowly until they are very tender.
4. Add the pasta cut into small pieces and cook for a few minutes. Serve with olive oil and a twist of pepper.

Pasta e ceci del Federico

Federico's Pasta and Chickpeas

00:30 Soaking time for peas 12:00 — 02:30 00:50 using canned peas

American	Ingredients	Metric/Imperial
¾ lb	Chickpeas or	350 g / 12 oz
1 can	Boiled chickpeas	1 can
5 tbsp	Vegetable oil	4 tbsp
2	Garlic cloves	2
3	Rosemary leaves	3
2	Stock cubes	2
½ lb	Ditalini pasta	225 g / 8 oz
	Salt and pepper	

1. Put the chickpeas in to soak the night before or, if you prefer, use canned cooked chickpeas, which will save time.
2. Heat the oil in a large pot, add garlic and rosemary; allow to brown, remove garlic when brown.
3. Add the drained chickpeas and flavor them for 10 minutes or so in the oil, then add a little hot water and finish cooking the chickpeas. (It will take around 2 hours for fresh peas and 20 minutes for the ready-cooked ones.)
4. When cooked, pass the peas and rosemary through a vegetable sieve or blender to obtain a smooth creamy mixture.
5. Add 2 crumbled stock cubes to 2 quarts [2 litres / 3½ pints] water, pour in the chickpea purée and the pasta. Cook the pasta until 'al dente', season with salt and pepper and serve this fragrant dish in earthenware bowls.

Zuppa di trippa alla trentina

Trentino Tripe Soup

00:30 | 02:10

American	Ingredients	Metric/Imperial
2 lb	*Tripe (partly cooked)*	*1 kg / 2 lb*
1 quart	*Stock*	*1 litre / 1¾ pint*
¼ tsp	*Chopped marjoram*	*¼ tsp*
¼ tsp	*Chopped thyme*	*¼ tsp*
¼ tsp	*Chopped chives*	*¼ tsp*
¼ tsp	*Rosemary*	*¼ tsp*
1	*Celery stalk*	*1*
	Parsley	
1	*Bay leaf*	*1*
2	*Carrots*	*2*
2	*Onions*	*2*
2	*Medium-sized potatoes*	*2*
1 tbsp	*Oil*	*1 tbsp*
1 tbsp	*Butter*	*1 tbsp*
3 tbsp	*Bread crumbs*	*2 tbsp*
3 tbsp	*Tomato purée*	*2 tbsp*
1	*Slice of bread*	*1*
	Salt and pepper	

1. Cut the tripe into strips and cook it for 1 hour in stock with the marjoram, thyme, chives, rosemary, celery, parsley and bay leaf added.
2. Peel and chop all other vegetables.
3. Heat the oil and butter and gently cook diced carrots, onion and potatoes for 5 minutes, add the tripe and 1 cup [225 ml / 8 fl oz] tripe stock. Simmer for a further 5 minutes.
4. Add bread crumbs, tomato purée and some bread cubes, pour over the remaining stock.
5. Cook the soup for 1 hour on a moderate heat; taste and season with salt and pepper if necessary. Serve hot accompanied by crusty bread.

Zuppa di trippa aretina

Areto Tripe Soup

00:30 | 02:15

American	Ingredients	Metric/Imperial
2¾ lb	*Partly cooked tripe*	*1.2 kg / 2¾ lb*
3	*Garlic cloves*	*3*
5	*Sprigs of parsley*	*5*
3	*Celery stalks*	*3*
3	*Carrots*	*3*
¼ tsp	*Chopped basil*	*¼ tsp*
¼ tsp	*Rosemary*	*¼ tsp*
Scant ¼ cup	*Vegetable oil*	*3 tbsp*
1	*Large onion*	*1*
2 quarts	*Meat stock*	*2 litres / 3½ pints*
1 lb	*Canned peeled tomatoes*	*500 g / 1 lb*
	Salt and pepper	
½ tsp	*Paprika*	*½ tsp*
5 tbsp	*Grated parmesan*	*4 tbsp*
1 tbsp	*Olive oil*	*1 tbsp*

1. Wash and drain the tripe, cut into strips. Chop the garlic and parsley and cut the celery and carrots into large pieces. Chop the basil and rosemary together very finely.
2. Heat oil in a large pan, add the chopped onion, the parsley and the garlic; let it brown stirring often, then add the prepared vegetables and fry for a further 10 minutes.
3. Add the meat stock, the tripe, the peeled tomatoes, and season with salt, pepper and paprika. Cover and cook for 2 hours, stirring from time to time over a low heat.
4. Taste for seasoning then add 1 tablespoon of olive oil and parmesan.

Zuppa di asparagi

Asparagus Soup

00:10 | 00:40

American	Ingredients	Metric/Imperial
¼ cup	*Butter*	*50 g / 2 oz*
1	*Onion*	*1*
	Slices of bread	
1 quart	*Stock*	*1 litre / 1¾ pints*
¾ lb	*Asparagus tips*	*350 g / 12 oz*
½ cup	*Grated parmesan cheese*	*50 g / 2 oz*

1. Heat the butter in a pan until brown, add the chopped onion, then brown the slices of bread.
2. Bring stock to the boil, drop in the asparagus tips, simmer until cooked for about 20 minutes.
3. Place the slices of bread and the parmesan in an ovenproof dish. Top with asparagus when cooked.
4. Preheat the oven to 400°F / 200°C / Gas Mark 6.
5. Pour a little stock over the bread and put in the oven shortly before serving. Bake until the parmesan has browned. Serve the asparagus with the soup poured over it.

Minestra di riso e piselli

Rice and Pea Soup

00:20 | 01:00

American	Ingredients	Metric/Imperial
¼ cup	*Butter*	*50 g / 2 oz*
1	*Onion*	*1*
14 oz	*Fresh or frozen peas*	*400 g / 14 oz*
5 oz	*Cooked ham*	*150 g / 5 oz*
1½ quarts	*Stock*	*1.5 litres / 2½ pints*
⅔ cup	*Rice*	*150 g / 5 oz*
2	*Egg yolks*	*2*
½ cup	*Grated parmesan cheese*	*50 g / 2 oz*
	Pepper	
	Croûtons	

1. Gently heat half the butter in a saucepan. Chop the onion, add to the pan with peas, ham cut into strips and stir well.
2. Cover with the stock, cook for 30 minutes on a moderate heat, then add the rice and continue until the rice is cooked.
3. Beat the egg yolks in a bowl with the parmesan and a pinch of pepper. When the soup is cooked, remove from the heat and pour in the beaten egg mixture gradually, stirring vigorously. Serve with croûtons fried in the remaining butter.

Lentil soup

Zuppa di lenticchie

Lentil Soup

Preparation 00:25 (Soaking time 01:00) — Cooking 01:30

American	Ingredients	Metric/Imperial
14 oz	*Lentils*	*400 g / 14 oz*
2 oz	*Ham fat*	*50 g / 2 oz*
2	*Celery stalks*	*2*
1	*Small onion*	*1*
1	*Garlic clove*	*1*
2 or 3	*Sage leaves*	*2 or 3*
2 or 3	*Rosemary leaves*	*2 or 3*
3 tbsp	*Vegetable oil*	*2 tbsp*
2 tbsp	*Butter*	*25 g / 1 oz*
4	*Salted anchovies*	*2*
15 oz	*Canned tomatoes*	*450 g / 15 oz*
4	*Slices bread*	*4*
¾ cup	*Grated pecorino cheese*	*50 g / 2 oz*

1. Wash lentils and put them to soak in warm water for 1 hour. Discard those which have floated to the surface. Drain the others and put them in 2 quarts [2 litres / 3½ pints] lightly salted water to cook.
2. Chop the ham fat, celery, onion, garlic and a few leaves of sage and rosemary together and fry them gently in heated oil and half the butter. When the vegetables have softened, add the rinsed anchovies, boned and chopped into small pieces. Allow to mix in well, stirring all the time, then add the tomatoes mixed with a few drops of water.
3. Drain the lentils and put them in the sauce you have prepared, season well. Do not throw away the cooking water. Simmer lightly until a thick broth is formed, add some lentil cooking water if too thick.
4. Preheat the oven to 350°F / 180°C / Gas Mark 4.
5. Cover the bottom of 4 small oven dishes with slices of bread fried in butter. Taste the soup for seasoning, then pour over the bread, sprinkle with grated pecorino and put in the oven to brown.

Minestra e fegatini

Chicken Liver Soup

Preparation 00:15 — Cooking 01:00

American	Ingredients	Metric/Imperial
1 quart	*Chicken stock*	*1 litre / 1¾ pints*
	Salt and pepper	
11 oz	*Chicken livers*	*200 g / 11 oz*
¼ cup	*Butter*	*50 g / 2 oz*
2	*Eggs*	*2*
⅔ cup	*Rice*	*150 g / 5 oz*
3	*Sprigs of parsley*	*3*

1. Prepare a strong stock, preferably chicken.
2. Bring a small pan of salted water to the boil, add the chicken livers and leave to cook for 5 minutes. Drain and dice the livers.
3. Heat the butter in a fairly large saucepan over a medium heat, add the chicken livers and brown lightly. Hard-cook (boil) the eggs, shell them, break into pieces and salt lightly.
4. Bring the stock to the boil and pour in the rice. Stir and cook.
5. Chop the parsley very finely, add to the cooked rice, remove from the heat, season, stir and let it rest for 2-3 minutes. Pour the soup into a large tureen, stir in the chicken livers and the eggs before serving.

Cook's tip: as a variation you could add to the soup, with the rice, a chopped carrot and onion and bouquet garni.

Pancotto alla calabrese

Calabrian Bread Soup

Preparation 00:30 — Cooking 00:45

American	Ingredients	Metric/Imperial
¼ cup	*Olive oil*	*50 ml / 2 fl oz*
½ lb	*Tomatoes*	*225 g / 8 oz*
4	*Sprigs of parsley*	*4*
2	*Bay leaves*	*2*
1	*Garlic clove*	*1*
1	*Celery stalk*	*1*
	Salt and pepper	
4	*Stale bread rolls*	*4*
4	*Eggs*	*4*
	Grated pecorino cheese	

1. Put the oil in a large pan and heat gently, add the chopped tomatoes, a little parsley, the bay leaves, a clove of garlic and the sliced celery. Cook for 3 minutes.
2. Pour in 1½ quarts [1.5 litres / 2½ pints] of water, and salt and pepper, bring to the boil and simmer for 30 minutes. Drain off the stock into a clean saucepan.
3. Toast the sliced rolls in the oven or under the grill. Let them soften for a few minutes, add to the stock for 2 minutes, then remove them with a slotted spoon and place in the soup plates.
4. Break each egg into the boiling soup; when it is poached, remove it, still using the slotted spoon, and place it on the bread in the plates. Sprinkle with pecorino cheese and serve with the soup.

Coulis di Nizza

French Tomato Soup

00:30 00:40

American	Ingredients	Metric/Imperial
½ lb	Onions	200 g / 8 oz
¼ cup	Butter	50 g / 2 oz
¼ cup	Flour	25 g / 1 oz
1 lb	Tomatoes	450 g / 1 lb
2 tsp	Chopped tarragon	2 tsp
1 quart	Stock	1 litre / 1¾ pint
1 tbsp	Chopped parsley	1 tbsp
1 cup	Cream	225 ml / 8 fl oz

1. Cut the peeled onions into thin slices, heat the butter in a saucepan and gently fry until soft, sprinkle with flour and brown the onion rings on a low heat, stirring all the time.
2. Add the peeled chopped tomatoes and the tarragon with the stock. Cook over a moderate heat for 30 minutes, then strain through a fine sieve, reheat and stir in the cream just before serving. Finally add the chopped parsley and some tarragon to garnish the soup.

Brodo d'estate dei veneziani

Venetian Summer Broth

This is an ancient and fortifying recipe of the Venetian Maritime Republic.

00:10 00:30

American	Ingredients	Metric/Imperial
3	Egg yolks	3
1	Lemon	1
	Salt and pepper	
2½ cups	Cold stock	600 ml / 1 pint
	Croûtons	

1. Beat the egg yolks well, adding the lemon juice, drop by drop, in a medium-sized pan, then season with salt and pepper. Continuing to beat, add the cold stock a little at a time.
2. Place the pan on a low flame and continue stirring until the mixture is thick and creamy. Serve in cups or small bowls with croûtons fried in butter. Remember that it must not be allowed to boil.

Zuppa alla bolognese

Bolognaise Soup

00:25 00:45

American	Ingredients	Metric/Imperial
2 oz	Mortadella	50 g / 2 oz
4	Eggs, separated	4
1 cup	Grated parmesan cheese	100 g / 4 oz
⅔ cup	Semolina	100 g / 4 oz
	Nutmeg	
	Salt	
6 tbsp	Butter	75 g / 3 oz
1 quart	Meat stock or consommé	1 litre / 1¾ pints

1. Preheat the oven to 350°F / 180°C / Gas Mark 4.
2. Finely chop the mortadella. Put the egg yolks in a bowl together with the parmesan, the semolina (retaining 1 teaspoon), and a pinch each of nutmeg and salt; mix the ingredients together with the mortadella. Add the softened butter, cream well and then fold in the stiffly beaten egg whites. Butter a mold, dust with the remaining semolina, pour in the mixture and place the dish in the oven.
3. When the mixture is cooked, allow to cool and cut it into cubes. Heat the well flavored stock or consommé and as soon as it starts to boil put in the cubes. Cook for a further 5 minutes and then serve.

Zuppa spagnola

Spanish Soup

00:20 00:40

American	Ingredients	Metric/Imperial
1	Onion	1
3 tbsp	Oil	2 tbsp
1	Garlic clove	1
1 tbsp	Chopped parsley	1 tbsp
14 oz	Can of tomatoes	400 g / 14 oz
3 tbsp	Tomato purée	2 tbsp
2 lb	Assorted fish	1 kg / 2 lb
	Salt and pepper	
½ cup	White wine	125 ml / 4 fl oz

1. Finely chop the peeled onion. Heat the oil in a saucepan, add the onion and crushed garlic, cook over a low heat until transparent. Add chopped parsley, tomatoes cut into pieces, tomato purée mixed with juice from the can of tomatoes. Allow to simmer for 10 minutes.
2. Add the various fish, well washed and scaled, the larger ones first, cut into pieces.
3. Bring to the boil. Season with salt and pepper, add wine, cook for a further 15 minutes. Serve with toast or hot crusty bread.

Zuppa ricca della Valsusa

Rich Valsusa Soup

00:20 00:45 to 01:00

American	Ingredients	Metric/Imperial
5 oz	Hard rye bread	150 g / 5 oz
¼ cup	Butter	50 g / 2 oz
5 oz	Goat's milk cheese	150 g / 5 oz
2¼ cups	Stock	500 ml / 18 fl oz
1	Onion	1
4	Juniper berries	4
¼ tsp	Pepper	¼ tsp
¼ tsp	Nutmeg	¼ tsp

1. Take some rye bread and crumble it carefully, then put it in a saucepan. Add the butter and cheese in small pieces and stir, adding some stock and the same amount of water. Cook over a low flame, stirring all the time, very carefully.
2. Chop the peeled onion and add it to the remaining heated butter with the juniper berries, a pinch of pepper and nutmeg; cook for 5 minutes. When the soup is cooked, season it with the onion mixture.

Crema di pomodoro

Cream of Tomato Soup

00:15 01:00

American	Ingredients	Metric/Imperial
2 lb	*Tomatoes, canned or fresh plum*	*1 kg / 2 lb*
1	*Stock cube*	*1*
½ cup	*Butter*	*100 g / 4 oz*
	Salt and pepper	
1	*Mozzarella cheese*	*1*
3 tbsp	*Milk*	*2 tbsp*
1 cup	*Grated parmesan cheese*	*100 g / 4 oz*
1 cup	*Coffee (single) cream*	*225 ml / 8 fl oz*
4	*Eggs*	*4*
1 tsp	*Fresh basil*	*1 tsp*

1. Blend the tomatoes to form a thick, smooth sauce. Dissolve stock cube in 1 quart [1 litre / 1¾ pints] of water, together with half the butter, salt and a little pepper. Simmer and add the tomatoes.
2. Break the mozzarella into small pieces, place it in a bowl with the milk, and work until it mixes well, then add it to the soup. Add the parmesan a little at a time, stirring well, and finally the cream, keeping the heat low.
3. Using the remaining butter, make four small, thin omelettes from the eggs. Roll them up and cut into strips.
4. Chop the basil. Just before serving, place the strips of omelette in the bottom of the soup plates, pour over the soup and sprinkle with the basil.

Crema di sedano 

Cream of Celeriac Soup

00:20 01:30

American	Ingredients	Metric/Imperial
1	*Large white celeriac*	*1*
1 tbsp	*Vegetable oil*	*1 tbsp*
2	*Potatoes*	*2*
	Salt and pepper	
2	*Egg yolks*	*2*
1 cup	*Coffee (single) cream*	*225 ml / 8 fl oz*

1. Take the celeriac, peel it, wash it very carefully under cold water, and cut it into small pieces. Drop into a pot of boiling salted water and blanch for 15 minutes.
2. Remove from the pot, drain and rinse under cold running water. Drain again and dry it very carefully with absorbent kitchen paper.
3. Put the oil in a saucepan to heat, add pieces of celeriac and leave over a low heat until the vegetable has completely absorbed the oil. Stir carefully.
4. Peel and thoroughly wash the potatoes, cut them into pieces and put them in the saucepan, adding 1 quart [1 litre / 1¾ pints] of cold water and a little salt. Put a lid on the saucepan and cook on a very low heat for about 1 hour.
5. Pass the contents through a vegetable sieve, blender or food processor, and heat again, remembering to keep the heat low.
6. Beat the egg yolks in a bowl together with the cream, sprinkle with pepper, add a little hot soup, taking care to stir all the time. Mix the egg and cream into the soup and serve hot.

Passato di castagne

Chestnut Purée

01:00 00:10

American	Ingredients	Metric/Imperial
2 lb	*Chestnuts*	*1 kg / 2 lb*
2	*Celery stalks*	*2*
	Sage or other herbs	
	Salt and pepper	
¼ cup	*Butter*	*50 g / 2 oz*
½ cup	*Milk*	*125 ml / 4 fl oz*

1. Peel the chestnuts and cook them in salted water to which you have added some celery, a sprig of sage and any other herbs and seasonings you wish. When the chestnuts are cooked, drain them, remove the inner skin and sieve or blend them.
2. Melt the butter in a large saucepan, add the chestnut purée, dilute with milk and then add water until the mixture is just the right thickness.
3. Boil for a few moments more and then pour into bowls and serve with croûtons fried in butter.

Crema di rape

Cream of Turnip Soup

00:39 01:00

American	Ingredients	Metric/Imperial
¼ cup	*Butter*	*50 g / 2 oz*
½ cup	*Flour*	*50 g / 2 oz*
1 quart	*Stock*	*1 litre / 1¾ pints*
	Salt and pepper	
¼ tsp	*Cinnamon*	*¼ tsp*
1	*Onion*	*1*
1	*Garlic clove*	*1*
4	*Large turnips*	*4*
1¼ cups	*Milk*	*300 ml / ½ pint*
2	*Fresh eggs*	*2*
1 tsp	*Brandy*	*1 tsp*
½ cup	*Grated parmesan cheese*	*50 g / 2 oz*
1 tbsp	*Chopped parsley*	*1 tbsp*

1. Prepare a béchamel base with the butter and flour (see page 162). Add the stock gradually, then put it on to simmer gently, adding a little salt, pepper and a little powdered cinnamon.
2. Add the whole onion and crushed garlic.
3. Clean and peel the turnips, pass through a food processor or slice thinly. Add the turnips and the milk to the thick, simmering stock, keeping the heat low, stirring from time to time until the turnips are cooked. At this point, remove the garlic or onion.
4. Meanwhile beat the eggs with the brandy, adding the parmesan a little at a time.
5. Finally add a little hot soup to the egg. Switch off the heat, add the beaten egg mixture to the soup and stir with a whisk so that the eggs thicken.
6. Pour the soup into soup plates and garnish with a sprinkling of chopped parsley.

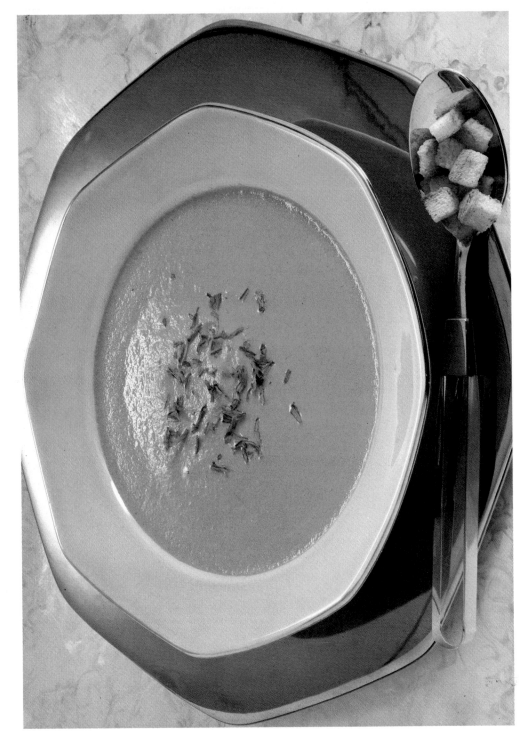

Cream of carrot soup

Crema di carote

Cream of Carrot Soup

00:30 | 00:40

American	Ingredients	Metric/Imperial
2 lb	*Baby carrots*	1 kg / 2 lb
2	*Small onions*	2
½ cup	*Butter*	100 g / 4 oz
Scant ¼ cup	*All purpose (plain) flour*	3 tbsp
1 quart	*Stock*	1 litre / 1¾ pints
	Salt and pepper	
¼ tsp	*Nutmeg*	¼ tsp
½ cup	*Single cream*	100 ml / 4 fl oz

1. Wash and scrape carrots, grate most of them and cut the rest into small dice. Peel and finely chop the onions. Heat half the butter in a saucepan, add the onion and cook over a low heat until transparent, then remove from the butter with a draining spoon.
2. Sprinkle the remaining butter with the flour and stir well to form a roux, then gradually add stock, whisking constantly to avoid lumps. When the mixture is thoroughly blended, add grated carrots, onion and the diced carrots.
3. Continue simmering, stirring often, until the diced carrots are cooked, season with salt, pepper and nutmeg.
4. Remove from heat, gently stir in the cream and allow the soup to rest for 10 minutes before serving. The soup can also be garnished with small cooked pasta shapes.

Zuppa di zucca

Pumpkin Soup

It is the custom in some areas to serve this soup sprinkled with sugar.

00:25 | 00:45

American	Ingredients	Metric/Imperial
2 lb	*Pumpkin*	1 kg / 2 lb
¼ cup	*Butter*	50 g / 2 oz
	Salt	
1 quart	*Milk*	1 litre / 1¾ pints
4	*Slices of bread*	4

1. Peel the pumpkin, remove the seeds from the flesh, and cut into small pieces.
2. Heat a saucepan with a little butter and, when it begins to foam, add the pumpkin and some salt. Cook for about 30 minutes and, if necessary, add a little water.
3. Sieve or blend the pumpkin, collecting it in a second saucepan.
4. Return the pumpkin to the heat, mixing in a few tablespoons of water, and cook for 10 minutes, then add the boiling milk.
5. Stir well and pour the purée into bowls in which you have previously placed the slices of bread.

Fonduta

Cheese Fondue

02:00 00:30

American	Ingredients	Metric/Imperial
¾ lb	*Fontina cheese*	350 g / 12 oz
2¼ cups	*Milk*	½ litre / 18 fl oz
6 tbsp	*Butter*	75 g / 3 oz
3	*Egg yolks*	3
	Grated black truffle	

1. Cut the cheese into small cubes and cover it with milk in the top of a double boiler, allow to soak in the milk for 2 hours. Add butter and egg yolks to cheese.
2. Place the pan in the base of the double boiler containing water which has been brought to the boil.
3. Work the cheese with a large wooden spoon. At first the cheese will become rather stringy, then it will become more liquid, and finally thicken. When the mixture has thickened and is perfectly smooth, remove from the heat and serve piping hot. Garnish the fondue with the grated black truffle. Vegetables such as chard or fennel, cooked and puréed with butter can also be added to the fondue.

Crema Aurora

Cream Aurore

00:20 00:40

American	Ingredients	Metric/Imperial
1 lb	*Fleshy, ripe tomatoes*	500 g / 1 lb
5 tbsp	*Vegetable oil*	4 tbsp
2	*Medium sized onions*	2
1	*Small bunch of thyme*	1
7	*Parsley sprigs*	7
	Salt and pepper	
1 quart	*Vegetable stock*	1 litre / 1¾ pints
3 tbsp	*Cream*	2 tbsp

1. Scald the tomatoes, remove the skin and pips, and put the chopped flesh on one side.
2. Heat the oil in a saucepan. Thinly slice the onion and gently fry until transparent, then add the flesh of the tomatoes, the thyme and parsley, tied together in a bundle.
3. Stir, season with salt and pepper, add the stock and cook for about 30 minutes over a medium heat. Remove the herbs, allow to cool and put through a blender or food processor.
4. Return the purée to a gentle heat with enough stock to make a fairly smooth cream, if liked stir in 2-3 tbsp cream. The soup can be accompanied by small pieces of bread fried in butter and sprinkled with grated parmesan cheese.

Cheese fondue

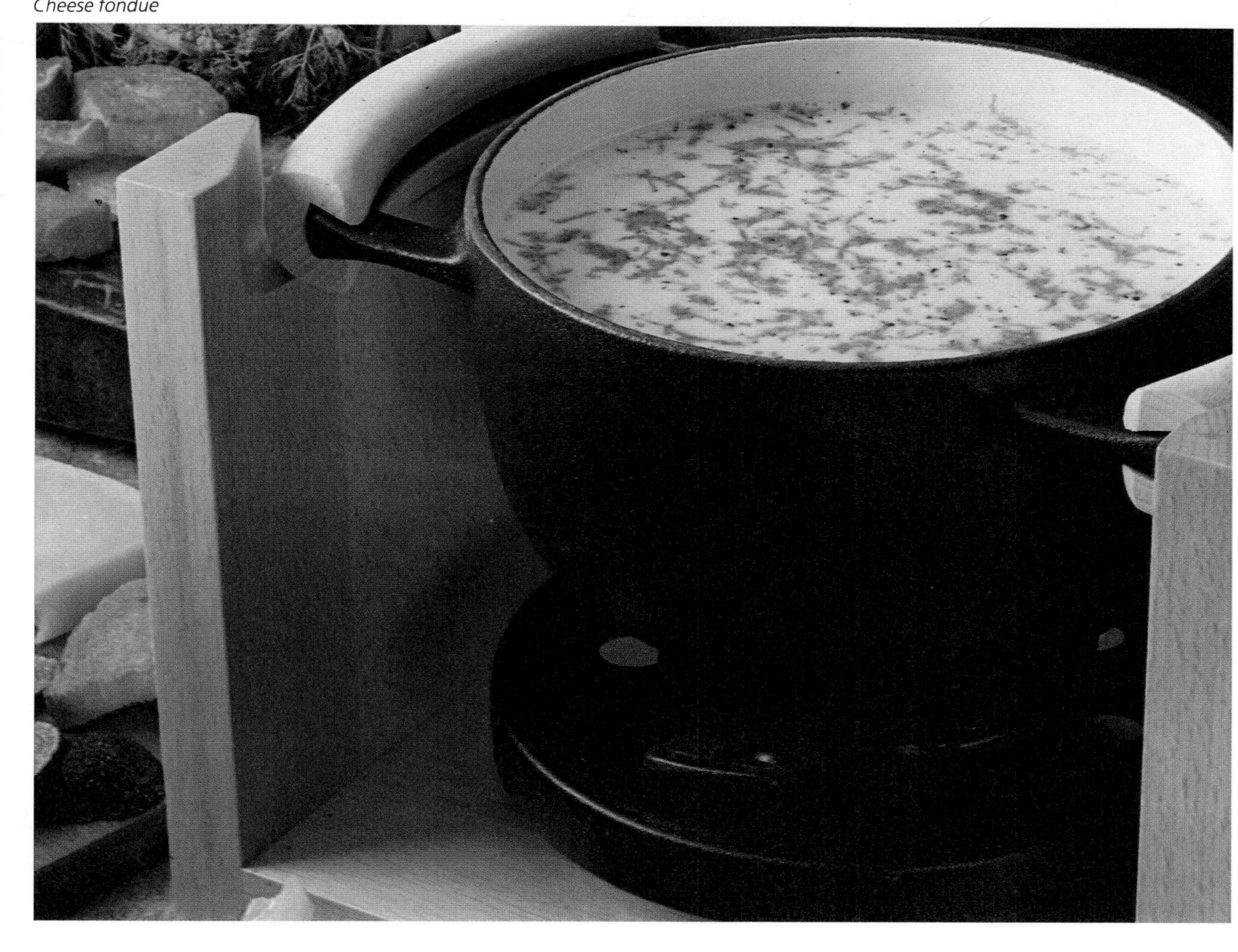

Crema di cavolfiore Du Barry

Cream of Cauliflower Du Barry

00:15 00:40

American	Ingredients	Metric/Imperial
1	*Cauliflower*	1
⅓ cup	*Butter*	40 g / 1½ oz
1 cup	*Cream*	225 ml / 8 fl oz
	Salt and pepper	
1 tbsp	*Cornstarch (cornflour)*	1 tbsp
⅔ cup	*Milk*	150 ml / 5 fl oz

1. Wash the cauliflower thoroughly, divide into florets and cook in 2 cups [600 ml / 1 pint] boiling salted water for about 30 minutes. Drain but retain some of the cooking water. Sieve or blend to obtain cauliflower purée, moisten with the cooking water.
2. Add all the butter, cream and season away from the heat. If the soup seems too thin, thicken by adding 1 tablespoon of cornstarch dissolved in cold milk. Add to the hot soup, bring back to almost boiling for 2-3 minutes, stirring all the time carefully.
3. Pour the soup into a heated soup tureen, sprinkle with plenty of grated parmesan cheese and garnish with croûtons.

Crema di porri

Cream of Leek Soup

00:30 00:30

American	Ingredients	Metric/Imperial
2 lb	*Fresh leeks*	1 kg / 2 lb
1 quart	*Stock*	1 litre / 1¾ pints
	Salt and pepper	
¼ tsp	*Nutmeg*	¼ tsp
2	*Potatoes*	2
3 tbsp	*White wine*	2 tbsp
½ cup	*Butter*	100 g / 4 oz
3 tbsp	*Coffee (single) cream*	2 tbsp
1	*Lemon*	1
2	*Egg yolks*	2

1. Thoroughly wash and finely chop the leeks, except for two which should be sliced thinly. Put the stock on the heat, add all the leeks, both chopped and sliced, and simmer until they are almost cooked.
2. Season with salt, pepper and nutmeg, add peeled and finely grated potatoes, white wine and the butter, simmer for 10 minutes.
3. Add the cream, a little at a time, stirring carefully. Beat the egg yolks with lemon juice and place on one side.
4. Taste and if the vegetables are well cooked, remove from the heat. Allow to cool a little, then add the eggs beaten with the lemon juice and stir well with a whisk.

Crema di tacchino

Cream of Turkey Soup

00:30 00:30

American	Ingredients	Metric/Imperial
½ lb	*Roast turkey meat*	225 g / 8 oz
1 quart	*Chicken or turkey stock*	1 litre / 1¾ pints
1	*Onion*	1
1	*Bay leaf*	1
1 cup	*Coffee (single) cream*	225 ml / 8 fl oz
	Salt and pepper	
4	*Slices of bread*	4

1. Put the turkey meat through the grinder (mincer) twice, adding a few tablespoons of stock or blend finely.
2. Put the remaining stock in a saucepan with the onion and bay leaf and bring to the boil. Add the turkey to the saucepan, remove from the heat and pass through a sieve or blender. Collect the purée in a saucepan and season. Dilute it with the cream, whipping with a small whisk.
3. When the soup is half-thick, put it on the heat and bring it almost to the boil, stirring all the time. Season with salt and pepper.
4. Cut the sliced bread into small squares and toast in the oven. Transfer the soup to a tureen and serve immediately with the toasted bread.

Soups for all occasions

Spanish chilled vegetable soup

1. *To make the soup in a blender, roughly chop most of the cucumber, 3 tomatoes, some pepper. Finely dice the rest. Hard-cook (boil) 2 eggs and dice.*

2. *Put the roughly chopped vegetables in the blender with the garlic, onions and parsley.*

3. *Add the oil, tomato and lemon juice. Blend.*

4. *Serve croûtons as a garnish with diced vegetables and eggs.*

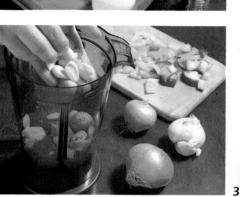

1

2

3

4

Gazpacho 

Spanish Chilled Vegetable Soup

00:20 Chilling time 02:00 | 00:00

American	Ingredients	Metric/Imperial
1	*Garlic clove*	1
1	*Cucumber*	1
4	*Large, ripe tomatoes*	4
½	*Sweet yellow pepper*	½
½	*Sweet green pepper*	½
1	*Onion*	1
3 tbsp	*Chopped parsley*	2 tbsp
5 tbsp	*Olive oil*	4 tbsp
1 cup	*Tomato juice*	225 ml / 8 fl oz
3 tbsp	*Lemon juice*	2 tbsp
	Salt and pepper	

1. Rub the inside of a soup tureen with a crushed clove of garlic. Chop the cucumber into small dice and arrange in the tureen. Skin and slice the tomatoes, deseed the peppers and peel the onion. Cut all vegetables into matchsticks or dice. Chop the parsley finely and mix with the oil, tomato and lemon juice. Stir well, season and pour over the vegetables.

2. The soup may be made by roughly chopping the ingredients in a blender or food processor. Chill and serve with croûtons.

Orzo d'agosto

August Barley

01:00 Standing time 24:00 | 02:00

American	Ingredients	Metric/Imperial
1⅔ cups	*Pearl barley*	250 g / 9 oz
1	*Garlic clove*	1
5	*Sprigs of parsley*	5
¼ cup	*Olive oil*	4 tbsp
1 lb	*White, floury potatoes*	500 g / 1 lb
2	*Italian sausages*	2
	Salt and pepper	

1. Soak the barley for at least a day, changing the water often; it should double in volume.

2. Chop the garlic and parsley together and fry gently in half the heated olive oil in a large pan. Pour in the barley, stir, then add plenty of water (including part of the soaking water). At first leave the pan uncovered until it comes to the boil, then lower the heat and cover.

3. After about 1 hour of cooking, put in the diced potatoes and the chopped sausage. Continue cooking until the barley is completely cooked when tasted.

4. Add the remaining oil and season with salt and a little freshly ground black pepper.

5. Remove from heat and leave until cold. Serve in small earthenware bowls, cold but not chilled.

FISH

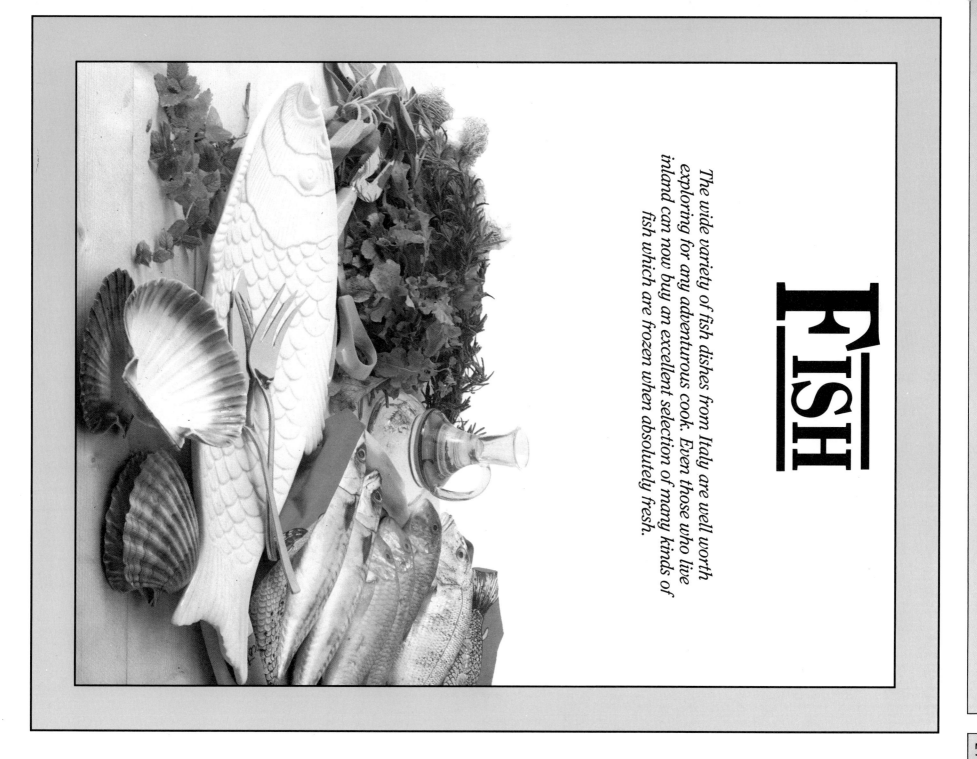

The wide variety of fish dishes from Italy are well worth exploring for any adventurous cook. Even those who live inland can now buy an excellent selection of many kinds of fish which are frozen when absolutely fresh.

Selecting and cooking fish

Make sure that fish and shellfish are really fresh when purchased. Look for bright eyes, stiff flesh and a shiny carpace in shellfish. Dull eyes accompanied by limp flesh and even the faintest whiff of ammonia indicate staleness.

Try to buy fish on the day it is going to be cooked and eaten. If storing in the refrigerator, cover loosely. It is best to cook and eat the fish within 24 hours.

Cooking fish

Deep frying

Many of the fish recipes in this book use this method as it is a popular way of eating fish in Italy. As frying requires boiling oil there are some simple but essential points to keep in mind.

- Use a deep pan and do not fill with oil. The oil should come no more than two-thirds of the way up the pan.
- Do not allow naked flames to lick up the side of the pan as even a splash of fat can cause a fire.
- If, by any unfortunate chance, the fat does catch fire never use water to douse flames. Turn off the heat immediately and cover the flames and pan, to exclude air, with a metal lid. Try not to move the pan as this can result in injury.

Food is usually coated before frying to prevent the fish breaking up and the fat soaking through the food. This can be done with flour or egg and breadcrumbs used as a coating, or by dipping the fish in batter. The fat must be heated to a high temperature to seal the outside or the result will be unappetizing. Heat the oil to 325°-375°F / 170°-190°C depending on the amount of fish which is being cooked at one time. Do not fill the pan with too much food as this lowers the temperature of the oil.

To test the temperature of the oil without a thermometer, drop a cube of stale bread into the oil; it should rise to the surface evenly browned in 1 minute.

Shallow frying or sautéing

This is a method of cooking food in a shallow frying pan with oil which reaches half way up the food to be cooked. Again the oil must be hot to seal the fish.

Broiling (grilling)

This is a good and fast method of cooking whole fish, large fillets and fish steaks. Heat the broiler (grill) before starting to cook the fish, brush with oil before cooking. It is better to make slits across the backs of whole fish such as trout before cooking, as this allows the heat to cook the fish evenly. Cooking time will depend on the size and thickness of the fish, an average-sized fish ¾ lb / 350 g will take about 10 minutes.

Poaching

This method is used for cooking whole fish, fish fillets and fish steaks in liquid which can be water, fish stock or milk. Poached fish is gently cooked over a low heat to ensure that the fish keeps its delicate flavor. It should not be boiled.

Baking

Whole fish and fish fillets can be baked in the oven with oil butter and herbs at 350°F / 180°C / Gas Mark 4. Sometimes wine or sauce is added during cooking.

Fish stock

Any liquid which has been used to cook fish becomes a stock and should be retained for use in sauces or cooking other fish. It is worth freezing if not required within a short time.

To make a good fish stock trimmings are used, so it is wise to ask the fishmonger to give you the trimmings if you are having fish filleted. Bring the fish trimmings to the boil with a chopped onion, carrot, bay leaf, bouquet garni, a few peppercorns, some white wine or white wine vinegar and 1 quart [1 litre / 1¾ pints] water. Lower the heat when the mixture boils and simmer for 25-30 minutes. Unlike beef stock, fish stock should not be cooked for hours otherwise it becomes bitter. Strain the stock and use as required.

Useful equipment for cooking fish: thermostatically controlled fryer, deep fat pan with basket, thick frying pans, fish slice.

Preparing shellfish

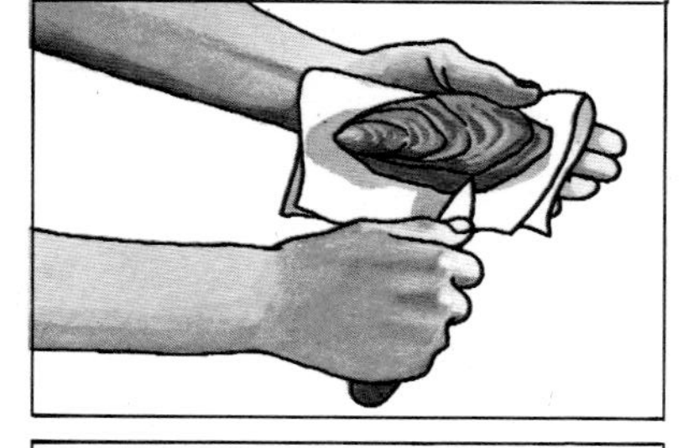

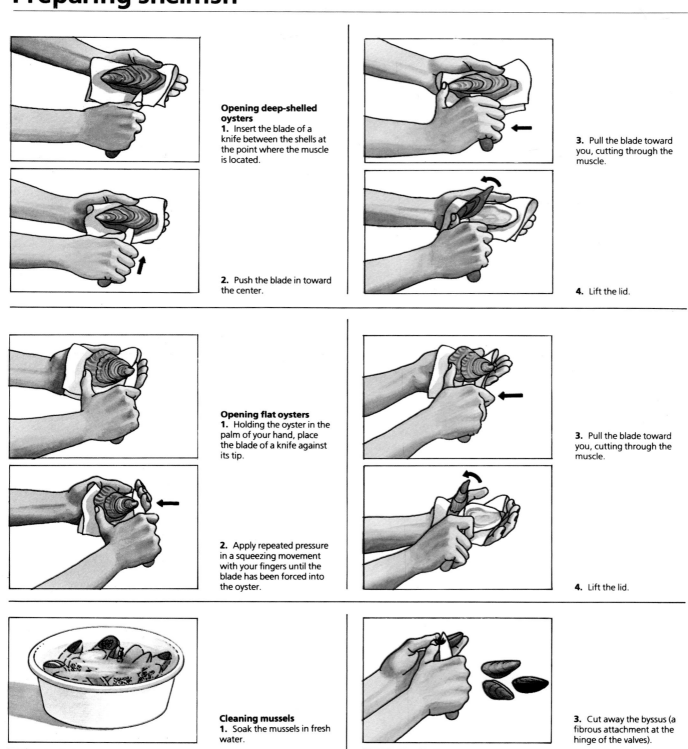

Opening deep-shelled oysters
1. Insert the blade of a knife between the shells at the point where the muscle is located.

2. Push the blade in toward the center.

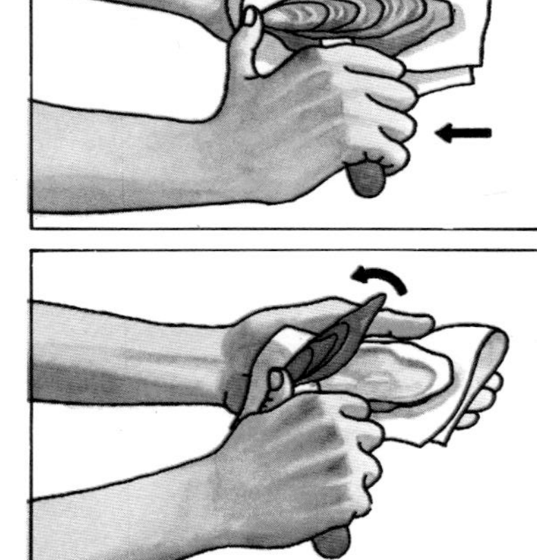

3. Pull the blade toward you, cutting through the muscle.

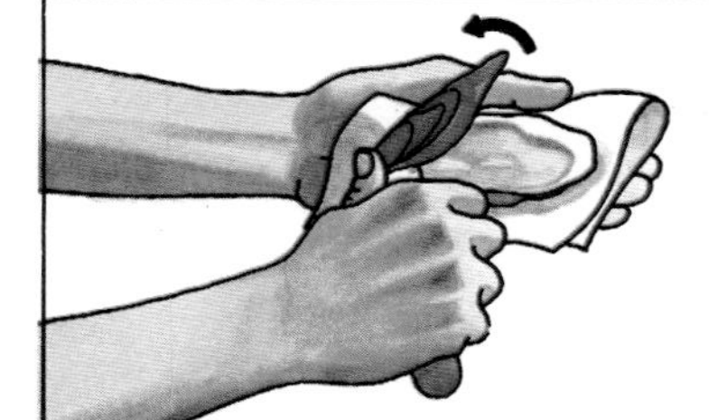

4. Lift the lid.

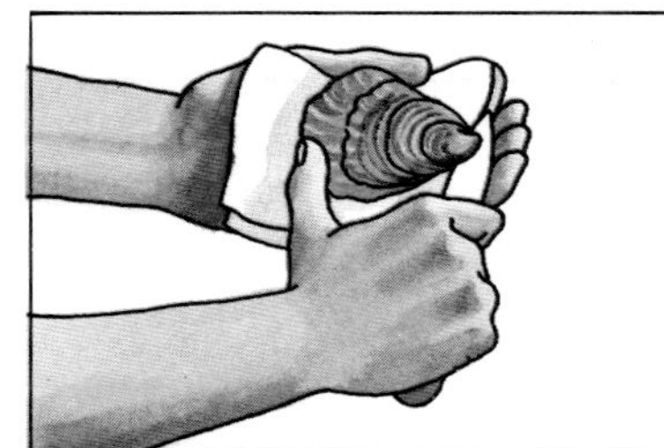

Opening flat oysters
1. Holding the oyster in the palm of your hand, place the blade of a knife against its tip.

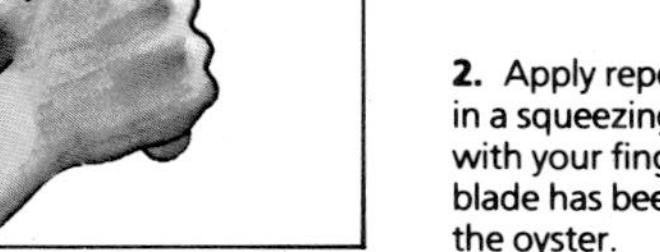

2. Apply repeated pressure in a squeezing movement with your fingers until the blade has been forced into the oyster.

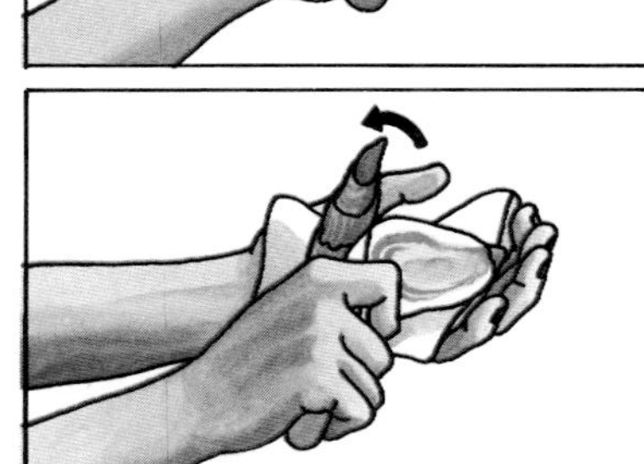

3. Pull the blade toward you, cutting through the muscle.

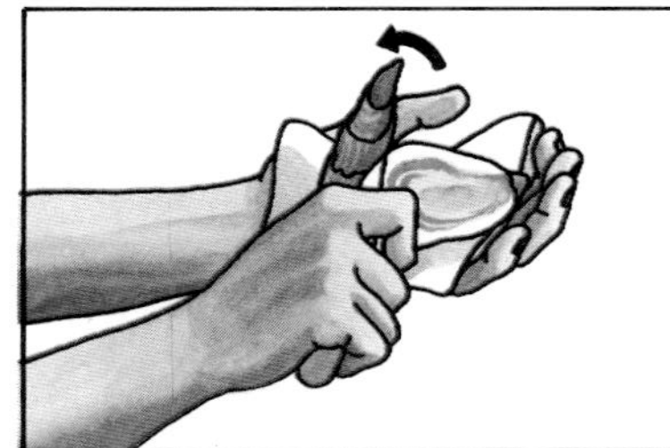

4. Lift the lid.

Cleaning mussels
1. Soak the mussels in fresh water.

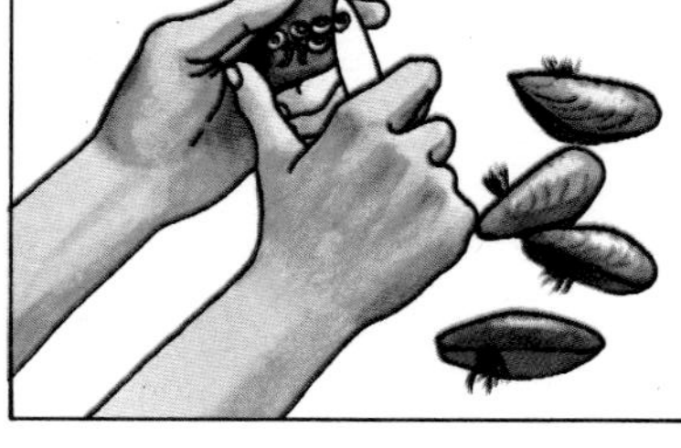

2. Scrape them with a small, pointed knife.

3. Cut away the byssus (a fibrous attachment at the hinge of the valves).

4. Rinse the mussels quickly in a colander without leaving them to soak. (Although usually sold cleaned, mussels will need to be washed again before cooking.)

To prepare and cook a lobster

1. Sever the nerve cord with the point of a sharp knife or skewer where the head meets the body. Secure the claws with rubber bands. Place in a pan of boiling water and cook for 15 minutes for the first 1 lb / 450 g and 10 minutes for each additional 1 lb / 450 g.
2. Hold the cooled drained lobster and cut through the shell and flesh as far as the tail. Remove the stomach which is near the head. Open the tail and loosen the flesh.
3. Remove the meat from the tail. Crack open the claws and remove the flesh.
4. The khaki colored liver can be served in a mayonnaise sauce. Fill the two halves with dressed meat, arrange the two halves together as a whole lobster and garnish with the tail flesh cut into slices.

1

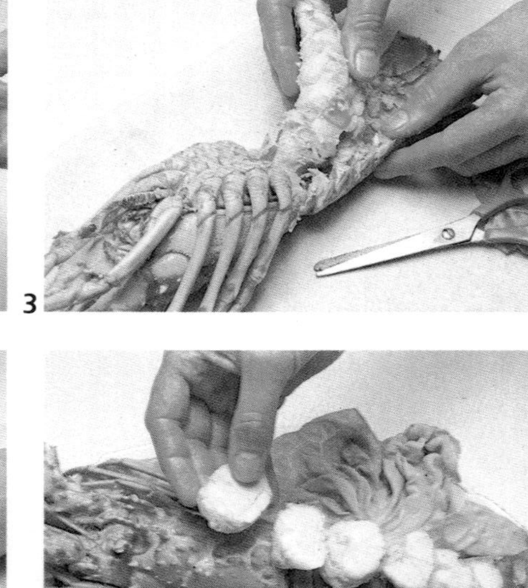
3

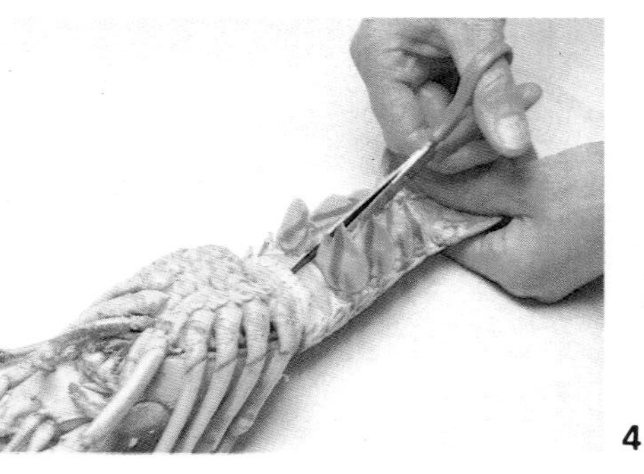
2

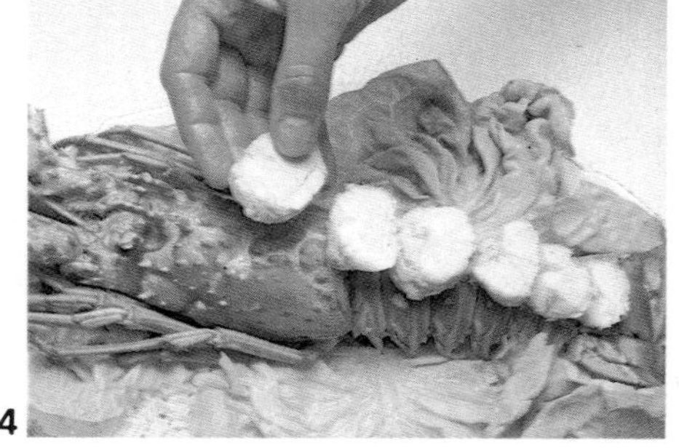
4

Preparing fish

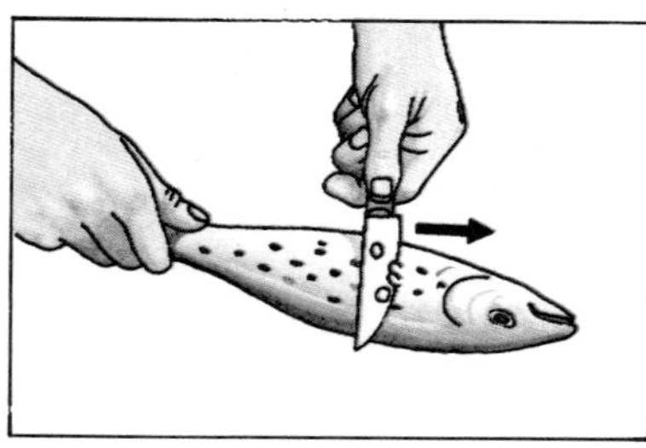

Scaling
Hold the fish by the tail and with the blade of a knife scrape off the scales, working toward the head.

Trimming
Using the scissors, cut off the back fin and the side, lower and tail fins.

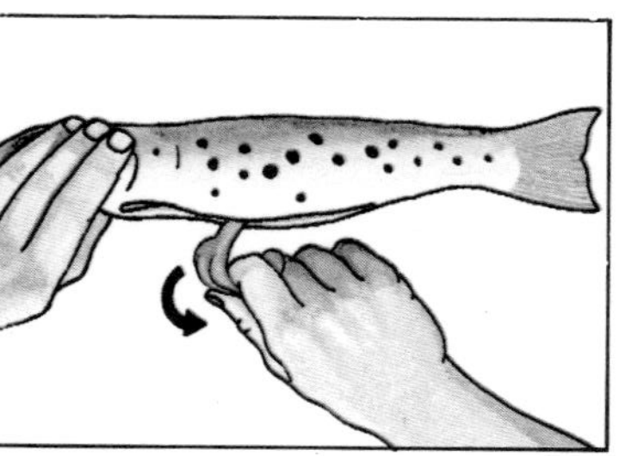

Gutting the fish through the belly
With a sharp knife, make an incision through the belly of the fish. Grasp the end of the intestine nearest the head and pull it away along the length of the slit. Cut the intestine at the tail end.

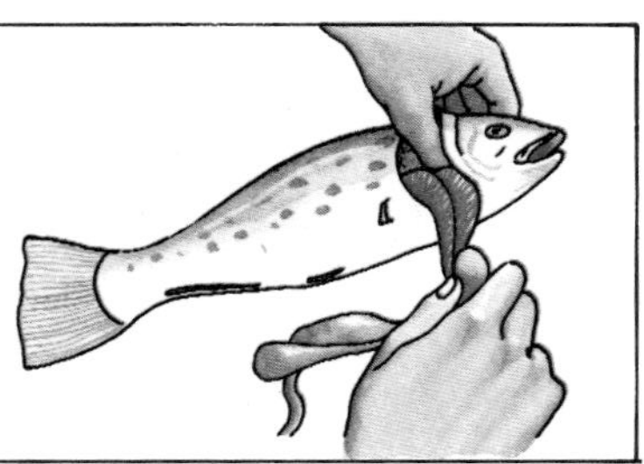

Gutting the fish through the gills
Slip your index finger into the gills, bending it to make a hook, and gently pull out the intestine. Draw out the gills and the guts.

Skinning a flat fish
1. Cut off the fins on both sides. Lay the fish flat on a chopping board, brown side up, and score the skin with your fingernail or a sharp knife along the lines where tail and fins meet body.

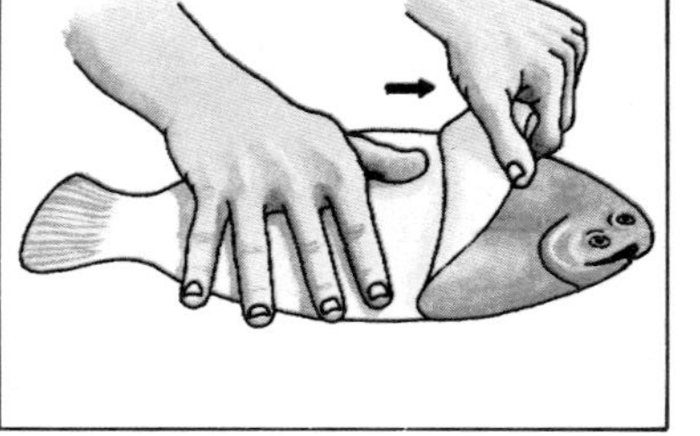

2. Insert your thumb between the flesh and the skin at the tail end and use to work the skin free. Hold the flesh steady with one hand and use the other to pull the brown skin. It will come off all at once. When you reach the head, remove the second (white) skin by detaching it under the jaw and sliding your thumb along underneath to lift it. Repeat on the white side.

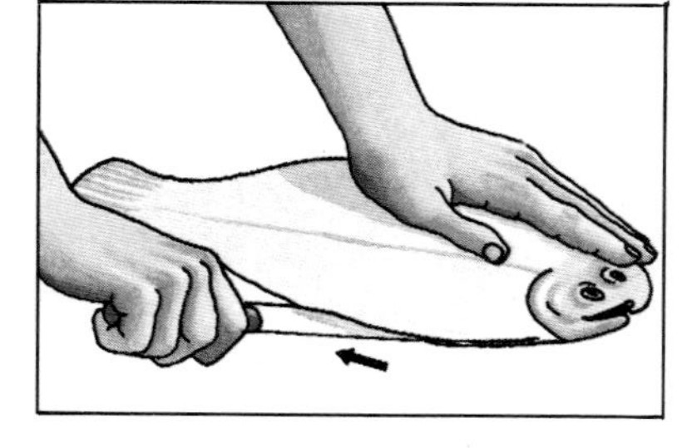

Filleting a flat fish

1. Lay the fish flat on a chopping board. Mark out the fillets with a flexible knife, sliding the blade between the pinkish edges and the whiter flesh.

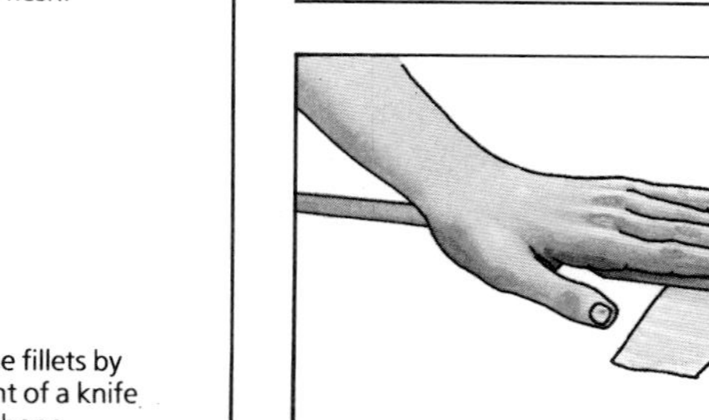

2. Separate the fillets by sliding the point of a knife along the backbone.

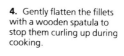

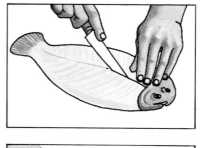

3. Lift the fillets by sliding the blade of the knife underneath them and cutting gently along the backbone. Turn the fish over and repeat.

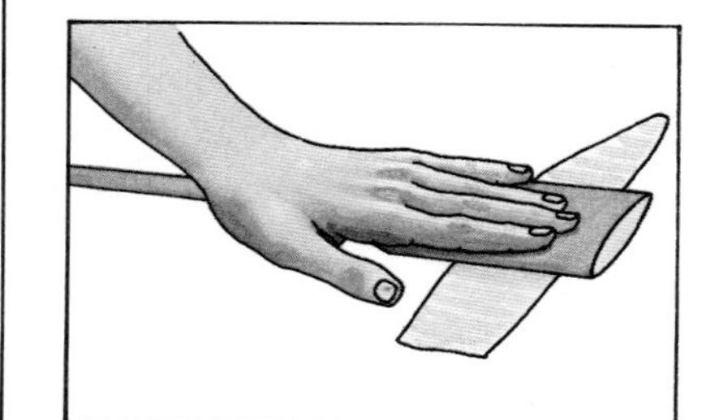

4. Gently flatten the fillets with a wooden spatula to stop them curling up during cooking.

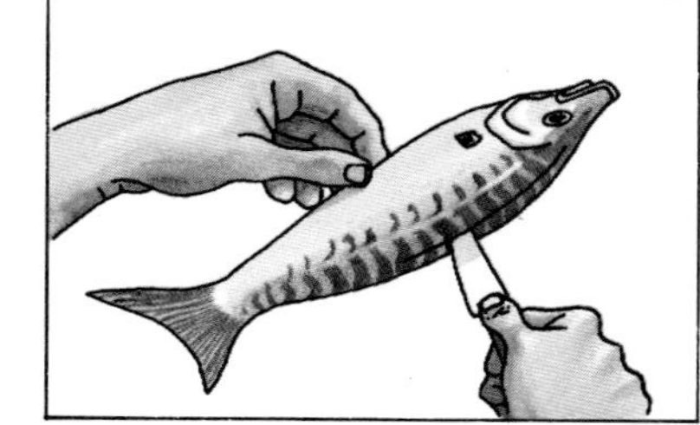

Filleting a round fish

1. Place the cleaned fish on its right side. Holding the fish by its belly, insert the point of a knife in the back, close to the head. Cut all along the back fin.

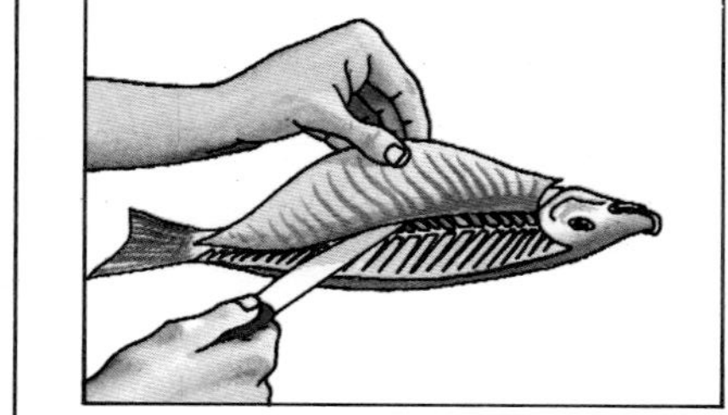

3. To remove the lower fillet, turn the fish over and slide the blade of a knife along the backbone in the same way.

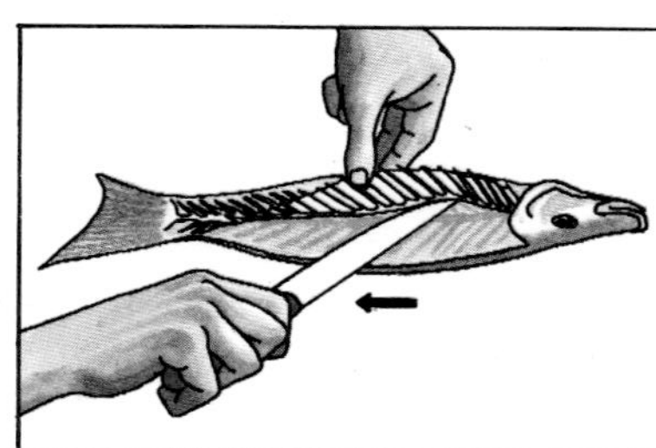

2. Make a deep cut just behind the head. Starting at the head, insert a knife between the flesh and the backbone and remove the fillet by sliding the knife gently toward the tail.

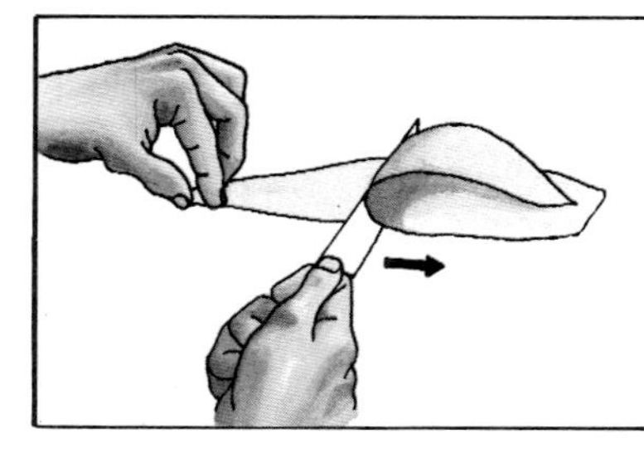

4. To skin the fillets, place them skin side downward on a cutting board and slide the blade of a knife, angled at a slant, between the skin and the flesh.

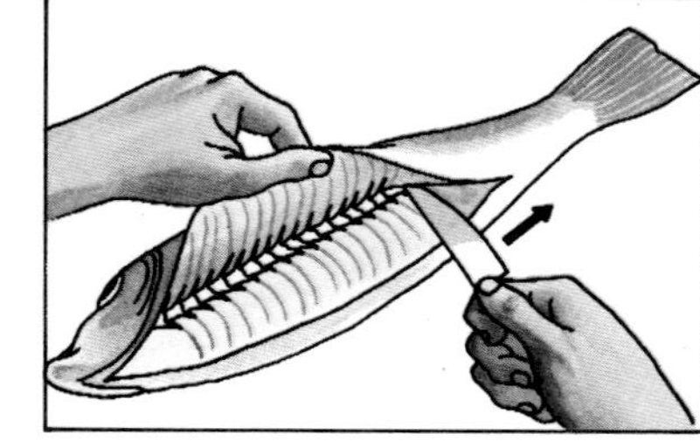

Boning a round fish

1. Gut and trim the fish. Use a small pointed knife to extend the belly slit from the anal orifice to the tail.

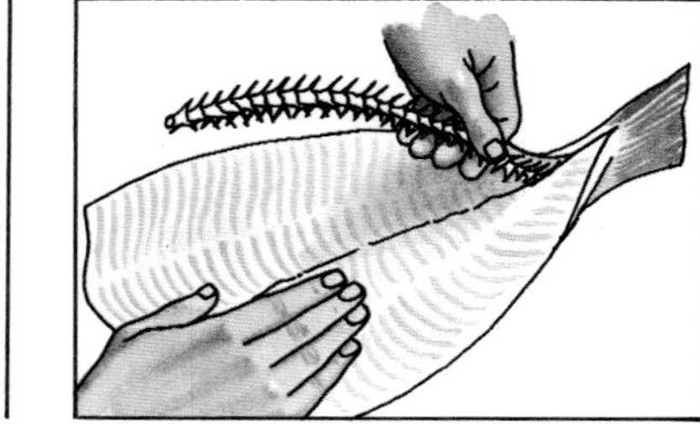

2. Pull the two halves of the fish apart and remove the ribs (break them to detach them from the backbone). Then remove the backbone.

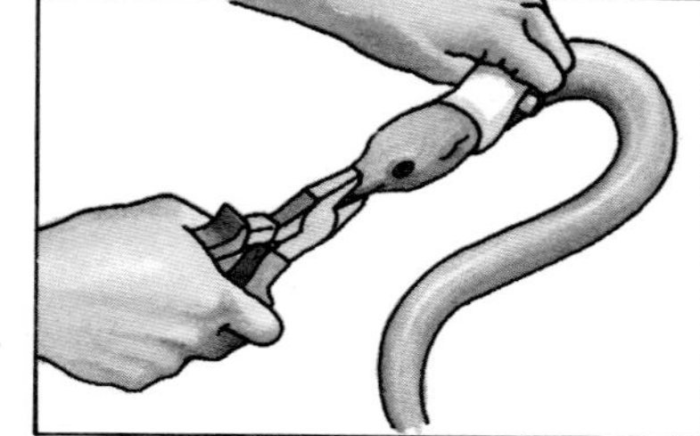

Skinning an eel

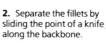

1. Make a cut right around the neck behind the head. Pull back the skin at this point (this is not easy; you may find it helps to hold the head in a pair of pliers).

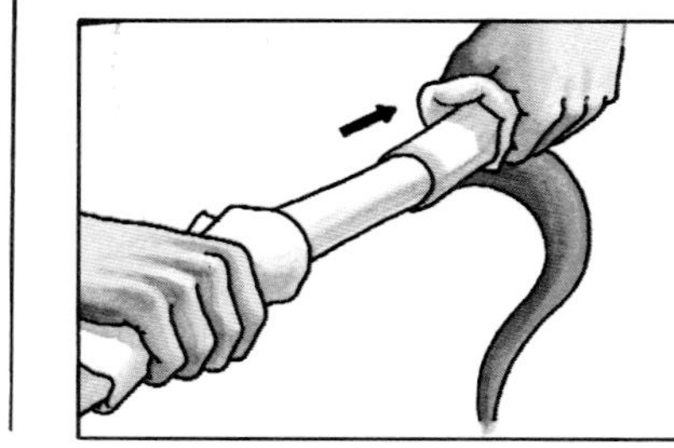

2. Hold the eel and skin with a cloth and pull the skin off backwards. It will come off all at once. Slide the knife under the intestine and remove the guts.

Grilled lobster

Aragosta ai ferri

Grilled Lobster

01:00 00:40

American	Ingredients	Metric/Imperial
1 (2 lb)	*Live lobster*	*1 (1 kg / 2 lb)*
1	*Celery stalk*	*1*
1	*Onion*	*1*
1	*Carrot*	*1*
1	*Bay leaf*	*1*
1½	*Lemons*	*1½*
	Salt and pepper	
1	*Sprig of rosemary*	*1*
2	*Garlic cloves*	*2*
½ cup	*Dry white wine*	*125 ml / 4 fl oz*
1 cup	*Vegetable oil*	*225 ml / 8 fl oz*
2 oz	*Capers*	*50 g / 2 oz*
1	*Hard-cooked (boiled) egg*	*1*

1. Put enough water to cover the lobster well in a saucepan with the celery, onion, carrot, bay leaf, half a lemon, sliced, and salt. When the water boils, plunge the lobster into it, cover immediately and cook for 25 minutes. Allow to cool in the liquid.
2. Wash the sprig of rosemary, strip the leaves from the stem and chop them very finely, mix with 1 crushed clove of garlic. Put the mixture into a bowl, add the wine, salt and pepper and stir in 4-5 tablespoons of oil.
3. Preheat the broiler (grill).
4. Cut the cooked lobster in half, brush with oil and broil for 10 minutes, basting with the oil and wine mixture.
5. Chop the capers and put into a cup with the sieved yolk of the hard-cooked egg. Heat the remaining oil in a very small saucepan and sauté the remaining garlic clove. As soon as the garlic colors, discard, take the pan off the heat and mix with the capers, egg yolk mixture, remaining basting liquid, some pepper and the juice of 1 lemon. Taste and add more salt if necessary. Transfer the grilled lobster to a dish and pour this sauce over the top.

Spiedini di scampi

Scampi on Skewers

00:30 00:40

American	Ingredients	Metric/Imperial
16	*Large scampi*	*16*
2 oz	*Ham*	*50 g / 2 oz*
24	*Sage leaves*	*24*
⅓ cup	*Margarine or butter*	*75 g / 3 oz*
1	*Sprig of rosemary*	*1*
2 cups	*Dry white wine*	*450 ml / ¾ pint*

1. While raw, remove the tails of the scampi. With a pair of scissors, cut open the hard shell part, remove the tail and wrap the middle of each tail with a slice of ham. Thread the tails onto skewers, alternating with sage leaves.
2. Melt the margarine or butter in a frying pan with a sprig of rosemary and put in the skewers. As soon as the scampi have browned, pour over the dry white wine and allow to simmer over a moderate heat. When cooked, drain and keep them hot. Serve with the pan juices.

Gamberoni in agrodolce

Prawns in Sweet and Sour Sauce

00:45 00:20

American	Ingredients	Metric/Imperial
20	*Large prawns*	20
	Salt	
2	*Slices of lemon*	2
1	*Anchovy in oil*	1
2 tbsp	*Vegetable oil*	1½ tbsp
2 tbsp	*Butter*	25 g / 1 oz
1	*Garlic clove*	1
3 tbsp	*Capers*	2 tbsp
3 tbsp	*White vinegar*	2 tbsp
2 tsp	*Sugar*	2 tsp
2 tbsp	*Chopped parsley*	1½ tbsp

1. Wash the prawns thoroughly in running water, then place into a saucepan with cold water to cover, salt and 2 slices of lemon. Bring to the boil and cook for about 15 minutes.
2. Prepare the sauce, sauté the anchovy lightly in heated oil and butter, add the crushed garlic and chopped capers, and then vinegar and sugar. Bring to the boil, stir, then turn off the heat and allow to cool slightly.
3. Drain the prawns, arrange on a dish, pour the sauce over the top and sprinkle liberally with chopped parsley. Refrigerate for 30 minutes before serving.

Aragosta all'arancia

Lobster in Orange Cream

00:30
Chilling time 02:00
00:35

American	Ingredients	Metric/Imperial
1 (2 lb)	*Lobster*	1 (1 kg / 2 lb)
1	*Onion*	1
1	*Carrot*	1
1	*Celery stalk*	1
1	*Bunch of herbs*	1
½ cup	*Dry white wine*	125 ml / 4 fl oz
¼ cup	*Butter*	50 g / 2 oz
¼ cup	*Cognac*	50 ml / 2 fl oz
	Salt and pepper	
2	*Eggs*	2
3	*Oranges*	3
1 cup	*Whipping (double) cream*	225 ml / 8 fl oz

1. Wash the live lobster. Put the vegetables into a saucepan containing enough water to cover the lobster well, add herbs, salt, white wine and bring to the boil. Drop in the lobster and cook for 20 minutes. Allow to cool slightly in liquid.
2. Drain, remove the meat from the shell and cut into fairly thin slices. Melt butter in a saucepan, add the slices of lobster, shake the pan, add cognac, set alight. Shake again over the heat, then season with salt and pepper.
3. Beat the eggs with the juice of the oranges until frothy, add this to the saucepan, then add the cream; whisk over a low heat. Arrange the lobster on a serving dish and refrigerate for at least 2 hours. Serve cold.

Prawns in sweet and sour sauce

Scampi con riso pilaff

Scampi with Rice Pilaff

00:20 01:00

American	Ingredients	Metric/Imperial
1 lb	Scampi	500 g / 1 lb
½ cup	Vegetable oil	125 ml / 4 fl oz
	White flour	
1	Onion	1
½ cup	Butter	100 g / 4 oz
3 tbsp	Cognac	2 tbsp
⅔ cup	Coffee (single) cream	150 ml / ¼ pint
	Salt	
1 quart	Stock	1 litre / 1¾ pints
2 cups	Rice	400 g / 14 oz

1. Preheat oven to 375°F / 190°C / Gas Mark 5.
2. Shell the scampi and wash them in running water, drain and dry them in a clean cloth. Heat the oil in a frying pan.
3. Dip the scampi in flour and fry over a medium heat until golden. Remove them from the oil and drain on kitchen towels to absorb the oil.
4. Finely chop half the onion and brown in half the butter. Add the scampi and allow the flavors to mingle for a few minutes. Sprinkle with cognac. When the cognac has evaporated, pour the cream over the scampi, season with salt and cook for a further 10 minutes over a low heat.
5. Heat stock to make a rice pilaff. In a large pan fry half an onion in a little butter until it is dry. Pour in the rice, stir and cover with the stock. Put the lid on the pan and put in the oven. Leave the rice in the oven, without opening the door, for 20 minutes.
6. When cooked, the rice will have completely absorbed the stock. Combine remainder of the butter with the rice. Heat the scampi and serve with the rice pilaff.

Granchi alla bordolese

Crabs in White Wine

00:30 01:00

American	Ingredients	Metric/Imperial
1	Carrot	1
1	Onion	1
1	Shallot	1
2 tbsp	Chopped parsley	1½ tbsp
½ cup	Butter	100 g / 4 oz
2	Sprigs of thyme	2
2	Bay leaves	2
20	Crabs	20
½ cup	Chopped tomatoes	125 ml / 4 fl oz
¼ cup	Cognac	50 ml / 2 fl oz
	Salt and pepper	
1 cup	Dry white wine	225 ml / 8 fl oz
2	Egg yolks	2

1. Finely chop the carrot, onion, shallot and parsley, mix together.
2. Heat half the butter in a pan and when it starts to foam, add the chopped vegetables, thyme and bay, cook over a low heat for about 15 minutes. The vegetables should be very soft. Remove the pan from the heat and put aside.
3. Clean the crabs, removing the inedible parts, and put them into a pan containing remaining hot butter. Cover and cook, shaking continuously, until they have turned red (about 10 minutes). Purée the tomatoes and keep hot.
4. When the crabs are ready, pour in the cognac and flame. Add the tomatoes, the cooked vegetable mixture, season with pepper, tip in wine, cover and cook for 20 minutes.
5. Arrange the crabs on a heated serving dish. Reduce the contents of the pan by boiling for 5-6 minutes. Stir in the egg yolks and a little water. Add the remaining butter to the sauce, let it melt and then pour all the sauce over the crabs.

Granceola gratinata

Spider-Crab au Gratin

00:30 00:30

American	Ingredients	Metric/Imperial
4	Spider-crabs	4
¼ cup	Cognac	50 ml / 2 fl oz
1 cup	Béchemal sauce (see page 162)	225 ml / 8 fl oz
2	Egg yolks	2
¼ cup	Butter	50 g / 2 oz
½ cup	Grated emmental cheese	50 g / 2 oz

1. Preheat the oven to 400°F / 200°C / Gas Mark 6.
2. Poach the crabs in plenty of salted water for 15 minutes. Cut open with a knife, scoop out the insides and put the edible parts (meat and roe) into a bowl with the cognac. Wash the shells thoroughly.
3. Prepare a béchamel sauce and add the egg yolks and the crabmeat soaked in cognac.
4. Butter the shells, pile the crabmeat preparation inside them, top with dabs of butter and the grated cheese and place in a hot oven for 10 minutes. Serve very hot.

Mitili ripieni

Stuffed Mussels

00:30 00:30

American	Ingredients	Metric/Imperial
1¾ lb	Mussels	800 g / 1¾ lb
2	Garlic cloves	2
5	Sprigs of parsley	5
¼ cup	Bread crumbs	25 g / 1 oz
1	Egg	1
	Salt and pepper	
3 tbsp	Vegetable oil	2 tbsp

1. Preheat the oven to 425°F / 220°C / Gas Mark 7.
2. Carefully wash the very fresh mussels, scraping them well. Then open the shellfish by plunging in boiling water until shells open, discard any which remain closed.
3. Crush the garlic and parsley, add the bread crumbs, egg, salt and pepper and mix with the oil. Stuff the mussels with this mixture, and close them again.
4. Put the stuffed mussels in a large foil bag, close and cook in a very hot oven for 25 minutes. Serve hot.

Muscoli alla Villeroy

Mussels Villeroy

00:30 00:30

American	Ingredients	Metric/Imperial
2 lb	Uncooked mussels	1 kg / 2 lb
3 tbsp	Butter	40 g / 1½ oz
⅓ cup	Flour	40 g / 1½ oz
2¼ cups	Milk	500 ml / 18 fl oz
	Salt and pepper	
4	Eggs	4
¾ cup	Bread crumbs	75 g / 3 oz
2½ cups	Oil	600 ml / 1 pint

1. Wash the mussels and rinse well under cold running water. Place in a large pan with a little water and shake over a high heat until the shells open.
2. Remove the mussels from their shells and drain.
3. Make a béchamel sauce (see page 162) with butter, flour, milk and seasoning. It must be fairly thick and should be bound with raw egg yolk.
4. Beat the remaining eggs in one basin and put the bread crumbs in another. Heat some oil in the frying pan. Dip each mussel in the béchamel sauce, then the bread crumbs, the beaten eggs and again in the bread crumbs. Fry in the oil and serve hot with slices of lemon.

Cozze gratinate all'aglio

Baked Mussels with Garlic Topping

00:20 00:20

American	Ingredients	Metric/Imperial
1¾ lb	Large mussels	800 g / 1¾ lb
4	Garlic cloves	4
3 tbsp	Chopped parsley	2 tbsp
	Salt and pepper	
½ cup	Butter	100 g / 4 oz
½ cup	Bread crumbs	50 g / 2 oz
3 tbsp	Vegetable oil	2 tbsp
	Sprigs of parsley	

1. Preheat the oven to 450°F / 230°C / Gas Mark 8. Scrub the mussels well and drop into boiling water until they have all opened. Discard any closed shells.
2. Chop the parsley and garlic very finely, add salt and pepper and blend thoroughly with softened butter until the mixture is creamy. Place a spoonful of this butter in each half-shell containing a mussel and top with plenty of bread crumbs.
3. Arrange the prepared mussels on an oiled baking tray and bake in a hot oven for 20 minutes. Serve very hot, decorated with sprigs of parsley.

1

2

3

4

1. Put the washed mussels in a large pan with the butter, some parsley and a bay leaf.
2. Add a glass of white wine.
3. Shake the pan over a high heat until the mussel shells open. Discard any that do not open.
4. Thicken the pan juices with a teaspoon each of butter and flour mixed together and blended into the juices. Stir over gentle heat.

Capesante gratinate

Scalloped Mussels

00:25 00:25

American	Ingredients	Metric/Imperial
¾ lb	*Sweetbreads*	350 g / 12 oz
	Flour	
1	*Small onion*	1
2 tbsp	*Butter*	25 g / 1 oz
⅓ cup	*Olive oil*	75 ml / 3 fl oz
1 lb	*Mussels*	450 g / 1 lb
1	*Bay leaf*	1
1	*Garlic clove*	1
	Salt and pepper	
¼ cup	*Dry white wine*	50 ml / 2 fl oz
½ tsp	*Cornstarch (cornflour)*	½ tsp
⅓ cup	*Whipping (double) cream*	75 ml / 3 fl oz

1. Skin the sweetbreads then scald in boiling water for 5 minutes; drain, cut into small pieces and toss in flour.
2. Preheat the oven to 425°F / 220°C / Gas Mark 7.
3. Chop the onion and sauté in butter and oil; when it has colored slightly, add the sweetbreads and cook until golden, then the mussels (with shells properly scrubbed and washed), the bay leaf and clove of garlic. Sauté these for a few minutes, shake over the heat, then season with a little salt and pour in the wine. Cook for another 5 minutes.
4. Remove the bay leaf and garlic and thicken the sauce with cornstarch. Pour in the cream, add freshly ground black pepper, stir well and spoon the preparation into scallop shells. Crisp in a very hot oven for 10 minutes. The mussels may be removed from the shells before being cooked in the oven.

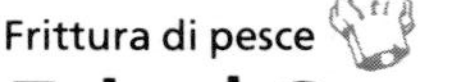

Frittura di pesce

Fried Seafood Platter

01:00 00:30

American	Ingredients	Metric/Imperial
4	*Small lemon sole*	4
4	*Mullet*	4
5 oz	*Whitebait*	150 g / 5 oz
½ lb	*Scampi*	225 g / 8 oz
1 lb	*Mussels*	500 g / 1 lb
½ lb	*Sea-strawberries (tiny squid)*	225 g / 8 oz
1	*Bunch of parsley*	1
1	*Garlic clove (optional)*	1
1 cup	*Vegetable oil*	225 ml / 8 fl oz
¼ cup	*Butter*	50 g / 2 oz
3 tbsp	*Cognac*	2 tbsp
2	*Lemons*	2

1. Skin, gut, wash and drain the soles. Remove the scales from the mullet and gut, wash and drain. Clean and wash the whitebait and squeeze to remove the innards. Shell the scampi.
2. Scrub the mussels, put them into boiling water until they open, then remove the meat and discard the shells. Clean and wash the sea-strawberries.
3. Wash and chop the parsley with the clove of garlic.
4. Flour all the fish and toss in a sieve to remove any excess.
5. Heat plenty of oil in a large frying pan until very hot, then fry the fish one batch at a time. When the first batch is cooked, transfer to a sheet of absorbent kitchen paper to drain. Sprinkle with salt and keep warm while the remainder of the fish is being cooked.
6. When all the fish have been fried, keep warm.
7. Heat the butter and a little oil in a small pan and sauté most of the bunch of parsley, chopped, add cognac and a few drops of lemon juice.
8. Arrange the fish on a heated serving dish, keeping the varieties separate, pour the sauce over them and serve very hot garnished with lemon slices and sprigs of parsley.

Fried seafood platter

Gamberi della Camargue

Crayfish Poached in Wine

00:20 00:25

American	Ingredients	Metric/Imperial
2 (¾ lb)	*Crayfish*	2 (350 g / 12 oz)
3 cups	*Dry white wine*	700 ml / 1¼ pints
¼ cup	*Calvados*	50 ml / 2 fl oz
	Salt and pepper	
8	*Slices of crusty bread*	8

1. Wash the crayfish very carefully and dry with a clean cloth.
2. Heat the wine and calvados in a saucepan with salt and pepper to taste. When the liquid boils, throw in the crayfish, reduce the heat, cover and simmer for at least 15 minutes.
3. Remove, drain and arrange on a dish. Serve with toasted slices of crusty bread.

Cook's tip: retain cooking liquid to use as stock for cooking other fish or for a fish soup.

Peoci alla bulgara

Fried Mussels

00:30 | 00:30

American	Ingredients	Metric/Imperial
2 lb	*Washed mussels*	1 kg / 2 lb
2	*Eggs*	2
½ cup	*Bread crumbs*	50 g / 2 oz
2	*Onions*	2
1¼ cups	*Oil for frying*	300 ml / ½ pint
2	*Lemons*	2

1. Put the well washed mussels into a large pan with 2-3 tablespoons water, shake over a high heat until shells open.
2. Remove mussels from shells, dip each one in beaten egg and then in bread crumbs.
3. Cut the onions into rings and dip in egg and bread crumbs. Fry the mussels and rings in batches in very hot oil, a few at a time, drain on absorbent paper towels. Serve on a heated dish with slices of lemon.

Omelette della festa

Festive Omelette

00:10 | 00:10

American	Ingredients	Metric/Imperial
¾ lb	*Shrimps*	350 g / 12 oz
6	*Eggs*	6
	Salt and pepper	
2 tbsp	*Butter*	25 g / 1 oz

1. To make this omelette, use either potted shrimps (they are very small and delicate, but do not have very much flavour), or fresh or frozen shelled shrimps. Put fresh shrimps in boiling water for 5 minutes and remove the shells.
2. Beat the eggs with salt and a pinch of pepper. Heat a large piece of butter in a frying pan, pour in the eggs and heat until they are just setting. Quickly add the shrimp filling. Season with salt and pepper. Fold over the omelette, heat for a moment or two more and serve.

Conchiglie Saint Jacques 

Coquilles St. Jacques

00:35 | 00:30

American	Ingredients	Metric/Imperial
¾ lb	*Sweetbreads*	350 g / 12 oz
½ cup	*Butter*	100 g / 4 oz
3	*Anchovies*	3
	or	
1 tsp	*Anchovy paste*	1 tsp
1	*Large bunch of parsley*	1
12	*Scallops*	12
1 tbsp	*White vinegar*	1 tbsp
¾ lb	*Mushrooms*	350 g / 12 oz
1 cup	*Béchamel sauce (see page 162)*	225 ml / 8 fl oz
	Salt and pepper	
½ cup	*Grated parmesan cheese*	50 g / 2 oz
½ cup	*Bread crumbs*	50 g / 2 oz

Festive omelette

1. Cook the sweetbreads for 20 minutes in salted water to which vinegar has been added, drain and chop.
2. Make a paste by beating the butter, anchovies (or anchovy paste) and some finely chopped parsley together.
3. Wash the scallops well (leaving the white meat and coral in place), sprinkle with vinegar and spread with the paste.
4. Heat the oven to 425°F / 220°C / Gas Mark 7.
5. Wash the mushrooms, slice finely and sauté with butter and remaining chopped parsley.
6. Make the béchamel sauce; stir in the grated parmesan, the sweetbreads and mushrooms, season with salt and pepper. Pile this mixture on top of the scallops.
7. Sprinkle bread crumbs over each scallop and place in a hot oven for 10 minutes before serving.

Pagelli profumati

Fragrant Porgies (Sea Bream)

00:10 00:25

American	Ingredients	Metric/Imperial
4	*Porgies (sea bream)*	4
12	*Sprigs of mint*	12
½ cup	*Vegetable oil*	125 ml / 4 fl oz
	Salt and pepper	

1. Preheat oven to 400°F / 200°C / Gas Mark 6.
2. Have the fishmonger clean and scale the porgies. Put 2 sprigs of mint in the belly of each fish and 1 small sprig in the gills.
3. Grease a baking pan with oil and arrange the fish in a row lightly seasoned with salt and pepper and brushed over with the oil. Put in a hot oven for 20 minutes or until cooked and serve immediately with a salad.

Orata in arrosto

Baked (Gilthead) Porgy

00:20 01:00

American	Ingredients	Metric/Imperial
1 (2 lb)	*Porgy (Gilthead bream)*	1 (1 kg / 2 lb)
	Salt	
Scant ¼ cup	*Vegetable oil*	3 tbsp
⅓ cup	*Butter*	75 g / 3 oz
¼ cup	*Dry white wine*	50 ml / 2 fl oz
1 tbsp	*Chopped parsley*	1 tbsp

1. Preheat oven to 400°F / 200°C / Gas Mark 6.
2. Clean the fish, make a few incisions to help even cooking. Season with salt, rub with oil, put in an oiled heat-resistant dish and pour a little oil over the fish. Bake in a hot oven. It is best to begin cooking using oil.
3. After 10 minutes, remove and pour over half the melted butter. Cook for a further 30 minutes, remove from the oven, and move fish carefully on to a serving dish.

Dentex (perch) served on a bed of sliced potatoes

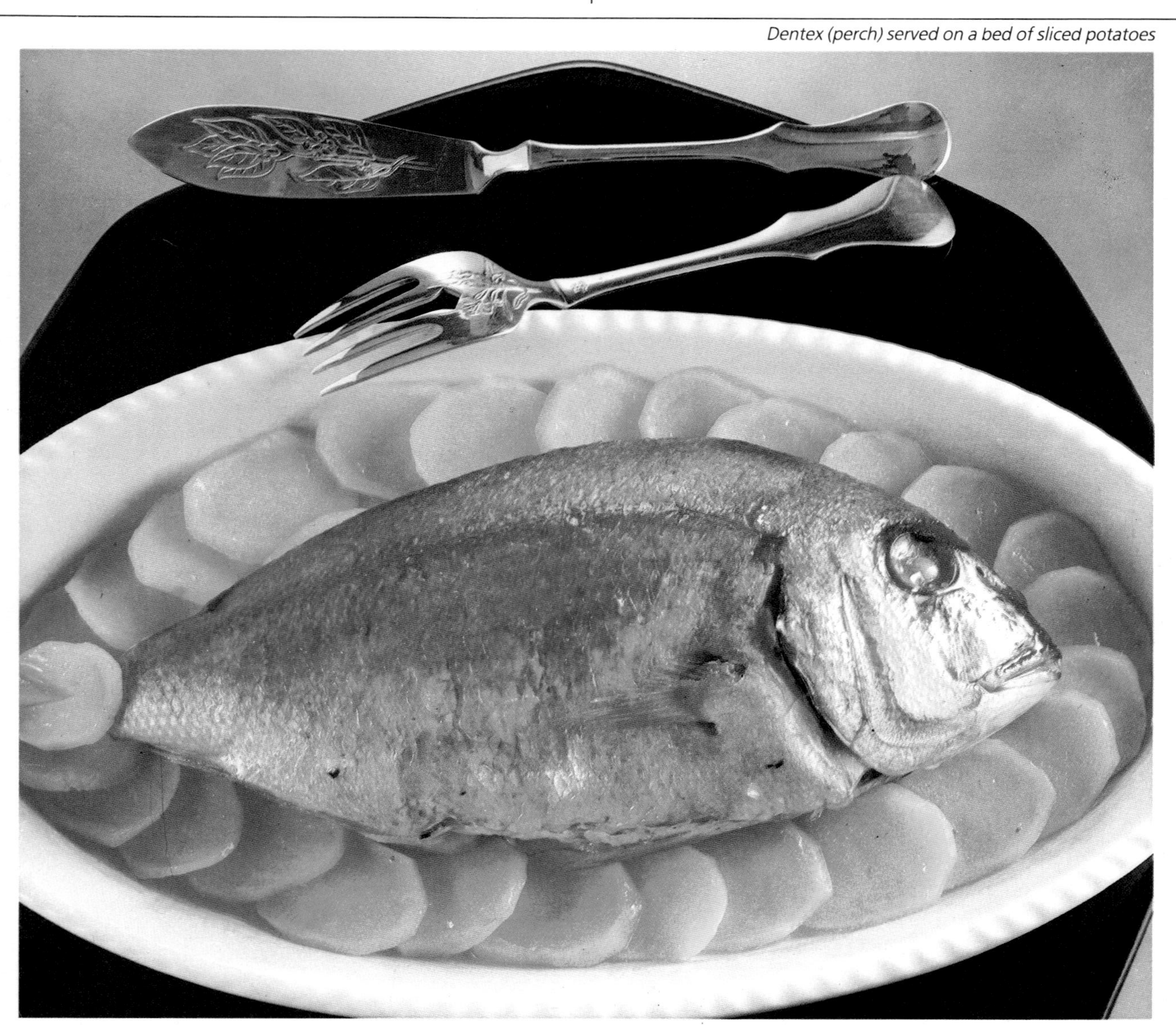

4. Ladle out the cooking juices into a pan and add a little white wine. Heat for a few minutes. Finally away from the heat, add some butter and parsley. Pour this sauce over the hot fish.

Merluzzetti in verde

Striped Bream in Green

00:20 00:25

American	Ingredients	Metric/Imperial
2 lb	*Striped bream*	*1 kg / 2 lb*
2	*Lemons*	*2*
1	*Carrot*	*1*
3 or 4	*Peppercorns*	*3 or 4*
Scant ¼ cup	*Vegetable oil*	*3 tbsp*
	Salt and pepper	
1	*Sweet yellow pepper*	*1*
5 tbsp	*Capers in brine*	*4 tbsp*
1 tsp	*Chopped chives*	*1 tsp*
5	*Sprigs of parsley*	*5*

1. Thoroughly clean the striped bream and wash them in running water. Immerse in cold water in a pan and cook on a low heat adding 2 slices of lemon, 1 scraped and sliced carrot and a few peppercorns.
2. As soon as the fish are cooked, drain, remove the skin and bones, chop up into small pieces and put in a bowl while still hot, flavor with oil, lemon juice, salt and pepper, beaten together.
3. Cut open the sweet pepper, remove the seeds and membrane, cut into thin strips and mix with the fish.
4. Wash the capers, chop and add to the fish. Mix well, then place on a large plate or in an earthenware dish. Sprinkle with a little chopped chives and sprigs of parsley. Put in the refrigerator for 30 minutes before serving.

Boghe fritte alla San Fruttuoso

Fried Porgy (Bream)

00:15 00:20

American	Ingredients	Metric/Imperial
2 lb	*Porgy (Bream)*	*900 g / 2 lb*
2	*Eggs*	*2*
	Pepper	
½ cup	*Bread crumbs*	*50 g / 2 oz*
¼ cup	*Oil*	*50 ml / 2 fl oz*
2	*Garlic cloves*	*2*
	Sprigs of basil	
1	*Onion*	*1*

1. Clean and cut the porgy, remove the fins and scrape off the scales. Wash and dry, then dip into seasoned beaten egg, and then into bread crumbs.
2. Heat the oil in a heavy pan with 2 crushed cloves of garlic. When hot, add the fish and cook for 10 minutes before turning. Turn only once, fry until golden, drain on absorbent kitchen towels and serve very hot. Garnish with sprigs of fresh basil and thin raw onion rings.

Sarago con funghi

Porgies (White Bream) with Mushrooms

00:35 01:00

American	Ingredients	Metric/Imperial
1 (1¾ lb)	*Porgies (white bream)*	*1 (800 g / 1¾ lb)*
2 tbsp	*Chopped parsley*	*1½ tbsp*
1	*Garlic clove*	*1*
1	*Small onion*	*1*
¼ tsp	*Oregano*	*¼ tsp*
	Salt and pepper	
½ cup	*Vegetable oil*	*125 ml / 4 fl oz*
½ cup	*Dry white wine*	*125 ml / 4 fl oz*
2½-3 cups	*Mushrooms*	*275 g / 10 oz*
3 tbsp	*Butter*	*40 g / 1½ oz*
1	*Lemon*	*1*
2 tbsp	*White flour*	*2 tbsp*

1. Trim the fins, cut open on the belly side and remove the intestines, wash thoroughly under running water.
2. Make 2 or 3 parallel cuts with a knife to make cooking more even.
3. Preheat the oven to 350°F / 180°C / Gas Mark 4.
4. Chop the parsley, garlic and onion very finely. Arrange half the onion on the bottom of an ovenproof dish. Place the fish on it with half the parsley and a pinch of oregano. Season with salt and pepper and some of the oil and the wine.
5. Put the fish in a moderate oven, occasionally basting with the sauce collecting at the bottom of the dish.
6. Clean the mushrooms, wash them and cut into slices. Heat about two thirds of butter and 2 tablespoons [25 ml / 1 fl oz] of oil in a small frying pan. Add the remaining parsley. Fry gently for a moment, then put in the mushrooms, season with salt and pepper, stir and cook over a moderate heat for about 10 minutes then add to the fish, sprinkle with lemon juice and finish cooking.
7. When the fish is cooked, take the dish out of the oven, place fish on the heated serving dish, arrange the mushrooms around it and keep hot.
8. Strain the contents of the ovenproof dish, collecting it in a small saucepan. Make a paste from the flour and some butter, add it to the juice. Put the saucepan over a low heat, and stirring continuously, boil the sauce for 2 minutes, taste it and add salt, if necessary. Pour onto the serving dish and serve.

Branzino in bellavista

Sea Bass in Aspic

01:00 Setting time 01:30 — 00:50

American	Ingredients	Metric/Imperial
1 (2 lb)	*Sea bass*	*1 (1 kg / 2 lb)*
1	*Carrot*	*1*
1	*Onion*	*1*
1	*Celery stalk*	*1*
1	*Bay leaf*	*1*
	Salt	
1 envelope	*Gelatin*	*1 sachet*
12	*Olives*	*12*
4	*Gherkins*	*4*
2	*Lemons*	*2*

1. Clean and gut the fish.
2. Put carrot, onion, celery and bay leaf into a saucepan containing 2 quarts [2 litres / 3½ pints] of water, bring to the boil and simmer for 20 minutes. Add salt and the fish, simmer for a further 20 minutes, then turn off the heat and allow the fish to cool in the liquid.
4. Prepare the gelatin according to the maker's instructions or by sprinkling on to 3 tablespoons boiling, strained fish stock. When dissolved make up to 1¼ cups [300 ml / ½ pint] with strained fish liquid.
5. Pour some of the gelatin onto a serving dish and set in the refrigerator.
6. Handling the fish with great care, drain and remove part of the skin, lay on the dish of prepared gelatin.
7. Decorate with olives and gherkins, then pour some of the remaining gelatin over. Refrigerate for 30 minutes, pour more gelatin over and chill. Continue until all gelatin is used. Serve garnished with lemon wedges or slices.

Merluzzo fritto

Fried Cod

00:20 — 00:25

American	Ingredients	Metric/Imperial
	Salt	
1 lb	*Cod*	*500 g / 1 lb*
½	*Garlic clove*	*½*
3	*Fresh tomatoes*	*3*
2	*Large onions*	*2*
Scant ¼ cup	*Oil for frying*	*3 tbsp*
1	*Sweet red pepper*	*1*
3 tbsp	*Chopped parsley*	*2 tbsp*

1. Place a pan of salted water over a low heat, without allowing to boil. Carefully place the cod in the pan. As soon as it is cooked, turn off the heat and leave it in the water for about 15 minutes to cool.
2. Peel and crush the garlic, cut the skinned tomatoes into large pieces and chop the onions very thinly.
3. Remove the cod from the pan, take out the bones and skin, cut into large pieces.
4. Put the oil into a thick-bottomed frying pan, brown the onions and tomatoes, add the pieces of fish, the crushed garlic, the salt and the very finely deseeded chopped red pepper. Cover and cook for a further 10 minutes over a low heat. Wash and finely chop the parsley and sprinkle over the fish before serving.

Baccalà alla portoghese

Portuguese Salt Codfish

00:30 Soaking time: 12:00 — 00:40

American	Ingredients	Metric/Imperial
2 lb	*Salt codfish*	*1 kg / 2 lb*
2 cups	*Milk*	*450 ml / ¾ pint*
4	*Onions*	*4*
¼ cup	*Vegetable oil*	*50 ml / 2 fl oz*
2 lb	*Potatoes*	*1 kg / 2 lb*
1	*Garlic clove*	*1*
	Pepper	
½ tsp	*Oregano*	*½ tsp*
¼ tsp	*Nutmeg*	*¼ tsp*
⅔ cup	*Black olives*	*100 g / 4 oz*
2 tbsp	*Chopped parsley*	*1½ tbsp*

1. Leave the codfish in cold water for at least 12 hours, then put it into boiling water, cover and cook for about 20 minutes.
2. Drain, remove the skin and all the bones, cut the fish up and soak in milk for about 1 hour.
3. Preheat the oven to 350°F / 180°C / Gas Mark 4.
4. Chop the onions finely and gently sauté in the heated oil until they are soft but not brown. Slice the potatoes, add to the onions, cook for 10 minutes and then add the codfish, crushed garlic, pepper, oregano and a pinch of nutmeg. Stir and put the dish in the oven for 20 minutes or until potatoes are cooked.
5. Stone the olives. Sprinkle the olives and chopped parsley over the codfish just before serving. Serve very hot.

Baccalà 'speciale estivo'

Summer Codfish

01:00 Soaking time 08:00 — 00:20

American	Ingredients	Metric/Imperial
1¾ lb	*Dried codfish*	*800 g / 1¾ lb*
14 oz	*New potatoes*	*400 g / 14 oz*
1	*Garlic clove*	*1*
1	*Bunch of parsley*	*1*
⅔ cup	*Olive oil*	*150 ml / ¼ pint*
1	*Lemon*	*1*
	Salt and pepper	
2	*Firm tomatoes*	*2*
6	*Radishes*	*6*
6	*Porcini mushrooms in oil*	*6*

1. Soak the codfish overnight, put it into a saucepan, cover with water and boil for about 20 minutes.
2. Wash the potatoes and boil in a separate saucepan until cooked. Cool, peel and cut into cubes.
3. Crush the garlic and chop parsley; put into a bowl and add the olive oil and lemon juice.
4. Drain the codfish, cool, then cut into fairly small pieces. Mix into the parsley sauce with the potatoes and season with salt and pepper.
5. Transfer to a salad dish, decorate with sliced tomatoes, radishes and mushrooms, chill before serving.

Seppie in umido con riso

Stewed Cuttlefish with Rice

00:25 00:30

American	Ingredients	Metric/Imperial
1 lb	*Cuttlefish*	500 g / 1 lb
⅓ cup	*Vegetable oil*	5 tbsp
1 tbsp	*Chopped parsley*	1 tbsp
1	*Garlic clove*	1
½ lb	*Peeled tomatoes, fresh or canned*	225 g / 8 oz
	Salt and pepper	
1 ½ cups	*Long grain rice*	300 g / 11 oz

1. Skin and wash the cuttlefish, discard the sac containing the inky liquid. Cut lengthways into a large number of strips.
2. Heat the oil, finely chop the parsley and garlic, and brown in the oil. Add the cuttlefish. Crush the peeled tomatoes with a fork and add to the fish. Season with salt, sprinkle with pepper and cook for 20 minutes.
3. Meanwhile cook the rice 'al dente' in lightly salted water, drain and arrange in a large soup-tureen or heated casserole. Pour the cuttlefish and sauce over the rice.

Seppie ripiene alla Corsaro Nero

Stuffed Cuttlefish Corsaro Nero

00:30 00:50

American	Ingredients	Metric/Imperial
1 ½ lb	*Cuttlefish*	700 g / 1 ½ lb
Scant ¼ cup	*Vegetable oil*	3 tbsp
1	*Onion*	1
1	*Garlic clove*	1
2 tbsp	*Chopped parsley*	1 ½ tbsp
2 oz	*Crustless bread*	50 g / 2 oz
¼ cup	*Milk*	50 ml / 2 fl oz
½ cup	*Dry white wine*	125 ml / 4 fl oz
	Salt and pepper	
1 ¼ cups	*Béchamel sauce (see page 162)*	300 ml / ½ pint
2	*Hard-cooked (boiled) eggs*	2
3 tbsp	*Grated cheese*	2 tbsp
4	*Tomatoes*	4

1. Using scissors, cut open the belly side of the cuttlefish and clean thoroughly. Discard the sac of inky liquid, the eyes and mouth. Wash carefully under cold running water and drain, belly downwards on a cloth.
2. Heat the oil in a saucepan and brown the chopped onion, crushed garlic and parsley. Soak the crustless bread in milk, squeeze it, crumble and add to the fried onion. Sprinkle with the dry white wine, season with salt and allow the sauce to thicken.
3. Prepare a béchamel sauce, season well, remove from the heat, add finely chopped hard-cooked eggs to the sauce together with the grated cheese. Stir thoroughly, adjusting the seasoning.
4. Preheat the oven to 350°F / 180°C / Gas / Mark 4.
5. Fill the cuttlefish with this mixture. Wash the tomatoes and cut in half. Close the opening of each cuttlefish with half a tomato and arrange them in an ovenproof dish.
6. Pour béchamel sauce over the fish, cover with oiled parchment (greaseproof paper) and cook in a moderate oven for about 40 minutes. If the cuttlefish becomes rather dry, add a little stock or dry white wine.

Palombo ai piselli

Dogfish with Peas

00:10 00:25

American	Ingredients	Metric/Imperial
1	*Onion*	1
2 tbsp	*Vegetable oil*	1 ½ tbsp
2 tbsp	*Butter*	25 g / 1 oz
4	*Dogfish (rock salmon) slices*	4
	Salt and pepper	
6	*Tomatoes*	6
¼ tsp	*Oregano*	¼ tsp
1 cup	*Garden peas*	150 g / 5 oz

1. Slowly fry a very finely chopped onion in a large frying pan with oil and butter. As soon as it begins to turn brown, add the slices of dogfish and season with salt and pepper.
2. Skin the tomatoes (canned tomatoes may be used) and chop up finely. Add tomatoes, oregano and drained peas to the fish. Cover and cook over a moderate heat for 20 minutes.

Palombo fritto 

Fried Dogfish

00:15 00:15

American	Ingredients	Metric/Imperial
1	*Small bunch of parsley*	1
4	*Dogfish (rock salmon) slices*	4
½ cup	*Milk*	125 ml / 4 fl oz
½ cup	*Flour*	50 g / 2 oz
	Oil for frying	
1	*Lemon*	1

1. Wash and drain the parsley. Wash and fry the fish and immerse in milk for 5 minutes. Dip the fish slices in flour, shake to remove any excess.
2. Heat plenty of oil in a fryer or in a large frying pan. When it begins to haze, put in the slices of dogfish. Brown the fish on both sides. Drain and wipe off the excess oil with kitchen towels.
3. Pick good sprigs of parsley and toss them in the boiling oil for a few seconds. Serve the fried dogfish on a serving dish garnished with the fried parsley (be careful not to burn it) and slices of lemon.

Palombo alla francese

Dogfish French-Style

00:30 00:30

American	Ingredients	Metric/Imperial
1	*Small onion*	*1*
3	*Anchovies in brine*	*3*
1 tbsp	*Chopped parsley*	*1 tbsp*
1	*Garlic clove*	*1*
⅔ cup	*Vegetable oil*	*150 ml / ¼ pint*
½ cup	*Dry white wine*	*125 ml / 4 fl oz*
1	*Lemon*	*1*
4 drops	*Worcester sauce*	*4 drops*
	Salt and pepper	
4 (6 oz)	*Dogfish (rock salmon) slices*	*4 (175 g / 6 oz)*
⅓ cup	*White flour*	*40 g / 1½ oz*

1. Chop the onion into very thin slices. Wash and bone the anchovies. Chop the parsley very finely together with the garlic.
2. Heat a small saucepan containing half the oil, onion and the anchovies. Allow to brown, using a fork to help them break down properly. Then add the parsley and pour the white wine into the pan. Boil over a moderate heat until the wine almost evaporates, then add lemon juice and a few drops of Worcester sauce. Season with salt and pepper, mix well and remove the sauce from the heat.
3. While the sauce is cooking, dip the slices of dogfish in flour and fry in very hot oil until golden brown on both sides. Drain off almost all the oil, pour the sauce into the pan, cover and cook over a moderate heat for 10 minutes, occasionally shaking the pan so that the food does not stick to the bottom.
4. Serve the slices of dogfish piping hot on a serving dish with the remaining sauce in the pan poured over them, accompanied by boiled potatoes.

Pesce in agrodolce Shangai

Fish in Shanghai Sweet and Sour Sauce

00:15 00:35

American	Ingredients	Metric/Imperial
¼ cup	*Vegetable oil*	*50 ml / 2 fl oz*
2 tbsp	*Vinegar*	*1½ tbsp*
¼ cup	*White wine*	*50 ml / 2 fl oz*
3 tbsp	*Soy sauce*	*2 tbsp*
1 tbsp	*Sugar*	*1 tbsp*
1 tbsp	*Cornstarch (cornflour)*	*1 tbsp*
1¾ lb	*White fish in slices*	*800 g / 1¾ lb*
1	*Onion*	*1*
1	*Sweet pepper*	*1*

1. Preheat oven to 350°F / 180°C / Gas Mark 4.
2. In a saucepan put the oil, vinegar, white wine, soy sauce, sugar and flour dissolved in a little water. Stir well and bring to the boil, continuing to stir, then lower the heat and cook until the mixture begins to thicken. Remove from the heat and allow to cool.
3. Fry the slices of fish dipped in flour and when they are golden brown on both sides, remove and keep warm.
4. Slice the onion and pepper and fry for a few moments in the oil in which the fish was fried. Line an ovenproof dish with foil, place the fish on it and pour over the sweet and sour sauce, cover with the sliced onion and pepper. Close the foil, forming a bag, and put in the oven for 15 minutes.

Frittelle di pesce

Fish Fritters

01:00 00:40

American	Ingredients	Metric/Imperial
Filling		
14 oz	*Porgy (sea bream)*	*400 g / 14 oz*
2	*Slices of bread*	*2*
2	*Garlic cloves*	*2*
¼ cup	*Milk*	*50 ml / 2 fl oz*
1	*Sweet pepper*	*1*
2	*Fresh tomatoes*	*2*
	Salt and pepper	
Sauce		
2	*Large onions*	*2*
1 cup	*Tomato sauce (see page 171)*	*225 ml / 8 fl oz*
1	*Sweet pepper*	*1*
¼ cup	*Vegetable oil*	*50 ml / 2 fl oz*
Pastry		
4 cups	*All purpose (plain) flour*	*450 g / 1 lb*
¼ tsp	*Salt*	*¼ tsp*
½ oz	*Active dry yeast*	*15 g / ½ oz*
For frying		
2½ cups	*Olive oil*	*600 ml / 1 pint*

1. To make the filling; skin and bone the fish and chop into fairly small pieces. Soak the bread in a little warm milk. Crush the garlic. Wash sweet pepper, remove the seeds and chop finely. Skin the tomatoes and scoop out all the seeds and juice. Pour all these ingredients together into a mixing bowl, add salt and pepper and work them into a smooth paste with a wooden spoon.
2. To make the sauce; chop the onions and sauté in a little heated oil. Add tomato sauce (or crushed tomatoes) and sweet pepper, deseeded and chopped. Cook for 10 minutes then put aside.
3. To make the pastry; mix flour, salt, yeast, a pinch of salt and a little tepid water and knead until smooth. Roll out on a floured board and, using a pastry cutter, cut into rounds with a diameter of 1½-2 in / 3-4 cm.
4. Put a spoonful of filling on each pastry round, damp edges slightly and close with another round, pressing the edges firmly together.
5. Half-fill a large frying pan with olive oil and allow to become hot, lower the fritters into the oil and fry until they are an even golden-brown. Lift with a slotted spoon and drain on absorbent kitchen towels.
6. Reheat the sauce for a few minutes, then serve the fritters hot with the sauce served separately in a jug.

Cook's tip: use the dried yeast which is now available to mix dry with the flour, otherwise follow instructions on the packet.

Fish fritters

Nasello alla Onassis

Onassis-Style Hake

This is a very appetizing dish which comes from Greece.

00:40 00:45

American	Ingredients	Metric/Imperial
1 (1¾ lb)	Hake	1 (800 g / 1¾ lb)
4	Onions	4
3 tbsp	Vegetable oil	2 tbsp
1 cup	Dry white wine	225 ml / 8 fl oz
6	Tomatoes	6
5 oz	Raw ham	150 g / 5 oz
1 tsp	Mixed herbs	1 tsp
	Salt and pepper	
1 tbsp	Pine kernels	1 tbsp

1. Clean the hake, leaving it whole, apart from removing the scales and entrails.
2. Place the cleaned hake in a heat-resistant dish on a bed of chopped onions, then sprinkle with a little oil and half cover with the white wine.
3. Begin cooking over a low heat and turn the hake after 15 minutes. Do this carefully without breaking. Continue to cook over a low heat.
4. Prepare a fresh tomato purée by skinning and chopping the tomatoes, add the ham in small cubes, herbs, pepper, salt and pine kernels.
5. Pour the purée over the fish after the first 30 minutes of cooking, then turn up the heat, cook for a further 10 minutes over a moderate heat and serve piping hot.

Tortini di nasello al gratin

Hake Pie au Gratin

01:00 00:45

American	Ingredients	Metric/Imperial
1¼ lb	Hake (fresh or frozen)	600 g / 1¼ lb
1	Onion	1
1	Carrot	1
1	Bay leaf	1
1	Celery stalk	1
	Pinch of thyme	
3 or 4	Mushrooms	3 or 4
2 tbsp	Vegetable oil	1½ tbsp
1	Garlic clove	1
1 tbsp	Butter	1 tbsp
½ cup	Bread crumbs	50 g / 2 oz

1. Prepare a stock for the fish by boiling 2 cups [600 ml / 1 pint] of water with a chopped onion, carrot, bay leaf, celery and thyme for 30 minutes, cool. Cook the fish in the stock by bringing to the boil and simmering for 15 minutes. Drain and remove the bones and skin.
2. Wash the mushrooms and cut into thin slices. Heat oil with the crushed garlic, add the mushrooms, season with salt and pepper and cook over a very low heat for 15 minutes.
3. Cut up the fish, put in a clean bowl and add the mushrooms. Melt 1 tablespoon [15 g / ½ oz] of butter, without browning, and add to the fish. Put the mixture in a sealed bowl and refrigerate. Preheat the oven to 400°F / 200°C / Gas Mark 6.
4. Remove the mixture from the refrigerator and divide out amongst 8 large washed shells. Sprinkle bread crumbs over the surface and cook for about 20 minutes.

Trancio di nasello alla toscana

Hake Tuscan-Style

00:15 00:20

American	Ingredients	Metric/Imperial
1 lb	*Hake fillets*	500 g / 1 lb
	Salt	
¼ cup	*Butter*	50 g / 2 oz
1	*Sprig of sage*	1

1. Steam or boil the hake fillets for about 10-15 minutes until cooked, season with salt, then drain and arrange on a serving dish.
2. In a frying pan heat butter until brown with a few chopped sage leaves and pour over the fillets. This is a dish with a delicate flavor and it is essential to serve it very hot.

Aringa affumicata alla bismarck

Smoked Herring Fillets on Garlic Bread

00:15 00:00

American	Ingredients	Metric/Imperial
¾ lb	*Smoked herring*	350 g / 12 oz
¾ lb	*Brown bread*	350 g / 12 oz
2 tbsp	*Butter*	25 g / 1 oz
2	*Garlic cloves*	2
	Chilli sauce or pickle	

1. Cut each herring into half and divide into fillets, removing the bone.
2. Slice the bread. Mix crushed garlic with butter, spread on the slices of bread, lay the herring fillets on top with skin and roe. Serve cold, accompanied by chilli sauce or pickle.

Coda di rospo con pomodoro e olive

Monkfish Tail with Tomato and Olives

00:20 00:40
using a pressure cooker

American	Ingredients	Metric/Imperial
¼ cup	*Vegetable oil*	50 ml / 2 fl oz
14 oz	*Monkfish tail*	400 g / 14 oz
Scant ¼ cup	*Chopped tomatoes (no seeds or juice)*	3 tbsp
⅓ cup	*Green olives, stoned*	50 g / 2 oz
	Salt	

1. Put 1 cup [225 ml / 8 fl oz] of water into the pressure cooker. Into the pan supplied with the cooker, put some oil and then the fish, surround the fish with the chopped tomatoes and halved green olives and season with a little salt.
2. Close the cooker and bring up to pressure on a high heat, reduce the heat when pressure has been reached and continue to cook over minimum heat, for 10 minutes.
3. Reduce the pressure, remove the pan and thicken the sauce by boiling, uncovered, for a few minutes.

Triglie al cartoccio Portofino

Mullet Portofino-Style

00:10 00:35

American	Ingredients	Metric/Imperial
4 (7 oz)	*Mullet*	4 (200 g / 7 oz)
1	*Roll*	1
2 tbsp	*Vinegar*	1½ tbsp
6 oz	*Capers*	175 g / 6 oz
1	*Hard-cooked (boiled) egg*	1
½ tsp	*Chopped sage*	½ tsp
½ tsp	*Chopped rosemary*	½ tsp
	Salt and pepper	
2 tbsp	*Vegetable oil*	1½ tbsp
½ lb	*Peeled shrimps*	225 g / 8 oz
½ lb	*Shelled mussels*	225 g / 8 oz
8	*Basil leaves*	8
4	*Sprigs of parsley*	4
12	*Black or green olives*	12

1. Clean the mullet, removing the scales and make an incision under the belly. Wash and remove the guts.
2. To make the stuffing soak the inside of a bread roll with a little vinegar. Add some chopped capers, a crumbled hard-cooked egg, a generous pinch of chopped sage and rosemary, salt, pepper and a little oil; mix well. Fill the bellies of the mullet with this mixture and press down gently.
3. Preheat the oven to 400°F / 200°C / Gas Mark 6.
4. Spread out 4 sheets of foil or buttered wax paper (grease-proof) on the chopping board. On each sheet, lay one stuffed mullet, a few raw washed shrimps and mussels, and a few basil leaves. Close the cases, leaving a loose parcel to enable the steam to circulate. When the fish are wrapped, lay them on a baking sheet and put in a hot oven for 35 minutes.
5. Take out the cases, put on a heated serving dish. Each diner can open a case. Garnish with sprigs of parsley and if desired, some black or green olives. Serve with a mixed salad or boiled potatoes with parsley.

Triglie alla livornese

Mullet Leghorn-Style

00:30 00:35

American	Ingredients	Metric/Imperial
12	*Mullet*	12
	Flour	
	Salt and pepper	
½ cup	*Vegetable oil*	125 ml / 4 fl oz
3 tbsp	*Chopped parsley*	2 tbsp
3	*Garlic cloves*	3
1¼ cups	*Tomato sauce (see page 171)*	300 ml / ½ pint

1. Preheat oven to 400°F / 200°C / Gas Mark 6.
2. Clean, wash and dry the mullet, dip in seasoned flour. Heat the oil in a roasting pan, arrange the fish in the hot oil and brown in the oven for 10 minutes. Remove and turn the fish over carefully with a fish slice.
3. Season with salt, pepper, chopped parsley and crushed garlic. Return to the oven for 10 minutes, then add tomato sauce and cook for a further 15 minutes.
4. Serve piping hot with some sauce on each fish.

Mullet Leghorn-Style

Cernia lessata con salsa mousseline

Poached Grouper with Mousseline Sauce

00:40 00:40

American	Ingredients	Metric/Imperial
1 (2½ lb)	*Grouper*	1 (1.2 kg / 2½ lb)
10	*Peppercorns*	10
1	*Onion*	1
1	*Carrot*	1
1	*Celery stalk*	1
3	*Lemons*	3
2 cups	*Dry white wine*	450 ml / ¾ pint
	Salt and pepper	
12	*Scampi*	12
For the sauce		
1 cup	*Butter*	225 g / 8 oz
4	*Eggs*	4
1 cup	*Wine vinegar*	225 ml / 8 fl oz
1	*Lemon*	1
1 cup	*Whipping (double) cream*	225 ml / 8 fl oz

1. Clean and wash the fish thoroughly and place in a large pan (preferably a fish kettle) with peppercorns, chopped onion, carrot, celery, 1 lemon cut in half, the wine and enough water to cover the fish. Season, cover, bring to the boil and simmer for about 30 minutes.
2. Wash and cook the scampi, remove the heads and add the tails to the fish kettle 5 minutes before the cooking time is up.
3. Make the mousseline sauce (see page 178) with the butter, eggs, vinegar, 1 lemon, salt and pepper in a double boiler.
4. Whip the cream until stiff, fold into the sauce carefully, pour into a warm jug or sauceboat.
5. Transfer the fish without breaking to a heated serving dish, surround with the scampi and lemon slice. Serve accompanied by the mousseline sauce.

Razza in salsa mousseline

Skate in Cream Sauce

00:15 00:30

American	Ingredients	Metric/Imperial
1¾ lb	*Skate*	800 g / 1¾ lb
2 tbsp	*Butter*	25 g / 1 oz
1 cup	*Cream*	225 ml / 8 fl oz
1 tsp	*Mixed herbs*	1 tsp
½ cup	*Dry white wine*	125 ml / 4 fl oz
1 tbsp	*Cognac*	1 tbsp
	Salt and pepper	
1½ cups	*Cooked and buttered spinach*	300 g / 11 oz

1. Clean and wash the fish. Heat the butter in a fish kettle and place the skate in the kettle.
2. Cover with the cream, add the chopped herbs and begin cooking over a low heat, without stirring. After 15 minutes, turn the fish over (it doesn't matter if it breaks). Sprinkle with white wine and brandy, then lightly season with salt and pepper on the surface. Cook for a further 15 minutes, still covered and over a very low heat. Keep warm.
3. Prepare on the heated serving dish a bed of cooked, buttered spinach. Place the fish and the sauce it was cooked in on top of the spinach. Serve hot.

Pescetti in carpione

Soused Small Fish

00:15 Standing time 24:00 00:40

American	Ingredients	Metric/Imperial
1 lb	*Small fish*	450 g / 1 lb
	White flour	
½ cup	*Vegetable oil*	125 ml / 4 fl oz
1	*Large onion*	1
1 tbsp	*Butter*	1 tbsp
	Salt	
1 cup	*Red wine vinegar*	225 ml / 8 fl oz
1	*Bay leaf*	1
2	*Peppercorns*	2

1. Carefully wash the small fish, dry them gently with a towel or on absorbent kitchen towel. Flour lightly and shake off the excess, then fry in plenty of hot vegetable oil.
2. Remove the fish from the oil and drain on a plate covered with kitchen towels.
3. Cut the onion into thin rings and fry gently over a low heat with oil and butter. In a dish with a lid arrange the fried fish in layers, each seasoned with salt and covered with the onion. Continue until the fish is used up.
4. Boil good quality red wine vinegar, flavored with a bay leaf and two peppercorns. When the vinegar reaches boiling point, remove the pepper and pour over the fish to cover them. Leave to stand until the next day.

Pesce spada alla messinese

Messina Swordfish

01:30 01:00

American	Ingredients	Metric/Imperial
⅔ cup	*Vegetable oil*	150 ml / ¼ pint
1	*Large onion*	1
1	*Celery stalk*	1
⅓ cup	*Green olives, stoned*	50 g / 2 oz
1 tbsp	*Capers*	1 tsbp
6	*Tomatoes*	6
14 oz	*Swordfish*	400 g / 14 oz
	Salt and pepper	
3	*Small pumpkins*	3
	White flour	
½ lb	*Pizza dough (see page 156)*	225 g / 8 oz
	Butter	
¼ tsp	*Chopped thyme*	¼ tsp
¼ tsp	*Chopped oregano*	¼ tsp

1. Chop onion finely and fry slowly in a little oil in a covered pan for a few minutes. Add the chopped celery, a little water and continue cooking. Put the olives in the frying pan together with the capers, cook for 3 minutes. Add the tomatoes, peeled and crushed with a fork, and the swordfish, skinned and cut into small pieces. Season with salt and cook covered over a very low heat for 20 minutes.
2. Wash and wipe the small pumpkins, cut into small sticks, dry and dip in white flour. Fry in plenty of hot oil and leave to drain on a plate covered with kitchen towels.
3. Preheat the oven to 400°F / 200°C / Gas Mark 6.
4. Roll out the risen dough with a rolling pin, forming a thin disc. Line a well buttered and floured pie dish with the rolled dough. Spread the fried pumpkins over the dough and add the swordfish with the juice that is left after cooking. Sprinkle with thyme and oregano and put in a hot oven for about 30 minutes. Serve hot.

Stoccafisso alla vicentina

Stockfish Vicentina-Style

In Italian, this dish is also, though erroneously called 'baccala alla vicentina' (dried salt cod). 'Baccala' is a preserved fish, dried and salted, whereas stockfish does not contain salt.

00:25 01:00

American	Ingredients	Metric/Imperial
2 lb	*Stockfish*	*1 kg / 2 lb*
	Flour	
½ cup	*Grated parmesan cheese*	*50 g / 2 oz*
	Salt and pepper	
½ tsp	*Cinnamon*	*½ tsp*
¼ cup	*Vegetable oil*	*50 ml / 2 fl oz*
1	*Scallion (spring onion)*	*1*
1	*Garlic clove*	*1*
4	*Anchovies*	*4*
1 tbsp	*Chopped parsley*	*1 tbsp*
1 cup	*Dry white wine*	*225 ml / 8 fl oz*
2½ cups	*Milk*	*600 ml / 1 pint*
2 tbsp	*Butter*	*25 g / 1 oz*

1. Buy stockfish ready softened, but if this is difficult and you have to buy it dried, leave to soak for 48 hours, renewing the water very frequently, after beating with a wooden mallet to break up the flesh and help the absorption of water.
2. Once it is softened, cut the stockfish into four rather large pieces, without removing the skin. Flour lightly and place in a single layer in a casserole. The casserole is not greased.
3. Preheat the oven to 350°F / 180°C / Gas Mark 4.
4. Generously sprinkle the fish with parmesan, salt and pepper, cinnamon and flour. Heat the oil in a pan, chop the onion and garlic, lightly fry until they have turned golden, add the anchovies, washed and broken into pieces. Blend the anchovies with the other ingredients in the frying pan with the aid of a wooden spoon. Then add the chopped parsley and the dry white wine.
5. Allow to boil down almost completely, add the milk and top up with butter. As soon as this has dissolved, pour the sauce over the stockfish, being careful to cover it completely. Cover and bake in the oven until the liquid covering the fish has almost disappeared.
6. This dish can be served with slices of buckwheat polenta.

Spiedini misti al limone

Seafood Skewers with Lemon

00:25 00:20

American	Ingredients	Metric/Imperial
1¼ lb	*Swordfish, fresh tuna, or angler fish or a fish with firm flesh*	*600 g / 1¼ lb*
1	*Lemon*	*1*
8	*Wooden skewers*	*8*
8	*Pickled onions*	*8*
2 tbsp	*Butter*	*25 g / 1 oz*
2	*Bay leaves*	*2*
	Salt and pepper	
¼ cup	*Dry white wine*	*50 ml / 2 fl oz*

1. Preheat the oven to 425°F / 220°C / Gas Mark 7.
2. Cut the flesh of the fish into cubes and place in an earthenware dish. Remove the rind from a lemon, together with the white part, leaving the whole peeled fruit.
3. Cut the lemon into slices, dividing into 4. Prepare the fish on the wooden skewers, alternating 2 pieces of fish with 1 slice of lemon and 1 pickled onion at either end of the skewer.
4. Arrange the skewers on a well-buttered ovenproof dish together with a few bay leaves, salt and pepper. Put in a very hot oven for 10 minutes, then sprinkle with dry white wine and continue cooking in the oven for a further 10 minutes. Serve on a heated serving dish, sprinkled with the cooking juices.

Storione al cartoccio

Sturgeon in Cases

00:30 00:35

American	Ingredients	Metric/Imperial
1 tbsp	*Chopped parsley*	*1 tbsp*
1	*Garlic clove*	*1*
¼ tsp	*Thyme*	*¼ tsp*
¼ tsp	*Oregano*	*¼ tsp*
	Vegetable oil	
8	*Thin slices of bacon*	*8*
4	*Slices of sturgeon fish*	*4*
	Salt and pepper	
⅓ cup	*Butter*	*75 g / 3 oz*

1. Preheat the oven to 350°F / 180°C / Gas Mark 4.
2. Chop the parsley together with half a clove of garlic, put in an ovenproof earthenware dish and add a pinch of thyme and oregano. Mix well.
3. Prepare 4 oval pieces of wax paper (greaseproof) paper, brushed with oil and put a slice of bacon in the middle. Coat the slices of fish in the prepared herbs, making sure that they are well-covered, season with salt and pepper on both sides.
4. Arrange the fish on the slices of bacon, cover with the remaining bacon, dot each slice of fish with small pieces of butter. Wrap in the paper parcels, cutting a small slit on the top of each.
5. Arrange the 4 cases on a baking sheet and put in a moderate oven for 35 minutes. The cases will swell up during cooking. Unwrap the paper, lift the fish on to a heated serving dish and serve immediately.

Fillets of sole served with pan juices

Sogliole Hélène

Sole Hélène

00:45 | 01:30

American	Ingredients	Metric/Imperial
1 cup	*White flour*	100 g / 4 oz
1 cup	*Cornstarch (cornflour)*	100 g / 4 oz
	Salt	
⅔ cup	*Butter*	175 g / 6 oz
3 tbsp	*Milk*	2 tbsp
½ cup	*Vegetable oil*	125 ml / 4 fl oz
8	*Sage leaves*	8
½ lb	*Mushrooms*	225 g / 8 oz
1	*Garlic clove*	1
1	*Egg*	1
1 ¼ lb	*Sole fillets*	600 g / 1 ¼ lb
1 tbsp	*Chopped parsley*	1 tbsp

1. Prepare some short crust pastry by sifting the flour, cornstarch and a pinch of salt in a bowl. Add ⅔ cup [150 g / 5 oz] butter, rub fat into flour until mixture resembles fine bread crumbs, mix with 6 tablespoons water and the milk. Knead for 2 minutes on a floured board and rest in the refrigerator for 20 minutes.
2. Wash and dry the fillets of sole, flour lightly and fry until they are golden brown in heated oil, the remaining butter and a few sage leaves. Brown on both sides, remove from the seasoning and drain on kitchen towels.
3. Preheat oven to 400°F / 200°C / Gas Mark 6.
4. Clean the mushrooms and cut them into thin slices. Heat oil and a crushed clove of garlic in a large pan, add the mushrooms, cook for 3 minutes, add 1 cup [225 ml / 8 fl oz] of water and continue cooking for 30 minutes.
5. Roll out the pastry with a rolling pin and line a buttered, floured pie-dish. Arrange the sole fillets on the pastry, cover with the mushrooms and pour over an egg beaten with a pinch of salt and chopped parsley. Top with remaining pastry, brush with beaten egg, put in a hot oven and cook for about 40 minutes.

Sogliole alla panna

Sole with Cream

00:30 | 00:25

American	Ingredients	Metric/Imperial
2	*Eggs*	2
	Salt and pepper	
8	*Sole fillets*	8
½ cup	*Bread crumbs*	50 g / 2 oz
⅔ cup	*Vegetable oil*	150 ml / ¼ pint
3 tbsp	*Parsley*	2 tbsp
1	*Lemon*	1
1 tbsp	*Fresh chopped chives*	1 tbsp
1 cup	*Double (whipping) cream*	225 ml / 8 fl oz

1. Beat the eggs well with salt and pepper and pour into a shallow dish. Immerse the sole fillets in this batter and leave to stand for 10 minutes.
2. Drain the fillets and cover carefully with bread crumbs. Heat some oil in a frying pan and when it is very hot, put in the sole fillets, stomach side down, and brown on both sides. Lift out with a fish slice and drain them on kitchen towels to remove the excess grease.
3. Chop some parsley, add grated lemon rind and some very finely chopped chives, mix this with the lightly whipped cream to obtain a smooth sauce.
4. Arrange the fried fillets on a serving dish, spread the sauce over them and serve immediately. Alternatively serve cream separately in a sauceboat and garnish with lemon wedges or thin slices of lemon.

Fette di pesce alla casalinga

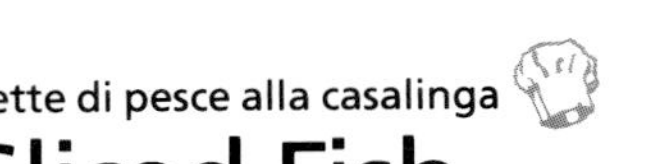

Sliced Fish Housewife-Style

00:30 | 00:40

American	Ingredients	Metric/Imperial
1	*Celery stalk*	1
1	*Carrot*	1
1	*Onion*	1
1 tbsp	*Parsley*	1 tbsp
1	*Salted anchovy*	1
¾ lb	*Ripe plum tomatoes*	350 g / 12 oz
2 (14 oz)	*Dogfish or swordfish slices*	2 (400 g / 14 oz)
½ cup	*Vegetable oil*	125 ml / 4 fl oz
2 tbsp	*Butter*	25 g / 1 oz
	Salt and pepper	

1. Chop the celery, carrot, onion and parsley very finely, wash and bone the anchovy and chop coarsely. Skin the tomatoes and remove the seeds.
2. Wash and skin the fish and put into a pan with plenty of heated oil; brown lightly on either side, then tip off most of the oil and add the vegetables, anchovy, tomatoes and butter to the pan. Season with salt and pepper, stir gently and simmer for 30 minutes, turning the fish once only and taking great care that it does not stick to the pan.
3. Arrange the fish on a serving dish, pour all the residue from the pan over it and serve hot.

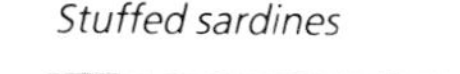

Stuffed sardines

Sardine ripiene

Stuffed Sardines

00:25 00:25

American	Ingredients	Metric/Imperial
8	*Sardines*	8
1	*Roll*	1
	Milk	
1 tbsp	*Chopped parsley*	1 tbsp
2	*Shallots*	2
	Salt and pepper	
1 cup	*Béchamel sauce (see page 162)*	225 ml / 8 fl oz
	Butter	

1. Preheat the oven to 400°F / 200°C / Gas Mark 6.
2. Wash and scrape the sardines with a knife, cut open from head to tail, remove the backbone and place each open sardine on the chopping-board.
3. Prepare the filling with the soft part of the roll soaked in milk, the chopped parsley, the finely chopped shallot and salt and pepper.
4. Prepare the béchamel sauce. Pour the filling onto 4 opened sardines, in a buttered heatproof dish, with the inside facing upwards, and cover with the other 4 sardines. Pour over the béchamel sauce and bake in the oven for 25 minutes.

Sardine fritte con verdure

Fried Sardines with Salad

00:30 00:10

American	Ingredients	Metric/Imperial
20	*Fresh sardines*	20
	Salt	
	Tomatoes	
2	*Fresh chilli peppers*	2
1	*Cucumber*	1
2	*Small onions*	2
¼ cup	*Olive oil*	50 ml / 2 fl oz
2 tbsp	*Vinegar or lemon juice*	1½ tbsp
	Cayenne pepper	
1 cup	*Vegetable oil*	225 ml / 8 fl oz

1. Scale the sardines, holding them by the tail and using a sharp knife. Make an incision along the belly and remove the backbone.
2. Put the fish in a large bowl and sprinkle with salt, leave to stand for about 10 minutes.
3. Prepare the vegetables for the mixed salad. Wash and slice the tomatoes, cut the deseeded chilli into fine strips and the cucumber and onions into thin rings.
4. Put the vegetables in a salad bowl and season with olive oil, a little vinegar, or lemon juice, according to taste, salt and ground cayenne pepper.
5. Remove the excess salt from the sardines with absorbent paper towels. Heat the oil in a large frying pan, cook the fish, turning them to make sure of even cooking. Cook the fish for about 8 minutes.
6. Serve the hot sardines immediately with the vegetable salad and crusty bread.

Fried sardines

Crema di pesce in umido

Creamed Fish Soup

00:40 | 00:25

American	Ingredients	Metric/Imperial
1¾ lb	*Selection of fish suitable for soup*	800 g / 1¾ lb
3	*Onions*	3
1	*Carrot*	1
1	*Celery stalk*	1
1	*Bunch of herbs*	1
¾ cup	*Vegetable oil*	175 ml / 6 fl oz
1 lb	*Sweet peppers*	500 g / 1 lb
1 lb	*Ripe, peeled tomatoes*	500 g / 1 lb
½ cup	*Dry red wine*	125 ml / 4 fl oz
	Salt and pepper	
¼ tsp	*Paprika*	¼ tsp
8	*Slices of crusty bread*	8
	Sprigs of parsley	

1. Clean and bone the fish very thoroughly and put all the flesh together in a large bowl.
2. Chop the onions finely, slice the carrot, celery and the herbs. Put these into a wide, shallow pan with ½ cup [125 ml / 4 fl oz] of oil and cook, stirring frequently for 10 minutes.
3. Wash the peppers, remove the seeds and cut the flesh into narrow strips. Sieve the tomatoes and blend with the fish using an electric blender or food processor. The result should be a thick, creamy consistency.
4. Add this cream and the peppers cut into strips to the vegetables and herbs in the pan and continue to cook. Pour in the red wine, season with salt, pepper and a pinch of paprika, remove from the heat but keep very warm.
5. Prepare some slices of bread by cutting off the crusts and frying the slices in very hot oil; drain well and place 2 slices on each soup plate or individual ovenproof bowl. Ladle the creamed soup over the bread, stand the plates (or bowls) in a hot oven for a few minutes, decorate each plate with a sprig of parsley and serve piping hot.

Creamed fish soup

Tonno con piselli

Tuna with Peas

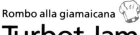

00:25 — 00:45

American	Ingredients	Metric/Imperial
1¼ lb	Fresh peas	600 g / 1¼ lb
1	Onion	1
1 tbsp	Butter	1 tbsp
1 tbsp	Vegetable oil	1 tbsp
1 tbsp	Chopped parsley	1 tbsp
14 oz	Tuna fish	400 g / 14 oz

1. Shell the peas, put them in a heatproof dish, cover with water and simmer for 10 minutes. Drain, retaining ⅔ cup [150 ml / ¼ pint] of water.
2. Chop the onion finely and lightly fry in heated butter and oil. As soon as it begins to brown, add some chopped parsley, the peas and the retained liquid. Simmer over a low heat. Season well, add the slices of fresh tuna and continue cooking for about 20 minutes.

Tonno al cartoccio

Tuna Fish in Cases

00:15 — 00:25

American	Ingredients	Metric/Imperial
4	Slices of tuna fish	4
4	Sheets of foil	4
	Salt and pepper	
	Vegetable oil	
4	Slices of lemon	4
16	Black olives	16
4	Rolled-up anchovies with a caper in the middle	4

1. Preheat the oven to 425°F / 220°C / Gas Mark 7.
2. Remove the skin from the slices of tuna and arrange on 4 sheets of foil, seasoned with salt and pepper and sprinkled with a little oil.
3. On each slice of tuna place a slice of lemon, 4 black olives and a rolled-up anchovy. Close the foil cases and bake in a hot oven for 25 minutes. Open the foil and transfer the fish on to heated plates. This dish may be served with avocado sauce (see page 176) or mustard sauce (see page 178).

Rombo alla giamaicana

Turbot Jamaica-Style

00:20 Standing time 12:00 — 00:00

American	Ingredients	Metric/Imperial
14 oz	Turbot	400 g / 14 oz
2 tbsp	Vegetable oil	25 ml / 1 fl oz
	Salt and pepper	
2	Lemons	2
1 tbsp	Chopped parsley	1 tbsp
½	Garlic clove	½
1 tbsp	Brandy	1 tbsp

1. Clean the turbot, remove the bones and chop the flesh into small pieces. In a bowl, working with a wooden spoon, mix the fish with a little oil and salt. Add a pinch of pepper, pour lemon juice over and leave to steep overnight in the refrigerator.
2. Chop the parsley with a little garlic and add 1 tablespoon of brandy. Sprinkle the surface of the dish with this sauce and serve.

Cook's tip: skate can also be prepared in this way.

'Il pesce' 

Fish Mold

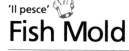

00:15 Chilling time 02:00 — 00:20

American	Ingredients	Metric/Imperial
1 lb	Potatoes	500 g / 1 lb
¾ lb	Canned tuna	350 g / 12 oz
2	Eggs	2
	Salt and pepper	
1 tbsp	Chopped parsley	1 tbsp
⅓ cup	Cream	75 ml / 3 fl oz
½ cup	Grated parmesan cheese	50 g / 2 oz
6	Olives	6
2	Gherkins	2
5	Sprigs of parsley	5

1. Boil, peel and rub the potatoes through a sieve, collecting purée in a bowl. Drain the tuna, put in a blender, together with the whole eggs, a little salt and pepper, the parsley and cream. Blend for a few minutes until a soft cream is obtained.
2. Pour into the bowl containing the mashed potato, add the grated parmesan and mix thoroughly together. Take a fish-shaped mold and pour the mixture into it, levelling the surface with the blade of a knife. Cover with foil and put in the refrigerator for about 2 hours. Turn out onto an oval dish and garnish with olives, gherkins and sprigs of parsley.

Merlani alla Caen

Caen-Style Whiting

00:30 — 00:15

American	Ingredients	Metric/Imperial
4	Whiting	4
¾ cup	Flour	75 g / 3 oz
1 tbsp	Vegetable oil	1 tbsp
½ cup	Butter	100 g / 4 oz
1 tsp	Parsley	1 tsp
1 tsp	Dill	1 tsp
1	Shallot	1
1	Lemon	1
	Salt and pepper	
½ cup	Cider	125 ml / 4 fl oz

1. Preheat oven to 400°F / 200°C / Gas Mark 6.
2. Fillet the whiting, wash, pat dry and dip in flour. Heat the oil and some of the butter in the frying pan, then put in the whiting and brown them on both sides.
3. Chop up the herbs and the shallot very finely. Cut a lemon into slices, arrange on each fish together with the chopped herbs.
4. Season with salt and pepper to taste, pour over the cider and finally dot the fish with small pieces of butter. Place, covered, in a hot oven, to bake for 15 minutes before serving.

Anchovy bake

Alici in tortiera

Anchovy Bake

00:35 00:40

American	Ingredients	Metric/Imperial
1½ lb	*Fresh whole anchovies*	700 g / 1½ lb
¼ cup	*Vegetable oil*	50 ml / 2 fl oz
½ cup	*Fresh bread crumbs*	25 g / 1 oz
1 tsp	*Oregano*	1 tsp
	Salt and pepper	
1 lb	*Sieved fresh tomatoes*	450 g / 1 lb
8	*Garlic cloves*	8

1. Preheat oven to 350°F / 180°C / Gas Mark 4.
2. Prepare the anchovies by removing the heads, slitting along the underside and opening flat; remove guts and bones, wash and dry.
3. Arrange an even layer of anchovies in a well-oiled pie dish; sprinkle with bread crumbs, oregano, salt and pepper. Spoon some of the sieved or blended tomatoes over the top. Repeat these layers until the dish is full and top with plenty of oil and several cloves of garlic.
4. Bake the anchovies in the oven for 40 minutes, remove garlic and serve hot.

Acciughe in cotoletta

Anchovy Cutlets

00:40 00:15
Chilling time: 24:00

American	Ingredients	Metric/Imperial
1 lb	*Fresh anchovies*	450 g / 1 lb
1	*Egg*	1
	Salt and pepper	
	Flour	
1 cup	*Lard*	225 g / 8 oz
2	*Garlic cloves*	2
1 tbsp	*Chopped basil*	1 tbsp
4	*Walnuts (shelled)*	4
1 oz	*Pine kernels*	25 g / 1 oz
¼ cup	*Vegetable oil*	50 ml / 2 fl oz
3 tbsp	*White wine vingar*	2 tbsp
3 tbsp	*Cognac (optional)*	2 tbsp

1. Wash and dry the anchovies. Remove the heads and tails, split open and remove the backbone and all the smaller bones from the anchovies.
2. Coat in the beaten egg seasoned with salt and pepper, then drain and dip in flour.
3. Melt the lard or heat frying oil in a pan and when the fat is smoking hot, fry the anchovies and cook on both sides. Lift out with a fish slice and drain thoroughly on absorbent kitchen towels.
4. Meanwhile, chop the garlic and basil together, preferably in a blender or food processor and combine into a sauce with the walnuts, pine kernels, a little oil and the vinegar and cognac if desired.
5. Lay the anchovies in a single layer on a china (not metal) plate, spread the sauce over them, cover the dish with film and put in a cool place for 24 hours.

Cook's tip: this is a very good luncheon dish.

Leccia del Golfo Paradiso

Rudderfish (Amberjack) in Garlic and Lemon

01:00 00:30
Marinade time 04:00

American	Ingredients	Metric/Imperial
½ cup	*Oil*	125 ml / 4 fl oz
1¾ lb	*Rudderfish (amberjack)*	800 g / 1¾ lb
½ tsp	*Chopped parsley*	½ tsp
½ tsp	*Sage*	½ tsp
2	*Garlic cloves*	2
	Pepper	
2	*Lemons*	2
¼ cup	*Dry white wine*	50 ml / 2 fl oz

1. Brush oil all over the thick slice of fish.
2. Chop parsley and sage leaves with the cloves of garlic and sprinkle these into the fish-kettle with a thin layer of oil. Lay the fish on top and sprinkle with freshly-ground pepper. Leave for 2 hours, then turn, sprinkle again with pepper and leave for a further 2 hours.
3. Pour the juice of 2 lemons over the fish and commence cooking over a very low heat. If the fish shows any signs of sticking, put in some of the white wine which you may have chosen to serve with the meal. After 15 minutes, turn the fish and cook for a further 15 minutes.
4. Serve very hot, straight from the pan. The rudderfish is a very fine fish with a delicate flavor, no salt is needed when it is cooked by this method.

Cook's tip: moray eel can be cooked in exactly the same way making the tender white flesh delicious.

Alborelle in carpione

Soused Sprats

00:20 00:40
Marinating time 2 days

American	Ingredients	Metric/Imperial
2 lb	*Sprats*	1 kg / 2 lb
	Flour	
½ cup	*Vegetable oil*	125 ml / 4 fl oz
	Salt	
1 cup	*Wine vinegar*	225 ml / 8 fl oz
2	*Medium-sized onions*	2
1	*Celery stalk*	1
4	*Basil leaves*	4
½ tsp	*Chopped thyme*	½ tsp
2	*Bay leaves*	2

1. Cut, wash and dry the fish; coat with flour, eliminating the excess by tossing in a large sieve.
2. Heat some oil in a frying pan and cook the fish over a high heat for 2 minutes each side.
3. Drain on absorbent paper then put into a deep bowl and season with salt, shaking to ensure an even distribution.
4. Slice the onions into thin rings, put into a saucepan with the vinegar, ⅔ cup [150 ml / ¼ pint] water and bring to the boil. Add the celery (with leaves), basil, thyme, bay leaves and any other herbs you choose. Allow the vinegar to boil until the vegetables are cooked, then strain, still boiling hot, over the fish and cover immediately. Leave for at least 2 days before serving.

Alborelle arrosto

Fried Sprats

00:20 00:25

American	Ingredients	Metric/Imperial
2 lb	*Sprats*	*1 kg / 2 lb*
2 tbsp	*Butter*	*25 g / 1 oz*
½ cup	*Olive oil*	*125 ml / 4 fl oz*
2	*Sprigs of rosemary*	*2*
	Salt and pepper	
½ cup	*Dry white wine*	*125 ml / 4 fl oz*
2	*Lemons*	*2*

1. Gut and clean the fish, wash well under the tap and dry with a cloth. Heat the oil and butter in a shallow pan with a sprig of rosemary.
2. Make some small transverse cuts on the backs of the fish and fry on all sides.
3. Season with salt and pepper. When the fish are crisp and golden, sprinkle the wine over them and allow it to evaporate completely.
4. Arrange the fish on a dish, garnish with lemon slices and serve with a crisp salad.

Sarde caramellate alla giapponese

Caramelized Sprats Japanese-Style

00:20 00:30

American	Ingredients	Metric/Imperial
½ cup	*Vegetable oil*	*125 ml / 4 fl oz*
1 lb	*Sprats*	*450 g / 1 lb*
1 cup	*Sugar*	*225 g / 8 oz*
⅓ cup	*Soy sauce*	*5 tbsp*

1. Preheat oven to 350°F / 180°C / Gas Mark 4.
2. Put the oil in a frying pan, add the sprats and cook until golden brown, drain on kitchen towels.
3. Put the sugar in a saucepan, cook over a low heat until caramelized. Add the soy sauce, combine with the caramel and continue to cook over a low heat for a few minutes. Immerse the sprats in the caramel, then lay each fish on a foil lined baking sheet. Cook in the oven for 15 minutes and serve.

Frittata di bianchetti

Whitebait Frittata

00:15 00:15

American	Ingredients	Metric/Imperial
½ cup	*Flour*	*50 g / 2 oz*
	Salt and pepper	
4	*Eggs*	*4*
¼ cup	*Milk*	*50 ml / 2 fl oz*
¾ lb	*Whitebait (or bianchetti)*	*350 g / 12 oz*
2 cups	*Vegetable oil*	*450 ml / ¾ pint*

1. Sift flour with salt and pepper, make a well in the centre, drop in the eggs and milk, mix well.
2. Beat the egg mixture together with the whitebait.
3. Pour into a large pan containing plenty of boiling oil. When one side is cooked, either turn the *frittata* (difficult and dangerous!) or remove from the pan and slide it under the broiler (grill) to brown the top.
4. This delicious *frittata* can be served either hot or cold, cut into thin slices.

Anguilla alla veneta

Venetian Eel

This is a traditional Venetian dish which appealed so much to the Austrians during their occupation of the region that they 'adopted' it.

00:45 Marinating time 2 days 01:00

American	Ingredients	Metric/Imperial
¾ lb	*Eel*	*350 g / 12 oz*
4 tbsp	*Flour*	*25 g / 1 oz*
½ cup	*Vegetable oil*	*125 ml / 4 fl oz*
1	*Onion*	*1*
1	*Carrot*	*1*
1	*Garlic clove*	*1*
2	*Sprigs of sage*	*2*
1 cup	*Wine vinegar*	*225 ml / 8 fl oz*
	Salt and pepper	

1. Clean the eel and wipe it well with a damp cloth. Remove the internal organs and the gills, wash thoroughly then chop into pieces and coat with flour, shake off excess.
2. Using a cast-iron pan, heat a generous half of the oil and when this is very hot, add the eel and cook, stirring frequently. Drain and transfer to a bowl.
3. Slice the scraped carrot and peeled onion thinly, chop the garlic and sage and sauté all together in remaining heated oil.
4. Allow to brown slightly, add a little vinegar, a small quantity of water and some freshly ground pepper. Simmer for 20 minutes then pour over the eel. Marinate for 2 days, then serve cold.

Anguilla allo spiedo

Spit-Roasted Eel

00:25 00:15

American	Ingredients	Metric/Imperial
1 (1½ lb)	*Eel*	*1 (700 g / 1½ lb)*
8	*Slices of crusty bread*	*8*
8	*Bay leaves*	*8*
	Salt and pepper	
4 tbsp	*Vegetable oil*	*3 tbsp*

1. Clean and wash the eel thoroughly, then chop into pieces about 2½ in / 6 cm long.
2. Thread the rotisserie skewers with small thick slices of bread, bay leaves and pieces of eel, season with salt and pepper, brush with oil and cook under a hot broiler (grill) until the eel is well done, brushing with oil from time to time during cooking.

Traditional Italian eel

Capitone della tradizione italiana

Traditional Italian Eel

00:15 00:40

American	Ingredients	Metric/Imperial
1 (2 lb)	*Eel*	*1 (1 kg / 2 lb)*
¼ cup	*Vegetable oil*	*50 ml / 2 fl oz*
2 tbsp	*Butter*	*25 g / 1 oz*
4	*Anchovy fillets*	*4*
½ tsp	*Chopped rosemary*	*½ tsp*
2	*Bay leaves*	*2*
¼ cup	*Rum*	*50 ml / 2 fl oz*
½ cup	*Dry white wine*	*125 ml / 4 fl oz*
1 cup	*Cream*	*225 ml / 8 fl oz*
	Sprigs of parsley	

1. Clean and wash the eel and chop it into pieces about 4 in / 10 cm.
2. Heat a little oil and butter in a frying pan and sauté together the anchovy fillets and pieces of eel. Add the herbs and the rum. Flame, and when this dies down add the wine and a little cream. Continue to cook for 15 minutes over a low heat. Serve very hot, garnished with sprigs of parsley.

Capitone marinato

Marinated Eel

00:30 Marinating time 2 days 00:40

American	Ingredients	Metric/Imperial
1 (2 lb)	*Eel*	*1 (1 kg / 2 lb)*
1	*Garlic clove*	*1*
	Salt and pepper	
2 or 3	*Bay leaves*	*2 or 3*
1 cup	*Vegetable oil*	*225 ml / 8 fl oz*
1 cup	*Wine vinegar*	*225 ml / 8 fl oz*

1. Skin the eel by hanging up by the head, make a slit around the neck and then roll the skin downwards, using a coarse cloth to help grip. Gut, wash and dry, then coil the body around the head and lay it in a casserole pot. The coiled up eel should fit into the base of the casserole.
2. Sprinkle with salt, pepper, crushed garlic and a few bay leaves, then pour the oil and vinegar over, making sure that the eel is completely immersed.
3. Cover and cook over very low heat. When the eel is cooked, the juices should have been almost absorbed. Cool in the liquor and leave to marinate for several days before serving.

Capitone alla livornese

Leghorn Eel

00:30 00:30

American	Ingredients	Metric/Imperial
1	*Onion*	*1*
1	*Carrot*	*1*
1	*Celery stalk*	*1*
1	*Lemon*	*1*
1 (2 lb)	*Eel*	*1 (1 kg / 2 lb)*
	Salt and pepper	
2 tbsp	*Wine vinegar*	*1½ tbsp*
1 tbsp	*Tomato paste*	*1 tbsp*
4	*Slices of bread*	*4*
2 tbsp	*Butter*	*25 g / 1 oz*
2 tbsp	*Oil*	*1½ tbsp*

1. Prepare, wash and chop the vegetables into even-sized pieces. Cook in 1¼ cup [300 ml / ½ pint] water, adding the rind of a lemon.
2. Clean, wash and slice the eel.
3. When the vegetables are cooked, drain, retaining the vegetable water. Place alternate layers of eel and vegetables into a large pan until all ingredients are used. Season with salt and pepper, pour over vegetable water, add more warm water if necessary to cover, and simmer gently for about 20 minutes.
4. When the eel is cooked, add vinegar and tomato paste. Continue to simmer for 5 minutes.
5. Fry the slices of bread in butter and oil, then lay them on a heated serving dish and spoon the eel on top.

Squid in ink

Calamari neri

Squid in Ink

00:40 00:45

American	Ingredients	Metric/Imperial
2 lb	*Squid (inkfish)*	1 kg / 2 lb
	Salt and pepper	
	Flour	
¼ cup	*Corn oil*	50 ml / 2 fl oz
1	*Onion*	1
½ cup	*Dry white wine*	125 ml / 4 fl oz
2	*Garlic cloves*	2
1	*Sweet red pepper*	1
	Sprigs of parsley	
1	*Lemon*	1

1. Prepare the squid by removing the head with a sharp knife. Open the body and discard the internal organs, retain the ink sac.
2. Wash the squid, cut into strips and dip in seasoned flour.
3. Heat the oil in a frying pan and sauté the peeled chopped onion lightly; add the squid, stir for 3 minutes, pour in the white wine and season with salt and pepper, cook gently for 30 minutes.
4. Crush the garlic, deseed and chop sweet pepper and add with the ink-sac to the pan. Stir well, cook for a further 10 minutes and serve garnished with sprigs of parsley and lemon wedges.

Calamari in salsa rossa

Squid in Tomato Sauce

01:00 02:10

American	Ingredients	Metric/Imperial
2 lb	*Squid*	1 kg / 2 lb
2	*Garlic cloves*	2
1	*Sprig of rosemary*	1
½ cup	*Vegetable oil*	125 ml / 4 fl oz
1¼ lb	*Ripe tomatoes*	600 g / 1¼ lb
	Salt and pepper	
¼ cup	*Butter*	50 g / 2 oz
	Cornstarch (cornflour)	

1. Clean the squid carefully (retaining the ink sacs), wash and cut into strips then allow to drain in a colander.
2. Chop the garlic and rosemary finely, then put into a saucepan with the oil. Heat the oil and sauté the herbs for 2 minutes, then add the squid and continue to cook, stirring frequently over a moderate heat.
3. Wash and sieve or blend the tomatoes and add them to the pan together with the ink sacs, some salt and a few twists of pepper. Cover with really tight-fitting lid and simmer very gently for 2 hours (the liquid should only just bubble). Open the saucepan as little as possible, but from time to time to check that the pan is not drying up.
4. Add the butter and if the sauce is too thin, thicken it slightly with a little flour, check the seasoning and serve very hot.

Cacciucco alla livornese

Leghorn Fish Stew

Suitable fish for this recipe include conger eel, dog fish, sea hen, *cicale di mare, scorfani* or similar North Sea varieties.

01:00 01:00

American	Ingredients	Metric/Imperial
4½ lb	*Coarse fish plus squid and octopus*	*2 kg / 4½ lb*
1	*Red chilli pepper*	*1*
1	*Onion*	*1*
1	*Celery stalk*	*1*
2 tbsp	*Chopped parsley*	*1½ tbsp*
½ tsp	*Chopped basil*	*½ tsp*
1 cup	*Olive oil*	*225 ml / 8 fl oz*
2	*Garlic cloves*	*2*
	Salt and pepper	
½ cup	*Dry white wine*	*125 ml / 4 fl oz*
¾ lb	*Peeled tomatoes*	*350 g / 12 oz*
8-12	*Slices of crusty bread*	*8-12*

1. Wash and generally prepare all the fish. Cut the squid and octopus into strips.
2. Chop the deseeded chilli pepper, onion, celery, parsley and basil.
3. Heat the olive oil in a large, deep pan with 1 clove of garlic, the deseeded chilli pepper and the chopped vegetable and a little salt and pepper. Cook lightly, then add strips of squid and octopus, cover and simmer until tender.
4. Stir in the white wine and allow this to evaporate. Add the peeled tomatoes, 1¼ cups [300 ml / ½ pint] water, stir well and then add the rest of the fish and cook until tender.
5. Prepare 2-3 slices of bread per person, rubbing with crushed garlic and either frying in oil, toasting under the broiler (grill) or in the oven. Put the bread on the individual plates and pour over the fish stew.

Moscardini alla camoglina

Octopus Camoglina-Style

01:00 01:30

American	Ingredients	Metric/Imperial
1¾ lb	*Octopus*	*800 g / 1¾ lb*
⅓ cup	*Vegetable oil*	*75 ml / 3 fl oz*
3	*Garlic cloves*	*3*
⅓ cup	*White wine*	*75 ml / 3 fl oz*
5 oz	*Chopped tomatoes*	*140 g / 5 oz*
1 tbsp	*Tomato purée*	*1 tbsp*
2	*Bay leaves*	*2*
½	*Chilli pepper*	*½*
1	*Sweet red pepper*	*1*
	Salt and pepper	

1. Carefully clean the octopus. If they are rather large, cut them in half. Wash thoroughly, drain and brown in a large frying pan with heated oil and crushed cloves of garlic.
2. Cook until all the water has disappeared, sprinkle with white wine, evaporate and add the tomatoes and purée, bay leaves, a large piece of chilli, the deseeded sweet red pepper cut in four, salt and pepper. Cover and cook very gently for about 1¼ hours. During cooking, ensure that the juice does not dry up too much and, if necessary, add a little water.
3. When the cooking is over, the juice must be thick and very red. Remove the garlic, red pepper and chilli.

Cook's tip: this dish is also suitable for freezing.

Polipi alla Marianna

Octopus Marianna

00:15 02:30

American	Ingredients	Metric/Imperial
1¾ lb	*Octopus*	*800 g / 1¾ lb*
¾ cup	*Vinegar*	*175 ml / 6 fl oz*
2	*Onions*	*2*
2	*Garlic cloves*	*2*
2	*Cloves*	*2*
¼ cup	*Vegetable oil*	*50 ml / 2 fl oz*
	Salt and pepper	
3 tbsp	*Brandy*	*2 tbsp*

1. Preheat oven to 350°F / 180°C / Gas Mark 4.
2. Clean the octopus, remove eyes and vesicles. Wash them thoroughly under a cold tap and then in a mixture of cold water and a ¼ cup [50 ml / 2 fl oz] vinegar. Cut the octopus into large pieces.
3. Finely chop the onion and garlic. Put the octopus in an ovenproof dish, add the chopped garlic and onion, 2 cloves, the oil and the rest of the vinegar. Season generously with salt and pepper, add just enough water to cover all the ingredients. Cover with the lid and then cook in a moderate oven for about 2 hours.
4. Turn the oven up to 425°F / 220°C / Gas Mark 7.
5. Remove the casserole from the oven, sprinkle the brandy over the octopus, put the lid back on the casserole and return to the oven for 20 minutes.

Polipetti e seppioline affogati

Stewed Octopus and Cuttlefish

00:10 00:30

American	Ingredients	Metric/Imperial
1¼ lb	*Octopus and cuttlefish*	*600 g / 1¼ lb*
2	*Garlic cloves*	*2*
¼ cup	*Vegetable oil*	*50 ml / 2 fl oz*
5	*Fresh tomatoes*	*5*
½	*Sweet pepper*	*½*
	Salt and pepper	
5 tbsp	*White wine (optional)*	*4 tbsp*
1 tbsp	*Chopped parsley*	*1 tbsp*

1. Buy the octopus and cuttlefish ready cleaned or frozen. In a stew pot or casserole lightly fry the cloves of garlic in oil, remove the garlic and add the cuttlefish and octopus (if the cuttlefish are large, cut them into rings).
2. Allow fish to cook for a few minutes in the oil, add the tomatoes, peeled and seeded, a piece of sweet pepper, salt and a pinch of pepper, and if liked the white wine. Cover, lower the heat and cook for at least 20 minutes. Serve sprinkled with chopped parsley.

Carpa alla birra

Carp Cooked in Beer

00:30 00:25

American	Ingredients	Metric/Imperial
1 (1¾ lb)	*Carp (freshwater fish)*	*1 (800 g / 1¾ lb)*
¼ cup	*Butter*	*50 g / 2 oz*
2 tbsp	*Vegetable oil*	*1½ tbsp*
¼ tsp	*Chopped rosemary*	*¼ tsp*
¼ tsp	*Chopped sage*	*¼ tsp*
¼ tsp	*Mixed herbs*	*¼ tsp*
¼ tsp	*Chopped bay leaves*	*¼ tsp*
¼ tsp	*Chopped thyme*	*¼ tsp*
¼ tsp	*Chopped marjoram*	*¼ tsp*
1 quart	*Beer*	*1 litre / 1¾ pints*

1. Clean the carp thoroughly, removing the fins and gutting it. Wash and dry.
2. Heat the butter and oil in a pan, add chopped rosemary, sage and herbs and then add the carp.
3. Chop the bay leaves, thyme and marjoram. Turn up the heat under the pan, add the chopped herbs and all the beer together. Reduce the heat to moderate and continue to cook, turning the fish once only.
4. When the fish is cooked, the liquid in the pan should have reduced by half.
5. Transfer the carp to a heated serving dish, sieve the sauce, reheat and pour over the fish. Serve either hot or cold.

Carpa alla Chaplin con riso e salsa

Carp in Sauce with Rice

01:00 01:00

American	Ingredients	Metric/Imperial
1 (2 lb)	*Carp*	*1 (1 kg / 2 lb)*
	Salt and pepper	
3	*Garlic cloves*	*3*
2	*Cloves*	*2*
¼ tsp	*Powdered bay leaves*	*¼ tsp*
¼ tsp	*Powdered thyme*	*¼ tsp*
4	*Lemons*	*4*
1	*Onion*	*1*
1	*Carrot*	*1*
2 tbsp	*Chopped parsley*	*1½ tbsp*
2 tbsp	*Butter*	*25 g / 1 oz*
¼ cup	*Flour*	*25 g / 1 oz*
1 cup	*Rice*	*200 g / 7 oz*

1. Clean the carp, remove the scales, wash and cut into slices, lay these in a deep dish and sprinkle with salt.
2. In a mortar, pound 1 clove of garlic, 1 clove and the powdered bay and thyme, gradually add the juice of 1 lemon and pour this mixture over the fish. Leave for 20 minutes, stirring from time to time.
3. Chop the other clove of garlic, the onion, carrot and parsley and put into a pan with 2½ cups [600 ml / 1 pint] of water. Add 1 clove, the juice of a lemon, some shavings of lemon peel and a little pepper, bring to the boil and simmer until the vegetables are cooked. Add 2½ cups [600 ml / 1 pint] of cold water and strain into a heatproof casserole. Transfer the fish from the marinade into the casserole, bring the liquid to the boil and simmer for 15 minutes.
4. Remove the fish and place on a heated serving dish, taking care that it does not break. Remove half the liquid, reduce the remainder and thicken by adding the butter mixed with flour in small pieces, whisk until smooth.
5. Surround the fish with boiled or steamed rice, pour some of the sauce over the fish and serve the rest separately in a sauceboat.

Conchiglie di pesce gratinato

Scalloped Dentex au Gratin

00:30 00:20

American	Ingredients	Metric/Imperial
14 oz	*Dentex (perch)*	*400 g / 14 oz*
¼ cup	*Butter*	*50 g / 2 oz*
¼ cup	*Cognac*	*50 ml / 2 fl oz*
1 cup	*Béchamel sauce (see page 162)*	*225 ml / 8 fl oz*
1	*Egg yolk*	*1*
2 tbsp	*Grated parmesan cheese*	*1½ tbsp*
½ cup	*Bread crumbs*	*50 g / 2 oz*
4	*Scallop shells*	*4*

1. Preheat oven to 400°F / 200°C / Gas Mark 6.
2. Poach the fish, drain and remove the skin and bones.
3. Dice the flesh and sauté lightly in butter. Sprinkle with a little cognac.
4. Prepare the béchamel sauce, then stir in an egg yolk and the grated cheese.
5. Butter the scallop shells and spoon a little béchamel into each; then lay the fish on it and cover with another layer of sauce. Top with bread crumbs and crisp in the oven for a few minutes.

Dentici alle mandorle

Dentex with Almonds

00:20 01:00

American	Ingredients	Metric/Imperial
2	*Dentex (perch)*	*2*
2	*Lemons*	*2*
12	*Peppercorns*	*12*
	Salt	
1	*Carrot*	*1*
1	*Celery stalk*	*1*
1	*Small bunch of parsley*	*1*
½ cup	*Flaked almonds*	*50 g / 2 oz*
¼ cup	*Vegetable oil*	*50 ml / 2 fl oz*
1	*Onion*	*1*
2 tbsp	*Flour*	*15 g / ½ oz*
Scant ¼ cup	*Tomato paste*	*3 tbsp*
1½ cups	*Green olives*	*225 g / 8 oz*
2 tbsp	*Capers*	*1½ tbsp*
½ tsp	*Anchovy paste*	*½ tsp*
¼ cup	*Wine vinegar*	*50 ml / 2 fl oz*
1 tsp	*Sugar*	*1 tsp*

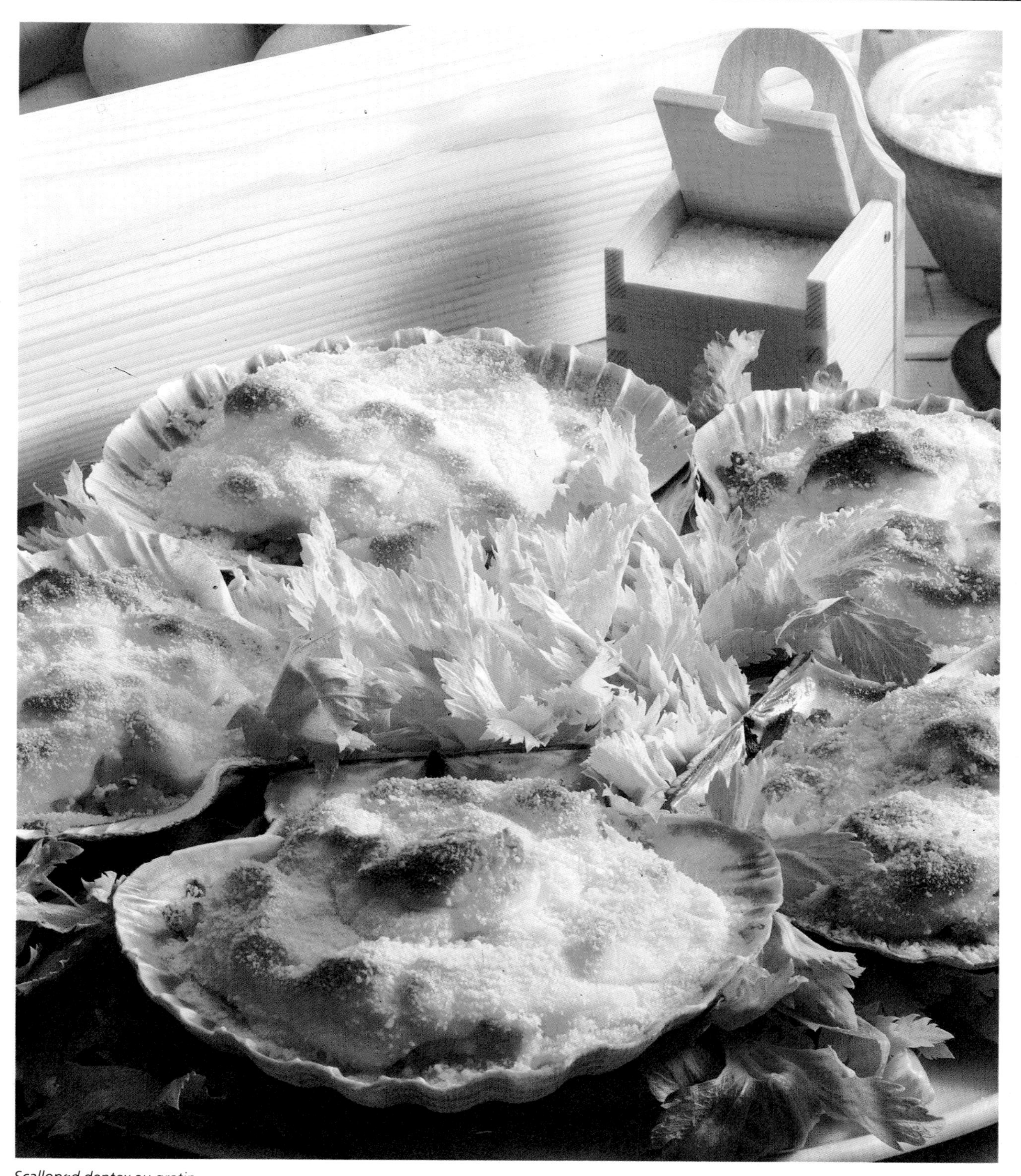

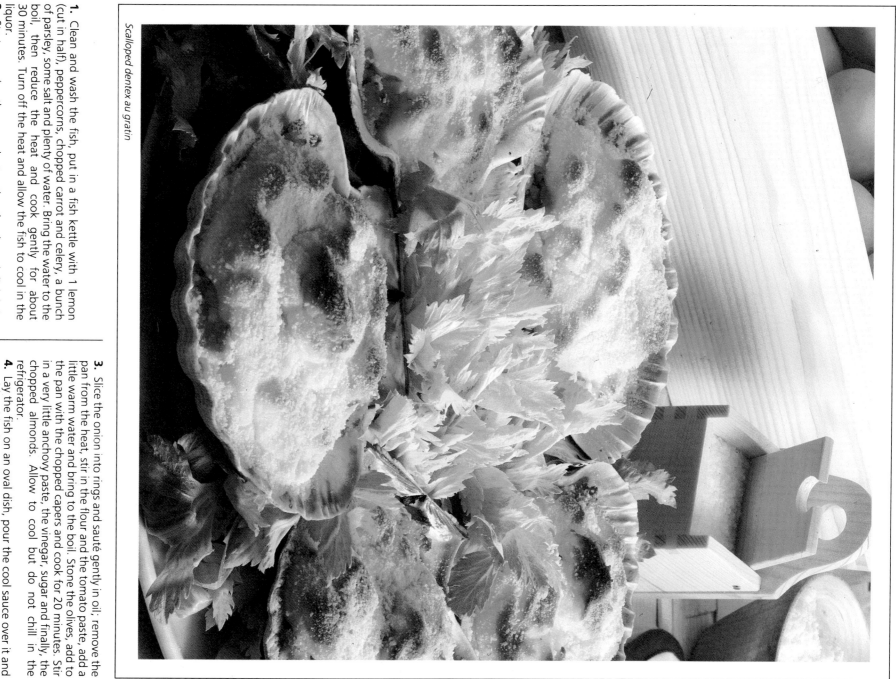

Scalloped dentex au gratin

1. Clean and wash the fish, put in a fish kettle with 1 lemon (cut in half), peppercorns, chopped carrot and celery, a bunch of parsley, some salt and plenty of water. Bring the water to the boil, then reduce the heat and cook gently for about 30 minutes. Turn off the heat and allow the fish to cool in the liquor.
2. Start preparing the sauce by toasting the almonds lightly in the oven.
3. Slice the onion into rings and sauté gently in oil; remove the pan from the heat, stir in the flour and the tomato paste, add a little warm water and bring to the boil. Stone the olives, add to the pan with the chopped capers and cook for 20 minutes. Stir in a very little anchovy paste, the vinegar, sugar and finally, the chopped almonds. Allow to cool but do not chill in the refrigerator.
4. Lay the fish on an oval dish, pour the cool sauce over it and garnish with slices of lemon and toasted almonds arranged alternately.

Perch rolls

Involtini di pesce persico

Perch Rolls

00:30 | 00:30

American	Ingredients	Metric/Imperial
8	*Perch*	8
4	*Salted anchovies*	4
1	*Small bunch of parsley*	1
1	*Garlic clove*	1
	Salt and pepper	
16	*Sage leaves*	16
¼ cup	*Flour*	25 g / 1 oz
¼ cup	*Butter*	50 g / 2 oz
¼ cup	*Vegetable oil*	50 ml / 2 fl oz
1	*Lemon*	1

1. Clean the perch carefully, split each one into half and remove all the bones.
2. Wash, split and bone the anchovies, then cut each half into two.
3. Chop the garlic with half the parsley and sprinkle this mixture onto the fish halves. Add pepper, a leaf of sage and a piece of anchovy. Roll the perch around the anchovy and herb filling and secure with a toothpick. Flour the rolls.
4. Heat the oil and butter in a heavy pan, then slip in the fish rolls and cook over medium heat.
5. When the fish are cooked on all sides, sprinkle with the remaining chopped parsley, the juice of a lemon, salt and pepper. Leave them in the pan for 1 minute, then serve hot.

Cotolette di pesce persico

Fried Fillets of Perch

00:30 | 00:10
Marinating time 02:00

American	Ingredients	Metric/Imperial
1	*Egg*	1
1	*Lemon*	1
4	*Fillets of perch*	4
1	*Large bunch of sage*	1
¼ cup	*Butter*	50 g / 2 oz
¼ cup	*Vegetable oil*	50 ml / 2 fl oz
1 cup	*Bread crumbs*	100 g / 4 oz
2	*Sweet red peppers*	2

1. Beat the egg and lemon juice together until the mixture becomes a pale yellow cream. Immerse the fillets of perch in this mixture, completely cover with sage leaves and marinate for 2 hours, turning once only.
2. Heat the butter and oil in a frying pan, sauté some sage leaves for 1-2 minutes, then discard the sage.
3. Coat the marinated fillets, one at a time, with bread crumbs, slip them into the pan and cook for 8-9 minutes, only turning once.
4. Serve hot with the deseeded sliced sweet red peppers.

Salmone in salsa verde

Salmon in Green Sauce

02:00 — 01:00

American	Ingredients	Metric/Imperial
1 cup	*White wine*	*225 ml / 8 fl oz*
	Bouquet garni	
2	*Carrots*	*2*
1	*Onion*	*1*
4	*Slightly crushed peppercorns*	*4*
2 lb	*Salmon*	*1 kg / 2 lb*
5 tsp	*Gelatin*	*5 tsp*
3 tbsp	*Port*	*2 tbsp*
4	*Eggs*	*4*
1	*Bunch of parsley*	*1*
1	*Bunch of watercress*	*1*
1	*Small bunch of tarragon*	*1*
1	*Gherkin*	*1*
1	*Anchovy fillet*	*1*
½ cup	*Butter*	*100 g / 4 oz*
¼ cup	*Vegetable oil*	*50 ml / 2 fl oz*
2 tbsp	*Vinegar*	*1½ tbsp*
	Salt and pepper	
2	*Tomatoes*	*2*

1. Prepare a court-bouillon by bringing the white wine and an equal quantity of water to the boil with bouquet garni, sliced carrots, onions and peppercorns. Lower the heat, cover and simmer for 30 minutes, then allow to cool.
2. Clean and wash the pieces of salmon and put them in a saucepan with the court-bouillon. Cover and bring back to the boil. Lower the heat and simmer for 30 minutes
3. Lift the fish carefully from the liquid using a fish slice and place on a serving dish. Strain the liquid through a fine sieve or muslin and retain.
4. Prepare a gelatin by sprinkling on top of 3 tablespoons boiling water; dissolve completely. Add to this 2½ cups [600 ml / 1 pint] of the fish liquid, with the port; mix well.
5. Hard-cook (boil) 3 eggs, rinse in cold water, separate yolk from white in remaining egg.
6. Wash the parsley, watercress and tarragon and chop in a blender with the gherkin and anchovy fillet.
7. Soften the butter and add to the blender gradually with 1 raw egg yolk and 1 hard-cooked egg yolk. Switch on the machine again, add the oil, vinegar, salt and pepper, blending all together. Transfer to a sauceboat.
8. Cover the fish with the jelly allowing it to run on to the serving dish. Coat fish several times with wine jelly.
9. Garnish the serving dish and fish with slices of tomato, sliced hard-cooked eggs and the jelly, on the plate, roughly chopped with a knife.

Salmone del ghiottone

Salmon Filler

00:30 — 00:15

American	Ingredients	Metric/Imperial
½ lb	*Potatoes*	*225 g / 8 oz*
Scant ¼ cup	*Milk*	*3 tbsp*
2 tbsp	*Butter*	*25 g / 1 oz*
7 oz can	*Salmon*	*200 g / 7 oz can*
	Salt and pepper	
⅔ cup	*Mayonnaise (see page 175)*	*150 ml / ¼ pint*
2	*Hard-cooked (boiled) eggs*	*2*
4	*Gherkins*	*4*
1 tsp	*Capers*	*1 tsp*
6	*Olives*	*6*

1. Peel, quarter and cook 2 large potatoes, drain and mash with milk and a knob of butter.
2. Drain the salmon and remove the bones. Put the mashed potatoes and salmon together in a bowl, add salt and pepper and combine until the mixture is smooth and uniform. Cover and cool.
3. Choose an oval dish, shape the mixture into the form of a fish and garnish with mayonnaise, slices of hard-cooked (boiled) egg, gherkins, capers and olives. Serve with rice or potato salad and green salad.

Trotelle salmonate

Young Salmon Trout

00:35 — 00:40

American	Ingredients	Metric/Imperial
4	*Young trout*	*4*
1	*Celery stalk*	*1*
1	*Onion*	*1*
2	*Carrots*	*2*
	Salt	
¼ cup	*Cream*	*50 ml / 2 fl oz*
1 cup	*Béchamel sauce (see page 162)*	*225 ml / 8 fl oz*
1 tsp	*Herb mustard*	*1 tsp*
1 cup	*Mayonnaise (see page 175)*	*225 ml / 8 fl oz*
1	*Lemon*	*1*
1	*Sprig of parsley*	*1*

1. Wash, gut and clean the fish. Place in a saucepan.
2. Pour enough cold water to cover the fish into the saucepan and put in all the washed roughly chopped vegetables. Season with salt.
3. Bring to the boil and simmer gently for 15 minutes, remove from the water carefully with a fish slice, place on a serving dish and allow to cool.
4. Make a thick cream by mixing together the cream, béchamel sauce, mustard and the mayonnaise.
5. Remove the skin from the young trout and cover completely with the savoury sauce. The fish can be garnished with slices of lemon and sprigs of parsley. Serve with boiled potatoes and sliced zucchini (courgettes) or green beans.

Tinche alla piemontese

Piedmontese Tench

00:15 | 00:35

American	Ingredients	Metric/Imperial
6	*Tench (freshwater fish)*	6
¾ cup	*Flour*	75 g / 3 oz
	Salt and pepper	
3 tbsp	*Butter*	40 g / 1½ oz
1	*Onion*	1
½ tsp	*Sage*	½ tsp
3 tbsp	*Vinegar*	2 tbsp
3 tbsp	*Grape juice*	2 tbsp

1. Thoroughly clean the tench and dip in flour, season with salt and pepper.
2. In a frying pan heat the butter, fry the fish on both sides and keep warm.
3. Put the finely chopped onion and the sage in the cooking juices, cook for 4 minutes until the onion is soft and transparent, add the vinegar and grape juice. Boil for 4 minutes, pour the sauce over the fish and serve hot.

Tench Piedmontese

Trout in cases

Trota al cartoccio

Trout in Cases

00:20 | 00:35

American	Ingredients	Metric/Imperial
4	*Trout*	4
½ tsp	*Chopped thyme*	½ tsp
½ tsp	*Chopped marjoram*	½ tsp
½ tsp	*Chopped rosemary*	½ tsp
	Salt and pepper	
1	*Lemon*	1
2	*Garlic cloves*	2
½ cup	*Olives, stoned*	75 g / 3 oz
1 tbsp	*Chopped parsley*	1 tbsp
¼ cup	*Butter*	50 g / 2 oz
½ lb	*Tomatoes*	225 g / 8 oz
½ cup	*Flour*	50 g / 2 oz
½ cup	*Dry white wine*	125 ml / 4 fl oz

1. Clean, gut and wash the trout, then stuff the stomachs with a mixture of thyme, marjoram, rosemary, salt, pepper and the juice of the lemon.
2. Crush the garlic, chop the olives and mix with the chopped parsley.
3. Heat 1 tablespoon [15 g / ½ oz] butter in a pan and add the garlic, parsley and olives with the peeled chopped tomatoes and cook gently for 10 minutes.
4. Dip the trout in flour, shake off excess, heat the remaining butter, cook the trout until golden on each side.
5. Preheat the oven to 350°F / 180°C / Gas Mark 4.
6. Place each trout on a sheet of foil, sprinkle with white wine, cover with the olive and tomato sauce and season with salt and pepper. Close the foil cases, arrange on a baking sheet and cook in the oven for about 20 minutes.
7. Unwrap the foil cases and serve on heated plates.

Trotelle ripiene

Stuffed Young Trout

01:00 00:35

American	Ingredients	Metric/Imperial
4	*Young trout*	*4*
3 oz	*Mild provolone cheese*	*75 g / 3 oz*
1	*Small bunch of parsley*	*1*
4	*Crayfish tails*	*4*
	Salt and pepper	
4 drops	*Worcester sauce*	*4 drops*
3 tbsp	*Cognac*	*40 ml / 1½ fl oz*
1	*Egg*	*1*
4	*Whole crayfish*	*4*
¼ cup	*Dry white wine*	*50 ml / 2 fl oz*
1 tbsp	*Vegetable oil*	*1 tbsp*
½	*Lemon*	*½*
⅔ cup	*Cream*	*150 ml / ¼ pint*
2 tbsp	*Flour*	*15 g / ½ oz*
1 tbsp	*Tomato purée*	*1 tbsp*
3 tbsp	*Butter*	*40 g / 1½ oz*

1. Clean the trout, cut them half open with scissors, then remove the backbone with all the bones, being careful not to remove the head.

2. Grate the cheese. Chop the parsley. Thoroughly wash all the crayfish and remove just the flesh from the shell of the four tails.

3. In an earthenware dish put the provolone, the parsley, a little salt, a good pinch of pepper, 2 drops of Worcester sauce, 2 teaspoons of cognac and a little less than a whole egg. Stir well and blend together. Spread the prepared mixture onto each trout, and place a crayfish tail on top, then roll up the trout, starting with the tail, keeping it tightly against the crayfish.

4. Preheat the oven to 400°F / 200°C / Gas Mark 6.

5. Arrange the fish in a high-sided container, add the remaining crayfish, season with salt and pepper, sprinkle with white wine and 1 tablespoon of oil. Add remaining cognac and the juice of half a lemon. Put a sheet of oiled parchment paper or foil over the container and bake in a hot oven for 25 minutes. When cooked, lift the trout on to a serving dish and keep warm.

6. Strain the remaining juice of the fish container into a pan, add the cream in which 2 tablespoons [15 g / ½ oz] flour, has been blended. Put the pan on the heat and stirring continuously, bring to the boil. Add 1 tablespoon of tomato purée and a few drops of Worcester sauce. Taste and if necessary, add salt. Blend in the butter, pour the sauce into a sauceboat and serve with the fish.

Stuffed young trout

MEAT

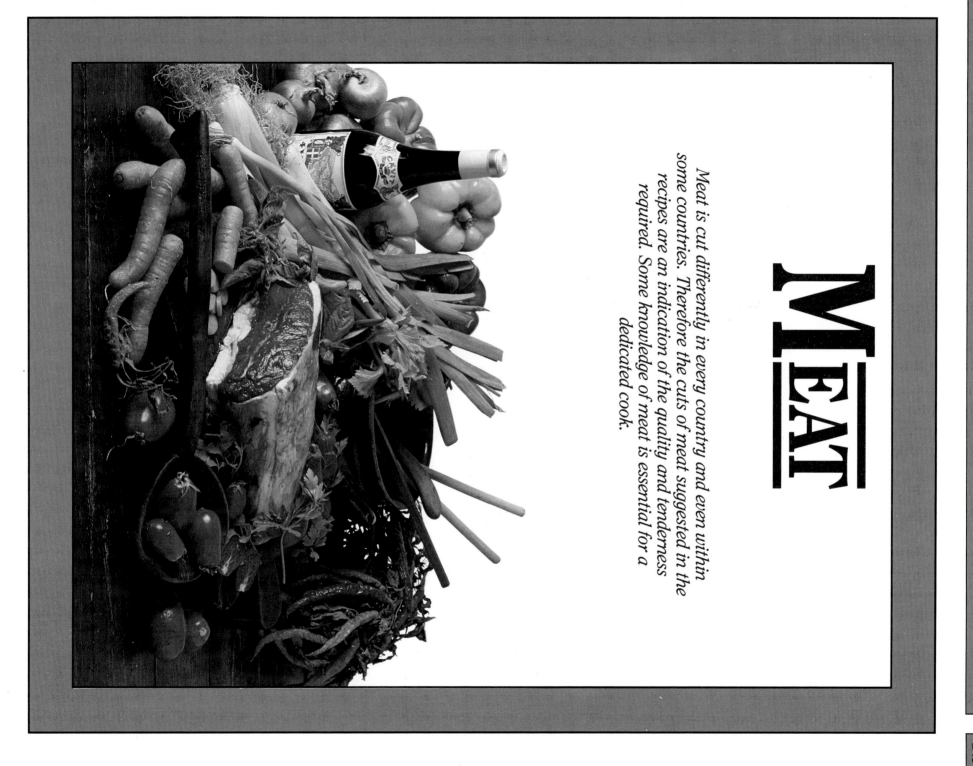

Meat is cut differently in every country and even within some countries. Therefore the cuts of meat suggested in the recipes are an indication of the quality and tenderness required. Some knowledge of meat is essential for a dedicated cook.

Meat

The most tender cuts of meat come from those sections of the animal where the least movement occurs, the hindquarters, and these are usually cooked by dry heat methods, such as roasting, broiling (grilling), pan roasting, sautéing and shallow frying. The parts of the animal which have the most muscular work to do in moving around are the forequarters. Tenderize these cuts with moist heat methods such as stewing, braising and poaching or deep frying.

Beef should be of a bright red color perhaps with a slight brownish tinge. Dark red meat may have been exposed to the air for some time but it could also be because it comes from an older animal. Look for firm flesh with a slight marbling of fat and this should be cream to dark cream depending on the feeding methods.

Veal should have pale pink flesh and firm, white fat.

Lamb should have reddish pink flesh with white to cream fat.

Pork will have pale pink flesh and white fat.

Avoid any flabby cuts of meat tinged with gray.

Beef cuts

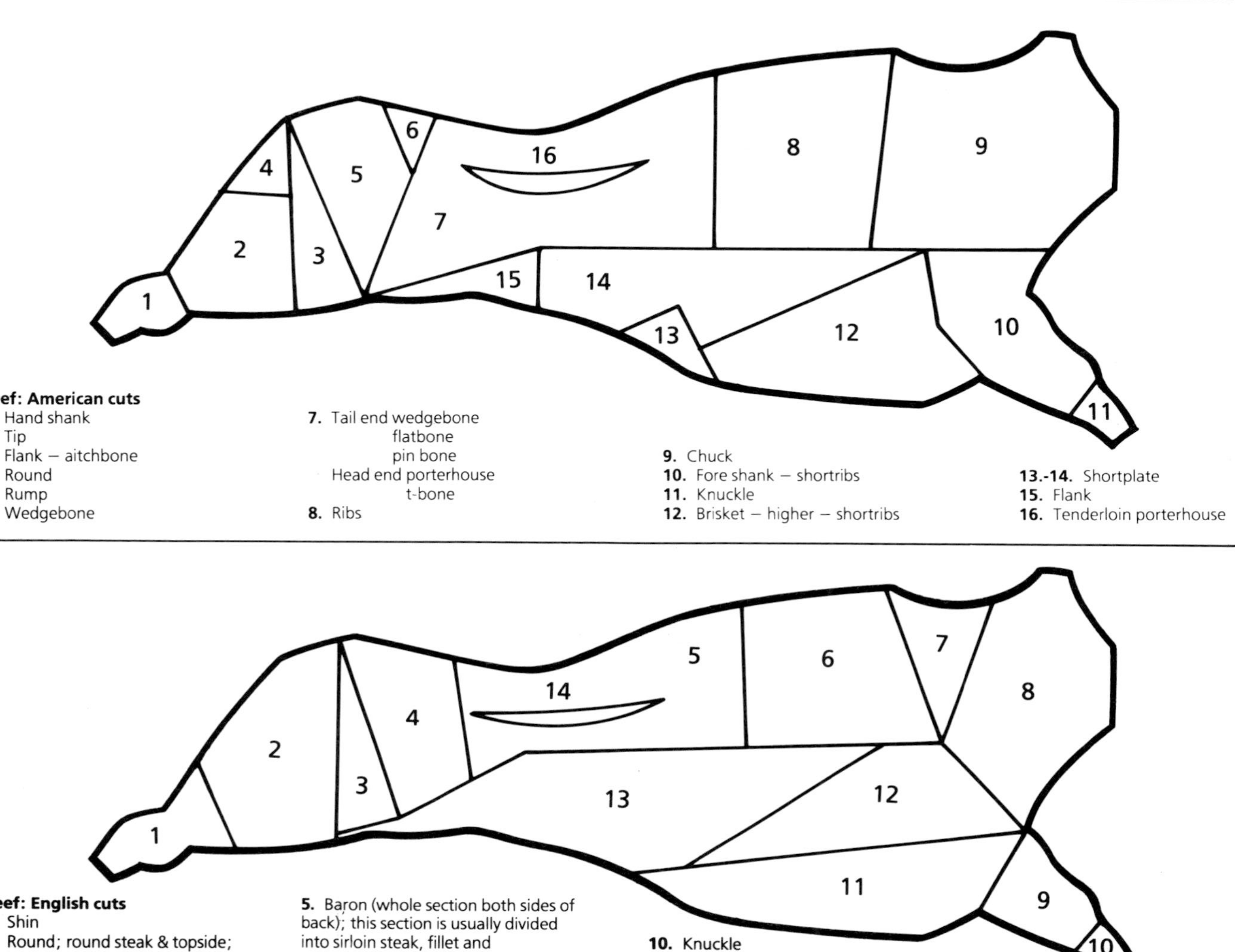

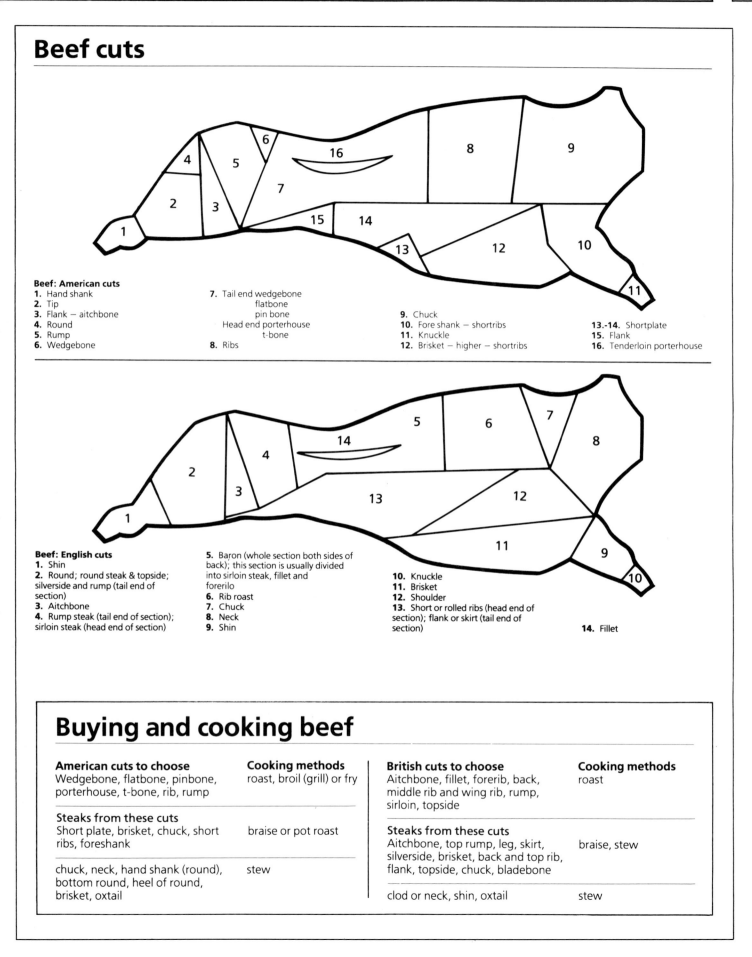

Beef: American cuts
1. Hand shank
2. Tip
3. Flank – aitchbone
4. Round
5. Rump
6. Wedgebone
7. Tail end wedgebone
flatbone
pin bone
Head end porterhouse
t-bone
8. Ribs
9. Chuck
10. Fore shank – shortribs
11. Knuckle
12. Brisket – higher – shortribs
13.-14. Shortplate
15. Flank
16. Tenderloin porterhouse

Beef: English cuts
1. Shin
2. Round; round steak & topside; silverside and rump (tail end of section)
3. Aitchbone
4. Rump steak (tail end of section); sirloin steak (head end of section)
5. Baron (whole section both sides of back); this section is usually divided into sirloin steak, fillet and forerilo
6. Rib roast
7. Chuck
8. Neck
9. Shin
10. Knuckle
11. Brisket
12. Shoulder
13. Short or rolled ribs (head end of section); flank or skirt (tail end of section)
14. Fillet

Buying and cooking beef

American cuts to choose	Cooking methods
Wedgebone, flatbone, pinbone, porterhouse, t-bone, rib, rump	roast, broil (grill) or fry
Steaks from these cuts Short plate, brisket, chuck, short ribs, foreshank	braise or pot roast
chuck, neck, hand shank (round), bottom round, heel of round, brisket, oxtail	stew

British cuts to choose	Cooking methods
Aitchbone, fillet, forerib, back, middle rib and wing rib, rump, sirloin, topside	roast
Steaks from these cuts Aitchbone, top rump, leg, skirt, silverside, brisket, back and top rib, flank, topside, chuck, bladebone	braise, stew
clod or neck, shin, oxtail	stew

Bollito freddo alla ligure

Ligurian Cold Boiled Beef

00:30 — Serves 6 — 03:00

American	Ingredients	Metric/Imperial
3¼ lb	*Beef brisket*	*1.5 kg / 3¼ lb*
1	*Carrot*	*1*
1	*Celery stalk*	*1*
1	*Onion*	*1*
1	*Bunch of parsley*	*1*
6	*Hard crackers (biscuits)*	*6*
1 cup	*Red wine*	*225 ml / 8 fl oz*
¼ cup	*Vegetable oil*	*50 ml / 2 fl oz*
2 tbsp	*Vinegar*	*1½ tbsp*
4	*Anchovies*	*4*
1 tbsp	*Capers*	*1 tbsp*
Scant ¼ cup	*Olive oil*	*3 tbsp*
1 tbsp	*Mustard*	*1 tbsp*
1	*Hard-cooked (boiled egg)*	*1*
	Salt and pepper	
	Pickled onions	
	Gherkins	

1. Put the rolled beef in a saucepan with the peeled carrot, celery, onion and a bunch of parsley, cover with water, bring to the boil and simmer for about 3 hours (or 40 minutes in a pressure cooker). When cooked, drain the beef from the stock (use stock for soup) and cool.
2. Cut the beef into small pieces and put it in a large pot. Crumble the hard crackers (biscuits) over and cover with strong red wine.
3. Beat the oil and vinegar together in a cup as for making a salad dressing, and pour over the meat. Return to the heat and simmer slowly until all the liquid has reduced; then cool.
4. Prepare a sauce by chopping and pounding (or make in a blender or food processor) the desalted and boned anchovy fillets and the capers, and dilute with olive oil. Add mustard, chopped hard-cooked (boiled) egg, salt and pepper and blend until you obtain a smooth sauce.
5. Remove the meat from the pot, place it on a serving dish and cover it with the sauce; allow to stand in a cool place but do not chill. Serve the beef decorated with pickled onions and gherkins.

Roast beef classico

Sirloin of Beef Pan-Roasted

00:15 — 00:32

American	Ingredients	Metric/Imperial
3¼ lb	*Beef tip (sirloin) joint*	*1.5 kg / 3¼ lb*
	Salt and pepper	
1 cup	*Olive oil*	*225 ml / 8 fl oz*
1	*Sprig of rosemary*	*1*
2	*Garlic cloves*	*2*

1. Wipe the meat well, roll and tie with string or ask the butcher to do this for you. Season with salt and pepper.
2. Put the olive oil into a heavy frying pan with rosemary and the cloves of garlic, remove these as soon as they have colored.
3. When the oil begins to smoke, add the meat and turn continuously for exactly 30 minutes, turn heat down to moderate after 5 minutes each side.
4. Remove and stand between two plates with a weight on top. Leave for 10 minutes to allow the juices to drain out, collect and return juice to the pan. Heat gently to boiling point and tip into a sauceboat.
5. Remove the string from the joint, carve into wafer-thin slices and serve immediately.

Arrosto vecchio Piemonte

'Old Piedmont' Roast

00:30 — 00:40

American	Ingredients	Metric/Imperial
¾ lb	*Shortcrust pastry*	*350 g / 12 oz*
1¼ lb	*Sirloin beef, in a single slice*	*600 g / 1¼ lb*
7 oz	*Prague ham*	*200 g / 7 oz*
¼ cup	*Béchamel sauce (see page 162)*	*50 ml / 2 fl oz*
1 tsp	*Mixed spice*	*1 tsp*
½ cup	*Butter*	*100 g / 4 oz*
2 or 3	*Sage leaves*	*2 or 3*

1. Preheat the oven to 350°F / 180°C / Gas Mark 4.
2. Roll out the pastry and lay the well beaten slice of beef on top. Put the ham on top of the meat, spread over a little béchamel and sprinkle with spice. Roll up the pastry with the meat filling. Damp and press the edges so that they are well sealed.
3. Place in a buttered baking pan, pour over the melted butter and add a few sage leaves. Put in a preheated oven and cook for 40 minutes, occasionally turning the roll carefully until it has taken on a good rosy color. If the cooking juice becomes too dry, add a little more butter.
4. Remove from the oven, let it cool, then cut into thick slices, putting two or three slices on each plate. Put the plates in a hot oven for a few moments before serving.

Costata alla campagnola

Country Sirloin

This is a stew of country origin, where the pot in the centre of the table invites drinking and lively conversation.

00:10 — 01:00 to 01:30

American	Ingredients	Metric/Imperial
Scant ¼ cup	*Vegetable oil*	*3 tbsp*
¼ cup	*Butter*	*50 g / 2 oz*
1	*Onion*	*1*
1	*Bunch of parsley*	*1*
1	*Celery stalk*	*1*
1	*Carrot*	*1*
3 lb	*Piece of sirloin*	*1 kg / 3 lb*
	Salt and pepper	
⅔ cup	*Dry white wine*	*150 ml / ¼ pint*
1	*Stock cube*	*1*

Country sirloin

1. Put oil and butter into a high sided heatproof pan, prepare and chop the vegetables; add the sirloin, boned and rolled. Brown on all sides.
2. Season with salt and pepper and moisten with good dry white wine. Add about 1 cup [225 ml / 8 fl oz] of stock made from a cube and boil on a vigorous heat until the wine and stock are almost absorbed.
3. Reduce the heat and cook for about 1 hour, turning the meat from time to time and, if necessary, adding more stock.
4. When the meat is cooked, place on a dish, return the pan to the heat with the strained sauce, add a little more white wine and reduce the heat to low. Cut the meat into thick slices, put it back into the sauce and serve immediately in the pan or casserole.

Roast beef allo champagne

Rib of Beef Cooked in Champagne

00:10 Standing time 00:20 — 00:20

American	Ingredients	Metric/Imperial
2 lb	*Rolled rib of beef*	*1 kg / 2 lb*
½ cup	*Butter*	*100 g / 4 oz*
Scant ¼ cup	*Oil*	*3 tbsp*
2 cups	*Dry champagne*	*450 ml / ¾ pint*
	Pepper	
1	*Stock cube*	1

1. Have bones removed by the butcher and the meat rolled. Wipe the meat and remove any membranes.
2. Melt the butter in a saucepan, then add the oil and brown the meat, turning continually for the first 10 minutes. Pour the champagne (other sparkling wine can be used) over the meat and continue to cook for a further 5 minutes, then add a few twists of pepper and the stock cube dissolved in ⅔ cup [150 ml / ¼ pint] hot water.
3. After 18 minutes, transfer the beef to a dish, cover and place a weight on top. Leave for 20 minutes to allow some of the juices to run out. Tip these back into the saucepan, reduce if necessary and serve separately. Carve a few slices from the joint and arrange on a heated serving dish together with the uncut portion. Surround the meat with fried or baked potatoes, warm through for a few seconds in a hot oven and serve.

Bocconcini di manzo piccanti

Spicy Beef Bouchées

00:25 — 01:20

American	Ingredients	Metric/Imperial
2	*Large onions*	2
¼ cup	*Vegetable oil*	*50 ml / 2 fl oz*
¼ cup	*Butter*	*50 g / 2 oz*
1½ lb	*Lean braising beef*	*700 g / 1½ lb*
	Salt and pepper	
½ tsp	*Paprika*	*½ tsp*
1	*Beef stock cube*	1
15 oz	*Peeled plum tomatoes*	*425 g / 15 oz*
2 or 3	*Potatoes*	*2 or 3*
1 tbsp	*Chopped parsley*	*1 tbsp*

1. Cut the onions into rings. Heat the oil and butter in a pan over a low heat and cook the onions for 6 minutes.
2. Cut meat into cubes and add to the onions, which can be pushed to the side of the pan, with salt and a generous sprinkling of paprika. Raise the heat and stir for a further 5 minutes.
3. Add 2½ cups [600 ml / 1 pint] water with the stock cube dissolved in it, the tomatoes and the peeled, thickly sliced potatoes. Bring to the boil and simmer for 1 hour. Test meat to make sure it is tender.
4. Taste and adjust the seasoning, add more paprika if necessary. Remove from the heat and leave covered for 10 minutes. Stir round with a wooden spoon to break down the potato and thicken the beef mixture. Sprinkle with parsley. Serve hot, with boiled rice or crusty bread.

Rib of beef cooked in champagne

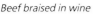

Beef braised in wine

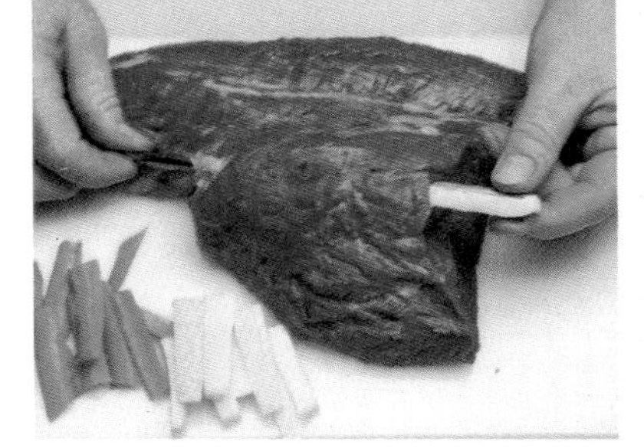

Brasato ubriaco

Beef Braised in Wine

00:15 Marinating time 12:00 | 01:45

American	Ingredients	Metric/Imperial
1¾ lb	Rump steak	800 g / 1¾ lb
1 (70 cl)	Bottle of Barolo wine	1 (70 cl)
2	Cloves	2
1	Onion	1
2	Carrots	2
2	Celery stalks	2
	Salt and pepper	
¼ tsp	Nutmeg	¼ tsp
⅓ cup	Butter	75 g / 3 oz
2	Bay leaves	2

1. Marinate the meat in red wine with the cloves stuck in the onion, the scraped carrots, cut into 4, and the washed celery. Before covering, add pepper and a sprinkling of nutmeg, leave to soak for 6 hours. Turn the meat and allow the other side to marinate.
2. Melt the butter in a saucepan with the bay leaves, put in the meat with the vegetables and fry gently for a few minutes, then cover with the red wine from the marinade, season with salt, cover and cook very slowly for 1½ hours or until meat is tender.
3. Rub the sauce through a sieve with the vegetables and collect it in the saucepan, slice the meat and lay on a heated serving plate; cover with the sauce. Serve with a green vegetable or polenta.

Rindsgulasch

Beef Goulash

00:40 | 01:30

American	Ingredients	Metric/Imperial
¾ lb	Onions	350 g / 12 oz
¾ lb	Tomatoes	350 g / 12 oz
2	Garlic cloves	2
1¾ lb	Chuck roast beef (chuck)	800 g / 1¾ lb
¼ cup	Butter	50 g / 2 oz
¼ tsp	Chopped marjoram	¼ tsp
½ tsp	Cumin	½ tsp
1	Bay leaf	1
2 tsp	Paprika	2 tsp
1 tbsp	Wine vinegar	1 tbsp
	Salt and pepper	
1	Beef stock cube	1

1. Chop the onions finely, skin the tomatoes, peel the garlic.
2. Cut the meat into 1½ in / 3½ cm squares.
3. Heat the butter, fry the onions and the crushed garlic for 4 minutes, push to one side.
4. Add the meat, stir until brown then add tomatoes, marjoram, cumin, a crumbled bay leaf, paprika and wine vinegar; season with salt and pepper. After cooking over a low heat for 30 minutes, add 2½ cups [600 ml / 1 pint] hot water in which the stock cube has been dissolved. Continue to cook until the meat is tender, by which time the liquid should be considerably reduced and very thick.

Brasato alle salsicce

Braised Meat with Sausages

00:30 | 01:30

American	Ingredients	Metric/Imperial
2 lb	*Topround (topside) beef*	1 kg / 2 lb
Scant ¼ cup	*Vegetable oil*	3 tbsp
¼ cup	*Butter*	50 g / 2 oz
4	*Onions*	4
1	*Garlic clove*	1
1	*Bouquet garni*	1
4	*Sausages*	4
¾ lb	*Small onions*	350 g / 12 oz

1. Ask the butcher to prepare beef or roll the boned meat tightly, tying it with string or thread, and brown it in oil and butter on a medium heat. When it is well browned on all sides add the finely chopped onions, the crushed garlic, and the bouquet garni.
2. Moisten with a ladleful of water and continue cooking for 1¼ hours with the heat low and the lid on the pan.
3. Meanwhile begin cooking the sausages in another pan. Brown on both sides, then plunge into boiling water and simmer for 3 minutes. Discard the cooking water. Peel, if necessary, and cut them into fairly thick slices, adding to the meat while it is cooking.
4. Now scald and peel the small onions, then add them to the meat and leave until they are cooked. Test the meat and season. Serve when tender.

Cook's tip: This dish is excellent eaten immediately but even better the next day! You can make this dish with braising beef, or with pork, even if it is fatty, as this cooking method uses up the meat fat. If using pork, remember that it should be served very hot.

Pilau sardo

Beef with Rice

00:10 | 02:00

American	Ingredients	Metric/Imperial
2 lb	*Joint of beef brisket*	1 kg / 2 lb
⅔ cup	*Oil*	150 ml / ¼ pint
¼ tsp	*Chopped thyme*	¼ tsp
¼ tsp	*Chopped bay leaf*	¼ tsp
¼ tsp	*Chopped rosemary*	¼ tsp
¼ tsp	*Garlic powder*	¼ tsp
½ cup	*Dry white wine*	125 ml / 4 fl oz
Scant 2 cups	*Stock*	450 ml / ¾ pint
1	*Egg yolk*	1
1	*Lemon*	1
	Salt and pepper	

1. Put the meat into a saucepan containing heated oil, add a ¼ teaspoon of thyme, bay, rosemary and garlic powder; pour over the wine gradually; when this has evaporated completely, add the stock. Cover and simmer until the meat is tender, which will take 1½-2 hours.
2. Remove from the pan. Strain the cooking juices, mix in the egg yolk and lemon juice and taste for seasoning.
3. Slice the meat, pour over some gravy, serving the rest in a sauceboat and serve with boiled rice.

Polpa alla bourguignonne

Italian Beef Bourgignon

00:30 | 01:15

American	Ingredients	Metric/Imperial
1 lb	*Shallots or small onions*	500 g / 1 lb
Scant ¼ cup	*Oil*	3 tbsp
¼ cup	*Butter*	50 g / 2 oz
1¼ lb	*Chuck eye beef (chuck) cubed*	600 g / 1¼ lb
	Salt and pepper	
½ cup	*Full-bodied red wine*	125 ml / 4 fl oz
½ lb	*Peeled plum tomatoes*	225 g / 8 oz
1	*Bay leaf*	1
1	*Stock cube*	1

1. Wash the onions, plunge into boiling water for 5 minutes, drain and skin. Transfer to a saucepan containing heated oil and butter. Brown lightly then add the cubed meat and plenty of salt and pepper. When the meat is slightly browned, add the red wine and allow to evaporate.
2. Add the tomatoes with the bay leaf and moisten with 2½ cups [600 ml / 1 pint] hot water in which the stock cube has been dissolved, taking care that the sauce does not stick to the pan.
3. Cook for at least 1 hour: the meat should then be tender and the sauce very thick. Serve with polenta or thick slices of crusty bread.

Cook's tip: This dish may be prepared in large quantities and will freeze well for up to 6 months.

Magatello in salsa del Don

Beef in 'Don' Sauce

00:30 | 00:00

American	Ingredients	Metric/Imperial
1¼ lb	*Fillet steak*	600 g / 1¼ lb
Sauce		
2	*Egg yolks*	2
¼ cup	*Oil*	50 ml / 2 fl oz
1	*Lemon*	1
3 tbsp	*Chopped black olives*	2 tbsp
½ tsp	*Anchovy paste*	½ tsp
1 tsp	*Mustard*	1 tsp
	Salt and pepper	

1. Have your butcher slice the beef very thinly (with the meat slicer) and then arrange the slices on a serving dish.
2. Put the egg yolks into the blender, switch on, add oil gradually and when you can see that it is well beaten, add the lemon juice, the chopped black olives, the anchovy paste, the mustard, and salt and pepper to taste. Blend again to obtain a smooth sauce. Transfer to a bowl and place in the refrigerator for 30 minutes.
3. Cover the fillet of beef with the sauce and garnish the dish with black olives.

Beef in 'Don' sauce

Meat, egg and spinach roll

Rollé verde e giallo

Meat, Egg and Spinach Roll

00:40 00:55

American	Ingredients	Metric/Imperial
1½ lb	Top round (topside) beef, in a slice	700 g / 1½ lb
1½ cups	Cooked spinach	300 g / 11 oz
¼ cup	Butter	50 g / 2 oz
¼ cup	Grated parmesan cheese	25 g / 1 oz
1 cup	Thick béchamel sauce (see page 162)	225 ml / 8 fl oz
5	Eggs – 3 hard-cooked (boiled)	5
11 oz	Ricotta (curd cheese)	300 g / 11 oz
1	Lemon	1
	Salt and pepper	
¼ tsp	Nutmeg	¼ tsp
2 or 3	Sprigs of rosemary	2 or 3
1	Onion	1
½ cup	Dry white wine	125 ml / 4 fl oz

1. Preheat the oven to 350°F / 180°C / Gas Mark 4.
2. Beat the beef flat, taking care not to tear it.
3. Mix the spinach with the butter, grated parmesan, béchamel sauce, 2 whole eggs, ricotta and grated rind of lemon. Season with salt, pepper and nutmeg.
4. Spread this mixture on the steak to within ¾ – 1¼ in / 2 – 3 cm of the edge. Place the 3 hard-cooked (boiled) eggs in the middle. Roll up carefully, ensuring that the filling stays in place and tie with kitchen string. Insert a few sprigs of fresh rosemary under the string.
5. Melt some butter in a casserole, add a chopped onion and then the meat roll; turn frequently so that the roll browns evenly. Sprinkle with white wine.
6. Transfer to the oven and bake, turning from time to time, for 45 minutes. To serve, cut the roll into fairly thick slices, arrange on a serving dish, strain and re-heat the cooking juices to pour over the meat.

Filetto in salsa

Beef Fillet in Sauce

00:25 00:20 to 00:30

American	Ingredients	Metric/Imperial
1½ lb	Fillet beef	700 g / 1½ lb
1	Garlic clove	1
1 oz	Bacon	25 g / 1 oz
2 tbsp	Chopped parsley	1½ tbsp
3 tbsp	Butter	40 g / 1½ oz
1 tsp	Curry powder	1 tsp
½ cup	Cream	125 ml / 4 fl oz

1. Spread out and beat the open fillet to form a single slice, lay on top a crushed clove of garlic, a little bacon cut into strips and a little chopped parsley. Roll up the slice of meat, then sew it with white thread or secure with toothpicks.
2. Melt a little butter in a frying pan and cook for about 20 minutes, finally adding the curry powder, the parsley and a little cream. Place on a heated serving dish and serve very hot.

Bollito misto

Boiled Mixed Meats

This famous dish comes from Piedmont and is ideal for a large family party.

01:00 03:00 to 04:00
Serves 10
Plus 06:00 soaking

American	Ingredients	Metric/Imperial
2 lb	Short ribs of beef	1 kg / 2 lb
2 lb	Bottom round of beef	1 kg / 2 lb
1 lb	Breast of veal, trimmed	450 g / 1 lb
1½ lb	Shoulder of lamb	700 g / 1½ lb
1	Calf's foot	1
½ lb	Belly of pork, trimmed	225 g / 8 oz
½ lb	Sausage	225 g / 8 oz
1	Ox tongue, soaked for 6 hours	1
1	Onion	1
2	Cloves	2
1	Garlic clove	1
2	Tomatoes, peeled and drained	2
2	Sprigs of parsley	2
8	Sprigs of thyme	8
2	Bay leaves	2
	Salt and pepper	
1 lb	New potatoes	450 g / 1 lb
24	Small onions	24
1 lb	Cabbage	450 g / 1 lb
1 lb	Zucchini (courgette)	450 g / 1 lb
1 lb	Carrots	450 g / 1 lb
1 lb	Green beans	450 g / 1 lb
1 quart	Béchamel sauce (see page 162)	1 litre / 1¾ pints
2½ cups	Green sauce (see page 69)	600 ml / 1 pint

1. Place all the meat in a very large pot with the soaked tongue, do not add the sausage at this stage. Cover with cold water, add the onion stuck with cloves, garlic, tomatoes, parsley, thyme and bay leaves.
2. Bring to the boil slowly and remove the scum as it rises to the surface.
3. Season with salt and pepper and simmer for 2-3 hours. Remove each joint of meat as it becomes tender; the veal and lamb will be cooked first. Add the sausage. Continue to skim the fat and scum from the surface as cooking progresses. The tongue will take longest to cook; drain it and skin when cooked.
4. At the end of 2½ hours start cooking the vegetables in a little stock from the meat or water, as preferred. Make sure that the vegetables are crisp. Keep warm.
5. Make the béchamel sauce with half meat broth and half and half milk and cream. Make the green sauce.
6. Carve the meats on a large heated serving platter and keep warm covered with foil in a low oven, adding a little meat stock from time to time. Garnish with parsley sprigs.
7. Serve the cooked vegetables on several platters covered with the béchamel sauce. Serve the green sauce separately, in a sauceboat.

Cook's tip: allow the stock to cool and skim for use in soups and sauces. Left-over meat can be served with a selection of salads for other meals.

Manzo brasato al barolo

Beef Braised in Red Wine

00:30 02:00

American	Ingredients	Metric/Imperial
1½ oz	*Cooked ham*	*40 g / 1½ oz*
3 lb	*Brisket beef*	*1.4 kg / 3 lb*
2 tbsp	*Lard*	*25 g / 1 oz*
Scant ¼ cup	*Oil*	*3 tbsp*
3 tbsp	*Butter*	*40 g / 1½ oz*
	Salt and pepper	
1 (70 cl)	*Bottle of Barolo wine*	*1 (70 cl)*
2	*Carrots*	*2*
2	*Onions*	*2*
4	*Celery stalks*	*4*
1	*Stock cube*	*1*
	Potatoes	

1. Dice the ham and insert it around the outside of the beef. Rub all over with lard.
2. Choose a heavy saucepan with a lid, add the oil and butter, allow to bubble and then lay the meat in the pan. Season with salt and pepper, pour in the wine, which should cover the meat completely.
3. Prepare and chop the vegetables, and when most of the wine has evaporated add them to the saucepan together with a stock cube made up with 2½ cups [600 ml / 1 pint] of water. Cover and braise for at least 2 hours.
4. Prepare boiled potatoes to serve with the meat. Remove the beef to a carving board, slice it and arrange on a heated dish, surrounded by the vegetables. Serve hot with cooking liquid in a sauceboat.

Brasato all'acciuga

Braised Beef with Anchovies

00:15 02:00

American	Ingredients	Metric/Imperial
3	*Slices of bacon*	*3*
Scant ¼ cup	*Vegetable oil*	*3 tbsp*
1¾ lb	*Chuck steak*	*800 g / 1¾ lb*
	Salt and pepper	
½ tsp	*Nutmeg*	*½ tsp*
3	*Anchovies, desalted and boned*	*3*
1	*Stock cube*	*1*
2 or 3	*Sprigs of parsley*	*2 or 3*

1. Chop the bacon into small pieces and put it in a pan with the heated oil, brown slightly, then add the piece of meat, season with salt and pepper and sprinkle with nutmeg. When the meat is browned on all sides, lower the flame and begin cooking.
2. Add the chopped anchovies and the parsley, mix in the 2½ cups [600 ml / 1 pint] stock made from the cube, cover and cook on a slow heat for about 2 hours.
3. Turn from time to time, add more stock if necessary, and check seasoning. Serve the meat in slices with boiled rice.

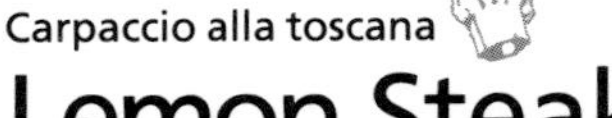

Carpaccio alla toscana

Lemon Steak

01:00 00:00

American	Ingredients	Metric/Imperial
1¼ lb	*Thin slices of fillet steak*	*600 g / 1¼ lb*
3	*Lemons*	*3*
	Salt and pepper	
8	*Small mushrooms (porcino)*	*8*
2 oz	*Grana cheese*	*50 g / 2 oz*
2 tbsp	*Chopped parsley*	*1½ tbsp*

1. The meat must be sliced very thinly, as if it was ham; it is advisable to have the butcher cut it on a machine.
2. Arrange the thin slices of steak on a serving dish. Beat juice of lemons in a cup with salt and pepper and sprinkle the steak with the mixture.
3. After 30 minutes, when the meat has absorbed the dressing, slice the flesh of well cleaned raw mushrooms and lay them on top of the meat with some slices of grana cheese and chopped parsley. Serve immediately.

Filetto all'uva

Fillet Steak with Grapes

00:30 00:45

American	Ingredients	Metric/Imperial
1¾ lb	*Fillet steak*	*800 g / 1¾ lb*
3 oz	*Raw ham, cut into strips*	*75 g / 3 oz*
¼ cup	*Butter*	*50 g / 2 oz*
1 lb	*Ripe white grapes*	*500 g / 1 lb*
Scant ¼ cup	*Brandy*	*3 tbsp*
½ cup	*Coffee (single) cream*	*125 ml / 4 fl oz*
2	*Cloves*	*2*
1 cup	*Stock*	*225 ml / 8 fl oz*
	Salt and pepper	
1	*Sugar lump*	*1*
½	*Lemon*	*½*

1. Lard the meat with small pieces of raw ham. Then tie the meat as for preparing a roast.
2. Melt the butter in a casserole, put in the piece of meat and brown it on all sides. Remove stones from grapes or use a seedless variety.
3. Blend grapes (or mash with a fork) together with brandy, sieve the mixture and pour the sauce over the meat. Add the cream, the cloves, ⅔ cup [150 ml / ¼ pint] stock, salt and pepper. Cover the pan, lower the heat and cook for about 20 minutes.
4. Put a sugar lump in a small pan and caramelize it, dilute with the juice of half a lemon and a little hot stock, then pour over the meat. Continue cooking, still covered, for a further 10 minutes.
5. Remove the meat, slice it (remember to remove all the string) and place it onto a heated serving dish. Return the pan to the heat with the sauce, add butter and heat on a high flame so that it thickens; then pour it onto the meat. Garnish the edge of the dish with white grapes which can be fried in butter. Serve with sauté potatoes and a green salad.

Lemon steak

Fillet en croûte

Filetto en croûte

Fillet en Croûte

01:00 | 00:45

American	Ingredients	Metric/Imperial
2	Carrots	2
2	Onions	2
1	Sprig of rosemary	1
½ cup	Butter	100 g / 4 oz
	Salt and pepper	
2 oz	Fat bacon	50 g / 2 oz
2 lb	Fillet steak	1 kg / 2 lb
2 oz	Chicken livers	50 g / 2 oz
1 ½ oz	Cooked ham	40 g / 1 ½ oz
2	Eggs	2
3 tbsp	Brandy	2 tbsp
1 (8 oz)	Packet of pastry	1 (225 g / 8 oz)

1. Preheat oven to 425°F / 220°C / Gas Mark 7.
2. Finely chop the prepared carrots and onions, fry them with rosemary in a little butter, and season with salt and pepper.
3. Slice the bacon very thinly and rub the fillet with it.
4. Grind (mince) the chicken livers and the ham finely or put through a food processor to obtain a fine mixture. Add to the carrots and onions with the egg and brandy. Season the fillet with salt and pepper and spread prepared sauce on top.
5. Roll the flaky or puff pastry out on the table, place the fillet on top and close it, pressing the edges down well so that it is completely sealed. Make small holes in the pastry with a fork, and finally brush it with the beaten egg.
6. Put the fillet wrapped in pastry in an oven pan and place in the oven for 15 minutes. Reduce the temperature to 325°F / 170°C / Gas Mark 3 for about 30 minutes.
7. Remove from the oven, allow to cool a little, cut the meat into slices and arrange it on a serving dish.

Costata di manzo alla griglia

Grilled Sirloin Steak

00:30 Marinating time 00:30 | 00:12

American	Ingredients	Metric/Imperial
½ cup	Olive oil	125 ml / 4 fl oz
¼ tsp	Chopped sage	¼ tsp
½ tsp	Chopped mint	½ tsp
¼ tsp	Chopped tarragon	¼ tsp
	Salt and pepper	
4	Sirloin steaks	4
2	Tomatoes	2
1	Sweet pepper	1
Scant ¼ cup	Oil	3 tbsp

1. Pour olive oil into a bowl and add the sage, mint and tarragon leaves, washed and finely chopped, season with salt and pepper and put the steaks in to marinate for about 30 minutes.
2. Wash and halve the tomatoes and the deseeded peppers. Heat the oil in a frying pan and cook the tomatoes and peppers. Remove and keep warm in a heated dish.

3. Raise the heat, add the steaks drained of their marinade. Cook for just 4 minutes on each side, as the meat should remain quite red. Arrange the steaks on the heated serving dish, pour over a little of the oil flavored with the herbs, and garnish with the vegetables.

Bocconcini alla lombarda

Lombardy Bouchées

00:25 00:40

American	Ingredients	Metric/Imperial
1½ lb	*Rumpsteak*	800 g / 1½ lb
1	*Egg*	1
	Salt and pepper	
1 cup	*Bread crumbs*	100 g / 4 oz
¼ cup	*Vegetable oil*	50 ml / 2 fl oz
2	*Garlic cloves*	2
1 cup	*Cream*	225 ml / 8 fl oz
¼ tsp	*Nutmeg*	¼ tsp
1 tbsp	*Chopped parsley*	1 tbsp

1. Cut the beef into strips, trimming away gristle and fat. Coat in the egg beaten with a little salt and then in the bread crumbs, as for cutlets.
2. Heat the oil and fry meat on both sides. Drain the beef strips and keep warm in a covered dish.
3. Put the crushed garlic in a casserole (not a metal one) with a small amount of frying oil, and as soon as the garlic starts to brown add the pieces of meat and pour in all the cream. Turn down the heat and stir, otherwise the cream will burn, season with salt and pepper.
4. Stir from time to time and, turning the meat, carry on cooking for a further 20 minutes on an extremely low heat. Before serving sprinkle with nutmeg and chopped parsley. Serve accompanied by boiled rice.

Involtini tirolesi

Tyrolean Beef Potatoes

00:20 01:00

American	Ingredients	Metric/Imperial
8	*Slices of fillet beef*	8
	Salt	
¼ lb	*Cooked ham*	100 g / 4 oz
6	*Würstel (frankfurters)*	6
¼ cup	*Butter*	50 g / 2 oz
¼ cup	*Dry white wine*	50 ml / 2 fl oz
½	*Stock cube*	½
1¼ cups	*Aspic*	300 ml / ½ pint
	Pickles	

1. Have the meat sliced fairly thin, beat slices with a cutlet bat.
2. Salt the slices and place on each, 1 slice of cooked ham and half a frankfurter, scalded, with the skin removed. Roll the meat around the sausage to form an olive.
3. Heat the butter in a large frying pan and fry the olives until they are well browned. Moisten with white wine and evaporate it quickly. Add 1¼ cups [300 ml / ½ pint] of hot water with half a stock cube crumbled in and continue cooking on a low heat for about 45 minutes.

4. Prepare the aspic following the instructions on the packet and allow to cool, using cooking juices as part of the liquid. Drain the beef olives, arrange in an oval dish and decorate the space between the olives with pickles. Pour on the aspic, let it cool and place in the refrigerator. Serve with a salad.

Bistecche arrotolate

Rolled Steaks

00:10 00:10

American	Ingredients	Metric/Imperial
1¼ lb	*Beef steak (fillet or rump)*	600 g / 1¼ lb
4	*Anchovies*	4
16	*Green olives*	16
¼ cup	*Butter*	50 g / 2 oz
1 tbsp	*Oil*	1 tbsp
⅔ cup 3	*Tomato sauce (see page 171) or canned tomatoes*	150 ml / ¼ pint 3
½ tsp	*Chopped oregano*	½ tsp
	Salt and pepper	
1 tbsp	*Capers*	1 tbsp

1. Have the meat cut in approximately 6 in / 13 cm pieces and just over ¼ in / ½ cm thick.
2. Place an anchovy and 2 olives on each slice of meat. Fold the steak in half and close with a toothpick.
3. Heat butter and oil in a frying pan on a high heat and add the meat. Fry on both sides for 2 minutes, add the tomato sauce prepared in advance or the canned tomatoes crushed with a fork, oregano, pepper and salt, and cook slowly for 8 minutes.
4. Add chopped capers, cook for a further 2 minutes and serve hot.

Filetto estivo

Summer Steak

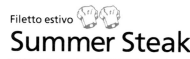

00:30 00:15

American	Ingredients	Metric/Imperial
1¾ lb	*Fillet steak*	800 g / 1¾ lb
1¼ cups	*Aspic*	300 ml / ½ pint
2 tbsp	*Vegetable oil*	1½ tbsp
¼ cup	*Butter*	50 g / 2 oz
	Salt	

1. Brown a piece of fillet steak in oil and butter on a very high heat. When it browns on all sides, add salt, then lower the heat for a few minutes, keeping the pan covered, then switch off the heat.
2. Put the well drained fillet on a chopping board and slice it thinly; pour the cooking juices into a cup and place it in the coldest part of the refrigerator.
3. Make a jelly with the aspic and let it cool. Take the cup with meat juices from refrigerator, remove the fat which will have formed on the surface and pour the cooking juices in to the jelly. Pour a little of it over the meat which has been arranged on a plate and return to the refrigerator.
4. Serve the meat, decorated with the aspic cut into cubes.

Involtini ai due sapori

Beef Olives with Two Different Flavors

01:00 | 01:00

American	Ingredients	Metric/Imperial
11 oz	*Round (top rump) steak, sliced*	*300 g / 11 oz*
11 oz	*Loin of pork, sliced*	*300 g / 11 oz*
¼ lb	*Bacon*	*100 g / 4 oz*
8	*Sage leaves*	*8*
2 oz	*Gruyère cheese*	*50 g / 2 oz*
¼ lb	*Cooked ham*	*100 g / 4 oz*
	Fennel seeds	
¼ cup	*Butter*	*50 g / 2 oz*
1 tbsp	*Oil*	*1 tbsp*
1	*Sprig of rosemary*	*1*
1	*Sprig of sage*	*1*
¼ cup	*Dry white wine*	*50 ml / 2 fl oz*
1	*Stock cube*	*1*
1 tsp	*Cornstarch (cornflour)*	*1 tsp*

1. Beat the slices of steak and pork until they are thin and flat, taking care not to tear them, remove any fat or gristle.
2. On each piece of steak place a slice of bacon, a sage leaf and a small strip of gruyère.
3. On each piece of the pork place a slice of ham, a sage leaf and 2 fennel seeds. Roll up each parcel and secure with a toothpick.
4. Melt some butter and oil in a heavy pan, add a sprig each of rosemary and sage. Place the olives in the pan and fry, browning them well on all sides. Add dry white wine and a twist of pepper and allow to cook slowly for 30-40 minutes, keeping the meat moist with water in which a stock cube has been dissolved. Remove the meat on to a heated serving dish.
5. Place the pan over the heat, add 2-3 tablespoons of water and warm through very gently. Thicken the cooking liquid with cornstarch and serve with a potato purée.

Polpettine alla béchamel

Beef Rissoles

00:30 | 00:06 each batch

American	Ingredients	Metric/Imperial
1 ½ cups	*Ground (minced) beef (cooked left-overs can be used)*	*350 g / 12 oz*
2	*Eggs*	*2*
1 ¼ cups	*Thick béchemal (see page 162)*	*300 ml / ½ pint*
2 tbsp	*Grated parmesan cheese*	*1 ½ tbsp*
¼ tsp	*Nutmeg*	*¼ tsp*
	Salt and pepper	
2 tbsp	*Flour*	*15 g / ½ oz*
	Bread crumbs	
1 cup	*Oil*	*225 ml / 8 fl oz*
	Lemon slices	

1. Combine the meat, eggs, béchamel sauce, parmesan, nutmeg, salt and pepper. Flour the hands and shape the rissoles into small, slightly flattened rounds. If time permits, chill for 30 minutes before coating.
2. Coat with bread crumbs and fry over a brisk heat in plenty of oil. Drain on paper towels to absorb the excess oil. Transfer to a warm serving dish and garnish with lemon slices.

Beef olives

Timballo alla giapponese

Japanese Timbale

00:30 00:40

American	Ingredients	Metric/Imperial
1⅔ cups	Rice	350 g / 12 oz
14 oz	Fillet of beef	400 g / 14 oz
½ cup	Dried mushrooms	50 g / 2 oz
3 tbsp	Vegetable oil	2 tbsp
1 tbsp	Sugar	1 tbsp
3 tbsp	Soy sauce	2 tbsp
9 oz	Fresh soy beans	250 g / 9 oz
	Salt and pepper	
Scant ¼ cup	Saki	3 tbsp

1. Preheat oven to 350°F / 180°C / Gas Mark 4. Line a deep ovenproof serving dish with foil.
2. Boil rice in plenty of salted water for 5 minutes, then drain. Cut the meat into cubes, soak mushrooms for 15 minutes in warm water and squeeze gently. Heat oil and fry meat together with mushrooms, sugar, soy sauce, fresh soy, salt and pepper. Add saki and evaporate, then pour over a little water and cook, stirring frequently for 20 minutes.
3. Pile rice onto foil in the dish, make a hollow in the centre and fill with meat and all the juices. Close foil and bake for 20 minutes, then serve very hot.

Trippa alla toscana

Tripe with Beans

00:10 01:50

American	Ingredients	Metric/Imperial
½ lb	Toscanelli or dried haricot beans	225 g / 8 oz
2 oz	Lean bacon	50 g / 2 oz
1	Onion	1
Scant ¼ cup	Oil	3 tbsp
1	Celery stalk	1
1	Carrot	1
1¾ lb	Tripe	800 g / 1¾ lb
	Salt and pepper	
1 tsp	Chopped marjoram	1 tsp
2	Bay leaves	2
2	Cloves	2
½ lb	Plum peeled tomatoes	225 g / 8 oz
1 quart	Stock	1 litre / 1¾ pints
3 tbsp	Grated parmesan cheese	2 tbsp

1. Soak the beans overnight in warm water, then drain.
2. Chop bacon and onion. Heat oil and sauté these lightly but without browning for 2 minutes. Add chopped celery and carrot and cook a further 2 minutes. Keeping heat very low, add tripe and season with pepper, marjoram, bay leaf and cloves.
3. Add tomatoes, beans and the stock, bring to the boil. Boil for 10 minutes then cover and simmer very gently for 1½ hours, making sure that there is always sufficient liquid in the pan.
4. Taste and adjust seasoning, sprinkle generously with freshly grated parmesan and serve.

Sartù

Neapolitan Bake

01:30 Serves 6 01:30

American	Ingredients	Metric/Imperial
1 cup	Ground (minced) beef	225 g / 8 oz
½	Bread roll	½
½ cup	Milk	125 ml / 4 fl oz
3	Eggs	3
½ cup	Grated cheese	50 g / 2 oz
	Salt and pepper	
3 tbsp	All purpose (plain) flour	2 tbsp
½ cup	Vegetable oil	125 ml / 4 fl oz
¼ cup	Butter	50 g / 2 oz
7 oz	Chicken livers	200 g / 7 oz
¼ tsp	Chopped sage	¼ tsp
¼ cup	White wine	50 ml / 2 fl oz
1 oz	Dried mushrooms	25 g / 1 oz
1	Garlic clove	1
¼ lb	Italian sausage	100 g / 4 oz
1	Onion	1
1½ cups	Rice	300 g / 11 oz
2 ¼ cup	Plum tomatoes or Tomato sauce (see page 171)	2 50 ml / 2 fl oz
½ cup	Stock	125 ml / 4 fl oz
1 tbsp	Dried bread crumbs	1 tbsp
1	Mozzarella cheese	1
¼ tsp	Nutmeg	¼ tsp

1. Mix the ground (minced) meat with the half bread roll soaked in milk (with the excess moisture squeezed out), 1 egg, 1 tablespoon of cheese, and salt and pepper to obtain a moist paste. It should not be too wet.
2. Shape the mixture into small balls, flour them and fry in heated oil and half the butter.
3. Clean and chop the chicken livers. Heat some butter in a pan with sage, add the livers and fry for 5 minutes. Add half the wine and cook for a further 5 minutes.
4. Soak mushrooms in water to cover for about 15 minutes.
5. In another frying pan heat the oil and put in the soaked, drained mushrooms, coarsely chopped, with the crushed garlic, pour in a little hot water, season with salt and pepper.
6. Keep the mushrooms to one side, then fry the sausage, cut into rounds. Drain off the fat when cooking is finished. Add to the pan with the chicken livers.
7. Preheat the oven to 400°F / 200°C / Gas Mark 6.
8. Gently fry in heated oil a very finely chopped onion, add the rice, moisten with the white wine and evaporate, add tomatoes or a little sauce and continue cooking the risotto, moistening with stock made from a cube. Cook the rice 'al dente', then remove it from the heat and add 1 tablespoon of grated cheese, a lightly beaten egg and a little milk.
9. Butter a timbale or a straight-sided mold and sprinkle it with bread crumbs, line the timbale sides and base with the risotto and in the centre alternate with the meatballs, mushrooms, chicken livers, sausage and mozzarella cut into pieces. When the ingredients are used up, add an egg beaten with last of the grated cheese, pepper, salt and a pinch of nutmeg. Cover with the remaining risotto and place in the preheated hot oven for 45 minutes.
10. Remove the mold from the oven, let it rest for a few minutes and turn it out onto a heated serving dish.

Stracotto di manzo

Stewed Beef

00:10 01:00

American	Ingredients	Metric/Imperial
1	Onion	1
1	Carrot	1
¼ cup	Butter	50 g / 2 oz
1 lb	Sirloin beef, boned and rolled	500 g / 1 lb
3 tbsp	Wine vinegar	2 tbsp
1 cup	Milk	225 ml / 8 fl oz
1 cup	Whipping (double) cream	225 ml / 8 fl oz
	Salt	

1. Peel and quarter onion, coarsely chop the carrot.
2. Heat butter in a heavy pan and, when foaming, add beef joint and brown meat all over. Add carrot and onion to pan and cook for 1-2 minutes.
3. Pour over vinegar and simmer for 5 minutes. Add milk and cream, cover and simmer for about 1 hour, adding more milk if required. Season with salt.
4. Remove joint, discard string, slice thickly and arrange on a hot serving plate. Pour sauce through a sieve over the meat and serve at once.

Polpettone fantastico

Decorated Meatloaf

00:45 03:10

American	Ingredients	Metric/Imperial
2½ cups	Ground (minced) beef or other meat	600 g / 1¼ lb
5 oz	Cooked ham	150 g / 5 oz
¼ lb	Italian sausage	100 g / 4 oz
	Chopped parsley	
4	Celery stalks	4
6	Eggs	6
¼ cup	Grated parmesan cheese	25 g / 1 oz
	Salt and pepper	
1 tbsp	Bread crumbs	1 tbsp
4	Carrots	4
1	Onion	1
1	Bouquet garni	1

1. Put the ground (minced) meat and ham into a large bowl with the ground (minced) sausage, some chopped parsley, 2 stalks of celery, finely chopped, 4 eggs and the parmesan cheese. Season with salt and pepper. Mix all these ingredients thoroughly until they form a sticky mixture, adding bread crumbs if the mixture is too wet. Use the food processor for this if possible.
2. Hard-cook (boil) 2 eggs and cool under running cold water, remove the shells.
3. Soak and wring out a clean white cloth and place the mixture on it, pressing it into the shape of a large salame sausage. Wash and peel 2 medium-sized carrots and lay them along the sides of a meatloaf; place one hard-cooked (boiled) egg at each end. Press these well into the meat so that they are covered, then wrap the cloth around the whole and sew up with white thread.
4. In a large saucepan bring 2 quarts [2 litres / 3½ pints] of water to the boil, add the onion, remaining celery and carrot. Immerse the meatloaf and cook for 3 hours over a medium heat. When quite cold, unwrap and cut into slices.

Cotolette di trita alla milanese

Milanese Minced Meat Cutlets

00:30 Chilling time 01:00 01:30

American	Ingredients	Metric/Imperial
1	Inside of bread roll	1
Scant ¼ cup	Milk	3 tbsp
1 lb	Ground (minced) meat (can be left-overs)	500 g / 1 lb
3	Eggs	3
1 tbsp	Grated parmesan cheese	1 tbsp
	Salt and pepper	
	Flour	
	Bread crumbs	
⅓ cup	Oil	75 ml / 3 fl oz
2 tbsp	Butter	25 g / 1 oz
1 tbsp	Chopped parsley	1 tbsp
2	Lemons	2

1. Soak the bread in warm milk, squeeze, then put through the grinder (mincer) together with the meat (if the meat you are using is already minced, put it through the grinder a second time), add 2 eggs, a little grated parmesan, salt and pepper. If the mixture is too soft add a few bread crumbs.
2. Shape into cutlets, flatten them and chill in the refrigerator for 1 hour.
3. Coat the cutlets in flour, the remaining egg and the bread crumbs. Heat oil and butter on a moderate heat and fry for 5 minutes on each side. Serve with a sprinkling of chopped parsley and lemon slices.

Scamone al forno

Roast Silverside

00:10 Cooling time 00:30 for joint 00:30

American	Ingredients	Metric/Imperial
1¾ lb	Top round beef (silverside)	800 g / 1¾ lb
⅓ cup	Mustard	4 tbsp
2 tbsp	Vegetable oil	1½ tbsp
2 tbsp	Butter	25 g / 1 oz
	Salt and pepper	
2	Sprigs of rosemary	2
3 tbsp	White wine	2 tbsp
1 tbsp	Brandy	1 tbsp
⅓ cup	Fresh cream	4 tbsp

1. Preheat oven to 475°F / 240°C / Gas Mark 9.
2. Choose a good quality joint of silverside, remove excess fat and smear the joint well with all but 1 tablespoon of the mustard. Place in a roasting pan with oil, butter, salt, pepper and rosemary.

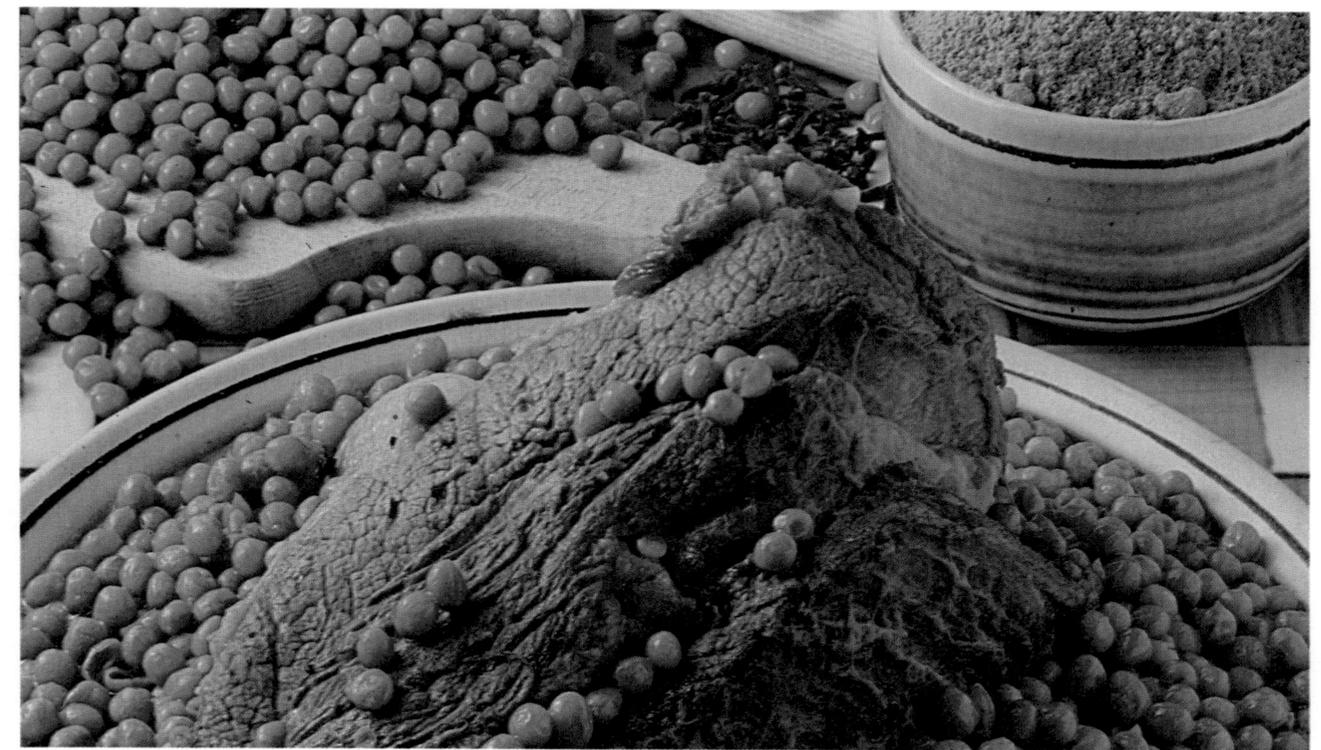

Roast silverside

3. Roast in the oven allowing 15 minutes per 1 lb / 450 g for a rare joint and 20 minutes per 1 lb / 450 g for a well done joint, turning from time to time and moistening occasionally with white wine if the meat appears to be getting too dry.
4. Remove from oven, cool slightly in the pan, then transfer to a serving dish, cover with foil and cool completely at room temperature.
5. Discard rosemary, pour meat juices into a saucepan and heat through. Put remaining mustard into a cup, add brandy and cream, mix well and add to juices in pan mixing well, then pour into a jug. Serve the beef thinly sliced, with the sauce.

Stufatino annegato

Spicy Beef Stew

00:20 02:15

American	Ingredients	Metric/Imperial
1½ lb	*Beef (flank)*	600 g / 1½ lb
7 oz	*Parma ham (single) piece*	200 g / 7 oz
11 oz	*Peas*	300 g / 11 oz
1	*Onion*	1
2	*Cloves*	2
⅔ cup	*Dry white wine*	150 ml / ¼ pint
1 quart	*Stock*	1 litre / 1¾ pints
¼ tsp	*Curry powder*	¼ tsp
	Salt and pepper	

1. Cut meat into 1 in / 2.5 cm cubes, trimming away fat. Put beef into a large saucepan, cube parma ham and pile, with the peas, around the meat; stud onion with cloves and add to pan. Pour over wine and cook over medium heat for 10 minutes.
2. Add stock and a pinch of curry powder. Cover and simmer for about 2 hours.
3. Just before serving add salt and pepper and serve hot.

Coda alla laziale

Lazio-Style Oxtail

00:30 03:30

American	Ingredients	Metric/Imperial
½	*Onion*	½
1	*Carrot*	1
1	*Leek*	1
1	*Celery stalk*	1
3	*Slices of raw ham*	3
Scant ¼ cup	*Oil*	3 tbsp
2 lb	*Oxtail*	1 kg / 2 lb
	Salt and pepper	
¼ tsp	*Chopped thyme*	¼ tsp
¼ tsp	*Chopped marjoram*	¼ tsp
2	*Bay leaves*	2
½ cup	*Dry white wine*	125 ml / 4 fl oz
14 oz	*Peeled plum tomatoes*	400 g / 14 oz
¼ tsp	*Nutmeg*	¼ tsp

1. Prepare the vegetables by peeling the onion, scraping the carrot and washing the leek and celery thoroughly. Chop the raw ham, onion, celery and carrot. Heat the oil in a casserole, add the vegetables and sweat over a low heat.
2. Cut the oxtail into small pieces and then cook it separately for 30 minutes in a pot of boiling salted water. Drain and add the meat to the vegetables. Allow the flavors to mingle for a few minutes by mixing well.
3. Add the herbs, season with salt and pepper and moisten with dry white wine. When the juice has evaporated, add the chopped tomatoes and sprinkle in some nutmeg.
4. Lower the heat and cook for 2 hours, adding a little water if the meat is drying out.
5. Serve very hot with mashed potatoes.

Cook's tip: the use of pressure cooker will reduce the cooking time by half, and also enhance the flavor.

1

2

3

1/2. Scoop seeds out of zucchini and fill with meat mixture.

3. Serve baked zucchini garnished with cucumber and carrot.

Turineisa di manzo

Stuffed Zucchini (Courgettes)

00:20 | 00:20

American	Ingredients	Metric/Imperial
8	*Small zucchini (courgettes)*	*8*
1½ cups	*Ground (minced) meat (left-overs will do)*	*350 g / 12 oz*
2 oz	*Continental sausage*	*50 g / 2 oz*
2	*Amaretti (small, hard macaroons)*	*2*
1	*Lemon*	*1*
1	*Pinch of nutmeg*	*1*
3 tbsp	*Seedless raisins*	*2 tbsp*
¼ cup	*Pine kernels*	*25 g / 1 oz*
¼ cup	*Grated parmesan cheese*	*25 g / 1 oz*
1	*Egg, beaten*	*1*
1	*Garlic clove*	*1*
	Salt and pepper	

1. Preheat oven to 350°F / 180°C / Gas Mark 4. Grease an ovenproof serving dish.
2. Wash zucchini, cut lengthwise and scoop out seeds.
3. In a large bowl, mix ground meat and finely chopped sausage, crushed amaretti, grated lemon rind, nutmeg, raisins, pine kernels, grated parmesan and beaten egg, add crushed garlic clove, pepper and salt.
4. Stuff zucchini with this mixture, lay in dish and bake for 20 minutes, then serve immediately.

Hamburger alla tedesca 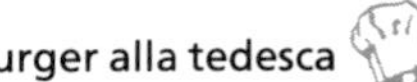

German-Style Hamburger

00:30 | 00:15

American	Ingredients	Metric/Imperial
14 oz	*Ground (minced) beef*	*400 g / 14 oz*
5	*Eggs*	*5*
	Grated zest of lemon	
1 tbsp	*Grated parmesan cheese*	*1 tbsp*
	Salt and pepper	
¼ tsp	*Nutmeg*	*¼ tsp*
	Flour	
	Bread crumbs	
¼ cup	*Butter*	*50 g / 2 oz*
¼ cup	*Oil*	*50 ml / 2 fl oz*

1. Preheat oven to 400°F / 200°C / Gas Mark 6.
2. Mix the meat with 1 egg, a little grated rind of lemon, parmesan, salt, pepper and nutmeg. Add as much flour as the mixture will absorb to make 4 firm hamburgers.
3. Coat the hamburgers generously with bread crumbs, heat the butter and oil and fry on a fairly high heat for 5-6 minutes each side.
4. Place on a heat resistant dish, with a little butter on each one and make a dent on the top with the back of a spoon. Slip 1 egg, which has been broken into a cup to make sure the yolk is whole, on to each hamburger. Place in a hot oven until the eggs are cooked. Serve surrounded by a mixed salad, according to taste.

German-style hamburger

Polpettone in salsa verde

Meat Loaf with Green Sauce

00:20 02:00

American	Ingredients	Metric/Imperial
1	*Onion*	1
¼ cup	*Oil*	50 ml / 2 fl oz
2 tbsp	*Butter*	25 g / 1 oz
1¼ lb	*Ground (minced) meat*	600 g / 1¼ lb
4	*Eggs*	4
½ cup	*Bread crumbs*	50 g / 2 oz
2 tbsp	*Chopped parsley*	1½ tbsp
2½ oz	*Ricotta (curd cheese)*	65 g / 2½ oz
½ tsp	*Chopped marjoram*	½ tsp
½ cup	*Grated parmesan cheese*	50 g / 2 oz
	Salt and pepper	
11 oz	*Floury potatoes*	300 g / 11 oz
1	*Stock cube*	1

1. Fry the onion in oil and butter, add the meat and brown. Remove from the heat, add the eggs, bread crumbs, chopped parsley, ricotta, marjoram and a generous amount of parmesan; season with salt and pepper.
2. Boil the potatoes, sieve and add to the other ingredients, mixing well.
3. Place the mixture on a clean baked cloth, shape into a large sausage, wrap and secure well.
4. Put the sausage into cold water or stock and boil for 2 hours.
5. When the loaf is cooked, drain and cool before removing the cloth.
6. Serve sliced with green sauce (see page 174).

Sciuscieddu siciliano

Baked Meatballs with Ricotta

00:20 01:00

American	Ingredients	Metric/Imperial
11 oz	*Ground (minced) meat*	300 g / 11 oz
1 tbsp	*Chopped parsley*	1 tbsp
3	*Eggs*	3
1 cup	*Grated parmesan cheese*	100 g / 4 oz
1	*Bread roll*	1
1 quart	*Stock*	1 litre / 1¾ pints
1½ lb	*Ricotta cheese*	700 g / 1½ lb

1. Preheat oven to 400°F / 200°C / Gas Mark 6. Butter an ovenproof serving dish.
2. Mix together ground (minced) meat, chopped parsley, 1 egg, some parmesan and the roll soaked in milk. Season and shape into meatballs; simmer in stock for 20 minutes.
3. Combine ricotta with remaining 2 eggs and rest of the parmesan. Place alternate layers of ricotta mixture and meatballs in the dish ending with a layer of meatballs; pour over a little stock, cover and cook in the oven for about 40 minutes.

Torta di fegatini

Chicken Liver Pie

00:30 01:45

American	Ingredients	Metric/Imperial
6	*Chicken livers*	6
¼ cup	*Butter*	50 g / 2 oz
6	*Sage leaves*	6
2	*Slices of ham*	2
½ cup	*Ground (minced) meat*	100 g / 4 oz
1	*Egg yolk*	1
1 cup	*Thick béchamel sauce (see page 162)*	225 ml / 8 fl oz
½ cup	*Mild grated provolone cheese*	50 g / 2 oz
¾ lb	*Puff pastry*	350 g / 12 oz

1. Preheat oven to 425°F / 220°C / Gas Mark 7 and then grease a 2 pint [900 ml / 1½ pint] pie dish.
2. Wash livers well and pat dry. Heat butter and fry livers and a few leaves of sage for 5 minutes. Chop coarsely and put aside. Chop ham.
3. Prepare some small meatballs mixing minced meat and egg yolk, fry these lightly to brown all over then put aside.
4. Prepare béchamel sauce using butter, flour and milk then add grated provolone.
5. Divide pastry in half, roll out one piece to an oblong and use to line pie dish. Spoon over meatballs and livers, and pour over the béchamel sauce. Roll out remaining pastry and use to cover pie. Bake in the oven for about 25 minutes. Reduce heat to 350°F / 180°C / Gas Mark 4 and cook for 1 hour, covering pie with wax (greaseproof) paper if browning too much.

Umido alla trentina

Meat and Vegetables Stewed in Beer

00:15 02:15

American	Ingredients	Metric/Imperial
1½ lb	*Beef, pork, lamb (any one or mixed)*	600 g / 1½ lb
2	*Onions*	2
2	*Carrots*	2
1	*Celery*	1
1	*Leek*	1
3 tbsp	*Vegetable oil*	2 tbsp
2 quarts	*Beer (preferably bitter)*	2 litres / 3½ pints
5 oz	*Continental sausage*	150 g / 5 oz
¼ lb	*Fat bacon (no lean)*	100 g / 4 oz
5 cups	*Fine white cornmeal for polenta*	600 g / 1¼ lb

1. Dice meat and chop vegetables. Heat oil and sauté meat until lightly browned. Remove and put on one side then sauté vegetables for 2-3 minutes. Return meat to pan.
2. Pour over beer, add chopped sausage and chopped bacon, cover and simmer for 2 hours.
3. Prepare polenta (see page 154). To serve, turn the polenta onto a hot, wide, deep serving dish, make a hollow in the centre and fill it with the stew.

Chicken liver pie

Veal cuts

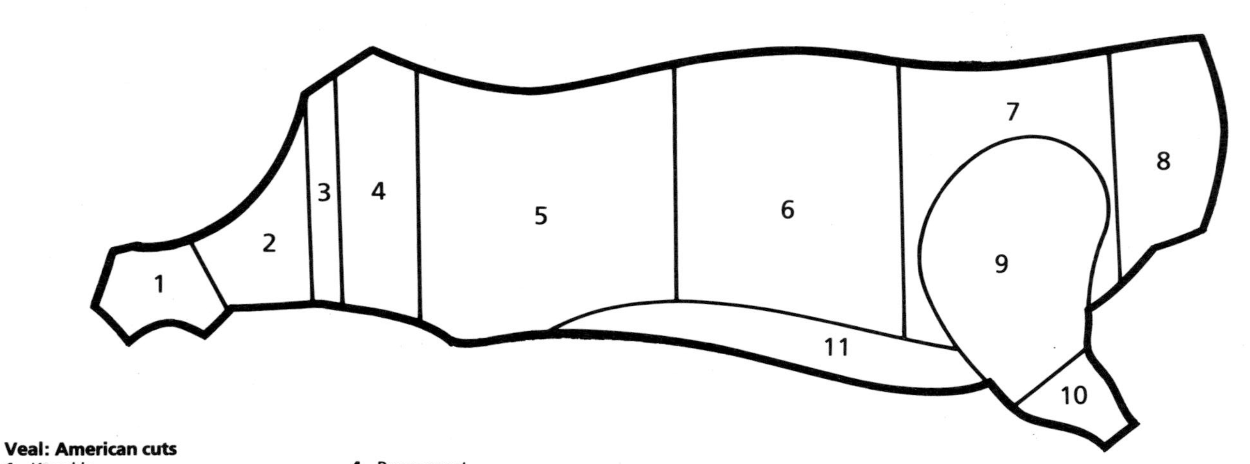

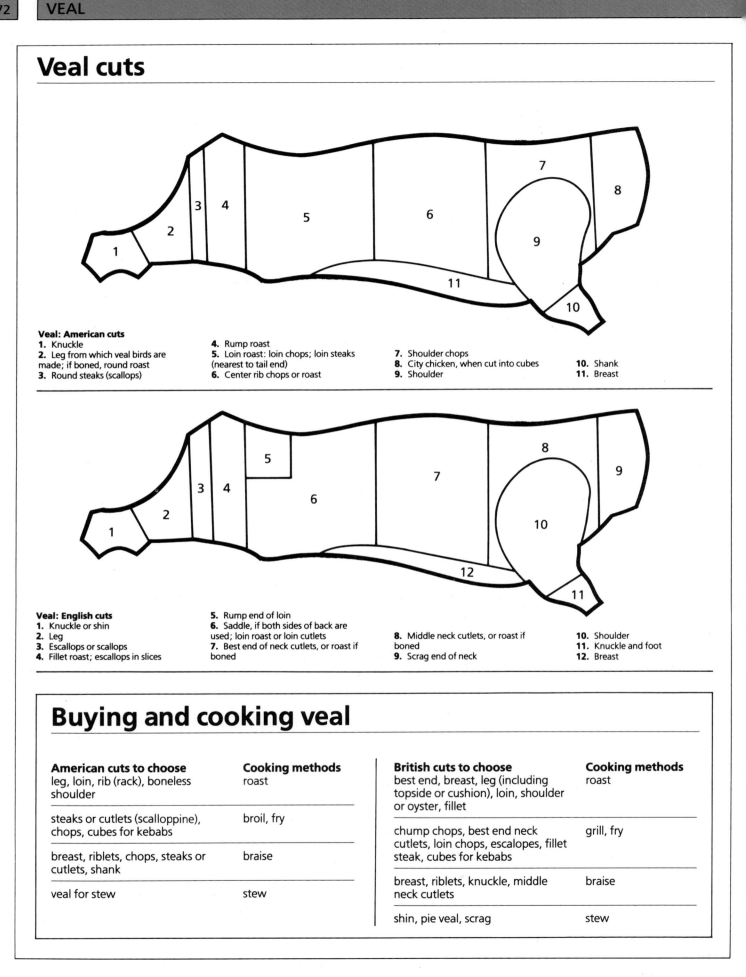

Veal: American cuts
1. Knuckle
2. Leg from which veal birds are made; if boned, round roast
3. Round steaks (scallops)
4. Rump roast
5. Loin roast: loin chops; loin steaks (nearest to tail end)
6. Center rib chops or roast
7. Shoulder chops
8. City chicken, when cut into cubes
9. Shoulder
10. Shank
11. Breast

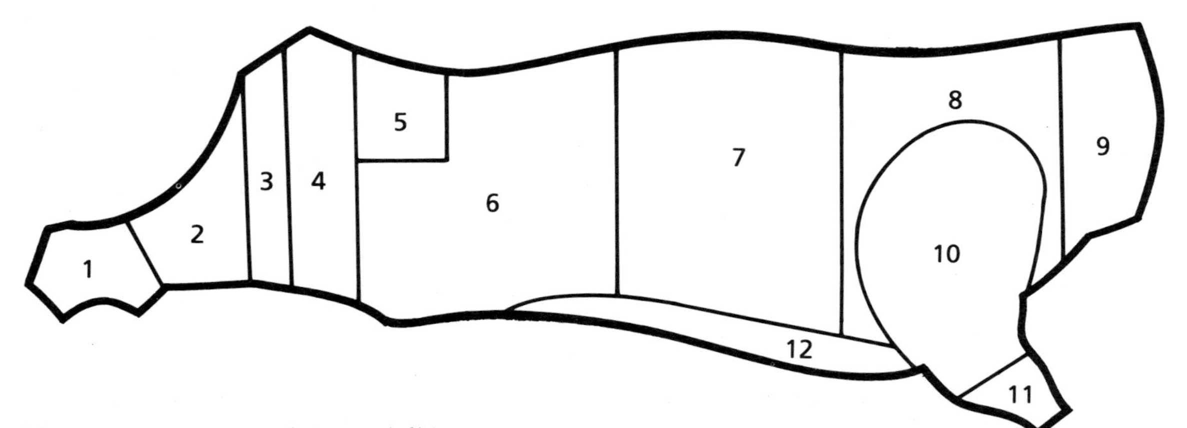

Veal: English cuts
1. Knuckle or shin
2. Leg
3. Escallops or scallops
4. Fillet roast; escallops in slices
5. Rump end of loin
6. Saddle, if both sides of back are used; loin roast or loin cutlets
7. Best end of neck cutlets, or roast if boned
8. Middle neck cutlets, or roast if boned
9. Scrag end of neck
10. Shoulder
11. Knuckle and foot
12. Breast

Buying and cooking veal

American cuts to choose	Cooking methods
leg, loin, rib (rack), boneless shoulder	roast
steaks or cutlets (scalloppine), chops, cubes for kebabs	broil, fry
breast, riblets, chops, steaks or cutlets, shank	braise
veal for stew	stew

British cuts to choose	Cooking methods
best end, breast, leg (including topside or cushion), loin, shoulder or oyster, fillet	roast
chump chops, best end neck cutlets, loin chops, escalopes, fillet steak, cubes for kebabs	grill, fry
breast, riblets, knuckle, middle neck cutlets	braise
shin, pie veal, scrag	stew

Uccellini 'scappati'

Lark Kebabs

00:15 00:30

American	Ingredients	Metric/Imperial
16 (weighing ¾ lb altogether)	Small slices tender veal or pork fillet	16 (weighing 350 g / 12 oz altogether)
	Salt and pepper	
16	Sage leaves	16
¼ lb	Smoked bacon or ham	100 g / 4 oz
8	Small slices of crusty bread	8
1	Thick slice of liver	1
	Oil for brushing	
½ cup	Juniper berries	50 g / 2 oz
3 tbsp	White wine	2 tbsp
2 tbsp	Flour	15 g / ½ oz
2 tbsp	Butter	15 g / ½ oz

1. Preheat oven to 425°F / 220°C / Gas Mark 7.
2. Pound slices of veal or pork and season with salt and pepper.
3. On each veal slice, lay a sage leaf and a small slice of bacon or ham, using both fat and lean.
4. Thread 8 short skewers with 2 rolls of meat, a slice each of bread and bacon and a piece of liver. Lay in a fireproof casserole dish, brush with oil, season and sprinkle with crushed juniper berries. Cover and cook in the oven for about 30 minutes.
5. When kebabs are done, transfer to a warm serving dish. Heat juices, loosening the residue with white wine.
6. Beat butter and flour together to form a paste and gradually whisk into the juices in the casserole dish until sauce has thickened, then pour over kebabs and serve.

Testina di vitello alla provenzale

Calf's Head Provençale

00:15 02:45

American	Ingredients	Metric/Imperial
1¾ lb	Calf's head	800 g / 1¾ lb
2	Onions	2
2	Garlic cloves	2
2	Celery heads	2
1	Lemon	1
	Salt and pepper	
1 lb	Fresh tomatoes	500 g / 1 lb
¼ cup	Vegetable oil	50 ml / 2 fl oz
½ tsp	Chopped marjoram	½ tsp

1. Boil calf's head in salted water for 15 minutes. Remove and cool. Refill saucepan with cold water, add 1 onion, 1 garlic clove, 3 chopped stalks of celery and lemon juice. Add calf's head and season with salt. Cover and simmer for 2 hours.
2. Meanwhile chop remaining onion, celery and garlic. Skin and deseed tomatoes. Heat oil and fry onion, celery and garlic for 3 minutes, then add tomatoes, season with salt, pepper and marjoram. Cover and simmer for 30-40 minutes until sauce has thickened.
3. Serve calf's head with tomato sauce poured over.

Vitello tonnato

Cold Veal in Tuna Sauce

00:20 02:00

American	Ingredients	Metric/Imperial
1½ lb	Veal joint, preferably top round	600 g / 1½ lb
1	Carrot	1
1	Onion	1
1	Celery stalk	1
7 oz	Tuna	200 g / 7 oz
4	Anchovies	4
2 tsp	Capers	2 tsp
1	Hard-cooked (boiled) egg yolk	1
1 tbsp	Vegetable oil	1 tbsp
⅔ cup	Consommé	150 ml / ¼ pint
1	Lemon	1

1. Simmer veal for 2 hours in salted water with carrot, onion and celery. Leave to cool in the liquid taking care it is completely covered.
2. Meanwhile prepare sauce. Drain tuna and put in a blender with anchovies and capers, blend on high speed for a few seconds. Put mixture into a bowl and add sieved egg yolk. Mix well, then beat in a little oil and the consommé, finally, add juice of lemon. The sauce should be light and frothy.
3. Drain veal well, slice thinly, lay on a serving dish and pour sauce over.
4. Cover dish with a sheet of cling wrap to prevent sauce discoloring and refrigerate for 24 hours before serving straight from the refrigerator.

Vitello in peperonata

Veal with Peperonata

Peperonata is a delicious sauce made from sweet peppers.

00:20 01:30

American	Ingredients	Metric/Imperial
1¾ lb	Shoulder veal	800 g / 1¾ lb
1 tbsp	Vegetable oil	1 tbsp
1 tbsp	Butter	1 tbsp
	Salt and pepper	
¼ cup	Dry red wine	50 ml / 2 fl oz
1 quart	Stock (cubes dissolved in hot water)	1 litre / 1¾ pints
4	Sweet yellow or red peppers	4
2	Tomatoes	2

1. Dice veal. Heat the oil and butter in a pan and sauté meat for 2-3 minutes. Season with salt and pepper, then add wine. Cover and cook for about 1 hour, adding stock from time to time.
2. Meanwhile, prepare peperonata. Chop peppers and remove seeds. Skin tomatoes and put with the peppers into a saucepan over a high heat, then lower and simmer for 20 minutes, adding hot water if required.
3. Season with salt and add to the meat. Simmer to reduce sauce to a good consistency, then serve hot.

Trippa alla contadina

Tripe Peasant-Style

A substantial main dish which needs only to be served with a salad or cheese board to complete the meal.

00:10 02:10

American	Ingredients	Metric/Imperial
1¾ lb	*Veal tripe*	*800 g / 1¾ lb*
¼ lb	*Parma ham*	*100 g / 4 oz*
1	*Small onion*	*1*
3	*Celery stalks*	*3*
1	*Carrot*	*1*
1	*Sprig of parsley*	*1*
⅓ cup	*Butter*	*75 g / 3 oz*
1 tbsp	*Tomato purée*	*1 tbsp*
1	*Clove*	*1*
¼ tsp	*Nutmeg*	*¼ tsp*
	Salt and pepper	
4	*Slices of white bread*	*4*
½ cup	*Grated parmesan cheese*	*50 g / 2 oz*

1. Wash tripe very thoroughly in several changes of water, blanch and cut into narrow strips.
2. Chop ham, onion, celery, carrot and parsley. Heat half the butter and fry ham and vegetables for 2-3 minutes. Add tripe and fry a further few minutes, stirring constantly.
3. Dissolve tomato purée in a little hot water, add to pot together with clove and a pinch of nutmeg. Cover and simmer for about 2 hours, adding salt and pepper only towards the very end.
4. Heat remaining butter and fry bread slices. Put one slice in each soup bowl, pile with tripe and vegetables and a good sprinkling of freshly grated parmesan.

Veau aux amandes

Veal with Almonds

00:10 00:35

American	Ingredients	Metric/Imperial
11 oz	*Veal fillet*	*300 g / 11 oz*
2 cups	*Shelled almonds*	*275 g / 10 oz*
3 tbsp	*Butter*	*40 g / 1½ oz*
¼ tsp	*Chopped sage*	*¼ tsp*
1 tsp	*Cornstarch (cornflour)*	*1 tsp*
⅔ cup	*Dry white wine*	*150 ml / ¼ pint*
	Salt and pepper	
¼ tsp	*Curry powder*	*¼ tsp*
1½ cups	*Italian rice*	*300 g / 11 oz*

1. Preheat oven to 400°F / 200°C / Gas Mark 6. Grease a large piece of foil and place on a baking sheet.
2. Dice veal, blanch almonds and mix the two together. Heat butter and sauté meat and almonds for 5 minutes with sage.
3. Blend cornstarch (cornflour) with wine and add to pan, stirring. Season with salt and pepper and a pinch of curry powder. Leave to simmer over a low heat.
4. Meanwhile boil rice until just tender, pile onto foil, make a hollow in the centre and fill with meat mixture. Close foil and cook in the oven for 10 minutes. Serve very hot.

Fegato alla francese

French-Style Liver

00:20 Marinating time 12:00 01:00

American	Ingredients	Metric/Imperial
1 lb	*Calf's liver*	*500 g / 1 lb*
¼ lb	*Bacon*	*100 g / 4 oz*
1 tsp	*Chopped sage*	*1 tsp*
	Salt and pepper	
1 tbsp	*Fine granulated (castor) sugar*	*1 tbsp*
1 quart	*White wine*	*1 litre / 1¾ pints*
2 or 3	*Bay leaves*	*2 or 3*

1. Buy the calf's liver in a single piece, remove the skin.
2. Dip the slices of bacon in chopped sage, season with salt and plenty of pepper.
3. Wrap the liver in the bacon, sprinkle sugar over the surface and place in an earthenware bowl, covering it with white wine and a few bay leaves. Leave to soak for at least 12 hours.
4. Transfer the liver to an ovenproof dish, add some of the marinade and cook in the oven for 1 hour. Slice and serve with boiled potatoes garnished with parsley.
5. This dish can also be served cold.

Lingua di vitello in salsa piccante

Calf's Tongue in a Piquant Sauce

00:15 Soaking time 01:00 02:20

American	Ingredients	Metric/Imperial
1½ lb	*Calf's tongue*	*700 g / 1½ lb*
	Salt	
3 tbsp	*Butter*	*40 g / 1½ oz*
1	*Large onion*	*1*
1	*Garlic clove*	*1*
5	*Anchovy fillets*	*5*
1 tbsp	*Capers*	*1 tbsp*
2 tsp	*Wine vinegar*	*2 tsp*
1	*Bunch of parsley*	*1*
4	*Pickled gherkins*	*4*
1 tsp	*French mustard*	*1 tsp*

1. Steep the tongue in salted water for at least 1 hour.
2. Place the tongue in salted water, bring to the boil and simmer briskly for about 2 hours.
3. Melt the butter in a wide, heavy pan and fry the finely-chopped onion and the crushed garlic, add the anchovy fillets and mix well with a wooden spoon, then add the capers, the vinegar and ½ cup [125 ml / 4 fl oz] water.
4. Remove the tongue from the water, drain and cool slightly. Cut into the slices and put into the sauce to flavor the tongue, over the heat, for about 15 minutes. Cook gently. Transfer the tongue to a heated serving dish and keep warm.
5. Chop the parsley and gherkins and add to the sauce with the mustard. (For a rather milder sauce, reduce the quantity of mustard.) Mix well, pour the hot sauce over the meat and serve immediately.

Veal stew with vegetables

Spezzatino all'ortolana 

Veal Stew with Vegetables

00:20 01:10

American	Ingredients	Metric/Imperial
1½ lb	*Lean veal, diced*	650 g / 1½ lb
	Salt and pepper	
	White flour	
¼ cup	*Vegetable oil*	50 ml / 2 fl oz
¼ cup	*Butter*	50 g / 2 oz
⅔ cup	*Dry white wine*	150 ml / ¼ pint
14 oz	*Peeled plum tomatoes*	400 g / 14 oz
1 quart	*Stock*	1 litre / 1¾ pints
1	*Celery stalk*	1
1	*Carrot*	1
1	*Onion*	1
2	*Zucchini (courgettes)*	2
½ tsp	*Chopped rosemary*	½ tsp
1	*Bay leaf*	1

1. Dip veal in seasoned flour. Heat half the oil and butter in a heavy-based pan and brown veal all over. Add wine and evaporate quickly over a high heat, then add chopped tomatoes and stock. Cover and leave to simmer.

2. Meanwhile, wash and chop vegetables. Heat remaining oil and butter in another pan, fry vegetables with rosemary, bay leaf and pepper. After 10 minutes, transfer vegetables with a slotted spoon to the pan containing the meat. Stir well and simmer for about 1 hour.

3. Transfer to a hot casserole dish and serve.

Rostin negaa (arrostino annegato)

Veal Scallopine Drowned in Wine

A traditional Milanese dish.

00:10 00:20

American	Ingredients	Metric/Imperial
1¼ lb	*Tender sliced veal (leg)*	600 g / 1¼ b
¼ lb	*Cooked ham*	100 g / 4 oz
½ cup	*Butter*	100 g / 4 oz
1 cup	*Dry white wine and white vinegar, mixed half and half*	225 ml / 8 fl oz
	Salt and pepper	

1. Pound the veal slices flat, cover each one with a slice of ham, roll and secure with fine kitchen string or toothpick.

2. Heat the butter in a frying pan and when it foams slip in the meat and brown over a high heat. Sprinkle with vinegar and wine, cover and simmer. Season with salt and pepper.

Fegato all'italiana in salsa

Italian-Style Liver in Sauce

00:15 00:20

American	Ingredients	Metric/Imperial
1 lb	*Calf's liver*	*500 g / 1 lb*
	Flour	
	Salt and pepper	
¼ cup	*Butter*	*50 g / 2 oz*
3 oz	*Raw ham*	*75 g / 3 oz*
1	*Small onion*	*1*
2 or 3	*Sage leaves*	*2 or 3*
1	*Bunch of parsley*	*1*
2 tsp	*Cornstarch (cornflour)*	*2 tsp*
1	*Stock cube*	*1*
3 tbsp	*Marsala*	*2 tbsp*

1. Cut the liver into slices and dip in seasoned flour, shake off excess.
2. Heat the butter, add the liver and fry for 5 minutes. Remove the slices and keep warm.
3. Chop the ham, a small onion, a few sage leaves and a bunch of parsley, and fry them in the same butter over a low heat for 6 minutes.
4. Add cornstarch dissolved in 1¼ cups [300 ml / ½ pint] stock with a small glass of marsala, and simmer for 10 minutes. Put the liver back in the sauce for a few minutes. Serve hot, adding seasoning at the last minute.

Cotolettine di vitello gratinate

Veal Cutlets au Gratin

00:20 Soaking time 01:00 00:25

American	Ingredients	Metric/Imperial
8	*Small veal loin steaks (cutlets)*	*8*
3 tbsp	*White flour*	*2 tbsp*
2	*Eggs*	*2*
1 cup	*Bread crumbs*	*100 g / 4 oz*
½ cup	*Butter*	*100 g / 4 oz*
8	*Slices of ham*	*8*
8	*Slices of fontina cheese*	*8*
½ tsp	*Nutmeg*	*½ tsp*
	Salt and pepper	

1. Beat the cutlets on either side, flour lightly and soak in beaten egg for 1 hour. Coat in bread crumbs, pat the crumbs with the flat of the hand.
2. Heat the butter in a pan and fry the meat until golden brown each side, drain on absorbent kitchen towels.
3. Cool the cutlets and arrange in an ovenproof dish, place a slice of raw ham, without the fat, and a very thin slice of fontina on each cutlet.
4. Preheat the oven to 425°F / 220°C / Gas Mark 7.
5. Sprinkle with nutmeg, pepper and salt, and dot with butter. Place in a hot oven for 15 minutes and serve as soon as the cheese has melted.

Vitello al curry

Veal in a Curry Sauce

00:10 01:40

American	Ingredients	Metric/Imperial
2 lb	*Veal loin*	*1 kg / 2 lb*
	Seasoned flour	
1	*Onion*	*1*
1	*Apple*	*1*
¼ cup	*Butter*	*50 g / 2 oz*
2	*Cloves*	*2*
1 tbsp	*Flour*	*1 tbsp*
1 tsp	*Curry powder*	*1 tsp*
2 cups	*Stock*	*450 ml / ¾ pint*
½	*Lemon*	*½*
	Salt	

1. Dice veal and toss in seasoned flour. Chop onion, peel and dice apple, melt butter and when foaming, sauté apple and onion for 2-3 minutes, add meat and cloves and brown meat all over, then lower the heat.
2. Blend flour and curry powder with a little water to a smooth paste, and add to pan. Pour over stock, stirring all the time, cover and simmer gently for 1½ hours. When meat is tender, add juice of lemon and salt.
3. Serve piping hot with apple chutney and a potato purée seasoned with a pinch of nutmeg.

Frittata di vitello alla salvia

Veal Omelette with Sage

00:15 00:18

American	Ingredients	Metric/Imperial
1 lb	*Roast veal*	*450 g / 1 lb*
5	*Eggs*	*5*
1	*Bunch of sage leaves*	*1*
1 tbsp	*Milk*	*1 tbsp*
1 tsp	*Flour*	*1 tsp*
1 tbsp	*Cognac*	*1 tbsp*
	Salt and pepper	
1 cup	*Vegetable oil*	*225 ml / 8 fl oz*
2 – 3 tbsp	*Béchamel sauce (see page 162)*	*1½ – 2 tbsp*

1. Chop the roast meat very finely or grind (mince) or put through a food processor. Add the beaten egg yolks, the stiffly whipped whites, and a handful of whole sage leaves. Beat with milk and flour to obtain a smooth mixture. Mix in the cognac and season with salt and pepper to taste.
2. Put oil in a frying pan and when it is smoking pour in the mixture, lowering the flame and shaking the pan so that it does not stick. Turn as for an ordinary omelette or if preferred cook the top under the broiler (grill) under a high heat.
3. Preheat the oven to 350°F / 180°C / Gas Mark 4.
4. Transfer the omelette to an ovenproof serving dish lined with aluminium foil. Close the foil by folding and place in the oven for 12 minutes. Pour béchamel over the omelette.

Cook's tip: if using a food processor, chop meat and mix the egg yolks, sage, milk, flour, cognac, salt and pepper. Fold in stiffly beaten egg whites after the other ingredients have been processed.

Veal in a curry sauce

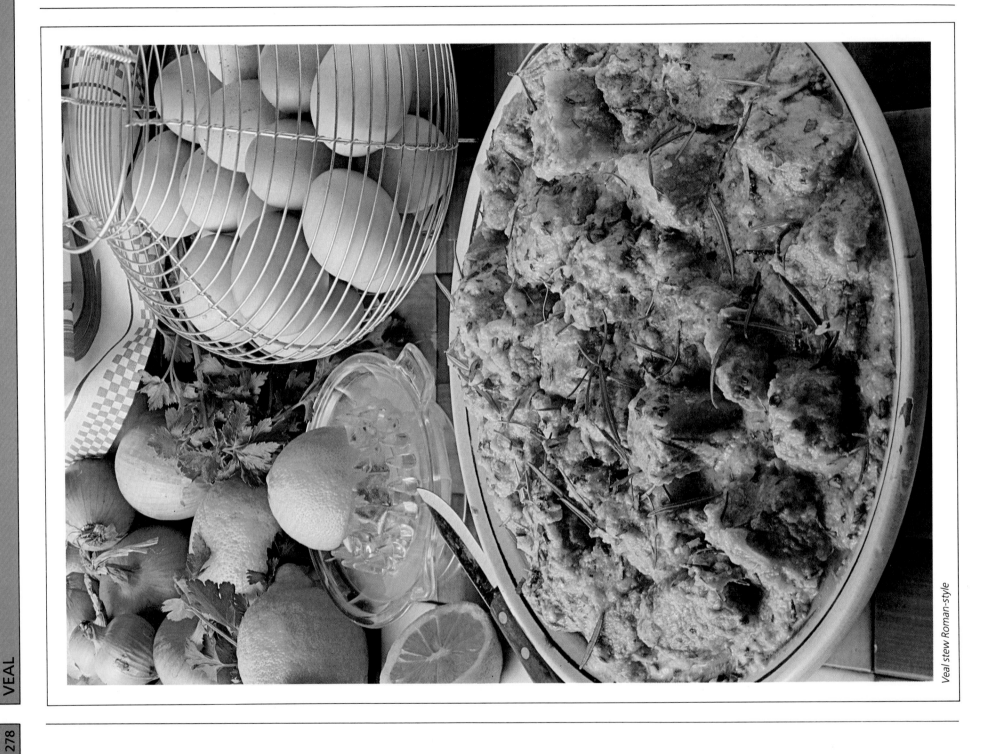

Veal stew Roman-style

Spezzatino alla romana

Veal Stew Roman-Style

00:10 02:00

American	Ingredients	Metric/Imperial
1	*Onion*	*1*
2	*Cloves*	*2*
¼ cup	*Butter*	*50 g / 2 oz*
1¾ lb	*Veal (breast or shoulder) diced*	*800 g / 1¾ lb*
½ tsp	*Chopped rosemary*	*½ tsp*
1 quart	*Stock*	*1 litre / 1¾ pints*
3	*Eggs*	*3*
1 tbsp	*Wine vinegar*	*1 tbsp*
1	*Lemon*	*1*
	Salt and pepper	
1 tbsp	*Chopped parsley*	*1 tbsp*

1. Slice the onion, stick cloves into one of the slices. Heat butter and, when very hot, sauté onion and cloves for 2-3 minutes, then add meat and brown, stirring all the time. Sprinkle with rosemary and pour over stock, cover and simmer for about 2 hours.
2. Meanwhile, put eggs, vinegar and lemon juice into a bowl, season with salt and pepper and beat well.
3. When meat is tender, pour over egg sauce and stir until the eggs begin to solidify. Serve on a hot serving dish sprinkled with chopped parsley.

Busecca 

Tripe and Vegetables

00:35 01:40

American	Ingredients	Metric/Imperial
1 lb	*Veal tripe*	*450 g / 1 lb*
	Salt and pepper	
1	*Potato*	*1*
1	*Celery stalk*	*1*
1	*Leek*	*1*
1	*Carrot*	*1*
1	*Onion*	*1*
½	*Savoy cabbage*	*½*
¼ lb	*Tomatoes*	*100 g / 4 oz*
¼ lb	*Green beans*	*100 g / 4 oz*
¼ cup	*Butter*	*50 g / 2 oz*
2 oz	*Bacon, chopped*	*50 g / 2 oz*
2	*Stock cubes*	*2*
2 tbsp	*Chopped parsley*	*1½ tbsp*
½	*Garlic clove*	*½*
2	*Sage leaves*	*2*
1 cup	*Grated parmesan cheese*	*100 g / 4 oz*

1. Take the veal tripe, remove the fat, scrape and wash thoroughly. Place in boiling salted water and simmer for 20 minutes. Drain, cool slightly and cut it into strips.
2. Chop a large peeled potato, the celery heart, the leek, carrot, onion, cabbage, tomatoes and the beans very finely.
3. Heat the butter in a pan, add the chopped bacon and cook for 5 minutes.
4. Prepare a stock with 2½ cups [600 ml / 1 pint] water and the cubes and put it on one side.
5. Mix the tripe with bacon. Then add the stock and cook for a further 40 minutes.
6. Add the vegetables and cook for another 20 minutes.
7. Add finely chopped parsley together with the crushed garlic, sage leaves and a good twist of pepper. Sprinkle with plenty of grated parmesan. Cook for a further 10 minutes or until the vegetables are cooked and taste for seasoning. Serve very hot.

Frittata di cervella e ricotta

Brains and Ricotta Omelette

00:10 00:10

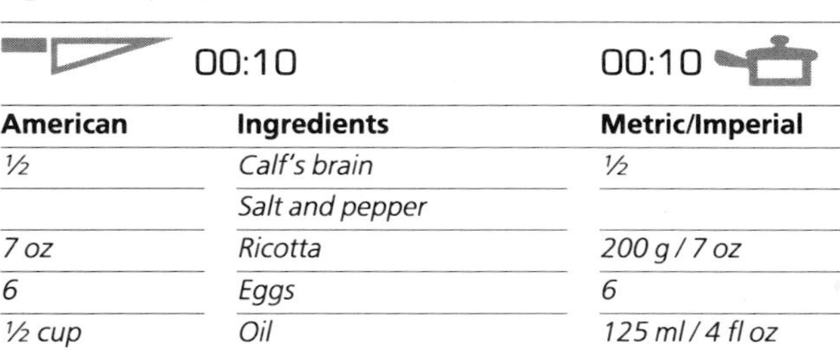

American	Ingredients	Metric/Imperial
½	*Calf's brain*	*½*
	Salt and pepper	
7 oz	*Ricotta*	*200 g / 7 oz*
6	*Eggs*	*6*
½ cup	*Oil*	*125 ml / 4 fl oz*

1. Wash and skin the brains, bring to the boil in salted water and simmer for 10 minutes, drain them and allow to cool. Cut into small pieces or blend.
2. Sieve the ricotta, add the brains and beat or blend to obtain a smooth mixture.
3. Beat the eggs in a bowl, add a pinch of salt and pepper, then little by little mix in the brains and ricotta mixture. Beat as though making an ordinary omelette mixture.
4. Heat the oil in an iron frying pan, when it is hot, pour in the mixture and continue cooking as for a normal omelette. Turn by slipping the omelette onto a plate and return to the pan upside down to cook the other side.
5. Lay it on a serving dish and cut into slices. Serve hot with salad or buttered spinach.

Scaloppine al whisky

Veal Scallopine with Whisky

00:05 00:07

American	Ingredients	Metric/Imperial
	Flour	
1 lb	*Veal scallopine (escalopes)*	*500 g / 1 lb*
¼ cup	*Butter*	*50 g / 2 oz*
	Salt	
	Freshly ground pepper	
¼ cup	*Whisky*	*50 ml / 2 fl oz*

1. Flour the scallopine, pressing well to make the flour stick to the meat.
2. Melt the butter in a heavy-bottomed frying pan and allow to color slightly. When butter is foaming, slip in the scallopine and on a fairly high heat, fry on both sides for 5 minutes, season with salt and a twist of ground black pepper, add the whisky, cover and simmer for 5 minutes. Serve very hot with freshly cooked vegetables.

1 2 3

Kidneys in cream sauce

1. *Skin kidneys, slice and remove cores.*
2. *Wash and soak for a few minutes in cold salt water. Remove the kidneys and pat dry in absorbent kitchen towels. Toss in seasoned flour.*
3. *Fry the floured kidneys in butter over medium heat for 6 minutes. Add chopped onion, garlic and thyme.*
4. *Add the wine and raise the heat for 2 minutes. Reduce the heat and add cream.*
5. *Add the juniper berries, cook for 8 minutes, season well and add parsley.*

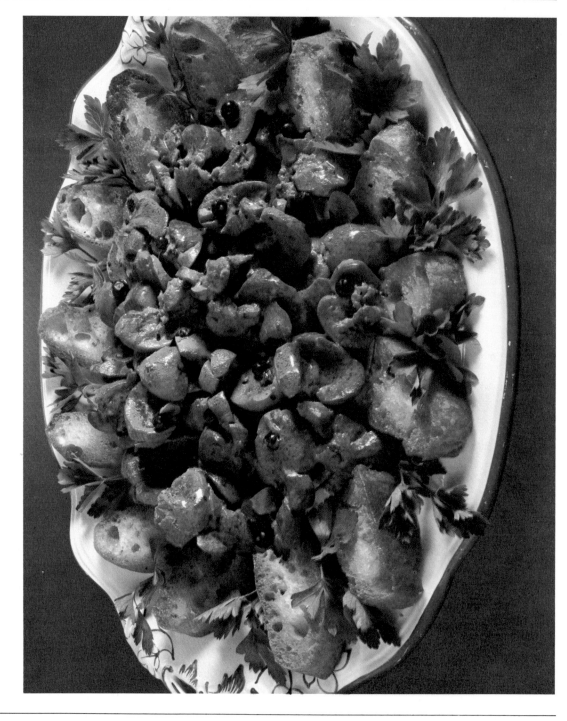

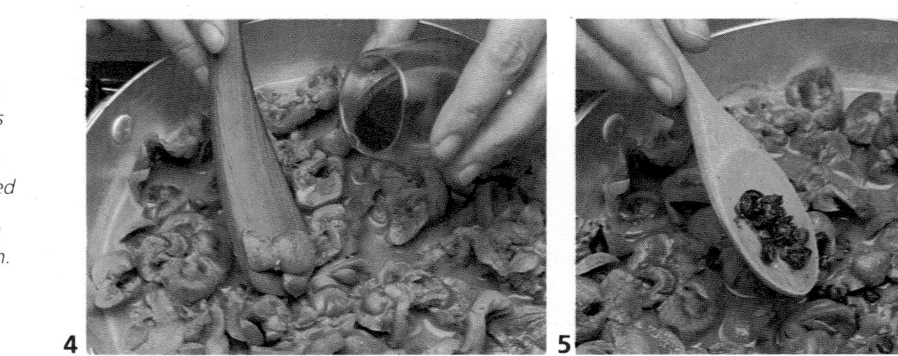

4 5

Rognoni di vitello

Kidneys in Cream Sauce

00:20 00:15

American	Ingredients	Metric/Imperial
1 ½ lb	*Veal or lamb's kidneys*	700 g / 1 ½ lb
3 tbsp	*Flour*	2 tbsp
½ cup	*Butter*	50 g / 2 oz
2	*Medium-sized onions*	2
1	*Small garlic clove*	1
¼ tsp	*Thyme*	¼ tsp
½ cup	*Red wine*	125 ml / 4 fl oz
	Salt and pepper	
½ cup	*Cream*	6 tbsp
12	*Slices small crusty loaf*	12
	Oil for frying	
1 tbsp	*Chopped parsley*	1 tbsp
1 tsp	*Juniper berries*	1 tsp

1. Prepare the kidneys by removing the skin and the core.
2. Flour the kidneys and fry in butter over medium heat. Add chopped onion, garlic and thyme. Cook for 6 minutes.
3. Add the wine, raise the heat for 2 minutes. Reduce the heat to low and stir in cream and juniper berries. Cook for a further 8 minutes and season well.
4. Fry the sliced bread in oil until crisp, drain on absorbent kitchen towels. Wash the parsley, chop finely and add to the kidneys.
5. Pour the kidneys into a heated serving dish, surround with fried bread and garnish with sprigs of parsley.

Rognone e riso in umido

Braised Calves' Kidneys with Rice

00:40 00:35

American	Ingredients	Metric/Imperial
1 lb	*Calves' kidneys*	500 g / 1 lb
3 tbsp	*Vinegar*	2 tbsp
½ cup	*Butter*	100 g / 4 oz
	Salt and pepper	
½ cup	*Dry white wine*	125 ml / 4 fl oz
2	*Garlic cloves*	2
1 tbsp	*Chopped parsley*	1 tbsp
1 tsp	*Rosemary*	1 tsp
1 cup	*Rice*	200 g / 7 oz

1. Slice the kidneys finely and remove all the fat; soak in vinegar and water for about 30 minutes.
2. Melt the butter in a heavy pan and when it is hot add the kidneys, brown and season.
3. Add the wine and allow it to evaporate, continue to cook for 15 minutes over a low heat.
4. Crush the garlic, chop the parsley and rosemary and mix.
5. Cook the rice in salted water until 'al dente', drain.
6. Place the kidneys in the middle of a heated serving dish, sprinkle with the garlic and rosemary mixture, surround with the rice and serve.

Panada del fattore

Veal and Whole Wheat Bread Stew

00:25 01:00

American	Ingredients	Metric/Imperial
11 oz	*Crusty whole wheat bread*	300 g / 11 oz
14 oz	*Veal shoulder or breast, cubed*	400 g / 14 oz
2 cups	*Stock*	450 ml / ¾ pint
2 tbsp	*Oil*	1 ½ tbsp
½ tsp	*Cinnamon*	½ tsp
	Salt and pepper	
2 tbsp	*Grated parmesan cheese*	1 ½ tbsp
2	*Eggs yolks*	2

1. Lay the bread, sliced thickly, in a saucepan, distribute the pieces of veal on the bread and pour on stock.
2. Cook over a medium heat, add oil, cinnamon, salt and pepper but do not stir.
3. Turn heat to low and allow the pan to cook slowly at an even temperature for about 50 minutes.
4. Towards the end of the cooking time test the meat with a fork, when tender, turn off the heat and sprinkle with grated parmesan.
5. Before serving, add the egg yolks, stir vigorously and serve in heated bowls.

Scaloppe alla Carlo Porta

Veal Scallopine Cooked in Foil with Spinach

00:25 00:30

American	Ingredients	Metric/Imperial
8	*Veal scallopine (escalopes)*	8
8	*Slices of fontina cheese*	8
8	*Slices of parma ham*	8
¼ tsp	*Chopped sage*	¼ tsp
1	*Shallot or small onion*	1
¼ cup	*Butter*	50 g / 2 oz
Scant 2 cups	*Cooked spinach*	400 g / 14 oz
1 cup	*Fresh cream*	225 ml / 8 fl oz
¼ cup	*Grated parmesan cheese*	25 g / 1 oz

1. Preheat the oven to 350°F / 180°C / Gas Mark 4.
2. Pound the scallopine flat and cover each one with a slice of fontina cheese and one of parma ham; add a small pinch of sage and roll up, securing with a toothpick.
3. Chop the shallot and fry in the butter, add the veal rolls and brown on a medium heat.
4. Put the spinach into another pan, add the cream and heat through gently. Sprinkle with parmesan cheese and stir well.
5. Spread the spinach mixture on a sheet of baking foil, lay the rolls of veal on top, close the foil and bake in the oven for 15 minutes.

Spezzatino alla greca al cartoccio

Veal Cooked in Foil

00:25 01:00

American	Ingredients	Metric/Imperial
1 ¼ lb	*Veal (not too lean)*	*600 g / 1 ¼ lb*
½ cup	*Butter*	*100 g / 4 oz*
1	*Onion*	*1*
1 oz	*Capers*	*25 g / 1 oz*
¼ lb	*Black olives*	*100 g / 4 oz*
1 cup	*Ouzo or dry grappa*	*225 ml / 8 fl oz*
1 tbsp	*Tomato purée*	*1 tbsp*
1	*Stock cube*	*1*
1 tsp	*White wine vinegar*	*1 tsp*
	Salt and pepper	
¼ tsp	*Paprika*	*¼ tsp*

1. Preheat the oven to 350°F / 180°C / Gas Mark 4.
2. Cut the veal into 2 in / 5 cm pieces. Choose a large, heavy saucepan, heat the butter, add the onion, chopped, and cook for 4 minutes, then add the veal.
3. Rinse the capers and add to the meat together with ⅔ cup [150 ml / ¼ pint] of water. Stir, keeping the heat low.
4. When the liquid has evaporated, add the black olives and liqueur. Continue to cook, stirring from time to time.
5. Dilute some tomato purée with a little water and add to the meat. Stir, cover and simmer. Dissolve the stock cube in ⅔ cup [150 ml / ¼ pint] boiling water (too much liquid would turn the dish into a stew) and add to the pan. When the meat is cooked, sprinkle with a little white wine vinegar, check for seasoning, add a pinch of paprika, stir and turn off the heat.
6. Wrap the entire contents of the pan in foil and cook in the oven for about 30 minutes. Serve immediately.

Involtini alla sarda

Veal in Tomato Sauce

00:20 00:30

American	Ingredients	Metric/Imperial
1 ¼ lb	*Veal (from the shoulder)*	*600 g / 1 ¼ lb*
½ cup	*Parmesan cheese*	*50 g / 2 oz*
2 tsp	*Sage, chopped*	*2 tsp*
½ cup	*Soft bread crumbs*	*25 g / 1 oz*
1	*Egg*	*1*
¼ lb	*Cooked ham*	*100 g / 4 oz*
	Flour	
¼ cup	*Butter*	*50 g / 2 oz*
	Salt and pepper	
3 tbsp	*Marsala*	*2 tbsp*
3	*Ripe tomatoes*	*3*
1	*Stock cube*	*1*

1. Try to slice the meat in such a way that each piece is of uniform size and thickness, flatten thick slices by beating.
2. Grate cheese onto sage, mix with bread crumbs and egg and season. Lay a slice of cooked ham on each piece of meat and spread the mixture over. Roll and secure with a toothpick, then dip into flour.
3. Heat the butter in a frying pan, add more sage then brown the rolled meat. Sprinkle with salt, pepper and marsala.
4. Preheat the oven to 350°F / 180°C / Gas Mark 4.
5. Skin and deseed tomatoes, chop and put into saucepan with a little stock and season. Place the veal in a casserole, cover with tomato sauce and cook for 20 minutes in the oven.

Veal cooked in foil

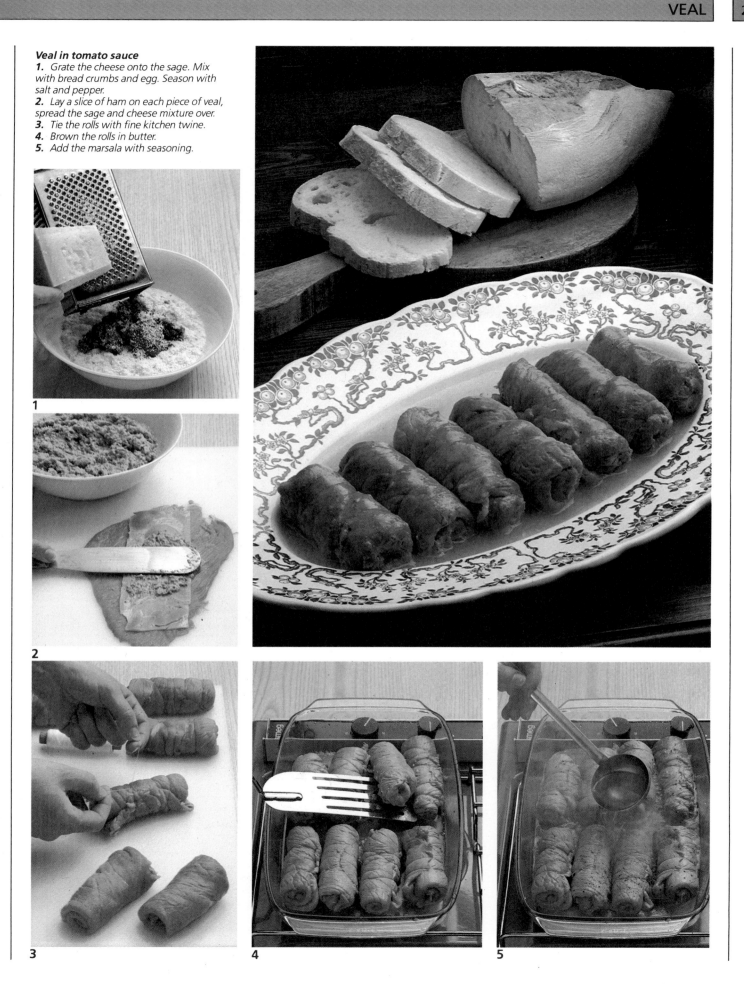

Veal in tomato sauce

1. Grate the cheese onto the sage. Mix with bread crumbs and egg. Season with salt and pepper.
2. Lay a slice of ham on each piece of veal, spread the sage and cheese mixture over.
3. Tie the rolls with fine kitchen twine.
4. Brown the rolls in butter.
5. Add the marsala with seasoning.

1

2

3

4

5

Hamburger alla Bismarck

Rissoles with Meat and Anchovies

00:20 Serves 6 | 00:25 to 00:30

American	Ingredients	Metric/Imperial
1 ¼ lb	*Mixed raw meats (veal, pork, beef)*	600 g / 1 ¼ lb
7 oz	*Bread crumbs, soaked in milk*	200 g / 7 oz
1 ¼ tsp	*Anchovy fillets or Anchovy paste*	1 ¼ tsp
2	*Egg yolks*	2
5 tbsp	*Bread crumbs*	4 tbsp
¼ cup	*Oil*	50 ml / 2 fl oz
2 tbsp	*Butter*	25 g / 1 oz
¼ tsp	*Chopped sage*	¼ tsp
¼ tsp	*Chopped rosemary*	¼ tsp
2 tbsp	*Chopped parsley*	1 ½ tbsp
4	*Eggs*	4
	Salt and pepper	

1. Grind (mince) the meat twice. Add to the bread crumbs and anchovy and mix well.
2. Place in a bowl, add egg yolks and enough extra bread crumbs to make a firm mixture; shape into 4 round, flat rissoles.
3. Heat some oil and butter in a frying pan, adding a little sage and rosemary.
4. Place the rissoles in the hot fat and cook for 3 minutes each side to brown and then reduce heat to low or medium to cook for another 7 minutes on each side.
5. Preheat the oven to 400°F / 200°C / Gas Mark 6.
6. Transfer to an oven-to-table dish, sprinkle with parsley and place a raw egg upon each rissole, taking care not to break the yolk. Cover immediately and put in the oven for 5 minutes or until the eggs are ready.
7. Serve immediately, adding salt and pepper at the table.

Ossobuco milanese

Stewed Shin of Veal

00:30 | 02:00

American	Ingredients	Metric/Imperial
6 x 3 in	*Veal shin bones*	6 x 7½ cm / 3 in
¼ cup	*Flour*	25 g / 1 oz
½ cup	*Butter*	100 g / 4 oz
1	*Onion*	1
1	*Carrot*	1
1	*Celery stalk*	1
2	*Garlic cloves*	2
3 – 4	*Sprigs of marjoram*	3 – 4
1	*Bay leaf*	1
1	*Lemon*	1
½ cup	*Dry white wine*	125 ml / 4 fl oz
6	*Ripe or canned tomatoes*	6
1 ¼ cups	*Stock*	300 ml / ½ pint
	Salt and pepper	
½ cup	*Chopped parsley*	6 tbsp

1. Ask the butcher to saw the shin of veal into the correctly sized pieces, dip in flour and shake off the excess.
2. Melt the butter over a medium heat in a large heavy pan and brown the veal shin on all sides. Remove onto a plate.
3. Chop the onion, carrot and celery into fine dice and crush the cloves of garlic. Cook in the pan over a low heat in the butter used for the veal for 5 minutes.
4. Stand the veal on its end, upright to prevent the marrow in the bone coming out. Add the marjoram and bay leaf with a small piece of lemon peel and the dry white wine. Cook on a high heat for 5 minutes.
5. Add the chopped tomatoes and stock, season well, bring to the boil, lower the heat, cover and cook for 1½ hours on a low heat. Add a little boiling water if the pan seems to be drying out during cooking.
6. Prepare the 'gremolata' which is an essential part of this dish by grating the remaining lemon peel finely, crush the other clove of garlic, mix with the lemon rind and the chopped parsley. When the dish is cooked, sprinkle with the lemon and parsley mixture.

Cook's tip: this dish is traditionally served with risotto Milanese.

Ossibuchi della festa

Braised Shin of Veal

00:30 | 01:30

American	Ingredients	Metric/Imperial
1	*Shin of veal sawn into 4 sections of 2 in / 5 cm*	1
3 tbsp	*Flour*	2 tbsp
¼ cup	*Oil*	50 ml / 2 fl oz
3 tbsp	*Butter*	40 g / 1 ½ oz
1	*Onion*	1
½ cup	*Dry white wine*	125 ml / 4 fl oz
2 lb	*Italian tomatoes fresh or canned*	1 kg / 2 lb
	Salt and pepper	
	Ground nutmeg	
½ lb	*Petit pois*	225 g / 8 oz
¼ lb	*Dried mushrooms*	100 g / 4 oz

1. Remove the skin surrounding the shins, flour them lightly, shaking off the excess.
2. Put oil and butter into a wide, heavy pan with a close fitting lid, heat and add the onion chopped very fine.
3. Turn the heat to low and add a little water if necessary to prevent the onion coloring too much. Slip in the shin bones and brown on both sides, taking care that they do not stick to the pan. Sprinkle with a little white wine and add the tomatoes, peeled and mashed with a fork.
4. Season with salt, pepper and a pinch of nutmeg, cover and cook for about 1 hour.
5. Meanwhile, soak the dried mushrooms in warm water for at least 15 minutes, remove from the water and squeeze gently.
6. Drain the peas and add them to the contents of saucepan. After 10 minutes, add the dried mushrooms. Continue to cook slowly with the lid on for a further 15 minutes.
7. The veal may either be left in the saucepan to serve or transferred to a container suitable for the refrigerator and any excess fat removed when cold.
8. Reheat very gently, stirring carefully to avoid separating the marrow from the bone. Serve hot.

Ossobuco (braised shin of veal)

Fagottini di banana

Stuffed Veal Olives with Banana

00:20 Serves 6 — 00:25

American	Ingredients	Metric/Imperial
12	*Small slices of leg of veal*	*12*
6	*Small bananas*	*6*
1	*Lemon*	*1*
	Salt and pepper	
1 tsp	*Mixed herbs*	*1 tsp*
¼ cup	*Butter*	*50 g / 2 oz*
¼ cup	*White wine*	*50 ml / 2 fl oz*
1 cup	*Coffee (single) cream*	*225 ml / 8 fl oz*
1 tbsp	*Chopped parsley*	*1 tbsp*

1. Beat the slices of veal thoroughly and spread on a wooden board.
2. Peel the bananas and put the flesh in a bowl with the lemon juice, a pinch of salt, pepper and mixed herbs. Mix well and spread the mixture on the slices of meat, roll them round the banana mixture and fasten them with toothpicks.
3. Cook the veal olives in a pan with the heated butter for 10 minutes, adding a little white wine and some cream from time to time.
4. Cook on a gentle heat for a further 15 minutes. Serve sprinkled with chopped parsley accompanied by a selection of freshly cooked vegetables.

Crocchette di vitello

Veal Croquettes

00:35 — 00:35

American	Ingredients	Metric/Imperial
½ lb	*Raw ground (minced) ham*	*225 g / 8 oz*
½ lb	*Ground (minced) veal*	*225 g / 8 oz*
2	*Eggs*	*2*
1	*Lemon*	*1*
½ cup	*Soft bread crumbs*	*50 g / 2 oz*
¼ cup	*Grated parmesan cheese*	*25 g / 1 oz*
½ tsp	*Chopped basil*	*½ tsp*
	Salt and pepper	
1 cup	*Dried bread crumbs*	*100 g / 4 oz*
1 cup	*Vegetable oil*	*225 ml / 8 fl oz*

1. Mix the ground ham and veal with the eggs, grated lemon rind, bread crumbs, parmesan, basil, salt and pepper, shape into croquettes and coat them in the dried bread crumbs.
2. Preheat the oven to 350°F / 180°C / Gas Mark 4.
3. Put the oil in a frying pan and fry the croquettes until golden brown.
4. Place on absorbent kitchen towels to drain. Arrange hot croquettes on a piece of foil, sprinkle with lemon juice, fold the foil to close and cook in the oven for 15 minutes. Serve immediately with rice and a green salad.

Cook's tip: if time allows it is advisable to chill croquette mixtures after coating and before frying. This helps to stop them from breaking up during cooking.

Noce di vitello arrosto

Roast Veal

00:15 Serves 6 — 01:20

American	Ingredients	Metric/Imperial
3¼ lb	*Round roast (leg) of veal*	*1.5 kg / 3¼ lb*
2	*Garlic cloves*	*2*
¼ lb	*Bacon*	*100 g / 4 oz*
¼ cup	*Oil*	*50 ml / 2 fl oz*
2 tbsp	*Butter*	*25 g / 1 oz*
1	*Bunch of parsley*	*1*
2	*Sprigs of rosemary*	*2*
	Salt and pepper	
2 cups	*Dry red wine*	*450 ml / ¾ pint*

1. Preheat the oven to 350°F / 180°C / Gas Mark 4.
2. Pierce the veal with a small sharp knife, and insert slivers of garlic and bacon.
3. Heat the oil and butter in a casserole and on a high heat brown the meat on all sides.
4. Chop the parsley and rosemary and add to the pot together with salt, several twists of pepper and the red wine. Cover and cook in the oven for 1¼ hours adding a little warm water, only if necessary. When the meat is cooked, transfer it to a board and cut into thin slices. Arrange on a heated serving dish.
5. Add a little water to the juice in the casserole and heat through to loosen the residue; sieve the liquid, reheat and serve with the roast.

Roast veal

Roast loin of veal

Punta di vitello arrosto

Roast Loin of Veal

Lombardy produces excellent veal and roast veal is a traditional dish of the district around Pavia.

00:10 01:30

American	Ingredients	Metric/Imperial
5 oz	*Bacon*	*150 g / 5 oz*
½ cup	*Oil*	*125 ml / 4 fl oz*
1	*Onion*	*1*
1	*Garlic clove*	*1*
3¼ lb	*Loin of veal (boned and rolled)*	*1.5 kg / 3¼ lb*
2 cups	*Stock*	*450 ml / ¾ pint*
½ cup	*Dry white wine*	*125 ml / 4 fl oz*
8	*Thin slices of fat pork for larding*	*8*
	Pepper to taste	

1. Preheat the oven to 400°F / 200°C / Gas Mark 6.
2. Chop the bacon into small pieces and fry in a casserole with heated oil and finely chopped onion. Add the crushed clove of garlic and continue to fry over gentle heat until the bacon begins to brown.
3. When the bacon has browned, turn up the heat and add the joint of veal, browning quickly on all sides. Add the stock (which can be made using stock cubes, if you wish) a little at a time, then the wine.
4. Lard the meat by placing 4 thin strips of fat pork over the joint.
5. Roast in the oven for 1 hour, turning the joint once and larding again with the remaining slices of fat pork to ensure a good color.
6. Sprinkle with pepper and add a little water if the meat shows signs of sticking to the pan.
7. Roast veal can be served either hot, garnished with strips of cooked mixed vegetables such as carrot, onion and green pepper, or cold with a variety of salads.

Pancetta di vitello in gelatina

Jellied Breast of Veal

00:45 02:10

American	Ingredients	Metric/Imperial
¼ lb	*Cooked ham*	*100 g / 4 oz*
¼ lb	*Mortadella*	*100 g / 4 oz*
3	*Eggs*	*3*
2 tbsp	*Grated parmesan cheese*	*1½ tbsp*
	Salt and pepper	
2 lb	*Breast of veal*	*1 kg / 2 lb*
3	*Carrots*	*3*
1	*Onion*	*1*
1	*Celery stalk*	*1*
1	*Bunch of chopped parsley*	*1*
5 tsp	*Gelatin*	*5 tsp*

1. Chop the ham and mortadella, put into a bowl with the eggs, parmesan, salt and pepper and mix well.
2. Wipe and trim excess fat from breast of veal, open out flat.
3. Stuff the breast of veal with the ham mixture, press down firmly and sew up with fine string, or secure with skewers.
4. Chop the carrots, onion, celery and parsley and put them in a large saucepan with plenty of water. Bring to the boil.
5. Wrap the breast of veal in a clean boiled cloth or muslin and secure firmly, lower into the boiling water and allow to cook for about 2 hours.
6. Remove from the pan, drain reserving 2½ cups [600 ml / 1 pint] stock. Unwrap the veal and put between 2 plates with a weight on top while it is cooling.
7. Dissolve the gelatin by sprinkling it on to 4-5 tablespoons boiling meat stock. Mix into the reserved stock and cool. Replace the vegetables.
8. Slice the veal and arrange on a deep serving dish, spoon gelatin and vegetables over the slices and refrigerate. Serve when meat and jelly have set. Some jelly can be chopped for decoration.

Veal, like beef, can be cooked in pastry *(see page 262)*

Pancetta di vitello ripiena

Stuffed Breast of Veal

00:25 02:00 to 02:30

American	Ingredients	Metric/Imperial
2 oz	*Cooked ham*	50 g / 2 oz
2 oz	*Mortadella*	50 g / 2 oz
¾ lb	*Ground (minced) meat (left-overs will do)*	350 g / 12 oz
3	*Eggs*	3
¼ cup	*Grated parmesan cheese*	25 g / 1 oz
	Salt and pepper	
2 lb	*Breast of veal*	1 kg / 2 lb
1	*Onion*	1
2	*Carrots*	2
2	*Bay leaves*	2
1	*Bouquet garni*	1

1. Chop the ham and mortadella and mix with the ground meat, eggs, parmesan, salt and pepper.
2. Stuff the breast of veal with this mixture and sew up firmly with coarse kitchen string.
3. Chop the vegetables and put into a large saucepan with the bay leaves and bouquet garni with plenty of water, add the veal, wrapped in a boiled muslin cloth. Cook for at least 2 hours.
4. Remove from the pan, drain and allow to cool before unwrapping and slicing.

Hamburger fantasiosi

Rissoles with Ham and Red Chilli

00:20 00:20

American	Ingredients	Metric/Imperial
1 lb	*Ground (minced) beef or veal*	500 g / 1 lb
1	*Egg yolk*	1
¼ lb	*Cooked ham, finely chopped*	100 g / 4 oz
1 tbsp	*Olive oil*	1 tbsp
	Salt and pepper	
1	*Red chilli pepper*	1
	Flour	
	Oil for frying	

1. Put the ground (minced) meat, egg yolk, finely chopped ham into a large bowl, add olive oil and season with salt and pepper.
2. Deseed the red chilli pepper, chop and mix with other ingredients until all are thoroughly blended.
3. Dust the hands lightly with flour and shape the mixture into 4 flattish rissoles.
4. Either fry the rissoles in oil, cooking them for 3 minutes each side in hot fat to brown and then reducing the heat to low or medium to cook for another 7 minutes on each side. Or cook them under the broiler (grill). If broiling, turn them so that the rissoles brown on both sides.
5. Serve at once with rice and green salad.

Polpettone di vitello

Veal Meatloaf in a Béchamel Sauce

00:30 01:00

American	Ingredients	Metric/Imperial
¾ lb	*Ground (minced) veal*	350 g / 12 oz
½ lb	*Ricotta (curd cheese)*	225 g / 8 oz
3	*Eggs*	3
⅓ cup	*Grated parmesan cheese*	40 g / 1½ oz
	Salt and pepper	
¼ tsp	*Nutmeg*	¼ tsp
½ cup	*Butter*	100 g / 4 oz
½ tsp	*Chopped sage*	½ tsp
½ tsp	*Chopped rosemary*	½ tsp
	Bread crumbs	
2 tbsp	*Marsala*	1½ tbsp
3 cups	*Thin béchamel sauce (see page 162)*	700 ml / 1¼ pints

1. Preheat the oven to 350°F / 180°C / Gas Mark 4.
2. Mix together in a bowl the veal, ricotta, 1 whole egg, 2 egg yolks and some of the parmesan; season with salt, pepper and a pinch of nutmeg.
3. Heat a little butter in a pan and add sage and rosemary, cook for 1 minute, pour into a small loaf pan (tin) coating the sides and bottom.
4. Shape the meat mixture into a loaf and coat with the bread crumbs and mold into the pan. Pour over the marsala, sprinkle with parmesan cheese and cook in a moderate oven for 1 hour.
5. Prepare the béchamel sauce making sure it is not too thick.
6. When the meatloaf is cooked, transfer it to a serving dish and allow it to cool before pouring the béchamel sauce over it, adding another liberal sprinkling of parmesan. To serve, cut into medium-sized slices and accompany with roast potatoes.

Frittura piccata prigioniera

Fillet of Veal 'Prigioniera'

00:15 00:15

American	Ingredients	Metric/Imperial
14 oz	*Fillet of veal, in slices*	400 g / 14 oz
	Flour	
2 tbsp	*Butter*	25 g / 1 oz
1 cup	*Cream*	225 ml / 8 fl oz
1	*Lemon*	1
3 tbsp	*Marsala*	2 tbsp
	Salt and pepper	

1. Cut thin slices of veal, beat well. Dip in flour, shake off excess.
2. Heat the butter in a large frying pan, fry meat on both sides over a medium heat then turn the heat low and add cream. The veal slices should remain a pinkish color.
3. Sprinkle with grated lemon rind, continue cooking, turning the veal gently and moistening with the marsala. Season with salt and pepper when cooking is finished. Arrange meat on a heated serving dish.
4. The cooking sauce should be smooth and creamy, serve poured over the meat. Garnish with slices of the lemon.

Lamb cuts

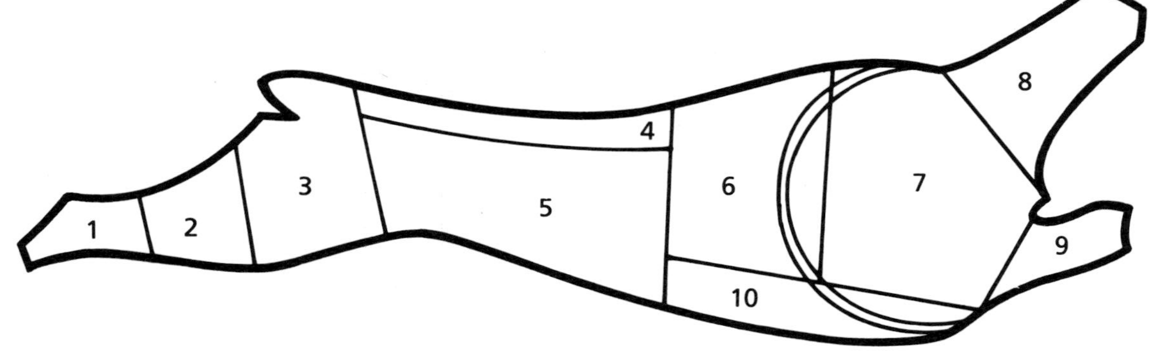

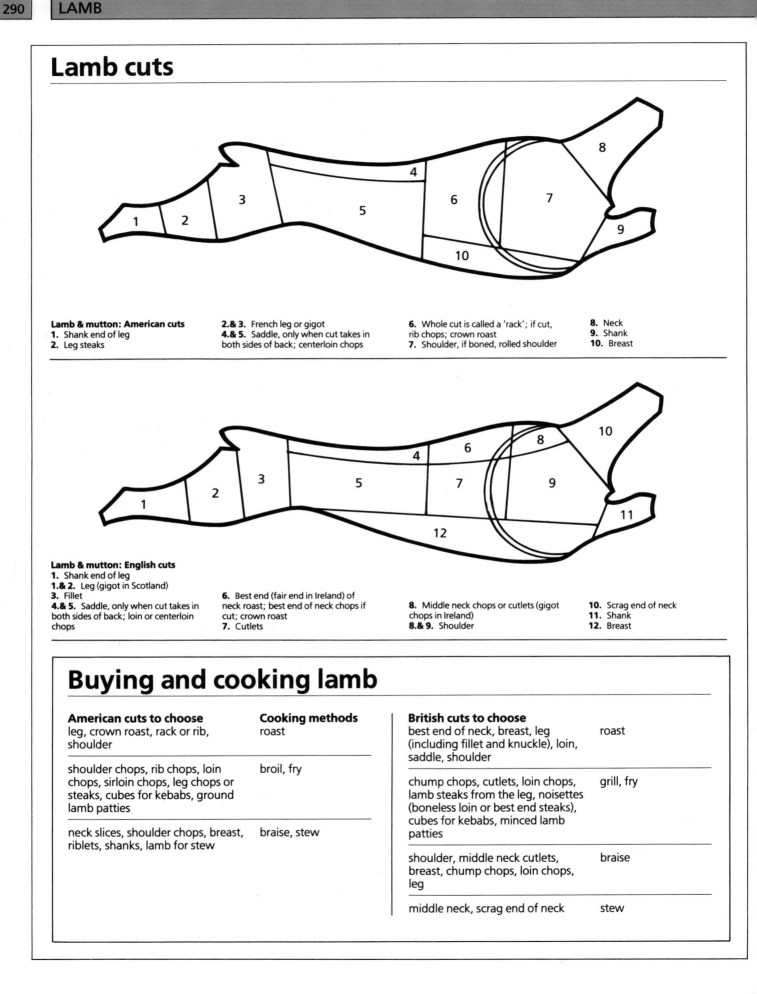

Lamb & mutton: American cuts
1. Shank end of leg
2. Leg steaks
2.& 3. French leg or gigot
4.& 5. Saddle, only when cut takes in both sides of back; centerloin chops
6. Whole cut is called a 'rack'; if cut, rib chops; crown roast
7. Shoulder, if boned, rolled shoulder
8. Neck
9. Shank
10. Breast

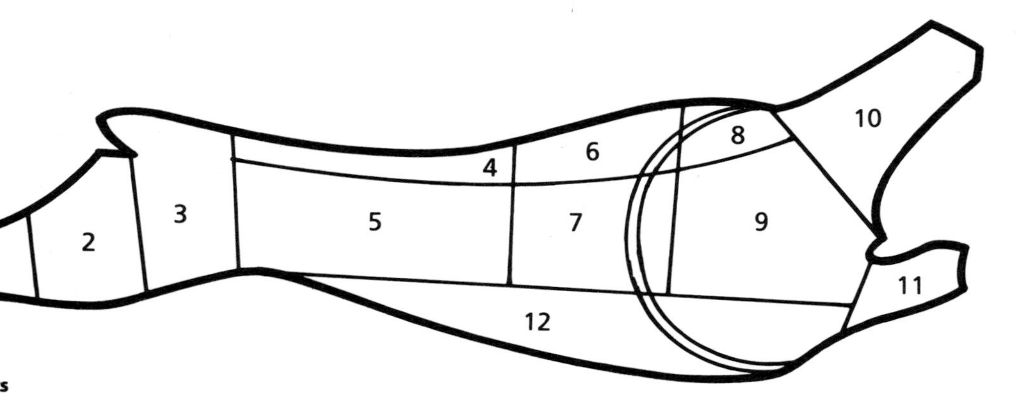

Lamb & mutton: English cuts
1. Shank end of leg
1.& 2. Leg (gigot in Scotland)
3. Fillet
4.& 5. Saddle, only when cut takes in both sides of back; loin or centerloin chops
6. Best end (fair end in Ireland) of neck roast; best end of neck chops if cut; crown roast
7. Cutlets
8. Middle neck chops or cutlets (gigot chops in Ireland)
8.& 9. Shoulder
10. Scrag end of neck
11. Shank
12. Breast

Buying and cooking lamb

American cuts to choose	Cooking methods
leg, crown roast, rack or rib, shoulder	roast
shoulder chops, rib chops, loin chops, sirloin chops, leg chops or steaks, cubes for kebabs, ground lamb patties	broil, fry
neck slices, shoulder chops, breast, riblets, shanks, lamb for stew	braise, stew

British cuts to choose	
best end of neck, breast, leg (including fillet and knuckle), loin, saddle, shoulder	roast
chump chops, cutlets, loin chops, lamb steaks from the leg, noisettes (boneless loin or best end steaks), cubes for kebabs, minced lamb patties	grill, fry
shoulder, middle neck cutlets, breast, chump chops, loin chops, leg	braise
middle neck, scrag end of neck	stew

Montone all'abruzzese

Casserole of Mutton with Wine and Herbs

00:20 02:10

American	Ingredients	Metric/Imperial
2 lb	*Mutton (shoulder or neck)*	1 kg / 2 lb
Scant ¼ cup	*Oil*	3 tbsp
4	*Bay leaves*	4
½ tsp	*Chopped basil*	½ tsp
½ tsp	*Chopped rosemary*	½ tsp
2	*Garlic cloves*	2
	Salt and pepper	
½	*Chilli pepper*	½
2 cups	*Dry white wine*	450 ml / ¾ pint

1. Dice the meat, heat the oil in a saucepan or casserole over a medium heat, add meat, turning until brown.
2. Chop the bay leaves, basil and rosemary, sprinkle over the meat, which should be stirred frequently.
3. Add crushed garlic, salt, several twists of pepper, a piece of chilli, the wine, and 1 cup [225 ml / 8 fl oz] water, cover and cook gently for 2 hours either on top of the stove or in a medium oven.

Montone al pilaff

Mutton Pilaff

00:20 01:00

American	Ingredients	Metric/Imperial
⅔ cup	*Oil*	150 ml / ¼ pint
2	*Garlic cloves*	2
1¼ lb	*Stewing mutton*	600 g / 1¼ lb
3	*Onions*	3
1½ cups	*Rice*	350 g / 12 oz
10	*Strands of saffron*	10
3 tbsp	*Rosewater*	2 tbsp
	Salt and pepper	
1 tsp	*Sugar*	1 tsp
1 quart	*Stock*	1 litre / 1¾ pints
¼ cup	*Raisins*	40 g / 1½ oz
1 tsp	*Chopped mint*	1 tsp
1 tsp	*Chopped sage*	1 tsp
1½ oz	*Pine kernels*	40 g / 1½ oz

1. Choose a large pan with a lid. Heat the oil and fry the garlic cloves, remove when brown.
2. Cut the mutton into small dice and put in the oil, cook for about 10 minutes until brown. Add roughly chopped onions, the washed and drained rice. When the rice has become transparent, add the saffron, dissolved in rosewater, the salt, pepper, sugar and stock. Stir well and cover.
3. When the rice has absorbed all the liquid, test the meat then add the raisins, chopped mint and sage. Remove the pan from the stove and allow it to stand for a few minutes in a warm place. Pile pilaff onto a heated serving dish and garnish with lightly toasted pine kernels.
4. This dish must be served piping hot.

Cotolettine di agnello al verde

Lamb Chops in Green Sauce

00:05 00:20

American	Ingredients	Metric/Imperial
2 tbsp	*Vegetable oil*	1½ tbsp
2 tbsp	*Butter*	25 g / 1 oz
6	*Sprigs of rosemary*	6
1¾ lb	*Small lamb chops*	800 g / 1¾ lb
½ cup	*White wine*	225 ml / 8 fl oz
⅔ cup	*Green olives, pitted (stoned)*	100 g / 4 oz
3 tbsp	*Capers*	2 tbsp

1. Heat oil and butter over a brisk heat in a large frying pan with the rosemary; add the lamb chops to the pan and brown on both sides.
2. Moisten with the white wine and cook for a further 10 minutes on a medium heat.
3. Remove the rosemary from the pan, add the finely chopped olives and capers and cook over a low heat for a few minutes. Serve hot accompanied by boiled rice or potatoes.

Scottadito 

Lamb Chops Fried in Pecorino Batter

00:30 00:10

American	Ingredients	Metric/Imperial
1	*Rack (best end neck) of young spring lamb*	1
2	*Eggs*	2
¼ cup	*Grated pecorino (sheep's milk cheese)*	25 g / 1 oz
	Salt and pepper	
1 tbsp	*Chopped parsley*	1 tbsp
½ cup	*Very fine bread crumbs*	50 g / 2 oz
2	*Garlic cloves*	2
2 tbsp	*Vegetable oil*	2 tbsp
6	*Lemon slices*	6

1. Ask the butcher to remove the corner bone and backbone, leaving just the rib. Using a very sharp knife, lay bone bare up to the level of the fillet (but not cutting through the meat). Take this strip of meat, wrap it around the fillet and secure with a cocktail stick. Flatten into a cutlet shape.
2. Preheat oven to 300°F / 150°C / Gas Mark 2.
3. Prepare batter by beating eggs and adding grated pecorino, chopped parsley, salt and pepper. Dip cutlets in this mixture and then coat with bread crumbs.
4. Cut cloves of garlic in half, heat oil in the frying pan and sauté garlic for 1 minute, then remove. Add cutlets to the pan and fry, browning well on both sides. Remove with a slotted spoon and drain on absorbent kitchen towels. Put on a serving dish and keep warm in the oven.
5. Cut 6 strips of kitchen foil, about 2 × 2¾ in / 5 × 7 cm, fringe and wrap around exposed bones of cutlets.
6. Serve cutlets garnished with lemon slices accompanied with artichoke hearts fried in bread crumbs.

Costolette di agnello con patate al vino

Lamb Cutlets with Potatoes in Wine

00:40 Serves 6 | 00:20

American	Ingredients	Metric/Imperial
12	*Lamb cutlets*	12
¼ cup	*Flour*	25 g / 1 oz
½ cup	*Butter*	100 g / 4 oz
4	*Garlic cloves*	4
4	*Sage leaves*	4
½ cup	*Dry white wine*	125 ml / 4 fl oz
2 lb	*Potatoes*	1 kg / 2 lb
¾ cup	*Olive oil*	175 ml / 6 fl oz
2	*Onions*	2
	Salt	
½ tsp	*Hot paprika*	½ tsp

1. Coat the cutlets in flour, heat the butter in a pan and fry until golden brown for about 3 minutes each side.
2. Add the crushed garlic and sage, pour in the wine and cook on a low heat for 10 minutes.
3. Peel the potatoes and cut into thick slices (alternatively if they are small to medium-sized, cut into quarters), cook in boiling salted water until tender but firm.
4. Heat the oil in a pan over a medium heat and cook the thinly sliced onions for 4 minutes.
5. Add the potatoes to the onion and fry, turning from time to time, without breaking the potatoes too much. Sprinkle with salt and paprika.
6. Serve the cooked cutlets on a heated serving dish garnished with potatoes and onions.

Frittura mista

Fried Mixed Grill

00:40 | 00:20

American	Ingredients	Metric/Imperial
1¼ cups	*Flour*	150 g / 5 oz
3 tbsp	*Olive oil*	2 tbsp
2	*Eggs*	2
	Salt and pepper	
3 tbsp	*Dry white wine*	2 tbsp
3	*Artichokes*	3
½	*Lemon*	½
5 oz	*Calf's brains*	150 g / 5 oz
5 oz	*Calf's liver*	150 g / 5 oz
¾ lb	*Zucchini (courgettes)*	350 g / 12 oz
4	*Lamb chops*	4
½ tsp	*Curry powder*	½ tsp
1¼ cups	*Vegetable oil for frying*	300 ml / ½ pint
1	*Bay leaf*	1
1	*Sage leaf*	1

1. Prepare the batter, putting the flour in a large bowl, add olive oil, the egg yolks and a pinch of salt. Mix carefully and add the white wine and sufficient water so that the batter is not too thick.
2. Clean the artichokes and cook them for 5 minutes in water with a little lemon juice. Immerse the carefully cleaned calf's brains and liver in boiling water; steep for 5 minutes.
3. Cut all the meat and vegetables into thin slices or small pieces. Whip the egg whites until they are stiff and fold them gently into the batter, taking care that they do not collapse, add a little curry powder, tip in the meat and vegetables and mix so that they are all well covered.
4. Heat the oil in a large deep frying pan with a bay leaf and a leaf of sage and put the ingredients into the pan in batches and fry until golden brown. Drain on absorbent kitchen towels.

Montone del capraio

Mutton with Bread and Onions

Traditionally, this dish was cooked in a low-burning wood-fired range using a copper pan with a very tight-fitting lid. Nowadays the pressure cooker makes an ideal substitute.

00:10 | 00:30 in a pressure cooker

American	Ingredients	Metric/Imperial
¼ cup	*Butter*	50 g / 2 oz
1	*Onion*	1
2 lb	*Stewing mutton*	1 kg / 2 lb
	Salt and pepper	
8	*Slices of crusty bread*	8

1. Melt the butter in the pressure cooker, fry the chopped onion. Cut the meat into small pieces, add to the onion, season with salt and pepper. Pour over 1 cup [225 ml / 8 fl oz] water, close the cooker lid, bring to pressure and cook for 20 minutes over moderate heat.
2. De-pressurize the cooker, remove the meat and serve on thick slices of toast with all the juices poured over it.

Fondue all'abbacchio

Lamb Fondue

02:30 | 01:00

American	Ingredients	Metric/Imperial
11 oz	*Fontina cheese*	300 g / 11 oz
2 cups	*Milk*	450 ml / ¾ pint
⅓ cup	*Butter*	75 g / 3 oz
3	*Egg yolks*	3
6	*Lamb cutlets*	6
½ cup	*Stock*	125 ml / 4 fl oz
1 tbsp	*Lemon juice*	1 tbsp
3 tbsp	*Gin*	2 tbsp

1. Prepare the fondue in the usual way (see page 207) for the basic recipe.
2. Heat half the butter in a pan, add the cutlets and fry gently for 3 minutes each side, then moisten with hot stock. Finish cooking with the pan covered for about 20 minutes. Add the gin and the lemon juice.
3. Arrange the cutlets on a metal dish and place on a hotplate, cover with the fondue and serve hot.

Fried mixed grill

Rognoni alla senape

Kidneys in Mustard Sauce

00:20 | 00:00

American	Ingredients	Metric/Imperial
8	*Lambs' kidneys*	8
¼ cup	*Butter*	50 g / 2 oz
2	*Garlic cloves*	2
1 cup	*Dry white wine*	225 ml / 8 fl oz
1 tbsp	*Mustard*	1 tbsp
4 drops	*Worcester sauce*	4 drops
Scant ¼ cup	*Chopped parsley*	3 tbsp

1. Skin and core the kidneys, scald in boiling water for a few minutes and drain. Slice or halve the kidneys.
2. Heat the butter in a heavy pan with the garlic, add kidneys and fry over a medium heat for 5 minutes, then add the white wine and turn the heat up to allow it to evaporate.
3. Reduce the heat to moderate and continue cooking for another 10 minutes, add the mustard and a few drops of Worcester sauce. Stir well, sprinkle with parsley and serve hot with a purée of potatoes.

Abbacchio e carciofi

Lamb with Artichokes

01:00 | 01:00

American	Ingredients	Metric/Imperial
2	*Whole lamb loins*	2
¼ cup	*Butter*	50 g / 2 oz
¼ cup	*Vegetable oil*	50 ml / 2 fl oz
6	*Sage leaves*	6
6	*Sprigs of rosemary*	6
	Salt and pepper	
1 cup	*Dry white wine*	225 ml / 8 fl oz
8	*Small artichokes*	8
2	*Eggs*	2
1 cup	*Bread crumbs*	100 g / 4 oz
½	*Lemon*	½
	Oil for deep frying	

1. Preheat the oven to 400°F / 200°C / Gas Mark 6.
2. Wash and thoroughly dry the lamb. Heat the butter and oil in a roasting pan, adding a few sage leaves, rosemary and seasoning with salt and pepper. Put the lamb in the pan and brown on all sides in the oven.
3. Moisten the lamb with the white wine, adding a little at a time so that one amount is absorbed before adding another.
4. While the lamb is cooking, clean the artichokes, remove the tough leaves, chokes and thorns, and boil them for 10 minutes or so. Remove them from the heat and drain upside down on a wire rack to extract all the water.
5. Cut the artichokes in two, dry them well, then coat them with the beaten eggs and the bread crumbs. Fry them on a brisk heat in plenty of oil.
6. Squeeze a few drops of lemon juice onto the artichokes, when cooked, then remove them from the pan and put to dry on a sheet of kitchen towel which will soak up the excess grease; then sprinkle with grated lemon rind.

Kidneys in mustard sauce

7. Finish cooking the lamb; there should be no juices left at the end of cooking. Place in the centre of a heated serving dish and surround with the fried artichokes.

Agnello al limone

Lamb with Lemon

00:30 Marinating time 02:00 Serves 6 | 01:00

American	Ingredients	Metric/Imperial
3 lb	*Leg of lamb*	1.4 kg / 3 lb
2	*Garlic cloves*	2
2	*Lemons*	2
	Salt and pepper	
¾ cup	*Vegetable oil*	175 ml / 6 fl oz
½ tsp	*Chopped sage*	½ tsp
½ tsp	*Chopped rosemary*	½ tsp
2½ cups	*White wine*	600 ml / 1 pint
½ cup	*Wine vinegar*	125 ml / 4 fl oz
14 oz	*Plum tomatoes, fresh or canned*	400 g / 14 oz
1 cup	*Black olives*	175 g / 6 oz
	New potatoes	

1. Cut meat into 1 in / 2½ cm cubes, mix with the crushed garlic and lemon juice and pour over the lamb with salt and pepper. Marinate for 2 hours.
2. Heat the oil in a large frying pan, add the chopped sage and rosemary. When the fat is hot, brown the pieces of lamb well on all sides. Moisten a little at a time with the white wine mixed with the vinegar, then cover with the tomatoes, which can be broken down with a wooden spoon, and add the black olives.
3. Cook over a low heat, or continue cooking in the oven at 325°F / 170°C / Gas Mark 3.
4. Remove the meat from the pan when it is well cooked with a slotted spoon. Sieve the sauce, if necessary thickening it with a little flour or thinning with a little wine. Reheat and serve very hot, surrounded by boiled new potatoes.

Umido alla pugliese

Lamb Stew with Pasta

00:15 | 01:30

American	Ingredients	Metric/Imperial
1¾ lb	*Stewing lamb*	*800 g / 1¾ lb*
2	*Onions*	*2*
1¼ lb	*Tomatoes*	*600 g / 1¼ lb*
3 tbsp	*Vegetable oil*	*2 tbsp*
1 tbsp	*White flour*	*1 tbsp*
⅔ cup	*Red wine*	*150 ml / 5 fl oz*
2	*Lemons*	*2*
1 lb	*Orecchiette or other pasta*	*450 g / 1 lb*
	Sprigs of parsley	
	Salt and pepper	

1. Dice meat, peel and chop onions, peel tomatoes. Heat oil and sauté meat and onions for 3-4 minutes until meat is brown.
2. Add flour to pan then cook for 1 minute. Remove from the heat and pour over wine, lemon juice and stir in tomatoes. Return to heat, cover and simmer for about 1¼ hours, stirring from time to time.
3. Meanwhile cook pasta in plenty of boiling salted water until 'al dente'. Stir cooked pasta into stew.
4. Spoon stew into an earthenware dish, garnish with sprigs of parsley, add a sprinkling of black pepper or powdered capsicum and serve.

Agnello arrosto del Nilo

Roast Lamb of the Nile

01:00 | 01:00
Marinating time 01:00

American	Ingredients	Metric/Imperial
3¼ lb	*Leg of lamb*	*1.5 kg / 3¼ lb*
1 cup	*Vegetable oil*	*225 ml / 8 fl oz*
	Salt and pepper	
¼ cup	*Butter*	*50 g / 2 oz*
2	*Onions*	*2*
½ cup	*White wine*	*125 ml / 4 fl oz*
	Stock	
4	*Potatoes*	*4*
1 lb	*Artichokes*	*450 g / 1 lb*
1	*Lemon*	*1*
3 tbsp	*Chopped parsley*	*2 tbsp*

1. Cut the leg of lamb into 1 in / 2½ cm cubes and marinate in oil, salt and pepper for 1 hour.
2. Heat the butter and oil from the marinade in a large pan, sweat thinly sliced onions over a low heat. Remove the onions to a plate, raise the heat and fry the meat until brown.
3. Return the onions to the lamb, mix well and moisten with the white wine and stock. Continue cooking on a moderate heat, covered, for about 30 minutes. When the lamb is cooked through, turn off the heat, leaving the pan covered.
4. Peel the potatoes and cut them into thin wedges; peel and trim the artichokes and cut them into slices after coating them with lemon juice. Slowly heat the lamb and add the potatoes and artichokes as soon as the cooking juices are hot. Cook for a further 30 minutes or until the vegetables are tender. Serve sprinkled with chopped parsley.

Abbacchio aglio e aceto

Lamb with Garlic and Vinegar

00:30 | 01:30

American	Ingredients	Metric/Imperial
2 lb	*Lamb (neck, shoulder, breast)*	*1 kg / 2 lb*
¼ cup	*Vegetable oil*	*50 ml / 2 fl oz*
6	*Garlic cloves*	*6*
6	*Sprigs of rosemary*	*6*
	Salt and pepper	
2	*Boned anchovies*	*2*
½ cup	*Vinegar*	*125 ml / 4 fl oz*

1. Preheat the oven to 350°F / 180°C / Gas Mark 4.
2. Wash and thoroughly dry the meat, cut in pieces, then put in an ovenproof dish to brown with oil, 2 crushed cloves of garlic and rosemary in the oven for 15 minutes, turning from time to time. Season with pepper and a very little salt.
3. Crush the anchovies in a mortar or blender with 4 cloves of garlic, dilute the pulp with red or white vinegar, according to taste, to obtain a generous quantity of sauce.
4. When the lamb is well browned on all sides, pour over the sauce with 1 cup [225 ml / 8 fl oz] water and continue cooking on a medium heat on the stove or in the oven, as you wish.
5. Remove the meat from the pan to a heated serving dish. Dilute the sauce with a little water if it has reduced too much, pour into a sauceboat and serve separately with the lamb.

Agnello con le melanzane

Lamb Stew with Eggplant

00:30 | 02:00
Serves 6

American	Ingredients	Metric/Imperial
3½ lb	*Lamb, shoulder or breast*	*1.6 kg / 3½ lb*
1 cup	*Vegetable oil*	*225 ml / 8 fl oz*
¼ lb	*Chopped bacon*	*100 g / 4 oz*
2	*Garlic cloves*	*2*
5	*Eggplant (aubergines)*	*5*
	Salt and pepper	
1 cup	*Light red wine*	*225 ml / 8 fl oz*
2 tbsp	*Chopped parsley*	*1½ tbsp*

1. Trim and cut the lamb into pieces.
2. Heat oil in a frying pan, add chopped bacon, crushed garlic, cook for 2 minutes, then put in the lamb and cook until brown on a medium heat.
3. Slice the eggplant (aubergines) lengthwise to obtain slices which are not too thin, salt and put the slices between two plates at an angle to drain. Place oil in another pan over a high heat and fry the slices until golden. Drain on kitchen towels.
4. Lower the heat under the pan with the lamb and pour in the wine and the same amount of water a little at a time, turning the meat to stop it sticking.
5. Drain any excess grease from the eggplant and, when the lamb is cooked, mix it with the fried eggplant slices, add plenty of chopped parsley and switch off the heat. Leave covered for a further 10 minutes, then serve, giving the dish a final stir.

Pork cuts

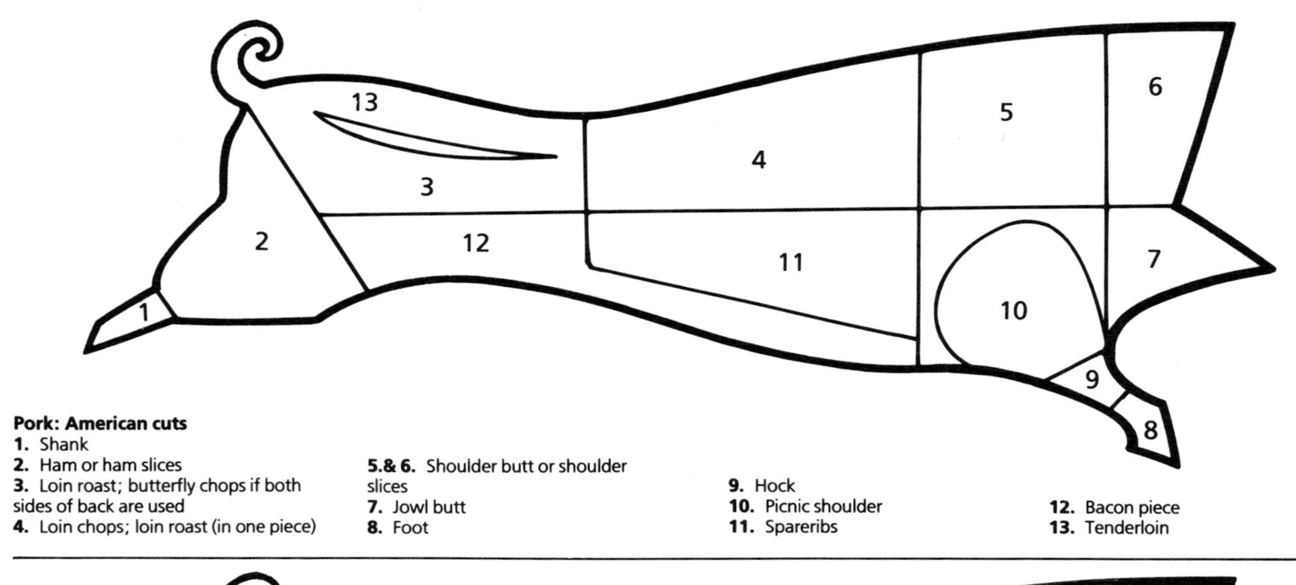

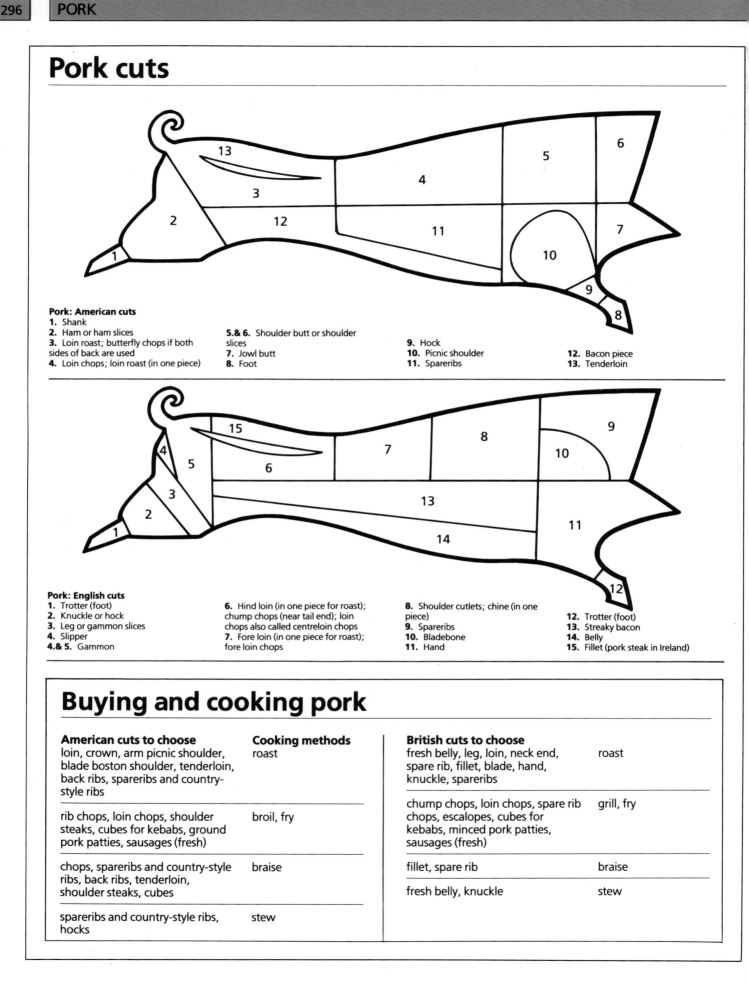

Pork: American cuts
1. Shank
2. Ham or ham slices
3. Loin roast; butterfly chops if both sides of back are used
4. Loin chops; loin roast (in one piece)
5.& 6. Shoulder butt or shoulder slices
7. Jowl butt
8. Foot
9. Hock
10. Picnic shoulder
11. Spareribs
12. Bacon piece
13. Tenderloin

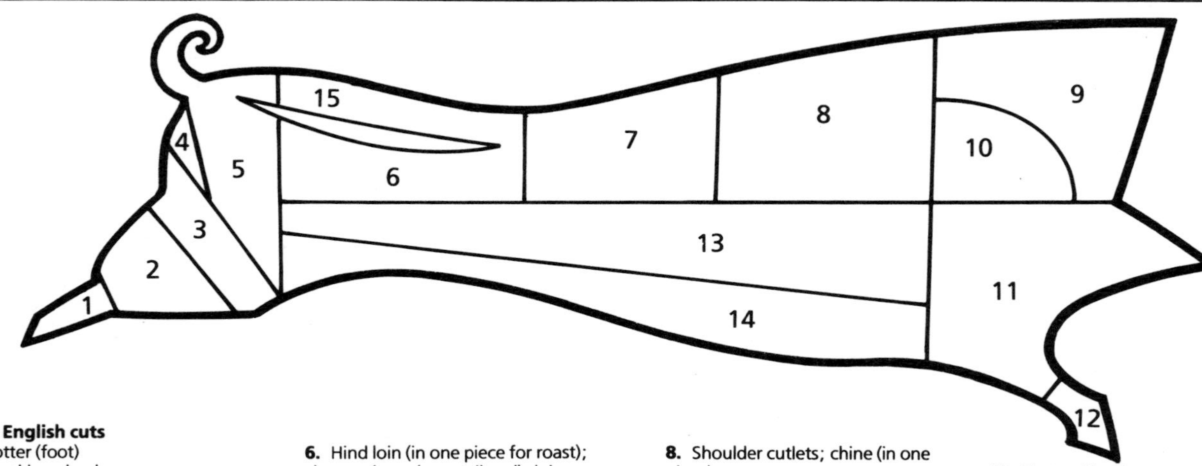

Pork: English cuts
1. Trotter (foot)
2. Knuckle or hock
3. Leg or gammon slices
4. Slipper
4.& 5. Gammon
6. Hind loin (in one piece for roast); chump chops (near tail end); loin chops also called centreloin chops
7. Fore loin (in one piece for roast); fore loin chops
8. Shoulder cutlets; chine (in one piece)
9. Spareribs
10. Bladebone
11. Hand
12. Trotter (foot)
13. Streaky bacon
14. Belly
15. Fillet (pork steak in Ireland)

Buying and cooking pork

American cuts to choose	Cooking methods
loin, crown, arm picnic shoulder, blade boston shoulder, tenderloin, back ribs, spareribs and country-style ribs	roast
rib chops, loin chops, shoulder steaks, cubes for kebabs, ground pork patties, sausages (fresh)	broil, fry
chops, spareribs and country-style ribs, back ribs, tenderloin, shoulder steaks, cubes	braise
spareribs and country-style ribs, hocks	stew

British cuts to choose	
fresh belly, leg, loin, neck end, spare rib, fillet, blade, hand, knuckle, spareribs	roast
chump chops, loin chops, spare rib chops, escalopes, cubes for kebabs, minced pork patties, sausages (fresh)	grill, fry
fillet, spare rib	braise
fresh belly, knuckle	stew

Arista di maiale alla panna

Pork Ribs with Cream

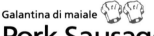

Preparation 00:25 — Cooking 01:15

American	Ingredients	Metric/Imperial
3¼ lb	*Pork shoulder butt (chine)*	1.5 kg / 3¼ lb
4	*Garlic cloves*	4
10	*Cloves*	10
½ cup	*Vegetable oil*	125 ml / 4 fl oz
3 or 4	*Sprigs of rosemary*	3 or 4
1 cup	*Whipping (double) cream*	225 ml / 8 fl oz
½ cup	*Cognac, rum or grappa*	125 ml / 4 fl oz
	Salt and pepper	

1. Preheat oven to 400°F / 200°C / Gas Mark 6.
2. Insert into the meat the cloves of garlic (cut in pieces) and alternate with the cloves; brush with oil. Tie a few sprigs of rosemary to the meat with thin white thread. Put the pork in an ovenproof dish, pour oil over it and put in the oven.
3. After 10 minutes cooking, turn the meat and roast it well on all sides.
4. Beat cream in a bowl with a glass of spirits (cognac, rum or grappa according to your own preference).
5. When the pork has been cooking for 30 minutes, lower the oven to 325°F / 170°C / Gas Mark 4 and moisten with the cream and liquor, pouring it all over the meat at once. Continue cooking for a further 30 minutes, taking care that the cooking juices do not dry out too much and turning the meat from time to time. If the sauce reduces too much, add a very little warm water.
6. Test the sauce and season with salt and pepper to taste. Remove the meat from the pan, strain sauce, slice the meat, cover it with the sauce and place the serving dish in the oven for a few moments before serving very hot.

Galantina di maiale 

Pork Sausage

Preparation 01:00 — Cooking 03:00

American	Ingredients	Metric/Imperial
1	*Piece of pig's intestine*	1
¼ lb	*Tongue, in a single slice*	100 g / 4 oz
¼ lb	*Cooked ham, in a single slice*	100 g / 4 oz
10	*Pistacchio nuts*	10
	Salt and pepper	
	Nutmeg	
¼ cup	*Marsala*	50 ml / 2 fl oz
¼ tsp	*Powdered truffle*	¼ tsp
1¼ lb	*Lean pork (ham slices)*	600 g / 1¼ lb
¼ lb	*Fat bacon*	100 g / 4 oz
1	*Bunch of herbs*	1

1. Soak the intestine in warm water so that it softens thoroughly.
2. Cut half the tongue and lean part of the ham into very small cubes. Mix well with the shelled pistacchio nuts, salt and pepper and a little grated nutmeg, marsala and a little powdered truffle, then keep cold and covered.
3. Grind (mince) the remaining meat, the fat from the ham and the fat bacon, add to the other ingredients and work together until thoroughly combined.
4. Drain the intestine from the water, dry it well with a cloth, spread on a chopping board and roll the mixture in it tightly, giving it the shape of a large sausage. Fold at the two ends, then wrap in a cloth, tying it in the middle and at the sides.
5. Boil in plenty of salted water with the bunch of herbs for 3 hours. When it is cooked, remove and cool with a weight on top.

Cook's tip: This dish is quickly and easily made in a food processor.

Fettine agrodolci

Sweet and Sour Pork Sauce

Preparation 00:30 — Cooking 00:50

American	Ingredients	Metric/Imperial
2	*Pippin apples*	2
8 oz	*Canned tomatoes*	225 g / 8 oz
⅓ cup	*Vegetable oil*	4 tbsp
⅓ cup	*Dry white wine*	4 tbsp
1	*Stock cube*	1
½ tsp	*Mustard*	½ tsp
4	*Shoulder slices of pork*	4
	Flour	
	Salt and pepper	

1. Peel the pippin apples, grate coarsely and collect the flesh in a frying pan. Add the well drained and puréed tomatoes to the apples, stir well, then add oil, dry white wine, and the stock cube dissolved in a little boiling water. Simmer the sauce for 20 minutes so that it blends and thickens well.
2. Beat the meat well, make up a little strong mustard and spread it sparingly on the pork slices; flour them lightly.
3. When the sauce seems cooked, check seasoning, taste, add the meat and cook for 15 minutes on each side. Serve hot.

Polpettone al cognac

Meatloaf with Cognac

Preparation 00:10 — Cooking 00:30

American	Ingredients	Metric/Imperial
1 lb	*Ground (minced) pork*	450 g / 1 lb
5 oz	*Ricotta (curd cheese)*	150 g / 5 oz
1	*Egg*	1
3 tbsp	*Grated parmesan cheese*	2 tbsp
	Salt and pepper	
¼ tsp	*Nutmeg*	¼ tsp
3 tbsp	*Cognac*	2 tbsp
3 tbsp	*Oil*	2 tbsp
1 tbsp	*Butter*	15 g / ½ oz

1. Mix all the ingredients (except the cognac, oil and butter) thoroughly, then press them firmly into one large round.
2. Sprinkle some of the cognac over the meatloaf, then heat the oil and butter and fry in a wide, heavy pan, add the meat, turn every now and then, taking great care that it does not stick to the bottom of the pan.
3. Continue to sprinkle with the cognac (the taste combines well with pork and ricotta). This meatloaf is a good choice for a picnic, but can be served hot.

Spiedini di fegato nella rete

Liver Kebabs in Caul

00:40 00:15

American	Ingredients	Metric/Imperial
1	*Piece of caul*	*1*
1 lb	*Pig's liver*	*½ kg / 1 lb*
	Slices of bread	
8	*Bay leaves*	*8*
	Oil	
	Salt and pepper	
8	*Lemon slices*	*8*
	Parsley	

1. Soften caul fat in tepid water for 30 minutes then drain.
2. Cut liver into thick slices and wrap each piece in caul fat.
3. Thread skewers with slices or bread, liver and bay leaves. Brush with oil, season and place under a medium broiler (grill). Cook for 10-15 minutes, turning skewers from time to time.
4. Put skewers on a hot serving dish and garnish with lemon slices and parsley sprigs.

Rostiscianna con polenta

Mixed Meat Stew with Polenta

01:00 01:30

American	Ingredients	Metric/Imperial
½ lb	*Pork*	*225 g / 8 oz*
½ lb	*Beef*	*225 g / 8 oz*
½ lb	*Italian sausage*	*225 g / 8 oz*
½ lb	*Pork spare rib*	*225 g / 8 oz*
¼ cup	*Butter*	*50 g / 2 oz*
¼ cup	*Oil*	*50 ml / 2 fl oz*
2 or 3	*Onions*	*2 or 3*
1	*Carrot*	*1*
1	*Celery stalk*	*1*
1½ cups	*Dry red wine (Barbera)*	*350 ml / 12 fl oz*
14 oz	*Peeled tomatoes*	*400 g / 14 oz*
2 lb	*Red onions*	*1 kg / 2 lb*
	Salt	
¾ lb	*Coarse-grained corn meal for polenta*	*350 g / 12 oz*

1. Cut all the meat into pieces of roughly equal size and place in a saucepan with heated butter, oil and 2 or 3 chopped onions. Add the chopped carrot and celery.
2. Stir and brown slightly then add the wine and, when it has been absorbed, the tomatoes.
3. Stir then add the chopped onions, and cook with the lid on for 20 minutes. Stir again and leave to simmer covered, until the meat is done.
4. Prepare the polenta by bringing 1½ quarts [1.5 litres / 2½ pints] of salted water to the boil and then adding the corn meal in a slow, steady, thin trickle, stirring constantly with a wooden spoon. Continue to stir for the full 20 minutes the polenta takes to cook. Add a little oil at the last moment.
5. Warm a large, deep serving dish. To serve, turn out the polenta onto the warmed dish, make a hollow in the centre and fill this with the piping hot meat stew.

Spiedini in padella

Fried Kebabs

00:20 00:20

American	Ingredients	Metric/Imperial
11 oz	*Pork fillet*	*300 g / 11 oz*
7 oz	*Italian sausage*	*200 g / 7 oz*
7 oz	*Liver*	*200 g / 7 oz*
1	*Onion*	*1*
1	*Sweet pepper*	*1*
	Sage leaves, as required	
1 tsp	*Chopped rosemary*	*1 tsp*
1 tbsp	*Vegetable oil*	*1 tbsp*
1 tbsp	*Butter*	*1 tbsp*
1 quart	*Stock (cubes dissolved in hot water)*	*1 litre / 1¾ pints*
1 tbsp	*Brandy*	*1 tbsp*
	Salt and pepper	

1. Cut up all the meat into fair-sized chunks, peel and slice onion and deseed and slice sweet pepper.
2. Thread meat and vegetables onto prepared skewers, alternating the varieties, e.g. pork fillet, sausage, liver and sage, finishing with a slice of onion and one of sweet pepper.
3. Heat oil and butter in a large frying pan and brown skewers all over. Add stock and cook a further 10 minutes. Season with salt and pepper, increase heat and pour over brandy.
4. Remove skewers and put in a deep serving dish. Pour over some sauce and serve remaining sauce separately.

Polpettone all'alsaziana

Meatloaf with Sauerkraut

This dish is typical of those from the region of Alsace.

00:30 01:00

American	Ingredients	Metric/Imperial
1¼ lb	*Lean pork*	*600 g / 1¼ lb*
7 oz	*Smoked ham*	*200 g / 7 oz*
2	*Eggs*	*2*
¼ tsp	*Salt*	*¼ tsp*
¼ tsp	*Nutmeg*	*¼ tsp*
½ cup	*Bread crumbs*	*50 g / 2 oz*
⅓ cup	*Oil*	*75 ml / 3 fl oz*
2	*Garlic cloves*	*2*
2	*Sprigs of rosemary*	*2*
11 oz	*Sauerkraut (see page 302)*	*300 g / 11 oz*
1 cup	*Vinegar*	*225 ml / 8 fl oz*

1. Preheat the oven to 450°F / 220°C / Gas Mark 8.
2. Grind (mince) the pork and ham, mix with the eggs, some salt and grated nutmeg and work the mixture with bread crumbs as needed into a shape like a large sausage.
3. Heat the oil in a casserole with a lid, add meatloaf, garlic and rosemary and bake for 1 hour or until cooked.
4. When the meatloaf is cooked, cool, slice and arrange on a serving dish.
5. Prepare the sauerkraut by boiling in water and vinegar Cover the meatloaf with the sauerkraut just before serving.

Kebabs

Maialetto di Paolo

Cold Loin of Pork with Tuna Sauce

00:20 01:00

American	Ingredients	Metric/Imperial
2 lb	*Loin of pork without bones or fat*	1 kg / 2 lb
9 oz	*Tuna in oil*	250 g / 9 oz
1	*Onion*	1
4	*Anchovies*	4
	Salt and pepper	
2 cups	*White wine*	450 ml / ¾ pint
2 tsp	*Cognac*	2 tsp
¼ cup	*Vegetable oil*	50 ml / 2 fl oz
2	*Lemons*	2

1. Bone the loin of pork or buy one boned and discard all the fat. (The bones may be used next day for stock and pork fat is always useful for frying.)
2. Put the meat into a large saucepan with the chopped tuna, the thinly sliced onion, the washed, boned and broken up anchovies, salt, pepper, white wine and cognac. Cover and cook over moderate heat. Test the pork by inserting a toothpick, when it enters easily, the meat is cooked.
3. Transfer the pork, sliced, to a large serving dish and tip the remaining contents of the saucepan into a large bowl, mix oil and lemon juice and pour over the meat. Decorate with chopped gherkins.

Cook's tip: This dish must be prepared at least 12 hours in advance to allow the pork to absorb the flavor of the sauce. It will keep well in the refrigerator for several days.

Maiale alla bresciana

Pot-Roast of Pork with Artichoke Hearts

00:30 01:30

American	Ingredients	Metric/Imperial
1	*Onion*	1
1	*Celery stalk*	1
1	*Carrot*	1
¼ cup	*Oil*	50 ml / 2 fl oz
¼ cup	*Butter*	50 g / 2 oz
8	*Artichoke hearts*	8
¼ tsp	*Chopped rosemary*	¼ tsp
3 lb	*Loin of pork, boned and rolled*	1.4 kg / 3 lb
1 cup	*Red wine*	225 ml / 8 fl oz
	Salt and pepper	
14 oz	*Small potatoes*	400 g / 14 oz
1	*Stock cube*	1
Sauce (optional)		
2 tbsp	*Mustard*	1½ tbsp
1	*Egg yolk*	1
4	*Anchovy fillets*	4
1 cup	*Coffee (single) cream*	225 ml / 8 fl oz

1. Chop the onion, celery and carrot and fry lightly in oil and butter. Add the artichoke hearts and a little rosemary. Remove and set the vegetables aside on a plate, put the meat into the pan; brown quickly over a high heat, turning constantly.
2. Pour some red wine over the meat and allow to evaporate, season with salt and pepper. Now tip the vegetables into the pan with the meat and add the peeled potatoes; reduce the heat and add some stock made with the stock cube dissolved in boiling water.
3. Cook for about 1 hour, adding a small quantity of wine from time to time.
4. When the meat is cooked, cut it into thick slices and place on a heated serving dish. Arrange the potatoes around it and sieve or blend the vegetables and remaining liquid which can either be served separately or poured over the meat.
5. Serve with mustard or, if preferred, with a sauce made from mustard, egg yolk, a few chopped anchovy fillets and single cream beaten together.

Carré della Maremma

Loin of Pork 'Maremma'

00:30 01:30

American	Ingredients	Metric/Imperial
2 lb	*Loin of pork, boned*	1 kg / 2 lb
¼ lb	*Fat bacon*	100 g / 4 oz
	Salt and pepper	
3 or 4	*Cloves*	3 or 4
¼ cup	*Vegetable oil*	50 ml / 2 fl oz
6	*Sage leaves*	6
3	*Sprigs of rosemary*	3
½	*Onion*	½
1	*Celery stalk*	1
1 tbsp	*Chopped parsley*	1 tbsp
¼ cup	*Butter*	50 g / 2 oz
½ cup	*Red wine*	125 ml / 4 fl oz
1	*Stock cube*	1
1	*Garlic clove*	1
¼ lb	*Canadian (lean) bacon*	100 g / 4 oz
1 lb	*Plum tomatoes*	500 g / 1 lb
2 lb	*Swiss chard*	1 kg / 2 lb

1. Have the butcher bone the pork for you, stick in pieces of fat bacon dipped in salt and pepper and a few cloves. Paint with oil, coat with coarse salt, sage and rosemary. Tie it tightly with white thread.
2. Chop the onion with a little celery and parsley. Heat oil and butter, cook vegetables gently on a low heat in a large casserole, adding the meat. Moisten with dry full-bodied red wine. Allow the wine to evaporate, add some stock made from the cube and continue cooking, adding more stock from time to time.
3. Fry crushed cloves of garlic in a small pan with a little oil, add a little finely chopped bacon and some chopped, peeled, tomatoes with the seeds removed; pour in a little hot water and cook very gently until a reduced sauce has formed.
4. Separately boil some Swiss chard, using only the white part. When cooked, drain and mix the chard with the tomato sauce, seasoning well.
5. Cut the meat into slices and arrange it on a heated dish covered with the cooking sauce and with the chard around it.

Maiale alla Kyoto

Eastern Pork Chops

00:15 Marinating time 02:00 — 00:25

American	Ingredients	Metric/Imperial
½ cup	*Soy sauce*	125 ml / 4 fl oz
½ cup	*Saki*	125 ml / 4 fl oz
2 tsp	*Sugar*	2 tsp
2 tsp	*Sesame seed oil*	2 tsp
1	*Garlic clove*	1
½	*Onion*	½
¼ tsp	*Ground ginger*	¼ tsp
	Salt	
4	*Large pork chops*	4

1. Make a marinade by beating together the soy sauce, saki, sugar and sesame seed oil and then adding the finely chopped crushed garlic, onion and ground ginger. Sprinkle salt on the chops, immerse them in the marinade and leave for 2 hours.
2. Preheat the oven to 300°F / 150°C / Gas Mark 2.
3. Broil (grill) chops, browning on each side and basting with the marinade, then wrap each one in foil and bake for 15 minutes in the oven. Serve very hot, accompanied either with steamed vegetables or boiled rice.

Fegato e peperoni alla russa

Liver and Peppers Russian-Style

00:40 Soaking time 02:00 — 00:30

American	Ingredients	Metric/Imperial
1 lb	*Pigs' liver*	500 g / 1 lb
⅔ cup	*Milk*	150 ml / ¼ pint
1 cup	*Vegetable oil*	225 ml / 8 fl oz
¼ cup	*Butter*	50 g / 2 oz
	Salt and pepper	
3 tbsp	*Red wine vinegar*	2 tbsp
2	*Onions*	2
3	*Sweet peppers*	3
5	*Ripe tomatoes (fresh or canned)*	5
1 tsp	*Cayenne pepper*	1 tsp
7 oz	*Stale bread cut into cubes*	200 g / 7 oz

1. Soak the pigs' liver in milk for 2 hours. Drain and dry with kitchen towels. Cook slices of liver in a pan with quarter of the oil and the butter. Season with salt and pepper, add red wine vinegar and let it evaporate. As soon as the liver is cooked, remove it from the pan and place it on a plate.
2. Heat remaining butter and some oil. Fry the onions in a high-sided pan.
3. Remove the seeds and pith from the peppers, cut into strips, add to the onions with the chopped tomatoes and cook over a brisk heat. Season with salt, pepper and plenty of cayenne pepper.
4. Add the liver and mix thoroughly with the sauce.
5. Fry the cubes of stale bread separately in the remaining heated oil, drain and serve round the liver.

Filetto di maiale alle mele

Roast Pork with Apples

00:15 — 00:40

American	Ingredients	Metric/Imperial
1 lb	*Tender loin of pork (fillet)*	500 g / 1 lb
Scant ¼ cup	*Vegetable oil*	3 tbsp
	Salt and pepper	
1¾ lb	*Cooking apples*	800 g / 1¾ lb
1 tbsp	*Honey*	1 tbsp
¾ cup	*White wine*	175 ml / 6 fl oz
½	*Stock cube*	½
2 tbsp	*Butter*	25 g / 1 oz

1. Preheat the oven to 350°F / 180°C / Gas Mark 4.
2. Trim the meat carefully and tie it with kitchen thread to keep it in shape. Lay it in a baking pan with oil, salt and pepper and cook in a moderate oven for about 30 minutes.
3. Peel and core the apples and slice them very thinly. Heat them for a few minutes in a separate pan with honey and white wine. Arrange the apples with their cooking syrup on a serving dish to make a bed for the roast pork.
4. After removing the string, slice the meat, arrange back together as though it were still whole.
5. Put the pan on the heat with the cooking juices from the meat, mixing them with boiling water mixed with half a stock cube. When the gravy has thickened a little, mix in a small piece of butter away from the heat. As soon as it has melted pour the hot sauce over the meat.

Maiale alla indonesiana

Curried Pork Indonesian-Style

00:30 Marinating time 02:00 — 01:00

American	Ingredients	Metric/Imperial
1 lb	*Lean pork*	500 g / 1 lb
3	*Lemons*	3
1 tbsp	*Curry powder*	1 tbsp
2	*Garlic cloves*	2
½ cup	*Oil*	125 ml / 4 fl oz
1	*Coconut*	1
2	*Sweet peppers*	2
1	*Red chilli pepper*	1
3 tbsp	*Wine vinegar*	2 tbsp
1 tbsp	*Cane sugar*	1 tbsp
	Salt	

1. Cut the pork into small cubes, and put in a basin together with the lemon juice, curry powder and crushed garlic. Mix well and leave to marinate for 2 hours.
2. Put the pork in pan, add the oil and the grated flesh of the coconut, cover and cook slowly for about 30 minutes.
3. Preheat the oven to 350°F / 180°C / Gas Mark 4.
4. Wash the peppers, remove the seeds, blanch and chop finely, put into a bowl. Deseed the chilli pepper, chop finely and add to the bowl with vinegar, sugar, a pinch of salt and mix.
5. Divide the meat mixture into portions and place each on a square of kitchen foil; sprinkle over the pepper mixture. Close the foil to form parcels. Bake in the oven for 30 minutes.

Croque Monsieur

Fried Cheese and Ham Sandwiches

Preparation 00:25 — Cooking 00:15

American	Ingredients	Metric/Imperial
1 tbsp	*Butter*	15 g / ½ oz
8	*Slices of sandwich loaf*	8
4	*Slices of gruyère cheese*	4
4	*Slices of cooked ham*	4
6	*Eggs*	6
	Salt and pepper	
½ cup	*Bread crumbs*	50 g / 2 oz
	Oil for frying	
1	*Truffle*	1

1. Butter the slices on one side only. Put a slice of gruyère and a slice of ham on each buttered side and close the sandwich.
2. Immerse these sandwiches in 2 beaten eggs, seasoned with salt and pepper and then coat in bread crumbs.
3. Heat oil in a pan over a high flame and fry sandwiches until golden on each side. Remove and keep warm in the oven.
4. Cook 4 eggs in the oil over a low heat.
5. Lay the fried sandwiches on individual plates and place a fried egg on top, taking care not to break the yolk. Add sliced truffle, if desired. Put in a hot oven for a few minutes and serve.

Costine con i crauti

Pork Ribs with Sauerkraut

Preparation 00:40 — Cooking 02:15

American	Ingredients	Metric/Imperial
3¼ lb	*Pork spare ribs*	1.5 kg / 3¼ lb
¼ cup	*Butter*	50 g / 2 oz
½ cup	*Dry white wine*	225 ml / 8 fl oz
	Salt and pepper	
1	*Stock cube*	1
1	*Large cabbage*	1
1	*Onion*	1
2 oz	*Smoked bacon*	50 g / 2 oz
¼ cup	*Vinegar*	50 ml / 2 fl oz

1. Cut the pork ribs into pieces and brown them in a little butter, then drain off the fat and place them in another pan.
2. Moisten with dry white wine, and when it has evaporated, season with salt and pepper. Add 2½ cups [600 ml / 1 pint] stock made from the cube and cook slowly for 2 hours.
3. Cut a firm cabbage into thin strips, wash and place in a pan, pour over 2½ cups [600 ml / 1 pint] boiling water and cook for 10 minutes.
4. Gently cook the chopped onion in a very large saucepan with a little butter and the chopped smoked bacon, add the well drained cabbage, season with salt and pepper and cook covered for about 30 minutes, adding stock from time to time.
5. After 20 minutes add the vinegar and allow to evaporate over a brisk heat.
6. Add the sauerkraut to the pork ribs and let them cook together for a further 15 minutes. Serve very hot with mustard.

Mini-pig allo spiedo

Spit-Roasted Suckling-Pig

Preparation 00:30 — Cooking 02:30

American	Ingredients	Metric/Imperial
1	*Suckling-pig (small, lean piglet)*	1
1 cup	*Oil*	225 ml / 8 fl oz
	Salt and pepper	
2	*Onions*	2
½ cup	*Cognac*	125 ml / 4 fl oz
1	*Garlic clove*	1
3	*Bay leaves*	3

1. Choose a very small piglet, weighing no more than 22 lb [10 kg]. Season the inside with oil, salt and pepper, rub with onions and pour in the cognac. Using strong kitchen string, tie the feet close to the body. Rub oil over the entire skin surface then impale the piglet on the spit.
2. Put oil, salt and pepper into a cup and beat well; add a crushed clove of garlic and some crumbled bay leaves.
3. Start roasting over a good heat. The small piglet will take at least 2 hours to roast and it must be continually brushed with the oil mixture.

Spezzatino tirolese

Tyrolean Stew

Preparation 00:30 — Marinating time 01:00 — Cooking 01:30

American	Ingredients	Metric/Imperial
2 lb	*Pork loin*	1 kg / 2 lb
1 cup	*Red wine*	225 ml / 8 fl oz
Scant ¼ cup	*Vegetable oil*	3 tbsp
	Salt and pepper	
3	*Cloves*	3
2	*Bay leaves*	2
2 oz	*Bacon*	50 g / 2 oz
1	*Onion*	1
1 tbsp	*Butter*	15 g / ½ oz
11 oz	*Italian sausage*	300 g / 11 oz
8 oz	*Peeled tomatoes*	225 g / 8 oz
3	*Potatoes*	3
½	*Stock cube*	½

1. Trim fat and cut the pork into small pieces, marinate in an earthenware pot with the red wine, oil, salt, pepper, cloves, and bay leaves. Cover and leave at room temperature for 1 hour.
2. Chop the bacon and onion very finely and fry gently in a little butter and oil for 4 minutes, then add the sausage cut into small pieces and fry it so that the fat melts a little.
3. Add the marinated meat and fry it over a high heat, stir in the marinating juices with the cloves and bay leaves and evaporate. Moisten with 2 cups [450 ml / ¾ pint] of hot water and add the tomatoes.
4. Cover and cook on a moderate heat for about 45 minutes.
5. Add the peeled potatoes, cut into small pieces, check the seasoning and if necessary add either half a stock cube or a little salt, or both. Cook for a further 50 minutes.
6. Accompany this dish with polenta or with thick slices of crusty brown bread.

Spit-roasted suckling pig

Roast pork with orange

Arista alla francese

Loin of Pork French-Style

00:20 01:20

American	Ingredients	Metric/Imperial
2 tbsp	Butter	25 g / 1 oz
¼ cup	Vegetable oil	50 ml / 2 fl oz
1½ lb	Loin of pork (chine)	700 g / 1½ lb
1	Onion	1
2	Potatoes	2
6	Sage leaves	6
2	Sprigs of rosemary	2
2	Garlic cloves	2
3	Juniper berries	3
¼ tsp	Chopped thyme	¼ tsp
2 cups	Milk	450 ml / ¾ pint
1	Stock cube	1
1	Zest of lemon	1
1 tbsp	Mustard	1 tbsp
1	Egg yolk	1
1 tbsp	Worcester sauce	1 tbsp
	Salt and pepper	

1. Heat butter and oil in a large pan, add the pork ribs with the onion cut into four, potatoes cut into wedges, sage, rosemary, crushed cloves of garlic, juniper berries and a pinch of thyme. Brown slowly on all sides.
2. Add the milk and the stock cube dissolved in a little boiling water and cook slowly for 1 hour. Strain the cooking juices. Remove the meat and keep warm.
3. Return to the heat adding the lemon zest, and reduce. Slice the meat and place it on a heated ovenproof dish.
4. Add mustard, the egg yolk and Worcester sauce to the cooking juices and mix well; adjust the seasoning and pour the sauce over the meat.

Cosciotto di maiale alla grappa

Leg of Pork with Grappa

00:25 02:00

American	Ingredients	Metric/Imperial
1	Carrot	1
1	Celery stalk	1
1	Bay leaf	1
4	Sprigs of parsley	4
3	Garlic cloves	3
¼ cup	Vegetable oil	50 ml / 2 fl oz
2 tbsp	Butter	25 g / 1 oz
10 oz	Leeks	275 g / 10 oz
2 lb	Loin of pork (chine)	1 kg / 2 lb
½ cup	Vinegar	125 ml / 4 fl oz
½ cup	Dry white wine	125 ml / 4 fl oz
1	Stock cube	1
	Pepper	
¼ cup	Grappa	50 ml / 2 fl oz

1. Prepare a bouquet garni with carrot, celery, bay leaf and parsley tied together. Put the whole cloves of garlic in a large saucepan and fry them in the oil and the butter; add the vegetables which you have tied together, the leeks cut into rings and finally the meat. Brown and moisten with a little vinegar and then the dry white wine.
2. When the vegetables have softened and the wine has evaporated, add stock made with a cube and 2½ cups [600 ml / 1 pint] water and plenty of pepper.
3. Cover the pan and cook on a very low heat for about 2 hours, adding a little hot water from time to time whenever the sauce becomes too dry.
4. When the meat is quite tender, remove it from the heat and place it on one side. Strain the sauce and return it to the pan together with the meat. On a medium heat add the grappa; cook for another 10 minutes.
5. When the pork is cooked, cut it into thick slices and serve it with the sauce and an accompaniment of steamed potatoes or white rice.

Arrosto di maiale all'arancia

Roast Pork with Orange

00:35 02:10
Serves 6

American	Ingredients	Metric/Imperial
1	Onion	1
1	Garlic clove	1
½ cup	Vegetable oil	125 ml / 4 fl oz
1 tsp	Lard	1 tsp
1	Sweet red pepper	1
4-6	Oranges	4-6
	Salt	
1 tsp	Sugar	1 tsp
4 lb	Boned leg of pork	2 kg / 4 lb
½ tsp	Powdered thyme	½ tsp
½ tsp	Chopped rosemary	½ tsp
½ tsp	Chopped mint	½ tsp
¼ tsp	Cayenne pepper	¼ tsp
1⅓ cups	Rice	250 g / 9 oz
⅓ cup	Olives	50 g / 2 oz
3 tbsp	Rum	2 tbsp

1. Preheat the oven to 350°F / 180°C / Gas Mark 4. Prepare the sauce, which will be used to moisten the roast.
2. Finely chop the onion and garlic and put in half the heated oil and the lard to brown for 4 minutes. Add the deseeded, chopped red sweet pepper, the grated peel of 2 oranges and the juice of 4 ripe oranges. Season with a little salt and sugar.
3. Rub the pork with a mixture of salt, remaining oil, powdered thyme, chopped fresh rosemary, chopped mint and a little cayenne pepper. Place the spiced meat on an oiled rack in a preheated oven.
4. During cooking brush the meat frequently with the sauce. If it becomes too thick add a little more orange juice. Cook for about 2 hours.
5. Cook rice until 'al dente', drain and keep warm in the oven.
6. When the roast is well cooked, remove from the oven and leave for 10 minutes, then cut into slices about ¼ in / 5 mm in thickness and arrange them on a serving dish. Garnish with slices of 2 oranges and olives and cover with the sauce, diluted with a little orange juice and a little rum. Serve surrounded by boiled rice.

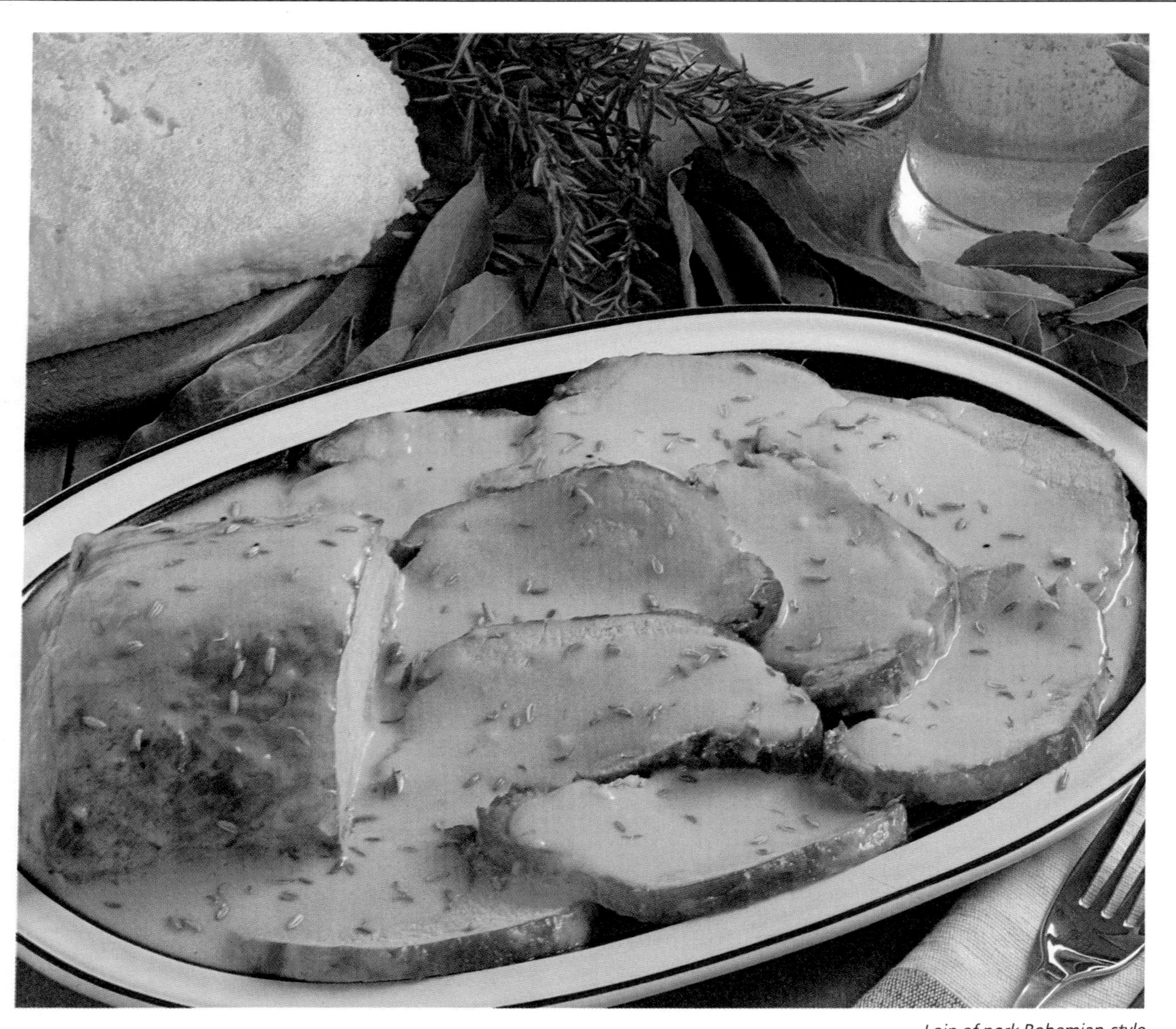

Loin of pork Bohemian-style

Carré di maiale alla boema

Loin of Pork Bohemian-Style

This is a typical recipe from Bohemia, where it is usually accompanied by boiled vegetables in season and by light, foaming local beer.

00:30 01:30

American	Ingredients	Metric/Imperial
2 lb	*Onions*	*1 kg / 2 lb*
2 lb	*Pork loin (chine)*	*1 kg / 2 lb*
2 tbsp	*Vegetable oil*	*25 ml / 1 fl oz*
3 tbsp	*Butter*	*40 g / 1½ oz*
1 quart	*Light beer*	*1 litre / 1¾ pints*
¼ cup	*Flour*	*25 g / 1 oz*
6	*Fennel seeds*	*6*
¼ cup	*Coffee (single) cream*	*50 ml / 2 fl oz*
3 tbsp	*Gin*	*2 tbsp*

1. Put the onions, peeled and cut into slices, into a bowl and add sufficient cold water to cover and allow to rest for about 30 minutes.
2. Fry the pork in a large pan with the oil and 2 tablespoons [25 g / 1 oz] butter until it is browned on all sides. Add the drained onions to the pan with the pork and sweat them very gently for about 10 minutes.
3. Remove the pan from the heat and pour in the beer in a thin stream to cover the meat; return to the heat and bring to the boil. Cook uncovered on a medium high heat until the beer has completely evaporated, taking care not to let the meat stick to the bottom of the pan.
4. When the meat is tender, remove it from the heat and put it on a plate; strain the cooking liquid and put it in a separate pan with remainder of butter, flour, a few fennel seeds, cream and the gin.
5. Return the meat to the pan and continue cooking over a gentle heat for 10 minutes.
6. Cut the meat into slices, place them on a serving dish and cover with the sauce.
7. Serve accompanied with boiled vegetables garnished with parsley and glasses of beer.

Il 'burischio'

Black Pudding

This recipe is a speciality of several regions of Italy where a peasant culture remains strong. The important ingredient for the success of this dish is fresh pig's blood.

00:40 03:00

American	Ingredients	Metric/Imperial
1 quart	*Fresh pig's blood*	*1 litre / 1¾ pints*
1	*Bunch of fennel grass*	*1*
	Salt and pepper	
¼ tsp	*Nutmeg*	*¼ tsp*
½ lb	*Pork scraps ('friccioli')*	*225 g / 8 oz*
18 in	*Pig's intestine*	*50 cm / 18 in*
1	*Bunch of herbs for the stock*	*1*
2 lb	*Turnip tops*	*1 kg / 2 lb*
2	*Garlic cloves*	*2*
½ cup	*Vegetable oil*	*125 ml / 4 fl oz*
3 tbsp	*Tomato purée*	*2 tbsp*
1	*Hot chilli pepper*	*1*

1. Place the blood in a bowl, add a handful of fennel and a little salt, pepper and nutmeg.
2. Put the pork scraps in a frying pan and fry on a lively heat for about 10 minutes until they are golden brown. Remove them from the heat and place on one side.
3. At this point you will need about 18 in / 50 cm of pig's intestine, cut into 3 pieces to make three sausages. Make a knot at one end and tie it with string, then put a funnel in the other end and pour in some of the blood with a ladle. Stop before it is half full and put in some of the pork scraps; continue to fill with blood, stopping every now and then to add some pieces of meat.
4. Finish by tying the end of the sausage tightly and wrapping it in a cloth, which is also tied.
5. Put it in a pan of cold water with a bunch of herbs and boil it for about 30 minutes.
6. Prepare the turnip tops, boiling and draining them and rolling them into balls. Fry cloves of garlic in a pan of very hot oil, put in the turnip tops to flavor them. Add tomato purée dissolved in a little cold water with a small piece of hot chilli pepper.
7. Add the black pudding cut into thick slices and leave on a medium heat long enough for it to become well flavored. Serve very hot.

Black pudding

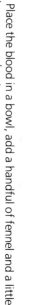

Cassoeula o posciandra o bottaggio

Pork and Sausage Casserole

00:00 03:00

American	Ingredients	Metric/Imperial
1	*Onion*	1
1	*Large slice of fat bacon*	1
2 tbsp	*Vegetable oil*	25 ml / 1 fl oz
2 tbsp	*Butter*	25 g / 1 oz
1	*Carrot*	1
1	*Celery stalk*	1
1 lb	*Pork ribs*	500 g / 1 lb
1	*Pig's head (snout and ear)*	1
7 oz	*Pork rind*	200 g / 7 oz
1 tbsp	*Tomato purée*	1 tbsp
1	*Stock cube*	1
	Salt and pepper	
2	*Savoy cabbages*	2
7 oz	*Thin budello sausage*	200 g / 7 oz
½ tsp	*Spices (optional)*	½ tsp

1. Chop the onion finely and brown it with chopped fat bacon or with oil and butter.
2. When the ingredients have softened, add the carrot and celery, also chopped very finely, and cook on a gentle heat, moistening with water if it is really necessary.
3. Boil separately the ribs, snout and rind until tender then cut into large pieces. Retain stock.
4. When the vegetables have softened, add the ribs, the snout and the rind, add the tomato purée diluted with a little warm water, pour in 2½ cups [1 pint / 600 ml] of stock made with the cube and cook through on a low flame, covered.
5. Preheat the oven to 325°F / 160°C / Gas Mark 3.
6. Strip the leaves from the cabbages, eliminating the tougher parts, rinse the leaves under running water, shred coarsely and mix with the meat, a little at a time. Season with salt and pepper and spices.
7. Cut the sausage into pieces, put it into a baking pan adding a drop of water and place it in the oven, covered and at a low heat. When the fat has melted, add the sausage to the casserole, cook for 1 hour in the oven. Serve piping hot with crusty bread.

Lonza profumata

Pork in Brandy Sauce

00:20 00:15

American	Ingredients	Metric/Imperial
1¾ lb	*Loin of pork*	800 g / 1¾ lb
8	*Round slices of bacon*	8
20	*Sage leaves*	20
½ tsp	*Rosemary leaves, chopped*	½ tsp
¼ cup	*Butter*	50 g / 2 oz
3 tbsp	*Oil*	2 tbsp
¼ cup	*Brandy*	50 ml / 2 fl oz
½	*Stock cube*	½

1. Cut the pork in thin slices, (about 2 per head) removing all excess fat. Lay a slice of bacon and two sage leaves on each piece of meat, roll up and secure with a toothpick.
2. Put the butter and oil into a wide pan and add remaining sage and the rosemary; as soon as the fat has heated, add the meat and pour on the brandy. Allow to cook for 10 minutes, moistening from time to time with boiling water in which a stock cube has been dissolved.
3. Strain the cooking juices into a sauceboat and serve with the meat and accompany with purée potatoes.

Rognoni trifolati alla panna

Kidneys in Cream Sauce

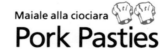

00:20 00:35
Soaking time 02:00

American	Ingredients	Metric/Imperial
3	*Pigs' kidneys*	3
¼ cup	*Vinegar*	50 ml / 2 fl oz
½ cup	*Butter*	100 g / 4 oz
1	*Onion*	1
	Salt and pepper	
¾ lb	*Mushrooms*	350 g / 12 oz
1	*Bunch of parsley*	1
⅔ cup	*Single (coffee) cream*	150 ml / ¼ pint

1. Skin and wash the kidneys, cut in half lengthwise and discard the fat. Place in a bowl with plenty of water and vinegar and leave to soak for 2 hours. Rinse well under the tap, dry and cut into fairly small pieces.
2. Melt the butter in a saucepan and fry the finely chopped onion for 4 minutes, add the kidneys and cook for 10 minutes, uncovered, over a medium heat. Season with salt and freshly ground black pepper.
3. Add the mushrooms, washed and sliced, continue cooking for a further 15 minutes and remove the pan from the heat. Chop the parsley, sprinkle over and then add the cream.
4. Put the kidneys on a low heat, do not allow to boil but reheat thoroughly. Serve very hot.

Maiale alla ciociara

Pork Pasties

A speciality of the Frosinone region, this dish is filling and very tasty.

00:30 00:40

American	Ingredients	Metric/Imperial
3 tbsp	*Oil*	2 tbsp
¾ lb	*Ground (minced) pork*	350 g / 12 oz
2	*Eggs*	2
2	*Italian sausages*	2
1 cup	*Grated parmesan cheese*	100 g / 4 oz
2	*Potatoes, boiled and mashed*	2
¼ tsp	*Nutmeg*	¼ tsp
4	*Sage leaves*	4
½ lb	*Short crust pastry*	225 g / 8 oz
½ cup	*Butter*	100 g / 4 oz

Kidneys in cream sauce

1. Preheat the oven to 400°F / 200°C / Gas Mark 6.
2. Heat the oil in a pan and cook the pork for 8 minutes, drain on to a plate and allow to cool.
3. Put the ground (minced) pork, eggs, sausages, (skinned and chopped), parmesan and potatoes into a bowl and mix thoroughly. Add a little grated nutmeg and a few chopped sage leaves.
4. Divide the pastry into 4 portions. Roll each into a round. Divide the pork mixture into 4 and heap onto each pastry round. Damp and seal the edges.
5. Grease a baking tray, lay the pasties on the tray and bake in a hot oven for 15 minutes. Reduce the oven temperature to 325°F / 170°C / Gas Mark 3 and cook for a further 15 minutes. These pasties need only to be served with a green salad.

POULTRY

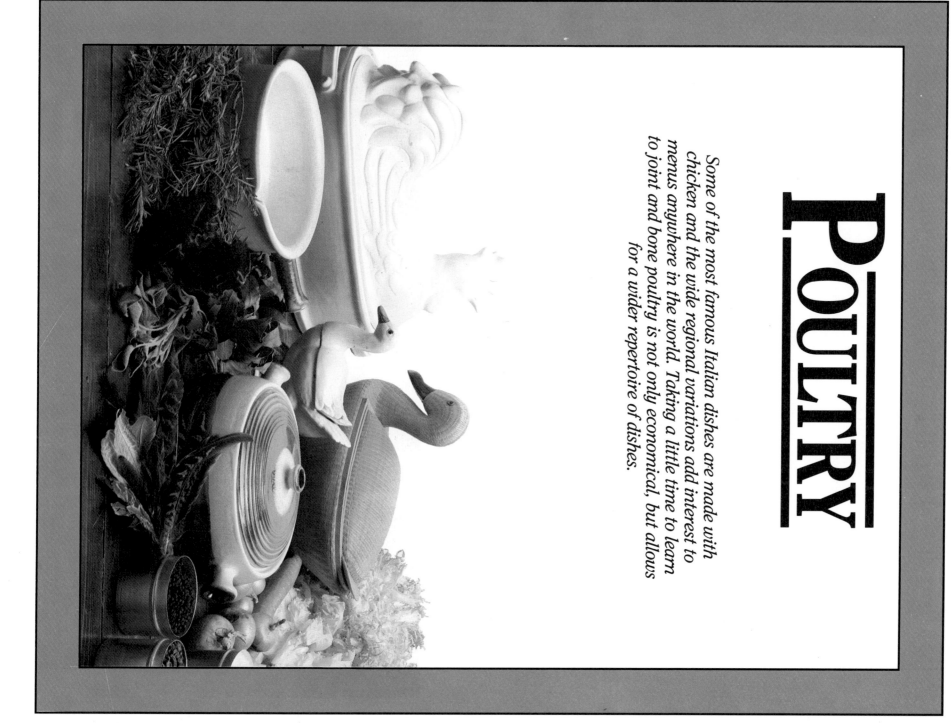

Some of the most famous Italian dishes are made with chicken and the wide regional variations add interest to menus anywhere in the world. Taking a little time to learn to joint and bone poultry is not only economical, but allows for a wider repertoire of dishes.

Preparing and storing poultry and game

Meat	Preparation	Freezing	To use
Poultry and game birds	**1.** Pluck and clean the bird. Cut off the neck and feet. **2.** Leave whole or cut up.	**1.** Whole (place a foil plug inside): wrap in foil. Place in freezer bag. Expel the air. Seal and label. **2.** In pieces: wrap each piece in foil and place the individual packages in one bag. Will keep: duck, pheasant: 6–12 months depending on its fat. turkey: 6–8 months. goose: 3–5 months. game fowl: 10 months. chicken: 10 months.	**1.** Before cooking, with the meat still in the package, thaw in the refrigerator 24 hours for whole birds or 12 hours for pieces. **2.** Cook without delay to avoid deterioration.
Game animals (venison, wild boar)	Prepare pieces with a view to future use (roast, chops, braising meats, etc).	**1.** Wrap in foil. **2.** Place in individual bags and seal, expelling the air. Label. Will keep 7 months.	**1.** For braising pieces: thaw in a marinade for 24 hours in refrigerator (you will not be able to use the marinade liquid to make a sauce). **2.** For roasting pieces: with the meat still in its packing, thaw in refrigerator for 24 hours.
Rabbits and hares	**1.** Skin and clean the animal. **2.** Cut off the head and feet. **3.** Cut into pieces or leave whole. **4.** Leave raw or prepare in cooked dishes without too much flavoring.	**1.** Whole: wrap in foil and place in a freezer bag. Seal, expelling the air. Label. **2.** In pieces: wrap each piece in foil. Place in freezer bags and seal, expelling the air. Label. **3.** Cooked: place in plastic containers. Cover and label. Will keep: rabbit: 10 months hare: 6 months	**1.** Raw: remove from package and thaw in refrigerator for 24 hours or in a marinade. **2.** Cooked: do not thaw but cook in the oven or in a casserole.

Jointing a chicken

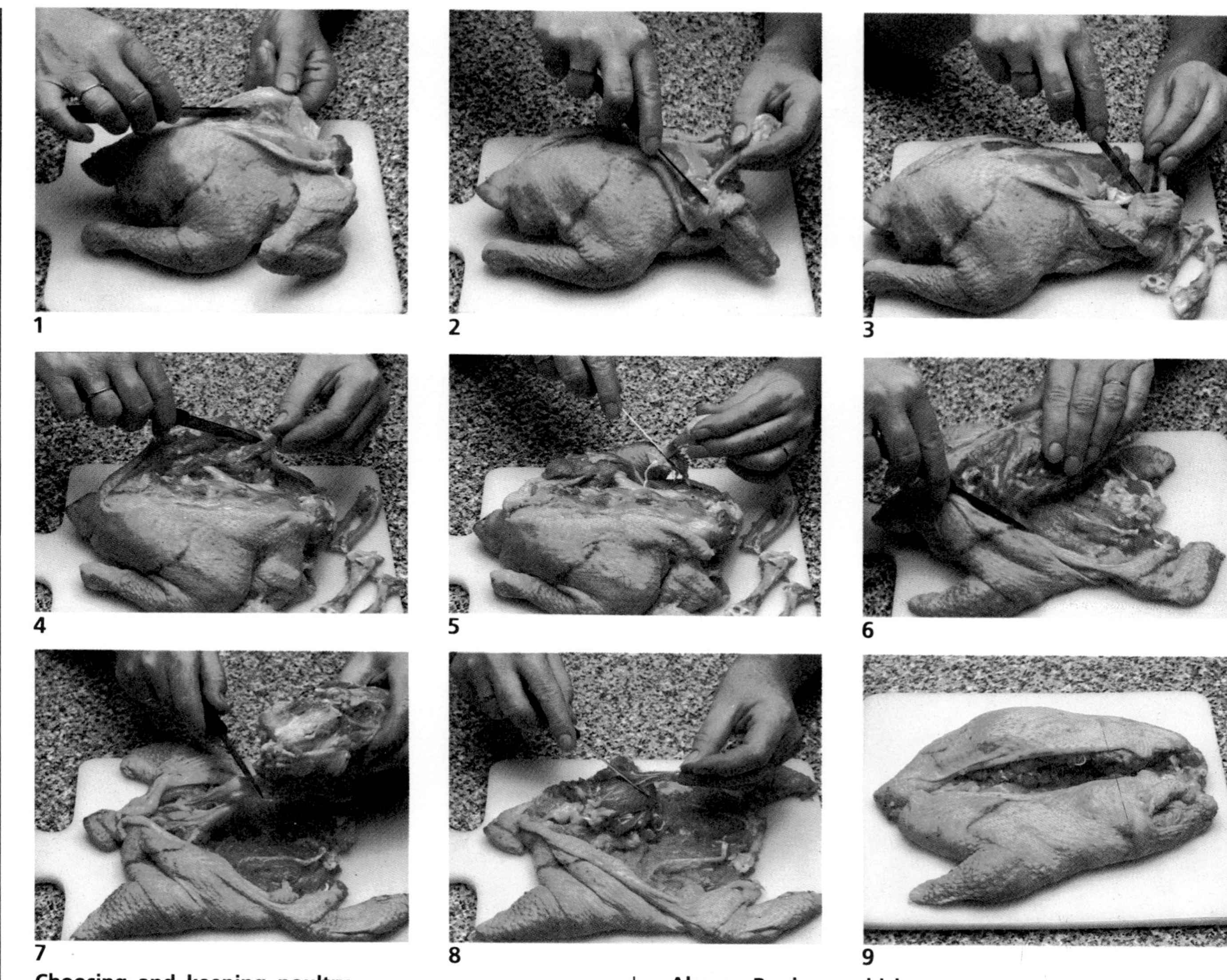

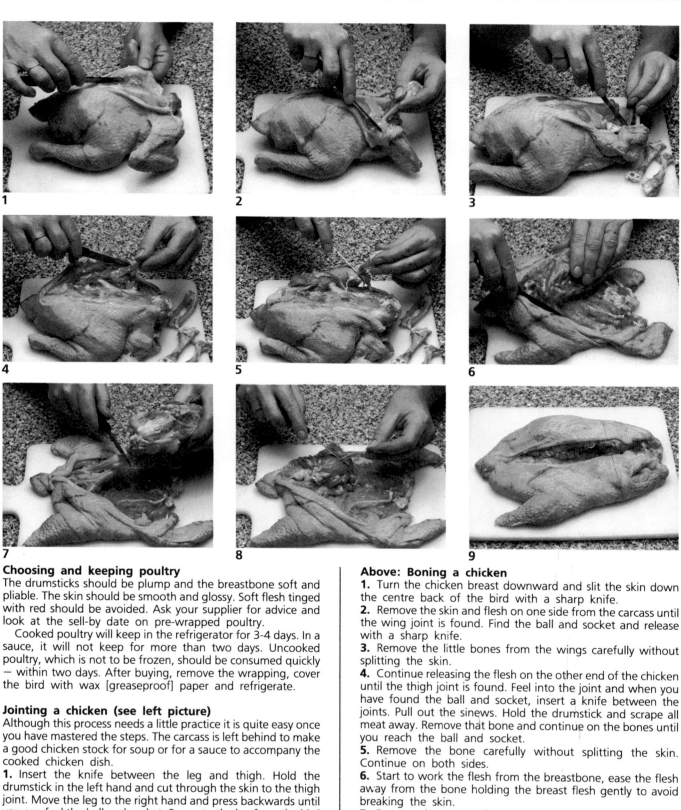

Choosing and keeping poultry

The drumsticks should be plump and the breastbone soft and pliable. The skin should be smooth and glossy. Soft flesh tinged with red should be avoided. Ask your supplier for advice and look at the sell-by date on pre-wrapped poultry.

Cooked poultry will keep in the refrigerator for 3-4 days. In a sauce, it will not keep for more than two days. Uncooked poultry, which is not to be frozen, should be consumed quickly – within two days. After buying, remove the wrapping, cover the bird with wax [greaseproof] paper and refrigerate.

Jointing a chicken (see left picture)

Although this process needs a little practice it is quite easy once you have mastered the steps. The carcass is left behind to make a good chicken stock for soup or for a sauce to accompany the cooked chicken dish.

1. Insert the knife between the leg and thigh. Hold the drumstick in the left hand and cut through the skin to the thigh joint. Move the leg to the right hand and press backwards until you can feel the ball and socket. Separate the leg from the bird by cutting through the ball and socket.
2. Separate the thigh and the drumstick by cutting through the joint between.
3. Remove the wing joints by twisting back. If necessary use scissors for this step.
4. With a pair of scissors, or a sharp knife, cut along the rib cage on both sides to separate the breast from the back.
5. Divide the breast in two halves by cutting down each side of the breast bone.

Above: Boning a chicken

1. Turn the chicken breast downward and slit the skin down the centre back of the bird with a sharp knife.
2. Remove the skin and flesh on one side from the carcass until the wing joint is found. Find the ball and socket and release with a sharp knife.
3. Remove the little bones from the wings carefully without splitting the skin.
4. Continue releasing the flesh on the other end of the chicken until the thigh joint is found. Feel into the joint and when you have found the ball and socket, insert a knife between the joints. Pull out the sinews. Hold the drumstick and scrape all meat away. Remove that bone and continue on the bones until you reach the ball and socket.
5. Remove the bone carefully without splitting the skin. Continue on both sides.
6. Start to work the flesh from the breastbone, ease the flesh away from the bone holding the breast flesh gently to avoid breaking the skin.
7. Remove the carcass from the chicken in one piece gently cutting away any flesh.
8. Remove any small bones from the flesh which have not come away with the boning, remove any sinews which are still visible but take care not to break the skin.
9. The boned chicken, complete with whole skin, can then be stuffed and sewn up.
10. At this stage the bird can either be roasted or cooked in stock for a galantine to be served cold with a dressing of mayonnaise and aspic.

Roasting poultry

POULTRY	WEIGHT	HOW TO COOK	TEMPERATURE	TIME	FOIL ROASTING	ACCOMPANIMENTS
Poussin	Baby chicken 6-8 weeks ¾ lb / 350 g – 1¼ lb / 550 g	Grill or roast	350°F / 180°C / Gas Mark 4	30-40 mins	50 mins	Green salad or as chicken
Spring chicken	3 months old 2 lb / 1 kg	Grill or roast	350°F / 180°C / Gas Mark 4	50-60 mins	30 mins – 1 lb / 450 g	Slightly thickened gravy, crispy bacon rolls. Chipolata sausages, bread sauce, savory stuffing
Roasting chicken or broiler	6-12 months old 3-4 lb / 1½-2 kg	Fry, roast, sauté, casserole, poach	400°F / 200°C / Gas Mark 6	20 mins- 1 lb / 450 g + 20 mins	30 mins- 1 lb / 450 g	
Boiling fowl	Over 1 year old 4 lb / 2 kg and over	Boil, stew, casserole		Up to 5 lb / 2 kg bring to the boil and simmer 1¼ hrs. Over 5 lb / 2½ kg at least 2 hrs		
Capon	Young cock bird 7-10 months old 5½-9 lb / 2½-4 kg	Roast, casserole, poach	400°F / 200°C / Gas Mark 6	25 mins- 1 lb / 450 g + 20 mins	25 mins- 1 lb / 450 g	As chicken
Turkey	7-12 lb / 3½-5½ kg	Roast whole	425°F / 220°C / Gas Mark 7 reducing to 325°F / 170°C / Gas Mark 3	15 mins- 1 lb / 450 g + 15 mins	25 mins- 1 lb / 450 g	Thickened gravy made with giblets. Cranberry sauce, chestnut or sausage meat stuffing, bread sauce
Duck	3½-5½ lb / 1¾-2½ kg	Roast whole or joint	400°F / 200°C / Gas Mark 6	20 mins- 1 lb / 450 g + 20 mins	30-35 mins- 1 lb / 450 g	Slightly thickened gravy (red wine added is delicious). Apple sauce, sage and onion stuffing
Goose	9-13 lb / 4-6 kg	Roast whole	425°F / 220°C / Gas Mark 7 reducing to 350°F / 180°C / Gas Mark 4	For 15 mins reducing to 15 mins- 1 lb / 450 g + 15 mins	30 mins- 1 lb / 450 g	Orange salad, cherries as a garnish. Thickened gravy, apple sauce, celery and apple or sage and onion stuffing

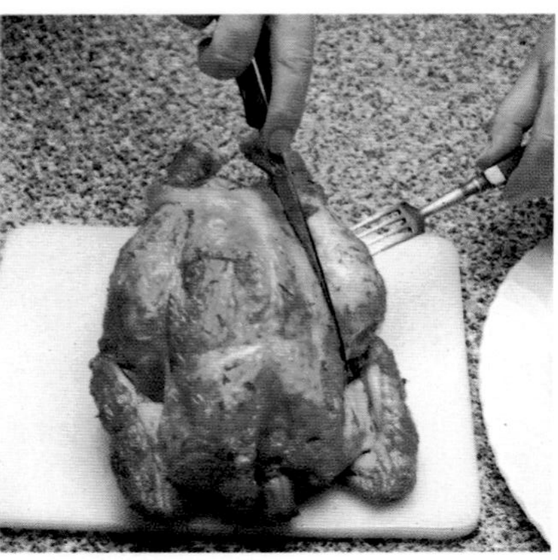

To carve a chicken
1. *Secure with a carving fork in leg. Place knife between leg and body.*

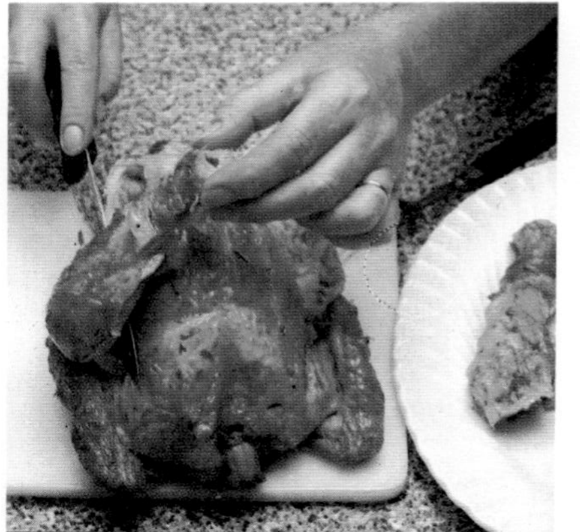

2. *Remove drumstick and thigh in one piece. Cut into two pieces. Continue on other side removing drumstick and thigh.*

3. *Carve the wing joints on each side by finding the joint and cutting through.*

To barbecue chicken

Chicken, turkey and duck are all suitable for cooking on a barbecue. Whole chicken and duck can be spit roasted, turkey is more suitable cut into portions.

A whole bird, about 4 lb / 2 kg, will need about 2 hours over a good fire. Portions will take anything from 25 to 30 minutes for drumsticks, to 1 hour for large pieces.

All poultry will have a better flavor if marinated for several hours before cooking. Baste the poultry meat with either melted butter or oil during cooking but only baste with marinade toward the end of the cooking time.

Red wine marinade

Mix 1¼ cups [150 ml / ¼ pint] red wine with 2 tablespoons lemon juice; 1 small onion, peeled and sliced; 1 bay leaf; few sprigs fresh parsley, thyme, oregano. Season with freshly ground pepper and mix with ½ cup [125 ml / 4 fl oz] oil. Pour over the poultry joints in a dish and leave to marinate for several hours or overnight in the refrigerator. One way to ensure the marinade seeps round the joints is to place the joints with the marinade in a large plastic bag. Turn every few hours allowing the mixture to flow round the joints. Retain the liquid for basting toward the end of cooking.

***4.** Turn the bird upside down and cut through the bottom. Loosen the breast carefully with the knife.*

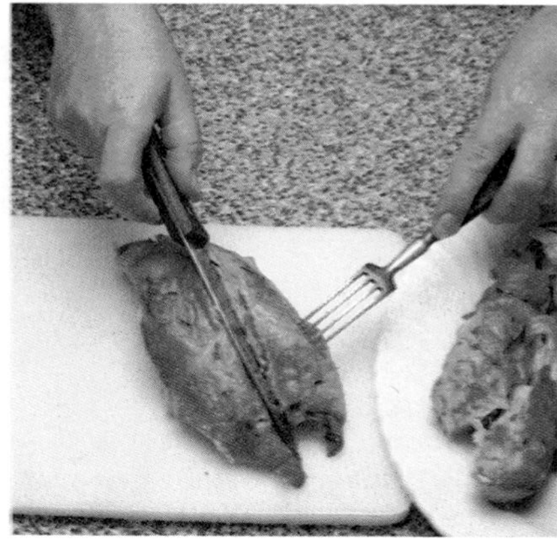

***5.** Remove the breast as a whole piece, carve as desired.*

***6.** Arrange chicken in original shape on a heated serving plate, keep warm and serve when convenient.*

Braised capon

Cappone al brunello

Capon Braised in Red Wine

00:20 Marinating time 06:00 | 02:15

American	Ingredients	Metric/Imperial
1 (4½ lb)	Medium-sized young capon	1 (2 kg / 4½ lb)
1	Onion	1
2	Carrots	2
1	Celery stalk	1
1	Bay leaf	1
1	Sprig of thyme	1
2	Cloves	2
	Salt and pepper	
1 (70 cl)	Bottle of red wine	1 (70 cl)
3 tbsp	Butter	40 g / 1½ oz
2 oz	Bacon	50 g / 2 oz
1 cup	Chicken stock	225 ml / 8 fl oz
3 tbsp	Cognac	2 tbsp

1. Wash and dry the capon. Prepare a marinade with sliced onion, carrots and celery, bay leaf, sprig of thyme, 2 cloves, pepper and the wine. Put the capon in a large plastic bag with the marinade and leave for 5 to 6 hours.
2. Remove from the marinade and transfer to a large, heavy saucepan containing melted butter and the diced bacon. Brown the capon, add the strained vegetables from the marinade.
3. Remove all the fat from the pan and pour in the wine used for marinating. When this has evaporated, add the chicken stock and simmer for 2 hours. Alternatively cook in the oven at 375°F / 190°C / Gas Mark 5.
4. Remove the capon to a heated dish, allow to stand for 10 minutes before carving.
5. Add the cognac to the sauce and stir well, sieve and serve in a sauceboat.

Cappone ripieno

Stuffed Capon

00:30 Serves 6 | 01:30

American	Ingredients	Metric/Imperial
1 (4½ lb)	Capon	1 (2 kg / 4½ lb)
¼ lb	Stale bread	100 g / 4 oz
⅔ cup	Milk	150 ml / ¼ pint
2 oz	Cooked ham	50 g / 2 oz
1 oz	Capers	25 g / 1 oz
½ tsp	Chopped sage	½ tsp
¼ tsp	Chopped rosemary	¼ tsp
1	Egg	1
	Salt and pepper	
1	Lemon	1
¼ cup	Butter	50 g / 2 oz
½ cup	Red wine	125 ml / 4 fl oz

1. Preheat the oven to 375°F / 190°C / Gas Mark 5.
2. Wash and dry the capon. Soak the bread in the milk, squeeze out the excess moisture and combine it with the diced ham and the capon's liver, washed and chopped. Chop the capers and a little sage and rosemary together and add with a beaten egg to the bread and milk mixture. Season well.
3. Stuff the capon carefully, sew up the aperture and sprinkle with a mixture of lemon juice and chopped sage.
4. Heat the butter in a large casserole, brown the capon well on all sides, pour in the red wine and cook in the oven for 1½ hours. Carve and keep warm.
5. Make a gravy with the cooking juices and little water if necessary, season and serve in a sauceboat.

Timballo di caccia

Timbale of Game

00:30 | 02:00

American	Ingredients	Metric/Imperial
14 oz	Ground (minced) game or chicken	400 g / 14 oz
¼ lb	Chicken livers	100 g / 4 oz
5 oz	Raw ham	150 g / 5 oz
4	Eggs	4
1½ cups	Grated parmesan cheese	175 g / 6 oz
	Salt and pepper	
½ tsp	Nutmeg	½ tsp
1	Truffle	1
8	Slices of fat bacon to line the mold	8

1. Preheat the oven to 325°F / 170°C / Gas Mark 3.
2. Put the ground meat into a bowl, add washed, chopped chicken livers and chopped raw ham. Mix well adding the egg yolks, the grated cheese, salt, pepper, nutmeg and truffle. Finally, add the egg whites beaten to a stiff froth.
3. Line a small loaf pan with slices of fat bacon, so that they adhere properly. Pour the mixture into the pan, cover with the ends of fat bacon linings and a piece of foil.
4. Place the loaf pan in a roasting pan, pour boiling water carefully into the roasting pan until it reaches half way up the loaf pan.
5. Cook for 2 hours, remove from oven and allow to cool. Turn out and serve with crusty bread or toast.

Ruspante alla sabinese

Sabine-Style Chicken

00:25 01:15

American	Ingredients	Metric/Imperial
1 (3 lb)	*Chicken*	*1 (1.4 kg / 3 lb)*
2	*Whole salt-cured anchovies*	*2*
⅓ cup	*Green olives, stoned*	*50 g / 2 oz*
1	*Red chilli pepper*	*1*
1 tbsp	*Capers*	*1 tbsp*
Scant ¼ cup	*Olive oil*	*3 tbsp*
½ cup	*Dry frascati*	*125 ml / 4 fl oz*
	Salt	
½	*Stock cube*	*½*

1. Preheat the oven to 375°F / 190°C / Gas Mark 5.
2. Prepare the chicken, wash and dry thoroughly.
3. Wash and bone the anchovies and chop together with the olives, deseeded chilli and capers.
4. Heat the oil in a casserole until very hot, then add the whole chicken, turning to brown evenly.
5. Pour in the frascati and allow to bubble for 2 minutes. Turn down the heat and add the chopped anchovies, olives, chilli and capers. Season lightly with salt.
6. Cover and transfer to the oven for 30 minutes. Check to see if juice is drying out, add ½ cup [125 ml / 4 fl oz] chicken stock. Cook for a further 30 minutes.
7. Carve and serve with olive sauce poured over.

Pollo alla birra

Chicken Braised in Ale

00:25 01:10

American	Ingredients	Metric/Imperial
1 (3 lb)	*Chicken*	*1 (1.4 kg / 3 lb)*
3 tbsp	*Flour*	*2 tbsp*
2 tbsp	*Vegetable oil*	*1½ tbsp*
3 tbsp	*Butter*	*40 g / 1½ oz*
	Salt and pepper	
2 oz	*Pork fat*	*50 g / 2 oz*
2	*Onions*	*2*
3 cups	*Light ale*	*700 ml / 1¼ pints*

1. Wash the chicken, then cut into quarters and flour lightly.
2. Heat the oil and butter and sauté the chicken until brown on all sides. Season with a sprinkling of salt and pepper.
3. Preheat the oven to 350°F / 180°C / Gas Mark 4.
4. Chop the pork fat into small pieces and slice the onions finely. Put all the pork fat and some of the onions into a casserole, dust lightly with flour and lay the chicken on top, followed with another layer of onions.
5. Heat the ale in a pan with the cooking juices from the chicken, pour over the chicken. Cover and cook in the oven for about 45 minutes. Check for seasoning.
6. Transfer the chicken to a heated serving dish and keep warm. Sieve the sauce, thicken if necessary, pour into a sauceboat and serve with the chicken.

Pollo al cartoccio

Chicken Baked in Foil

00:15 01:25

American	Ingredients	Metric/Imperial
1 (3 lb)	*Chicken*	*1 (1.4 kg / 3 lb)*
1	*Garlic clove*	*1*
1	*Sprig of rosemary*	*1*
2 or 3	*Sage leaves*	*2 or 3*
¼ cup	*Olive oil*	*50 ml / 2 fl oz*
	Salt and pepper	
3 or 4	*Slices of fat tuscany ham*	*3 or 4*
¼ cup	*Sherry or brandy*	*50 ml / 2 fl oz*

1. Preheat the oven to 350°F / 180°C / Gas Mark 4.
2. Wash and dry the chicken thoroughly. Place the garlic and herbs inside, rub all over with olive oil, sprinkle lightly with salt and pepper and cover with the slices of ham, securing with thread or fine string.
3. Place on a sheet of foil, moisten with sherry or brandy, close the foil and bake in a moderate oven for about 1¼ hours or until cooked.
4. Carve and serve hot or cold with a mixed salad.

Fegatini al pompelmo in coppa

Liver in Grapefruit Cups

00:30 00:30

American	Ingredients	Metric/Imperial
4	*Large grapefruits*	*4*
1¾ lb	*Chicken livers*	*800 g / 1¾ lb*
	Salt	
1 tbsp	*Flour*	*1 tbsp*
Scant ¼ cup	*Olive oil*	*3 tbsp*
2 tbsp	*Butter*	*25 g / 1 oz*
2 tbsp	*Marsala*	*1½ tbsp*
	Pepper	

1. Cut off the top quarter of the grapefruits. Hollow out the insides and scrape out all the flesh without breaking the peel, which will subsequently act as a cup. Squeeze juice from grapefruit flesh.
2. Clean the livers, chop into pieces, season with salt and dip in the flour.
3. Heat the oil in a pan with butter, brown the chicken livers.
4. Sprinkle with marsala and pepper, turn from time to time, then add the juice of the grapefruit.
5. Serve liver mixture in the grapefruit cups.

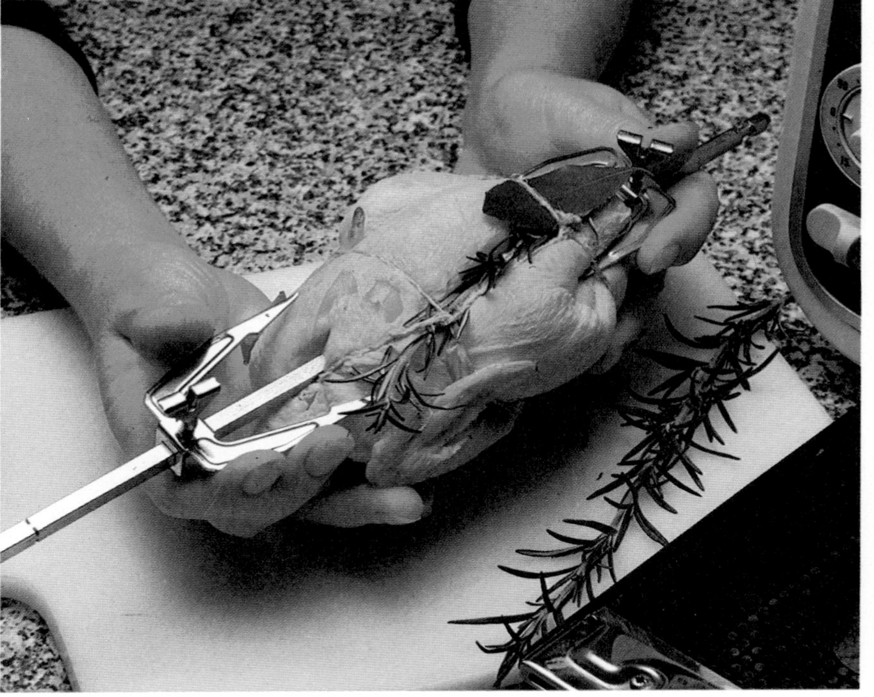

Spit-roasted spring chicken

Prosciuttini di pollo

Chicken Hams

This delicious recipe comes from Sergio Lorenzi who uses it with great success in his Pisa restaurant 'Da Sergio', which is very popular for its excellent cuisine.

00:40 — 01:00

American	Ingredients	Metric/Imperial
8	*Chicken thighs*	*8*
1 cup	*Ground (minced) veal*	*225 g / 8 oz*
¼ lb	*Parma ham*	*100 g / 4 oz*
½ cup	*Grated parmesan cheese*	*50 g / 2 oz*
	Salt and pepper	
Scant ¼ cup	*Olive oil*	*3 tbsp*
¼ cup	*Dry white wine*	*50 ml / 2 fl oz*
1 cup	*Cream*	*225 ml / 8 fl oz*

1. Bone the thighs, (this is a tricky job that requires some patience). Use a very sharp, slim knife and slide it between the bone and the flesh, turning the flesh back on itself as you loosen it and taking great care not to cut the skin. Hopefully there will be 8 little empty bags at the end of this operation ready for the stuffing.
2. Preheat the oven to 350°F / 180°C / Gas Mark 4.
3. Make a stuffing for the chicken thighs by mixing together the ground veal, chopped parma ham and grated parmesan. Add salt and pepper and mix well.
4. Stuff the thighs and sew them up carefully to resemble miniature hams.
5. Flour the 'little hams' (prosciuttini). Heat the olive oil in a shallow frying pan and sauté the chicken thighs until golden on each side. Season with salt and a few twists of freshly ground black pepper.
6. When golden transfer to a roasting pan and put in the moderate oven for 30 minutes to complete the cooking.
7. Transfer the chicken to a heated serving dish and keep warm. Reheat the pan juices, add the wine and cream, stir over a low heat until the sauce has acquired a good consistency.
8. Pour the sauce over the chicken and serve with green peas or carrots tossed in butter.

Galletti allo spiedo

Spit-Roasted Spring Chicken

00:25 — 01:00 to 01:25

American	Ingredients	Metric/Imperial
2 (3¼ lb)	*Spring chickens*	*2 (1.5 kg / 3¼ lb)*
2	*Small onions*	*2*
4	*Cloves*	*4*
1 tsp	*Sage*	*1 tsp*
2	*Bay leaves*	*2*
½ tsp	*Rosemary*	*½ tsp*
	Salt and pepper	
Scant ¼ cup	*Vegetable oil*	*5 tbsp*

1. Buy the chickens with the giblets, wash thoroughly.
2. Stick the onions with cloves and place in the stomach cavity of each chicken.
3. Chop the giblets, add sage, bay leaves and rosemary; stuff the chicken crop end with this mixture, season with salt and pepper. Close the openings with skewers or sew with kitchen thread.
4. Thread the birds onto the spit, sprinkle liberally with salt and pepper and brush with oil. While roasting, continue to baste or brush with oil to crisp the skin.
5. Test by inserting a skewer into the thigh joint, if juice is still pink, continue cooking until it is clear.
6. Remove from spit and carve.

Fegatini al cartoccio

Chicken Livers in Foil

00:25 00:30

American	Ingredients	Metric/Imperial
1¼ lb	*Chicken livers*	600 g / 1¼ lb
1	*Garlic clove*	1
1 tbsp	*Chopped parsley*	1 tbsp
¼ tsp	*Fennel seeds*	¼ tsp
	Salt and pepper	
12	*Slices of lean bacon*	12
2 tbsp	*Butter*	25 g / 1 oz
1 tbsp	*Vegetable oil*	1 tbsp

1. Preheat the oven to 425°F / 220°C / Gas Mark 7.
2. Wash the livers and chop finely. Chop the garlic and herbs, season with salt and pepper and sprinkle over the liver.
3. Flatten the de-rinded bacon slices on a board, divide the chopped liver and herbs onto each slice. Roll and wrap 3 slices at a time in foil lightly greased with oil and butter.
4. Place on a baking sheet and cook for about 30 minutes in a hot oven, turning the foil parcels once.
5. To serve, place the foil envelopes on individual plates, open and accompany with pickled onions and crusty bread.

Bignés di pollo

Chicken Vol-au-Vents

00:20 00:40

American	Ingredients	Metric/Imperial
½ lb	*Chicken livers*	225 g / 8 oz
¼ cup	*Butter*	50 g / 2oz
1¼ cups	*Béchamel sauce (see page 162)*	300 ml / ½ pint
⅔ cup	*Whipping (double) cream*	150 ml / ¼ pint
16	*Vol-au-vent cases, cooked*	16

1. Wash the chicken livers and chop finely. Sauté in a little butter for 15 minutes.
2. Prepare a béchamel sauce, allow to cool slightly, add the cream, stir well.
3. Preheat the oven to 350°F / 180°C / Gas Mark 4.
4. Add some of the béchamel to the livers and continue to cook for a further 5 minutes.
5. Fill the cases with the chicken liver mixture, topping up with the rest of the béchamel sauce.
6. Reheat in the oven for about 15 minutes before serving.

Chicken vol-au-vents

Petti di pollo in carpione

Soused Chicken Breasts

00:45 Chilling time 02:00 — 00:20

American	Ingredients	Metric/Imperial
1½ lb	Chicken breasts	700 g / 1½ lb
	Flour	
2	Eggs	2
½ cup	Bread crumbs	50 g / 2 oz
3 tbsp	Vegetable oil	2 tbsp
¼ cup	Butter	50 g / 2 oz
	Salt and pepper	
2	Onions	2
1 cup	Wine vinegar	225 ml / 8 fl oz
½ tsp	Chopped rosemary	½ tsp
2	Bay leaves	2
8	Radishes	8
4	Carrots	4

1. Slice the chicken breasts very thinly, dip into flour, then the beaten eggs and finally coat with bread crumbs.
2. Heat oil and butter in a large frying pan and sauté the chicken on both sides. Drain on absorbent kitchen towels and transfer to a deep serving dish; sprinkle with salt and pepper.
3. Slice the onions very thinly into rings, and sauté gently in some butter until soft, then turn up the heat and allow to color slightly. Remove with a slotted spoon and lay on top of the chicken.
4. Put the vinegar into a pan with rosemary and bay leaves, heat to boiling point and pour over the chicken. Cover and put in a cool place for 2 hours.
5. Check to see if the chicken has absorbed the vinegar. If it has been absorbed completely, heat a little more and add to the dish, allow to cool again.
6. Decorate with radishes and carrot flowers and serve.

Insalata di petti e soia

Chicken and Beansprout Salad

00:30 — 00:17

American	Ingredients	Metric/Imperial
2	Chicken breasts	2
⅔ cup	Chicken stock	150 ml / ¼ pint
¼ lb	Fontina cheese	100 g / 4 oz
1 lb	Beansprouts	450 g / 1 lb
2 cups	Mayonnaise (see page 175)	450 ml / ¾ pint
2 tbsp	Tomato ketchup	1½ tbsp
¼ cup	Milk	50 ml / 2 fl oz
¼ lb	Cooked pasta	100 g / 4 oz

1. Simmer the chicken breasts in stock. Allow to cool and slice thinly (use stock for sauce or soup).
2. Slice the fontina cheese into thin strips. Scald the beansprouts in boiling water for exactly 1 minute and drain completely.
3. Mix the chicken with the beansprouts and cheese. Mix the mayonnaise with the bottled tomato ketchup and the milk. Stir gently until the sauce, vegetable ingredients and pasta are well combined. Serve with slices of toast.

Pollo in umido alla contadina

Country-Style Braised Chicken

00:30 — 01:00

American	Ingredients	Metric/Imperial
1½ oz	Dried mushrooms	40 g / 1½ oz
1 (3¼ lb)	Medium-sized chicken	1 (1.5 kg / 3¼ lb)
3 tbsp	Flour	2 tbsp
	Salt and pepper	
¼ cup	Butter	50 g / 2 oz
¾ lb	Button onions	350 g / 12 oz
1	Carrot	1
1	Celery stalk	1
¼ cup	Dry red wine	50 ml / 2 fl oz
5	Peeled tomatoes	5
½ cup	Cream	125 ml / 4 fl oz

1. Soak the mushrooms for 15 minutes in warm water.
2. Joint the chicken (see page 313) and lightly coat with seasoned flour. Shake floured pieces in a sieve to remove excess.
3. Melt the butter in a large pan and sauté the onions lightly. As soon as they start to color add the washed and finely chopped carrot and celery. Continue to cook for 5 minutes, moistening with a little water if necessary.
4. Add the chicken pieces, brown well, then pour in the wine and tomatoes, mash the tomatoes down with a wooden spoon. Season with salt and pepper, cover and simmer very gently.
5. Drain the mushrooms and add them to the pan. Continue to cook for 45 minutes – 1 hour, or until chicken is tender, on a fairly low heat or in the oven at 350°F / 180°C / Gas Mark 4.
6. Remove chicken to a heated serving dish. Add the cream to the sauce, mix well on a low heat and pour over the chicken.

Petti di pollo alla valdostana

Chicken Breasts with Fontina

00:15 — 00:20

American	Ingredients	Metric/Imperial
4	Chicken breasts	4
½ cup	Milk	125 ml / 4 fl oz
	Flour	
2 tbsp	Butter	25 g / 1 oz
2 tbsp	Vegetable oil	1½ tbsp
	Salt and pepper	
½ cup	Dry white wine	125 ml / 4 fl oz
4	Thick slices of fontina cheese	4

1. Flatten the chicken breasts by pounding, soak them in milk for 10 minutes, drain and then flour.
2. Heat the butter and oil in a frying pan (with a lid), and when really hot, slip in the chicken and brown on both sides.
3. Season well, pour in the wine and allow to evaporate. Lay 1 slice of fontina cheese on each piece of chicken.
4. Cover the pan and continue to cook until the cheese has melted. Serve very hot.

Chicken breasts with fontina

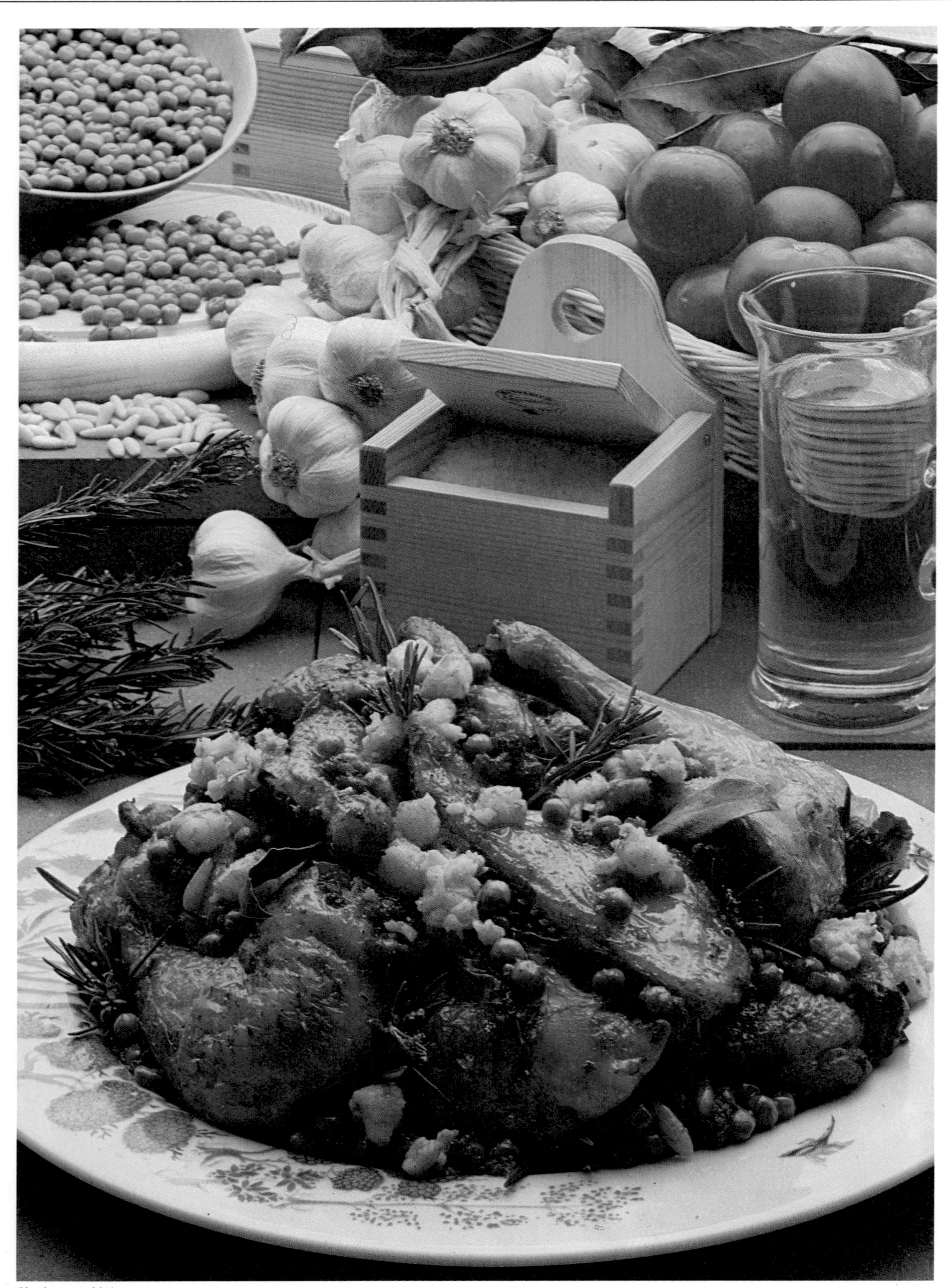

Chicken and lobster

Pollo con aragostina

Chicken and Lobster

01:00 | 01:20

American	Ingredients	Metric/Imperial
1 (3 lb)	Young chicken	1 (1.4 kg / 3 lb)
2 tbsp	Vegetable oil	1½ tbsp
½ cup	Butter	100 g / 4 oz
1	Onion	1
1	Garlic clove	1
	Salt and pepper	
1	Bay leaf	1
¼ cup	Dry white wine	50 ml / 2 fl oz
4	Ripe tomatoes	4
1	Sprig of rosemary	1
¼ cup	Pine kernels	25 g / 1 oz
1 cup	Green peas	150 g / 5 oz
1 (1¼ lb)	Cooked lobster	1 (600 g / 1¼ lb)
3 tbsp	Cognac	2 tbsp

1. Wash and dry a prepared chicken, cut into pieces of roughly equal size. Heat the oil and half the butter and sauté the chicken joints for 5 minutes each side.
2. Add the onion, chopped and crushed clove of garlic, season with salt and pepper, add the bay leaf, pour in the wine, bubble for 2 minutes, then lower the heat. Add the chopped tomatoes and rosemary. Cover and cook for 45 minutes.
3. Add the chopped pine kernels and the peas. Complete the cooking, check the seasoning, remove from the heat and keep warm.
4. Extract the meat from the boiled lobster, using a sharp knife to remove the meat from the tail. Break the claws with a small hammer and remove the meat with a skewer. Chop all the meat.
5. Heat the remaining butter in a pan, sauté the lobster pieces then douse with cognac, set alight, and season with salt and pepper. Combine the chicken and lobster in the pan with all the juices and serve hot with boiled rice.

Pollo alla boscaiola

Chicken with Mushrooms and Tomatoes

00:30 | 01:00

American	Ingredients	Metric/Imperial
1 (4½ lb)	Large chicken	1 (2 kg / 4½ lb)
3 tbsp	Flour	2 tbsp
1	Onion	1
2	Garlic cloves	2
Scant ¼ cup	Oil	3 tbsp
⅓ cup	Butter	75 g / 3 oz
½ cup	Dry white wine	125 ml / 4 fl oz
	Salt and pepper	
2	Sprigs of thyme	2
14 oz	Ripe tomatoes	400 g / 4 oz
1	Stock cube	1
½ lb	Mushrooms	225 g / 8 oz
1 tbsp	Chopped parsley	1 tbsp

1. Preheat the oven to 350°F / 180°C / Gas Mark 4.
2. Wash and dry the chicken, then joint into 6 pieces (see page 313) and flour lightly.
3. Chop the onion into dice, crush 1 clove of garlic and sauté in half the heated oil and butter.
4. As soon as they have colored slightly, remove to a casserole. Add the chicken pieces to the pan, brown lightly on all sides then pour in the wine and turn up the heat to reduce the wine. Season with salt and pepper and add to the casserole with the pan juices and thyme.
5. Skin the tomatoes, remove the seeds and chop coarsely, add them to the chicken with 1¼ cups [300 ml / ½ pint] stock, made from the cube, then cover and put in the oven for 30 minutes.
6. Wash and slice the mushrooms and cook in remaining oil and butter with 1 crushed clove of garlic for 10 minutes; add half the chopped parsley.
7. Remove the chicken from the oven, add the cooked mushrooms, stir well and return for a further 30 minutes.
8. Remove sprigs of thyme and serve piping hot, sprinkled with remaining parsley.

Pollanca ripiena arrosto

Stuffed and Roasted Spring Chicken

00:30 | 02:00
Serves 6

American	Ingredients	Metric/Imperial
1 (4½ lb)	Spring chicken	1 (2 kg / 4½ lb)
3	Slices of bread (less crust)	3
1 cup	Stock	225 ml / 8 fl oz
	Chicken livers	
2 oz	Bacon	50 g / 2 oz
2 oz	Italian sausage	50 g / 2 oz
1	Garlic clove	1
1	Shallot	1
1	Small onion	1
1	Egg	1
	Salt and pepper	
2 tbsp	Butter	25 g / 1 oz
2 tbsp	Vegetable oil	1½ tbsp
½ cup	Dry white wine	125 ml / 4 fl oz

1. Preheat oven to 400°F / 200°C / Gas Mark 6.
2. Wash and dry the chicken thoroughly.
3. Prepare a stuffing by soaking the bread in the stock. Chop the chicken liver, the bacon, sausage, garlic, shallot and onion very finely. Mix all together in a bowl and add the soaked bread (squeezed out), egg, salt and pepper. The stuffing can be made in the food processor to save time. Mix thoroughly and stuff the chicken.
4. Sprinkle a little salt on the chicken and rub with butter and oil, place on roasting pan brushed with oil and roast in the oven for 1 hour.
5. Turn the heat down to 325°F / 170°C / Gas Mark 3. Remove the bird from the oven and baste with the wine and stock. Return and cook for a further 1 hour, basting from time to time.
6. Remove the bird to a board and leave to stand for 10 minutes before carving.
7. Make a gravy with the pan juices to serve with the roast chicken.

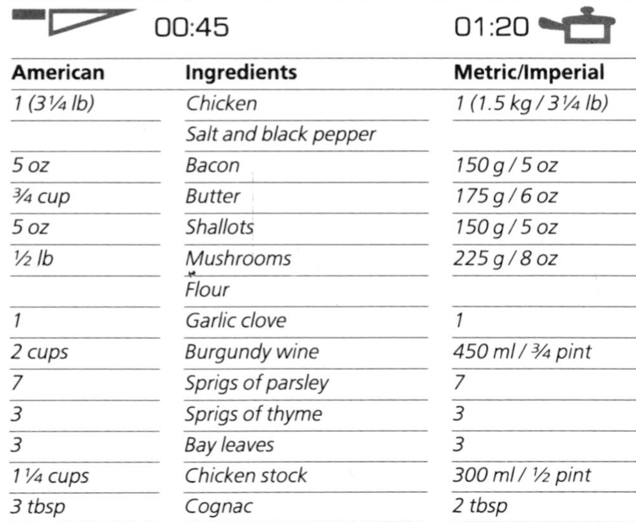

Coq au vin

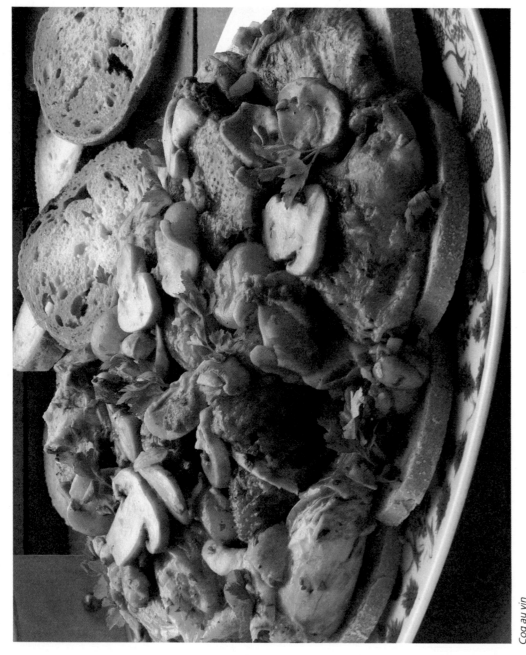

Coq au vin alla borgognona

Coq au Vin

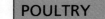

00:45 01:20

American	Ingredients	Metric/Imperial
1 (3¼ lb)	*Chicken*	*1 (1.5 kg / 3¼ lb)*
	Salt and black pepper	
5 oz	*Bacon*	*150 g / 5 oz*
¾ cup	*Butter*	*175 g / 6 oz*
5 oz	*Shallots*	*150 g / 5 oz*
½ lb	*Mushrooms*	*225 g / 8 oz*
	Flour	
1	*Garlic clove*	*1*
2 cups	*Burgundy wine*	*450 ml / ¾ pint*
7	*Sprigs of parsley*	*7*
3	*Sprigs of thyme*	*3*
3	*Bay leaves*	*3*
1¼ cups	*Chicken stock*	*300 ml / ½ pint*
3 tbsp	*Cognac*	*2 tbsp*

1. Preheat the oven to 350°F / 180°C / Gas Mark 4.
2. Joint the chicken into pieces (see page 313). Put them on a plate with all the edible giblets except the liver; season with salt and freshly-ground black pepper.
3. Dice the bacon, drop into boiling water for 5 minutes, then drain.
4. Heat a third of the butter in a large, heavy pan, sauté the bacon. As soon as it has colored, remove from the pan with a slotted spoon and put aside on a plate.
5. Boil the shallots for 5 minutes. Meanwhile, slice the mushrooms, sauté in the same pan as the bacon, then add the parboiled shallots. Leave for only a few minutes, then transfer both mushrooms and shallots, with a small quantity of juice, to the bowl containing the bacon and keep warm.
6. Flour the pieces of chicken and sauté in a third of the butter in a large casserole with the crushed garlic over moderate heat until brown. Pour in the wine and bring to the boil; add the herbs (tied in a bunch), bacon, shallots, mushrooms and sufficient stock to cover. Cook with the lid on in a moderate oven for 45 minutes.
7. Remove the chicken and vegetables with a slotted spoon, place on a serving dish and keep warm. Replace the pan on the stove and bring the sauce to the boil, then lower the heat, add 2 tablespoons [25 g / 1 oz] of butter mixed with a little flour and whisk over a moderate heat until the sauce has thickened.
8. Check the seasoning, then pour the sauce over the chicken. At the last moment, heat the cognac, pour over the whole dish and set alight. Serve immediately.

Corona di pollo e olive

Chicken and Olive Ring

02:00 01:15

American	Ingredients	Metric/Imperial
1 (3¼ lb)	Small chicken	1 (1.5 kg / 3¼ lb)
Scant ¼ cup	Vegetable oil	3 tbsp
2 tbsp	Butter	25 g / 1 oz
2	Sprigs of rosemary	2
2	Eggs	2
5 oz	Piece of tongue	150 g / 5 oz
1¼ cups	Gelatin	300 ml / ½ pint
¼ lb	Green olives	100 g / 4 oz
¼ lb	Black olives	100 g / 4 oz
1	Lettuce	1
1	Bunch of watercress	1

1. Pot-roast the chicken with oil, butter and rosemary for 1¼ hours.
2. Remove from the pot, allow to cool slightly, skin and remove flesh from the bones.
3. Hard-cook (boil) eggs, cool in cold water, remove shells. Cut the tongue into strips, discarding any fat.
4. Prepare the gelatin according to the maker's instructions and put a little of it in a mold (preferably a ring mold with a hole in the middle) and refrigerate. When the gelatin in the mold has set, arrange on it the chicken, tongue, olives and the sliced or quartered eggs. Top up with the cool gelatin and refrigerate. To serve, plunge the mold quickly into water and then turn onto a serving dish lined with lettuce leaves and watercress and remove the mold.

Budellette di pollo al limone

Chicken Livers with Lemon

00:30 00:40

American	Ingredients	Metric/Imperial
1 lb	Chicken giblets and chicken livers	450 g / 1 lb
1	Onion	1
1	Carrot	1
1	Celery stalk	1
¼ lb	Mortadella	100 g / 4 oz
¼ cup	Butter	50 g / 2 oz
	Salt and pepper	
2½ cups	Chicken stock	600 ml / 1 pint
2	Egg yolks	2
1	Lemon	1
3 tbsp	Chopped parsley	2 tbsp

1. Wash the giblets well in hot water, chop finely.
2. Slice the onion, carrot and celery and cut the mortadella into thin strips; sauté in the heated butter. Add the giblets and season with salt and pepper. Cover with stock, bring to the boil then lower the heat and simmer for about 35 minutes.
3. Beat the egg yolks, add lemon juice and a little of the cooking liquid, mix well. Pour into the pan with the livers.
4. Stir well, remove from the heat and serve immediately, sprinkled with chopped parsley. Serve with rice or toast.

Pollo al formaggio

Chicken in Cheese Sauce

00:40 01:00

American	Ingredients	Metric/Imperial
1 (3 lb)	Chicken	1 (1.4 kg / 3 lb)
	Flour	
3 tbsp	Olive oil	2 tbsp
2 tbsp	Butter	25 g / 1 oz
	Salt	
1 tsp	Paprika pepper	1 tsp
2 cups	Stock	450 ml / ¾ pint
1 cup	Dry white wine	225 ml / 8 fl oz
5 oz	Emmental cheese	150 g / 5 oz
¼ tsp	Nutmeg	¼ tsp
1 tbsp	Chopped parsley	1 tbsp

1. Wash the chicken, dry carefully and cut into quarters. Flour lightly.
2. Heat the oil and butter in a pan, add the chicken, brown all over, and sprinkle with a little salt and paprika pepper. As soon as the chicken has colored, cover with stock, turn down the heat to moderate and simmer, covered, for 30 minutes.
3. Add the wine, vaporize and continue to cook until the meat is tender, taking care that the liquor neither dries up nor darkens. Transfer the chicken to a dish and keep warm.
4. Grate the emmental and add it to the pan, away from the heat, then replace the pan on the stove over a gentle heat and add the rest of the wine. Stir the sauce, which should remain liquid and smooth. Check the seasoning and, at the last moment, add a pinch of grated nutmeg and a spoonful of chopped parsley. Serve immediately poured onto the chicken.

Coppette Stefania

Chicken and Cream Salad

00:35 00:15

American	Ingredients	Metric/Imperial
2	Filleted chicken breasts	2
¼ cup	Butter	50 g / 2 oz
½ tsp	Chopped sage	½ tsp
2 cups	Beanshoots	100 g / 4 oz
¼ lb	Gruyère cheese	100 g / 4 oz
1 cup	Mayonnaise (see page 175)	225 ml / 8 fl oz
3 tbsp	Brandy	2 tbsp
2 tbsp	Tomato purée	1½ tbsp
½ cup	Cream	125 ml / 4 fl oz
	Salt and pepper	
1	Lettuce	1

1. Sauté the chicken breasts in butter and sage for 6 minutes each side on a gentle heat. Cool and cut into narrow strips.
2. Plunge the beanshoots into boiling water for 1 minute then drain well. Cut the gruyère into matchstick pieces.
3. Place the chicken, beanshoots and cheese in a bowl.
4. Prepare the sauce by blending the mayonnaise, brandy, tomato paste and cream together until the mixture is light and frothy, then fold into the other ingredients and season.
5. Cover the bowl and refrigerate until required. Serve in individual bowls each lined with a few crisp leaves of lettuce.

Petti di pollo allo sherry

Chicken Breasts in Sherry Sauce

00:35 00:25

American	Ingredients	Metric/Imperial
4	*Chicken breasts*	4
	Salt	
1 tbsp	*Flour*	1 tbsp
3 oz	*Parma ham*	75 g / 3 oz
3 oz	*Fontina cheese*	75 g / 3 oz
1	*Black truffle*	1
2 tbsp	*Olive oil*	1½ tbsp
2 tbsp	*Butter*	25 g / 1 oz
1	*Small onion*	1
½ cup	*Dry sherry*	125 ml / 4 fl oz
1 cup	*Stock*	225 ml / 8 fl oz

1. Choose 4 plump breasts of chicken. Using a thin, sharp knife, open up each breast laterally to form a pouch. Flatten by pounding, season with salt and flour lightly.
2. Place 2 slices of ham (cut to fit), a thin slice of fontina and a sliver of truffle inside each one. Close and secure with toothpicks.
3. Heat the oil and butter in a large frying pan, chop the onion and sauté for 4 minutes. When the onion starts to color, add the chicken breasts and brown on both sides.
4. Pour in the sherry and allow to evaporate. Continue to cook, moistening the chicken from time to time with a little stock for a further 15 minutes. Make a gravy to serve with the chicken, using the juices from the pan.

Petti di pollo fritti

Chicken Breasts Fried in Batter

00:30 Marinating time 01:30 00:08

American	Ingredients	Metric/Imperial
½ tsp	*Chopped bay leaves*	½ tsp
½ tsp	*Chopped rosemary*	½ tsp
1	*Garlic clove*	1
⅔ cup	*Olive oil*	150 ml / ¼ pint
1	*Lemon*	1
	Salt and pepper	
4	*Chicken breasts*	4
½ cup	*All purpose (plain) flour*	50 g / 2 oz
1	*Egg*	1
½ cup	*Milk*	125 ml / 4 fl oz
	Vegetable oil for frying	
	Lemon wedges	

1. Chop bay leaves and rosemary, crush the garlic and put in a bowl with the olive oil, lemon juice, salt and pepper.
2. Immerse the chicken breasts and marinate for 1½ hours turning from time to time.
3. Prepare a fairly thick batter by whisking flour, beaten egg and milk with a pinch of salt.
4. Coat the chicken breasts with batter. Heat some vegetable oil in a deep frying pan and when it is really hot slip in the chicken breasts and cook until crisp and brown. Drain on absorbent kitchen towels.
5. Serve hot with lemon wedges and grilled tomatoes.

Pollo in gelatina

Chicken in Home-Made Aspic Jelly

00:40 04:00

American	Ingredients	Metric/Imperial
2	*Calves' feet*	2
1 or 2	*Celery stalks*	1 or 2
2	*Carrots*	2
2	*Onions*	2
1	*Egg white*	1
1 (3 lb)	*Chicken*	1 (1.4 kg / 3 lb)
1½ oz	*Pistachio nuts*	40 g / 1½ oz
⅔ cup	*Black and green olives*	100 g / 4 oz
	Pickled onions	
	Gherkins	

1. You can buy aspic granules ready prepared, but the home-made variety is always superior.
2. Boil 2 calves' feet, celery, carrots and onions in 2 quarts [2 litres / 3½ pints] of water for 3 hours. When the liquid has reduced by half, strain through a cloth; add slightly beaten egg white and crushed shell, boil for another 5 minutes, strain through muslin again, this time into a bowl. Cool and refrigerate.
3. Cook the chicken by boiling or roasting depending on type. Allow 20 minutes to each 1 lb / 450 g plus 20 minutes over for roasting. A genuine boiling fowl of this size will take 2 hours.
4. Cool completely and carve with an eye to the appearance. Arrange on a serving dish and garnish with green and black olives and pistachio nuts.
5. Pour the cold jelly over the meat and decorate with pickled onions and gherkins.

Galletti al vino

Spring Chicken in Red Wine

00:25 01:20

American	Ingredients	Metric/Imperial
1 (3 lb)	*Spring chicken*	1 (1.4 kg / 3 lb)
2 oz	*Bacon*	50 g / 2 oz
¼ cup	*Vegetable oil*	50 ml / 2 fl oz
¾ lb	*Button onions*	350 g / 12 oz
	Salt and pepper	
	Flour	
¼ cup	*Butter*	50 g / 2 oz
3 tbsp	*Cognac*	2 tbsp
½ cup	*Red wine*	125 ml / 4 fl oz
2	*Bay leaves*	2
2	*Cloves*	2
1 cup	*Chicken stock*	225 ml / 8 fl oz
1 tbsp	*Chopped parsley*	1 tbsp

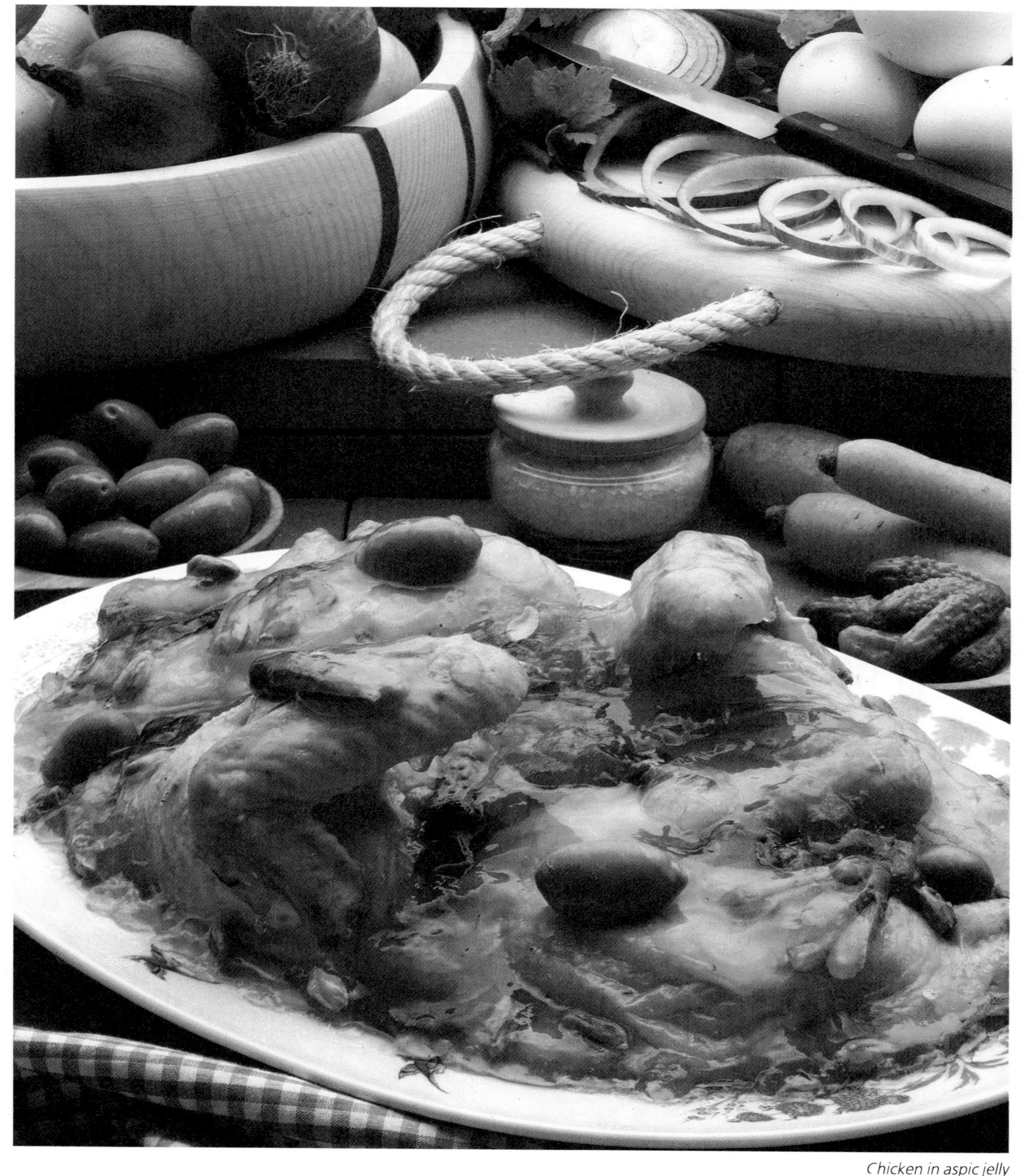

Chicken in aspic jelly

1. Wash and dry the chicken thoroughly and joint into small pieces (see page 313).
2. Chop the bacon and sauté in a little oil; add the button onions and season with salt and pepper.
3. Flour the chicken pieces lightly. Melt most of the butter in a second pan, add the chicken and sauté until golden on all sides.
4. Transfer the onions and bacon to the pan with the chicken, stir and check seasoning. Add the cognac; flame, then add the wine, bay leaves and cloves.
5. As soon as the wine boils, add the stock, lower the heat and simmer gently for about 45 minutes.
6. When the chicken is cooked, transfer to a heated serving dish with the onions using a slotted spoon.
7. Thicken the sauce by gradually adding 2 teaspoons flour mixed with the remaining butter, beat until smooth and creamy.
8. Pour over the chicken and arrange the onions around it. Sprinkle with parsley.

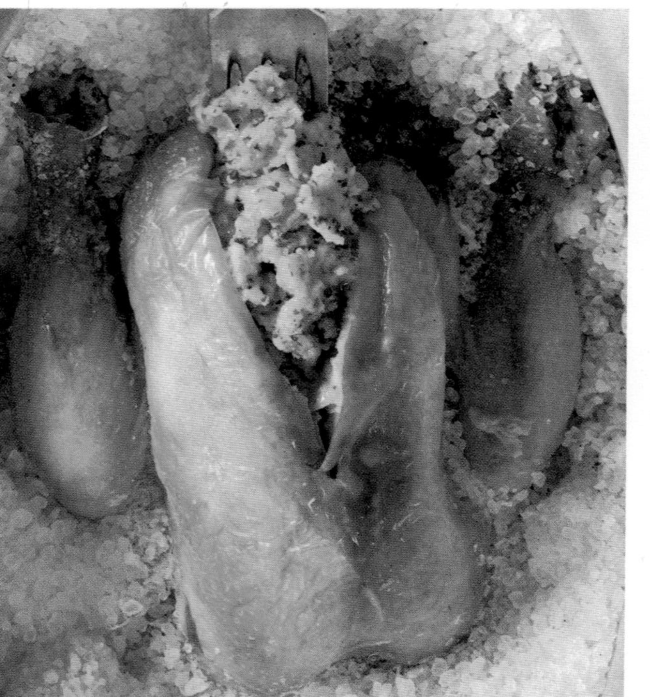

Stuffed and boiled chicken

Gallina ripiena

Stuffed and Boiled Chicken

00:30 01:30

American	Ingredients	Metric/Imperial
1 (3 lb)	Small chicken	1 (1.4 kg / 3 lb)
	Chicken giblets	
¼ cup	Butter	50 g / 2 oz
½ tsp	Chopped sage	½ tsp
7 oz	Cooked ham	200 g / 7 oz
¼ lb	Italian sausage	100 g / 4 oz
2	Slices of bread	2
¼ cup	Milk	50 ml / 2 fl oz
1	Egg	1
3 tbsp	Grated parmesan cheese	2 tbsp
	Salt and pepper	
¼ tsp	Nutmeg	¼ tsp
1	Carrot	1
1	Onion	1
1	Celery stalk	1
1	Bouquet garni	1
4	Tomatoes	4

1. Wash and dry the chicken inside and out.
2. Sauté the liver and heart in heated butter and sage. Finely chop the ham, skin the sausage and soak the bread in the milk. Put all the chopped ingredients together, add the bread (well squeezed out), the egg, grated cheese, salt, pepper and a pinch of nutmeg. Mix thoroughly.
3. Stuff the chicken with this mixture and sew up to secure.
4. Place the carrot, onion, celery and bouquet garni in a large pan of boiling salted water, add the chicken and boil for about 1 hour. Drain, slice and serve garnished with tomato slices.

Coscette di pollo alla boscaiola

Chicken Thighs Braised with Mushrooms

00:15 00:50

American	Ingredients	Metric/Imperial
4	Chicken thigh portions	4
¼ lb	Bacon	100 g / 4 oz
½ tsp	Chopped thyme	½ tsp
½ tsp	Chopped rosemary	½ tsp
	Salt and pepper	
2 tbsp	Vegetable oil	1½ tbsp
¼ cup	Butter	50 g / 2 oz
1	Onion	1
1	Carrot	1
1	Celery stalk	1
¼ cup	Dry white wine	50 ml / 2 fl oz
1 cup	Stock	225 ml / 8 fl oz
¾ lb	Mushrooms	350 g / 12 oz
14 oz	Peeled plum tomatoes	400 g / 14 oz
1 cup	Coffee (single) cream	225 ml / 8 fl oz
1 tbsp	Parsley	1 tbsp

1. Bone the chicken portions carefully, wash and dry; insert a slice of bacon into each with a pinch of thyme and rosemary and a little pepper. Secure with a toothpick.
2. Sauté gently in heated oil and butter until golden.
3. Chop the onion, carrot and celery and add these to the pan on a medium heat, cook for 6 minutes.
4. Moisten with white wine, allow to bubble for 1 minute and then add the stock and the sliced mushrooms, stir well. After a few minutes add the pulped tomatoes. Cook over medium heat for 30 minutes.
5. Remove the toothpicks and check the seasoning. (This part of the dish can be prepared well ahead of time.)
6. To serve, heat through very gently, adding a little extra pepper if necessary and pour the cream into the sauce a few moments before serving. Sprinkle with chopped parsley.

Tacchino alla salvia

Turkey with Sage

00:25 00:35

American	Ingredients	Metric/Imperial
3 tbsp	Seedless raisins	2 tbsp
1 lb	Turkey breast	500 g / 1 lb
2 oz	Sliced bacon	50 g / 2 oz
4	Sage leaves	4
3 tbsp	Butter	40 g / 1½ oz
2 tbsp	Vegetable oil	1½ tbsp
	Salt and pepper	

1. Preheat the oven to 350°F / 180°C / Gas Mark 4.
2. Put the raisins to soak in warm water.
3. Stretch the turkey out flat and lay the sliced bacon and sage leaves on top. Roll and tie.
4. Heat the butter and some oil in a pan, add the turkey and brown well all over.

5. Transfer to a small casserole dish, season with salt and pepper and add the raisins. Cover with foil or a lid and cook for 15 minutes. Remove the cover and cook for a further 15-20 minutes.
6. Cut into slices and serve hot.

Cotolette di tacchino e speck

Turkey Rissoles

00:30 Plus chilling — 00:16

American	Ingredients	Metric/Imperial
3	*Thick slices of white bread*	3
¼ cup	*Milk*	50 ml / 2 fl oz
1¼ lb	*Turkey meat*	600 g / 1¼ lb
3 oz	*Fat bacon*	75 g / 3 oz
2	*Eggs*	2
1 tbsp	*Grated parmesan cheese*	1 tbsp
1 tsp	*Worcester sauce*	1 tsp
½ tsp	*Cayenne pepper*	½ tsp
½ tsp	*Mixed herbs*	½ tsp
1 tbsp	*Flour*	1 tbsp
½ cup	*Dried bread crumbs*	50 g / 2 oz
⅔ cup	*Frying oil*	150 ml / ¼ pint
	Salt and pepper	

1. Soak the bread in the milk, squeeze out the excess moisture.
2. Grind (mince) the turkey and the bacon fat together, add 1 beaten egg, grated parmesan cheese, Worcester sauce, cayenne pepper, mixed herbs and mix well with the bread. Form into 8 rissoles using floured hands.
3. Now beat the remaining egg with 2 tablespoons [1½ tablespoons] water on a flat plate and sprinkle the bread crumbs on another plate. Dip the rissoles in the egg and then in bread crumbs and chill in the refrigerator for 30 minutes.
4. Heat the oil in a frying pan over a high heat, slip in 4 rissoles and reduce heat slightly. Fry for 4 minutes each side, drain onto absorbent kitchen towels and keep warm. Reheat the oil and fry the remaining rissoles. Season and serve with lemon wedges.

Cook's tip: A quick dish which can be made from left-over pieces of turkey, chicken or game. Mix in the food processor to save time.

Tacchino fiorito

Turkey Flower

02:00 — 00:45

American	Ingredients	Metric/Imperial
1	*Rolled turkey breast*	1
	Salt	
1	*Carrot*	1
1	*Onion*	1
1	*Celery stalk*	1
1	*Sprig of parsley*	1
2½ tsp	*Gelatin*	2½ tsp
8	*Radishes*	8
1	*Bunch of watercress*	1

1. Place the turkey in a saucepan just covered with slightly salted water containing a roughly chopped carrot, onion, stalk of celery and sprig of parsley.
2. Bring to the boil and simmer for 45 minutes or until cooked, cool and then cut into 6 even slices.
3. With scissors cut each slice into a petal shape.
4. Strain the vegetables and reserve the stock. Heat a few tablespoons until boiling, add gelatin, make up to 1¼ cups [300 ml / ½ pint] with remaining stock and cool.
5. Chill in ice-making compartment of the refrigerator or in the freezer for 15 minutes.
6. Arrange the turkey slices on a large plate in the shape of a flower, brush them several times over with the gelatin and decorate with radishes cut into flowers. Chop the rest of the gelatin and pile between the petals. Garnish with watercress.

Cook's tip: the turkey petals can be decorated with canned pimentos cut into petals, small flowers and cucumber peel for stalks. Surround with thinly sliced cucumber for a special, eye-catching buffet dish.

Rotolo di tacchino ripieno

Stuffed Turkey Roll

00:35 Plus cooling time Serves 6 — 01:30

American	Ingredients	Metric/Imperial
1 (3 lb)	*Roll of turkey meat*	1 (1.4 kg / 3 lb)
¼ lb	*Sliced mortadella*	100 g / 4 oz
2	*Eggs*	2
1 tbsp	*Grated parmesan cheese*	1 tbsp
1 tbsp	*Milk*	1 tbsp
	Salt and pepper	
3	*Slices of cheese*	3
2	*Sprigs of rosemary*	2
¼ tsp	*Nutmeg*	¼ tsp
3 tbsp	*Vegetable oil*	2 tbsp
¼ cup	*Butter*	50 g / 2 oz
4	*Sage leaves*	4
½ cup	*Dry white wine*	125 ml / 4 fl oz
1 cup	*Stock*	225 ml / 8 fl oz
4	*Tomatoes*	4
12	*Olives*	12
8	*Gherkins*	8

1. Discard the string around the turkey roll, open out the meat and cover with slices of mortadella (with the skin removed).
2. Beat the eggs with the grated cheese, milk, salt and pepper; cook, as for an omelette, on both sides. The safest way of cooking the upper side is to slide the pan under a hot broiler (grill) for a few seconds.
3. Cool the omelette completely then lay it on the slices of mortadella, cover with the sliced cheese and sprinkle with chopped rosemary and a pinch of nutmeg. Roll up tightly and tie securely with kitchen string. Sew up the ends so that the melting cheese will not ooze out or cover with foil.
4. Preheat the oven to 375°F / 190°C / Gas Mark 5.
5. Heat some oil and butter in a large casserole, add rosemary and a few sage leaves. Brown the roll over a low heat, turning to achieve an even color. Pour wine over the meat, then continue to cook in a moderate oven basting with a little stock from time to time for 1½ hours.
6. Remove from the pan, cool completely. Slice and lay on a large serving dish. Garnish with tomatoes, olives and gherkins.

Tacchino al melograno

Turkey with Pomegranates

This dish is a native of the region around Venice, where pomegranate juice is available all the year round.

00:30 02:30

American	Ingredients	Metric/Imperial
1 (6¾ lb)	Young turkey hen	1 (3 kg / 6¾ lb)
2½ oz	Sliced bacon	65 g / 2½ oz
	Salt and pepper	
2 tbsp	Vegetable oil	1½ tbsp
¼ cup	Butter	50 g / 2 oz
3	Pomegranates	3

1. Preheat the oven to 350°F / 180°C / Gas Mark 4.
2. Choose a young hen turkey that has been well hung. Have it cleaned and wash thoroughly.
3. Lard with slices of bacon, especially over the breast. Season lightly with salt and pepper, then place in a pan with heated oil and butter. Cook for 2½ hours in the oven, basting with the strained juice of 2 pomegranates.
4. Prepare the sauce by chopping the giblets very finely, mixing with the juice of the remaining pomegranate, some oil, ½ cup [125 ml / 4 fl oz] stock, salt and pepper. Simmer over a very low heat, stirring constantly.
5. When the turkey is cooked, allow to stand for 10 minutes, then slice and serve accompanied with this delicious pomegranate sauce, strained or blended.

Cook's tip: if pomegranate juice is not available, use grapefruit. Add a few drops of red vegetable coloring to deepen the color of the sauce.

Tacchino alla diavola

Devilled Turkey

00:30
Marinating time 06:00
Serves 6
01:00

American	Ingredients	Metric/Imperial
1 (3 lb)	Turkey joint	1 (1.4 kg / 3 lb)
⅔ cup	Olive oil	150 ml / ¼ pint
2	Garlic cloves	2
1	Sprig of parsley	1
	Salt and pepper	
Scant ¼ cup	Spicy mustard	3 tbsp
1	Onion	1
4 – 8	Large fresh mushrooms	4 – 8

1. Marinade the turkey joint in olive oil with the crushed garlic cloves, a chopped sprig of parsley and seasoning.
2. Leave for at least 6 hours, turning several times.
3. Preheat the oven to 400°F / 200°C / Gas Mark 6. Oil a baking pan and cook the turkey for 30 minutes.
4. Remove from the oven and brush with a mixture of spicy mustard and finely chopped onion. Reduce heat to 350°F / 180°C / Gas Mark 4.
5. Surround the turkey with mushrooms brushed with remaining marinade and cook for a further 30 minutes.

Fesa di tacchino alla valdostana

Turkey Breasts with Ham and Cheese

00:30 00:30

American	Ingredients	Metric/Imperial
1¼ lb	Turkey breasts	600 g / 1¼ lb
1	Egg	1
½ cup	Dried bread crumbs	50 g / 2 oz
¼ cup	Butter	50 g / 2 oz
Scant ¼ cup	Oil	3 tbsp
¼ lb	Parma ham	100 g / 4 oz
¼ lb	Fontina cheese	100 g / 4 oz
	Salt and pepper	
1 tsp	Thyme	1 tsp

1. Divide the turkey breasts into 4 escalopes, flatten with a cutlet bat, add to the beaten egg and leave to soak for 30 minutes.
2. Preheat the oven to 350°F / 180°C / Gas Mark 4.
3. Coat the turkey carefully with bread crumbs, patting the crumbs in place. Sauté in the heated butter and oil on a medium heat until golden.
4. Drain on absorbent kitchen towels then lay in an oven-proof dish. Place a slice of ham and several thin slivers of cheese on each piece of turkey, sprinkle with a pinch of salt, pepper and thyme and place in the hot oven until the cheese has melted – about 20 minutes. A little grated truffle makes a tasty but optional garnish.

Scaloppe di tacchino Cordon Bleu

Scallopine of Turkey Cordon Bleu

00:20 00:25

American	Ingredients	Metric/Imperial
4	Turkey scallopine (escalopes)	4
	Salt and pepper	
	Flour	
4	Slices of lean cooked ham	4
4	Thin slices of fontina cheese	4
½ cup	Button mushrooms	75 g / 3 oz
⅓ cup	Butter	75 g / 3 oz
3 tbsp	Olive oil	2 tbsp
1 tbsp	Chopped parsley	1 tbsp
1 cup	Chicken stock	225 ml / 8 fl oz
	Sprigs of parsley	

1. Pound the scallopine lightly to flatten, season with salt and pepper and dust with flour.
2. Cut the ham and fontina into slices the same size as the scallopine.
3. Wash and dry the mushrooms and slice thinly. Heat a little of the butter in a small pan and sauté the mushrooms lightly; set them aside.

4. Heat the remainder of the butter and all the olive oil in a pan large enough to accommodate the scallopine. Cook them for 6-7 minutes on each side.
5. Lay a slice of ham on each scallopine, scatter with mushroom slices and sprinkle with chopped parsley and a little pepper, top with slices of fontina.
6. Heat the stock and pour it over the scallopine, cover the pan and simmer for 8 to 10 minutes, by which time the cheese should have melted.
7. Serve at once, decorated with sprigs of parsley.

Tacchinella tartufata

Turkey with Truffle

00:40 03:00

American	Ingredients	Metric/Imperial
1 (6 lb)	*Young hen turkey*	*1 (2.7 kg / 6 lb)*
	Salt and pepper	
¼ lb	*Pork fat*	*100 g / 4 oz*
½ cup	*Ground (minced) veal*	*100 g / 4 oz*
½ cup	*Ground (minced) pork*	*100 g / 4 oz*
1	*Truffle*	*1*
¼ cup	*Butter*	*50 g / 2 oz*
Scant ¼ cup	*Olive oil*	*3 tbsp*

1. Preheat the oven to 400°F / 200°C / Gas Mark 6.
2. Wash and dry the turkey, sprinkle salt and pepper inside.
3. Prepare a stuffing either by chopping or make in the food processor. Chop the pork fat and combine it with the ground (minced) veal and pork, the turkey liver and half the truffle, finely sliced.
4. Stuff the turkey and sew up the aperture.
5. Cut the rest of the truffle into slivers and insert these under the skin of the bird, spacing them as evenly as possible. Rub the entire surface with butter.
6. Cook in a roasting pan in the oil and butter for 3 hours, basting from time to time with the pan juices. Remove from the oven, allow to stand for 10 minutes, carve and serve hot with roast potatoes and gravy made from pan juices.

Anatra al porto

Duck with Port

00:15 01:00

American	Ingredients	Metric/Imperial
1	*Medium-sized duck*	*1*
3 tbsp	*Vegetable oil*	*2 tbsp*
¼ cup	*Butter*	*50 g / 2 oz*
1	*Onion*	*1*
1	*Carrot*	*1*
1	*Celery stalk*	*1*
	Salt and pepper	
1½ cups	*Port (or dry marsala)*	*350 ml / 12 fl oz*
¼ lb	*Mushrooms*	*100 g / 4 oz*
½ cup	*Chicken stock*	*125 ml / 4 fl oz*
1	*Egg*	*1*
1 tsp	*Cornstarch (cornflour)*	*1 tsp*
1	*Lemon*	*1*

1. Singe, wash and joint the duck.
2. Heat the oil and butter and sauté the duck with chopped onion, carrot and celery; season with salt and pepper. When the vegetables start to color, add the port or marsala and simmer for 20 minutes.
3. Slice the washed mushrooms, add to the pan and continue to cook gently, adding more port or a little stock if necessary. When the duck is tender, take out of the pan and place on a heated serving dish.
4. Beat the egg with the cornstarch, add the lemon juice and pour this mixture over the duck juices. Mix well on a very low heat for 2-3 minutes, then pour the sauce over the duck. Serve with roast potatoes, and spinach or peas.

Germano reale alla tedesca

German-Style Mallard

00:30 01:40

American	Ingredients	Metric/Imperial
1	*Mallard duck*	*1*
⅓ cup	*Butter*	*65 g / 2½ oz*
½ lb	*Marrons glacés*	*225 g / 8 oz*
2	*Onions*	*2*
3	*Apples*	*3*
¼ cup	*Cognac*	*50 ml / 2 fl oz*
6	*Cloves*	*6*
3 tbsp	*Vegetable oil*	*2 tbsp*
2½ cups	*Beer*	*600 ml / 1 pint*
¾ lb	*Plum tomatoes, peeled*	*350 g / 12 oz*
¾ lb	*Brussels sprouts, washed and halved*	*350 g / 12 oz*
1 cup	*Béchamel sauce (see page 162)*	*225 ml / 8 fl oz*
1	*Lemon*	*1*
	Salt and pepper	
1 tsp	*Horse-radish powder (optional)*	*1 tsp*

1. Clean, singe and thoroughly wash and dry the mallard. Mix a large knob of butter with the marrons glacés, cut into pieces, 1 chopped onion, 2 apples, sliced or cut into small pieces and put the mixture into the stomach. Place the bird so that the opening is uppermost and pour in the cognac. Close the opening with an onion studded with cloves.
2. Put the oil and remaining butter in a large heatproof casserole on a medium heat and brown the mallard all over.
3. Preheat the oven to 375°F / 190°C / Gas Mark 5.
4. Sprinkle the duck with beer and after 10 minutes cooking on the stove, add the chopped tomatoes and sprouts, cover and cook in the oven for a further 40 minutes, turning the mallard several times. Remove it from the sauce and keep warm in the oven and put all the sauce in an electric blender or rub through a sieve.
5. Reduce oven heat to 325°F / 170°C / Gas Mark 3. Put the mallard back in the sauce, continue cooking for another 30 minutes.
6. Prepare a well-seasoned béchamel sauce and add to it the grated flesh of 1 apple and the juice of the lemon. Season the sauce with some salt and pepper and add a pinch of hot powdered horse-radish, if you wish. Pour it in to a sauceboat and keep warm.
7. Carve the mallard, serve hot in its stock accompanied by the apple béchamel sauce.

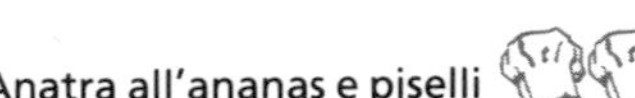

Duck with orange sauce

Anatra all'arancia

Duck with Orange Sauce

00:35 — 01:15

American	Ingredients	Metric/Imperial
1 (4½ lb)	*Medium-sized duck*	*1 (2 kg / 4½ lb)*
3 tbsp	*Olive oil*	*2 tbsp*
¼ cup	*Butter*	*50 g / 2 oz*
	Salt	
1 cup	*Vegetable stock*	*225 ml / 8 fl oz*
1	*Lemon*	*1*
6	*Oranges*	*6*
2	*Sugar cubes*	*2*
3 tbsp	*Wine vinegar*	*2 tbsp*

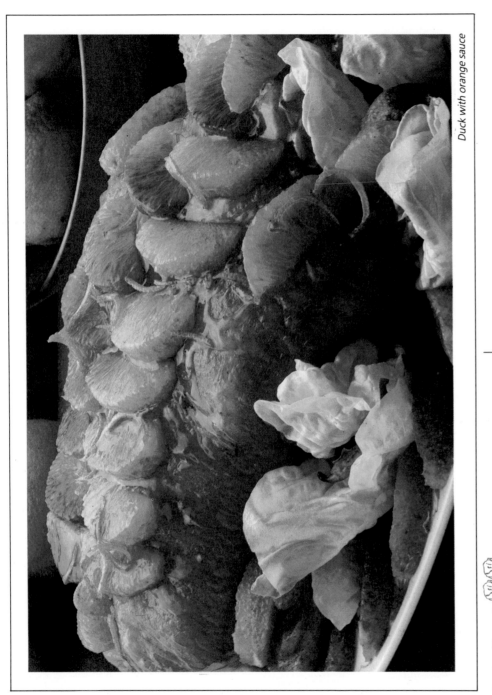

1. Preheat the oven to 400°F / 200°C / Gas Mark 6.
2. Singe, clean and wash the duck, dry very thoroughly.
3. Heat oil and butter in a casserole and brown the duck all over; add salt, pour in the stock mixed with a little lemon juice and cook in the oven for 20 minutes. Turn the heat down to 350°F / 180°C / Gas Mark 4 and cook until tender. Transfer to a plate and keep warm.
4. Squeeze 2 oranges and strain the juice. Cut the zest of the lemon into thin strips and soften by immersing in boiling water for 1 minute.
5. Sieve the cooking juices and add the orange juice and lemon zest.
6. In a small saucepan, make a caramel by melting 2 sugar cubes which have been rubbed with orange peel and adding a little vinegar.
7. Tip the sauce with the cooking juices into the caramel and heat gently, stirring, over a low heat without allowing the mixture to boil.
8. Carve the duck and arrange on a heated serving dish. Garnish with the remaining oranges, peeled, sliced and with the pips removed.

Anatra all'ananas e piselli

Duckling with Pineapple and Green Peas

00:30 — 01:00

American	Ingredients	Metric/Imperial
1 (3 lb)	*Duckling*	*1 (1.4 kg / 3 lb)*
Scant ¼ cup	*Vegetable oil*	*3 tbsp*
¼ cup	*Butter*	*50 g / 2 oz*
1	*Onion*	*1*
1	*Garlic clove*	*1*
¼ cup	*Flour*	*25 g / 1 oz*
¾ lb	*Canned pineapple*	*350 g / 12 oz*
	Salt and pepper	
3	*Tomatoes*	*3*
¼ lb	*Mushrooms*	*100 g / 4 oz*
½ lb	*Peas, frozen*	*225 g / 8 oz*

1. Wash and dry the duckling, cut into 4 portions with poultry shears.
2. Put into a pan with hot oil and brown all over. Turn the heat down and turn to cook evenly.
3. Carve the joints and remove as much of the flesh as possible from the bones.
4. Heat the butter in the same pan, sauté the chopped onion and a crushed clove of garlic for 4 minutes then add the duck meat. Sprinkle with flour and stir well.
5. Add the juice of the pineapple, mix and season well. Tip in the skinned, mashed tomatoes and the sliced mushrooms; simmer for 30 minutes.
6. Lightly cook the peas. Dice the pineapple chunks and add, with the peas, to the pan. Cook for a further 15 minutes and serve piping hot.

Duckling with pineapple and green peas

Anatra arrosto

Pot-Roasted Duckling

00:20 01:15

American	Ingredients	Metric/Imperial
1 (4½ lb)	Duckling	1 (2 kg / 4½ lb)
1	Onion	1
1	Bunch of herbs	1
2 tbsp	Butter	25 g / 1 oz
7 oz	Sliced bacon	200 g / 7 oz
¼ cup	Vegetable oil	50 ml / 2 fl oz
¼ tsp	Chopped thyme	¼ tsp
¼ tsp	Chopped marjoram	¼ tsp
2	Bay leaves	2
	Salt and pepper	
1	Lemon	1
1 cup	Red wine or marsala	225 ml / 8 fl oz
1	Egg yolk	1
	Lemon or orange slices	

1. Wash and dry the duckling. Chop the giblets with the onion and a small bunch of herbs, mix with a knob of butter and place in the cavity. Cover with slices of bacon and truss firmly.
2. Heat the oil in a pan large enough to take the duckling; add thyme, marjoram, the bay leaves, salt and pepper. Put the duckling in the pan and when it has browned all over, drain off the fat. Sprinkle with lemon juice and then pour in the wine or marsala. Cook until tender, then transfer to an oven-proof serving dish.
3. Preheat the oven to 400°F / 200°C / Gas Mark 6.
4. Cut duckling carefully into portions, then put together in the original shape, brush with egg yolk, secure the joins with toothpicks and put in a hot oven for 15 minutes. The egg yolk will form a glaze that conceals the cuts.
5. Remove duckling and garnish with lemon or orange slices.
6. Dilute pan juices with a little water, heat until boiling and strain into a sauceboat.

Oca con le mele renette

Roast Goose with Apples

00:15 02:15

American	Ingredients	Metric/Imperial
1	Medium-sized goose	1
2 lb	Canadian apples	1 kg / 2 lb
¼ cup	Olive oil	50 ml / 2 fl oz
1 cup	Dry white wine	225 ml / 8 fl oz
	Salt and pepper	

1. Preheat the oven to 350°F / 180°C / Gas Mark 4.
2. Singe, clean, wash and dry the goose. The skin may be removed which will considerably reduce the fat content.
3. Peel, core and dice half the apples and place them in the cavity of the goose. If you have left the skin on, sew up the aperture; if not, bind with a strip of foil.
4. Place in an oiled roasting pan and roast, baste occasionally.
5. After 1½ hours, pour wine over the goose, vaporize, season with salt and pepper and return to the oven. Continue to baste from time to time for a further 30 minutes or until cooked.
6. Peel, core and slice the remaining apples, boil in very slightly salted water, strain and sieve. Serve the goose, sliced, with this apple sauce.

Oca con salsa di peperoni

Goose with Sweet Pepper Sauce

00:30 01:35

American	Ingredients	Metric/Imperial
1	*Small goose*	*1*
3 tbsp	*Vegetable oil*	*2 tbsp*
2 tbsp	*Butter*	*25 g / 1 oz*
6	*Sage leaves*	*6*
6	*Sprigs of rosemary*	*6*
½ cup	*Dry white wine*	*125 ml / 4 fl oz*
	Salt and pepper	
¼ lb	*Salami*	*100 g / 4 oz*
2	*Large sweet peppers*	*2*

1. Preheat the oven to 400°F / 200°C / Gas Mark 6.
2. Clean and skin the goose (this is not too difficult if you have a sharp knife and a little patience). Reserve the liver and the emptied and cleaned stomach (optional).
3. Place the goose in a roasting pan with the oil and rub with butter, sage and rosemary. Brown all over in oven and season.
4. Allowing 15 minutes cooking time per 1 lb / 450 g and 15 minutes extra continue to cook until tender. Moisten with wine from time to time.
5. Carve the goose into 8 pieces and place on a dish in a warm place. Retain the cooking juices, you will need them for the sauce.
6. Chop the salami finely, together with the bird's stomach, (optional), liver, and the peppers, deseeded. Skim off as much fat as possible from the cooking juices, strain and add the chopped ingredients; cook over a medium heat for 15 minutes.
7. Add the finely chopped goose liver and a few twists of the pepper mill. Check the seasoning and stir until all the ingredients are cooked.
8. Serve the goose accompanied by the hot sauce.

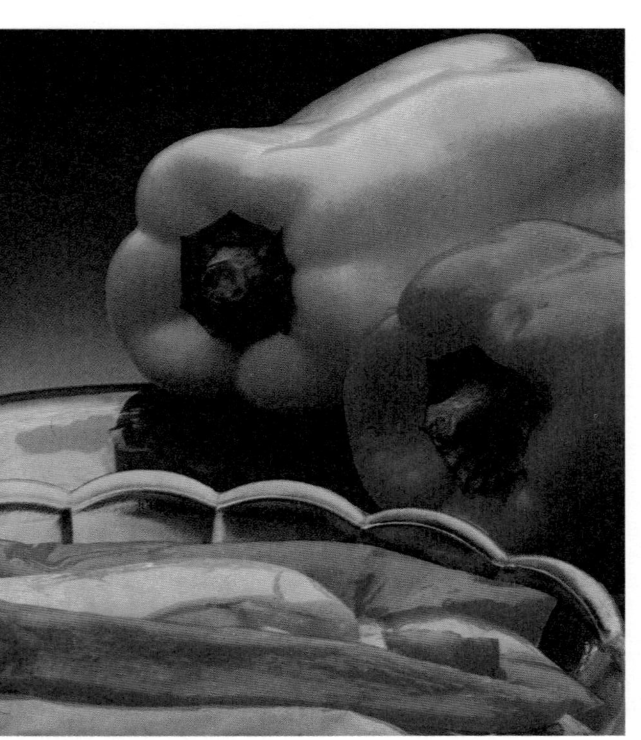

Sweet peppers

Oca arrostita alla lorenese

Roast Goose

00:25 02:00 to 02:30

American	Ingredients	Metric/Imperial
1	*Small goose*	*1*
¼ lb	*Bacon*	*100 g / 4 oz*
6	*Sage leaves*	*6*
3	*Sprigs of rosemary*	*3*
¼ cup	*Butter*	*50 g / 2 oz*
3 tbsp	*Vegetable oil*	*2 tbsp*
	Freshly ground pepper	

1. Preheat the oven to 350°F / 180°C / Gas Mark 4.
2. Scald, pluck and clean the goose. Flatten slightly by pounding. Cut half the bacon into strips and put some inside the goose and some on the breast and legs, securing with toothpicks.
3. Using the prongs of a fork to make little holes, insert sage leaves and rosemary under the skin.
4. Place the goose in a roasting pan with several knobs of butter and some oil. Roast for 2 hours, baste from time to time.
5. Test by pricking with a fork; if any liquid runs out, you will need to cook the bird a little longer.
6. Transfer to a warm serving dish, dust with freshly-ground pepper and serve with roast potatoes.

Oca al vino

Goose Braised in Wine

00:15 02:00

American	Ingredients	Metric/Imperial
1 (3¼ lb)	*Young goose*	*1 (1.5 kg / 3¼ lb)*
	Salt and pepper	
1	*Small onion*	*1*
1	*Sprig of sage*	*1*
1	*Sprig of rosemary*	*1*
	Oil	
4	*Lemons*	*4*
2½ cups	*Dry red wine*	*600 ml / 1¾ pints*
1	*Bunch of mixed herbs*	*1*
2 tbsp	*Cornstarch (cornflour)*	*3 tbsp*

1. Preheat the oven to 350°F / 180°C / Gas Mark 6.
2. Wash the goose well, season the cavity with salt, place an onion and a sprig each of sage and rosemary inside.
3. Rub all over with oil, place in a large roasting pan, sprinkle with lemon juice and roast for about 2 hours. Turn after 30 minutes.
4. Bring the wine to the boil in a saucepan with a bunch of mixed herbs.
5. Strain and add to the goose at the end of 1 hour. Turn the bird twice during the next hour.
6. Carve the goose before serving and sprinkle with salt and pepper, but only in moderation as the goose is already highly flavored. Put the goose in the oven while you make the sauce. The goose should be served very hot.
7. Strain fat from cooking juices and thicken with cornstarch blended with a little water. Pour into a sauceboat and serve at once with the carved goose.

Goose braised in wine

GAME

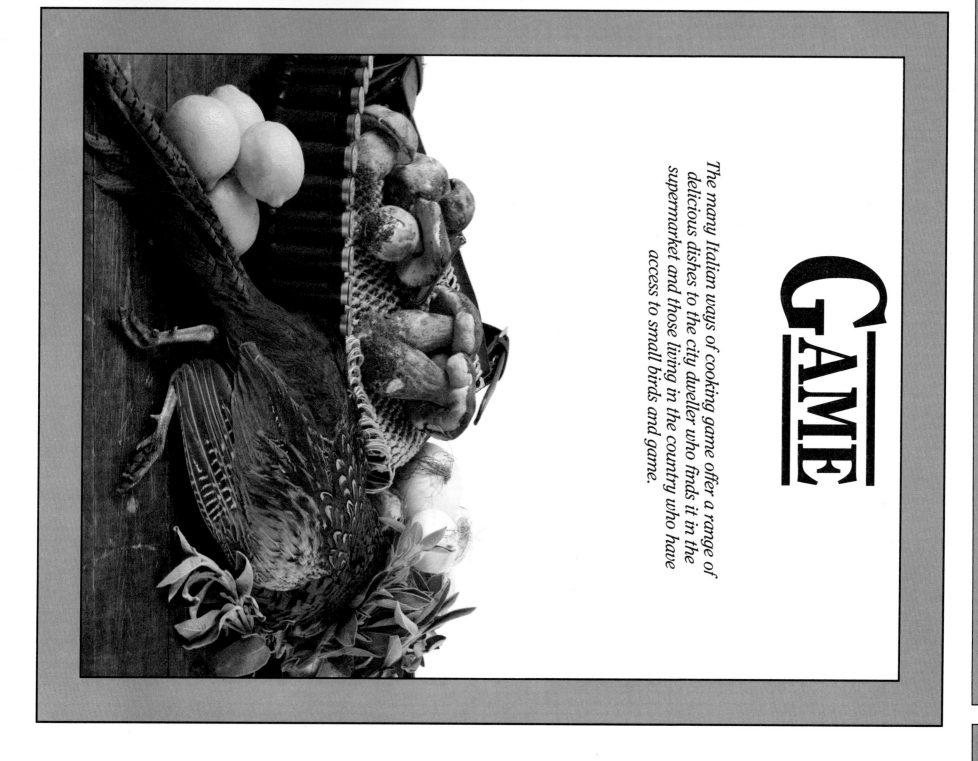

The many Italian ways of cooking game offer a range of delicious dishes to the city dweller who finds it in the supermarket and those living in the country who have access to small birds and game.

Game

Game	Temperature	Foil roasting	Accompaniments
CAPERCAILLIE	40-45 mins 400°F / 200°C / Gas Mark 6	70 mins	Serve on pieces of fried bread
GROUSE	30-40 mins 400° F / 200°C / Gas Mark 6	40 mins	Serve on fried bread with thin gravy. Garnish with watercress.
PARTRIDGE	30-40 mins 400°F / 200°C / Gas Mark 6	40 mins	Serve with bread sauce, garnish with watercress. Apple and celery salad
PHEASANT	15 mins 400° / 200° / Gas Mark 6 reducing to 350°F / 180°C / Gas Mark 4	60-70 mins Useful for older birds	Thin gravy, fried bread crumbs, game chips, watercress, various stuffings
PIGEON	30-35 mins 400°F / 200°C / Gas Mark 6	50-60 mins	Slightly thickened gravy
SNIPE	25 mins 400°F / 200°C / Gas Mark 6	40 mins	Thin gravy, game chips
TEAL	30-35 mins 400°F / 200°C / Gas Mark 6	40 mins	Green salad, garnish with watercress

Game	Temperature	Foil roasting	Accompaniments
WOODCOCK	25 mins 400°F / 200° / Gas Mark 6	40 mins	Thin gravy, game chips
HARE	40 mins 1 lb / 450 g 400°F / 200°C / Gas Mark 6	50 mins	Roast saddle, back and legs. Marinate 24 hours before roasting. Chestnut or sausagemeat stuffing, red currant jelly.
RABBIT	45 mins 1 lb / 450 g 350°F / 180°C / Gas Mark 4		
VENISON	15-20 mins 1 lb / 450 g 400°F / 200°C / Gas Mark 6	20-25 mins per 1 lb / 450 g	Roast loin and haunch. Marinate for 12-14 hours. Red currant or rowan jelly, chestnut purée

Small game birds are fairly lean and do not require long cooking times. However they do need to be barded with thin layers of pork fat or bacon to add moisture during the cooking period, venison also benefits from barding. Arrange the fat over the birds and tie with string or secure with a skewer. Remove the barding fat at least 10 minutes before the end of the roasting time to allow the birds to brown and crisp before serving.

Birds prepared for the oven (left to right)
Top: hen pheasant, guinea fowl, chicken, oven ready turkey.
Centre: grey legged partridge, red legged partridge, wild duck, grouse.
Bottom: ideal for individual portions, small quail, wood pigeon and poussin.

Cedrone al barolo

Grouse in Barolo Wine

00:20 01:00

American	Ingredients	Metric/Imperial
2	*Dressed wood grouse*	*2*
1	*Onion*	*1*
1	*Carrot*	*1*
1	*Celery stalk*	*1*
1	*Shallot*	*1*
¾ lb	*Mushrooms*	*350 g / 12 oz*
¼ cup	*Vegetable oil*	*50 ml / 2 fl oz*
1 quart	*Barolo wine*	*1 litre / 1¾ pints*
¼ tsp	*Cinnamon*	*¼ tsp*
	Salt and pepper	
4	*Cloves*	*4*

1. Cut grouse in half, peel and chop onion, carrot, celery and shallot. Wash mushrooms in warm water and drain.
2. Heat oil and, when very hot, brown grouse, then drain and put on one side. Add onion to pan and sauté for 2 minutes. Pour over wine, remaining vegetables (not mushrooms) cinnamon, salt, pepper and cloves. Return grouse to pan, cover and cook on hob over a low heat for 1 hour.
3. Add mushrooms 10 minutes before end of cooking time, then arrange grouse on a dish, spoon over sauce and serve.

Faraona alla Giobatta

Guinea-Fowl in Walnut Sauce

00:30 01:00 to 01:15

American	Ingredients	Metric/Imperial
1 (2 lb)	*Guinea-fowl*	*1 (1 kg / 2 lb)*
¼ cup	*Vegetable oil*	*50 ml / 2 fl oz*
1 oz	*Capers*	*25 g / 1 oz*
2	*Garlic cloves*	*2*
¼ tsp	*Chopped rosemary*	*¼ tsp*
¼ tsp	*Chopped sage*	*¼ tsp*
¼ tsp	*Chopped basil*	*¼ tsp*
1 cup	*Dry red wine*	*225 ml / 8 fl oz*
	Salt and pepper	
1 cup	*Stock*	*225 ml / 8 fl oz*
¼ cup	*Butter*	*50 g / 2 oz*
1 tbsp	*Cognac*	*1 tbsp*
¼ cup	*Flour*	*25 g / 1 oz*
½ cup	*Walnuts, shelled and chopped*	*50 g / 2 oz*
½ cup	*Milk (optional)*	*125 ml / 4 fl oz*

1. Wash and dry the guinea-fowl, put into a large saucepan with oil and brown quickly over a fairly high heat.
2. Chop the capers, garlic, rosemary, sage and basil and sprinkle over the bird, then add the wine and season with salt and pepper.
3. Lower the heat, add stock and simmer until tender.
4. Prepare the sauce by melting the butter in small pan, then, away from the heat, add the cognac, flour, chopped walnuts and a pinch of salt. Return the pan to the heat and cook this mixture for a few minutes adding stock from the bird and the milk. Mix well and heat through for a further 2 minutes.
5. Arrange the guinea-fowl on a heated serving dish, carve and pour the walnut sauce over the bird.

Faraona nel coccio

Guinea-Fowl Casseroled in Terracotta

This dish is regularly prepared by Giorgio Gioco at the '12 Apostles' restaurant in Verona; for an accompanying vegetable he suggests roasted or plain boiled potatoes.

00:30 01:20

American	Ingredients	Metric/Imperial
1 (3 lb)	*Guinea fowl*	*1 (1.4 kg / 3 lb)*
⅓ cup	*Butter*	*75 g / 3 oz*
	Salt	
24	*Button onions*	*24*
¼ lb	*Button mushrooms*	*100 g / 4 oz*
½ cup	*Port wine*	*125 ml / 4 fl oz*

This dish requires a terracotta casserole that is fireproof.
1. Draw, singe, wash and dry the fowl, cut into quarters.
2. Heat half the butter in the casserole, sauté the bird until golden brown all over, add salt and cover. Lower the heat and cook gently for 15 minutes.
3. Sauté peeled onions with some butter in one pan and mushrooms in yet another. Add both, with their juices, to the casserole. Pour in the port wine, bubble for 2 minutes, adjust the seasoning. Cover and continue to cook gently until done.

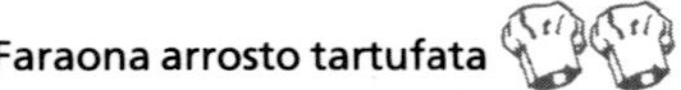

Faraona arrosto tartufata

Roast Guinea-Fowl with Truffles

00:20 01:00

American	Ingredients	Metric/Imperial
1 (3 lb)	*Guinea-fowl*	*1 (1.4 kg / 3 lb)*
2	*Black truffles*	*2*
2 tbsp	*Butter*	*25 g / 1 oz*
	Salt and pepper	
Scant ¼ cup	*Marsala wine*	*3 tbsp*
1	*Lemon*	*1*

1. Preheat the oven to 400°F / 200°C / Gas Mark 6.
2. Rinse the inside of the guinea-fowl under running water.
3. Peel the truffles thinly and slice. Put a few raw slices in the cavity of the fowl and under the skin.
4. Sauté the remaining slices in butter with salt and pepper, moistening with marsala. Remove the pan from the heat and allow the mixture to cool before using it to stuff the fowl. Sew up both apertures.
5. Butter a sheet of baking foil, place the fowl on it, sprinkle lightly with salt, pepper and lemon juice. Wrap in the foil and cook in a moderately hot oven.
6. After 45 minutes, unwrap the foil and allow the bird to brown. Remove to a carving board, allow to stand for 10 minutes and carve.

Guinea-fowl casseroled in terracotta

Guinea-fowl with cream and marsala

Faraona alla panna

Guinea-Fowl in Fresh Cream Sauce

00:25 01:30

American	Ingredients	Metric/Imperial
1 (3¼ lb)	*Guinea-fowl*	*1 (1.5 kg / 3¼ lb)*
¼ lb	*Bacon or parma ham with fat*	*100 g / 4 oz*
½ cup	*Butter*	*100 g / 4 oz*
1	*Celery stalk*	*1*
2	*Small carrots*	*2*
1	*Onion*	*1*
¼ tsp	*Chopped rosemary*	*¼ tsp*
¼ tsp	*Chopped thyme*	*¼ tsp*
¼ tsp	*Chopped marjoram*	*¼ tsp*
2	*Bay leaves*	*2*
	Salt and pepper	
½ cup	*Dry white wine*	*125 ml / 4 fl oz*
1 cup	*Stock*	*225 ml / 8 fl oz*
1 cup	*Coffee (single) cream*	*225 ml / 8 fl oz*

1. Wash and dry the guinea-fowl and wrap the bacon or ham around it.
2. Melt the butter in a large, heavy pan, add the fowl and brown on all sides.
3. Chop the vegetables finely and add them, with the herbs to the pan. Season with salt and pepper. After a few minutes, add the wine and let it bubble, then add a little stock, lower the heat, cover and simmer for about 1¼ hours.
4. When the bird is cooked, transfer to a board, carve and then arrange on a heated serving dish.
5. Pour the cream into the pan, allow the sauce to thicken but not boil; sieve or blend, reheat and pour over the guinea-fowl.

Faraona alla panna e al marsala

Guinea-Fowl with Cream and Marsala

00:10 01:20

American	Ingredients	Metric/Imperial
1 (3 lb)	*Guinea-fowl hen*	*1 (1.4 kg / 3 lb)*
¼ cup	*Butter*	*50 g / 2 oz*
½ cup	*Marsala wine*	*125 ml / 4 fl oz*
	Salt and pepper	
1¼ cups	*Coffee (single) cream*	*300 ml / ½ pint*

1. Singe the guinea-fowl, wash and dry thoroughly both inside and outside.
2. Melt the butter in a heavy pan, add the fowl and brown all over, moistening with the marsala, a little at a time.
3. Allow the marsala to vaporize; season with salt and pepper and cook on a low heat for 50 minutes, adding the cream very gradually.
4. Remove guinea fowl and keep warm. Reduce the liquid in the pan slightly.
5. Cut the bird into 4 pieces, arrange on a heated serving dish and top with the fragrant sauce.

Starne arrosto

Roast Partridge

00:20 01:00 to 01:25

American	Ingredients	Metric/Imperial
2	*Partridges*	*2*
	Salt and pepper	
¼ lb	*Chicken livers*	*100 g / 4 oz*
1	*Slice of ham*	*1*
2 tbsp	*Butter*	*25 g / 1 oz*
1 tbsp	*Cognac*	*1 tbsp*
¼ tsp	*Chopped thyme*	*¼ tsp*
2	*Thin slices of fat bacon*	*2*
2	*Vine leaves*	*2*
	Fried bread	

1. Wipe the partridges and season the cavity.
2. Prepare the stuffing for the partridges by washing and chopping the chicken livers with those of the partridges.
3. Chop the ham, mix with the butter, chicken livers, the cognac, a pinch of thyme, salt and pepper. Put half of this mixture in each partridge and sew it up.
4. Wrap the birds in a thin slice of fat bacon and a vine leaf, then truss the partridges and cook on the spit or in a very hot oven (475°F / 240°C / Gas Mark 9.) When the partridges are almost cooked, remove the binding and bacon and brown over a brisk heat.
5. Cut in half and serve on slices of crisp fried bread.

Composta di piccioni

Pigeon Compote

00:25 01:15

American	Ingredients	Metric/Imperial
4	*Pigeons*	*4*
7 oz	*Pork fat*	*200 g / 7 oz*
	Butter	
2 tbsp	*White flour*	*15 g / ½ oz*
1 cup	*Stock*	*225 ml / 8 fl oz*
2	*Bay leaves*	*2*
2	*Sprigs of thyme*	*2*
5	*Sprigs of parsley*	*5*
	Salt and pepper	
16	*Small onions*	*16*
¼ lb	*Dried mushrooms*	*100 g / 4 oz*
1⅓ cup	*Green olives, stoned*	*225 g / 8 oz*

1. Wash the prepared pigeons. Heat the diced pork fat and butter, brown the pigeons.
2. Stir in the flour, allow it to color slightly then add the stock, bay leaves and sprigs of thyme and parsley; season with salt and pepper.
3. Add the onions, stir, cover and simmer on a low heat for about 40 minutes.
4. Wash the dried mushrooms and soak for at least 15 minutes in warm water. Add to the pigeons with the green olives, simmer for a further 20 minutes and remove herbs.
5. Serve the pigeons with boiled rice or pasta accompanied by a salad made from several different kinds of lettuce.

Piccioni selvatici con i funghi

Wild Pigeons with Mushrooms

00:30 00:60

American	Ingredients	Metric/Imperial
4	Pigeons	4
2 oz	Bacon	50 g / 2 oz
2 oz	Cooked ham	50 g / 2 oz
2 oz	Raw smoked ham	50 g / 2 oz
¼ cup	Butter	50 g / 2 oz
Scant ¼ cup	Oil	3 tbsp
3½ cups	Mushrooms	400 g / 14 oz
⅔ cup	Red wine	150 ml / ¼ pint
1 cup	Stock	225 ml / 8 fl oz
	Salt and pepper	

1. Pluck, clean, singe and cut the pigeons in half. Gut and cut them in half again lengthwise.
2. Chop the bacon and dice both the cooked and the raw ham. Fry in the heated oil and butter in a large pan together with the bacon. Simmer over a low heat.
3. Raise the heat, then put in the pigeon pieces and brown.
4. Wash and dry the mushrooms, slice and add to the pan. Allow to absorb the flavor and then put in the wine. As soon as the wine has evaporated, add salt, pepper and pour in the boiling stock. Cover the pan and simmer over a low heat for another 40 minutes before serving.

Piccioni alle cipolle

Pigeons in Onion Sauce

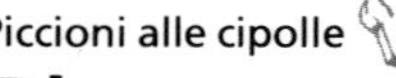

00:30 01:30

American	Ingredients	Metric/Imperial
4	Young pigeons	4
Scant ¼ cup	Vegetable oil	3 tbsp
¼ cup	Butter	50 g / 2 oz
1¼ lb	Onions	600 g / 1¼ lb
	Salt and pepper	
1	Sprig of thyme	1
1	Bay leaf	1
14 oz	Canned tomatoes	400 g / 14 oz

1. Wash the pigeons, cut each one into half, lengthwise. Heat the oil and butter in a large pan and brown the halved pigeons on either side.
2. Lower the heat and continue to cook slowly for 15 minutes. Remove from the pan and keep warm.
3. Chop the onions and put them into the same pan with a little more oil and allow to color slightly. Return the pigeons to the pan, season well with salt and pepper and crumble in the thyme and bay leaf, add tomatoes and break down with a spoon. Cover and cook over moderate heat for about 30 minutes, stirring from time to time.
4. As soon as the pigeons are done, arrange on a heated serving dish with the sauce poured over the top. A little water or stock may be added to clear the pan juices for the sauce.

Cook's tip: This dish requires less attention if cooked in the oven for 40 minutes until pigeons are tender at 325°F / 170°C / Gas Mark 3 from stage 3.

Piccioni alla Farnese

Stuffed Pigeons Braised in Wine

01:00 01:15

American	Ingredients	Metric/Imperial
8	Pigeons	8
1	Onion	1
½ cup	Butter	100 g / 4 oz
1 cup	Rice	225 g / 7 oz
2½ cups	Meat stock	600 ml / 1 pint
1 cup	Grated parmesan cheese	100 g / 4 oz
7 oz	Parma ham, diced	200 g / 7 oz
7 oz	Cooked peas	200 g / 7 oz
1 cup	Ground (minced) meat	225 g / 8 oz
¼ lb	Sausage, skinned and chopped	100 g / 4 oz
	Salt and pepper	
1 cup	Dry red wine	225 ml / 8 fl oz
1 cup	Cream	225 ml / 8 fl oz
1	Bunch of watercress	1

1. Bone the bodies of the pigeons, leaving only the bones in the legs and feet.
2. Chop the onion finely and sauté in a little butter; add the rice and sauté it for 5 minutes, stirring constantly. Moisten with stock, a little at a time and continue to cook over a moderate heat, uncovered, for 10 minutes.
3. Allow to cool then add the grated parmesan, diced parma ham, cooked peas, ground meat and sausage. Mix well and season with salt and pepper.
4. Stuff the pigeons with this mixture and sew up the aperture with kitchen thread.
5. Heat the remainder of the butter in a large pan and add the pigeons, brown on both sides. Add the red wine gradually, sprinkling it over the birds. When the wine has evaporated add a little hot stock and simmer gently for 45 minutes.
6. Remove the birds from the pan on to a board, cut each one into half and arrange on a hot serving dish. Keep warm while you prepare the sauce.
7. Strain the cooking liquid, add cream, reheat and pour over the pigeons.
8. Serve immediately garnished with watercress.

Colombacci alle olive

Wood Pigeons with Olives

00:20 00:55

American	Ingredients	Metric/Imperial
3	Medium-sized wood pigeons	3
¼ cup	Butter	50 g / 2 oz
¼ cup	Vegetable oil	50 ml / 2 fl oz
	Salt and pepper	
½ cup	Red wine	125 ml / 4 fl oz
⅔ cup	Green olives in brine, stoned	100 g / 4 oz
3 tbsp	Chopped parsley	2 tbsp

1. Wash and dry wood pigeons. Cut each in half, heat butter and oil in a flameproof dish and brown pigeons all over. Sprinkle with salt and pepper and cook over a low heat for 35 minutes.
2. Add the wine and allow to evaporate over a medium heat for 20 minutes. Add olives and parsley. Cook a further 5 minutes.
3. Transfer to a hot serving dish and serve.

Colombacci alla francese

Wood Pigeons French-Style

00:20 Marinating time 12:00 — 00:40

American	Ingredients	Metric/Imperial
3	*Wood pigeons*	3
	Salt and pepper	
2	*Garlic cloves*	2
2 tsp	*Chopped basil*	2 tsp
1	*Lemon*	1
½ cup	*Grappa*	125 ml / 4 fl oz
12	*Cloves*	12
¼ cup	*Flour*	25 g / 1 oz
3 tbsp	*Butter*	40 g / 1½ oz
½ cup	*Dry white wine*	125 ml / 4 fl oz
1 oz	*Bacon*	25 g / 1 oz
	Stock if required	

1. Thoroughly clean wood pigeons, including insides, then marinate for 12 hours with salt, pepper, garlic, basil, juice of the lemon, grappa and cloves. Remove from marinade, dry and coat in flour.
2. Heat butter and brown pigeons all over. Add marinade, wine and finely chopped bacon, cover and cook for 30 minutes over a medium heat, adding stock if necessary. Serve at once.

Piccioni alla Marengo

Pigeons Braised with Chicken Livers

00:30 — 01:10

American	Ingredients	Metric/Imperial
4	*Small pigeons*	4
1	*Sprig of rosemary*	1
4	*Bay leaves*	4
	Salt and pepper	
½ cup	*Butter*	100 g / 4 oz
3 tbsp	*Vegetable oil*	2 tbsp
¼ lb	*Chicken livers*	100 g / 4 oz
1	*Small onion*	1
1 oz	*Bacon*	25 g / 1 oz
1	*Small truffle*	1
3 tbsp	*Brandy*	2 tbsp
1 cup	*Stock*	225 ml / 8 fl oz

1. Clean, draw, wash and dry the pigeons. Divide the sprig of rosemary into 4 and place one piece with 1 bay leaf and a pinch of salt and pepper inside each pigeon; truss.
2. Heat half the butter and the oil in a large pan and brown the pigeons over a moderate heat.
3. Rinse and chop the chicken livers.
4. Chop the onion and bacon very finely. Melt the remainder of the butter in a second pan and sweat the onion and bacon until transparent; stir in the chicken livers and mash with a fork.
5. Cut the truffle into slivers, add it to the pan with the chicken livers and stir; leave to cook slowly for 10 minutes.
6. Sprinkle the brandy over the pigeons and then immediately tip in the liver and truffle mixture with all the juice.
7. Turn the pigeons several times, season, add the stock and simmer for 30 minutes over a moderate heat.
8. Transfer the birds to a serving dish and pour over the sauce.

Pernici in salmì alla padovana

Salmis of Partridges Paduan-Style

01:00 Hanging time 8 days — 01:40

American	Ingredients	Metric/Imperial
4	*Partridges*	4
½ cup	*Butter*	100 g / 4 oz
3	*Carrots*	3
1	*Sprig of rosemary*	1
8	*Slices of fat bacon*	8
⅔ cup	*Olive oil*	150 ml / ¼ pint
1	*Head of celery*	1
1	*Onion*	1
2	*Bay leaves*	2
	Livers (from the partridges)	
¼ cup	*Marsala wine*	50 ml / 2 fl oz
¼ lb	*Mushrooms*	100 g / 4 oz
	Salt and pepper	
3 tbsp	*Red currant jelly*	2 tbsp

1. Draw the partridges, keeping the livers and hang for 8 days in a dark place.
2. Pluck, singe, wash and lightly salt the inside of the bird.
3. Stuff with a mixture of a little butter, finely chopped carrots, rosemary and cover with 2 slices of bacon.
4. Heat half the butter and oil and brown the birds.
5. Heat the remaining butter and oil and cook the rest of the chopped carrot, celery and the onion with 2 bay leaves. Then add the chopped livers and, after a few minutes, sprinkle with marsala, cover and cook for 15 minutes. Rub through a sieve or blend.
6. Preheat the oven to 400°F / 200°C / Gas Mark 6.
7. Arrange the partridges on an oiled baking pan or large casserole. Pour over the vegetables and liver, put in a hot oven for 15 minutes. Reduce the temperature to 350°F / 180°C / Gas Mark 4. Cover and cook for 1 hour.
8. Remove birds on to a heated serving dish and keep warm.
9. Add 1¼ cup [300 ml / ½ pint] water or stock to the dish and scrape all the juices, reduce to make a gravy.
10. Slice the mushrooms very thinly. Pour the sauce into a pan and heat with the mushrooms for 3 minutes, season, then add red currant jelly. Serve the birds hot with the sauce.

Partridges in sauce

Starne fra due fuochi

Partridges Between Two Fires

00:35 | 01:55

American	Ingredients	Metric/Imperial
2	*Partridges*	2
	Salt and pepper	
2	*Slices of veal fat*	2
2	*Slices of ham fat*	2
¼ cup	*Butter*	*50 g / 2 oz*
¼ cup	*Vegetable oil*	*50 ml / 2 fl oz*
1	*Onion*	1
½ cup	*Dry white wine*	*125 ml / 4 fl oz*
1 cup	*Stock*	*225 ml / 8 fl oz*
¼ cup	*Flour*	*25 g / 1 oz*
1	*Seville orange*	1
2 oz	*Chicken livers*	*50 g / 2 oz*

1. Preheat the oven to 350°F / 180°C / Gas Mark 4.
2. Prepare the partridges, season with salt and pepper and surround them with the veal fat and slices of ham fat.
3. Heat the butter and oil in a casserole and brown the birds, add onion, chopped. After 10 minutes, pour in the dry white wine, a little stock and cook slowly in the oven for 1½ hours.
4. Remove the veal and ham fat and keep the birds warm in a low oven.
5. Add washed chopped partridge and chicken livers to the cooking juices in the casserole, cook stirring for 3 minutes.
6. Add the stock and cook for a few minutes. Mix a knob of butter with the flour, whisk to thicken the sauce then add the juice of the orange. Bring to the boil, stirring all the time and strain into a sauceboat. Carve partridges and serve with sauce.

Pernici alla salsa

Partridges in Sauce

00:50 | 01:30

American	Ingredients	Metric/Imperial
2	*Partridges*	2
	Salt and pepper	
½ cup	*Butter*	*100 g / 4 oz*
½ cup	*Dry white wine*	*125 ml / 4 fl oz*
1	*Carrot*	1
1	*Onion*	1
	Partridge giblets	
1	*Bay leaf*	1
1	*Garlic clove*	1
1	*Truffle*	1
1¼ cups	*Chicken stock*	*300 ml / ½ pint*
1	*Lemon*	1
	Fried bread	

1. Preheat the oven to 350°F / 180°C / Gas Mark 4.
2. Clean and wash the partridges, truss them, season with salt and pepper.
3. Heat half the butter and brown the birds evenly in a large casserole, pouring a few tablespoons of wine over them and turning them so that they cook evenly all over.
4. Cook in the oven for 45 minutes basting and turning from time to time. Allow to cool and remove the wing tips and the skin. Add these to the cooking juices in the casserole with the diced carrot, chopped onion, the heart and liver of the partridges. Add the bay leaf, the clove of garlic, salt and pepper and half of the remaining butter.
5. Brown on a medium heat, pouring over the remaining wine a little at a time. Add the truffle in slices and 1 cup [225 ml / 8 fl oz] stock.
6. Cook over a moderate heat, stirring frequently, for about 30 minutes. Strain the sauce. Rub the remains through a sieve or blend and add to the sauce.
7. Cut the partridges in half, add to the sauce with a little more stock or wine if necessary and cook for 15 minutes over a low heat. Stir frequently.
8. Drain the birds on to a heated serving dish with a slotted spoon. Add the rest of the butter and lemon juice to the sauce, stir well and pour over the birds. Serve hot.

Pasticcio di fagiano 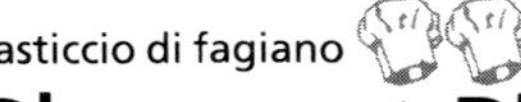

Pheasant Pie

01:00 | 01:45

American	Ingredients	Metric/Imperial
1 (2 lb)	*Pheasant*	*1 (1 kg / 2 lb)*
	Salt and pepper	
¼ cup	*Vegetable oil*	*50 ml / 2 fl oz*
⅓ cup	*Butter*	*75 g / 3 oz*
2 tbsp	*Chopped parsley*	*1½ tbsp*
1	*Celery stalk*	1
1	*Carrot*	1
1	*Onion*	1
¼ cup	*White wine*	*50 ml / 2 fl oz*
1 cup	*Béchamel sauce (see page 162)*	*225 ml / 8 fl oz*
3	*Eggs*	3
2 tsp	*Gelatin*	*2 tsp*
1¼ cups	*Stock*	*300 ml / ½ pint*
1	*Truffle*	1
1 oz	*Canned tongue*	*25 g / 1 oz*
1	*Lettuce*	1

1. Preheat the oven to 350°F / 180°C / Gas Mark 4.
2. Clean the pheasant, season with salt and pepper and brown in a mixture of half oil and half butter in a frying pan.
3. In a casserole put the parsley, some chopped celery, carrot, onion, sprinkle with wine and cook for 1 hour until the meat is tender.
4. Remove the pheasant meat from the bone and grind (mince) or put through a food processor.
5. Add the béchamel sauce to the ground meat, together with 3 egg yolks, blend well, then fold in 2 egg whites beaten to a very stiff froth.
6. Grease a pie mold with butter and line the inside with strips of parchment paper greased with butter. Pour in the mixture, so that the mold is three-quarters full, and shake it well. Cook over a bain-marie in a preheated oven and, when the mixture has solidified, allow it to cool in the mold. Turn out and remove the strips of paper.
7. Dissolve the gelatin in the stock. Clean the mold and pour in dissolved gelatin in a layer two fingers thick and refrigerate.
8. When the gelatin has set, garnish with slices of truffle and small cubes of tongue. Fill with more gelatin, set slightly and return the pie carefully on to the gelatin. Leave in the refrigerator to set. Unmold on to a bed of lettuce.

Fagiano alla piemontese

Pheasant Piedmont-Style

00:25 01:30

American	Ingredients	Metric/Imperial
1 (2 lb)	*Pheasant*	*1 (1 kg / 2 lb)*
⅓ cup	*Butter*	*75 g / 3 oz*
1	*Sprig of rosemary*	*1*
	Salt and pepper	
6	*Slices of bacon*	*6*
¼ cup	*Marsala wine*	*50 ml / 2 fl oz*
7 oz	*Black olives*	*200 g / 7 oz*

1. Preheat the oven to 350°F / 180°C / Gas Mark 4.
2. Clean the pheasant, wash carefully and dry.
3. Mix half the butter with the rosemary and season, place inside the pheasant. Wrap the bird in the slices of bacon and truss it. Put in an ovenproof dish with the remaining butter, cut into pieces. Cook until golden brown in the oven, basting occasionally with marsala wine and the cooking juices.
4. Remove the stones from the olives, take the bird from the oven, add the olives and cook for a further 30 minutes over a moderate heat on the stove.
5. Remove the pheasant, untie and carve on a board. Cut the bacon into pieces. Arrange the bird and bacon on a heated serving dish, add the olives and serve.

Fagiano alla cacciatora

Hunter's Pheasant

00:20 02:00

American	Ingredients	Metric/Imperial
¼ lb	*Fat bacon*	*100 g / 4 oz*
1	*Carrot*	*1*
2	*Celery stalks*	*2*
¼ lb	*Raw ham*	*100 g / 4 oz*
1	*Onion*	*1*
2 oz	*Dried mushrooms*	*50 g / 2 oz*
Scant ¼ cup	*Vegetable oil*	*3 tbsp*
1 tbsp	*Butter*	*1 tbsp*
2	*Oven-ready well hung pheasants*	*2*
½ cup	*Brandy*	*125 ml / 4 fl oz*
	Stock if needed	

1. Chop bacon, carrot, celery and ham finely, and slice onion. Soften dried mushrooms in tepid water, then drain.
2. Heat oil and butter in a large pan and sauté onion for 2 minutes. Add pheasants to pan and brown all over. Pour over brandy and add bacon, carrot, celery and ham to pan, with mushrooms.
3. Cover and cook over a low heat for about 2 hours, adding stock to the pan to prevent the ingredients drying out.
4. Transfer pheasants to a hot serving dish using a slotted spoon. Place vegetables around birds, pour juices over pheasants serve accompanied by puréed green vegetables tossed in butter.

Fagiano arrosto

Roast Pheasant

00:25 01:25

American	Ingredients	Metric/Imperial
1	*Pheasant*	*1*
¼ lb	*Fat bacon*	*100 g / 4 oz*
½ cup	*Butter*	*100 g / 4 oz*
1 cup	*Milk*	*225 ml / 8 fl oz*
3	*Slices of white bread*	*3*
3	*Cloves*	*3*
	Salt	
1	*Onion*	*1*

1. Pluck and singe the pheasant. Lard the breast and legs with the bacon, and put on the spit, moistening continually with melted butter.
2. Serve the pheasant accompanied simply by its cooking juices or by the following bread sauce.
3. Boil the milk and add the bread, the onion studded with cloves, salt, 1 tablespoon [15 g / ½ oz] of butter and cook for 15 minutes. Stir well, remove the onion and mix well.
4. Carve the pheasant and serve with the bread sauce, roast potatoes and steamed broccoli.

Fagiano alla romana

Roman-Style Pheasant

This dish can be served hot or cold.

00:25 01:30 to 02:00

American	Ingredients	Metric/Imperial
7 oz	*Sweetbreads*	*200 g / 7 oz*
1	*Onion*	*1*
7 oz	*Chopped veal*	*200 g / 7 oz*
¼ cup	*Melted butter*	*50 g / 2 oz*
½ tsp	*Chopped sage*	*½ tsp*
½ tsp	*Chopped rosemary*	*½ tsp*
1 tbsp	*Grated parmesan cheese*	*1 tbsp*
1	*Egg, beaten*	*1*
2	*Pheasants*	*2*
5 oz	*Fat bacon*	*150 g / 5 oz*
½ cup	*Vegetable oil*	*125 ml / 4 fl oz*
1 lb	*Boiled potatoes*	*450 g / 1 lb*

1. Preheat oven to 350°F / 180°C / Gas Mark 4.
2. Chop sweetbreads and onion and combine in a bowl with chopped meat, melted butter, sage, rosemary, parmesan and bind together with beaten egg. Stuff cavity of pheasants with forcemeat.
3. Cover pheasant breasts with fat bacon, place in a roasting pan, brush with oil and cook for about 1½ hours, basting with oil from time to time.
4. Pierce flesh of birds to check juices are clear, then remove stuffing in one piece. Joint pheasants into four, slice stuffing thickly. Place pheasant joints on a hot serving dish, surround with stuffing slices and boiled potatoes and pour over cooking juices. Serve hot.

Cook's tip: The dish can be refrigerated overnight and served cold the next day accompanied by a salad of several different kinds of lettuce and crusty bread.

Roast pheasant

Squab Mexican-style

Piccioncini alla messicana

Squab Mexican-Style

00:30 — 00:40

American	Ingredients	Metric/Imperial
4	Squab	4
3 tbsp	Soy sauce	2 tbsp
1 cup	Sesame seed oil	225 ml / 8 fl oz
2	Slices of smoked ham	2
1 tsp	Sugar	1 tsp
2 tbsp	Sherry	1½ tbsp
	Salt	
2 oz	Mushrooms	50 g / 2 oz
7 oz	Whole green beans	200 g / 7 oz
2 tsp	Cornstarch (cornflour)	2 tsp

1. Prepare the squab then split them but without severing the halves completely. Flatten slightly.
2. Moisten with two thirds of the soy sauce and sauté in sesame seed oil until crisp. Transfer to a casserole dish and stuff each squab with half a slice of smoked ham.
3. Mix the sugar and sherry together in a bowl, add a pinch of salt and the rest of the soy sauce. Pour this mixture over the squab, add ¼ cup [50 ml / 2 fl oz] boiling water, cover and simmer.
4. Slice the mushrooms, add to the casserole and continue to simmer for 15-20 minutes.
5. Preheat the oven to 325°F / 170°C / Gas Mark 3.
6. Cook the beans lightly in salted water; drain and place on a sheet of foil. Lift the squab with a slotted spoon and lay on top of the beans. Close the foil and place in the oven for 15 minutes.
7. Thicken the liquid in the casserole with the cornstarch (cornflour) and serve this sauce hot with the squab.

Beccacce alla re Enzo

King Enzo's Woodcocks

This is an ancient recipe dating back to King Enzo's imprisonment in Emilia.

00:25 — 01:15

American	Ingredients	Metric/Imperial
2	Onions	2
4	Garlic cloves	4
	The giblets	
½ cup	Lard	100 g / 4 oz
1 tsp	Chopped sage	1 tsp
1 tsp	Chopped rosemary	1 tsp
4	Dressed woodcocks	4
1 tbsp	Vegetable oil	1 tbsp
½ cup	Grappa	125 ml / 4 fl oz
1 cup	Whipping (double) cream	225 ml / 8 fl oz
¼ tsp	Pepper	¼ tsp
¼ tsp	Cinnamon	¼ tsp
¼ tsp	Unsweetened cocoa	¼ tsp
1 lb	Cooked potatoes for purée	450 g / 1 lb
1 cup	Milk	225 ml / 8 fl oz
½ cup	Butter	100 g / 4 oz
	Salt	
¼ tsp	Nutmeg	¼ tsp
1	Lemon	1

King Enzo's woodcocks

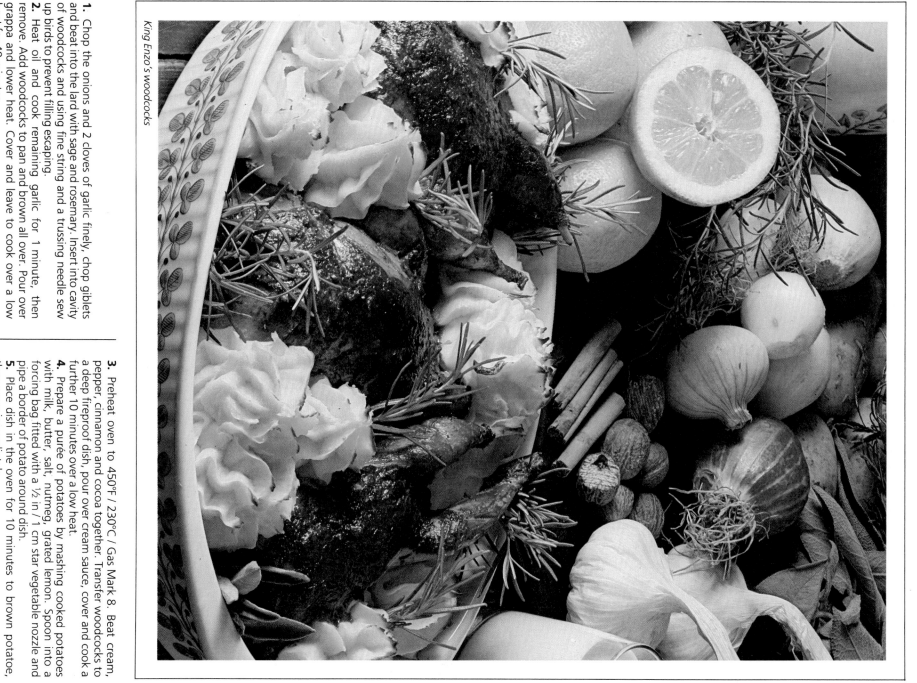

1. Chop the onions and 2 cloves of garlic finely, chop giblets and beat into the lard with sage and rosemary. Insert into cavity of woodcocks and using fine string and a trussing needle sew up birds to prevent filling escaping.
2. Heat oil and cook remaining garlic for 1 minute, then remove. Add woodcocks to pan and brown all over. Pour over grappa and lower heat. Cover and leave to cook over a low heat for 40 minutes.
3. Preheat oven to 450°F / 230°C / Gas Mark 8. Beat cream, pepper, cinnamon and cocoa together. Transfer woodcocks to a deep fireproof dish, pour over cream sauce, cover and cook a further 10 minutes over a low heat.
4. Prepare a purée of potatoes by mashing cooked potatoes with milk, butter, salt, nutmeg, grated lemon. Spoon into a forcing bag fitted with a ½ in / 1 cm star vegetable nozzle and pipe a border of potato around dish.
5. Place dish in the oven for 10 minutes to brown potatoe, then serve immediately.

Beccacce al crostone Montmartre

Woodcocks Montmartre-Style

00:20 Serves 8 — 00:40

American	Ingredients	Metric/Imperial
8	Dressed woodcocks	8
1 tsp	Chopped thyme	1 tsp
1 tsp	Chopped rosemary	1 tsp
1 tsp	Chopped sage	1 tsp
⅔ cup	Softened lard	150 g / 5 oz
12	Slices of fat bacon	12
2 tbsp	Vegetable oil	1½ tbsp
¼ lb	Chopped sausage	100 g / 4 oz
2 tbsp	Grated parmesan cheese	1½ tbsp
2	Egg yolks	2
½	Grated truffle	½
8	Large pieces of fried bread	8

1. Preheat oven to 375°F / 190°C / Gas Mark 5.
2. Chop giblets of birds. Chop thyme, rosemary and sage, then beat herbs into softened lard. Divide mixture into 12 balls placing a ball inside each bird.
3. Put birds in a large roasting pan (or 2 pans). Place a piece of bacon over each breast, glaze with half the oil, and bake for 40 minutes.
4. Meanwhile heat remaining oil in a pan, fry chopped giblets, sausage and parmesan until lightly browned. Pass through a strainer or blender, add yolks, grated truffle and beat in well.
5. Spread mixture over 8 pieces of fried bread, lay a game bird over each piece, place on a heated serving dish and serve.

Beccacce in salmì

Salmis of Woodcock

00:20 Marinating time 12:00 — 01:30

American	Ingredients	Metric/Imperial
2 quarts	Barbera wine	2 litre / 3½ pints
1	Carrot	1
1	Onion	1
1	Celery stalk	1
1 tbsp	Cinnamon	1 tbsp
1 tbsp	Peppercorns	1 tbsp
1 tbsp	Unsweetened cocoa	1 tbsp
4	Large dressed woodcocks	4
	or	
8	Small woodcocks	8
¼ cup	Butter	50 g / 2 oz
¼ cup	Vegetable oil	50 ml / 2 fl oz
1 tsp	Chopped sage	1 tsp
1 tsp	Chopped rosemary	1 tsp
14 oz	Peeled tomatoes, strained	400 g / 14 oz
1 tbsp	Cornstarch	1 tbsp

1. Prepare marinade by pouring in a bowl the red wine and chopped carrot, onion and celery, cinnamon, peppercorns and cocoa. Place woodcocks in marinade and leave overnight.
2. Drain off marinade and retain. Heat butter and oil in a large pan and sauté woodcocks, until lightly browned all over, with sage and rosemary. Then cover with strained tomatoes. Cover and cook for about 1½ hours over a low heat. Preheat oven to 300°F / 150°C / Gas Mark 2.
3. Remove cooked woodcocks and place on a hot serving dish, cover and keep warm in the oven. Add drained marinade to pan, stir into tomato mixture. Blend cornstarch with a little water, add to pan and bring to boil stirring all the time.
4. Pour sauce into a serving boat to accompany woodcocks and serve with boiled potatoes.

Beccaccia al cognac

Woodcocks in Cognac

00:15 — 00:50

American	Ingredients	Metric/Imperial
7 oz	Chicken livers	200 g / 7 oz
¼ cup	Vegetable oil	50 ml / 2 fl oz
4	Woodcocks	4
⅓ cup	Cognac	4 tbsp
4 tbsp	Stock	3 tbsp
1	Lemon	1

1. Preheat the oven to 300°F / 150°C / Gas Mark 2.
2. Wash and chop chicken livers.
3. Heat oil in a large frying pan and brown the trussed woodcocks all over, reduce heat, cover and cook a further 40 minutes. Remove birds from pan, and keep warm in oven on a large heatproof serving dish.
4. Brown livers in remaining fat in a pan, then pour over cognac. Set alight, then when flame has subsided, add stock and lemon juice and stir in well.
5. Pour the chicken liver sauce over woodcocks and serve immediately.

Coniglio selvatico in fricassea

Wild Rabbit Fricassée

00:20 — 01:30

American	Ingredients	Metric/Imperial
7 oz	Small onions	200 g / 7 oz
3 tbsp	Vegetable oil	2 tbsp
3 tbsp	Butter	40 g / 1½ oz
1 (2 lb)	Wild rabbit, jointed	1 (1 kg / 2 lb)
½ cup	White wine	125 ml / 4 fl oz
½ cup	Water	125 ml / 4 fl oz
	Salt and pepper	
2	Egg yolks	2
1 tsp	Cornstarch (cornflour)	1 tsp
1 tbsp	Lemon juice	1 tbsp
Scant ¼ cup	Whipping (double) cream	3 tbsp

1. Peel onions. Heat oil and butter in a large pan and sauté onions for 2-3 minutes. Remove and put on one side. Add rabbit joints to pan and cook until lightly browned all over. Return onion to pan.
2. Pour over wine, water, and season with salt and pepper. Cover and simmer for 1-1½ hours until rabbit is tender. Preheat oven to 300°F / 150°C / Gas Mark 2. Drain rabbit joints and onions and put on a hot serving dish. Cover with foil and keep warm in the oven.

3. Meanwhile prepare sauce: beat the egg yolks, cornstarch (cornflour), lemon juice and cream together. Pour into stock in pan and bring slowly to the boil stirring all the time.
4. Pour lemon cream sauce over rabbit and serve at once.

Coniglio selvatico alla sarda

Sardinian Wild Rabbit

00:20 01:20

American	Ingredients	Metric/Imperial
1 (1½ lb)	*Small rabbit, jointed*	*1 (700 g / 1½ lb)*
1	*Onion*	*1*
Scant ¼ cup	*Vegetable oil*	*3 tbsp*
	Salt and pepper	
½ cup	*Water*	*125 ml / 4 fl oz*
2 cups	*Dry white wine*	*450 ml / ¾ pint*

1. Joint rabbit and remove liver and chop. Peel and chop onion. Heat oil in a fireproof dish and sauté onion for 2-3 minutes to brown rabbit joint. Season with salt and pepper and cook over a low heat, adding water. Cover and cook for about 1 hour over a low heat.
2. Add liver to pan and white wine, cover and continue cooking for about 10 minutes.
3. Serve the rabbit on a hot serving dish, pour juices over.

Coniglio del cacciatore 

Huntsman's Rabbit

00:30 01:00
Marinading time 12:00

American	Ingredients	Metric/Imperial
1	*Rabbit*	*1*
1	*Carrot*	*1*
1	*Celery*	*1*
1	*Onion*	*1*
4	*Cloves*	*4*
4	*Bay leaves*	*4*
	Pepper	
¼ tsp	*Nutmeg*	*¼ tsp*
2½ cups	*Red wine*	*600 ml / 1 pint*
¼ cup	*Butter*	*50 g / 2 oz*
3 tbsp	*Vegetable oil*	*2 tbsp*
6	*Canned tomatoes*	*6*
	Rabbit liver	

1. Cut the skinned rabbit into pieces and, after washing it thoroughly, place it in a dish with a lid.
2. Add the carrot, peeled and cut into pieces, the celery, the onion with a few cloves stuck into it, bay leaves, pepper, nutmeg and the red wine. Marinate the rabbit for 12 hours.
3. After marinating, chop the vegetables from the marinade. Heat the butter and oil in a large saucepan, as soon as the onion starts to brown, add the rabbit joints. Allow the flavors to mingle and cover with the wine from the marinade. Cook slowly, allowing the wine to evaporate gently.
4. Halfway through cooking add the mashed tomatoes, the rabbit liver, if available, and adjust the seasoning.
5. Remove the rabbit from the cooking sauce to a heated dish, strain the sauce, with the liver, through a vegetable sieve or blender. Return the sauce and the rabbit to the pan and heat slowly. Serve piping hot with crusty bread.

Coniglio alla cacciatora

Rabbit Chasseur

00:20 01:15

American	Ingredients	Metric/Imperial
2	*Large onions*	*2*
Scant ¼ cup	*Vegetable oil*	*3 tbsp*
2 tbsp	*Butter*	*25 g / 1 oz*
1	*Young rabbit*	*1*
	Salt and pepper	
14 oz	*Peeled tomatoes*	*400 g / 14 oz*
1 tbsp	*Chopped parsley*	*1 tbsp*

1. Peel and wash the onions and cut them into thin rings.
2. Heat the oil and butter in a frying pan. Cook on a very low heat, the onions should break apart, but should not brown.
3. Clean and joint the rabbit. Raise the heat and push onions to one side, fry the rabbit joints until golden, season with salt and pepper.
4. Preheat the oven to 350°F / 180°C / Gas Mark 4.
5. Add the well mashed tomatoes and 1¼ cups [300 ml / ½ pint] water, cover and cook in the oven for 1 hour. Sprinkle with parsley before serving.

Coniglio in porchetta Valsavaranche

Stuffed Rabbit Valsavaranche

00:45 01:30

American	Ingredients	Metric/Imperial
1	*Small rabbit*	*1*
1½ cups	*Ground (minced) meat (can be left-overs)*	*350 g / 12 oz*
¼ tsp	*Chopped rosemary*	*¼ tsp*
¼ tsp	*Chopped sage*	*¼ tsp*
2 tbsp	*Grated parmesan cheese*	*1½ tbsp*
2	*Eggs*	*2*
	Salt and pepper	
2	*Garlic cloves*	*2*
1	*Onion*	*1*
⅓ cup	*Vegetable oil*	*4 tbsp*
1 cup	*Cream*	*225 ml / 8 fl oz*
Scant ¼ cup	*Vinegar*	*3 tbsp*

1. Open the rabbit lengthwise, making a cut under the belly so that you can clean it thoroughly.
2. Grind (mince) the edible rabbit offal together with the meat and a little rosemary and sage. Add the grated parmesan and eggs to obtain a soft stuffing mixture and season.
3. Fill the rabbit with the stuffing, sew up the opening well.
4. Preheat the oven to 325°F / 170°C / Gas Mark 3.
5. Crush the garlic and chop the onions and fry in heated oil for 5 minutes, push to one side.
6. Raise the heat, put in the rabbit and brown on all sides. Moisten a little at a time with the cream mixed with the vinegar to form a thick sauce, which should not stick. (If necessary dilute with a little stock or hot water.) Cover and cook the rabbit for 1 hour in the oven.
7. Place the rabbit on a heated serving dish. Strain the sauce through a sieve and serve in a sauceboat.

Coniglio in fricassea

Rabbit Fricassée

00:30 01:25

American	Ingredients	Metric/Imperial
3 tbsp	Vegetable oil	2 tbsp
¼ cup	Butter	50 g / 2 oz
½ lb	Onions	225 g / 8 oz
	Flour	
2	Forequarters rabbit	2
½ cup	White wine	125 ml / 4 fl oz
1 ¼ cups	Stock	300 ml / ½ pint
	Salt and pepper	
2	Egg yolks	2
1	Lemon	1
3 tbsp	Cream	2 tbsp
1 tbsp	Parsley	1 tbsp

1. Preheat the oven to 350°F / 180°C / Gas Mark 4. Heat oil and butter in a casserole, fry diced onions, drain and put aside.
2. Put the floured rabbit pieces into the same pan, brown them well, then replace the onions. Moisten with the white wine, add stock and season with salt and pepper. Cover and cook for 1 hour in the oven.
3. Beat egg yolks with the juice of a lemon and the cream.
4. Remove the rabbit and the onions with a slotted spoon on to a heated serving dish. Pour the egg mixture into the casserole on a very low heat, mix well with the cooking juices.
5. Pour the sauce over the rabbit and sprinkle with parsley.

Umido di coniglio alla francese

Casserole of Rabbit

00:10 02:15

American	Ingredients	Metric/Imperial
½	Cabbage	½
4	Onions	4
3½ cups	Mushrooms	400 g / 14 oz
1	Carrot	1
1	Celery stalk	1
1	Shallot	1
1	Tomato	1
1¾ lb	Rabbit	800 g / 1¾ lb
3 tbsp	Flour	2 tbsp
1 tbsp	Vegetable oil	1 tbsp
1 tbsp	Butter	1 tbsp
⅔ cup	Wine	150 ml / ¼ pint
¼ cup	Cognac	50 ml / 2 fl oz
	Salt and pepper	

1. Preheat oven to 325°F / 170°C / Gas Mark 3. Line a casserole dish with some cleaned cabbage leaves.
2. Chop the onions, mushrooms, carrot, celery, shallot and tomato. Cut rabbit into small pieces, toss in flour.
3. Heat oil and butter and sauté meat until lightly browned all over, drain and transfer to the casserole dish.
4. Add the onions and the mushrooms to pan and cook for 2-3 minutes, then place with the meat in the casserole. Add remaining vegetables, pour over wine and cognac and season. Cover with cabbage leaves and a lid. Bake for about 2 hours.

Coniglio tonné caldo alla còrsa

Corsican Hot Rabbit with Tuna

This is an ancient and exquisite dish from Ajaccio, and was introduced to the French Court by Letitia Bonaparte.

01:00 01:15

American	Ingredients	Metric/Imperial
1	Rabbit	1
1	Stock cube	1
1	Bouquet garni	1
1 cup	Mayonnaise (see page 175)	225 ml / 8 fl oz
¼ lb	Tuna	100 g / 4 oz
2	Anchovies	2
1 tsp	Capers	1 tsp
	Cabbage leaves	

1. Put the rabbit in a pan with 1 quart [1 litre / 1¾ pints] stock or water and a bouquet garni, bring to the boil and simmer for about 45 minutes. Cool in the liquid for 15 minutes.
2. Drain, remove the flesh from the bones, chop up the meat.
3. Mix the well-seasoned mayonnaise with the sieved or blended tuna, anchovies and chopped capers.
4. Line an ovenproof serving dish with boiled and drained cabbage leaves, and on top of the leaves arrange the chopped rabbit meat. Cover with the tuna sauce and let it rest, covered with foil for 2 hours. Then heat the oven to 350°F / 180°C / Gas Mark 4.
5. Put dish in oven for 10-15 minutes. Serve immediately.

Lepre in salmì alla panna

Jugged Hare with Cream

01:00 06:00
Marinating time 48:00

American	Ingredients	Metric/Imperial
1 (4½ lb)	Hare	1 (2 kg / 4½ lb)
2	Garlic cloves	2
3	Sprigs of rosemary	3
3	Sprigs of sage	3
2	Bay leaves	2
3	Sprigs of thyme	3
1	Small bunch of basil	1
¼ tsp	Nutmeg	¼ tsp
4	Cloves	4
1	Onion	1
1	Carrot	1
1	Head of celery	1
1 quart	Red wine	1 litre / 1¾ pints
¼ cup	Butter	50 g / 2 oz
½ cup	Vegetable oil	125 ml / 4 fl oz
1	Slice of fat bacon	1
1 quart	Stock	1 litre / 1¾ pints
	Salt and pepper	
1 tbsp	Sugar	1 tbsp
2 tbsp	Rum	1½ tbsp
1 tbsp	Unsweetened cocoa	1 tbsp
1 tbsp	White flour	1 tbsp
1 cup	Whipping (double) cream	225 ml / 8 fl oz

Jugged hare with cream

1. Clean and wash the skinned hare, collect the blood, cut into pieces.
2. Marinate the hare in all the garlic, finely chopped herbs, spices, vegetables and red wine for 48 hours.
3. Heat the oil and butter in a large pan, add chopped bacon fat, brown the jointed hare sprinkling with half of the marinade.
4. When the pot starts to become dry, add the other half of the marinade and stock and cook, covered, over a low heat for about 4 hours or in the oven preheated to 325°F / 170°C / Gas Mark 3.
5. When the meat is easily detached from the bone, add the blood and cook for a further 15 minutes or so, season well.
6. In a separate pan, melt some butter, add the sugar, allow it to melt, then add the rum, the cocoa and the flour. Stir well so that all the ingredients are absorbed by the butter, then add the pieces of hare, followed by the strained cooking juices.
7. Add the cream gradually, carefully stirring all the time. Simmer for 5 minutes and serve with polenta.

Leprotto alla siciliana

Sicilian Hare

00:30 01:00 to 01:30

American	Ingredients	Metric/Imperial
1	*Young hare*	1
¼ lb	*Grated ewe's milk cheese*	100 g / 4 oz
⅔ cup	*Sultanas*	100 g / 4 oz
7 oz	*Black olives*	200 g / 7 oz
½ cup	*Vegetable oil*	125 ml / 4 fl oz
	Bilberry sauce (optional)	
Sauce		
1 lb	*Bilberries*	225 g / 8 oz
1 tsp	*Mustard*	1 tsp
1	*Egg yolk*	1

1. Preheat the oven to 400°F / 200°C / Gas Mark 6.
2. Thoroughly clean a young hare.
3. Chop up the usable intestines, add ewe's milk cheese and washed sultanas. Stir the pitted (stoned) black olives into the mixture and fill the belly of the hare. Cooking can take place in a hot oven for 1 hour or on the spit for 1½ hours, whichever is preferred, basting with the oil.
4. The hare is served sprinkled with the very hot pan juices and accompanied by a sweet spicy bilberry sauce. Rub bilberries through a strainer with mustard and egg yolk and serve in a sauceboat.

Lepre alla cacciatora

Huntsman's Hare

00:20 00:45

American	Ingredients	Metric/Imperial
1 (2 lb)	*Saddle of hare*	1 (1 kg / 2 lb)
½ cup	*Vegetable oil*	125 ml / 4 fl oz
¼ cup	*Butter*	50 g / 2 oz
2 oz	*Bacon*	50 g / 2 oz
	Basil	
5	*Sprigs of parsley*	5
½ tsp	*Chopped rosemary*	½ tsp
12	*Juniper berries*	12
1	*Carrot*	1
1	*Celery stalk*	1
1	*Onion*	1
2 cups	*Stock*	450 ml / ¾ pint
4	*Peeled tomatoes*	4
1 tbsp	*Cornstarch (cornflour)*	1 tbsp
1 cup	*White wine*	225 ml / 8 fl oz
	Salt and pepper	

1. Cut the saddle into joints, wash and dry thoroughly. Heat a mixture of oil and butter in a large casserole, add cubed bacon, basil, parsley, rosemary, juniper berries, carrot, celery, onion. When the mixture has turned golden, push to one side and add the pieces of hare.
2. Continue cooking, turning occasionally. Add the stock and the tomatoes, thicken with cornstarch (cornflour) and finally put in the wine, salt and pepper. Cover and complete the cooking.
3. Serve piping hot sprinkled with parsley.

Lepre casalinga in salmì

Hare Marinaded in Red Wine

00:30 02:30
Marinating time 24:00

American	Ingredients	Metric/Imperial
1 (4½ lb)	*Hare, jointed*	1 (2 kg / 4½ lb)
1 (70 cl)	*Bottle red wine*	1 (70 cl)
3	*Onions*	3
1	*Carrot*	1
1	*Head of celery*	1
2	*Sprigs of thyme*	2
¾ cup	*Flour*	75 g / 3 oz
	Salt and pepper	
⅓ cup	*Butter*	75 g / 3 oz
	Vegetable oil	
2 oz	*Cooked ham*	50 g / 2 oz

1. Wash the pieces of hare very carefully and steep in red wine with a piece of onion and a finely chopped carrot.
2. Add half the chopped celery and thyme, make sure the pieces of hare are completely covered and remain in the marinade for at least 24 hours, in a cool place.
3. Drain the hare joints and dust with seasoned flour.
4. Heat the oil and butter in a large frying pan, cook the pieces of meat until golden on each side.
5. Add finely chopped onion, the remaining chopped celery, season with salt and pepper. Continue cooking until no more blood can be seen, about 15 minutes on a low to medium heat. Sprinkle with marinade, then add the chopped ham. Cover and cook over a low heat for 2 hours.
6. Remove hare joints on to a heated serving dish and keep warm. Strain or blend the sauce, reheat and pour over the hare.

Cosciotto di cervo alla aostana

Haunch of Venison Aosta-Style

00:25 03:00

American	Ingredients	Metric/Imperial
1	*Haunch of venison*	1
8	*Garlic cloves*	8
12	*Slices of bacon*	12
⅔ cup	*Vegetable oil*	150 ml / ¼ pint
	Salt and pepper	
½ cup	*Cognac*	125 ml / 4 fl oz

1. Prepare fire for spit roasting, or preheat oven to 400°F / 200°C / Gas Mark 6.
2. Stud a haunch of venison with garlic and small pieces of fat bacon, brush with oil and put on the spit, start cooking, allowing 1½ hours per 2 lb / 1 kg of meat, turning from time to time. Sprinkle with pepper and a little salt, since meat is already flavored, and use fat oozing out to baste.
3. When half-cooked, pour over cognac, then baste again. The meat is cooked when the juices run clear when it is pierced with a fork.
4. Serve the haunch whole, on a large wooden chopping board or on a broad metal dish. Carve at the table.

Daino alla castellana

Venison Castelli-Style

00:20 02:00

American	Ingredients	Metric/Imperial
2 lb	*Venison*	*1 kg / 2 lb*
1	*Onion*	*1*
2	*Garlic cloves*	*2*
¼ lb	*Bacon*	*100 g / 4 oz*
½ cup	*Vegetable oil*	*125 ml / 4 fl oz*
3	*Celery stalks*	*3*
3	*Carrots*	*3*
2 tbsp	*Chopped parsley*	*1½ tbsp*
3	*Tomatoes*	*3*
1	*Leek*	*1*
1 quart	*Red Barbera or Barola wine*	*1 litre / 1¾ pints*

1. Preheat oven to 300°F / 150°C / Gas Mark 2.
2. Cut meat into bite-size pieces, chop onion, garlic and bacon. Heat oil in a fireproof casserole dish and when very hot add meat to pan and brown all over. Add onion, garlic and bacon to pan and cook a further 2 minutes, stirring briskly. Remove from heat.
3. Finely chop celery, carrots, parsley, tomatoes and leeks, add to pan and cook for 10 minutes. Pour over wine, cover and cook in the oven for about 1½-2 hours and serve piping hot.

Capriolo alla crema

Venison with Cream

00:25 03:00

American	Ingredients	Metric/Imperial
1	*Onion*	*1*
1	*Celery stalk*	*1*
2 tbsp	*Vegetable oil*	*1½ tbsp*
½ cup	*Butter*	*100 g / 4 oz*
2	*Garlic cloves*	*2*
1	*Haunch of venison*	*1*
	Salt and pepper	
6	*Sage leaves*	*6*
2 cups	*Dry white wine*	*450 ml / ¾ pint*
2 cups	*Stock*	*450 ml / ¾ pint*
3 tbsp	*Flour*	*2 tbsp*
½ cup	*Whisky*	*125 ml / 4 fl oz*
½ cup	*Coffee (single) cream*	*125 ml / 4 fl oz*

1. Peel and slice onion, chop celery. Heat oil and butter together in a large pan and brown vegetables with garlic for 2-3 minutes, then remove from pan and keep on one side.
2. Add venison haunch to pan and over a brisk heat brown all over, seasoning with salt and pepper. Add sage leaves, wine and sautéd vegetables and cook for about 2 hours, or cook in the oven at 350°F / 180°C / Gas Mark 4.
3. Add stock to pan, cover and simmer for a further hour, then remove haunch and put on a hot plate.
4. Strain stock into a saucepan, blend flour and whisky together using a fork to remove lumps, pour into stock and bring to the boil stirring all the time. Off the heat, stir in cream.
5. Carve haunch and arrange on a hot serving dish. Pour over cream sauce and serve hot with a purée of potato.

Daino con riso

Venison with Rice

00:25 02:00

American	Ingredients	Metric/Imperial
1	*Shoulder of venison*	*1*
1	*Onion*	*1*
1	*Garlic clove*	*1*
2 oz	*Belly pork*	*50 g / 2 oz*
½ cup	*Vegetable oil*	*125 ml / 4 fl oz*
1 cup	*Stock*	*225 ml / 8 fl oz*
1	*Head of celery*	*1*
1	*Carrot*	*1*
1	*Bay leaf*	*1*
¼ tsp	*Chopped basil*	*¼ tsp*
	Salt and pepper	
2	*Plum tomatoes, peeled*	*2*
⅔ cup	*Rice*	*150 g / 5 oz*
¼ cup	*Grated cheese*	*25 g / 1 oz*
1 tbsp	*Chopped parsley*	*1 tbsp*
1	*Black truffle, sliced*	*1*

1. Cut the meat into bite-size pieces. Chop onion very finely together with the garlic clove. Dice belly pork. Heat oil and, when very hot, brown meat all over.
2. Add the onion, garlic and the belly pork to pan and cook a further 2 minutes, stirring briskly. Pour over stock, add chopped celery, carrot, bay leaf, basil, salt, pepper and sieved tomatoes.
3. Cover pan and cook for about 2 hours over a low heat. Meanwhile, boil rice and drain, then put into pan with venison.
4. Spoon venison and rice mixture onto a hot serving dish, sprinkle with grated cheese and parsley, garnish with black truffle and serve.

Capriolo in salsa di menta

Venison in Mint Sauce

00:20 01:00

American	Ingredients	Metric/Imperial
1¾ lb	*Venison*	*800 g / 1¾ lb*
½ cup	*Vegetable oil*	*125 ml / 4 fl oz*
	Salt and pepper	
1 tbsp	*Chopped mint*	*1 tbsp*
1 tbsp	*Chopped basil*	*1 tbsp*
2	*Garlic cloves*	*2*
2	*Egg yolks*	*2*
1 tsp	*Vinegar*	*1 tsp*
1 tbsp	*Butter*	*15 g / ½ oz*
	Chopped parsley	

1. Preheat oven to 400°F / 200°C / Gas Mark 6.
2. Cut venison into bite-size pieces and put into a roasting pan. Pour over oil, season, cover and bake for about 1 hour.
3. Chop mint and basil with garlic and put into a bowl. Add beaten egg yolks, vinegar and beat until frothy. Place bowl over a pan of water and cook over a medium heat, beating butter into sauce. When thickened pour into a sauceboat.
4. Spoon cooked venison onto a hot serving dish, garnish with chopped parsley and serve with herb sauce.

Daino o capriolo in crostini

Young Deer on Fried Bread

00:40 | 00:40

American	Ingredients	Metric/Imperial
2 lb	*Game*	*1 kg / 2 lb*
½ cup	*Vegetable oil*	*125 ml / 4 fl oz*
	Salt and pepper	
¾ lb	*Rolled smoked bacon, sliced thinly*	*350 g / 12 oz*
4	*Sprigs of rosemary*	*4*
1 tsp	*Powdered garlic*	*1 tsp*
8	*Whole slices of sandwich loaf*	*8*
½ cup	*Butter*	*100 g / 4 oz*
1 oz	*Goose liver paté*	*25 g / 1 oz*

1. Cut the deer into small uniform pieces. Steep in oil after seasoning it with salt and pepper for 20 minutes, then lard with thinly sliced bacon.
2. Preheat the oven to 400°F / 200°C / Gas Mark 6.
3. Tie up the slices of bacon tightly, forming small cases, and insert some sprigs of rosemary under the thread. Thread the pieces onto skewers and put them on an oiled baking pan; sprinkle with powdered garlic. Cook in the oven for 40 minutes. If necessary, sprinkle with a little oil beaten with an equal amount of water.
4. On slices of sandwich loaf, spread a cream made of butter and goose liver paté.
5. During the last 5 minutes of cooking the meat, heat the fried bread in the oven and arrange it on a heated serving dish. Place the skewers on the fried bread, without pulling off the meat, and serve piping hot.

Arrosto misto di selvaggina

Mixed Roast Game

00:20 | 00:20

American	Ingredients	Metric/Imperial
2 lb	*Mixed game : venison, hare, wild rabbit, young wild boar*	*1 kg / 2 lb*
	Seasoned flour	
¼ cup	*Vegetable oil*	*50 ml / 2 fl oz*
¼ cup	*Cognac*	*50 ml / 2 fl oz*
	Salt and pepper	
¼ tsp	*Paprika*	*¼ tsp*
2	*Lemons*	*2*
	Chopped parsley	

1. Preheat the oven to 425°F / 220°C / Gas Mark 7.
2. Cut game into equal sized pieces, toss in seasoned flour, thread onto a spit or large skewers. Brush with oil and place threaded skewers on a baking sheet.
3. Place in oven for 15-20 minutes, sprinkle with cognac from time to time, and turn occasionally.
4. Whisk pepper, salt and paprika into lemon juice. Put cooked skewers on a large hot ovenproof plate and pour lemon sauce over. Garnish with chopped parsley and serve.

Young deer on fried bread

Cinghialetto alla auvergnese

Wild Boar Auvergne-Style

00:30 Marinating time 02:00 — 03:00

American	Ingredients	Metric/Imperial
1 (4½ lb)	*Suckling wild boar*	*1 (2 kg / 4½ lb)*
18	*Slices of bacon*	*18*
10	*Garlic cloves*	*10*
1 tsp	*Sage, chopped*	*1 tsp*
1 tsp	*Rosemary, chopped*	*1 tsp*
2	*Onions, chopped*	*2*
1¼ cups	*Lard*	*275 g / 10 oz*
1 quart	*Brandy*	*1 litre / 1¾ pints*
1¼ cups	*Vegetable oil*	*300 ml / ½ pint*
	Salt and pepper	
4½ lb	*Russet apples*	*2 kg / 4½ lb*
4½ lb	*Canadian apples*	*2 kg / 4½ lb*
1 cup	*Fruit alcohol*	*225 ml / 8 fl oz*

1. Prepare fire for spit-roasting or preheat oven to 400°F / 200°C / Gas Mark 6.
2. Thoroughly clean wild boar and lard with bacon strips and garlic cloves inserted under skin.
3. Finely chop giblets and mix these with sage, rosemary, onion, three quarters of the lard and put into cavity of boar. Place boar in a large bowl, pour over brandy and leave for 2 hours, turning from time to time.
4. Thread boar on a spit, brush with oil beaten with salt and pepper. Cook over a medium heat allowing 1½ hours per 2 lb / 1 kg of meat, turning frequently.
5. Meanwhile slit skins of apples around centres and put in a roasting pan. Place in oven and bake for 25 minutes.
6. Place cooked boar on a large heated serving dish, surround with whole apples, then pour over fruit alcohol. Set this alight and serve boar immediately.

Cinghiale alla montenegrina

Wild Boar Montenegro-Style

00:40 — 02:00

American	Ingredients	Metric/Imperial
1	*Whole small wild boar*	*1*
	Salt	
5 tbsp	*Paprika*	*4 tbsp*
1 cup	*Vegetable oil*	*225 ml / 8 fl oz*
¾ lb	*Mustard seeds*	*350 g / 12 oz*
14 oz	*Carrots*	*400 g / 14 oz*
¾ lb	*Onions*	*350 g / 12 oz*
¾ lb	*Zucchini (courgettes)*	*350 g / 12 oz*
¾ lb	*Tomatoes*	*350 g / 12 oz*
2⅓ cups	*Raisins*	*400 g / 14 oz*
1	*Sweet red pepper*	*1*
	Stock	
½ cup	*Slivovitz*	*125 ml / 4 fl oz*

1. Put the small wild boar in an earthenware pot over a wood fire and flavor with salt and paprika.
2. Prepare a sauce with the oil, mustard seeds, carrots, onions, zucchini (courgettes), tomatoes, softened raisins, salt and sweet red pepper. Immerse all the ingredients in a little hot stock and cook for about 30 minutes stirring continuously.
3. Rub through a sieve and pour the sauce obtained over the wild boar, which is then sprinkled with slivovitz. Allow to marinate for a while, then serve at the table.

Cook's tip: small wild boar will be difficult to find. If necessary, you could replace it with a small suckling pig or one of the famous mini-pigs originating from Australia and now also bred in Italy and other countries.

Cinghiale agrodolce

Sweet and Sour Wild Boar

00:30 Marinating time 48:00 — 03:30

American	Ingredients	Metric/Imperial
¼ lb	*Onion*	*100 g / 4 oz*
1½ oz	*Shallot*	*40 g / 1½ oz*
¼ lb	*Carrot*	*100 g / 4 oz*
4	*Garlic cloves*	*4*
1	*Celery stalk*	*1*
¼ cup	*Vegetable oil*	*50 ml / 2 fl oz*
2	*Bay leaves*	*2*
3	*Sprigs of parsley*	*3*
½ tsp	*Chopped thyme*	*½ tsp*
6	*Peppercorns*	*6*
2	*Cloves*	*2*
1½ quarts	*White wine*	*1.5 litres / 2½ pints*
Scant ¼ cup	*Vinegar*	*3 tbsp*
¼ cup	*Butter*	*50 g / 2 oz*
4 lb	*Boned leg of wild boar*	*1.8 kg / 4 lb*
2 cups	*Red wine*	*450 ml / ¾ pint*
½ oz	*Grated plain chocolate*	*15 g / ½ oz*
2 tbsp	*Sugar*	*25 g / 1 oz*
2 tbsp	*Pine kernels*	*1½ tbsp*
3 tbsp	*Sultanas*	*2 tbsp*
¼ lb	*Candied fruit in pieces*	*100 g / 4 oz*
	Salt	

1. Peel and chop onion, shallot, carrot, garlic and celery. Heat oil and when very hot cook half the vegetables for 2-3 minutes with bay leaf, parsley, thyme, pepper and cloves.
2. Pour over the white wine with half vinegar and boil for 10 minutes and leave to cool. Place meat in a large bowl, pour over marinade, and leave for 48 hours turning meat from time to time. Strain, marinade and discard.
3. Heat butter in a large pan, fry remaining garlic, onion, celery and carrot. Push these to one side and add boar meat to pan and brown all over. Pour over red wine, remaining vinegar, bring to the boil, cover and cook until liquid has reduced by half, about 3 hours. Preheat oven to 300°F / 150°C / Gas Mark 2.
4. Take meat from pan, put aside and keep warm, covered with foil, in a low oven. Strain stock, return to pan and add remaining ingredients. Stir well and cook for 10 minutes until thickened slightly.
5. Return meat to pan and reheat for 10 minutes. Transfer to a hot serving dish and serve immediately.

Umido di cervo con polenta taragna

Venison Stew with Polenta Taragna

00:20 02:00

American	Ingredients	Metric/Imperial
1¾ lb	*Venison*	800 g / 1¾ lb
	Flour	
⅓ cup	*Vegetable oil*	4 tbsp
1 quart	*Stock*	1 litre / 1¾ pints
1	*Celery stalk*	1
1	*Carrot*	1
1	*Onion*	1
1	*Bouquet garni*	1
1¼ lb	*Corn meal and whole wheat flour, mixed and sieved together*	600 g / 1¼ lb
14 oz	*Grated cheese*	400 g / 14 oz

1. Cut the piece of venison into small pieces (you can also use wild boar) and dip the pieces in flour.
2. Heat the oil and brown the meat. Add stock and a mixture of a chopped celery, carrot, onion and a bouquet garni with lots of thyme. Stir and continue cooking, adding stock as necessary and keeping the heat low.
3. Prepare the polenta using half corn meal and half wholemeal flour (see page 154). The polenta must be firm. When the polenta is almost cooked, add the cheese, stir and pour it all into a large bowl.
4. Serve the polenta and venison stew separately, piping hot.

Daino allo spiedo

Venison on a Spit

00:20 Marinating time 02:00 01:00 to 02:00

American	Ingredients	Metric/Imperial
1	*Fillet of venison*	1
8	*Slices of fat bacon*	8
4	*Sage leaves*	4
½ tsp	*Rosemary*	½ tsp
1	*Sprig of myrtle*	1
1 tsp	*Chopped thyme*	1 tsp
½ tsp	*Chopped oregano*	½ tsp
½ tsp	*Chopped marjoram*	½ tsp
2	*Bay leaves*	2
1 cup	*Vegetable oil*	225 ml / 8 fl oz
1	*Lemon*	1
	Salt and pepper	

1. Wipe the venison with a clean cloth, lard with fat bacon.
2. Mix all the herbs in a bowl with oil and lemon juice, season with plenty of salt and pepper.
3. Allow to marinate for at least 2 hours turning in the liquid from time to time.
4. Put the venison on the spit over a very lively heat and paint with marinade from time to time. Turn frequently until the meat is perfectly cooked.

Cook's tip: This recipe can also be used for a small haunch in which case it should be marinated for 12 hours.

Cervo alla Vatel

Venison Vatel-Style

00:20 Marinating time 08:00 04:00

American	Ingredients	Metric/Imperial
4 quarts	*Red wine*	4 litres / 7 pints
1	*Large bunch of mixed herbs*	1
	Salt and pepper	
2 tsp	*Powdered cinnamon*	2 tsp
1	*Onion*	1
4½ lb	*Venison*	2 kg / 4½ lb
½ cup	*Coffee (single) cream*	125 ml / 4 fl oz
¼ cup	*Cognac*	50 ml / 2 fl oz

1. Pour red wine into a large bowl, add herbs, salt, pepper, cinnamon and sliced onion. Add venison to bowl and leave overnight to marinate.
2. Transfer venison and marinade to a fireproof casserole dish. Bring to boil, cover and simmer over a low heat for about 2 hours until liquid has reduced by a half. Remove meat and put on one side. Strain or purée sauce in a blender.
3. Return meat and sauce to casserole dish, cover and cook a further 2 hours over a low heat. Just before serving, season with salt and pepper, stir in cream and cognac and serve immediately.

Capriolo in umido alla pastora

Shepherd's Venison Stew

This typical game dish originates from the Val d'Aosta region, and makes a delicious autumn meal.

00:25 Standing time 12:00 03:00

American	Ingredients	Metric/Imperial
2 lb	*Pieces of venison*	1 kg / 2 lb
	Seasoned flour	
⅔ cup	*Vegetable oil*	150 ml / ¼ pint
	Salt and pepper	
¼ tsp	*Chopped thyme*	¼ tsp
2	*Bay leaves*	2
¼ tsp	*Chopped rosemary*	¼ tsp
¼ tsp	*Chopped sage*	¼ tsp
1 quart	*Red wine*	1 litre / 1¾ pints
4	*Carrots*	4
4	*Onions*	4
4	*Celery stalks*	4
2	*Potatoes*	2
2	*Leeks*	2
1	*Shallot*	1
14 oz	*Small button onions*	400 g / 14 oz

1. Cut venison into bite-size pieces, toss in seasoned flour. Heat oil in a fireproof casserole dish and, when very hot, brown meat all over with salt, pepper, thyme, bay leaves, rosemary and sage.
2. Pour over red wine, cover and simmer for 2 hours. Allow to cool and refrigerate overnight.

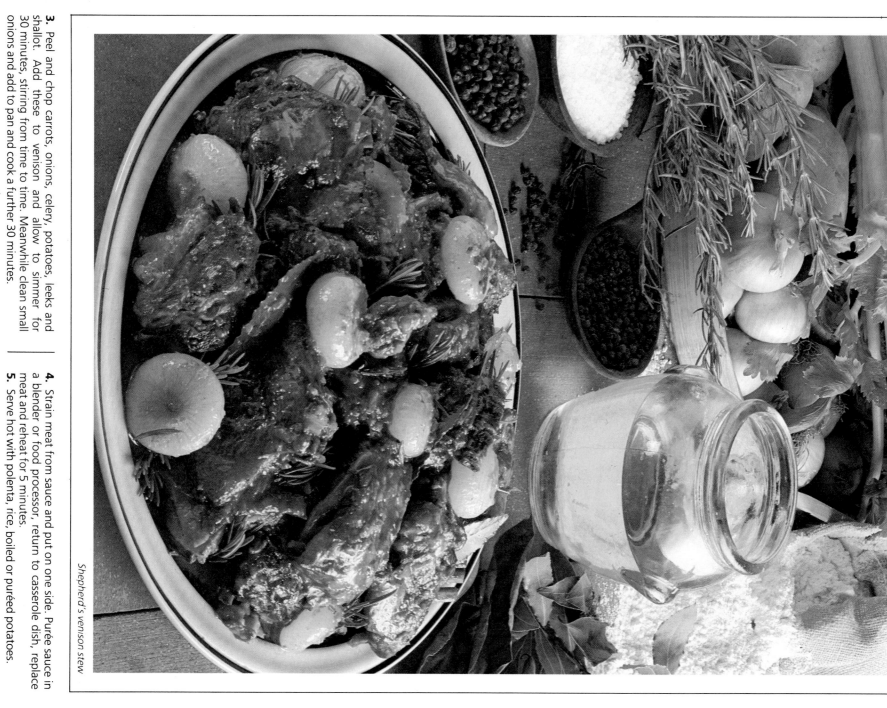

Shepherd's venison stew

3. Peel and chop carrots, onions, celery, potatoes, leeks and shallot. Add these to venison and allow to simmer for 30 minutes, stirring from time to time. Meanwhile clean small onions and add to pan and cook a further 30 minutes.

4. Strain meat from sauce and put on one side. Purée sauce in a blender or food processor, return to casserole dish, replace meat and reheat for 5 minutes.

5. Serve hot with polenta, rice, boiled or puréed potatoes.

Pheasant Vatel-style

Fagiano alla Vatel

Pheasant Vatel-Style

00:10 — 00:50

American	Ingredients	Metric/Imperial
1	*Onion*	1
1	*Oven-ready pheasant and liver*	1
¼ cup	*Softened butter*	50 g / 2 oz
1	*Canadian apple*	1
¼ cup	*White vinegar*	50 ml / 2 fl oz
¼ cup	*Red wine*	50 ml / 2 fl oz
	Salt and pepper	

1. Preheat oven to 350°F / 180°C / Gas Mark 4.
2. Chop onion and liver and mix in with half the butter. Place the stuffing inside bird and cover opening with apple. Place in a roasting tin.
3. Melt the remaining butter and use to brush bird. Combine vinegar and red wine and pour over pheasant. Season with salt and pepper and roast in the oven for about 50 minutes until cooked.
4. Transfer pheasant to a hot serving dish and serve with boiled rice or a potato purée.

Fagiano e cavolo

Pheasant and Cabbage

00:20 — 02:00

American	Ingredients	Metric/Imperial
1	*Firm white cabbage*	1
¼ cup	*Vegetable oil*	50 ml / 2 fl oz
¼ lb	*Fat bacon*	100 g / 4 oz
	Salt and pepper	
2	*Oven-ready pheasants*	2
¼ lb	*Sliced bacon*	100 g / 4 oz
¼ cup	*Whipping (double) cream*	50 ml / 2 fl oz

1. Wash and shred cabbage, par boil for 5 minutes, then drain. Heat half the oil in a pan and add cabbage and chopped fat bacon. Season with salt and pepper and cook for 30 minutes.
2. Truss pheasants, heat remaining oil in a large frying pan and brown birds all over. Cover breasts with bacon slices, then pour over thick cream, add cabbage to pan, cover and cook over a low heat for about 1½ hours.
3. Transfer pheasants to a hot serving dish, remove bacon, spoon cabbage around birds, pour creamy sauce over breasts, and serve.

Fantasia di pollo e quaglie

Chicken and Quail Surprise

00:25 — 00:45

American	Ingredients	Metric/Imperial
4	*Quails*	4
4	*Chicken breasts*	4
¼ cup	*Butter*	50 g / 2 oz
¼ cup	*Vegetable oil*	50 ml / 2 fl oz
2 oz	*Bacon*	50 g / 2 oz
½ tsp	*Chopped rosemary*	½ tsp
2 cups	*Mushrooms*	200 g / 7 oz
2 cups	*Béchamel sauce (see page 162)*	450 ml / ¾ pint

1. Cut the quails in half and cook with the chicken breasts, in a large pan with the heated butter and oil. Turn from time to time until golden on each side and cooked through. Add the chopped bacon and rosemary.
2. Wash the mushrooms, slice thinly and sauté in a small pan with a little butter for 5-6 minutes.
3. Prepare a béchamel sauce, add the mushrooms.
4. Arrange the chicken and quails on a serving dish, top with mushroom sauce and serve very hot surrounded by a garnish of triangles of toast.

Schidionata di quaglie

Quails on the Spit

00:35 — 00:15

American	Ingredients	Metric/Imperial
8	*Quails*	8
1 tsp	*Chopped basil*	1 tsp
1 tsp	*Chopped rosemary*	1 tsp
1	*Onion*	1
¼ cup	*Butter*	50 g / 2 oz
	Salt and pepper	
8	*Slices of bacon*	8
¼ cup	*Vegetable oil*	50 ml / 2 fl oz
	Rice	

1. Clean, singe and wash the quails. Dry and stuff with chopped basil, rosemary and onion mixed with butter.
2. Lightly season the quails with salt and pepper, then lard them by wrapping in thin slices of bacon secured with thread.
3. Put them on the spit and paint with vegetable oil. Brown the quails over a high heat, brush with the fat that falls into the dripping pan.

4. Remove from the spit at the end of the cooking time and serve with boiled rice, seasoning with the dripping pan juices.

Cook's tip: The same recipe can be used for cooking small pigeons and other small birds.

Quaglie alla cacciatora

Huntsman's Quails

00:30 00:45

American	Ingredients	Metric/Imperial
8	*Large quails*	8
½ cup	*Butter*	100 g / 4 oz
1 tsp	*Chopped sage*	1 tsp
8	*Cloves*	8
½ tsp	*Nutmeg*	½ tsp
4	*Garlic cloves*	4
8	*Slices of bacon*	8
¼ cup	*Brandy*	50 ml / 2 fl oz
8	*Slices of polenta*	8

1. Clean the quails, singe and remove their intestines.
2. Mix half the butter with the chopped sage, cloves, nutmeg and chopped garlic, divide into 4.
3. Place a portion inside each bird. Wrap the quails in the slices of bacon and secure with toothpicks.
4. Sauté them in a frying pan with butter, browning them evenly. Sprinkle with brandy, cover the pan and continue cooking for 15 minutes.
5. When the cooking is completed, put a lighted match to the pan and allow the excess alcohol to burn off completely.
6. Serve the quails immediately on slices of hot polenta on a heated serving dish.

Quaglie alla pavese

Quails Pavia-Style

00:30 01:00

American	Ingredients	Metric/Imperial
12	*Quails*	12
	Salt and pepper	
8	*Slices of bacon*	8
½ cup	*Vegetable oil*	125 ml / 4 fl oz
4	*Garlic cloves*	4
½ cup	*Red wine*	125 ml / 4 fl oz
1⅔ cups	*Rice*	350 g / 12 oz
1½ quarts	*Chicken stock*	1.5 litres / 2½ pints
2 oz	*Ox marrow*	50 g / 2 oz

1. Clean and singe the quails, season and cover them with slices of bacon.
2. Heat the oil, cook the birds with the crushed garlic until golden, sprinkle with the red wine as they turn brown.
3. Remove the quails after 25 minutes cooking and put them to one side.
4. Brown the rice in the pan juices from the quails, stirring frequently. As soon as the rice has browned, sprinkle with boiling stock and add the ox marrow. Continue cooking the rice so that it is 'al dente', then arrange it on the bottom of an ovenproof dish. Lay the quails on top of the rice, put in the oven or under the broiler (grill) for 5 minutes and serve immediately.

Quaglie arrosto alla foglia di vite

Roast Quails with Vine Leaves

00:40 00:25

American	Ingredients	Metric/Imperial
1 lb	*Grapes*	450 g / 1 lb
8	*Vine leaves*	8
8	*Large, unhung quails*	8
½ cup	*Butter*	100 g / 4 oz
	Salt and pepper	
8	*Thin slices of bacon*	8
1 cup	*White wine*	225 ml / 8 fl oz

1. Wash and dry grapes, halve and deseed them.
2. Wash the vine leaves very gently and dry them, taking care not to break them.
3. Pluck and draw the quails, singe, wash and dry them carefully. Brush all over with a little melted butter and season with a pinch of salt and pepper.
4. Put one grape, or more if they are small, inside each quail and wrap them first in a slice of bacon and then in a vine leaf. Truss them with white string.
5. Preheat the oven to 400°F / 200°C / Gas Mark 6.
6. Heat the remaining butter in a frying pan and cook the quails over a brisk heat for 5 minutes.
7. Arrange in a casserole, pour over the wine and 1 tablespoon water for each quail, season and cook for 20 minutes covered with foil. Add remaining grapes after 10 minutes.
8. Remove string, arrange quails on a serving dish surrounded by grapes. Pour over the pan juices. Serve accompanied by boiled rice.

Piccioni e piselli

Squab with Green Peas

00:15 01:15

American	Ingredients	Metric/Imperial
4	*Squab*	4
5 oz	*Pork fat*	150 g / 5 oz
2 tbsp	*Vegetable oil*	1½ tbsp
1	*Stock cube*	1
1 tbsp	*Cornstarch (cornflour)*	1 tbsp
1 lb	*Fresh (shelled) or frozen peas*	450 g / 1 lb
16	*Button onions*	16
	Salt and pepper	
2 tbsp	*Chopped parsley*	1½ tbsp

1. Prepare and wash the squab. Cut the pork fat into strips and fry in the heated oil; add the squab and brown all over.
2. After 10 minutes, remove the squab from the pan, add 1¼ cups [300 ml / ½ pint] stock made with the stock cube and stir in the cornstarch mixed with a little water. Bring to the boil, then add the peas, onions, salt and pepper.
3. Cover and simmer for 15 minutes, add the squab and simmer for a further 30 minutes. Add chopped parsley immediately before serving.

Cook's tip: serve these fledgling pigeons with a purée of potatoes seasoned with nutmeg or boiled potatoes.

VEGETABLES

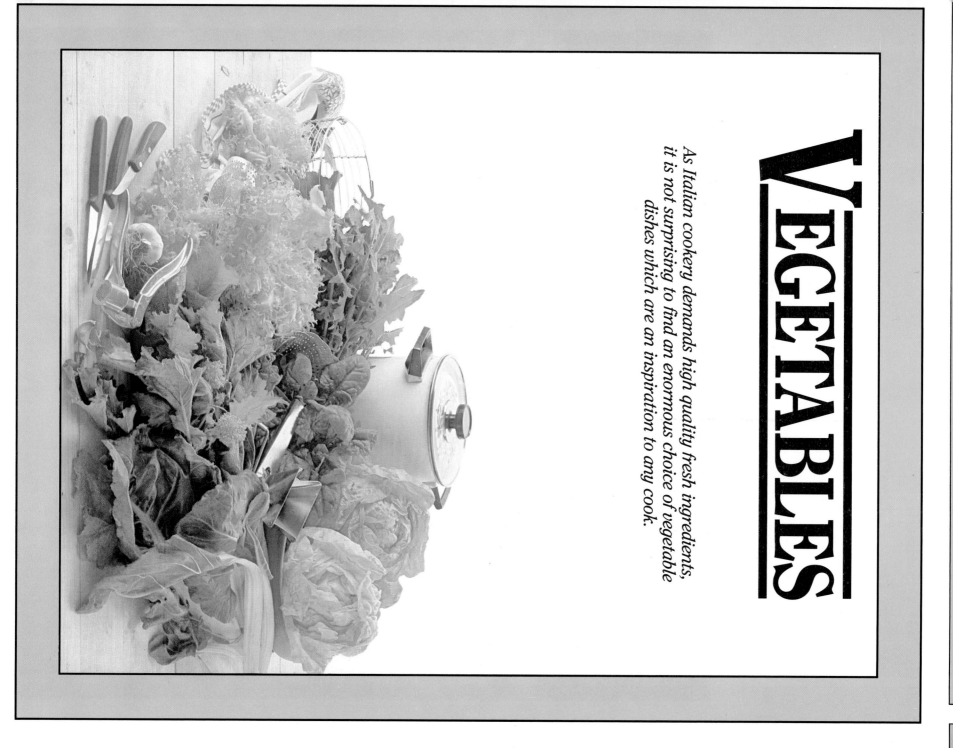

As Italian cookery demands high quality fresh ingredients, it is not surprising to find an enormous choice of vegetable dishes which are an inspiration to any cook.

Preparing salads

Crisp salads are not only enjoyable for their interesting textures and different color combinations of raw vegetables but they are also a valuable nutritional addition to the daily diet, providing some vitamin C and mineral salts. Green salads very often make excellent accompaniments to main dishes. The more varied salads, which include cooked vegetables, eggs, cheese or fish, can be served with perhaps a mayonnaise dressing, as a separate course or a light meal.

Cabbage
Remove the coarse outer leaves. Wash well to remove any earth or insects and shred with a sharp knife.

Celery
Cut off the root and separate the stalks. Remove any strings with a small sharp knife, wash well to remove any discolored parts from the grooves. Cut into small sticks or slices. Store in the vegetable drawer of the refrigerator. The color and texture of celery adds variation to many kinds of salad.

Cucumber
Make sure that the cucumber is fresh by pressing the stalk lightly. If it has any hint of softness, the cucumber will not keep. Cucumbers do not need to be peeled but this is a matter of individual taste. Store in a cool larder or in the salad drawer of the refrigerator. If the refrigerator is too cold, cucumber which has been cut will quickly turn icy and become mushy. This vegetable should be used as quickly as possible.

To prepare asparagus
1. *Cut off the thick and woody stalk. Scrape the white stem, wash well.*

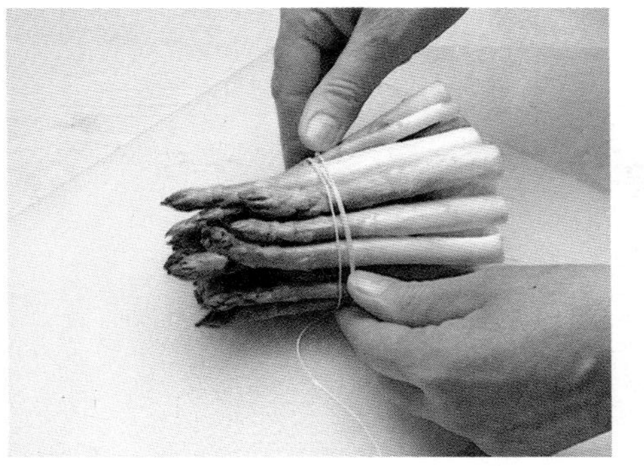

2. *Tie the bundles into even sizes. Cook upright in an asparagus pan, in 2½-3 in / 6-7 cm salted water.*

3. *Asparagus can take from 15-35 minutes to cook, depending on the thickness. To test, pierce the stalk with a sharp knife.*

To stuff eggplant (aubergines)
1. *Halve the eggplant lengthwise. Bring to the boil in a saucepan of water and blanch for 4 minutes, drain.*

2. *Remove the insides without piercing the skin. Chop the flesh and add to the chosen filling. Brush the eggplant shells with oil before adding the filling.*

3. *Arrange the shells in an ovenproof dish brushed with oil. Carefully spoon in the filling to cover the eggplant halves. Brush with oil and bake in the oven.*

Endive
Trim the root end away and remove the coarse outer leaves, wash and drain. Do not cut with a knife or it will discolor. Store in the salad compartment of the refrigerator.

Lettuce
There are various types of lettuce available and the choice will depend on individual taste. The preparation is similar for each variety. Remove the coarse outer leaves (these can be used for soup if carefully cleaned), separate the crisp leaves inside and wash well under cold running water. Drain in a colander or spinner to remove excess moisture. Pat dry with absorbent kitchen towels.

Do not cut lettuce leaves with a knife or scissors as this will bruise and blacken the edges. Tear the leaves into the salad bowl. Always be sure that lettuce which is to have a salad dressing is crisp and dry before you take it to the table. Toss in the dressing just before serving.

To store lettuces for several days, remove the soil and the outer leaves, pack in plastic bags, seal and store in the bottom of the refrigerator, unwashed until required. If refrigerator space is limited, lettuces can also be stored in a covered saucepan in a cool place for a short while.

Scallions (spring onions)
These should be firm and green, yellowing leaves indicate that they are not fresh. Remove the roots and the thin papery outer skin, cut the coarse tips away and wash well. Store in a sealed plastic bag or box or they will flavor other vegetables.

Tomatoes
Store unwashed in the salad drawer of the refrigerator. Wash before using and remove the stem. Small tomatoes are best used in salads with the skins on. Do not cut up tomatoes to add to a tossed green salad, because their juice will thin the dressing. It is better to dress them separately and use them to garnish the salad bowl just before you take it to the table. Alternatively, you can serve the tomatoes with their dressing as an accompaniment to the green salad.

To skin tomatoes, plunge into boiling water for 30 seconds and then into cold water. The skin will peel off easily, use as required.

Watercress
Buy fresh green watercress with no yellow leaves. If using for salad, pick over the stalks, rinse in cold water and pack in a plastic bag excluding the air. Keep in the salad compartment of the refrigerator.

Flavoring salads

It is well worth getting to know the characteristics of individual herbs, because they play a very important part in Italian cooking. It is much better to use one or two herbs sparingly so that you can really get to know their flavor rather than adding too many herbs to a dish. Fresh herbs such as mint, parsley, coriander, sage, thyme, marjoram, summer savory, basil, borage can be sparingly snipped with scissors over the salad bowl to add extra flavor. Garlic is often peeled, slightly crushed and used to rub over the salad bowl if only a hint of its flavor is required. Use fresh herbs to flavor salads and keep dried herbs for cooked dishes.

Cooking fresh vegetables

A helpful rule for cooking vegetables in water is that vegetables such as peas, beans and other greens which grow above the ground are put into boiling water. The root vegetables such as carrots, turnips and potatoes are best put into cold water and brought to the boil for even cooking.

If vegetables are cooked in a great deal of water much of the nutritive value is lost into the water. It is best, therefore, to cook vegetables in a covered pan in the minimum of water and use the cooking water to make soups and gravies. However, some vegetables such as tender young beans do need to be cooked in at least half a saucepan of water without a lid, for a short time, to prevent color loss. Vegetables which discolor such as artichokes, jerusalem artichokes, salsify, and cardoons, are best cooked with lemon juice added to the water.

Steaming

Cooking young tender vegetables in steam retains the nutrients and both the color and texture of fresh and frozen vegetables. Place the vegetables in a steamer over a pan of boiling water, so that the vegetables do not come into contact with the water. The steam will surround the vegetables but you will need to allow more time for cooking, usually about 10 minutes more than the time required to boil the vegetables.

Steaming saucepans are available which have an inside with holes to allow the steam to circulate. Alternatively, there are metal steaming baskets which stand on legs inside a saucepan.

It is possible to cook several types of vegetables together in a steamer providing they are wrapped in foil and are not packed tightly together. As water boils away in a steamer it is useful to have a kettle of boiling water ready to top up the water. Salt the vegetables, and not the water, lightly before cooking. More seasoning can be added at the table.

Using the microwave oven

This is an excellent method of cooking vegetables without loss of flavor or nutrients. Only a few spoons of water need to be sprinkled over the vegetables to retain moisture.

Pressure cooking

Although the principle of pressure cooking is the same for all cookers, the models vary and it is essential to follow the manufacturer's instructions for cooking vegetables. The pressure cooker retains the nutritive value of food and cooks more quickly, on average saving one-third of the total cooking time.

1. It is more nutritious to prepare potatoes when possible, leaving the skins on. Wash thoroughly and brush the skins clean.

2. Half fill a saucepan with cold salted water. Add the potatoes and bring to the boil. Cook until tender on a medium heat.

3. Skin and serve as boiled potatoes or cream with milk and butter. To sauté, cook for 10 minutes, drain, peel, slice and fry.

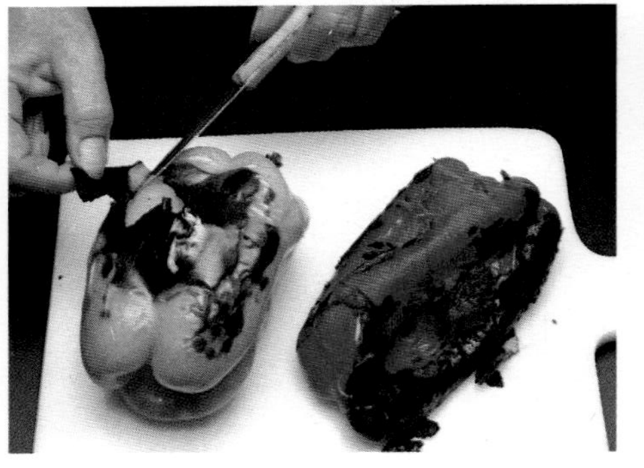

To skin sweet peppers

1. Put them in a very hot oven, or char under a broiler (grill). Peel off the thin outer skin.

2. Rinse the peppers under the cold tap to remove excess black pieces. Cut the stalk away, slit open, remove the seeds and wash.

3. Cut into strips and make into a salad. Here anchovies, capers and garlic are added This method provides a soft texture.

Dried legumes (pulses)

In Italy, dried peas and beans are often used in the hearty soups and stews of country origin. They are cheap and nutritious and will extend the meat or poultry content of the main dish.

Before being cooked, dried peas and beans require long soaking to replace the moisture removed during the drying process. Soak overnight or for about 4-5 hours for small beans and peas. Place in a large bowl with about 3 times as much water as there are beans. Rinse the beans after soaking.

Beans will take about 1 hour 15 minutes to cook for the smaller varieties to 2 hours for the large broad beans. They should be cooked in fast boiling water for 10 minutes at the beginning of the cooking time. If cooking in a casserole it is as well to partly cook them, as they will absorb all the juices from the vegetables and meat; this also prevents the meat from over-cooking while the beans are softening.

Chick peas will take about 2 hours to cook and dried peas from 1-2 hours with split peas cooking in 45 minutes.

Lentils and split peas do not need to be soaked but it is essential to wash well and remove any discolored seeds. Put lentils and split peas in a basin of water before soaking or cooking and remove any which float to the top of the bowl.

To cook and stuff artichokes

1. Trim the top and bottom. Loosen the inner leaves around the choke. Remove the choke without damaging the heart.

2. Place the artichoke cups in boiling salted water with 2 teaspoons lemon juice. Bring to the boil and cook until the outer leaves pull away easily (about 15 minutes).

3. Drain and place upside down on a wire rack for a few minutes. Fill with cooked stuffing and serve cold or fill and cook as directed in the recipe of your choice.

Salad of artichoke hearts, carrots and cheese

Insalata del mandorlo fiorito

Blossoming Almond Salad

01:00 00:10

American	Ingredients	Metric/Imperial
2 cups	*Parboiled rice*	400 g / 14 oz
5	*Mushrooms*	5
1	*Sweet red pepper*	1
3 tbsp	*Almonds*	2 tbsp
1 cup	*Frozen petit pois*	150 g / 5 oz
6 tbsp	*Vegetable oil*	5 tbsp
Scant ¼ cup	*White vinegar*	3 tbsp
	Salt and pepper	
2	*Garlic cloves*	2

1. Cook the rice keeping it 'al dente', rinse in cold water, drain it and leave to cool.
2. Clean the mushrooms well with a damp cloth and cut them into fine slices. Add with the rice to a salad bowl.
3. Divide the sweet red pepper into four, remove the white pith and the seeds, put it under a very hot broiler (grill) and cook well.
4. Shell the almonds, chop them finely and add to the rice. (Alternatively use flaked almonds.) Cook the frozen petit pois, drain them, add to the rice.
5. In a cup beat oil with white vinegar, add a pinch of salt, pepper and well crushed garlic. Beat the emulsion with a fork and pour over the rice, stirring carefully.
6. Put in the refrigerator for about 30 minutes only so that the salad is not too cold, then take it out and decorate the top with the red pepper, thinly sliced.

Insalatina primaverile

Little Spring Salad

00:15 Soaking time 00:05

American	Ingredients	Metric/Imperial
2	*Large Jerusalem artichokes* or	2
4	*Small artichokes*	4
2	*Carrots*	2
¼ lb	*Emmental*	100 g / 4 oz
	Salt and pepper	
Scant ¼ cup	*Olive oil*	3 tbsp
1	*Lemon*	1

1. Peel and trim the artichokes then soak them for some time in water acidulated with lemon juice so that they do not become black; drain them, discard all the woody or rough parts and then slice them finely.
2. Blanch the artichoke slices in boiling water for 5 minutes, drain and rinse in cold water.
3. Scrape and wash the carrots and use a large grater to obtain little pieces like matchsticks. Use the same utensil to grate the emmental.
4. Put the artichokes, carrot and cheese in a bowl, season with salt, pepper, olive oil and lemon juice and take at once to the table. This salad should always be prepared at the last moment and cannot be kept.

Parisian-style tomatoes

Pomodori alla parigina

Parisian-Style Tomatoes

00:45 00:12

American	Ingredients	Metric/Imperial
8	*Tomatoes*	8
	Salt	
¾ cup	*Peas*	100 g / 4 oz
1	*Carrot*	1
4	*Eggs*	4
1 cup	*Mayonnaise (see page 175)*	225 ml / 8 fl oz
1	*Lemon*	1
	Green and black olives	

1. Slice the tomatoes and empty out the pulp. Sprinkle with salt and let them drain for a few minutes. Now cook the peas and the scraped and diced carrot until tender, drain and leave to cool. Hard-cook (boil) the eggs, cool under running water and shell.
2. Pour the mayonnaise, juice of the lemon, the peas and the carrots into a bowl and mix thoroughly. Fill the tomatoes and garnish them with slices of hard-cooked egg and the green and black olives. Serve at once.

Sedano di Verona alla senape

Verona Celery with Mustard

00:20 Chilling time 01:00 00:00

American	Ingredients	Metric/Imperial
2	*Heads of celery*	2
1 tbsp	*Chopped parsley*	1 tbsp
3 tbsp	*Mild mustard*	2 tbsp
½ cup	*Vegetable oil*	125 ml / 4 fl oz
	Salt and pepper	
1 tsp	*Lemon juice*	1 tsp

1. Wash celery well, peel off strings with a sharp knife, slice it and put it on a serving dish. Sprinkle with parsley.
2. Prepare a dressing, in a bowl, with the mustard, the oil, salt and pepper, and a few drops of lemon juice.
3. Pour the sauce over the celery, then put it in bowls and leave to stand in lower part of refrigerator until served.

Insalata flamande

Flemish Salad

This is a typical very piquant Flemish salad, which is served with boiled pork and with any type of sausages.

00:30 00:25

American	Ingredients	Metric/Imperial
3	*Heads of Belgium endive*	*3*
1	*Bunch of parsley*	*1*
1	*Small onion*	*1*
1	*Carrot*	*1*
1	*Piece of white celery*	*1*
14 oz	*Dutch white asparagus (or canned)*	*400 g / 14 oz*
2	*Floury potatoes, boiled*	*2*
10	*Radishes*	*10*
1 cup	*Coffee (single) cream*	*225 ml / 8 fl oz*
	Salt and pepper	
2 tsp	*Mild mustard*	*2 tsp*
1	*Horseradish root*	*1*

1. Wash and finely chop the endive. Chop the parsley with the onion, finely slice raw scraped carrot, slice washed celery.
2. Parboil the white asparagus, if using fresh, and cut each one into 4 parts. Finely slice the cold boiled potatoes. Clean the radishes and cut them into little round slices.
3. Put all the vegetables in a large wooden salad bowl.
4. Mix the cream with salt and pepper, the mild mustard and mix with the vegetables. Horseradish is very pungent so only grate a small piece and scatter on top.

Insalata sivigliana

Sevillian Salad

00:20 00:00

American	Ingredients	Metric/Imperial
½ lb	*Lettuce head with firm leaves*	*225 g / 8 oz*
1	*Onion*	*1*
1 tbsp	*Vinegar*	*1 tbsp*
3	*Eggs*	*3*
1	*Can of sardines*	*1*
1	*Bunch of radishes*	*1*
5 oz	*Smoked mackerel*	*150 g / 5 oz*
½ cup	*Vegetable oil*	*125 ml / 4 fl oz*
	Salt and pepper	
1	*Lemon*	*1*

1. Clean the lettuce. Finely slice the onion and put it to soak with water and vinegar so that it loses a little of its sharpness.
2. Hard-cook (boil) the eggs and cool them under cold running water.
3. In a large earthenware dish or salad bowl collect the various ingredients: the sardines drained from oil and with the skins removed, the radishes washed and cut into little slices, the mackerel in small pieces, the hard-cooked eggs shelled and sliced, the onion drained from the water and vinegar, the lettuce well dried.
4. Prepare the sauce for the salad with oil, salt, pepper and lemon juice, beat the seasoning well until you obtain a smooth dressing and mix with the ingredients in the bowl.

Pallottoline di spinaci

Little Spinach Balls

00:30 00:40

American	Ingredients	Metric/Imperial
1 (½ lb pack)	*Frozen chopped spinach or*	*1 (225 g / 8 oz pack)*
1 lb	*Fresh spinach*	*450 g / 1 lb*
½ cup	*Butter*	*100 g / 4 oz*
2	*Eggs*	*2*
3 tbsp	*Grated parmesan cheese*	*2 tbsp*
¼ tsp	*Nutmeg*	*¼ tsp*
	Salt	
	Flour as required	
	Bread crumbs as required	
½ cup	*Oil*	*125 ml / 4 fl oz*

1. Put the frozen block of chopped spinach in a saucepan and defrost it completely. Let it absorb the water and leave it over the heat for no longer than 5 minutes. Drain it, squeeze well and then pass it through a vegetable-mill or food processor. You may also use fresh spinach but the preparation time will be doubled.
2. Put a little butter in a pan over a low heat and add the spinach, stirring thoroughly until it is well flavored and the moisture dried out. Remove from the heat, let it cool slightly, then add a whole egg, the grated parmesan, a little nutmeg and season with salt. Pour this mixture into a dish greased with butter and leave it to cool completely.
3. When it is quite cold and firm, take teaspoons of the mixture and shape into little balls the size of a walnut, dip it in the flour, then in beaten egg and then in the bread crumbs.
4. Fry all the spinach balls in a pan with plenty of butter and oil. Serve them hot or cold as part of a salad or use as a starter or as a side dish for a roast.

Tarato 

Eggplant [Aubergine] and Sweet Pepper Salad

00:30
Standing time 00:30
00:15

American	Ingredients	Metric/Imperial
2	*Eggplant (aubergines)*	*2*
	Salt and pepper	
2	*Sweet yellow peppers*	*2*
3 tbsp	*Vegetable oil*	*2 tbsp*
1 cup	*Natural yoghurt*	*225 ml / 8 fl oz*
2	*Garlic cloves*	*2*
½	*Lemon*	*½*

1. Cut the eggplant into slices, then sprinkle with salt, leave for 30 minutes until the bitter juice comes out.
2. Wash and dry the eggplant, then put under the broiler (grill) together with 2 peppers which have been cleaned and deseeded; brush with some of the oil. When they are cooked peel both the eggplant and the peppers and chop them finely.
3. Put them in a salad bowl. Mix the yoghurt, salt, black pepper, crushed cloves of garlic together with the oil and the juice of half a lemon. Pour over the vegetables and mix well. Chill before serving.

Little spinach balls

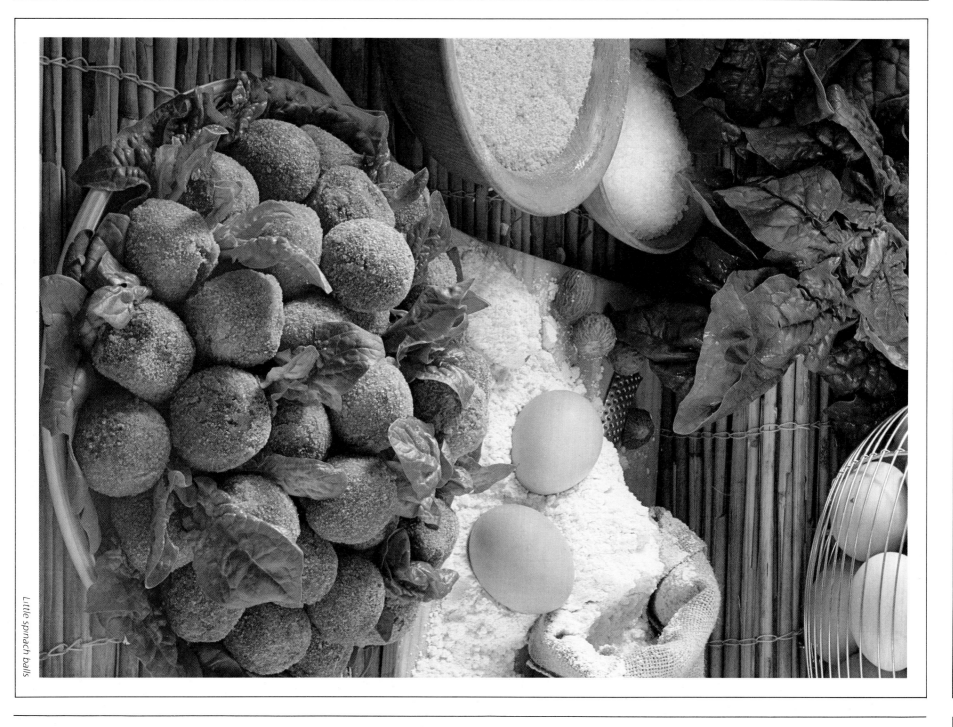

Sedano di Verona in insalata

Verona Celery in Salad

00:30 Soaking time 04:00 — 00:00

American	Ingredients	Metric/Imperial
1	*Head of celery*	1
1 cup	*Wine vinegar*	225 ml / 8 fl oz
1 cup	*Mayonnaise (see page 175)*	225 ml / 8 fl oz
1	*Lettuce*	1
12	*Black olives*	12
	Pepper	

1. Thoroughly clean the celery, removing the strings, then slice it very finely, using, if possible, a slicing machine to obtain thin slices of equal thickness. Put the slices in a non-metallic container and cover them with good wine vinegar.
2. Leave to infuse for 4 hours, then drain well and dry carefully with kitchen paper.
3. Mix the mayonnaise with the celery slices.
4. Line a salad bowl or a serving dish with well-washed and drained lettuce leaves. Arrange the seasoned celery on the leaves, decorate with black olives and sprinkle with plenty of freshly-ground pepper. Keep in the refrigerator until it is time to serve.

Insalata piemontese

Piedmontese Salad

00:10 Standing time 00:30 — 00:00

American	Ingredients	Metric/Imperial
1	*Head of celery*	1
1 tsp	*English mustard*	1 tsp
5	*Sprigs of parsley*	5
3	*Sprigs of chervil*	3
1 tsp	*Chopped chives*	1 tsp
½ cup	*Vegetable oil*	125 ml / 4 fl oz
1	*Lemon*	1

1. Clean the celery thoroughly and remove strings. Cut into thin slices and put into a salad bowl.
2. In a jug mix English mustard with finely-chopped parsley, chervil and chives, the oil and lemon juice.
3. Pour it all over the celery and leave to soak for 30 minutes. Serve cold.

Spinaci alla senape

Spinach with Mustard

00:30 — 00:10

American	Ingredients	Metric/Imperial
¾ lb	*Spinach*	350 g / 12 oz
3	*Eggs*	3
1 tbsp	*Vinegar or lemon juice*	1 tbsp
3 tbsp	*Olive oil*	2 tbsp
	Salt and pepper	
1 tsp	*Mustard*	1 tsp

1. For this salad very tender and fresh spinach is required. Clean carefully removing the roots and part of the stalks and wash several times to eliminate every trace of earth. Drain.
2. Hard-cook (boil) the eggs, cool them under running water, then shell them. Separate the yolks from the whites.
3. Drain the spinach well: a hand-spinner would be ideal for this. Tear it coarsely and put in a salad bowl. Season with a little white vinegar or lemon juice, olive oil, salt and fresh pepper, mixed with the mustard.
4. Chop separately the hard-cooked egg yolks and white and sprinkle the yolks in the centre and the whites round the outside of the spinach. Season with salt and pepper.

Barbabietole alla moda di Calais

Calais-Style Beetroot

00:20 — 00:25

American	Ingredients	Metric/Imperial
14 oz	*Potatoes*	400 g / 14 oz
	Salt and pepper	
2 tbsp	*Parsley*	1½ tbsp
1	*Garlic clove*	1
2	*Cooked beetroot*	2
¼ cup	*Vegetable oil*	50 ml / 2 fl oz
2 tbsp	*Vinegar*	25 ml / 1 fl oz
5	*Sprigs of parsley*	5
2	*Basil leaves*	2

1. Boil the potatoes in plenty of boiling, lightly salted water. Drain, cool and cut them into fairly small cubes.
2. Put the potatoes in a salad-bowl. Chop parsley and crush the garlic.
3. Cut the beetroot into cubes and add to the salad-bowl with the potatoes. Finally add the chopped mixture of parsley and garlic and mix together.
4. Season with oil, salt, pepper and a little vinegar. Stir well and serve garnished with the parsley and chopped basil leaves.

Insalata rustica

Rustic Salad

00:25 Chilling time 01:00 — 00:00

American	Ingredients	Metric/Imperial
½ lb	*Green asparagus*	225 g / 8 oz
1	*Very small cauliflower*	1
½ lb	*Green beans*	225 g / 8 oz
2	*Small potatoes*	2
1	*Small beetroot*	1
¼ lb	*Mortadella cut in a single slice*	100 g / 4 oz
1 cup	*Mayonnaise (see page 175)*	225 ml / 8 fl oz
1	*Lemon*	1
	Salt and pepper	

1. Separately, and using different timings, cook the washed asparagus tips, a small cauliflower, the green beans with stalks and strings removed and the potatoes.
2. Leave the vegetables till lukewarm and peel the potatoes, cutting them into large slices. Cut the beans into 2 or 3 and divide the cauliflower into sprigs, discarding the hard ribs. Collect the vegetables in a bowl which has an airtight seal, and chill in the refrigerator.

3. Remove the vegetables from the refrigerator, add the small red beetroot cut into dice and the mortadella cut into thin strips. Season with mayonnaise, lemon juice, salt and pepper.

La Sirenetta 

Seafood Salad

00:30 00:30

American	Ingredients	Metric/Imperial
1 lb	*Potatoes*	*500 g / 1 lb*
	Salt and pepper	
1 lb	*Frozen shrimps*	*500 g / 1 lb*
1	*Sweet red pepper*	*1*
1	*Head of celery*	*1*
½ cup	*Olive oil*	*125 ml / 4 fl oz*
1	*Lemon*	*1*
3	*Hard-cooked (boiled) eggs*	*3*
2 tbsp	*Chopped parsley*	*1½ tbsp*

1. Boil the potatoes in their skins in salted water, peel and cool before cutting into small sticks.
2. Cook the shrimps in boiling water, and drain well.
3. Put the red pepper under the broiler (grill).
4. Trim a head of celery, keep the heart and also the green stalks, chop into thin slices.
5. Put the potatoes in a salad-bowl, together with the celery and the shrimps; mix gently.
6. Peel the pepper, cut into small pieces and add to the bowl.
7. Season with a dressing made of olive oil, salt, pepper and the juice of a lemon, mix well.
8. Garnish with slices of hard-cooked (boiled) eggs and sprinkle with chopped parsley.

Insalata di mele e di soia

Apple and Soya Bean Salad

00:15 00:00

American	Ingredients	Metric/Imperial
1	*Head of lettuce*	*1*
2 cups	*Fresh soya bean sprouts*	*100 g / 4 oz*
2	*Apples*	*2*
2	*Oranges*	*2*
¼ lb	*Cheese*	*100 g / 4 oz*
¼ cup	*Vegetable oil*	*50 ml / 2 fl oz*
	Salt and pepper	
2	*Lemons*	*2*

1. Wash a head of lettuce and the fresh soya bean sprouts.
2. Peel the apples and cut them into slices. Peel the oranges removing the white pith and slice.
3. Cut the cheese into cubes.
4. Put the lettuce in the salad bowl. Mix the bean sprouts with the apples and oranges and cubed cheese.
5. Make a dressing by mixing the oil, salt and pepper with the lemon juice. Mix with the ingredients in the bowl and serve immediately.

Olive di Sicilia

Sicilian Olives

This is a typical dish of eastern Sicily and it is customary to prepare it in the late autumn when the olive trees are beaten. It is eaten at harvest suppers.

00:35 Plus 12 days 00:00

American	Ingredients	Metric/Imperial
1 lb or 3 cups	*Bitter green olives*	*500 g / 1 lb*
1	*Bunch of fennel*	*1*
3	*Garlic cloves*	*3*
1	*Bunch of mint*	*1*
	Salt	
¼ lb	*Celery*	*100 g / 4 oz*
Scant ¼ cup	*Olive oil*	*3 tbsp*
1 tbsp	*Red wine vinegar*	*1 tbsp*
1	*Sweet red pepper (optional)*	*1*

1. Bitter green olives are required for this salad. Squash them, take out the stones, then put them to soak in water for about a week changing the water every day.
2. At the end of the week put them back to soak in water adding fennel, crushed cloves of garlic, mint leaves and salt, leave to infuse for 3-4 days.
3. To prepare, take out the olives, drain them and put them in a large bowl with finely chopped mint and celery (include the leaves), season with olive oil, red wine vinegar and salt. You may also add some red pepper cut in very small pieces.

Misto gran sapore

Mediterranean Medley

01:00 00:40

American	Ingredients	Metric/Imperial
2	*Sweet peppers*	*2*
2	*Long eggplant (aubergines)*	*2*
	Salt and pepper	
3 tbsp	*Sunflower oil for frying*	*2 tbsp*
½ tsp	*Oregano*	*½ tsp*
2	*Garlic cloves*	*2*
3 tbsp	*Olive oil*	*2 tbsp*
4	*Basil leaves*	*4*

1. Preheat the oven to 400°F / 200°C / Gas Mark 6.
2. Arrange the washed and drained peppers in a pan, put in the oven and leave until the peppers have dried out; about 30 minutes.
3. Cut the eggplant into slices, sprinkle them with fine salt and leave until they sweat the bitter juice.
4. After about 30 minutes turn off the oven and leave the peppers in it until they become lukewarm.
5. Wash the eggplant under running water, dry lightly and put under the broiler (grill) for a little while; if you prefer, fry them quickly in seed oil. Drain them on a plate with absorbent paper and place in a large ovenproof dish.
6. Patiently peel the peppers, remove the seeds and arrange in alternate layers with eggplant. Sprinkle with pepper and salt.
7. Add oregano and crushed cloves of garlic to the olive oil, mix well and pour over the vegetables. Add some chopped fresh basil leaves and serve.

Insalata del Granduca

Grand Duke's Salad

01:00 00:40

American	Ingredients	Metric/Imperial
1	*Sweet yellow pepper*	1
1 cup	*Long grain rice*	200 g / 7 oz
2	*Gourds*	2
½ lb	*Fresh prawns*	225 g / 8 oz
7 oz	*Wurstëln*	200 g / 7 oz
⅔ cup	*Sultanas*	100 g / 4 oz
¼ cup	*Brandy*	50 ml / 2 fl oz
¼ lb	*Anchovies*	100 g / 4 oz
½	*Lemon*	½
½ tsp	*Tabasco sauce*	½ tsp
1 tbsp	*Vegetable oil*	1 tbsp
	Salt and pepper	
2	*Tomatoes*	2

1. Preheat the oven to 350°F / 180°C / Gas Mark 4.
2. Wash the pepper, put it in the oven to cook for 20 minutes. Take it out and peel it (you will see that the skin will come away very easily). Clear the seeds from the pepper and cut it into very thin strips.
3. Cook the rice and drain it when 'al dente', pass it quickly under cold water and drain well, put it in a salad bowl.
4. Separately boil the gourds, the prawns, and plunge the wurstëln in hot water for a few minutes. Wash the sultanas and soak in the brandy.
5. Chop the cleaned and boned anchovies finely and put in an earthenware dish. Mash them as much as possible, add a few drops of brandy, the juice of half a lemon and several drops of tabasco, beat well or put in a blender until you have a smooth sauce. Add the oil and seasoning.
6. Mix the anchovies with the rice in the salad bowl, add the drained prawns, the gourds cut into slices, the thin strips of pepper, the wurstëln cut into round slices and the sultanas. Stir well.
7. Garnish with some sliced fresh tomato and put in the refrigerator for 30 minutes before serving.

Insalata di ovoli

Royal Mushroom Salad

00:30 00:10

American	Ingredients	Metric/Imperial
½ lb	*Mushrooms*	225 g / 8 oz
2	*Eggs*	2
1 tsp	*Mustard*	1 tsp
	Salt and pepper	
¼ tsp	*Paprika*	¼ tsp
¼ cup	*Vegetable oil*	50 ml / 2 fl oz
1	*Lemon*	1
4 drops	*Tabasco sauce*	4 drops
1 tsp	*Worcester sauce*	1 tsp
3 tbsp	*Sherry*	2 tbsp
3 tbsp	*Coffee (single) cream*	2 tbsp
1	*Lettuce head*	1
12	*Cooked prawns (optional)*	12

1. Wipe or wash mushrooms and slice thinly.
2. Hard-cook (boil) eggs and rinse in cold water, put the yolks in an earthenware dish and crush them with a fork. Mix with mustard, a pinch of salt, the pepper and paprika. Now work the mixture with the oil, stirring continuously as if for a mayonnaise and sprinkling from time to time with lemon juice. When the mixture is creamy, add the tabasco and worcester sauce, then the sherry and cream and mix well.
3. Clean, wash and thoroughly drain a few choice lettuce leaves and use them to line 4 glasses. Blend a little sauce with the mushrooms, distribute them amongst the glasses and cover with the remaining sauce.

Cook's tip: if you wish to enrich this salad you may decorate the top with cooked shelled prawns. The white of the egg may be chopped or sieved to decorate the dishes.

Insalata alla creola

Creole-Style Salad

00:30 00:20

American	Ingredients	Metric/Imperial
1 lb	*Potatoes*	450 g / 1 lb
¼ lb	*Cooked ham*	100 g / 4 oz
¼ lb	*Canned pineapple, drained*	100 g / 4 oz
1 cup	*Mayonnaise (see page 175)*	225 ml / 8 fl oz
½ cup	*White wine*	125 ml / 4 fl oz
	Salt	
¼ tsp	*Paprika pepper*	¼ tsp
8	*Sprigs of parsley*	8

1. Boil the peeled potatoes in plenty of salted water, then cut into cubes together with the cooked ham and the pineapple. Put the ingredients in a salad bowl.
2. Place the mayonnaise in a bowl with white wine, salt and paprika pepper. Mix well.
3. Stir everything carefully to blend with the sauce, then serve garnished with sprigs of parsley.

Asticciole di sedano

Celery Stalks

00:20 Chilling time 02:00 00:00

American	Ingredients	Metric/Imperial
1	*Celery heart*	1
¼ lb	*Mascarpone cheese*	100 g / 4 oz
¼ lb	*Gorgonzola cheese*	100 g / 4 oz
	A little melted butter, (only if the mixture is rather dry)	
	Salt and pepper	

1. Take the heart of a fresh head of celery. Cut into pieces of about 4 in / 10 cm, wash and put into a bowl full of water and leave in the refrigerator until ready to serve. Then remove and dry.
2. Mix the mascarpone and the gorgonzola together with a fork, adding butter if necessary. Taste and add salt and pepper, if necessary. Spread the mixture in the channels of the dried pieces of celery, then put in the refrigerator for a few hours. Garnish with radishes and eat well chilled.

Creole-style salad

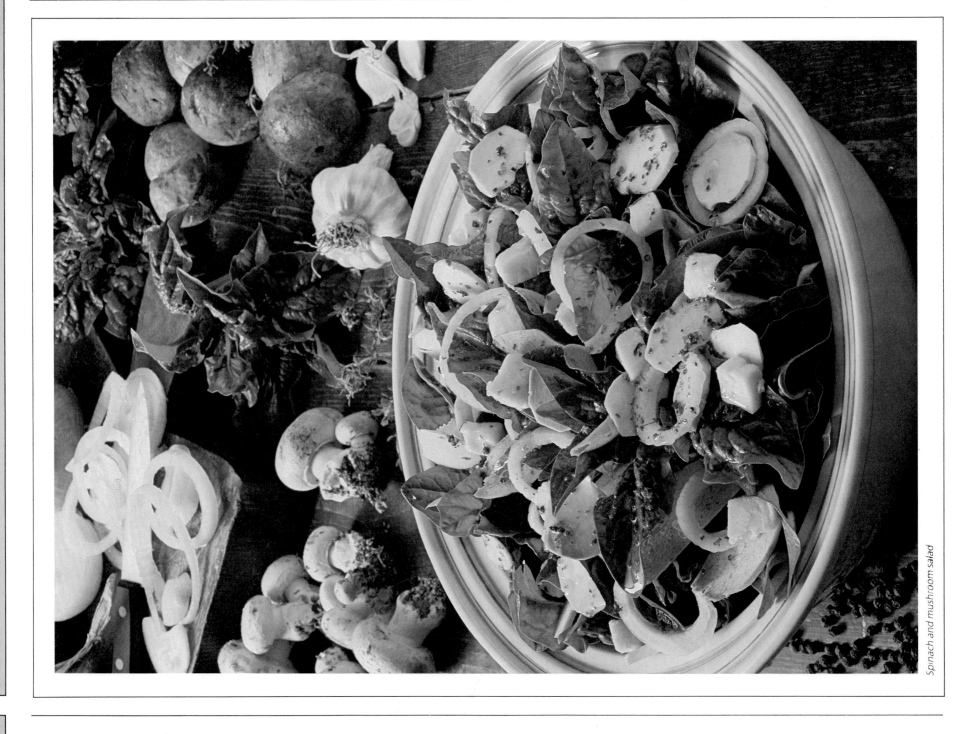

Spinach and mushroom salad

Insalata di spinaci e funghi

Spinach and Mushroom Salad

00:15 00:00

American	Ingredients	Metric/Imperial
14 oz	*Fresh spinach*	*400 g / 14 oz*
1-1½ cups	*Mushrooms*	*150 g / 5 oz*
1	*Red onion*	*1*
2½ oz	*Strong gorgonzola cheese*	*65 g / 2½ oz*
1	*Garlic clove*	*1*
1	*Sprig of thyme*	*1*
½ tsp	*Salt*	*½ tsp*
½ cup	*Olive oil*	*125 ml / 4 fl oz*
3 tbsp	*White vinegar*	*2 tbsp*
	Freshly ground white pepper	

1. Trim the spinach, wash in several changes of water and dry. Tear into pieces.
2. Wash the mushrooms, dry them and cut them into small slices.
3. Cut the onion into rings, crumble the gorgonzola and crush the garlic.
4. In a salad bowl put the spinach, the mushrooms, the onion and gorgonzola.
5. In a small glass jar with a screw-top lid put the garlic, the thyme, the salt, the oil and vinegar. Shake it vigorously and then pour the dressing over the salad. Mix gently to save crumpling the spinach leaves. Grind some pepper over and serve at once.

Insalata di riso golosa

Tempting Rice Salad

00:30 00:15

American	Ingredients	Metric/Imperial
2	*Heads of lettuce*	*2*
1 cup	*Rice*	*200 g / 7 oz*
4	*Eggs*	*4*
Scant ¼ cup	*Vegetable oil*	*3 tbsp*
2 tbsp	*Vinegar*	*1½ tbsp*
	Salt and pepper	
4	*Sardines in oil*	*4*

1. Carefully clean the lettuce removing the toughest leaves and cut the hearts in half. Cut most of the leaves into thin strips keeping a few large ones intact for garnishing the dish when it is served.
2. Boil the rice till 'al dente' and drain and rinse in cold water, drain again.
3. Hard-cook (boil) 4 eggs, cool in cold water and remove the shells.
4. Put the rice, strips of lettuce and the hearts in a salad bowl, mix and season with oil, vinegar, salt and pepper. Arrange the rice in the shape of a dome on a serving dish. Place the sardines on the rice.
5. Cut the eggs in half lengthways and place them around the rice. Arrange the large lettuce leaves between one piece of egg and the next.

Funghi con pomodoro

Mushrooms with Tomato

00:20 00:30

American	Ingredients	Metric/Imperial
1¾ lb	*Mushrooms*	*800 g / 1¾ lb*
1	*Garlic clove*	*1*
1	*Onion*	*1*
5 tbsp	*Vegetable oil*	*4 tbsp*
¼ cup	*Dry white wine*	*50 ml / 2 fl oz*
1 lb	*Peeled tomatoes*	*450 g / 1 lb*
	Salt and pepper	
1 tbsp	*Chopped parsley*	*1 tbsp*

1. Remove the stalks from the mushrooms (use in a sauce), wipe or wash the caps with a damp cloth and cut them into fairly thick slices.
2. Chop the garlic and the onion and brown them in a pan with the oil over a moderate heat. Add the mushrooms and when the pan juice has evaporated pour in the white wine and, over a moderate heat, leave it to evaporate.
3. Add the tomatoes, chopped up or passed through a vegetable-mill, the salt and pepper, and continue cooking for about 20 minutes. Sprinkle the mushrooms with the chopped parsley before serving cold.

Arlecchinata

Mixed Vegetable and Cheese Salad

01:00 00:00

American	Ingredients	Metric/Imperial
1	*Head of lettuce*	*1*
2	*Cucumbers*	*2*
	Salt	
1	*Bunch of radishes*	*1*
1	*Small cauliflower*	*1*
5 oz	*Gouda cheese*	*150 g / 5 oz*
1	*Lemon*	*1*
Scant ¼ cup	*Olive oil*	*3 tbsp*
½ tsp	*French mustard*	*½ tsp*
1 tbsp	*Anchovy paste*	*1 tbsp*

1. Prepare all the vegetables. Remove the oldest leaves from the lettuce, keeping the inner part, take off the leaves one by one and wash well.
2. Scrape the cucumbers well without removing their skin, wash and slice them (not too thick and not too thin), sprinkle with fine salt and drain off the juice by squeezing them between 2 tilting plates.
3. Wash the radishes well, remove the leaves and the bottom part, cut into slices. Divide the cauliflower into heads and soak in cold water. After 30 minutes drain and cut into florets.
4. Cut the cheese into small cubes. Prepare the seasoning in a bowl by putting in lemon juice, olive oil, mustard and a little anchovy paste. Blend well, using a fork.
5. On a serving dish first arrange the lettuce leaves, well dried, the cauliflower, then 1 slice of cucumber, well dried, and 1 of radish, so that the colors alternate. Put the cubes of cheese in the middle. Serve the seasoning separately.

Insalata Belzebù

Beelzebub's Salad

00:20 00:00

American	Ingredients	Metric/Imperial
1	*Head of lettuce*	1
3 cups	*Bean sprouts*	175 g / 6 oz
5 oz	*Emmental cheese*	150 g / 5 oz
4	*Anchovies in oil*	4
5 oz	*Cooked ham*	150 g / 5 oz
1 tbsp	*Capers*	1 tbsp
1	*Sweet yellow pepper*	1
1	*Sweet red pepper*	1
1	*Sweet green pepper*	1
10	*Small mushrooms*	10
1	*Hard-cooked (boiled) egg*	1
⅔ cup	*Olive oil*	150 ml / ¼ pint
	Salt and pepper	
¼ tsp	*Paprika*	¼ tsp
3 tbsp	*Soy sauce*	2 tbsp

1. Clean the lettuce and the bean sprouts by rinsing in cold water, drain, dry with absorbent kitchen towels and put in a salad bowl.
2. Add small pieces of emmental cheese, the anchovies in oil, the cooked ham cut into thin strips, capers, the sweet deseeded yellow, red and green peppers, cut into strips, a few sliced mushrooms and the sliced hard-cooked egg.
3. Season with a mixture of olive oil, a pinch of salt, pepper, paprika and soy sauce. Toss the ingredients well in the dressing and serve.

Lattughe e pomodori in salsa profumata

Lettuce and Tomatoes in Flavored Sauce

00:45 00:12
Chilling time 01:00

American	Ingredients	Metric/Imperial
2	*Small heads of lettuce*	2
4	*Tomatoes*	4
1 cup	*Mayonnaise (see page 175)*	225 ml / 8 fl oz
5 oz	*Tuna fish in oil*	150 g / 5 oz
1 oz	*Small pickled onions*	25 g / 1 oz
2	*Hard-cooked (boiled) eggs*	2
2	*Basil leaves*	2
8	*Sprigs of parsley*	8
7	*Mint leaves*	7
3 tbsp	*Vegetable oil*	2 tbsp
12	*Black olives*	12

1. Thoroughly clean the lettuce detaching the leaves one by one, pat dry.
2. Wash and dry the tomatoes, then slice and let them drain.
3. Prepare the sauce by putting in the blender the mayonnaise, then add the tuna fish crumbled, the small onions sliced, the hard-cooked eggs in little pieces, the basil, half the parsley, the mint and the oil. Switch on the blender and mix until you obtain a smooth and creamy sauce.
4. Arrange the lettuce leaves radiating from the centre on a serving dish, insert the slices of tomato between the leaves and pour the sauce on top.
5. Decorate with black olives and parsley. Keep in refrigerator for 1 hour before serving.

Beelzebub's salad

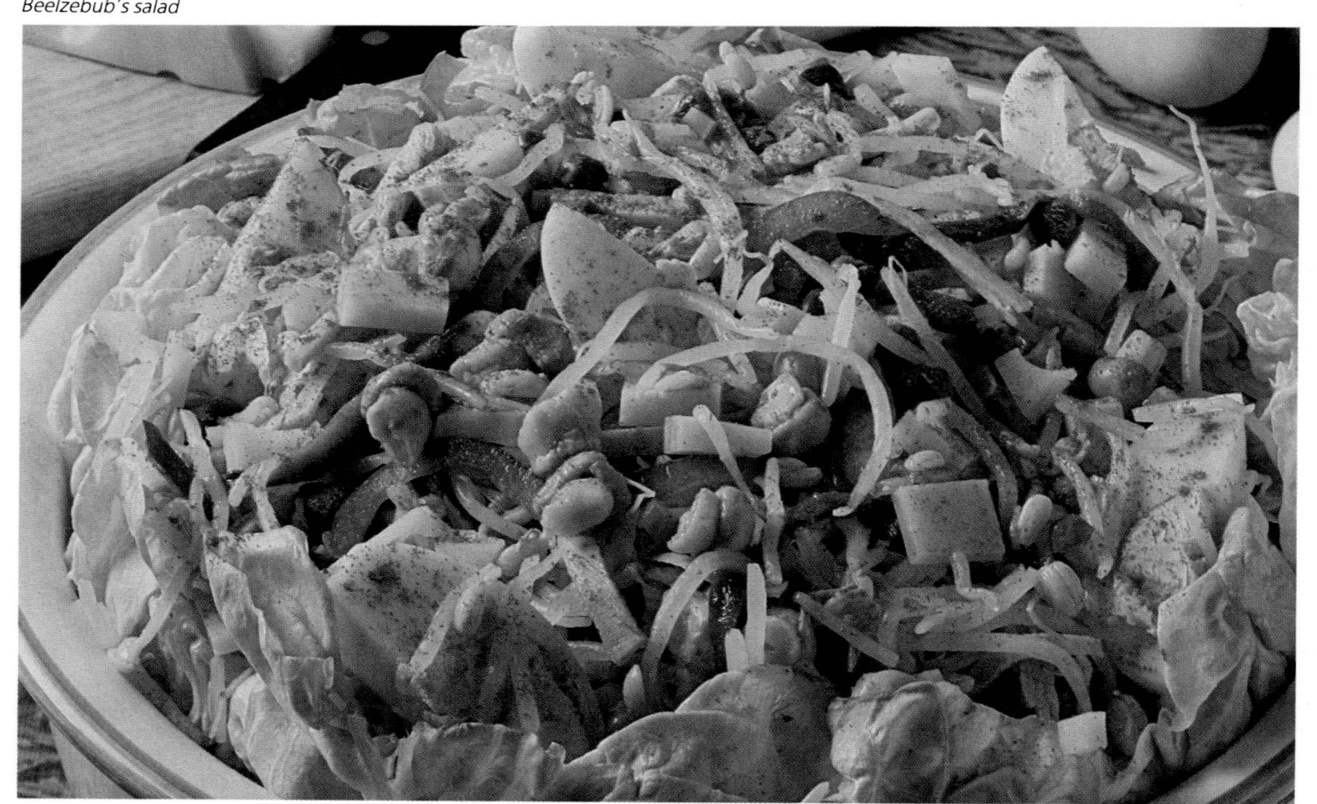

Orange salad

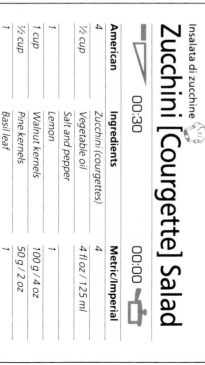

Insalata di arance

Orange Salad

Preparation 00:15 — Cooking 00:00

American	Ingredients	Metric/Imperial
4	*Oranges*	4
1	*Garlic clove*	1
	Salt	
1 tbsp	*Olive oil*	1 tbsp
1	*Small onion (optional)*	1

1. Using a very sharp small knife, remove the peel from the oranges and the white pith. Slice the orange as thinly as possible across the width.
2. Rub the sides of a glass salad bowl with a cut clove of garlic. Arrange the sliced oranges in the bowl. Season with salt, plenty of freshly-ground pepper, sprinkle with olive oil. Refrigerate for 30 minutes before serving.
3. Add the peeled onion, thinly sliced into rings, to the top of the orange if desired.

Insalata di zucchine

Zucchini [Courgette] Salad

Preparation 00:30 — Cooking 00:00

American	Ingredients	Metric/Imperial
4	*Zucchini (courgettes)*	4
½ cup	*Vegetable oil*	4 fl oz / 125 ml
	Salt and pepper	
1	*Lemon*	1
1 cup	*Walnut kernels*	100 g / 4 oz
½ cup	*Pine kernels*	50 g / 2 oz
1	*Basil leaf*	1

1. Thoroughly wash the zucchini, which must be fresh, then slice them very finelv. Put them in a large bowl and season with plenty of oil, salt, pepper and the juice of a lemon. Leave to stand for 1 hour, turning from time to time.
2. Remove brown skin from walnut kernels. Chop walnuts and pine kernels carefully with a half-moon cutter. Chop basil and mix with nuts into zucchini.

Cruda e cotta

Raw and Cooked Salad

00:40 00:20

American	Ingredients	Metric/Imperial
¾ lb	*Green beans*	350 g / 12 oz
	Salt and pepper	
2	*Potatoes*	2
2	*Small onions*	2
2	*Zucchini (courgettes)*	2
2	*Tomatoes*	2
1	*Cucumber*	1
2	*Egg yolks*	2
⅔ cup	*Vegetable oil*	150 ml / ¼ pint
2 tsp	*Light mustard*	2 tsp
1 tbsp	*Wine vinegar*	1 tbsp

1. Remove the strings from the green beans and then cut into 2 in / 5 cm pieces and cook in a little salted boiling water for 7 minutes.
2. Boil the potatoes until tender but firm. Add the onions for the last 10 minutes. Drain and dice.
3. Blanch the washed zucchini in some boiling salted water for 4 minutes, drain. Cut into slices.
4. Place the beans, diced potatoes, sliced onion and zucchini in a bowl, mix well.
5. Slice the tomatoes and finely slice a cucumber. Mix the raw vegetables with the cooked ones.
6. In a small bowl, mix the egg yolks with the oil, added gradually, mix in the mustard, salt and pepper. Flavor with wine vinegar or lemon juice.
7. Dress the salad with this mixture and refrigerate for a while so that it can be served slightly chilled.

Carote alla piacentina

Piacenza-Style Carrots

00:20 Standing time 01:00 00:10

American	Ingredients	Metric/Imperial
¾ lb	*New carrots*	350 g / 12 oz
2	*Lemons*	2
	Salt and pepper	
2	*Eggs*	2
2 tsp	*Chopped basil*	2 tsp
1	*Garlic clove*	1
3 tbsp	*Vegetable oil*	2 tbsp

1. Scrape the carrots well and slice them very finely, then season at once with the juice of 2 lemons and some salt. Leave them to soak for 1 hour.
2. Hard-cook (boil) 2 eggs, cool under running cold water, shell and cut them into slices.
3. Chop the basil very finely and mix with a crushed garlic clove, add to this the oil, salt and pepper.
4. Season the carrots with the herb and oil dressing. Arrange the carrots in a dish garnished with the slices of egg and serve.

Cook's tip: this can be served as a first-course.

Insalata al prosciutto

Ham Salad

00:25 00:00

American	Ingredients	Metric/Imperial
¾ lb	*Thick slice of cooked ham*	350 g / 12 oz
4	*Slices of pineapple, fresh or canned*	4
1	*Head of lettuce*	1
3 tbsp	*Brandy*	2 tbsp
½ cup	*Vegetable oil*	125 ml / 4 fl oz
1 tbsp	*Mustard*	1 tbsp
2	*Lemons*	2
	Salt and pepper	
2	*Bananas*	2

1. Remove all of the fat from the ham and cut the meat into small dice.
2. If you use fresh fruit, peel and divide up the pineapple into cubes. Drain it well if using canned fruit and cube if necessary.
3. Clean the lettuce discarding any damaged leaves and wash under running water. Shake the lettuce in a colander and line the salad bowl with it.
4. Mix the brandy in a small bowl with the oil, mustard, half the lemon juice, salt and pepper. Beat slightly with a fork to blend the seasoning.
5. Pour the dressing over the cubes of ham and pineapple, mix well, arrange them on the lettuce leaves.
6. Cut the bananas into rings, cover with remaining lemon juice and arrange round the salad.

Asparagi imperiali

Imperial Asparagus

00:30 00:15

American	Ingredients	Metric/Imperial
2	*Bundles of large asparagus*	2
	Salt	
1	*Lemon wedge*	1
1	*Truffle*	1
4	*Anchovies in brine, boned*	4
1¼ cups	*Mayonnaise (see page 175) or Mousseline sauce (see page 175)*	300 ml / ½ pint
2 tbsp	*Tomato purée*	1½ tbsp

1. Clean the asparagus well, scraping them one by one with a knife and cutting away the woodiest part. Cook in salted water with a lemon wedge, using the proper saucepan for asparagus, where they will be steamed without being reduced to a pulp. When cooked, take the asparagus out carefully and leave on one side to cool.
2. Arrange on an oval dish and sprinkle with thin slices of truffle. To do this properly and to obtain thin slices, use a truffle-slicer – a utensil that you will find in some kitchen shops, otherwise use a small sharp knife.
3. Decorate the dish with anchovy fillets, having trimmed and boned them.
4. Finally, cover the salad with well-seasoned mayonnaise mixed with tomato purée.

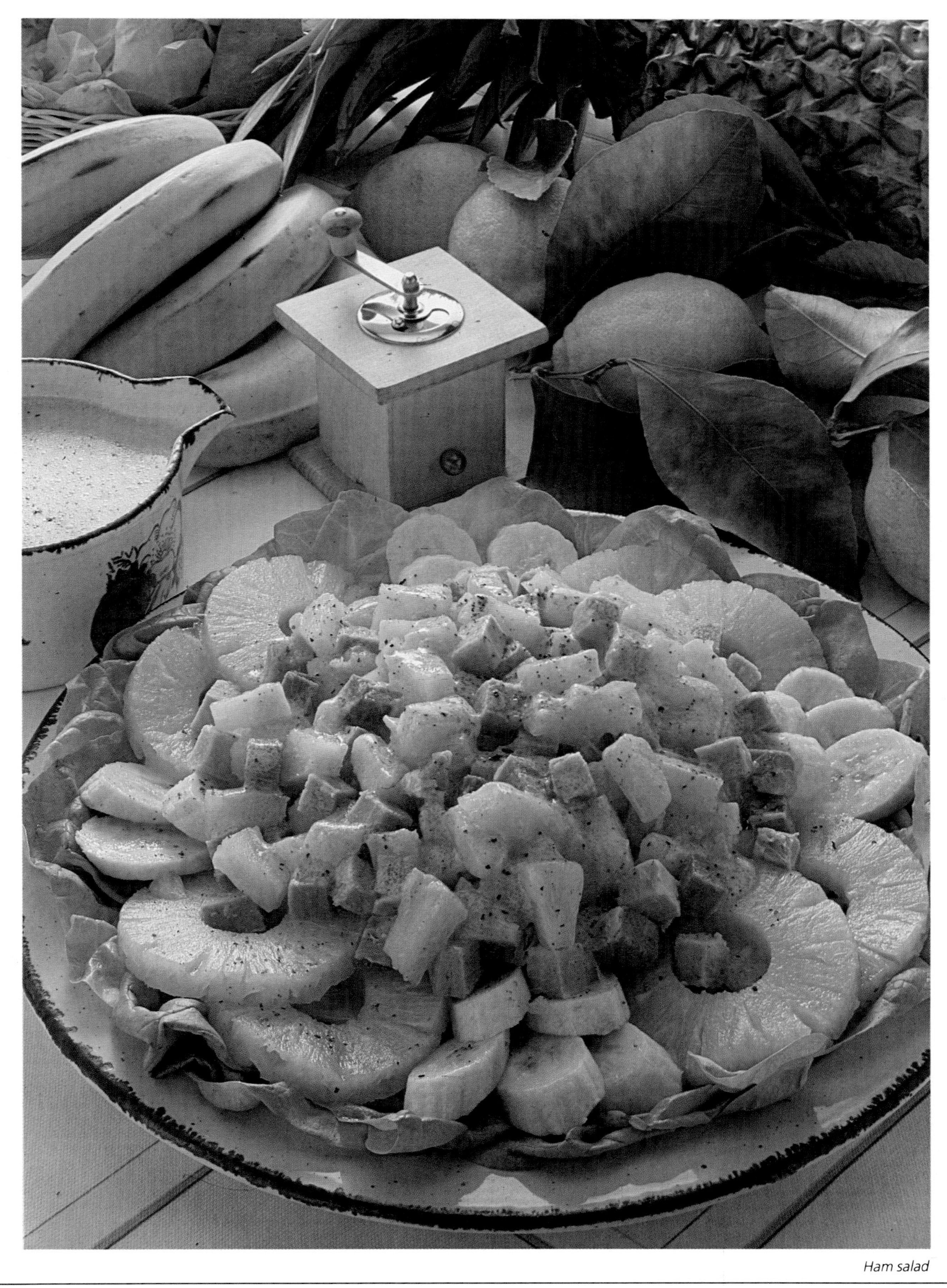

Ham salad

Insalata tropicale

Tropical Salad

00:20 | 00:10

American	Ingredients	Metric/Imperial
1	*Can of bean shoots*	1
3	*Small plants of Belgian endive*	3
¼ lb	*Gruyère cheese*	100 g / 4 oz
2	*Eggs*	2
½ cup	*Vegetable oil*	125 ml / 4 fl oz
	Salt and pepper	
¼ cup	*Vinegar*	50 ml / 2 fl oz
1	*Ripe avocado*	1

1. Drain the bean shoots, wash the Belgian endive plants well and then cut them into round slices. Cut the gruyère into small sticks.
2. Hard-cook (boil) the eggs, cool them under cold water and cut them into fairly thick slices.
3. Mix all ingredients together. Combine the oil, salt and pepper, and vinegar, together in a cup to make a dressing and mix into the salad.
4. Peel the avocado, cut in half, hollow out with a corer to make little balls, or with a coffee spoon to form flakes. Mix gently and serve immediately or avocados will discolor.

Insalata araba

Arab Salad

00:25 | 00:00

American	Ingredients	Metric/Imperial
2	*Large white onions*	2
1	*Juicy orange*	1
1	*Large sweet green pepper*	1
¼ lb	*Black olives, pitted (stoned)*	100 g / 4 oz
½ tsp	*Mustard*	½ tsp
½	*Lemon*	½
¼ cup	*Vegetable oil*	50 ml / 2 fl oz
1 tsp	*Honey*	1 tsp
	Salt and pepper	

1. Peel the mild white onions and cut into thin rings.
2. Remove the peel from the orange and also the white pith between segments, cut with a very sharp small knife.
3. Deseed the green pepper and, using a very sharp knife, slice into little thin strips.
4. Put the ingredients in an earthenware dish, add olives.
5. Mix the mustard with the lemon juice and oil, add thin honey, salt and pepper in a screw top jar. Put on the lid and shake well.
6. Pour onto the salad, mix and serve.

Arab salad

Fagiolini, cipolle e formaggio

Runner Beans, Onion and Cheese Salad

00:30 | 00:15

American	Ingredients	Metric/Imperial
14 oz	Runner beans	400 g / 14 oz
7 oz	Button onions	200 g / 7 oz
5 oz	Fontina cheese	150 g / 5 oz
1 tbsp	Capers	1 tbsp
2	Lemons	2
½ cup	Olive oil	125 ml / 4 fl oz
	Salt and pepper	
	Cream if desired	

1. Wash and remove any strings from the beans. Cook in a little boiling salted water for 6 minutes. Drain.
2. Cook the onions in boiling salted water for 5 minutes, drain.
3. Cut the fontina into small cubes. Wash the capers and chop. Mix all the ingredients together in a salad bowl.
4. In a separate bowl mix the lemon juice, olive oil, salt and pepper, pour on to the salad and mix well. An optional addition to the dressing is a little fresh cream.

Crescione e mele alla panna acida

Watercress and Apples with Sour Cream

00:25 | 00:00

American	Ingredients	Metric/Imperial
4	Bunches of watercress	4
2	Bunches of radishes	2
½ cup	Shelled almonds	65 g / 2½ oz
2	Golden delicious apples	2
2	Lemons	2
6 tbsp	Coffee (single) cream	5 tbsp
	Salt and pepper	

1. Clean the watercress thoroughly; wash it changing the water several times, drain.
2. Clean the radishes and cut into thin slices and slice the almonds finely.
3. Peel and core the apples, cut into small dice, sprinkle them with a little lemon juice to prevent them from turning black.
4. Arrange the watercress in a salad bowl. Add the slices of radish, the diced apples and the almonds.
5. Season the salad with a dressing made by mixing together the lemon juice and the cream with plenty of salt and pepper.

Insalata di cicoria al gorgonzola

Endive Salad with Gorgonzola

This is a refined variation of the old peasant custom of filling a long loaf of whole wheat bread with a smear of gorgonzola and a few leaves of wild endive.

00:15 | 00:00

American	Ingredients	Metric/Imperial
4	Bunches of endive	4
6 tbsp	Olive oil	5 tbsp
3 tbsp	Vinegar	2 tbsp
1 tsp	Mustard	1 tsp
1 tsp	Brandy	1 tsp
1 heaped tbsp	Gorgonzola cheese	1 heaped tbsp
	Salt and pepper	
4	Bread crusts	4
2	Garlic cloves	2

1. Trim the endive, wash it and cut thinly.
2. Place in a large bowl and season with a well mixed dressing made with olive oil, vinegar, mustard, a few drops of brandy, and the strong gorgonzola cheese, mashed with a fork, salt and pepper.
3. Add several crusts of dry bread rubbed with cut garlic and leave in the salad to give the flavor of garlic. Remove crusts before serving.

Giardinetto alla americana

American-Style Salad

00:25 | 00:03

American	Ingredients	Metric/Imperial
1	Carrot	1
1	Zucchini (courgette)	1
1	Small eggplant (aubergine)	1
1	Celery	1
1	Tomato	1
1	Canadian apple	1
1	Sweet red or yellow pepper	1
1	Small onion	1
3	Scallions (spring onions)	3
6	Fresh mint leaves	6
1	Banana	1
½ cup	Vegetable oil	125 ml / 4 fl oz
	Salt and pepper	
2	Lemons	2

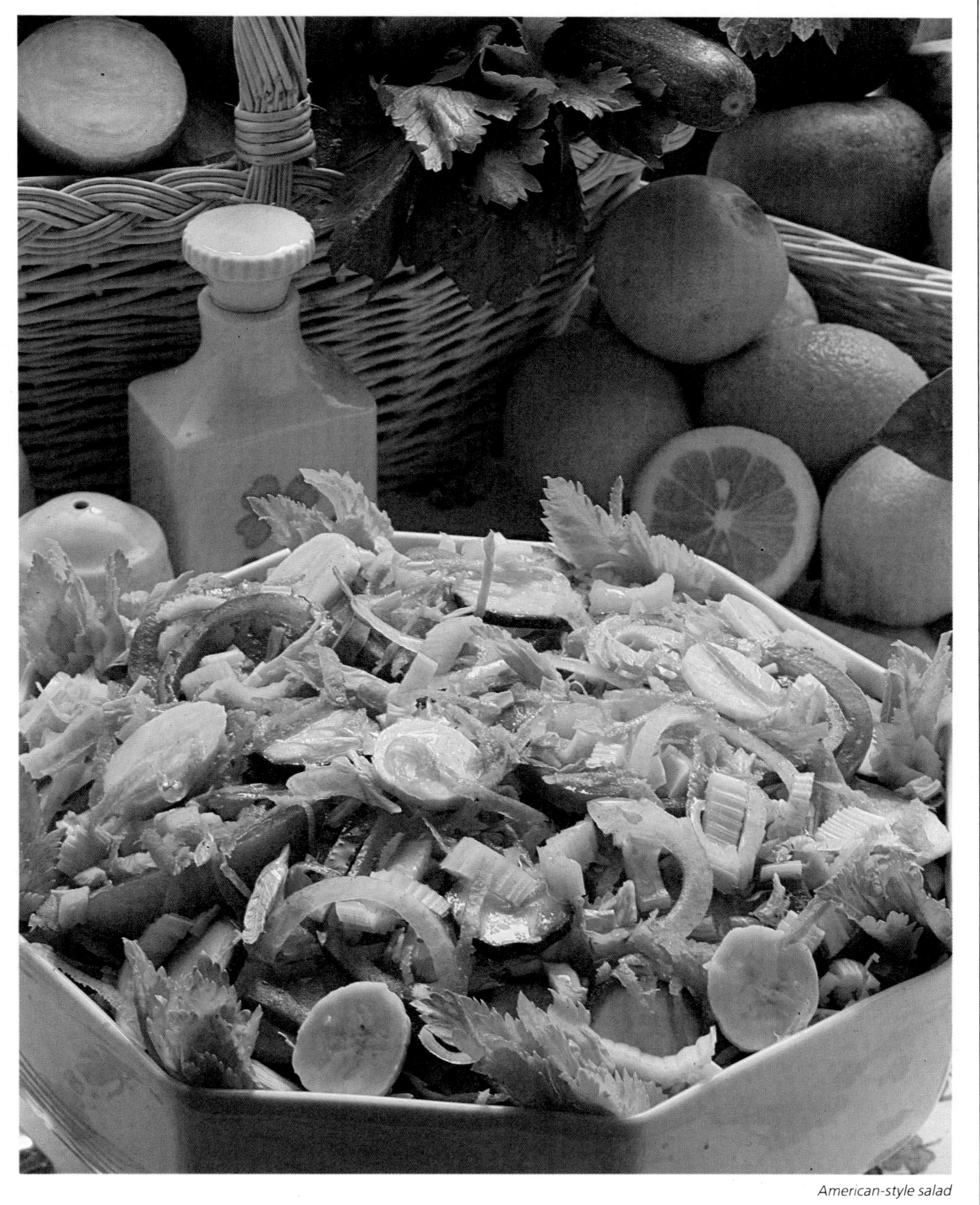

American-style salad

1. Finely grate the carrot, wash the zucchini, cut into thin round slices.
2. Peel and discard the skin from the eggplant. Slice the flesh finely. Blanch in boiling water for 3 minutes, drain and cool.
3. Cut the washed celery into rounds, the tomato and apple into slices and the deseeded pepper into pieces. Mix all the vegetables in a bowl and add the finely chopped onion, scallions, a few leaves of fresh mint and a sliced banana. Season with a well mixed oil, salt, pepper and lemon juice dressing. Stir round and serve immediately.

VEGETABLE DISHES

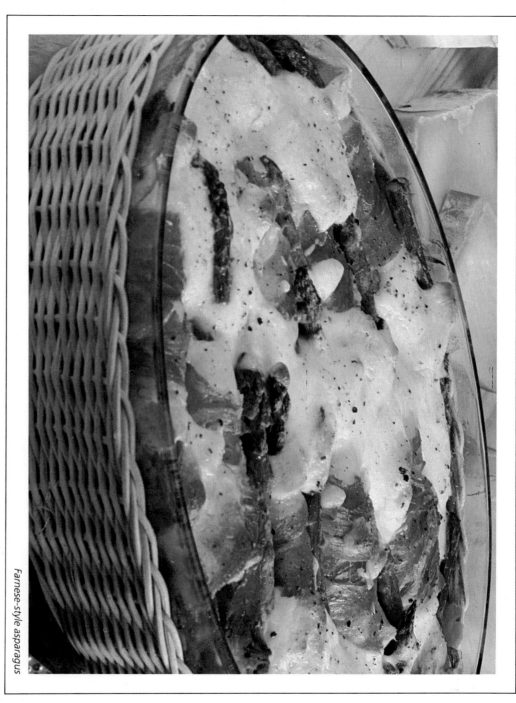

Farnese-style asparagus

Asparagi alla farnesina 

Farnese-Style Asparagus

00:35 00:20

American	Ingredients	Metric/Imperial
2 lb	*Asparagus*	*1 kg / 2 lb*
½ lb	*Fontina cheese*	*225 g / 8 oz*
½ lb	*Cooked ham*	*225 g / 8 oz*
1 cup	*Béchamel sauce (see page 162)*	*225 ml / 8 oz*
½ cup	*Butter*	*100 g / 4 oz*
	Salt and pepper	
¼ tsp	*Nutmeg*	*¼ tsp*

1. Prepare the asparagus, then half-cook them in boiling water. Drain and allow to cool.
2. Wrap the green part of the asparagus with 1 slice of fontina and 1 of cooked ham, securing them with half a toothpick.
3. Preheat the oven to 400°F / 200°C / Gas Mark 6.
4. Lay all the asparagus in a buttered ovenproof dish, cover with béchamel sauce and dot with butter. Sprinkle with salt, pepper and nutmeg. Put in a hot oven for 20 minutes and serve immediately.

Pasticcio di asparagi 

Asparagus Bake

00:30 00:30

American	Ingredients	Metric/Imperial
2 lb	*Asparagus*	*1 kg / 2 lb*
	Salt and pepper	
2½ cups	*Béchamel sauce (see page 162)*	*600 ml / 1 pint*
¼ cup	*Butter*	*50 g / 2 oz*
½ cup	*Grated parmesan cheese*	*50 g / 2 oz*
¼ lb	*Mozzarella cheese*	*100 g / 4 oz*

1. Preheat the oven to 400°F / 200°C / Gas Mark 6.
2. Prepare the asparagus and cook in boiling salted water for about 10 minutes or until tender.
3. Meanwhile make the béchamel sauce and season well.
4. Drain the asparagus and dry in a clean cloth. Place in a buttered ovenproof dish, add a few knobs of butter, sprinkle with grated parmesan, slices of mozzarella and freshly ground pepper.
5. Pour the béchamel sauce over the asparagus. Put in a hot oven for about 15 minutes.

Asparagi di Bassano in salsa

Bassano Asparagus in Sauce

00:30 00:20 to 00:30

American	Ingredients	Metric/Imperial
1½ lb	*Asparagus*	*700 g / 1½ lb*
3	*Eggs*	*3*
1½	*Lemons*	*1½*
½ cup	*Olive oil*	*125 ml / 4 fl oz*
	Salt and pepper	
1 tbsp	*Chopped parsley*	*1 tbsp*

1. Prepare asparagus and boil in salted water until tender.
2. Hard-cook the eggs, cool under running cold water, shell and chop both yolks and whites finely.
3. Pour the oil into a bowl, add the lemon juice and beat vigorously; season with salt and pepper and mix in parsley.
4. Arrange the asparagus on a heated oval serving dish with the tips turned inwards, then pour over the oil and lemon sauce. Wait for it to be partly absorbed, then sprinkle with the chopped egg.

Asparagi alla legnanese

Legnano-Style Asparagus

00:20 00:15

American	Ingredients	Metric/Imperial
1½ lb	*Asparagus*	*700 g / 1½ lb*
	Salt	
3	*Eggs*	*3*
	Ground black pepper	
½ cup	*Grated parmesan cheese*	*50 g / 2 oz*
½ cup	*Butter*	*100 g / 4 oz*

1. Prepare the asparagus, tie into bundles and cook in boiling salted water.
2. Hard-cook the eggs, cool under running cold water and shell them. Sieve the yolks and chop the whites finely.
3. Heat a serving dish and when the asparagus are properly cooked, arrange them on the dish. Sprinkle with a little freshly ground black pepper and parmesan. Pour on the melted butter and on top arrange the egg yolks and whites in alternate rows. Serve immediately.

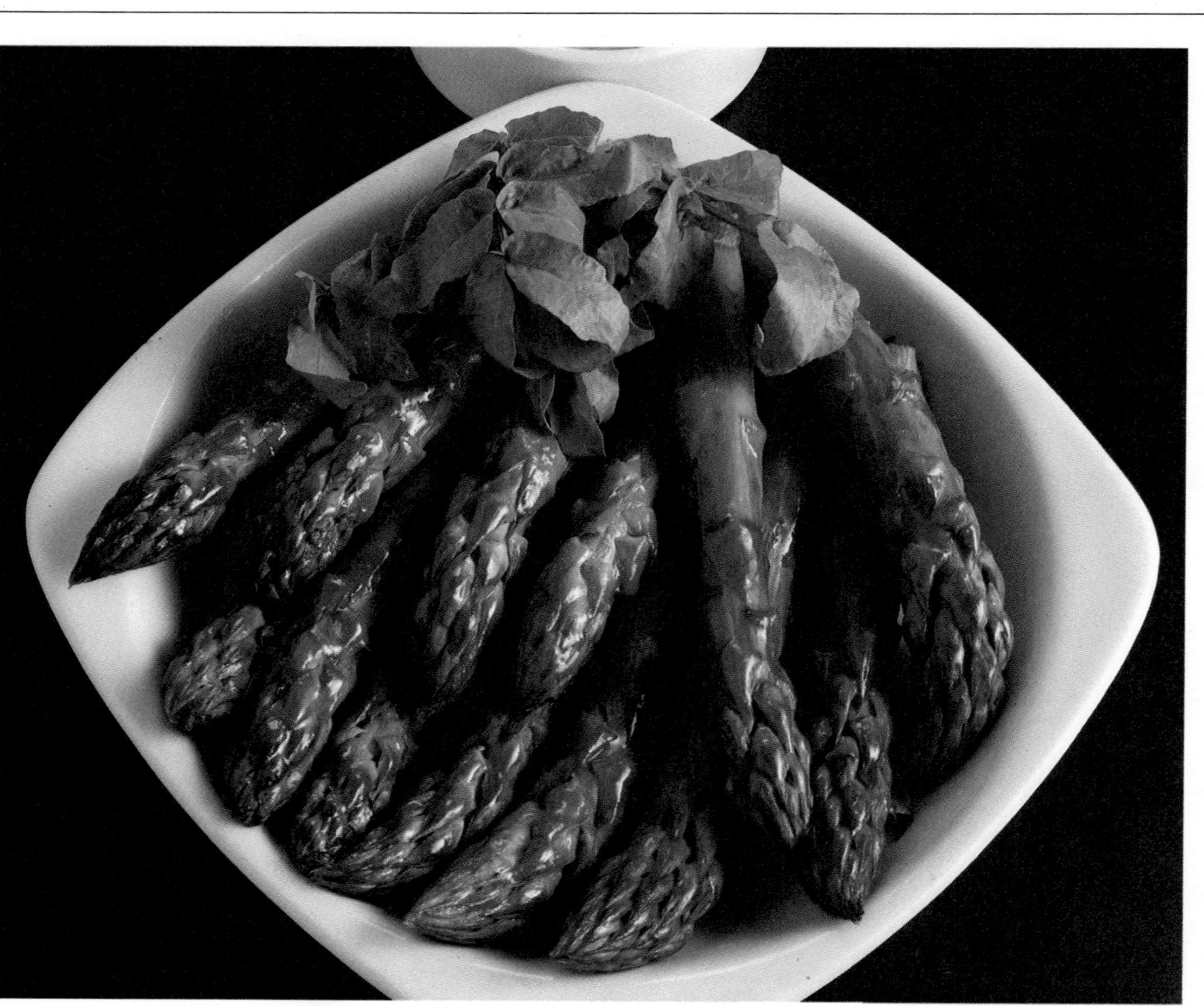

Bassano asparagus in sauce

Torta di asparagi

Asparagus Flan

00:40 00:50

American	Ingredients	Metric/Imperial
1 ¼ cups	*Béchamel sauce (see page 162)*	300 ml / ½ pint
1 lb	*Asparagus*	450 g / 1 lb
½ lb	*Shortcrust pastry (see page 452)*	225 g / 8 oz
	Salt and pepper	
½ cup	*Grated parmesan cheese*	50 g / 2 oz

1. Make the béchamel sauce and cover with film to prevent a skin forming.
2. Discard the tough part of the asparagus and cook in boiling salted water until tender.
3. Preheat the oven to 400°F / 200°C / Gas Mark 6.
4. Roll out the pastry on a floured board and line an 8 in / 20 cm flan ring. Trim the top and prick the bottom with a fork. Rest in the refrigerator for 10 minutes. Prepare a piece of wax (greaseproof) paper to fit the flan and cover with baking beans.
5. Cook the flan case for 15 minutes, remove the baking beans and cook for a further 5 minutes.
6. Reduce oven heat to 325°F / 170°C / Gas Mark 3.
7. Remove from the oven, allow to cool slightly, add the chopped asparagus, season, and cover with the béchamel sauce. Sprinkle with cheese and cook in the oven for 20 minutes. Serve hot.

Carciofi di Tivoli

Tivoli Artichokes

00:25 00:45

American	Ingredients	Metric/Imperial
8	*Large artichokes*	8
1	*Lemon*	1
½ lb	*Mushrooms*	225 g / 8 oz
10	*Slices of lean bacon*	10
½ cup	*Vegetable oil*	125 ml / 4 fl oz
3 tbsp	*Chopped parsley*	2 tbsp
4	*Garlic cloves*	4
	Salt and pepper	
¼ cup	*Dry white wine*	50 ml / 2 fl oz
½ cup	*Stock*	125 ml / 4 fl oz
	Sprigs of parsley	

1. Remove the prickles and the toughest leaves of the artichokes, wash very well both inside and out and spread out the leaves a little. Put in a pan with boiling water and lemon juice and parboil for 10-20 minutes depending on size.
2. Transfer them first into cold water, then upside down onto a plate to drain and dry.
3. Clean and wash the mushrooms. Cut into slices.
4. Chop up 2 slices of bacon, put in a frying pan with a little oil, bring to a medium heat and cook for 10 minutes with the mushrooms, parsley, crushed garlic, salt and pepper.
5. Carefully remove the choke from each artichoke and fill with the mushroom mixture. Cover with one of the remaining slices of bacon.
6. Preheat the oven to 425°F / 220°C / Gas Mark 7.
7. Tie up the artichokes with thick white thread and paint with oil, put them in an oiled ovenproof dish. Pour over the dry white wine and brown the artichokes in a hot oven for 10 minutes.
8. Lower the heat and sprinkle with the stock. Cook for a further 15 minutes then serve garnished with sprigs of parsley.

Sformato alla ligure

Ligurian Pudding

00:30 00:40

American	Ingredients	Metric/Imperial
4	*Artichoke hearts*	4
2 cups	*Béchamel sauce (see page 162)*	450 ml / ¾ pint
2	*Hard-cooked (boiled) eggs*	2
½ lb	*Shortcrust pastry*	225 g / 8 oz
¼ cup	*Grated parmesan cheese*	25 g / 1 oz

1. Preheat the oven to 400°F / 200°C / Gas Mark 6.
2. Cook the artichokes, take off the leaves and remove chokes.
3. Make the béchamel sauce and season well.
4. Slice the artichoke hearts and eggs.
5. Line an 8 in / 20 cm flan dish with two-thirds of the pastry.
6. Arrange the artichokes and hard-cooked eggs in the dish.
7. Pour the béchamel sauce over the artichokes and eggs. Sprinkle with grated parmesan.
8. Roll the remaining pastry to fit the top, damp the edges with cold water and seal. Make 3 slits on the top. Put in the oven for 25 minutes. Serve hot.

Cestini con fondi di carciofo

Baskets of Artichoke Bottoms

00:25 00:30

American	Ingredients	Metric/Imperial
4	*Deep soft rolls*	4
¼ cup	*Butter*	50 g / 2 oz
4	*Artichoke hearts (fresh or frozen)*	4
1 ¼ cups	*Béchamel sauce (see page 162)*	300 ml / ½ pint
2	*Slices of emmental cheese*	2
1	*Egg*	1
	Salt and pepper	
	Nutmeg	

1. Cut the tops of the rolls, hollow them out and brush the insides with melted butter.
2. Boil the artichoke hearts, then lightly fry in a frying pan with a little butter. Place an artichoke bottom in each roll.
3. Preheat the oven to 400°F / 200°C / Gas Mark 6.
4. Make some béchamel sauce and blend in the chopped emmental, egg yolk, salt, pepper and nutmeg. Finally, fold in the egg white, stiffly whipped and divide this mixture between the rolls.
5. Brush the outsides with melted butter and cook in a hot oven for about 15 minutes

Artichokes with garlic

Carciofi all'aglio

Artichokes with Garlic

Preparation 00:30 — Cooking 00:50

American	Ingredients	Metric/Imperial
8	*Artichokes*	8
1	*Lemon*	1
1	*Garlic clove*	1
⅔ cup	*Vegetable oil*	150 ml / ¼ pint
4	*Anchovies in oil*	4
⅓ cup	*Black olives, pitted (stoned)*	50 g / 2 oz
1 tsp	*Capers*	1 tsp
	Salt and pepper	
½ cup	*Bread crumbs*	50 g / 2 oz

1. Remove the toughest leaves from the artichokes, the prickles and the choke from inside. Cut into lengthwise pieces and cook in boiling water with a few drops of lemon. When the water comes back to the boil, cook for 10 minutes.
2. In another large pan, heat a clove of garlic in a little oil. Remove the garlic, add the drained anchovies, cut into small pieces, and stir until they have almost dissolved.
3. Add the drained artichokes and cook for 10 minutes.
4. Preheat the oven to 375°F / 190°C / Gas Mark 5.
5. Put the artichokes and anchovy sauce in an oiled ovenproof dish, add the olives, the chopped capers and sprinkle with salt and pepper and bread crumbs.
6. Pour over the oil in which the artichokes were cooked. Cook in the oven for about 20 minutes.

Melanzane ripiene di riso

Eggplant (Aubergines) Stuffed with Rice

Preparation 00:25 — Cooking 00:20

American	Ingredients	Metric/Imperial
1 cup	*Long grain rice*	200 g / 7 oz
1	*Stock cube*	1
4	*Eggplant (aubergines)*	4
¼ lb	*Raw ham*	100 g / 4 oz
½ cup	*Vegetable oil*	125 ml / 4 fl oz
¼ lb	*Fontina cheese*	100 g / 4 oz

1. Cook the rice until 'al dente' in 2½ cups [600 ml / 1 pint] stock made from a cube.
2. Wash the eggplant, cut in half lengthways and blanch in salted boiling water for 5 minutes. Drain and place on an absorbent kitchen towel.
3. Preheat the oven to 400°F / 200°C / Gas Mark 6.
4. Scoop out the flesh, taking care not to damage the skin. Cut the ham into small pieces and combine with the chopped flesh of the eggplant. Add the rice to this mixture. Paint the eggplant halves with oil inside and out and fill the skins with mixture.
5. Cut the fontina into thin slices. Cover the eggplant with the cheese. Place in an ovenproof dish and put in the oven until the cheese has melted.

Cook's tip: this dish can be served either hot or cold.

La parmigiana di melanzane

Eggplant (Aubergine) Pie

Preparation 02:00 (Standing time 00:40) — Cooking 00:40

American	Ingredients	Metric/Imperial
4	*Large round eggplant (aubergines)*	4
2 lb	*Tomatoes*	1 kg / 2 lb
	Salt and pepper	
2 tsp	*Basil*	2 tsp
2	*Eggs*	2
¼ lb	*Bologna sausage*	100 g / 4 oz
½ lb	*Mozzarella cheese*	225 g / 8 oz
	Butter	
½ cup	*Grated parmesan cheese*	50 g / 2 oz

1. Preheat the oven to 350°F / 180°C / Gas Mark 4.
2. Wash and cut the eggplant in half lengthways. Season with salt and keep under a weight for 30 minutes in order to expel the bitter juices.
3. Rinse and dry well. Blanch in boiling water for 4 minutes.
4. Make the fresh tomato sauce by boiling the tomatoes for 1 minute. Remove the skins and mash in a bowl with seasoning and basil.
5. Hard-cook (boil) 2 eggs, cut the Bologna sausage into thin slices and slice the mozzarella cheese.
6. Butter an ovenproof dish and place a layer of eggplant, tomato sauce, slices of Bologna sausage, slices of hard-cooked egg, slices of mozzarella cheese. Continue making layers until all the ingredients are used, and, finally, finish with a sprinkling of grated parmesan. Put in the oven for 30 minutes. Serve hot.

Tortino di melanzane

Eggplant (Aubergine) Bake

00:30 00:50

American	Ingredients	Metric/Imperial
4	Eggplant (aubergines)	4
1 cup	Vegetable oil	225 ml / 8 fl oz
¼ cup	Butter	50 g / 2 oz
1	Large onion	1
1 lb	Tomatoes	500 g / 1 lb
	Salt and pepper	
1	Bunch of basil	1
¼ lb	Mozzarella cheese	100 g / 4 oz
1 cup	Grated cheese	100 g / 4 oz

1. Wash and cut the eggplant into thick slices, lay out on a tray, sprinkle with salt, and allow to stand for 30 minutes until some of the bitter juice is released.
2. Heat the oil and butter in a pan and fry the finely chopped onion. When it turns golden brown, add peeled and deseeded tomatoes, stir, season with salt, cover and cook for about 20 minutes.
3. Prepare the basil, wash the leaves thoroughly and chop roughly. Cut mozzarella in slices.
4. Rinse and dry the eggplant with absorbent paper towels.
5. Preheat the oven to 375°F / 190°C / Gas Mark 5.
6. Heat a large thick pan with oil until very hot, fry the eggplant in batches.
7. Place a layer of eggplant in an ovenproof dish, cover with the tomato sauce, and sprinkle with grated cheese, basil, mozzarella, a pinch of salt and pepper. Put down another layer of eggplant and continue until all the ingredients are finished. Top with eggplant, a little sauce and plenty of cheese.
8. Cook in the oven for 30 minutes, serve hot.

La caponata 

Sweet and Sour Vegetables

01:00 01:00

American	Ingredients	Metric/Imperial
4	Round eggplant (aubergines)	4
2	Heads of green celery	2
Scant ¼ cup	Capers in brine	3 tbsp
⅔ cup	Green olives in brine, pitted (stoned)	100 g / 4 oz
½ cup	Vegetable oil	125 ml / 4 fl oz
1	Bunch of basil	1
3 tbsp	Pine kernels	2 tbsp
	Salt and pepper	
1 tbsp	Sugar	1 tbsp
¼ cup	White vinegar	50 ml / 2 fl oz

1. Wash the eggplant, dice without peeling, season with salt and place on a sloping board to allow the excess water to drain out for about 30 minutes. Then rinse and dry.
2. Wash celery and remove strings, cut into small sticks.

Eggplant (aubergine) bake

3. Bring to boil and simmer for 10 minutes. Wash the capers to remove the salt, cut green olives into small pieces.
4. Heat the oil in a pan until hot and fry the eggplant until golden, drain with a slotted spoon into another saucepan. Add the celery, capers, olives, coarsely chopped basil and pine kernels to the eggplant.
5. Add some of the oil in which the eggplant was cooked and cook over a very low heat for about 20 minutes. At the end of this time, adjust the salt and pepper seasoning, then add 1 tablespoon of sugar and the vinegar. The balance between the sugar and the vinegar is difficult to achieve, taste as it is added to obtain a good sweet and sour flavour. Serve the dish cold (but not chilled). Ideally best eaten the next day.

Pomodori al cartoccio 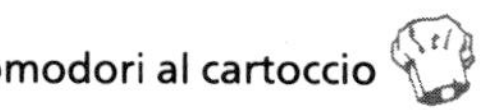

Tomato Parcels

00:35 00:30

American	Ingredients	Metric/Imperial
4	Tomatoes	4
	Salt and pepper	
¼ lb	Cooked ham	100 g / 4 oz
1 tbsp	Grated parmesan cheese	1 tbsp
1	Mozzarella cheese	1
1	Egg	1
1 tbsp	Chopped parsley	1 tbsp
¼ tsp	Nutmeg	¼ tsp
1 tbsp	Bread crumbs	1 tbsp
2 tbsp	Butter	25 g / 1 oz

1. Preheat oven to 350°F / 180°C / Gas Mark 4.
2. Cut the tomatoes in half, sprinkle them with salt and leave them to drain. Empty the pulp and cut it into very small pieces.
3. In a bowl mix the chopped cooked ham, the grated cheese, the mozzarella cut into tiny dice, the whole egg, the pulp of the tomatoes, the chopped parsley, some grated nutmeg, salt and pepper. Blend everything thoroughly and fill the tomatoes with this mixture, sprinkle with bread crumbs and put a dab of butter on each half.
4. Cover with foil and put in the oven for about 30 minutes. Serve hot or cold.

Zucchine alla mentuccia

Zucchini [Courgettes] with Pennyroyal

Preparation 00:30 | Cooking 00:20

American	Ingredients	Metric/Imperial
1 ¼ lb	*Small zucchini (courgettes)*	600 g / 1 ¼ lb
	Flour as required	
½ cup	*Sunflower oil*	125 ml / 4 fl oz
	Salt	
Scant ¼ cup	*Herb vinegar*	3 tbsp
1	*Small bunch of pennyroyal*	1
1	*Small onion*	1
	Freshly ground pepper	

1. Peel the zucchini, wash and dry them, then cut them into strips, dip in flour and fry in very hot oil. Drain on a sheet of paper to absorb the excess grease and sprinkle with salt.
2. Pour the vinegar into an earthenware dish, add the small bunch of pennyroyal chopped finely, a small onion also chopped and a little pepper. Beat with a fork to blend well.
3. Arrange zucchini on a serving-dish and pour over sauce.

Frittelle di fagioli

Bean Pancakes

Preparation 01:30 (Soaking time 12:00) | Cooking 01:20

American	Ingredients	Metric/Imperial
1 lb	*Dried haricot beans*	450 g / 1 lb
2	*Onions*	2
12	*Cloves*	12
2 tbsp	*Chopped parsley*	1 ½ tbsp
Scant ¼ cup	*Vegetable oil*	3 tbsp
½ cup	*Butter*	100 g / 4 oz
¼ cup	*Flour*	25g / 1 oz
½ cup	*Milk*	125 ml / 4 fl oz
1	*Egg*	1
	Salt and pepper	
½ cup	*Bread crumbs*	50 g / 2 oz

1. Soak the beans overnight in cold water.
2. Drain and put them in more water, bring to the boil, cover as tightly as possible and remove from the heat. Allow to stand for 1 hour: the beans will have become very swollen. Drain the water away, put in some fresh boiling water (do not salt), the onion studded with cloves, half the chopped parsley and 1 tablespoon of oil. Cook slowly for at least 1 hour until tender.
3. When the beans are cooked, drain and put them through a vegetable mill, blender or food processor.
4. Peel and chop the remaining onion finely and brown in a pot with a quarter of the butter.
5. Add half the flour, mix well, add the cold milk and stir in the mixture until it thickens.
6. Mix the bean purée, blend in the chopped parsley, the egg, the rest of the flour, salt and pepper.
7. Form into small flat cakes and coat in bread crumbs.
8. Heat the remaining butter and oil and fry the bean pancakes until golden brown.

Puré di fave

Bean Purée

Preparation 00:15 (Soaking time 12:00) | Cooking 01:00

American	Ingredients	Metric/Imperial
½ lb	*Dried haricot beans*	225 g / 8 oz
	Salt	
4 or 5	*Sage leaves*	4 or 5
¼ cup	*Butter*	50 g / 2 oz
4	*Scallions (spring onions)*	4

1. Put the beans to soak in cold water and leave overnight. Drain and put them in a saucepan, with cold water, salt and sage. Cook until soft.
2. Melt the butter in a frying pan and cook the chopped scallions (spring onions) over a very gentle heat. When they have become soft, mix butter and onions with the bean purée; sieve or blend. Adjust seasoning. This is an excellent side-dish for ragoût of oxtail.

Broccolini di Tropea

Whirlwind Broccoli

Preparation 00:25 | Cooking 00:25

American	Ingredients	Metric/Imperial
2	*Green broccoli*	2
5	*Anchovies in brine*	5
1 cup	*Black olives, pitted (stoned)*	175 g / 6 oz
1	*Onion*	1
3 oz	*Provolone cheese*	75 g / 3 oz
	Butter	
¼ cup	*Vegetable oil*	50 ml / 2 fl oz
½ cup	*Red wine*	125 ml / 4 fl oz

1. Thoroughly clean the broccoli removing the damaged leaves and thick stalks, wash and blanch for 4 minutes in boiling salted water. Drain well.
2. Bone the anchovies. Divide the black olives into 4 and cut the onions and cheese into thin slices.
3. Preheat the oven to 350°F / 180°C / Gas Mark 4.
4. Arrange on the bottom of a buttered ovenproof dish the broccoli, a little sliced onion, a little cheese, a few small pieces of anchovy and olive and sprinkle with oil. Proceed in layers until all the ingredients are used up, moistening with a little oil and seasoning.
5. Pour over the red wine, a little more oil, cover with foil and put in the oven until tender.

Castagne e cavoletti

Chestnuts and Sprouts

Preparation 01:00 | Cooking 00:45

American	Ingredients	Metric/Imperial
14 oz	*Chestnuts*	400 g / 14 oz
	Salt	
1	*Bay leaf*	1
1¾ lb	*Brussels sprouts*	800 g / 1¾ lb
⅓ cup	*Butter*	75 g / 3 oz

1. Put the chestnuts in salted cold water with a bay leaf, bring to the boil and simmer for 45 minutes. Drain, remove skins.
2. Wash and trim brussels sprouts and cook in a little boiling salted water for about 10 minutes until 'al dente'.
3. Melt the butter in a pan without browning, add the sprouts and chestnuts, shake over a low heat to mix and heat thoroughly before serving.

Cavoletti di Bruxelles gratinati

Brussels Sprouts au Gratin

00:15 00:30

American	Ingredients	Metric/Imperial
1 lb	*Brussels sprouts*	*500 g / 1 lb*
2 cups	*Thin béchamel sauce (see page 162)*	*450 ml / ¾ pint*
1 tbsp	*Butter*	*15 g / ½ oz*
	Salt and pepper	
7 oz	*Emmental cheese*	*200 g / 7 oz*

1. Trim the brussels sprouts, wash them and cook in a little boiling salted water.
2. Prepare a pouring béchamel sauce.
3. Preheat the oven to 425°F / 220°C / Gas Mark 7.
4. Butter an ovenproof dish and arrange the brussels sprouts in it in a single layer, very close together, salt and pepper them lightly and cover with béchamel. Sprinkle with the coarsely grated cheese and put in the oven for 10 minutes.
5. Heat the broiler (grill) for 5 minutes and finish the dish under the heat to form a golden crust. Serve hot.

Cook's tip: cooked cauliflowers, fennel, asparagus and Belgian endive can all be prepared in this way.

Cavolini di Bruxelles stufati

Stewed Brussels Sprouts

00:10 00:30

American	Ingredients	Metric/Imperial
2 lb	*Brussels sprouts*	*1 kg / 2 lb*
	Salt and pepper	
¼ cup	*Butter*	*50 g / 2 oz*
¼ lb	*Cooked ham*	*100 g / 4 oz*
½ cup	*Coffee (single) cream*	*125 ml / 4 fl oz*
1	*Vegetable stock cube*	*1*

1. Remove any damaged leaves from the brussels sprouts, trim the stalks. Wash well, then cook them in a saucepan containing a little boiling salted water for about 15 minutes, drain.
2. Melt the butter in a pan, add the sprouts and the cooked ham, cut into thin strips. Season well and allow to absorb the flavors, stirring from time to time.
3. In a small saucepan heat the cream and a crumbled stock cube, whisk until the cube has dissolved.
4. Pour over the brussels sprouts and leave to cook for a further 5-10 minutes over a low heat.
5. Serve hot sprinkled with freshly ground black pepper to accompany boiled or roast meats.

Verze ripiene alla Zia Tina

Aunt Tina's Stuffed Cabbage

00:30 00:40

American	Ingredients	Metric/Imperial
2	*Small savoy cabbages*	*2*
¼ cup	*Butter*	*50 g / 2 oz*
1 tbsp	*Chopped parsley*	*1 tbsp*
2	*Garlic cloves*	*2*
1 cup	*Ground (minced) veal*	*225 g / 8 oz*
½ lb	*Liver*	*225 g / 8 oz*
½ cup	*Mushrooms*	*50 g / 2 oz*
½ cup	*Stock*	*125 ml / 4 fl oz*
4	*Canned tomatoes*	*4*
1	*Egg*	*1*
1 oz	*Cheese*	*25 g / 1 oz*
1 cup	*Béchamel sauce (see page 162)*	*225 ml / 8 fl oz*

1. Discard the tough outer leaves and wash the savoy cabbages, and cook in boiling water for 7 minutes. Remove and drain upside down in a colander.
2. Put half the butter in a frying pan with some parsley and the crushed garlic. When it begins to brown, add the veal, the finely chopped liver and the washed and sliced mushrooms. Cook for 5 minutes adding a little stock and the sieved tomatoes.
3. Preheat the oven to 375°F / 190°C / Gas Mark 5.
4. Add an egg yolk, the cheese and the béchamel sauce to the meat. Mix well together and remove from the heat.
5. Open the cabbage leaves as wide as possible and fill with the meat mixture. Close up again.
6. Wrap the cabbage in buttered foil and place in an ovenproof dish. Cook for 20 minutes and serve from the folded-back foil.

Cavolfiore gratinato

Cauliflower au Gratin

00:05 00:30

American	Ingredients	Metric/Imperial
1	*Cauliflower*	*1*
1 tbsp	*Butter*	*15 g / ½ oz*
1 cup	*Béchamel sauce (see page 162)*	*225 ml / 8 fl oz*
	Salt and pepper	
3 tbsp	*Grated parmesan cheese*	*2 tbsp*

1. Preheat the oven to 375°F / 190°C / Gas Mark 5.
2. Cook the washed cauliflower in boiling salted water for about 10 minutes. Drain and, using a fork, divide into florets.
3. Butter an ovenproof dish and arrange the cauliflower in it.
4. Make the béchamel sauce and pour over the cauliflower, season well and sprinkle the surface with plenty of grated parmesan cheese.
5. Cook in the oven until it turns a pale golden color.

Cook's tip: for a rich cauliflower au gratin, add 2 egg yolks to the sauce. Whisk the whites until soft peaks stage and fold into the sauce.

Cavolo rosso

Red Cabbage

00:25 01:15

American	Ingredients	Metric/Imperial
2 lb	*Red cabbage*	*1 kg / 2 lb*
½ cup	*Lard*	*100 g / 4 oz*
⅓ cup	*Red vinegar*	*4 tbsp*
2 or 3	*Apples*	*2 or 3*
2 or 3	*Cloves*	*2 or 3*
	Salt	
2 tsp	*Sugar*	*2 tsp*
3 tbsp	*Red currant jelly*	*2 tbsp*

1. Remove the wrinkled outer leaves from the cabbage, wash, dry and shred.
2. Heat the lard in a large pan and add the cabbage, toss over a medium heat for 10 minutes.
3. Sprinkle with vinegar and allow to evaporate. Add the apples, peeled and cut into thin slices, the cloves, salt and the sugar and sprinkle with 1 cup [225 ml / 8 fl oz] water. Cover and leave to simmer over a low heat for 1 hour until the ingredients are well blended.
4. Beat the redcurrant jelly in a bowl sitting over hot water, to soften. Arrange the cabbage in a heated serving dish, pour over the jelly and mix through before serving.

Cook's tip: this dish originates from Denmark and is an excellent accompaniment for roast goose, ham or pork.

Salamini con le verze

Salami with Savoy Cabbage

00:20 00:20

American	Ingredients	Metric/Imperial
2	*Celery stalks*	*2*
1	*Large carrot*	*1*
⅔ cup	*Vegetable oil*	*150 ml / ¼ pint*
¼ cup	*Butter*	*50 g / 2 oz*
1	*Garlic clove*	*1*
2	*Savoy cabbages*	*2*
⅔ cup	*Red wine*	*150 ml / ¼ pint*
1	*Stock cube*	*1*
	Salt and pepper	
¼ tsp	*Mixed spice*	*¼ tsp*
½ lb	*Salami*	*225 g / 8 oz*

1. Chop the washed celery and scraped carrot. Heat the oil and butter with a crushed garlic clove. Add the vegetables and cook over a low heat for 5 minutes.
2. Discard the damaged leaves and wash the savoy cabbages well and remove the coarse stems. Drain and cut roughly into small pieces. Add to the pan a little at a time with the other fried vegetables as each batch is softened.
3. When all the vegetables are fairly dry, moisten with wine. Stir fry, moistening, if necessary, with water and stock until the vegetables are cooked to your taste.
4. Season well, add the spice and mix with the chopped salami. Serve hot.

Torta Gare-de-Lyon

Gare de Lyon Flan

00:30 00:45

American	Ingredients	Metric/Imperial
1 lb	*Meat (left-over roast or stewed meat)*	*450 g / 1 lb*
2	*Eggs*	*2*
1 tbsp	*Chopped parsley*	*1 tbsp*
2	*Onions*	*2*
3 tbsp	*White wine*	*2 tbsp*
½ tsp	*Marjoram*	*½ tsp*
½ tsp	*Nutmeg*	*½ tsp*
	Salt and pepper	
¼ cup	*Butter*	*50 g / 2 oz*
1	*Green cabbage*	*1*
¾ lb	*Shortcrust pastry*	*350 g / 12 oz*

1. Chop up the meat and add 1 egg plus 1 whisked egg white. Mix well, add the chopped parsley, the finely chopped onions, a little wine, marjoram, nutmeg, salt and pepper.
2. Melt the butter in a saucepan, pour in the mixture and cook for about 10 minutes, stirring well. Allow to cool.
3. Preheat the oven to 400°F / 200°C / Gas Mark 6.
4. Parboil the cabbage leaves in boiling salted water, drain and dry thoroughly.
5. Roll out the shortcrust pastry with a floured rolling pin, put the cabbage leaves on the pastry, top with the filling.
6. Roll up the pastry and place on a greased baking pan in the shape of a ring cake. Seal the edges well. Brush over the surface of the pastry with the remaining beaten egg yolk.
7. Cook in the oven for 30 minutes. Serve hot with mixed vegetables or cold with green salad.

Cavolfiore alla Franceschiello

Franceschiello's Cauliflower

This dish became internationally famous when it was introduced to the Imperial Court at Vienna and was much esteemed by the King of Naples, who was known for his gluttony.

00:10 00:30

American	Ingredients	Metric/Imperial
1	*Cauliflower*	*1*
1 tbsp	*Butter*	*15 g / ½ oz*
¼ cup	*Bread crumbs*	*25 g / 1 oz*
1 ¼ cups	*Béchamel sauce (see page 162)*	*300 ml / ½ pint*
4	*Ripe tomatoes*	*4*
½ tsp	*Oregano*	*½ tsp*
	Salt and pepper	

1. Preheat the oven to 400°F / 200°C / Gas Mark 6.
2. Cook a cauliflower 'al dente', remove the florets, place in a buttered ovenproof dish and sprinkle with bread crumbs.
3. Mix the béchamel sauce with the sieved tomatoes, a pinch of oregano, salt and pepper and pour over the cauliflower.
4. Cook in the oven for 20 minutes and serve hot.

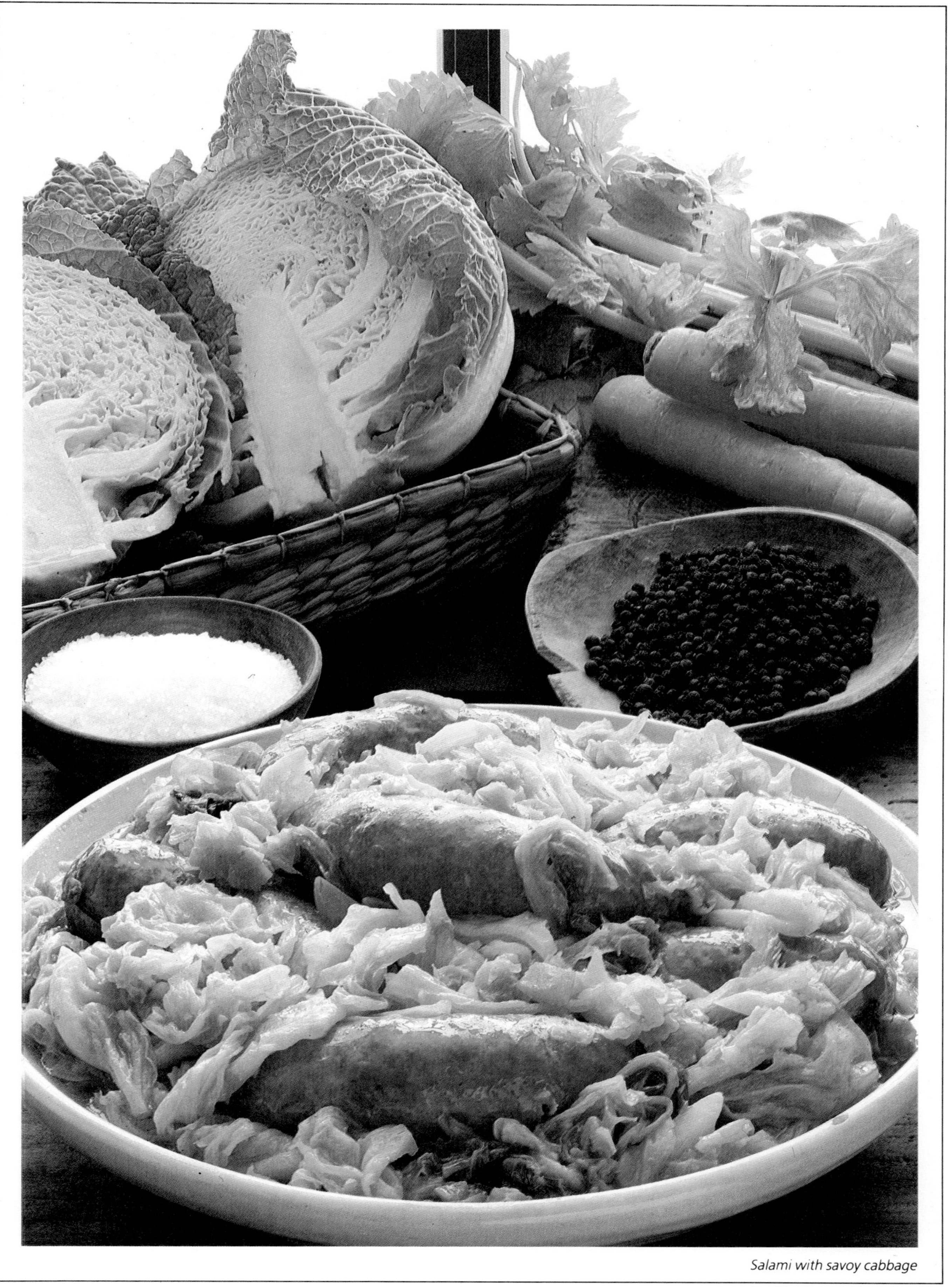

Salami with savoy cabbage

Carote bellavista

Bellavista Carrots

00:20 00:30

American	Ingredients	Metric/Imperial
1 lb	*Carrots*	*450 g / 1 lb*
¼ lb	*Celery*	*100 g / 4 oz*
3 tbsp	*Vegetable oil*	*2 tbsp*
1	*Lemon*	*1*
	Sugar	
	Salt and pepper	
1 cup	*Cream*	*225 ml / 8 fl oz*

1. Preheat the oven to 375°F / 190°C / Gas Mark 5.
2. Wash and scrape the carrots very carefully, then dry in a clean cloth and cut them into very fine slices.

Bellavista carrots

3. Trim the washed white celery cut into thin slices, and put into an ovenproof bowl. Add the carrots.
4. Season everything with a well mixed dressing of oil, lemon juice and a pinch of sugar, salt and pepper.
5. Put the bowl in a baking pan with boiling water coming halfway up the bowl in a moderate oven for 30 minutes.
6. After 15 minutes remove and add the cream, stir carefully and complete cooking. Arrange on a heated serving-dish and serve with a roast.

Cook's tip: unless you are using very young garden vegetables it is best to blanch the carrots in boiling water for 3-4 minutes in stage 2.

Bietole all'aglio e pomodoro

Beet with Garlic and Tomato

00:10 00:25

American	Ingredients	Metric/Imperial
1 lb	*Cooked beetroot*	*450 g / 1 lb*
¼ cup	*Vegetable oil*	*50 ml / 2 fl oz*
2	*Garlic cloves*	*2*
6	*Anchovy fillets*	*6*
1 cup	*Fresh tomato purée or peeled tomatoes*	*225 ml / 8 fl oz*
	Salt and pepper	

1. Clean the beetroot, remove the skin, rinse in cold water and cut into dice.
2. Heat the oil in a pan, add the garlic and allow to become golden.
3. Remove the garlic, add the anchovy fillets and crush with a wooden spoon in the oil. Add the sieved tomatoes, season with salt and pepper and cook over a low heat for about 10 minutes.
4. Tip in the beetroot, and allow to absorb the flavor for a further 10 minutes turning frequently. Serve on a heated serving dish as an ideal side dish for every type of meat.

Cardi all'astigiana

Cardoons Asti-Style

00:10 00:35

American	Ingredients	Metric/Imperial
2 lb	*Cardoons*	*1 kg / 2 lb*
1	*Lemon*	*1*
½ cup	*Butter*	*100 g / 4 oz*
	Salt and pepper	
2½ cups	*Béchamel sauce (see page 162)*	*600 ml / 1 pint*
¾ cup	*Grated parmesan cheese*	*75 g / 3 oz*

1. Remove the toughest stems from the cardoons, cut the others into pieces 2 in / 5 cm long and wash in water acidulated with the juice of the lemon.
2. Put a little butter in a frying pan and, when it begins to color, put in the cardoons, add salt and pepper to taste, cover and continue to cook.
3. Preheat the oven to 425°F / 220°C / Gas Mark 7.

4. Make the béchamel sauce.
5. Arrange the cardoons in a buttered ovenproof dish. Pour over the béchamel sauce and stir together thoroughly in order to flavor and coat the cardoons with the sauce. Sprinkle with plenty of grated parmesan cheese and put in a hot oven for 15 minutes. Serve immediately.

Indivia mascherata

Masked Chicory

00:20 | 00:10

American	Ingredients	Metric/Imperial
12	*Heads of chicory*	12
	Salt	
12	*Slices of cooked ham*	12
2 oz	*Emmental cheese*	50 g / 2 oz
12	*Black olives*	12

1. Remove the stem from each head of chicory and discard the damaged outer leaves. Then wash under running water and boil in salted water for about 10 minutes. Drain well on a cloth.
2. Spread out the slices of cooked ham on a wooden chopping-board. Place a head of chicory on each of them. Then wrap up the chicory, forming small cases, held together with a colored cocktail stick.
3. Thread a small cube of emmental and a black olive onto each end of the stick. Serve hot or cold.

Finocchi alla Cyrano

Cyrano's Fennel

This very delicate dish is linked with the restaurant frequented in Paris by the Cadetti (younger sons of nobles) of Gascony. To mark their well remembered exploits, this dish was dedicated by the chef/poet/pastry-cook, Raguenau, to the famous Cyrano de Bergerac.

00:20 | 00:35

American	Ingredients	Metric/Imperial
4	*Large fennel bulbs*	4
	Salt	
1 ¼ cups	*Béchamel sauce (see page 162)*	300 ml / ½ pint
2 oz	*Truffled mushrooms*	50 g / 2 oz
2 tbsp	*Chopped parsley*	1 ½ tbsp
	Bread crumbs	
¼ cup	*Butter*	50 g / 2 oz
1	*Mozzarella cheese*	1
½ tsp	*Nutmeg*	½ tsp
¼ cup	*Grated parmesan cheese*	25 g / 1 oz
	If desired, truffle essence can be added to the béchamel sauce	

1. Clean four fennel heads, cut in half and cook 'al dente' in salted water. Drain and put them to one side. Cut into slices.
2. Make the béchamel sauce and add the washed, sliced mushrooms and the chopped parsley.
3. Preheat the oven to 350°F / 180°C / Gas Mark 4.
4. Butter an ovenproof dish, sprinkle with bread crumbs and place a layer of fennel leaves on the bottom. Cover with a layer of béchamel and mushroom sauce, then add small pieces of mozzarella.
5. Continue with another layer of fennel, béchamel sauce and mozzarella, until all the ingredients are used. Sprinkle the top with nutmeg, finely grated parmesan cheese and finish by dotting the surface with butter.
6. Place in the middle of a hot oven for 25 minutes. Serve hot.

Finocchi in salsa cappuccina 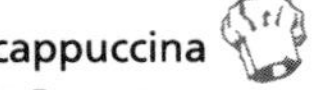

Fennel in Green Sauce

00:15
Standing time 01:00 | 00:10

American	Ingredients	Metric/Imperial
4	*Small fennel bulbs*	4
1 cup	*Green sauce (see page 174)*	225 ml / 8 fl oz
2	*Anchovies*	2
2	*Garlic cloves*	2
2	*Hard-cooked (boiled) eggs*	2
2 tsp	*Capers*	2 tsp
8	*Slices of bread fried in butter*	8

1. Thoroughly trim and finely slice the fennel.
2. Make the green sauce, mix with the finely chopped anchovies and the crushed cloves of garlic.
3. Mix the sauce together with the fennel and leave to stand for 1 hour. Before serving, add the sliced hard-cooked eggs and a few capers. Serve immediately with slices of fried bread.

Sfoglia fantasia

Fantasy Tart

00:35 | 00:25

American	Ingredients	Metric/Imperial
4	*Heads of fennel*	4
2 tbsp	*Butter*	25 g / 1 oz
	Salt and pepper	
¼ cup	*Grated cheese*	25 g / 1 oz
½ lb	*Frozen flaky pastry*	225 g / 8 oz
1 tbsp	*Flour*	1 tbsp
7 oz	*Cooked smoked ham*	200 g / 7 oz
1	*Large mozzarella cheese*	1
1	*Egg, beaten*	1

1. Cut the fennel into 4 pieces after removing the tough outside leaves. Wash thoroughly and boil in salted water for 15 minutes.
2. Drain and when slightly cooled, flavor with a little heated butter in a pan. Raise the heat and brown all over, sprinkle with salt, pepper and grated cheese. Turn off the heat and rest, covered.
3. Roll out the two-thirds of the thawed flaky pastry on a floured board to a round shape and line the sides and bottom of a buttered and floured flan or pie dish.
4. Preheat the oven to 425°F / 210°C / Gas Mark 7.
5. Spread the slices of ham, the sliced mozzarella sprinkled with pepper and finally the fennel over the pastry.
6. Roll the remaining pastry to fit the top of the dish. Damp the edges of the pastry with cold water and seal the lid with neat edges. Make 3 slits on top to allow the steam to escape. Brush with a little beaten egg.
7. Cook in the oven for 25 minutes until puffed and golden. Serve hot.

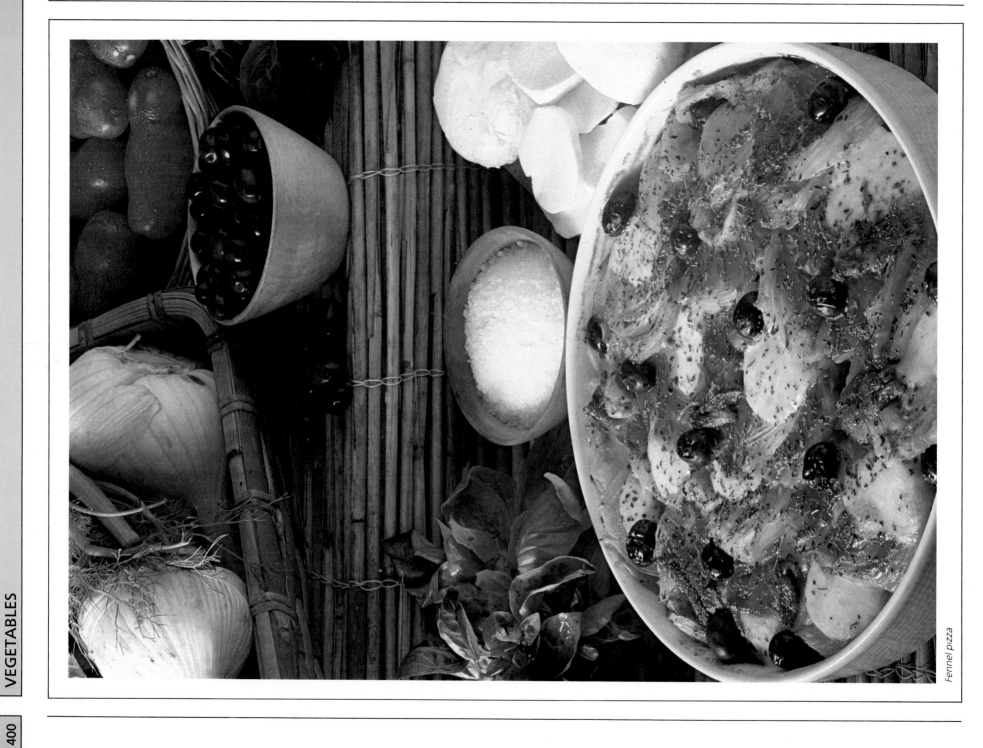

Fennel pizza

Finocchi in pizza

Fennel 'Pizza'

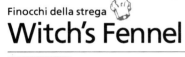

00:25 00:35

American	Ingredients	Metric/Imperial
2 lb	*Fennel bulbs*	1 kg / 2 lb
	Salt and pepper	
¼ lb	*Mozzarella cheese*	100 g / 4 oz
2	*Anchovies*	2
⅔ cup	*Black olives, pitted (stoned)*	100 g / 4 oz
1 lb	*Fresh tomatoes*	500 g / 1 lb
1 tsp	*Basil*	1 tsp
1 tbsp	*Oil*	1 tbsp
¼ tsp	*Oregano*	¼ tsp

1. Cook the fennel 'al dente' in plenty of salted water. Drain well and dry. Slice evenly.
2. Preheat the oven to 400°F / 200°C / Gas Mark 6.
3. Cut the mozzarella into slices, trim the anchovies and chop into small pieces, cut the olives into halves.
4. Put the tomatoes in a pan with ⅔ cup [125 ml / ¼ pint] water, boil for 10 minutes, add salt and a little basil. Sieve to obtain the juice.
5. In an oiled baking pan, arrange a layer of cooked fennel, season well. Place the anchovies and the mozzarella on top. Cover with the purée from the tomatoes. Arrange the olives on the top, sprinkle with chopped oregano and basil and brush with oil.
6. Cook in the oven for 10-15 minutes. Serve immediately.

Finocchi della strega

Witch's Fennel

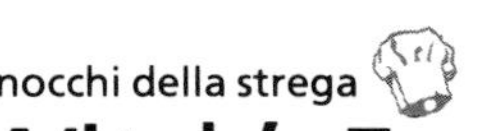

00:20 00:45

American	Ingredients	Metric/Imperial
4	*Fennel bulbs*	4
	Salt and pepper	
¼ cup	*Butter*	50 g / 2 oz
½ cup	*Grated parmesan cheese*	50 g / 2 oz
2½ cups	*Béchamel sauce (see page 162)*	600 ml / 1 pint
1 tsp	*Hot paprika*	1 tsp
4	*Slices of cheese*	4

1. Trim the fennel, cut into 4 and cook 'al dente' in plenty of salted water and drain.
2. Brown the fennel slices in a frying pan with half the melted butter for 4 minutes.
3. Sprinkle half the grated parmesan cheese over the fennel, stirring to mix well.
4. Preheat the oven to 350°F / 180°C / Gas Mark 4.
5. Make the béchamel sauce and add the paprika.
6. Butter an ovenproof dish and place the fennel in it. Put a slice of cheese on top of each piece, season well. Pour the béchamel sauce over, sprinkle with remaining parmesan and dot here and there with butter.
7. Put in the oven for about 30 minutes or until the cheese has formed a golden crust. Serve hot.

Polpette di lenticchie

Lentil Rissoles

00:20 01:30

American	Ingredients	Metric/Imperial
2 cups	*Dried lentils*	500 g / 1 lb
1 quart	*Stock*	1 litre / 1¾ pints
1	*Onion*	1
2 tbsp	*Butter*	25 g / 1 oz
1	*Egg*	1
3 tbsp	*Chopped parsley*	2 tbsp
	Salt and pepper	
	White flour	
	Oil for frying	

1. Pour boiling water on the lentils, allow to stand and remove any discolored lentils which come to the surface.
2. Put the lentils in a saucepan with the stock and bring to the boil, cover and leave to cook over a low heat for about 1 hour.
3. Peel and chop the onion, melt the butter in a pan and gently cook the onion until just colored.
4. Beat the egg and chop the parsley.
5. When the lentils are cooked, drain and blend or put through a food processor to make a purée. Add the purée to the onion, egg and parsley and season. Mix well until the mixture is smooth. This can also be done in the food processor. Leave for a few minutes in the refrigerator so that the mixture firms slightly.
6. Shape the rissoles from the mixture, flour lightly and leave to firm in the refrigerator or freezer while shaping the remainder.
7. Heat the oil in a large frying pan and cook the rissoles on both sides until golden, drain on absorbent kitchen towels. Serve with a charcuterie or broiled (grilled) meats or with a salad as a vegetarian dish.

Cook's tip: depending on type of lentils used you may have to add flour and bread crumbs to the mixture if it is not firm enough to shape.

Fagottini di lattuga

Sheaves of Lettuce

00:45 Frying time 00:05 for each batch of lettuce — 00:40

American	Ingredients	Metric/Imperial
16	*Large lettuce leaves*	16
1	*Thick slice of Dutch cheese*	1
Batter		
½ cup	*Flour*	50 g / 2 oz
	Salt	
1	*Egg*	1
1 tbsp	*Vegetable oil*	1 tbsp
Scant ¼ cup	*Milk*	3 tbsp
Sauce		
3 tbsp	*Vegetable oil*	2 tbsp
½	*Onion*	½
1	*Celery stalk*	1
1	*Small carrot*	1
1 lb	*Peeled tomatoes*	450 g / 1 lb
1	*Bay leaf*	1
½ tsp	*Oregano*	½ tsp
	Salt and pepper	
1	*Stock cube*	1
	Oil for frying	

1. Remove the largest undamaged leaves from the lettuces, wash and drain well. Cut the Dutch cheese into small cubes, divide amongst the lettuce leaves.
2. Fold the lettuce leaves into little parcels and secure with a toothpick.
3. Make some batter by sifting flour and salt into a bowl, beat in the egg, oil, and as much milk as necessary to make a thick batter. Cover and allow to stand for 10 minutes.
4. Prepare the sauce. Heat the oil in a pan, add the finely diced onion, celery and carrot, cook gently for 5 minutes.
5. Chop the peeled tomatoes, add to the vegetables with the bay leaf, oregano, salt and pepper. Add 2½ cups [600 ml / 1 pint] stock made with the cube. Simmer for 30 minutes.
6. Heat the oil in a deep frying pan.
7. Immerse the lettuce parcels in the batter, hold over the batter bowl to allow the excess to drain back into the bowl.
8. Cook 4 parcels in the heated oil, drain on absorbent kitchen towels. Continue with next batch. Serve hot with the sauce.

Funghi trifolati

Mushrooms with Garlic, Oil and Parsley

00:10 — 00:15

American	Ingredients	Metric/Imperial
1	*Garlic clove*	1
3 tbsp	*Butter*	40 g / 1½ oz
3 tbsp	*Vegetable oil*	2 tbsp
1 lb	*Mushrooms*	500 g / 1 lb
	Salt and pepper	
1 tbsp	*Chopped parsley*	1 tbsp

1. Crush the garlic and fry it lightly in a frying pan with the butter and a little oil.
2. Wash the mushrooms and chop into pieces. Add them to the frying pan, flavor with salt and ground pepper and cook for 10 minutes over a brisk heat, stirring gently with a wooden spoon.
3. Just before turning off the heat sprinkle with the chopped parsley and serve on a heated serving dish.

Cook's tip: this is an ideal accompaniment to grilled meats.

Boleti ripieni

Stuffed Mushrooms

00:30 — 00:30

American	Ingredients	Metric/Imperial
2 lb	*Large mushrooms*	1 kg / 2 lb
	Salt and pepper	
1	*Large bunch of parsley*	1
¼ cup	*Vegetable oil*	3 tbsp
¼ cup	*Butter*	50 g / 2 oz
4	*Tomatoes*	4
3 tbsp	*Bread crumbs*	2 tbsp

1. Wash and remove the stalks from the mushrooms. Chop the stalks. Wash the mushrooms and drain very thoroughly, place on a dish and sprinkle with salt.
2. Wash the parsley and chop.
3. Heat the oil and butter in a pan, add the parsley and cook for 2 minutes. Add the mushroom stalks and cook for a further 3 minutes.
4. Add the skinned and chopped tomatoes with 1 cup [225 ml / 8 fl oz] water. Season and simmer for 10 minutes.
5. Preheat the oven to 375°F / 190°C / Gas Mark 5.
6. Fill the caps with the mixture, sprinkle the bread crumbs on top and put in a buttered pan. Pour a little melted butter on top and cook for 15 minutes.

Funghialla panna

Creamed Mushrooms

00:10 — 00:35

American	Ingredients	Metric/Imperial
1¾ lb	*Mushrooms*	800 g / 1¾ lb
3 tbsp	*Butter*	40 g / 1½ oz
	Salt and pepper	
1	*Garlic clove*	1
1 cup	*Coffee (single) cream*	225 ml / 8 fl oz
1 tbsp	*Chopped parsley*	1 tbsp
	Triangles of toast	

1. Wash and dry the mushrooms with absorbent kitchen towels, trim the ends of the stalks, remove any bruised or damaged parts. Slice lengthwise.
2. Melt the butter in a thick pan, add the mushrooms, cook for a few minutes, until they become juicy, then season with salt, pepper and the crushed clove of garlic, continue cooking for a further 5 minutes.
3. Moisten the mushrooms with the cream and leave to simmer for about 10-15 minutes until the cream is absorbed. Serve, sprinkle with chopped parsley, surrounded by toast.

Sheaves of lettuce

Funghi ripieni al sapore di mare

Stuffed Mushrooms with a Tang of the Sea

00:45 00:30

American	Ingredients	Metric/Imperial
30	*Large mussels*	*30*
½ cup	*Dry sherry or marsala*	*125 ml / 4 fl oz*
8	*Medium-sized mushrooms*	*8*
1	*Garlic clove*	*1*
1 tbsp	*Chopped parsley*	*1 tbsp*
1 tbsp	*Chopped shallot*	*1 tbsp*
⅓ cup	*Butter*	*65 g / 2½ oz*
	Salt and pepper	
3 tbsp	*Olive oil*	*2 tbsp*
1 cup	*Fresh bread crumbs*	*50 g / 2 oz*

1. Thoroughly clean the mussels, wash them repeatedly under the cold running tap and put in a pan over the heat until they are all open (discard any which remain closed). Remove the mussels from the shells and keep them in a bowl, covered with sherry, for 1 hour.
2. Clean the mushrooms, detach the stalks from the caps. Chop the stalks and mix with the crushed garlic and the chopped parsley. Chop the shallot and cook this in 2 tablespoons [25 g / 1 oz] butter over a gentle heat with the mushroom stalks for 2 minutes. Add salt and pepper and keep warm.
3. Oil the mushroom caps and put them under the broiler (grill) for 5 minutes.
4. Preheat the oven to 425°F / 210°C / Gas Mark 7.
5. Divide the mixture between the caps, put 3 mussels on top, sprinkle with bread crumbs and pour melted butter over them. Cook the caps in a hot oven for 10 minutes and serve with lemon segments.

Sformato di pane

Savory Mushroom Bread Pudding

00:20 00:45

American	Ingredients	Metric/Imperial
¾ lb	*Fresh mushrooms*	*350 g / 12 oz*
3 tbsp	*Butter*	*40 g / 1½ oz*
1	*Garlic clove*	*1*
½ cup	*Stock*	*125 ml / 4 fl oz*
12	*Slices of presliced bread*	*12*
10	*Slices of emmental or fontina cheese*	*10*
2 oz	*Raw ham*	*50 g / 2 oz*
2	*Eggs*	*2*
2 cups	*Milk*	*450 ml / ¾ pint*
	Salt and pepper	

1. Preheat oven to 350°F / 180°C / Gas Mark 4.
2. Wash the mushrooms, slice and cook them in a pan with the butter and crushed garlic for about 10 minutes, add a little stock. Allow to cool.
3. Remove the crust from the slices of bread and put 6 in a large buttered ovenproof dish. Cover with the slices of cheese, arrange the mushrooms on top, the ham cut into strips and finish with the remaining slices of bread.
4. Beat the eggs in a bowl with the milk, salt and pepper, pour the liquid into the oven dish and allow to soak for 10 minutes, cover and keep cool.
5. Put the dish into a moderate oven for 30 to 35 minutes and serve hot.

Crostata di cipolle

Onion Tart

00:35 Resting time 00:20 00:40

American	Ingredients	Metric/Imperial
Pastry		
1½ cups	*Flour*	*175 g / 6 oz*
	Salt	
½ cup	*Butter*	*100 g / 4 oz*
Filling		
1 lb	*Onions*	*450 g / 1 lb*
⅓ cup	*Butter*	*75 g / 3 oz*
2	*Egg yolks*	*2*
1 tbsp	*Flour*	*1 tbsp*
⅔ cup	*Coffee (single) cream*	*150 ml / ¼ pint*
	Salt and pepper	

1. Prepare shortcrust pastry by sifting the flour and salt, add butter and a little water (see page 452). Knead the dough well with floured hands and allow to rest in the refrigerator for 20 minutes.
2. Peel the onions, wash and slice thinly.
3. Heat the butter in a pan and cook the onions over a low heat for 10 minutes.
4. Put the egg yolks in a bowl and mix without beating too much, add the flour and mix well. Thin the mixture by adding the cream a little at a time, making sure there are no lumps.
5. Remove the onions from the heat, blend the egg and cream mixture with them, season with salt and pepper and return to the heat for 4 minutes to thicken.
6. Preheat the oven to 400°F / 200°C / Gas Mark 6.
7. Roll out the short pastry on a floured board and line a pieshell (flan) ring, bottom and sides. Tip in the onion mixture and put into the oven for 25 minutes.

Cipolle alla sbirraglia

Spicy Stuffed Onions

00:30 00:35

American	Ingredients	Metric/Imperial
4	*Good quality red-skinned onions of the same size*	*4*
½ lb	*Italian sausages*	*225 g / 8 oz*
2 tbsp	*Parsley*	*1½ tbsp*
2	*Garlic cloves*	*2*
¼ cup	*Grated parmesan cheese*	*25 g / 1 oz*
2	*Eggs*	*2*
3 tbsp	*Flour*	*2 tbsp*
1 tsp	*Curry powder*	*1 tsp*
	Salt and pepper	

Spicy stuffed onions

1. Remove the first layer of skin from the onions and thoroughly clean the rest. Cut off the tops of the onions and put to one side. Hollow out with a sharp knife and remove all the inner flesh, leaving an outer shell with a thickness of about ¾ in / 2 cm.
2. Preheat the oven to 425°F / 220°C / Gas Mark 7.
3. Chop up the flesh of the onions, put in a bowl with the finely chopped sausage, the chopped parsley and crushed cloves of garlic. Add a little grated parmesan to the mixture, then 2 egg yolks and mix well.
4. Fill onions with this mixture, leaving a little space at the top.
5. Beat the egg whites to a froth. Sift the flour and curry powder together with salt and pepper and fold into the egg white with the remaining parmesan cheese. Season with salt and pepper.
6. Put this mixture into the top of the onions to complete the filling.
7. Place the onions on a heat-resistant tray or ovenproof dish. Pour a little water into the tray to prevent the onions burning while they are cooking.
8. Place in a hot oven for 35 minutes, then remove from the oven and serve hot.

Cipolle fritte

Fried Onion Rings

00:15 Soaking time 02:00 | 00:02 each batch

American	Ingredients	Metric/Imperial
4	*Medium-sized onions*	4
¼ cup	*Flour*	25 g / 1 oz
	Salt	
	Oil for frying	

1. Cut the peeled onions into fairly thin rings, put them to soak in cold water for 2 hours to lose some of the pungent flavor, then dry thoroughly with absorbent kitchen towels.
2. Sift the flour and salt onto a plate. Dip the onion rings in the flour and shake off excess.
3. Heat the oil in a heavy pan over a medium to high heat. Test with a small cube of bread for correct temperature, the bread should turn golden and rise to the surface in 30 seconds.
4. Toss in some of the onion rings and fry until golden, remove with a slotted spoon, drain and keep warm. Continue frying in batches. Sprinkle with salt and serve hot.

Pommes de terre alla noci

Potatoes with Walnuts

00:30 | 00:40

American	Ingredients	Metric/Imperial
6	*Potatoes*	6
2 tbsp	*Butter*	25 g / 1 oz
½ cup	*Walnuts*	50 g / 2 oz
2	*Eggs*	2
	Salt and pepper	
	Flour	
	Oil for frying	

1. Wash the potatoes, put in cold salted water, bring to the boil, cook for about 20 minutes.
2. Melt the butter in a pan.
3. Pass the potatoes through a ricer or vegetable-mill and add the butter, the chopped walnuts, the eggs to the purée and season with salt and pepper.
4. Beat the mixture well and with floured hands shape into little rissoles.
5. Fry in plenty of very hot oil until the rissoles are well browned on both sides.

Rösti

Fried Potatoes

00:10 | 00:25

American	Ingredients	Metric/Imperial
2 lb	*Potatoes*	1 kg / 2 lb
1	*Onion*	1
5 oz	*Smoked bacon*	150 g / 5 oz
1 cup	*Oil*	225 ml / 8 fl oz
	Salt and pepper	

1. Wash the potatoes and parboil in the skins. Peel and grate the potatoes, using the larger mesh of the grater.
2. Finely chop the onion and dice the bacon.
3. Heat the oil in a frying pan, brown the onion and bacon, then add the potatoes and season with salt and pepper. Cook for about 15 minutes until the base is golden brown, pressing down slightly with a slice.
4. Turn the mixture over and brown on the other side. Serve on a heated dish.

Palline di patate gustose

Savory Potato Balls

00:40 | 00:07 each batch

American	Ingredients	Metric/Imperial
1¾ lb	*Potatoes*	800 g / 1¾ lb
5 oz	*Cooked ham*	150 g / 5 oz
3	*Eggs*	3
5 oz	*Fontina cheese*	150 g / 5 oz
	Salt	
¼ tsp	*Nutmeg*	¼ tsp
2 tbsp	*Flour*	15 g / ½ oz
½ cup	*Bread crumbs*	50 g / 2 oz
	Vegetable oil for frying	

1. Boil the potatoes and mash or sieve to make a thick potato purée, leave it to cool.
2. Add the chopped ham, 2 egg yolks, the fontina cut into very small dice, fold in the egg whites beaten into stiff peaks, the salt and a little grated nutmeg. Beat the remaining egg on a plate.
3. Make some little balls the size of a mandarin orange, squash them slightly at the ends, roll in the flour, dip them in the beaten egg, then in the bread crumbs.
4. Heat oil in a large frying pan until really hot and fry the potato balls until they are golden brown on all sides. Drain them on absorbent kitchen towels and serve hot.

Gratin Re Sole

Sun King Gratin

00:30 | 00:40

American	Ingredients	Metric/Imperial
2 lb	*Potatoes*	1 kg / 2 lb
	Salt	
2	*Eggs*	2
½ cup	*Bread crumbs*	50 g / 2 oz
	Vegetable oil for frying	
2½ cups	*Curried béchamel sauce (see page 164)*	600 ml / 1 pint
7 oz	*Sliced cheese*	200 g / 7 oz

1. Boil the potatoes in salted water until almost cooked, drain. Peel and cut into slices and then into finger-sized pieces.
2. Dip in beaten eggs and then in bread crumbs and fry in hot oil. Drain on absorbent kitchen towels, and put to one side.
3. Preheat the oven to 350°F / 180°C / Gas Mark 4.
4. Oil an ovenproof dish and sprinkle with bread crumbs and cover the base with a layer of sliced potatoes.
5. Cover with a layer of curried béchamel sauce and a layer of sliced cheese. Continue layering the potatoes, sauce and cheese. Finish with a layer of béchamel sauce. Put the dish in the oven for 25 minutes.

Sun King gratin

Patate alla Regina Margherita

Queen Margherita's Potatoes

00:45 | 00:40

American	Ingredients	Metric/Imperial
4	*Large potatoes*	4
1 cup	*Béchamel sauce (see page 162)*	225 ml / 8 fl oz
¼ lb	*Mascarpone cheese*	100 g / 4 oz
¼ lb	*Fontina cheese*	100 g / 4 oz
¼ lb	*Gorgonzola cheese*	100 g / 4 oz
	Salt and pepper	
4	*Eggs*	4
	Butter	

1. Take some large good-quality potatoes of the same size. Boil without peeling them, drain and then peel carefully, taking care not to break them, and allow to cool.
2. Hollow out the insides, taking out about three-quarters of the flesh. Rub this through a sieve.
3. Make a pouring béchamel sauce, add the mascarpone and other cheeses, allowing them to melt over a low heat. Thoroughly mix together and season with salt and pepper.
4. Add the potato purée to this mixture and mix well. Put a large tablespoon of this mixture inside the potatoes, pressing down well with the spoon.
5. Preheat the oven to 375°F / 190°C / Gas Mark 5.
6. Fill the cavities with a whole egg. Butter an ovenproof dish, put the stuffed potatoes in it and pour round the remaining béchamel sauce.
7. Put in a hot oven for about 10 minutes or until the eggs have cooked. Serve very hot.

Cook's tip: apart from the cheeses indicated, you could also use the left-overs of other types of cheeses.

Patate trifolate

Sliced Potatoes with Parsley

00:10 | 00:30

American	Ingredients	Metric/Imperial
1½ lb	*Potatoes*	700 g / 1½ lb
½ cup	*Butter*	100 g / 4 oz
½ cup	*Vegetable oil*	125 ml / 4 fl oz
2	*Garlic cloves*	2
	Salt	
1	*Bunch of parsley*	1

1. Peel the potatoes, wash them and cut them into fairly even cubes.
2. In a frying pan heat butter and oil together with the garlic cloves. Dry the potatoes with absorbent kitchen towels, put them in the frying pan and cook them over a moderate heat for 20 minutes, until the potatoes are well browned. Season with salt. Stir carefully from time to time.
3. When the potatoes are cooked, remove garlic cloves, add the parsley chopped, and continue stirring gently for 2 minutes. Serve at once.

Patate Dauphine

Dauphine Potatoes

00:30 | 00:05 each batch

American	Ingredients	Metric/Imperial
2 lb	*Potatoes*	1 kg / 2 lb
⅓ cup	*Butter*	65 g / 2½ oz
	Salt and pepper	
¼ tsp	*Grated nutmeg*	¼ tsp
1 cup	*Flour*	100 g / 4 oz
4	*Eggs*	4
	Oil for frying	

1. Peel the potatoes and cut them into fairly large pieces and place in plenty of cold salted water. Bring to the boil and cook until soft but not mushy. Drain the potatoes well and leave them to dry off.
2. Put through a ricer or vegetable mill to purée.
3. In a thick-bottomed saucepan put 1 cup [225 ml / 8 fl oz] water, butter, salt, pepper and a sprinkling of grated nutmeg. Allow the butter to melt completely and add the flour, sprinkling it on to the boiling liquid. Work on a medium heat with a wooden spoon until a smooth paste is formed, which comes away easily from the sides of the saucepan.
4. Remove the mixture from the heat, blend in the 4 whole eggs, one at a time and add the potato purée.
5. Heat a pan of oil for deep frying until hot (350°F / 180°C) and drop in balls of the potato mixture.
6. Fry until golden on all sides and drain on absorbent kitchen towels. These potatoes make an excellent accompaniment to meat dishes, roasts or grills.

Torta di patate alla Carlina

Carlina-Style Potato Flan

01:30 | 01:10

American	Ingredients	Metric/Imperial
2 lb	*Potatoes*	1 kg / 2 lb
½ cup	*Butter*	100 g / 4 oz
½ cup	*Bread crumbs*	50 g / 2 oz
3	*Eggs*	3
½ lb	*Dried mushrooms*	225 g / 8 oz
3	*Chicken livers*	3
3	*Sausages*	3
	Salt and pepper	
¼ cup	*Flour*	25 g / 1 oz
½ cup	*Tomato sauce (see page 171)*	125 ml / 4 fl oz
1	*Slice of cooked ham*	1
1¼ cups	*Béchamel sauce (see page 162)*	300 ml / ½ pint

1. Boil the potatoes. Peel and cut into horizontal slices.
2. Take an ovenproof dish and spead all over with butter, sprinkle with bread crumbs, pour in a beaten egg yolk, mix thoroughly so that the egg is absorbed by the bread and add a second layer of bread crumbs to obtain a crisp crust. Hard-cook (boil) 2 eggs and shell.
3. Preheat the oven to 400°F / 200°C / Gas Mark 6.
4. Arrange the potatoes around the sides of the dish, leaving a hole in the middle for the filling.

5. Wash and slice the mushrooms. Heat the butter in a pan, add the mushrooms, together with the washed, chopped chicken livers and the sausages, cut into small pieces, and cook for 5 minutes, season with salt and pepper.
6. Add the flour, mix well and then add the tomato sauce and 1 cup [225 ml / 8 fl oz] of water and cook for 10 minutes.
7. Half-fill the dish with the mixture and cover with cooked ham and slices of hard-cooked egg. Cover with more potatoes. Press down carefully, sprinkle with parmesan, add some small pieces of butter. Turn into the ovenproof dish.
8. Pour over the béchamel sauce and place in a very hot oven for about 30 minutes.
9. Take out of the oven and allow to stand for a few minutes.

Crocchette alla parigina

Parisian-Style Croquettes

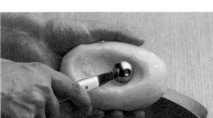

00:25 00:20
00:05 frying time each batch

American	Ingredients	Metric/Imperial
2 lb	*Potatoes*	*1 kg / 2 lb*
	Salt and pepper	
½ cup	*Butter*	*100 g / 4 oz*
3	*Eggs*	*3*
½ cup	*Milk*	*125 ml / 4 fl oz*
5 oz	*Cooked ham*	*150 g / 5 oz*
¼ lb	*Petit pois, cooked*	*100 g / 4 oz*
½ cup	*Grated parmesan cheese*	*50 g / 2 oz*
¼ tsp	*Nutmeg*	*¼ tsp*
½ cup	*Bread crumbs*	*50 g / 2 oz*
	Vegetable oil for frying	

1. Boil the peeled potatoes, drain them, season with pepper and pass while hot through ricer or potato-masher, collecting the mixture in a saucepan.
2. Blend the butter, 2 eggs and the milk with the potato purée and cook for several minutes over a low heat, stirring with a wooden spoon.
3. Add the cooked diced ham together with the petit pois and the grated parmesan. Season with salt and a little grated nutmeg and remove from the heat.
4. Beat the remaining egg on a plate and heat the oil in a deep pan for frying.
5. Shape the croquettes into small rolls. Dip in the beaten egg then in the bread crumbs and fry a few at a time until golden. Drain on absorbent kitchen towels, keep warm and serve hot.

Pomodori al gratin alla francese

Tomatoes au Gratin French-Style

00:25 00:30

American	Ingredients	Metric/Imperial
8	*Large ripe tomatoes of the same size*	*8*
1 cup	*Grated parmesan cheese*	*100 g / 4 oz*
1 cup	*Béchamel sauce (see page 162)*	*225 ml / 8 fl oz*
¼ lb	*Mozzarella cheese*	*100 g / 4 oz*
¼ cup	*Vegetable oil*	*50 ml / 2 fl oz*
¼ cup	*Bread crumbs*	*25 g / 1 oz*
8	*Sprigs of parsley*	*8*
	Lemon peel	

1. Cut off the tops of the tomatoes and with a small sharp knife, empty them out, leaving about 1 in / 2 cm of pulp. Chop up the pulp extracted from the tomatoes and add the finely grated parmesan cheese.
2. Make the béchamel sauce and add to the tomato pulp, stir in the mozzarella, cut into very small pieces.
3. Preheat the oven to 350°F / 180°C / Gas Mark 4.
4. Stuff the tomatoes with the mixture, taking care not to split them but pressing the filling down as far as possible so that they are properly stuffed.
5. Oil an ovenproof dish and arrange the tomatoes so that they are close together, brush over with oil.
6. Sprinkle the tops with fine bread crumbs, put in a preheated oven. Cook for 20 minutes, then replace the tops back on each of the tomatoes. Leave in the oven until the oven cools down, then remove the dish. Garnish with sprigs of parsley and lemon peel cut into spirals. Serve hot or cold.

Queen Margherita's potatoes
1. Hollow out the insides of the boiled potatoes.

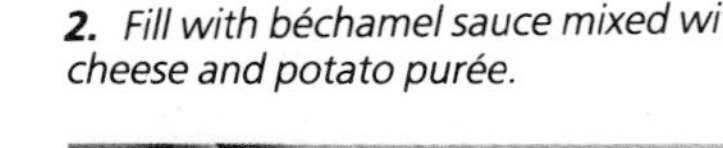

2. Fill with béchamel sauce mixed with cheese and potato purée.

3. Filled potatoes almost ready for the final stage of baking.

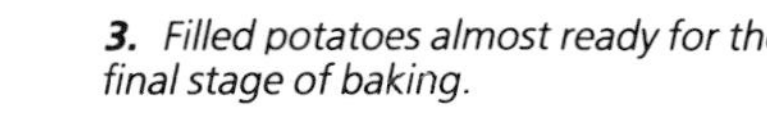

Cold carrot pudding

Budino freddo di carote

Cold Carrot Pudding

00:30 Setting time 03:00 | 00:15

American	Ingredients	Metric/Imperial
1¾ lb	Carrots	800 g / 1¾ lb
1	Potato	1
¼ lb	Green olives	100 g / 4 oz
¼ lb	Black olives	100 g / 4 oz
	Salt and pepper	
1 tsp	Mustard	1 tsp
½	Small onion	½
1 tbsp	Chopped parsley	1 tbsp
2½ cups	Aspic	600 ml / 1 pint
⅔ cup	Mayonnaise (see page 175)	150 ml / ¼ pint

1. Clean the carrots with a small knife, then boil them in salted water with a peeled potato until tender but firm. Drain, allow to cool slightly and cut into fine slices.
2. Place in an earthenware dish, add the green and black olives pitted (stoned) and chopped, season with salt and pepper, mustard, chopped onion and the parsley. Mix together well.
3. Make up the aspic according to the directions on the packet and allow to cool. Pour into a pudding mold and allow to set in the refrigerator.
4. Arrange the vegetables in the mold and pour in the remaining aspic. Set in the refrigerator for several hours.
5. Dip the mold quickly into a basin of warm water and turn it on to a plate.
6. Serve accompanied with a well seasoned mayonnaise flavored with mustard.

Scorzonera alla normanna 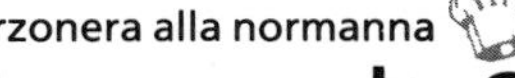

Normandy-Style Scorzonera

00:30 | 01:00

American	Ingredients	Metric/Imperial
1¼ lb	Scorzonera (black salsify)	600 g / 1¼ lb
	Salt and pepper	
1	Onion	1
2 cups	Béchamel sauce (see page 162)	450 ml / ¾ pint
	Butter	
¼ cup	Grated parmesan cheese	25 g / 1 oz
¼ cup	Bread crumbs	25 g / 1 oz

1. Scrape the scorzonera roots, wash them carefully, cut them into pieces 1¼ – 1½ in / 3 – 4 cm long and cook them in plenty of salted boiling water.
2. In a frying pan slowly cook a finely sliced onion in a little heated butter.
3. Drain the scorzonera and place it in the pan with the butter and onion. Season with salt and pepper and leave for a few minutes.
4. Preheat the oven to 400°F / 200°C / Gas Mark 6.
5. Prepare the béchamel sauce and season well with salt and freshly ground black pepper.
6. Put the scorzonera in a buttered ovenproof dish, pour the béchamel sauce over it and sprinkle with parmesan and bread crumbs, then put in a hot oven for about 30 minutes and serve piping hot.

Panzerotti di spinaci

Spinach Triangles

00:30 | 00:04 each batch

American	Ingredients	Metric/Imperial
1 lb	Spinach	450 g / 1 lb
3 tbsp	Olive oil	2 tbsp
	Salt and pepper	
2 cups	Flour	225 g / 8 oz
2	Eggs	2
	Oil for frying	

1. Wash and cook the spinach. Drain well, squeeze out excess water, arrange on a flat plate and cover with olive oil, add a pinch of salt and some freshly ground pepper.
2. In a bowl sift the flour and salt, add the eggs. Work the pastry mix together, gradually adding tepid water until a firm mixture is obtained.
3. Using a rolling pin, roll out the pastry into a fairly thin sheet and cut into squares about 2 in / 5 cm × 2 in / 5 cm. Fill each square with the seasoned spinach, damp the edges of the pastry with cold water, fold over to form triangles.
4. Heat the oil and fry the fritters until they are golden brown.
5. Drain on absorbent kitchen towels. Serve hot accompanied by tomato sauce (see page 171) if desired.

Coste alla mediterranea

Spinach Chilli Custard

00:15 | 00:35

American	Ingredients	Metric/Imperial
2 lb	Young fresh spinach	1 kg / 2 lb
	Salt and pepper	
1 tbsp	Butter	15 g / ½ oz
1¼ cups	Béchamel sauce (see page 162)	300 ml / ½ pint
3	Eggs	3
1	Red chilli pepper	1
1 cup	Grated parmesan cheese	100 g / 4 oz
½ cup	Bread crumbs	50 g / 2 oz

1. Clean the spinach, removing the toughest part of the stems, wash under running water, then cook for 5 minutes in very little boiling salted water. Drain well. Remove the water by squeezing slighlty, add the butter and mix well.
2. Prepare a pouring béchamel sauce and add half to the spinach, mix well. Put the spinach in an ovenproof dish or baking pan, pressing down on it slightly with a fork to ensure that it is properly crushed. Cover with the remaining béchamel sauce. Season well.
3. Preheat the oven to 400°F / 200°C / Gas Mark 6.
4. Beat the eggs, add a little finely chopped deseeded chilli pepper, grated parmesan and 1 tablespoon of bread crumbs. Pour this mixture, which must be thick but not too stiff, over the spinach. Sprinkle the surface with remaining bread crumbs.
5. Put the dish in a hot oven for 15 minutes so that it forms a golden crust. Serve hot with a main course.

Flan di spinaci

Spinach Savory

00:20 | 00:35

American	Ingredients	Metric/Imperial
1 ¼ lb	*Spinach*	*600 g / 1 ¼ lb*
2 tbsp	*Butter*	*25 g / 1 oz*
1	*Garlic clove*	*1*
2 cups	*Béchamel sauce (see page 162)*	*450 ml / ¾ pint*
	Salt and pepper	
2	*Eggs*	*2*

1. Wash and cook the spinach in a small amount of boiling salted water, drain and once it has cooled, squeeze the excess moisture out and put in a bowl with a little melted butter and a crushed clove of garlic.
2. Preheat the oven to 400°F / 200°C / Gas Mark 6.
3. Make the béchamel sauce, add to the spinach with salt and pepper.
4. Separate the eggs and add yolks to the spinach and mix. Whisk the egg whites and fold into the spinach mixture.
5. Tip the mixture into a deep buttered dish and cook in a bain-marie in the oven for about 20 minutes. Serve hot.

Cabiette

Nettle Gnocchi

00:40 | 01:15

American	Ingredients	Metric/Imperial
6 oz	*Nettles*	*175 g / 6 oz*
2 oz	*Fontina cheese*	*50 g / 2 oz*
2 lb	*Potatoes*	*1 kg / 2 lb*
2 cups	*Rye flour*	*225 g / 8 oz*
2	*Eggs*	*2*
1 ½ lb	*Onions*	*700 g / 1 ½ lb*
½ cup	*Butter*	*100 g / 4 oz*
	Salt and pepper	
½ cup	*Rye bread crumbs*	*50 g / 2 oz*

1. Wear an old pair of gloves to gather the nettles. Wash, squeeze and chop them finely, (the food processor is ideal for this).
2. Cut some fontina cheese into small pieces.
3. Peel, boil and mash the potatoes. Put the puréed potatoes in a bowl, add the nettles, the cheese, the sifted rye flour, mix together with the beaten eggs.
4. Cut the peeled onions into thin rings. Heat the butter in a pan and cook for 6 minutes over a gentle heat.
5. Form the potato mixture into small gnocchi (dumplings) and drop into boiling salted water. As soon as they have risen to the top of the pan, drain well.
6. Preheat the oven to 350°F / 180°C / Gas Mark 4.
7. Butter an ovenproof dish, place a layer of the potato dumplings on the bottom, then put some onions on top and sprinkle with melted butter. Continue adding another layer of gnocchi, seasoning well, until all the ingredients are used.
8. Sprinkle the final layer with bread crumbs. Put the dish in the oven for 45 minutes. Serve piping hot.

Stuffed mixed vegetables — eggplant, zucchini [courgettes], sweet pepper and onions

Crocchette di spinaci

Spinach Croquettes

00:45 | 00:05 each batch

American	Ingredients	Metric/Imperial
1 cup	*Thick béchamel sauce (see page 162)*	*225 ml / 8 fl oz*
2 lb	*Spinach or borage*	*1 kg / 2 lb*
	Salt and pepper	
½ cup	*Bread crumbs*	*50 g / 2 oz*
	Oil for frying	

1. Prepare a very thick béchamel sauce. Cook on a low heat, stirring continuously until really thick, allow to cool.
2. Wash the spinach, cook in a little boiling salted water, drain well and squeeze out excess moisture. Chop roughly and add to the béchamel sauce and allow to cool.
3. Form into croquettes the size of golf balls, dip in bread crumbs.
4. Heat the oil in a deep fat pan until very hot and fry the croquettes. When they are golden brown, remove from the fat and drain off the excess oil with absorbent kitchen towels.

Rape allo zucchero

Turnips with Sugar

00:15 00:15

American	Ingredients	Metric/Imperial
1 lb	Turnips	500 g / 1 lb
¼ cup	Butter	50 g / 2 oz
	Salt	
½ tsp	Sugar	½ tsp
1 tbsp	Flour	1 tbsp
2½ cups	Stock	600 ml / 1 pint

1. Peel and cut the turnips into slices, then into thin sticks of about 2 in / 5 cm long.
2. Melt a little butter in a pan, add the turnips, season them with salt and a pinch of sugar and sprinkle with flour, stir round for a few minutes.
3. Moisten with sufficient stock to cover the turnips and finish by cooking over a moderate heat.
4. When they are cooked, the sauce must have thickened enough to cover the turnips with a shiny film. Garnish with chopped parsley and serve with roast meat.

Misto ripieno

Stuffed Mixed Vegetables

00:30 00:30

American	Ingredients	Metric/Imperial
2	Large zucchini (courgettes)	2
2	Eggplant (aubergines)	2
2	Sweet pepper	2
2	Onions	2
	Salt and pepper	
7 oz	Roast meat	200 g / 7 oz
¼ lb	Italian sausage	100 g / 4 oz
1 tbsp	Chopped parsley	1 tbsp
½ cup	Grated cheese	50 g / 2 oz
1	Egg	1
3 tbsp	Bread crumbs	2 tbsp
1 tbsp	Butter	15 g / ½ oz
3 tbsp	Vegetable oil	2 tbsp

1. Top and tail the zucchini and eggplant and cut in half. Peel onion, cut pepper in half and deseed. Blanch for 5 minutes in boiling salted water.
2. Drain and, using a tablespoon, extract the middle flesh, chop and put in 2 different bowls.
3. Chop up the roast meat and the sausage, add the chopped parsley, the grated cheese, egg, the bread crumbs, salt and pepper. Mix well and divide this mixture between the zucchini, eggplant, onion and pepper.
4. Preheat the oven to 400°F / 200°C / Gas Mark 6.
5. Mix the filling and season well. Stuff the two different vegetables with the respective filling.
6. Arrange the zucchini and eggplant in an ovenproof dish rubbed over with a little butter and oil. Seal with foil and cook for 30 minutes.

Verdure in salsa al Grand Marnier

Vegetables in Grand Marnier Sauce

00:30 | 00:40

American	Ingredients	Metric/Imperial
½ lb	*Green beans*	225 g / 8 oz
3	*Small new potatoes*	3
	Salt and pepper	
4	*Zucchini (courgettes)*	4
1 lb	*Fresh or frozen asparagus*	450 g / 1 lb
Sauce		
3 tbsp	*White vinegar*	2 tbsp
	Salt and pepper	
3	*Egg yolks*	3
¾ cup	*Butter*	175 g / 6 oz
2	*Oranges*	2
2 tsp	*Grand Marnier*	2 tsp

1. Top and tail the beans, scrape the new potatoes. Wash the zucchini and cut into thick slices.
2. Cook the potatoes in cold salted water, bring to the boil and simmer briskly until tender but still firm.
3. Place the beans and zucchini in a little boiling salted water and cook for 5 minutes, drain well.
4. Cook the asparagus until tender but firm, according to type. (If using fresh see page 369).
5. Prepare the sauce by boiling together the vinegar, salt and pepper. Reduce by half. Add 1 tablespoon cold water. Blend in the 3 egg yolks and half the butter, cut into small pieces, mix well. Transfer the sauce to a bowl or double saucepan and cook over hot water. Do not let the sauce boil.
6. When the sauce begins to thicken, add the remaining butter a little at a time.
7. Remove from the heat, allow to cool down slightly, then add the juice of the oranges and the Grand Marnier.
8. Arrange the cooked vegetables on a heated platter, the potatoes may be sliced as liked, alternate the asparagus with the beans and zucchini.
9. Pour the sauce on top. For garnish a little grated orange rind may be sprinkled on top.

Misto di verdure al gratin

Mixed Vegetables au Gratin

04:00 | 00:40

American	Ingredients	Metric/Imperial
1	*Small cauliflower*	1
	Salt and pepper	
¼ cup	*Butter*	50 g / 2 oz
2	*Fennel bulbs*	2
14 oz	*Spinach*	400 g / 14 oz
¼ tsp	*Nutmeg*	¼ tsp
½ cup	*Grated cheese*	50 g / 2 oz
1 ¼ cups	*Béchamel sauce (see page 162)*	300 ml / ½ pint

1. Remove the green leaves and part of the stalk from the cauliflower and cook in a little salted water for about 15 minutes, drain. Cut off the florets and toss very quickly in half the heated, browned butter.
2. Drain off the fat and arrange the cauliflower in a large ovenproof dish.
3. Remove the tough outer leaves from the fennel and cook in boiling salted water. Drain and divide into 4 pieces.
4. Add the fennel to the dish with the cauliflower.
5. Remove the stalks from the spinach and tear into small pieces. Cook in a little boiling salted water for 5 minutes. Drain well, put in the dish with the fennel and cauliflower.
6. Preheat the oven to 400°F / 200°C / Gas Mark 6.
7. Sprinkle the vegetables with salt, pepper, nutmeg and half the grated cheese and cover with béchamel sauce. Dot the surface with butter and sprinkle with remaining grated cheese. Cook in the oven for at least 20 minutes.

Budino di verdure

Vegetable Pudding

00:50 | 01:25

American	Ingredients	Metric/Imperial
6 oz	*Green beans*	175 g / 6 oz
	Salt and pepper	
½ lb	*Asparagus*	225 g / 8 oz
2	*Scorzonera (black salsify)*	2
2	*Potatoes*	2
2	*Carrots*	2
1	*Small cauliflower*	1
3	*Artichokes*	3
½ cup	*Butter*	100 g / 4 oz
½ lb	*Thin slices of cooked lean ham*	225 g / 8 oz
2	*Eggs*	2
1 cup	*Grated parmesan cheese*	100 g / 4 oz

1. Choose some small, tender green beans, top and tail, wash and cook them whole in a little boiling salted water.
2. Remove and discard the white, woody part of the asparagus and steam them.
3. Scrape the scorzonera, wash, cut into pieces about the same size as the green beans and cook them in boiling salted water.
4. Cook the peeled, sliced potatoes and carrots 'al dente' like the other vegetables and drain them. Add to them the raw cauliflower, cut into florets.
5. Clean the artichokes, remove the tough outer leaves, the prickles and the choke, cut into pieces and add to the remaining vegetables.
6. Heat the butter, add all the vegetables and season with salt and pepper. Cook for 10 minutes.
7. Butter a 2 lb [1 kg / 2 lb] pudding mold and line the walls with slices of cooked ham. Fill with the mixed vegetables.
8. Beat the eggs well, add salt and pepper, the grated parmesan and pour all over the mixed vegetables, repeatedly banging the mold on the table so that the egg penetrates the spaces.
9. Put the mold into a bain-marie (or a baking pan filled with water to come halfway up the sides of the bowl) and cook for about 30 minutes. Turn out of the mold while it is still piping hot and serve immediately.

Cook's tip: unless young tender artichokes are available, it is probably better to use the canned variety.

Vegetable pudding

Vegetable strudel

Strudel di verdura

Vegetable Strudel

Preparation 01:00 (Standing time 00:30) — Cooking 01:00

American	Ingredients	Metric/Imperial
Pastry		
2 cups	*All purpose (plain) flour*	*225 g / 8 oz*
1	*Egg*	*1*
6 oz	*Ricotta cheese*	*175 g / 6 oz*
Stuffing		
1½ lb	*Cooked vegetables*	*700 g / 1½ lb*
¼ cup	*Butter*	*50 g / 2 oz*
½ cup	*Cream*	*125 ml / 4 fl oz*
1	*Egg*	*1*

1. Mix the sifted flour, the whole egg and the sieved or blended ricotta cheese. Knead well. Make into a ball, wrap in film and leave to stand for 30 minutes in a bowl, over a saucepan of hot water.
2. Trim and wash the vegetables of your choice – tomatoes, mushrooms, onions, asparagus, green beans, peppers, egg-plant (aubergines) etc – and partly cook them, separately, in salted water, or steam. When they are ready, drain and toss in half the butter.
3. Cover with the cream and leave to marinate for 30 minutes.
4. Preheat the oven to 400°F / 200°C / Gas Mark 6.
5. Smear some butter on a large sheet of waxed (greaseproof) paper and roll out the pastry thinly with a floured rolling pin. Arrange the vegetables on it with the cream marinade.
6. Roll up the pastry and place on an oiled baking pan. Brush the pastry with beaten egg and put in a hot oven for 40 minutes. Serve piping hot.

Pannocchi e patate alla griglia

Grilled Corn and Potatoes

Preparation 00:10 — Cooking 01:00

American	Ingredients	Metric/Imperial
8	*Potatoes*	*8*
4	*Fresh or canned corn on the cob*	*4*
¼ cup	*Butter*	*50 g / 2 oz*
	Salt and pepper	

1. Preheat the oven to 400°F / 200°C / Gas Mark 6.
2. Wash the potatoes thoroughly, vigorously brushing the skin clean, put in boiling water and cook for 10 minutes.
3. Drain and wrap in foil and then complete cooking in the oven for 45 minutes.
4. Blanch the corn on the cob in some boiling salted water for 5 minutes. Drain well and rub with butter.
5. Put the corn on the cob under the broiler (grill) and toast well on all sides, turning them frequently.
6. Serve the corn on the cob with melted butter passed separately, the potatoes with butter, salt and pepper. Alternatively, remove the tops of the potatoes still wrapped in foil and cover them with natural yoghurt. Serve as accompaniments to fish or meat or as vegetarian snacks.

Grilled corn and potatoes

Falsa torta di erbette

Mock Herb Flan

00:30 00:10 to 00:15

American	Ingredients	Metric/Imperial
1 lb	*Herbs (parsley, chervil, chives)*	*450 g / 1 lb*
6 oz	*Cooked ham*	*175 g / 6 oz*
3	*Eggs*	*3*
3 tbsp	*Cream*	*2 tbsp*
	Salt and pepper	
¼ cup	*Bread crumbs*	*25 g / 1 oz*
1 tbsp	*Butter*	*15 g / ½ oz*

1. Preheat oven to 350°F / 180°C / Gas Mark 4.
2. Wash the herbs, blanch in boiling water for 4 minutes, drain and squeeze well to remove the water.
3. Chop roughly in a blender or food processor and tip into a large bowl.
4. Add some chopped cooked ham, the whole eggs, the cream and season with salt and freshly ground pepper. Mix all the ingredients together.
5. Butter a 12 in / 30 cm pan or ovenproof dish, sprinkle with bread crumbs, remove the excess and pour in the mixture. Level the top of the mixture.
6. Cover the surface with bread crumbs and dot with butter. Put in the oven for 10 minutes or until lightly set. Do not let this dish overcook.

Romanian ratatouille

Peperoni alla turca

Turkish-Style Peppers

00:25 00:35

American	Ingredients	Metric/Imperial
4	*Large sweet yellow peppers*	*4*
⅓ cup	*Raisins*	*50 g / 2 oz*
½ cup	*Pine kernels*	*50 g / 2 oz*
7 oz	*Bologna sausage*	*100 g / 7 oz*
7 oz	*Fontina type cheese*	*200 g / 7 oz*
1 cup	*Bread crumbs*	*100 g / 4 oz*
3 tbsp	*Milk*	*2 tbsp*
1 tsp	*Chopped basil*	*1 tsp*
2 tbsp	*Chopped parsley*	*1½ tbsp*
2 tbsp	*Capers*	*1½ tbsp*
3	*Anchovy fillets*	*3*
Scant ¼ cup	*Vegetable oil*	*3 tbsp*
	Salt and pepper	

1. Preheat the oven to 375°F / 190°C / Gas Mark 5.
2. Blanch the peppers for 3 minutes in boiling salted water. Dry and remove the tops with a small knife. Empty out the peppers, removing all the seeds.
3. Soak the raisins in hot water for 10 minutes.
4. Prepare a stuffing with a mixture of softened raisins, pine nuts, chopped Bologna sausage, the cheese diced very small, bread crumbs and a little milk. Add the finely chopped basil, parsley, capers and anchovy fillets. Mix together well and divide amongst the peppers.
5. Put the peppers in a baking pan, sprinkle with a little oil, season with salt and pepper and cook for 35 minutes.

Ratatuia rumena

Romanian Ratatouille

00:30 01:00

American	Ingredients	Metric/Imperial
2	*Onions*	*2*
6	*Tomatoes*	*6*
2	*Sweet peppers*	*2*
1	*Eggplant (aubergine)*	*1*
4	*Zucchini (courgettes)*	*4*
2	*Turnips*	*2*
2	*Medium-sized potatoes*	*2*
2	*Carrots*	*2*
1	*Leek*	*1*
¼ lb	*French beans*	*100 g / 4 oz*
¼	*Small cauliflower*	*¼*
½	*Small cabbage*	*½*
¼	*Savoy cabbage*	*¼*
1	*Small bunch of parsley*	*1*
2	*Bay leaves*	*2*
2	*Sprigs of thyme*	*2*
1	*Bunch of white grapes, slightly sharp*	*1*
2	*Apples*	*2*
1	*Orange*	*1*
1 cup	*Vegetable oil*	*225 ml / 8 fl oz*
	Salt and pepper	

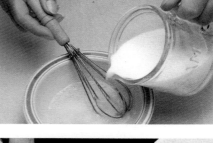

1. Preheat oven to 400°F / 200°C / Gas Mark 6.
2. Thoroughly wash all the vegetables and then trim and prepare as for all different types.
3. Cut onions into slices, peel tomatoes and cut into pieces, cut deseeded peppers into strips, the eggplant, zucchini, turnips and potatoes into dice. Cut the carrots and leek into rounds; chop the French beans, divide the cauliflower into florets and slice the cabbages.
4. Chop the parsley, bay leaves and thyme; peel and seed the grapes, peel and slice the apples, peel the orange and divide into segments. Put all these ingredients in layers into an earthenware pot, add the oil, 1¼ cup [300 ml / ½ pint] water and the salt and pepper.
5. Cover, put in a preheated oven and cook for about 1 hour without stirring. Serve hot with crusty bread.

Zucchine fritte

Fried Zucchini [Courgettes]

00:25 | 00:04 per batch

American	Ingredients	Metric/Imperial
1 lb	*Zucchini (courgettes)*	*500 g / 1 lb*
	Salt	
1 cup	*Flour*	*100 g / 4 oz*
1	*Egg*	*1*
⅔ cup	*Milk*	*150 ml / ¼ pint*
	Vegetable oil or lard for frying	

1. Wash and carefully dry the zucchini, cut lengthwise into slices and sprinkle with salt and lemon juice. Allow to stand for 15 minutes.
2. Prepare a batter. Sift the flour with a pinch of salt. Make a well in the centre of the flour and add beaten egg yolk and milk. Mix well. Whisk the egg white into a stiff peak and fold carefully into the batter.
3. Dip the zucchini in the batter to ensure that they are well covered.
4. Heat the oil in a deep pan and when hot (350°F / 180°C) pick the zucchini slices out with a fork, hold over the bowl to drain excess batter. Fry 4-6 slices at a time.
5. When golden and swollen, place on absorbent kitchen towels to drain and sprinkle with salt and serve hot and crisp.

Zucchini in crosta

Zucchini [Courgette] Pie

00:45 | 01:00

American	Ingredients	Metric/Imperial
1 lb	*Zucchini (courgettes)*	*500 g / 1 lb*
1	*Onion*	*1*
⅓ cup	*Butter*	*65 g / 2½ oz*
4 or 5	*Canned tomatoes*	*4 or 5*
½ tsp	*Chopped oregano*	*½ tsp*
	Salt and pepper	
4	*Eggs*	*4*
½ cup	*Grated cheese*	*50 g / 2 oz*
¼ lb	*Cooked ham*	*100 g / 4 oz*
½ lb	*Puff pastry*	*225 g / 8 oz*

1. Trim the zucchini and cut them vertically into quarters and then into small sticks; wash and drain well.
2. Gently fry a sliced onion in the butter in a large frying pan and, when it begins to turn golden, add the zucchini and stir to mix.
3. Add the canned tomatoes, a generous pinch of oregano, salt and pepper. Cover and continue cooking for about 20 minutes and if necessary, add a little water.
4. Beat 3 whole eggs in a bowl with a pinch of salt, the grated cheese and the chopped ham. Roll out the pastry fairly thinly to obtain a round to line the bottom and sides of an 8 in / 20 cm pie or flan dish and a smaller disc to cover it.
5. Preheat the oven to 425°F / 180°C / Gas Mark 7.
6. Butter and flour the dish, line it with the larger disc of pastry and fill with the zucchini, mixed well with the eggs and ham. Damp the edges with cold water, and place the smaller round on top. Seal the edges well, brush with beaten egg and make 3 slits to allow steam to escape. Place in a hot oven for 30 minutes.

Zucchini [courgette] pie
Top, left to right. Slice the zucchini finely. Add them to the frying pan. Beat the eggs in a bowl and add the milk.

Bottom, left to right: Mix the cooked zucchini with the eggs. Line a pie dish with the large disc of pastry; add the filling and the top covering of pastry. Glaze with egg.

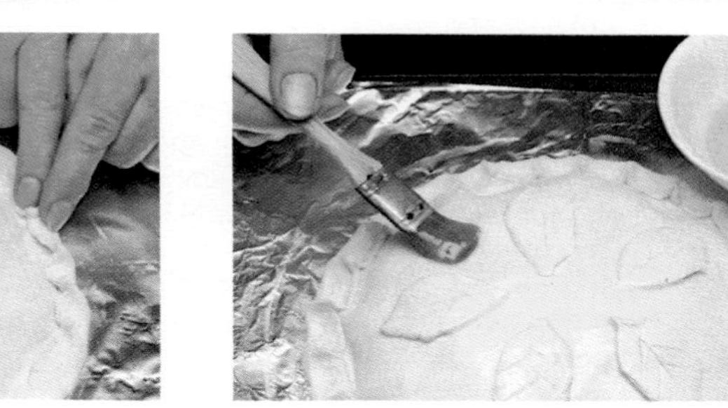

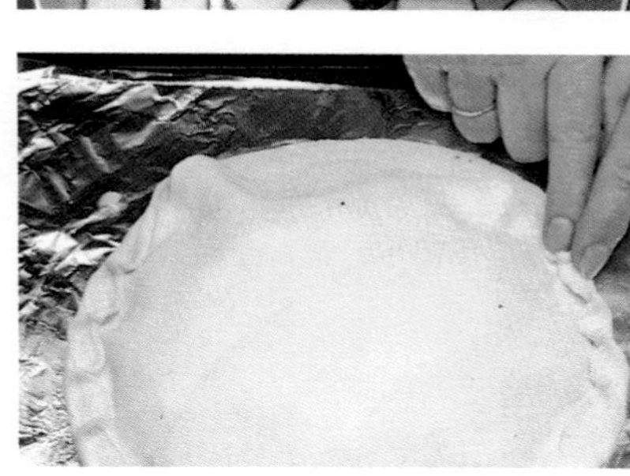

Zucchine Marseilles

Marseilles Zucchini [Courgettes]

00:45 00:05 each batch

American	Ingredients	Metric/Imperial
4	*Zucchini (courgettes)*	4
	Salt and pepper	
¼ cup	*Grated parmesan cheese*	25 g / 1 oz
1	*Egg*	1
3 tbsp	*Chopped parsley*	2 tbsp
2	*Basil leaves*	2
1½ cups	*Fresh bread crumbs*	75 g / 3 oz
	Flour	
½ cup	*Dried bread crumbs*	50 g / 2 oz
	Oil for frying	

1. Boil the zucchini, in salted boiling water for 5 minutes. Drain, allow to cool.
2. Dry and slice the zucchini and cut slices into 4. Put them in a bowl, then season with salt and pepper.
3. Add the parmesan, the beaten egg, parsley, chopped basil, fresh bread crumbs. Flour your hands and knead the mixture, then divide into small balls.
4. Dip in the dried bread crumbs and fry in the hot oil. Serve hot, as a starter or as an accompaniment to a main course.

Zucchine ai due colori

Zucchini [Courgettes] with Two Colors

00:35 00:35

American	Ingredients	Metric/Imperial
2½ cups	*Tomato sauce (see page 171)*	600 ml / 1 pint
8	*Zucchini (courgettes)*	8
⅔ cup	*Rice*	150 g / 5 oz
2 tbsp	*Butter*	25 g / 1 oz
1	*Onion*	1
2	*Eggs*	2
3 tbsp	*Cream*	2 tbsp
	Salt and pepper	
1 tbsp	*Vegetable oil*	1 tbsp

1. Prepare and cook the tomato sauce.
2. Wash the zucchini, cut them in half lengthways and empty out the flesh leaving the skins whole. Parboil the flesh for a few minutes in a little boiling salted water, then drain.
3. Cook the rice so that it remains 'al dente', flavor with half the butter and ⅔ cup [125 ml / ¼ pint] tomato sauce.
4. Preheat the oven to 350°F / 180°C / Gas Mark 4.
5. Chop the onion and flesh of zucchini. Beat the eggs and the cream, season with salt and pepper and add onion and zucchini. Heat a little oil and the remaining butter in a pan, pour in the egg and work with a fork until it is slightly set and creamy.
6. Fill the zucchini first with the flavored rice then with the scrambled egg mixture. Pour the remaining tomato sauce into an ovenproof dish, arrange the zucchini in the sauce and cook in the oven for 15 minutes.

Budino di zucchine

Zucchini [Courgette] Pudding

00:15 00:55

American	Ingredients	Metric/Imperial
2	*Carrots*	2
1	*Onion*	1
2 tbsp	*Chopped parsley*	1½ tbsp
1 tbsp	*Vegetable oil*	1 tbsp
¼ cup	*Butter*	50 g / 2oz
1 lb	*Zucchini (courgettes)*	500 g / 1 lb
	Salt and pepper	
¼ cup	*Grated parmesan cheese*	25 g / 1 oz
3	*Eggs*	3
1 cup	*Béchamel sauce (see page 162)*	225 ml / 8 fl oz

1. Preheat the oven to 350°F / 180°C / Gas Mark 4.
2. Make a chopped mixture with the carrots, the onion and the parsley and add to a pan with heated oil and butter.
3. Cut the tips off the zucchini, wash, dry and slice them. Add to the mixture in the pan. Season with salt and pepper and cook for 10 minutes.
4. Remove from the heat and add the parmesan, the beaten eggs and the béchamel sauce.
5. Pour the mixture into a buttered mold and cook in a roasting pan with water halfway up the mold for 45 minutes. Remove from the oven and serve hot.

Zucchine Tour d'Argent

Zucchini [Courgettes] Tour D'Argent

00:20 00:25

American	Ingredients	Metric/Imperial
8	*Zucchini (courgettes)*	8
¼ lb	*Cooked ham*	100 g / 4 oz
1	*Small onion*	1
1	*Egg*	1
1 cup	*Grated parmesan cheese*	100 g / 4 oz
2	*Slices of bread*	2
¼ cup	*Milk*	50 ml / 2 fl oz
	Salt and pepper	
⅔ cup	*Cooked long grain rice*	100 g / 4 oz
3 tbsp	*Butter*	40 g / 1½ oz

1. Thoroughly wash the zucchini, then cut them in half lengthways and remove some of the flesh. Blanch the flesh in boiling water for 2 minutes.
2. Mix the chopped ham with the finely chopped onion, the egg and most of the cheese. Soak the bread in milk, squeeze and add to the ham with salt, pepper, the cooked rice, the inside of the zucchini and thoroughly mix it all together.
3. Preheat the oven to 400°F / 200°C / Gas Mark 6.
4. Fill the zucchini with the mixture. Arrange them in a buttered ovenproof dish, sprinkle with parmesan cheese and put in a hot oven until the zucchini are cooked, then serve hot.

Zucchine ripiene

Stuffed Zucchini [Courgettes]

This is another attractive method of serving zucchini using the ingredients given in the recipe Zucchini Tour d'Argent opposite, but omitting the rice and adding extra sauce ingredients.

1. Cut the washed zucchini across the middle. Remove the flesh with a ball cutter or small spoon.
2. Cook the onion, finely diced, in a little butter, then add the cheese and the egg with the zucchini flesh.
3. Add the ham, finely chopped, to the mixture. Soak the bread in the milk. Squeeze the milk from 1 slice of bread, break into small pieces and mix well with the stuffing mixture. Season with salt and pepper.
4. Squeeze out the other slice of bread and use a small piece to seal one end of each halved zucchini. Stuff the mixture into the zucchini tubes.
5. Make a sauce with 1 small chopped onion, any excess zucchini flesh, 1 tablespoon chopped parsley and, if liked, 1 crushed garlic clove. Cook gently in 1 tablespoon oil for a few minutes in a large pan. Add 15 oz (425 g / 15 oz) peeled plum tomatoes mashed down with a spoon and salt and pepper. Cook the sauce for 5 minutes.
6. Add the zucchini halves to the pan, laying them on their sides. Poach gently for 15 minutes turning from time to time. Serve surrounded by sauce.

PUDDINGS

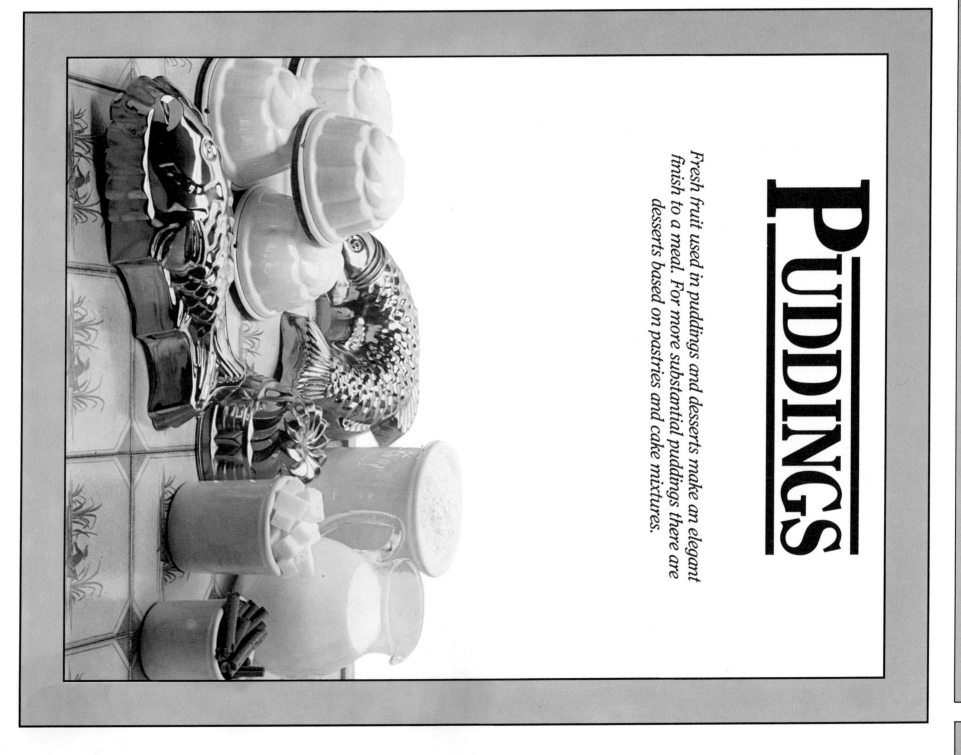

Fresh fruit used in puddings and desserts make an elegant finish to a meal. For more substantial puddings there are desserts based on pastries and cake mixtures.

Pudding di Natale

Christmas Pudding

Preparation 01:00 (Standing time 12:00) — Cooking 04:00

American	Ingredients	Metric/Imperial
1 cup	Ground almonds	150 g / 5 oz
5 oz	Candied fruit	150 g / 5 oz
1 cup	Currants	150 g / 5 oz
1 lb	Veal kidneys or	500 g / 1 lb
¼ lb	Prepared suet	100 g / 4 oz
½ cup	All purpose (plain) flour	50 g / 2 oz
2 tbsp	Sugar	25 g / 1 oz
1	Lemon	1
1	Orange	1
4	Eggs	4
1 tbsp	Brandy	1 tbsp
1 cup	Bread crumbs	100 g / 4 oz
	Milk to mix	

1. Put the almonds in a bowl. Slice or dice the candied fruit and soak the currants in warm water.
2. Skin the kidneys and remove the fat. Combine the sifted flour, sugar, candied fruit, juice and rind of 1 lemon, juice and rind of 1 orange, and the chopped kidney fat or suet. Mix thoroughly and allow to rest for 30 minutes.
3. Drain and dry the currants.
4. Add the beaten eggs, 1 tablespoon brandy, the currants and bread crumbs with enough milk to mix well. Allow to rest for a whole night, then turn into a well buttered mold or pudding basin, dusted with bread crumbs. Cover with foil and cook in a bain-marie for about 4 hours. Before serving, turn it onto a heated serving plate.

Omelette confiture

Jam Omelette

Preparation 00:25 — Cooking 00:25

American	Ingredients	Metric/Imperial
6	Eggs	6
¼ cup	Flour	25 g / 1 oz
½ cup	Milk	125 ml / 4 fl oz
1 tsp	Vanilla sugar	1 tsp
¼ tsp	Cinnamon	¼ tsp
½ cup	Butter	100 g / 4 oz
	Fine granulated (castor) sugar	
	Soft fruit jam	
¼ lb	Mascarpone cheese	100 g / 4 oz
	Candied fruit	
3 tbsp	Liqueur or cream	2 tbsp

1. Beat the eggs. Gradually blend in the flour and milk until you have a smooth mixture. Add vanilla sugar and cinnamon.
2. In a large cast iron frying pan melt the butter and as soon as it begins to smoke pour in the batter. The pancake must be very thin, therefore the frying pan has to be large. If the pan is small, make smaller pancakes. Turn the cooked pancake on to sugared paper and sprinkle with sugar.
3. Cover with a layer of fairly liquid jam (like bilberry, raspberry, etc), followed by a thin layer of mascarpone. Roll up.
4. If you have small pancakes, lay them on top of each other on a serving dish and proceed as before.
5. Decorate, if liked, with candied fruit, pour over some strong liqueur and serve flaming. Alternatively, decorate with rosettes of whipped cream and flakes of bitter chocolate.

Mele economiche

Baked Apples with Butter and Jam

Preparation 00:05 — Cooking 00:40

American	Ingredients	Metric/Imperial
4	Apples of equal size	4
4 tsp	Butter	4 tsp
8 tsp	Jam	8 tsp

1. Preheat the oven to 350°F / 180°C / Gas Mark 4.
2. Neatly core the apples. Fill each cavity with a knob of butter and 2 teaspoons of jam (any kind you like).
3. Place in an ovenproof dish with about 1 in / 2½ cm water on the bottom and bake in a preheated oven. When apples are cooked, the skin tends to become dry and break. Leave the apples in the oven until cold, then serve at once.

Pere alla piemontese

Piedmontese Pears

Preparation 00:45 — Cooking 00:30

American	Ingredients	Metric/Imperial
4	William pears	4
¼ cup	Sugar	50 g / 2 oz
½ cup	Sweet white wine	125 ml / 4 fl oz
¼ tsp	Cinnamon	¼ tsp
3 tbsp	Honey	2 tbsp
½ lb	Graham crackers (digestive biscuits)	225 g / 8 oz
¼ cup	Butter	50 g / 2 oz
¼ cup	Cornstarch (cornflour)	25 g / 1 oz
1 ¼ cups	Milk	300 ml / ¼ pint
3 tbsp	Sugar	2 tbsp
1 tbsp	Sweet or bitter cocoa	1 tbsp
1 tbsp	Bread crumbs	1 tbsp
	Candied cherries or violets for decorating	

1. Peel, core and finely slice the pears. In a small pan combine the pears, sugar, wine, with the cinnamon and honey. Cook until the mixture becomes smooth.
2. Allow to cool. When cool, add the crumbled crackers.
3. Preheat the oven to 350°F / 180°C / Gas Mark 4.
4. Prepare a sweet béchamel as follows: melt but do not brown most of the butter, add all the cornstarch and work it with a wooden spoon until it forms a ball. Gradually add the milk and blend thoroughly. When the béchamel is cooked, remove from the heat and stir until tepid. Add the sugar and cocoa and mix well. Combine the béchamel with the pears.
5. With the remaining butter rub over an ovenproof dish and sprinkle with bread crumbs. Pour in the mixture. Bake in a preheated oven until a golden crust has formed. Before serving, decorate with candied cherries or violets. This pudding is excellent served hot or cold.

Piedmontese pears

Pesche al forno della nonna

Grandmother's Baked Peaches

Preparation: 00:25 | Cooking: 00:30

American	Ingredients	Metric/Imperial
8	*Peaches*	*8*
6	*Amaretti biscuits*	*6*
1	*Egg yolk*	*1*
⅔ cup	*Sugar*	*150 g / 5 oz*
1 tbsp	*Liqueur*	*1 tbsp*
2 tbsp	*Butter*	*25 g / 1 oz*
¼ cup	*White wine*	*50 ml / 2 fl oz*

1. Preheat the oven to 350°F / 180°C / Gas Mark 4.
2. Choose good ripe peaches which are easily halved. Open them, remove the stones and with a teaspoon, scoop out some of the flesh.
3. Chop the flesh and combine with crumbled amaretti, the egg yolk, ¼ cup [50 g / 2 oz] sugar and 1 tablespoon of sweet liqueur (cointreau, amaretto, etc). Stir well to obtain a soft filling.
4. Spoon into the peaches and arrange in a buttered oven-proof dish. Add the wine and another ¼ cup [50 g / 2 oz] sugar. Dust the peaches with the remaining sugar.
5. Bake in a moderate oven for about 30 minutes. Take out of the oven and cool at room temperature.
6. Serve in the ovenproof dish and spoon, if you like, some ice cream, on each peach.

Mele alla parigina

French Apple Tart

Preparation: 00:30 | Cooking: 00:30

American	Ingredients	Metric/Imperial
6	*Apples*	*6*
1 tbsp	*Sweet liqueur*	*1 tbsp*
3 tbsp	*Sugar*	*2 tbsp*
¾ lb	*Shortcrust pastry (see page 452)*	*350 g / 12 oz*
	Butter	
1 cup	*Quick sweet béchamel sauce (see below)*	*225 ml / 8 fl oz*
3 tbsp	*Apricot jam*	*2 tbsp*

1. Preheat the oven to 400°F / 200°C / Gas Mark 6.
2. Peel and thinly slice the apples and combine with the liqueur and sugar.
3. Roll out the pastry and line the bottom and the sides of a buttered pie or flan dish with the shortcrust pastry, prick with a fork. Spread a layer of apples on the pastry.
4. Prepare a sweet béchamel and spread part of it on the apples. Keep on alternating apples and béchamel until the ingredients are used up, ending with the apples brushed over with sieved apricot jam. Bake in a hot oven for about 30 minutes.

Cook's tip: use the quick béchamel sauce recipe on page 162 . Omit salt and pepper, flavor with 1 teaspoon lemon juice, a few drops vanilla essence and 1 tablespoon sugar.

Charlotte di mele

Apple Charlotte

Preparation: 00:30 | Cooking: 00:50

American	Ingredients	Metric/Imperial
2 lb	*Canadian or Cox apples*	*1 kg / 2 lb*
⅓ cup	*Butter*	*75 g / 3 oz*
½ cup	*Brandy*	*125 ml / 4 fl oz*
1	*Lemon*	*1*
3 tbsp	*Sugar*	*2 tbsp*
1 tsp	*Vanilla sugar*	*1 tsp*
¼ tsp	*Cinnamon*	*¼ tsp*
¼ lb	*Apricot jam*	*100 g / 4 oz*
¼ cup	*Milk*	*50 ml / 2 fl oz*
¾ lb	*Savoy biscuits*	*350 g / 12 oz*

1. Peel, halve, core and finely slice the apples. Cook in half the butter with half the brandy, the lemon rind, sugar, vanilla and cinnamon. Place the pan over a medium heat and mix frequently until the apples are reduced to the consistency of a purée. Remove from the heat, leave to cool and stir in the apricot jam.
2. Preheat the oven to 350°F / 180°C / Gas Mark 4.
3. Pour the milk and the remaining brandy over half the savoy biscuits. Butter a 6 in / 15 cm soufflé dish (with straight sides) and cover the base and sides with the savoy biscuits.
4. Pour in the apple purée to fill the dish. Crumble the remaining savoy biscuits over the top and add the remaining melted butter. Bake in a moderate oven for 35 minutes.
5. Allow to cool for 10 minutes or so before turning out the charlotte or serve from the dish.

Mele fritte

Fried Apples

Preparation: 00:15 | Cooking: 00:04 each batch

American	Ingredients	Metric/Imperial
3	*Apples*	*3*
	Sugar	
2 tbsp	*Brandy*	*1½ tbsp*
1¼ cups	*Flour*	*150 g / 5 oz*
1	*Egg yolk*	*1*
½ cup	*Dry white wine*	*125 ml / 4 fl oz*
2	*Egg whites*	*2*
	Oil for frying	

1. Peel, core and then slice the apples to a thickness of about ¼ in / 1 cm. Marinate for a few minutes in a little sugar and brandy or any other liqueur.
2. Make the batter by sifting the flour into a bowl, make a well in the centre, add the egg yolk and wine, mix well. Whisk the egg whites until thick but not too stiff. Fold into the batter making sure there are no lumps.
3. Dip in the slices of apple one by one covering them all over with batter.
4. Heat oil in a deep pan to 350°F / 180°C and as soon as it begins to haze, fry the apple slices a few at a time. Fry both sides and leave to drain on a plate covered with kitchen towels to absorb the excess oil. Serve hot, sprinkled with sugar.

Fried apples

Apple strudel

Mele flambé al forno

Baked and Flambéd Apples

00:15 00:30

American	Ingredients	Metric/Imperial
4	*Sweet apples*	4
⅔ cup	*Sultanas*	100 g / 4 oz
4 tsp	*Peach or apricot jam*	4 tsp
½ cup	*Red wine*	125 ml / 4 fl oz
1 tbsp	*Sugar*	1 tbsp
1 tbsp	*Butter*	15 g / ½ oz
3 tbsp	*Aromatic liqueur*	2 tbsp
1 tsp	*Fruit brandy*	1 tsp

1. Preheat the oven to 400°F / 200°C / Gas Mark 6.
2. Wash and core the apples and arrange in an ovenproof dish.
3. Soak the sultanas in hot water and drain well. Fill the cavity of each apple with the sultanas and 1 teaspoon jam.
4. Pour the wine into an ovenproof dish, add the sugar and the butter and bake in the oven for at least 20 minutes.
5. Sprinkle the apples with a liqueur such as grand marnier or cointreau, and return to the hot oven. Before serving, add a few drops of fruit brandy and set alight. Serve with cream or ice cream.

Strudel di mele

Apple Strudel

01:00 01:05

American	Ingredients	Metric/Imperial
½ lb	*Frozen puff pastry (see page 453)*	225 g / 8 oz
3 tbsp	*Flour*	2 tbsp
Filling		
1 lb	*Apples*	500 g / 1 lb
1	*Lemon*	1
½ cup	*Melted butter*	100 g / 4 oz
3 tbsp	*Bread crumbs*	2 tbsp
⅓ cup	*Sultanas*	50 g / 2 oz
¼ cup	*Pine kernels*	25 g / 1 oz
¼ cup	*Ground almonds*	25 g / 1 oz
1 tsp	*Confectioner's (icing) sugar*	1 tsp
1 tsp	*Cinnamon*	1 tsp
1	*Egg yolk*	1

1. Allow the puff pastry to thaw. Roll out the pastry on a floured board and gently stretch out with your hands until the pastry is as thin as possible and oval in shape. Take care not to tear it.
2. Preheat the oven to 425°F / 220°C / Gas Mark 7.
3. Peel, core and slice the apples and place in a bowl of water with some lemon juice to prevent them turning brown. Brush the pastry with part of the melted butter and cover with the apples to within 1 in / 2½ cm from the edges.
4. Spread over the bread crumbs, softened, dried sultanas, pine kernels, ground almonds, sugar, cinnamon and grated lemon peel. Roll up the dough with the filling and seal the edges. Place on a buttered and floured baking sheet and brush with the rest of the butter mixed with the egg yolk.
5. Bake in a preheated oven for 15 minutes, lower the oven to 325°F / 170°C / Gas Mark 3 and bake for another 45 minutes.
6. Allow the strudel to cool, then dust with icing sugar and serve cut in slices.

Torta della zia Diana

Aunt Diana's Apple Flan

00:35 00:30

American	Ingredients	Metric/Imperial
¼ lb	*Shortcrust pastry (see page 452)*	100 g / 4 oz
1 lb	*Sweet apples*	450 g / 1 lb
1	*Lemon*	1
1	*Egg*	1
3 tbsp	*Sugar*	2 tbsp
⅔ cup	*Milk*	150 ml / ¼ pint
1 tbsp	*Rum*	1 tbsp
2 tsp	*Confectioner's (icing) sugar*	2 tsp

1. Make the shortcrust pastry and rest in the refrigerator.
2. Peel and slice the apples and cover with a little water and lemon juice.
3. Preheat the oven to 400°F / 180°C / Gas Mark 4.
4. Mix the egg with the sugar and the milk in a double boiler and whisk over a medium heat until it begins to thicken. Add the rum and mix well.
5. Line a 6 in / 15 cm pie dish with rolled out pastry and trim.
6. Arrange the drained apples on the pastry and cover with the creamy sauce and sprinkle with confectioner's (icing) sugar. Bake for 25-30 minutes, reducing the temperature to 325°F / 170°C / Gas Mark 3 after 10 minutes. Allow the top to form a golden brown crust, serve hot.

Torta di ribes

Red Currant Tart

01:00 00:30

American	Ingredients	Metric/Imperial
¼ lb	*Shortcrust pastry (see page 452)*	100 g / 4 oz
1 cup	*Sweet almonds*	150 g / 5 oz
1	*Egg yolk*	1
1 tbsp	*Confectioner's (icing) sugar*	1 tbsp
⅓ cup	*Cream*	4 tbsp
7 oz	*Red currant jam*	200 g / 7 oz
¾ lb	*Fresh red currants*	350 g / 12 oz

1. Preheat the oven to 400°F / 200°C / Gas Mark 6.
2. Line the pie or flan dish with the rolled out shortcrust pastry.
3. Blanch and grind the almonds in a blender or food processor. Combine with the egg yolk, sugar and cream and beat the mixture until smooth.
4. Spread the nut and cream mixture on the pastry and cover with a layer of red currant jam.
5. Bake in a hot oven for about 30 minutes.
6. Hull and wash the redcurrants, drain in a colander, then dry on a clean cloth.
7. Remove the tart from the oven and allow to cool. Cover with fresh red currants and serve at once.

Almond torte

Torta di mandorle

Almond Torte

Preparation 00:30 — Cooking 00:40

American	Ingredients	Metric/Imperial
4 cups	*All purpose (plain) flour*	*450 g / 1 lb*
2 tsp	*Baking powder*	*2 tsp*
½ cup	*Milk*	*125 ml / 4 fl oz*
1½ cups	*Confectioner's (icing) sugar*	*150 g / 6 oz*
½ cup	*Melted butter*	*100 g / 4 oz*
2 oz	*Honey*	*50 g / 2 oz*
2 cups	*Ground almonds*	*225 g / 8 oz*
Scant ½ cup	*Almonds, halved*	*50 g / 2 oz*

1. Sift flour in a bowl with the baking powder, make a well in the middle and pour in milk, sugar, melted butter and honey.
2. Preheat the oven to 375°F / 190°C / Gas Mark 5.
3. Blend together with a wooden spoon, then add the ground almonds, mixing well into a paste. Turn onto a floured board and keep on working for another 10 minutes. Shape the paste into a round the size of a cake pan. Place in a buttered, floured cake pan and bake for about 40 minutes.
4. To test whether it is cooked, insert a thin skewer which must come out perfectly clean. Remove from the oven and allow to cool. Decorate with almond halves.

Cook's tip: this mixture can be cooked in a baked pastry case in an 8 in / 20 cm flan ring. Any remaining pastry can be latticed on top.

Gubana

Fruit Plait

Preparation 01:00 — Cooking 00:35

American	Ingredients	Metric/Imperial
1 cup	*Sultanas and raisins*	*175 g / 6 oz*
½ cup	*Dry white wine*	*125 ml / 4 fl oz*
½ cup	*Pine kernels*	*50 g / 2 oz*
1 cup	*Walnuts*	*100 g / 4 oz*
3	*Dried figs*	*3*
3	*Dried prunes*	*3*
1	*Candied citron*	*1*
1 oz	*Chocolate chips*	*25 g / 1 oz*
1	*Orange*	*1*
1	*Lemon*	*1*
¼ cup	*Bread crumbs*	*25 g / 1 oz*
3 tbsp	*Butter*	*40 g / 1½ oz*
2	*Eggs, separated*	*2*
½ lb	*Puff pastry (see page 453)*	*225 g / 8 oz*
	Flour	
	Vanilla sugar	

1. Soak the raisins and sultanas in the wine for 30 minutes.
2. Preheat the oven to 425°F / 220°C / Gas Mark 7.
3. Grind (mince) the nuts, figs, prunes and candied citron; combine in a bowl with the well drained raisins and sultanas. Add the chocolate chips and the grated orange and lemon peel. Mix in a food processor, if liked.
4. Brown the bread crumbs in a pan with the heated butter and add to the mixture. Stir thoroughly.
5. Add 1½ lightly beaten egg yolks and fold in the stiffly beaten egg whites.
6. Roll out the puff pastry on a floured board and dust with flour. Put the filling in the centre of the pastry, cut strips on the sides and plait pastry over the top.
7. Brush with lightly beaten egg yolk mixed with ½ teaspoon water and bake on a buttered baking sheet for 35 minutes. Cover with waxed (greaseproof) paper if the pastry is browning too quickly. Dust with vanilla sugar before serving.

Budino à la flamme

Flambéd Pudding

Preparation 00:25 — Cooking 01:00

American	Ingredients	Metric/Imperial
1 cup	*Milk*	*225 ml / 8 fl oz*
½ lb	*Stale bread*	*225 g / 8 oz*
¼ cup	*Sugar*	*50 g / 2 oz*
¼ cup	*Rum*	*50 ml / 2 fl oz*
½ cup	*Chopped candied fruit*	*75 g / 3 oz*
2 oz	*Malaga grapes*	*50 g / 2 oz*
3	*Eggs*	*3*
3 tbsp	*Butter*	*40 g / 1½ oz*

1. Heat the milk to boiling point but take care not to let it boil.
2. Cut the bread into small pieces and put in a dish, pour over the hot milk with the sugar added. Set aside until all the liquid has been absorbed.
3. Mix together 1 tablespoon rum, the chopped candied fruit, the washed and mashed grapes and the beaten eggs. Mix well with the bread.
4. Preheat the oven to 350°F / 180°C / Gas Mark 4.
5. Butter a 1 quart [1 litre / 1¾ pint] pudding basin and pour in the mixture. Cook for 30 minutes over a saucepan of hot water and for another 30 minutes in the oven.
6. Heat the remainder of the rum without boiling. Turn the pudding onto a warmed serving dish, pour over the warm rum. Flambé at the table.

Torta di latte

Milk Pudding

Preparation 00:30 — Cooking 00:30

American	Ingredients	Metric/Imperial
1 lb	*Bread*	*500 g / 1 lb*
2 quarts	*Milk*	*2 litres / 3½ pints*
1 scant cup	*Sugar*	*200 g / 7 oz*
¼ cup	*Butter*	*50 g / 2 oz*
3	*Eggs*	*3*
30	*Blanched almonds*	*30*
1	*Lemon*	*1*
	Confectioner's (icing) sugar	

1. Preheat the oven to 350°F / 180°C / Gas Mark 4.
2. Cut up the bread and soak in a bowl with the milk. Add the sugar, knobs of softened butter, beaten egg and mix well.
3. Add blanched almonds, grated lemon peel and mix again.
4. Butter an ovenproof dish, fill with the mixture and bake until lightly browned. Cool and dust with confectioner's sugar.

Pineapple doughnuts

Struffoli di San Gennaro

Honeyed Cubes

Preparation 00:35 | Cooking 00:04 per batch

American	Ingredients	Metric/Imperial
3 cups	Flour	350 g / 12 oz
5	Eggs	5
	Salt	
1	Lemon	1
3 tbsp	Sugar	40 g / 1½ oz
3 tbsp	Brandy or liqueur	2 tbsp
	Oil for frying	
½ lb	Honey	225 g / 8 oz
1 tsp	Cinnamon	1 tsp
	Cake decorations	

1. Combine the sifted flour, eggs, a pinch of salt, grated lemon peel, sugar and alcohol into a fairly soft mixture.
2. Shape into strips about ½ in / 1 cm wide and cut into little cubes.
3. Heat the oil until hot and fry the cubes.
4. Warm up the honey, flavor with the cinnamon and pour over the cubes. Allow to soak.
5. Arrange in a ring on a serving dish, sprinkle with cake decorations, allow the honey to set and serve.

Bignés di ananas

Pineapple Doughnuts

Preparation 00:30 | Cooking 00:04 per batch

American	Ingredients	Metric/Imperial
2 cups	All purpose (plain) flour	225 g / 8 oz
½ tsp	Salt	½ tsp
2	Eggs, separated	2
½ cup	Beer	125 ml / 4 fl oz
½ cup	Milk	125 ml / 4 fl oz
1	Pineapple	1
¼ cup	Sugar	50 g / 2 oz
¼ cup	Rum	50 ml / 2 fl oz
	Oil for frying	

1. Sift the flour into a bowl with the salt and the egg yolks. Stirring all the while, add the beer and the milk, and a little water if necessary. Whisk the egg whites until stiff and fold into the batter.
2. Peel the pineapple and remove the hard centre. Chop into small cubes and put in a dish. Sprinkle with the sugar and pour on the rum, allow to marinate for about 10 minutes.
3. Heat the oil in a thick pan to 350°F / 180°C. Drain the pineapple chunks and mix with the batter. Remove with a slotted spoon and plunge into the hot oil in batches. Fry until golden brown.

Arancini dolci

Orange Pudding

00:40 01:15

American	Ingredients	Metric/Imperial
4	*Oranges*	*4*
1 cup	*Sugar*	*225 g / 8 oz*
2⅓ cups	*Round grain rice*	*500 g / 1 lb*
3 tbsp	*Flour*	*2 tbsp*
	Oil for frying	
3 tbsp	*Confectioner's (icing) sugar*	*2 tbsp*

1. Squeeze the oranges. Coarsely chop the peel and reserve.
2. Combine sugar, orange juice and 1½ quarts [1.5 litres / 2½ pints] water. Heat in a large saucepan to a rolling boil, then add the rice and the grated orange rind. Continue cooking on a low heat, stirring continuously, until all the liquid has been absorbed. Alternatively cook in a covered casserole in the oven at 350°F / 180°C / Gas Mark 4 for 1 hour. Stir from time to time.
3. Remove from the heat, allow to cool, then refrigerate for a few hours.
4. Roll the mixture in flour and knead to a dough. Shape small rounds from this.
5. Heat the oil in a deep pan, and when hot, 350°F / 180°C, put in the rounds of mixture. When they are golden brown, remove from the pan. Drain on absorbent kitchen towels and serve sprinkled generously with confectioner's sugar.

Torta Claudia 

Torta Claudia

02:00
Chilling time 03:00
00:00

American	Ingredients	Metric/Imperial
1	*Sponge cake (see page 454)*	*1*
½ cup	*Liqueur*	*125 ml / 4 fl oz*
2½ cups	*Whipped cream*	*600 ml / 1 pint*
1 cup	*Confectioner's (icing) sugar*	*100 g / 4 oz*
¼ lb	*Cocoa*	*100 g / 4 oz*
2	*Egg yolks*	*2*
3 tbsp	*Fine granulated (castor) sugar*	*2 tbsp*
Scant ¼ cup	*Marsala*	*3 tbsp*
2 oz	*Crushed caramelized almonds*	*50 g / 2 oz*

1. Slice the sponge cake into 3 equal rounds. Place the first in a round dish and moisten with liqueur.
2. Mix two-thirds of the whipped cream with the confectioner's sugar and divide in 2 parts.
3. Stir the cocoa into the first half in a bowl and spoon onto the round of sponge cake in the dish.
4. Moisten another round with liqueur and lay on top of the cream. Cover with the plain sweet cream. Lay the third and last round of cake, sprinkled with the remaining liqueur, on top and press lightly with the palm of the hand to even the cake. Refrigerate for 3 hours.
5. Prepare the zabaglione with eggs, sugar and marsala (see page 438). Remove cake from the refrigerator, cover the top and sides with the remaining cream, sprinkle with the crushed caramelized almonds, cover with the zabaglione and serve.

Cook's tip: to caramelize almonds spread toasted split almonds on an oiled baking pan. Caramelize sugar with a few drops of water, e.g. 3 tablespoons water to ½ cup [100 g / 4 oz] sugar and when it reaches a golden stage, pour over the almonds. Allow to set. Turn the almonds out of the pan and break up with a small hammer or rolling pin.

Alchechengi al cioccolato

Winter Cherries in Chocolate

00:50 00:10

American	Ingredients	Metric/Imperial
2 lb	*Cherries*	*1 kg / 2 lb*
½ lb	*Plain chocolate*	*225 g / 8 oz*
3 tbsp	*Milk*	*2 tbsp*

1. Choose large cherries. Divide the skin, which will be dry, into segments and, without detaching it from the fruit, peel it back to form a flower-like shape pointing away from the cherry.
2. Melt the chocolate in a bain-marie with the milk.
3. When the chocolate is creamy and smooth, dip the cherries, holding them by the cherry skin petals.
4. Spread out to dry on a marble slab greased with a drop of oil and as soon as the chocolate solidifies, arrange the cherries on a sweet dish.

Zuppa inglese casalinga

Plain Trifle

00:35 00:25

American	Ingredients	Metric/Imperial
½ cup	*Butter*	*100 g / 4 oz*
1 cup	*Flour*	*100 g / 4 oz*
¼ lb	*Cocoa*	*100 g / 4 oz*
½ cup	*Sugar*	*100 g / 4 oz*
1 quart	*Milk*	*1 litre / 1¾ pints*
10	*Amaretti biscuits*	*10*
⅔ cup	*Marsala*	*150 ml / ¼ pint*
1	*Packet of sponge fingers*	*1*

1. Melt the butter over a low heat, add the flour, cocoa and sugar and mix well. Gradually stir in the milk to avoid lumps. If necessary, remove the pan from the heat, stir and return it when everything is well mixed.
2. Cook slowly, stirring constantly, until the mixture has thickened. Crumble the amaretti biscuits and then add to the chocolate cream.
3. Moisten walls and bottom of a low, large mold with marsala. Moisten the sponge fingers with marsala diluted with a drop of milk or water. Line the bottom of the mold with sponge fingers; cover with a layer of cream, then another layer of sponge fingers. Continue in this way until all the ingredients are used up.
4. Serve as it is or unmold carefully and cover with whipped cream, crème patissiere or zabaglione. Refrigerate and serve well chilled.

Budino di cioccolata

Chocolate Pudding

00:35 01:00

American	Ingredients	Metric/Imperial
¼ lb	*Bitter chocolate*	100 g / 4 oz
2½ cups	*Milk*	600 ml / 1 pint
⅔ cup	*Sugar*	150 g / 5 oz
¼ lb	*Savoy biscuits*	100 g / 4 oz
½ cup	*Amaretto liqueur*	125 ml / 4 fl oz
3	*Eggs*	3
1	*Vanilla pod*	1

1. Grate the chocolate and heat it in the milk in a double boiler over a low heat until it melts.
2. Raise the heat and when the mixture boils, add a little less than half the sugar and crumble in the savoy biscuits. Cook for 15 minutes, stirring continuously. Strain through a sieve into a bowl. Add the amaretto liqueur and leave to cool.
3. Preheat the oven to 325°F / 170°C / Gas Mark 3.
4. In a separate bowl, beat the eggs and flavor with the vanilla. Combine with the milk mixture.
5. Dissolve the remaining sugar in a few drops of water until pale golden, pour into a pudding basin.
6. Add the chocolate mixture and cook in the oven sitting on a pan of water for 1 hour. Serve hot or cold.

Torta di noci

Nut Pudding

00:30 01:20

American	Ingredients	Metric/Imperial
4 cups	*Walnuts*	450 g / 1 lb
1 cup	*Almonds*	150 g / 5 oz
1 cup	*Pine kernels*	100 g / 4 oz
1 cup	*Pistachio nuts*	100 g / 4 oz
4¼ cups	*Sugar*	1 kg / 2 lb
1 cup	*Sultanas*	175 g / 6 oz
½ cup	*Butter*	100 g / 4 oz

1. Preheat the oven to 325°F / 170°C / Gas Mark 3.
2. Shell and grind the nuts in a blender. Put in a pan with the sugar and mix well. Heat and try to obtain a pale toffee consistency.
3. Butter a ring shaped mold well, quickly tip in the nuts, sultanas and any caramelized sugar left in the pan. Then bake for 1 hour.
4. Unmold onto a serving plate by putting the pan in boiling water for a few seconds before turning out. The consistency should be like soft toffee and it should be served at once.

Cook's tip: rum can be added to the mixture to give the pudding more flavor.

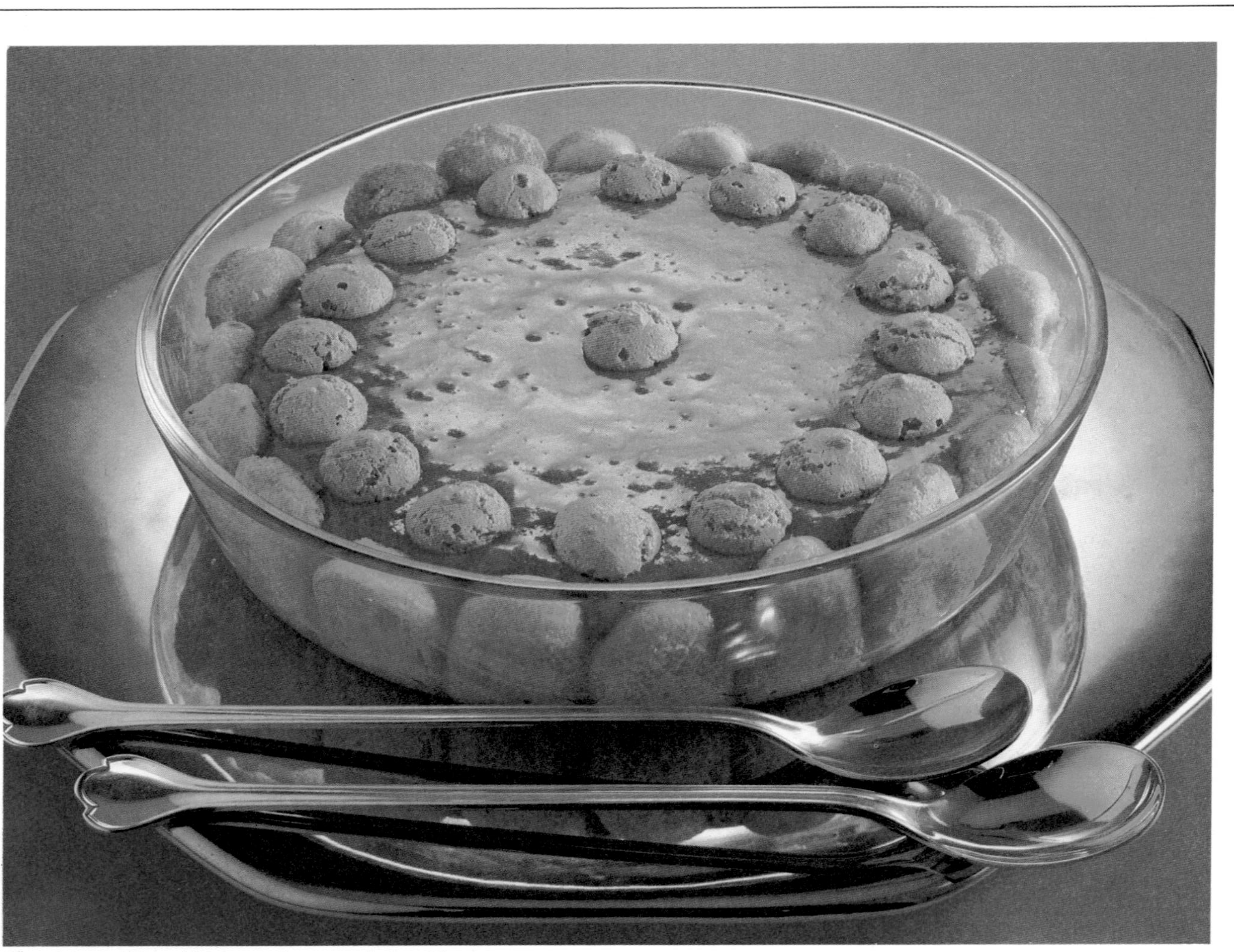

Chocolate pudding with sponge fingers and amaretti

Aspic di frutta

Fruit Jelly

00:25 Setting time 04:00 | 00:10

American	Ingredients	Metric/Imperial
6	*Oranges*	6
1	*Lemon*	1
10	*Sugar lumps*	10
14 oz can	*Pineapple*	420 g / 14 oz can
5 tsp	*Gelatin*	5 tsp
1½ lb	*Fresh fruit in season: strawberries, apricots, peaches, grapes, plums etc.*	700 g / 1½ lb

1. Cut the oranges and lemon in half and squeeze out the juice. Strain into a saucepan. Add sugar lumps and make up 2 cups [475 ml / ¾ pint] with pineapple juice (from the can) and water. Boil for a few minutes.
2. Dissolve the gelatin by sprinkling into a few tablespoons of boiling water, add this to the boiling liquid when the gelatin has dissolved completely.
3. Wash and chop the fruit, adding the canned pineapple. The jelly will have cooled a little by now.
4. Pour a little jelly into a mold and freeze for a few minutes. Stir the fruit into the remaining jelly and pour this into the mold. Refrigerate for a few hours.
5. Dip in warm water and turn out onto a plate.

Cook's tip: for a special occasion set the jelly in layers with carefully arranged slices of fruit of different colors on each layer of jelly. Allow each layer to almost set before adding the chopped fruit.

Macedonia nell'anguria

Fruit Salad in Watermelon

00:20 Chilling time 01:10 | 00:00

American	Ingredients	Metric/Imperial
1	*Average size watermelon*	1
8	*Yellow and purple plums*	8
2	*Ripe peaches*	2
1	*Orange*	1
1	*Lemon*	1
3 tbsp	*Maraschino or cointreau*	2 tbsp
1 tbsp	*Confectioner's (icing) sugar*	1 tbsp
½ lb	*Raspberries*	225 g / 8 oz

1. Cut the watermelon in half, scoop all the flesh into a bowl and patiently remove all the seeds. As the melon shell will be used as a container, even it out inside and wash it on the outside, drying well with absorbent kitchen towels.
2. Mix the melon flesh with the pitted (stoned) yellow and purple plums, the sliced peaches, orange and lemon juice, maraschino or cointreau and the sugar. Refrigerate for about 1 hour.
3. Carefully wash the raspberries and set aside. Turn the fruit salad into the melon shell, add the raspberries and return to the refrigerator for a few minutes to chill.
4. Serve within 30 minutes before the melon becomes watery, which would spoil the fruit salad.

Bavarese al caffè

Coffee Mousse

00:20 Chilling time 04:00 | 00:30

American	Ingredients	Metric/Imperial
1 cup	*Strong black coffee*	225 ml / 8 fl oz
5 tsp	*Gelatin*	5 tsp
1 cup	*Milk*	225 ml / 8 fl oz
⅔ cup	*Sugar*	150 g / 5 oz
1 cup	*Whipping (double) cream*	225 ml / 8 fl oz
2	*Eggs, separated*	2
1 tbsp	*Cornstarch (cornflour)*	1 tbsp
1 sachet	*Vanilla sugar*	1 sachet
2 or 3	*Small glasses of brandy*	2 or 3

1. Prepare some very strong coffee. Then sprinkle the gelatin on 3 tablespoons boiling water to dissolve.
2. Heat the milk. In a separate bowl pour the sugar, the egg yolks and cornstarch. Whisk thoroughly, adding the filtered coffee a little at a time. Continue whisking, add the boiling milk a little at a time to produce a creamy mixture.
3. Pour this into a double boiler, or place the bowl over a pan of boiling water on a medium heat. Reheat, and when it begins to thicken, add the vanilla sugar and allow to cool.
4. Add the brandy to the thoroughly dissolved gelatin and stir into the mixture. Strain into a bowl and stir several times.
5. Whisk the egg whites into soft peaks.
6. Whip the cream and fold gently into the mixture before it sets, then fold in the egg whites.
7. Pour into a mold, level it off and place a lightly buttered waxed (greaseproof) paper disc over the top. Refrigerate for 4 hours. To turn out, immerse in hot water for a few seconds.

Melone ripieno

Stuffed Melon

00:25 | 00:00

American	Ingredients	Metric/Imperial
1	*Large ripe melon*	1
1 lb	*Strawberries*	450 g / 1 lb
5 oz	*Ricotta*	150 g / 5 oz
2 tbsp	*Confectioner's (icing) sugar*	1½ tbsp
1	*Egg yolk*	1
1 tbsp	*Liqueur*	1 tbsp
1 cup	*Whipping (double) cream*	1

1. Cut the melon in half. Scoop out the flesh into a bowl, saving the empty melon shells.
2. Hull the strawberries, retain 8 for decoration, and soften them in water, drain and add to the chopped melon flesh. Combine with the ricotta and beat until the mixture is quite creamy. Blend in the confectioner's (icing) sugar, egg yolk and liqueur. This stage can all be done in a blender or food processor). Refrigerate for about 20 minutes.
3. Fill the melon halves with the mixture, whisk the cream and decorate the melon halves with whipped cream rosettes and whole strawberries. Refrigerate until ready to serve.

Zuccotto con amaretti

Amaretti Pudding

00:30 Chilling time 03:00 — 00:00

American	Ingredients	Metric/Imperial
4	*Eggs*	4
½ cup	*Sugar*	100 g / 4 oz
6	*Amaretti biscuits*	6
½ lb	*Mascarpone cheese*	225 g / 8 oz
¼ lb	*Sponge fingers*	100 g / 4 oz
⅔ cup	*Amaretto di Saronno liqueur*	150 ml / ¼ pint

1. Separate the eggs. Whisk yolks with sugar until very frothy.
2. Crumble the amaretti, add to the yolks and mix well. Add the mascarpone cheese little by little, mixing all the time.
3. Whisk the whites until very stiff and carefully fold into the mixture.
4. Line a mold with the sponge fingers soaked in the liqueur and pressed against the walls and bottom. Fill with the cream and cover with the remaining sponge fingers. Refrigerate for at least 3 hours before serving turned out.

Zuppa di amarene

Morello Cherry Trifle

00:25 Chilling time 02:00 — 00:20

American	Ingredients	Metric/Imperial
2 lb	*Morello cherries*	1 kg / 2 lb
1	*Cinnamon stick*	1
1	*Lemon*	1
3 tbsp	*Sugar*	2 tbsp
½ cup	*Red wine (optional)*	125 ml / 4 fl oz
6 – 8	*Slices of bread*	6 – 8

1. Wash, dry and pit (stone) the cherries. Put them into a saucepan with the cinnamon, lemon rind and the sugar. Add wine if liked. Cook until the cherries are wrinkled and give plenty of thick juice.
2. Slice the bread, line a 2½ cup [600 ml / 1 pint] pudding basin and add the cherries as soon as they are ready, removing the cinnamon stick.
3. Allow to cool before placing in the refrigerator. Serve the trifle well chilled.

Pesche rosé

Peaches in Rosé Wine

00:20 — 00:10

American	Ingredients	Metric/Imperial
8	*Large peaches*	8
1 tbsp	*Sugar*	1 tbsp
1	*Lemon*	1
1 (70 cl)	*Bottle of rosé wine*	1 (70 cl)
1	*Cinnamon stick*	1
¼ cup	*Confectioner's (icing) sugar*	50 g / 2 oz

1. Wash peaches and put in pan with about 1 in / 2½ cm of water and then 1 tablespoon sugar. Bring to the boil and simmer for about 10 minutes. Leave to cool, skin and slice.
2. In a container with a tight fitting lid put a layer of peaches and sprinkle with sugar and strips of lemon rind. Continue with the peaches, sugar and lemon rind until the fruit is used up.
3. Pour the bottle of rosé over the peaches and add a small cinnamon stick. Seal the container and refrigerate. Before serving remove the cinnamon and sprinkle with confectioner's sugar.

Torta di castagne

Chestnut Tart

00:25 — 00:30

American	Ingredients	Metric/Imperial
½ cup	*Butter*	100 g / 4 oz
1 tsp	*Flour*	1 tsp
1¼ lb	*Chestnuts*	600 g / 1¼ lb
	Salt	
3	*Eggs, separated*	3
½ cup	*Fine granulated (castor) sugar*	100 g / 4 oz
1 cup	*Ground almonds*	100 g / 4 oz
½	*Lemon*	½

1. Preheat the oven to 400°F / 200°C / Gas Mark 6. Butter and lightly flour an 8 in / 20 cm baking pan.
2. Shell the chestnuts and boil in slightly salted water until soft. Drain. Remove the inside skin and mash through a sieve or blender to obtain a fine purée.
3. In another bowl, cream the yolks with the sugar, add all the remaining softened butter in small knobs, the chestnut purée, ground almonds and grated lemon peel. Mix well.
4. Whisk the egg whites until stiff and carefully fold into the mixture. Turn into the buttered pan and bake in a hot oven for about 30 minutes. Pierce with a skewer to see whether the mixture is cooked: it should come out perfectly clean. Turn onto a wire rack, allow to cool and serve.

Cook's tip: if using canned chestnut purée, add more ground almonds or the mixture may be too wet.

Saint Louis Blues

Saint Louis Blues

00:40 Refrigeration time 01:00 to 02:00 — 00:20

American	Ingredients	Metric/Imperial
2	*Pineapples*	2
1 tbsp	*Rum*	1 tbsp
3 tbsp	*Sherry*	2 tbsp
Scant ¼ cup	*Rolled oats*	3 tbsp
1 cup	*Milk*	225 ml / 8 fl oz
Sauce		
1 cup	*Sugar*	225 g / 8 oz
10 oz	*Pineapple flesh*	275 g / 10 oz
¼ cup	*Sherry (optional)*	50 ml / 2 fl oz

1. Cut the pineapples in half lengthwise and scoop out the flesh, leaving about ½ in / 1 cm. Chop the flesh without wasting any of the juice and set aside.

Saint Louis blues

2. Fill shells with a mixture of rum, sherry and 3 [2] tablespoons sugar (taken from the sauce allowance), and refrigerate for 1-2 hours.
3. Cook the oats in milk for 20 minutes to make a firm porridge. Cool and combine with half the pineapple and juice.
4. To make a sauce, put the sugar in a pan with the remaining pineapple juice and flesh and, depending on taste, more sherry. Cook until the slightly fibrous flesh of the pineapple has become pulp. Strain and set aside.
5. Drain the juice in the pineapple shells into the sauce and fill them with the porridge mixture. Arrange on a serving plate or tray and pour the thick sauce over the preparation.

Zabaione

Zabaglione

Zabaglione is one of the most famous Italian puddings. It is very simple and quick to make.

00:05 00:10 to 00:15

American	Ingredients	Metric/Imperial
4	*Fresh egg yolks*	*4*
¼ cup	*Fine granulated (castor) sugar*	*50 g / 2 oz*
1 tsp	*Cornflour (cornstarch)*	*1 tsp*
¼ cup	*Marsala*	*50 ml / 2 fl oz*

1. Cream the yolks with the sugar and cornstarch (cornflour) (optional, but it prevents the yolks from curdling when being cooked) in a copper pan or bowl over a pan of hot water, making sure the bottom of the bowl does not touch the water. Whisk until pale and frothy and gradually whisk in the marsala.
2. Whisk over a moderate heat until the mixture is thick and creamy. Serve in wine glasses or small ramekin dishes.

Cook's tip: preparation and cooking time will depend on whether an electric mixer or hand whisk is being used.

Mandarini a sorpresa

Tangerine Surprise

00:25 00:00

American	Ingredients	Metric/Imperial
8	*Tangerines*	*8*
1 ¼ cups	*Fruit ice*	*300 ml / ½ pint*
1 cup	*Pistachio nuts*	*100 g / 4 oz*

1. Cut the tops from 8 tangerines, seedless if possible. Save the tops.
2. Scoop out the flesh taking great care not to break the skin.
3. Sieve the flesh through a coarse sieve to remove any seeds or pith, mix with the fruit ice (any kind you like) and chopped pistachio nuts. Fill the tangerines with the mixture, cover them again with their tops and then freeze for 30 minutes. Serve with plain biscuits or sponge fingers.

Cook's tip: step 3 may be mixed in seconds in a food processor and give even distribution of ingredients.

Monte Bianco

Mont Blanc

00:30 00:30

American	Ingredients	Metric/Imperial
14 oz	*Chestnuts*	*400 g / 14 oz*
2 cups	*Milk*	*450 ml / ¾ pint*
¼ cup	*Vanilla sugar*	*50 g / 2 oz*
1 tbsp	*Liqueur*	*1 tbsp*
1 cup	*Whipping (double) cream*	*225 ml / 8 fl oz*
½ tsp	*Vanilla essence*	*½ tsp*
4	*Marrons glacés*	*4*
4	*Candied violets*	*4*

1. Shell the chestnuts and boil them for a few minutes to remove any inside skin. When they are quite clean, simmer in milk and sugar until perfectly tender.
2. Mash twice through a sieve, blender, food processor, or food mill to get a smooth cream. Allow to cool.
3. Flavor with 1 tablespoon liqueur (grand marnier is excellent with chestnuts).
4. Arrange the chestnut cream in a mound on a serving dish, whip the cream and add the vanilla flavoring, pipe or spread over the chestnut mound. Decorate with small pieces or marrons glacés and candied violets.

Gelato pasticciato

Mixed Ice Cream

00:30 00:00
Freezing time 02:00
Serves 6

American	Ingredients	Metric/Imperial
2½ oz	*Plain chocolate*	*65 g / 2½ oz*
3 tbsp	*Milk*	*2 tbsp*
1 quart	*Ice cream*	*1 litre / 1¾ pints*
2 tbsp	*Cherry syrup*	*1½ tbsp*
3 tbsp	*Red currant syrup*	*2 tbsp*

1. Divide the ice cream into 3 parts in 3 bowls. Melt the chocolate with the milk, let it cool to avoid melting the ice cream and stir into the first bowl of ice cream. Turn into a mold and freeze.
2. Stir the cherry syrup into the second part, turn this on top of the first layer in the mold and return to the freezer.
3. Finally, stir the red currant syrup into the third part of the ice cream and turn on top of the other two. Freeze for 2 hours. Before serving, dip the mold into warm water quickly and turn out onto a serving dish.
4. The flavored ice cream can be decorated with cherries, whipped cream, candied fruit or melted chocolate.

Spiedini della Chiccolina

Fruit Kebabs

00:20 00:00

American	Ingredients	Metric/Imperial
2	*Apples*	*2*
3 tbsp	*Lemon juice*	*2 tbsp*
1 ¼ lb	*Strawberries (preferably large)*	*600 g / 1 ¼ lb*
¼ cup	*Fine granulated (castor) sugar*	*50 g / 2 oz*
3 tbsp	*Vinegar*	*2 tbsp*
8	*Brandy cherries*	*8*

1. Peel, core and cube the apples, cover with lemon juice.
2. Wash the strawberries and put into a bowl with the sugar and vinegar. Leave for 10 minutes. Besides giving an excellent juice which can be served separately, this method helps to preserve the true flavor and perfume of the strawberry.
3. On a small skewer thread a brandy cherry, a strawberry, a piece of apple, another strawberry, another piece of apple, finishing with a cherry.

Cook's tip: an excellent way to serve fresh fruit outdoors at barbecues and picnics.

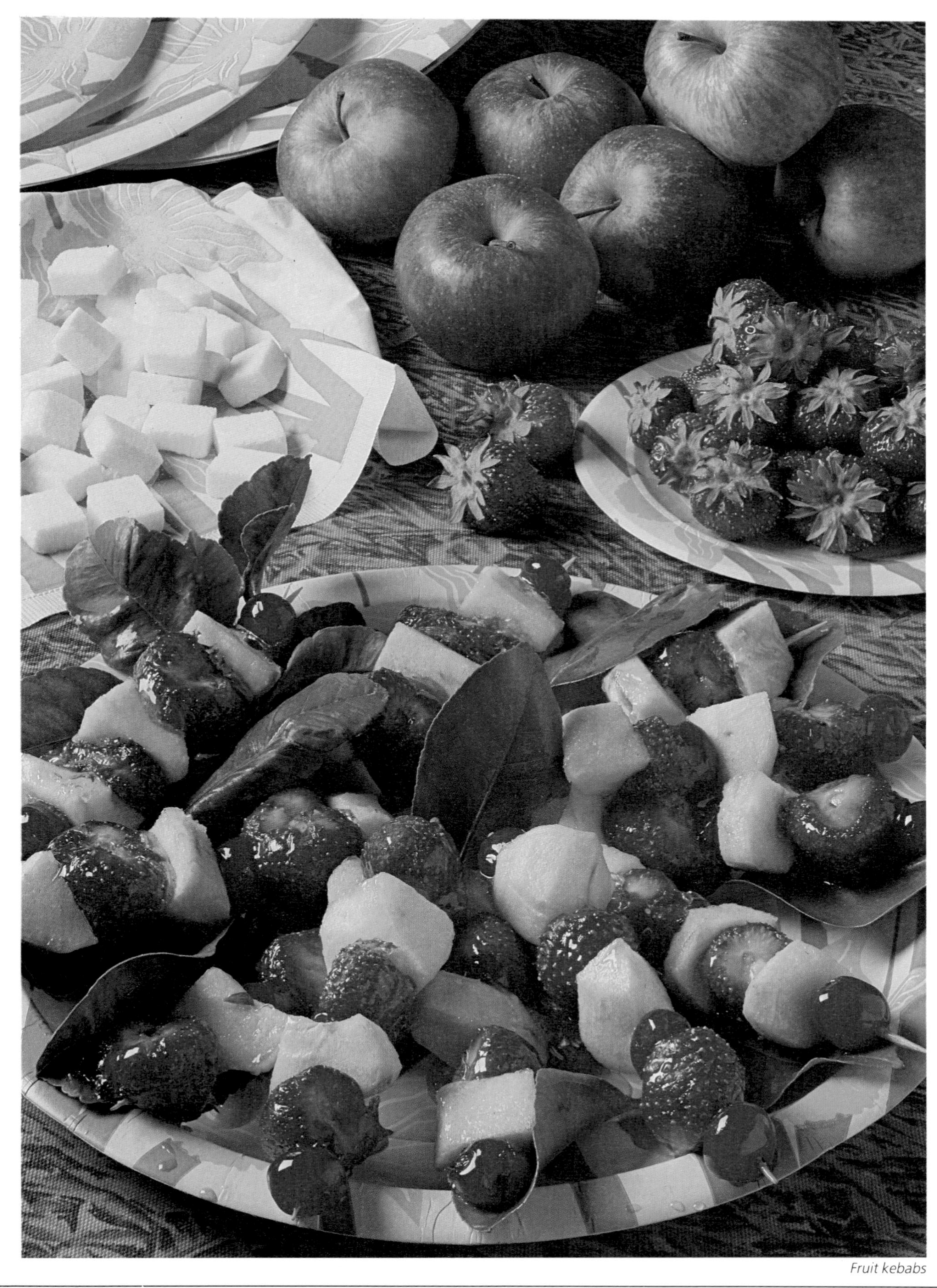

Fruit kebabs

Melon with port

Semifreddo al porto

Semifreddo with Port

00:45 — 00:15

American	Ingredients	Metric/Imperial
4	*Cooking apples*	4
⅓ cup	*Sugar*	65 g / 2½ oz
1	*Lemon*	1
½ cup	*White wine*	125 ml / 4 fl oz
1	*Sponge cake (see page 454)*	1
Sauce		
4	*Egg yolks*	4
½ cup	*Sugar*	100 g / 4 oz
½ cup	*Port*	125 ml / 4 fl oz
1 cup	*Whipped cream*	200 ml / 7 fl oz
5 oz	*Amaretti biscuits*	150 g / 5 oz

1. Peel, core and slice the apples. Put in a pan, sprinkle with sugar, lemon rind, wine and 3 tablespoons water and cook over a low heat for about 10 minutes until apples are soft and mushy and all liquid is absorbed.
2. Cream the egg yolks and the sugar well together until fluffy; add the port, pour into a bowl and cook over a saucepan of warm water, whisking until it thickens. Remove from the heat and keep on whisking, then carefully fold in the whipped cream.
3. Add the apple pureé and stir in the crushed amaretti.
4. Line a deep round cake pan on the bottom with wax (greaseproof) paper.
5. Cut the sponge cake in 3 horizontally, place one round on the bottom of the pan, cover with a layer of mixture and continue with the other 2 layers, using all the ingredients.
6. Decorate with 8 amaretti biscuits, then put into the freezer for 30 minutes to firm. Turn out onto a serving plate and store in the refrigerator.

Melone spagnolo al porto

Spanish Melon with Port

00:35 Chilling time 02:00 — 00:00

American	Ingredients	Metric/Imperial
2	*Green skinned Spanish melons*	2
	Salt and pepper	
½ cup	*Dry port*	125 ml / 4 fl oz

1. Cut the melons in half and remove the seeds. Scoop out some flesh and season the cavity with salt and pepper.
2. Refrigerate for 2 hours, then fill the cavity with a good dry port and allow to rest for 30 minutes. Serve with spoons suitable for scooping out melons.
3. For a special occasion place each melon in a bowl half filled with crushed ice.

Palle di neve

Snow Balls

00:20 — 00:02 per batch

American	Ingredients	Metric/Imperial
8	*Egg whites*	8
	Salt	
1¼ cups	*Milk*	300 ml / ½ pint
3 tbsp	*Vanilla sugar*	2 tbsp
	Chocolate cream (see page 453)	

1. Stir a pinch of salt into the egg whites and whisk until quite soft. Flavor the milk with vanilla sugar and bring to the boil.
2. Using a small rounded ladle, drop little even balls of egg white – a few at a time – into the boiling milk and leave there for about 2 minutes. Lift the balls out with a slotted spoon and dry on a clean cloth.
3. Make a chocolate cream with a little more milk and without macaroons, and spread it on a plate. Arrange the snow balls on this bed of chocolate cream and decorate with whipped cream or zabaglione.

Sorpresa di lamponi

Raspberry Surprise

00:40 Chilling time 12:00 — 00:05

American	Ingredients	Metric/Imperial
1 tbsp	*Kirsch*	1 tbsp
¼ lb	*Sponge fingers*	100 g / 4 oz
¾ lb	*Raspberries*	350 g / 12 oz
¼ cup	*Sugar*	50 g / 2 oz
Scant ¼ cup	*Red currant jelly*	3 tbsp

1. Pour the kirsch and the same amount of water into a soup plate and moisten the sponge fingers. Oil a mold and line with the moistened sponge fingers. Cover the sponge fingers with a layer of raspberries sprinkled with sugar, follow with another layer of sponge fingers until the mold is full.
2. Place a saucer on top of the pudding and press it down with a small weight. Leave in the refrigerator until the next day.
3. Melt the red currant jelly in a pan on a moderate heat. Turn out the pudding, pour the jelly over and serve.

Raspberry surprise

Cassata Siciliana

Sicilian Cassata

01:00 Chilling time 03:00 00:03

American	Ingredients	Metric/Imperial
1 scant cup	*Sugar*	*200 g / 7 oz*
2 tsp	*Vanilla sugar*	*2 tsp*
¾ lb	*Ricotta cheese*	*350 g / 12 oz*
¾ lb	*Mixed candied fruit*	*350 g / 12 oz*
2 oz	*Pistachio nuts*	*50 g / 2 oz*
¼ lb	*Bitter chocolate*	*100 g / 4 oz*
¼ cup	*Marsala wine*	*50 ml / 2 fl oz*
1	*Sweet tea loaf or brioche*	*1*
1 lb	*Apricot jam*	*450 g / 1 lb*
1¾ cups	*Confectioner's (icing) sugar*	*200 g / 7 oz*
	Orange flower water	

1. Dissolve the sugar and the vanilla sugar in a little water over a very low heat, stirring continuously.
2. Rub the ricotta through a sieve and add to the syrup. Chop the candied fruit and add half to the mixture.
3. Blanch, peel and cut the pistachio nuts in half and add these to the other ingredients.
4. Grate the chocolate, mix in thoroughly and pour in the marsala.
5. Cut the bread into thin slices. Line a cake pan with wax (greaseproof) paper and line this with slices of bread, spread with a little sieved apricot jam to bind it.
6. Pour the ricotta mixture into the cake pan and level the surface. Cover with more slices of bread, spread with apricot jam. Refrigerate for 2 hours.
7. Prepare the apricot glaze by combining the remaining sieved apricot jam, the confectioner's (icing) sugar and a little orange flower water in a saucepan over a moderate heat. Remove the cassata from the refrigerator and turn it upside down on a serving dish, removing the wax (greaseproof) paper. Brush with the apricot glaze and decorate with the remaining candied fruit. Refrigerate for 1 hour before serving.

Budino di fragole

Strawberry Pudding

01:00 Chilling time 04:00 00:15

American	Ingredients	Metric/Imperial
1 lb	*Strawberries*	*450 g / 1 lb*
½ cup	*Brandy*	*125 ml / 4 fl oz*
5 tsp	*Gelatin*	*5 tsp*
1 scant cup	*Sugar*	*200 g / 7 oz*
3	*Egg whites*	*3*
	Butter	

1. Clean the strawberries and arrange in a bowl. Pour over half the brandy and leave to marinate for 45 minutes.
2. Sprinkle the gelatin onto 3 tablespoons boiling water.
3. Pour the sugar into a saucepan and add about 2 cups [450 ml / ¾ pint] water. Place over a moderate heat to obtain a thick syrup. Do not allow the syrup to brown.
4. Remove from the heat and stir in the gelatin with the remaining brandy; continue stirring until the syrup has cooled.
5. Whisk the egg whites until stiff and fold into the syrup.
6. Butter a pudding basin and arrange a layer of strawberries on the bottom. Pour in half the mixture. If it is too runny, refrigerate until it is firmer. Make another layer of strawberries and pour on the remainder of the mixture. Refrigerate for about 4 hours.
7. To remove the pudding from the basin, immerse in hot water for a few seconds.

Torta di banane

Banana Tart

00:20 00:30

American	Ingredients	Metric/Imperial
1 cup	*All purpose (plain) flour*	*100 g / 4 oz*
2 tsp	*Baking powder*	*2 tsp*
	Salt	
½ cup	*Butter*	*100 g / 4 oz*
½ cup	*Sugar*	*100 g / 4 oz*
2	*Eggs*	*2*
3 – 4	*Bananas*	*3 – 4*
1	*Lemon*	*1*
1 tsp	*Sugar*	*1 tsp*
½ cup	*Chopped almonds*	*50 g / 2 oz*

1. Preheat the oven to 350°F / 180°C / Gas Mark 4.
2. Sift the flour, baking powder and salt on to a plate.
3. In a bowl, cream the butter and sugar until light and fluffy. Add the lightly beaten eggs and little by little fold in the flour mixture. Stir until well mixed and smooth. Turn into a buttered and floured 8 in / 20 cm cake pan and spread evenly.
4. Peel the bananas, slice lengthwise and arrange on the cake. Sprinkle with lemon juice, 1 teaspoon of sugar and chopped almonds. Bake in a preheated oven for 30 minutes or until set. Allow to cool before serving.

Orange mousse

Orange Mousse

00:30 Serves 8 00:20

American	Ingredients	Metric/Imperial
8	*Eggs*	*8*
1½ cups	*Sugar*	*350 g / 12 oz*
4	*Large oranges*	*4*
3 tbsp	*Cornstarch (cornflour)*	*2 tbsp*
5 tsp	*Gelatin*	*5 tsp*
1 cup	*Whipping (double) cream*	*225 ml / 8 fl oz*

1. Separate the eggs. In a bowl, cream the yolks with the sugar until light and fluffy over a pan of hot water. Add the strained juice of the oranges, grated rind of 2 oranges and the cornstarch (cornflour). Stir well.
2. Continue cooking over a low heat in a bain-marie whisking until the mixture thickens.
3. Sprinkle the gelatin over 2-3 tablespoons of boiling water, making sure it is dissolved. Whisk the cream until thick. Add gelatin to orange mixture.
4. Whisk the egg whites until fairly stiff and carefully fold into the mixture. Do the same with the whipped cream. Turn into 2 molds holding 4 portions, cover and freeze. Take out of the freezer 15 minutes before serving.

Macedonia di frutta secca e fresca

Fresh and Dried Fruit Salad

00:30 Chilling time 01:00 — 00:00

American	Ingredients	Metric/Imperial
1 ½ lb	Mixed fresh fruit in season	700 g / 1 ½ lb
½ lb	Dried fruit (apricots, figs, dates)	225 g / 8 oz
3 tbsp	Sugar	2 tbsp
1 tbsp	Brandy	1 tbsp
½ cup	Dry white wine	125 ml / 4 fl oz
	Ice	
	Cream	

1. Wash the fresh fruit, cut into small cubes, place in a bowl.
2. Break the dried fruit into small pieces and mix with the fresh. Add the sugar, brandy, dry white wine and mix well. Refrigerate for 1 hour.
3. Before serving, set the fruit salad bowl into a larger bowl filled with crushed ice. Serve if liked with a jug of cream.

Babà au rhum 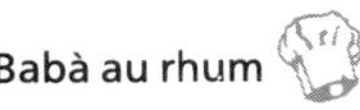

Rum Baba

01:15 including rising time — 00:20

American	Ingredients	Metric/Imperial
½ cup	Fine granulated (castor) sugar	100 g / 4 oz
½ cup	Milk	125 ml / 4 fl oz
¼ oz	Yeast	7 g / ¼ oz
	or	
1 tsp	Dried yeast	1 tsp
1 ¼ cups	Flour	150 g / 5 oz
½ tsp	Salt	½ tsp
2	Eggs	2
¼ cup	Butter	50 g / 2 oz
	Oil	
½ cup	Whipped cream	125 ml / 4 fl oz
2 oz	Candied fruit	50 g / 2 oz

1. Dissolve 1 teaspoon sugar in the warmed (bloodheat) milk and activate yeast by crumbling into the mixture or, if using dried yeast, reconstituting according to package instructions.
2. Sieve slightly warmed flour into a bowl with ½ teaspoon salt. Add the milk and yeast, beat well to form a smooth batter. Allow to rise for about 30 minutes.
3. Beat in the eggs and softened butter by hand to form a thick batter.
4. Brush the baba mold or several small molds with oil and half fill with mixture. Cover with cling wrap and allow mixture to rise to the top of the molds.
5. Preheat the oven to 425°F / 220°C / Gas Mark 7.
6. Bake the mixture for 15-20 minutes, the baba should spring back when touched lightly. Turn out on to a wire tray and allow to cool.
7. Dissolve the sugar in ⅔ cup [150 ml / ¼ pint] water over a low heat, do not stir. When the sugar is dissolved, boil until the mixture thickens to a syrup. Add the rum.
8. Soak the baba in the rum syrup, fill with whipped cream and decorate with candied fruit.

Margherita cup

Coppa Margherita

Margherita Cup

00:15 Chilling time 02:00 — 00:10

American	Ingredients	Metric/Imperial
¼ lb	Bitter chocolate	100 g / 4 oz
¼ cup	Cornstarch (cornflour)	25 g / 1 oz
2 cups	Milk	450 ml / ¾ pint
3 tbsp	Sugar	2 tbsp
1	Egg yolk	1
8	Savoy biscuits	8
3 tbsp	Cointreau	2 tbsp
½ cup	Whipped cream	125 ml / 4 fl oz
4	Cherries	4

1. Melt the broken pieces of chocolate in a bowl over a pan of water on a low heat.
2. Dissolve the cornstarch in the milk and add the sugar. Pour on to the melted chocolate and mix thoroughly. Raise the heat and boil until the mixture thickens.
3. Remove from the heat and add the egg yolk, stirring vigorously.
4. Soak the savoy biscuits in cointreau and place 2 in each cup. Pour in the chocolate cream and leave to cool in the refrigerator.
5. Before serving, decorate each cup with a swirl of whipped cream and a cherry. Serve at once.

Acini d'uva caramellati

Caramelized Grapes

00:25 | 00:15

American	Ingredients	Metric/Imperial
1½ lb	Grapes	700 g / 1½ lb
2 cups	Sugar	450 g / 1 lb
½ tsp	Cream of tartar	½ tsp
	Oil	

1. Cut the grapes from the bunch with a pair of pointed scissors, leaving a little stalk on each one. The grapes should be large, of good quality, and seedless with a firm skin.
2. Wash the grapes well and spread them out on a cloth to dry.
3. Combine the sugar with ½ cup [125 ml / 4 fl oz] of water and the cream of tartar in a saucepan and dissolve over a very low heat without stirring, then bring to the boil to obtain a thick syrup. Remove from the heat when the first tinge of color appears.
4. Immerse the grapes, one at a time. Stick each one on a toothpick, with the pointed end, piercing the grape. Lightly oil a plate to prevent the grapes from sticking and place the grapes on the plate to dry.

Caramelized grapes

Quick trifle

Zuppa inglese velocissima

Quick Trifle

00:20 Chilling time 02:00 | 00:10

American	Ingredients	Metric/Imperial
½ lb	*Dry crackers (biscuits) or sponge fingers*	*225 g / 8 oz*
½ cup	*Liqueur*	*125 ml / 4 fl oz*
1 lb	*Fresh mixed fruit*	*450 g / 1 lb*
¼ lb	*Walnuts or dried fruit*	*100 g / 4 oz*
1¼ cups	*Milk*	*300 ml / ½ pint*
1 tbsp	*Sugar*	*1 tbsp*
1 tbsp	*Cocoa*	*1 tbsp*
2	*Eggs*	*2*
½ tsp	*Vanilla essence*	*½ tsp*
1 cup	*Whipping cream*	*225 ml / 8 fl oz*
	Chocolate flake	

1. Line a glass dish with a layer of crackers.
2. Sprinkle with some liqueur and cover with fruit mixed with a few chopped walnuts or any dried fruit. Add a second layer of crackers and fruit juice or liqueur.
3. Prepare the custard. Whisk together milk, sugar, cocoa and eggs and cook in a double boiler until slightly thick. Flavor with vanilla.
4. Pour the custard over the trifle and, when cool, cover the surface with whipped cream decorated with chocolate flake. Chill in the refrigerator for at least 2 hours.

Melone mixed

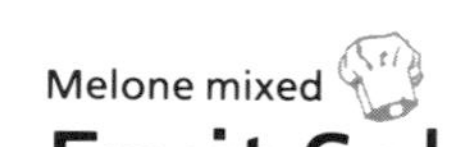

Fruit Salad in Melon Shells

00:30 | 00:00

American	Ingredients	Metric/Imperial
1	*Large sugar melon*	*1*
¼ lb	*Marrons glacés in pieces*	*100 g / 4 oz*
5 oz	*Candied citron*	*150 g / 5 oz*
1 cup	*Blanched, split almonds*	*100 g / 4 oz*
3	*Bananas*	*3*
1	*Lemon*	*1*
1 tbsp	*Sugar*	*1 tbsp*
3 tbsp	*Sweet liqueur*	*2 tbsp*

1. Cut the melon in half, scoop out the flesh, remove the seeds and cut the flesh into small cubes.
2. Mix the melon in a bowl with the marron glacés, finely chopped candied citron, split almonds, sliced bananas (sprinkled with lemon juice to stop them turning brown), a little sugar and 1 tablespoon of any liqueur.
3. Sprinkle a little liqueur inside the 2 melon shells and refrigerate. Just before serving, turn the fruit salad into the melon shells and place them on a plate or in a wide bowl on a bed of crushed ice. Serve cold.

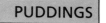

Macedonia colorata

Colored Fruit Salad

00:30 Chilling time 01:00 | 00:00

American	Ingredients	Metric/Imperial
2 lb	Watermelon	1 kg / 2 lb
2 lb	Honeydew melon	1 kg / 2 lb
2	Peaches	2
½ lb	Raspberries	225 g / 8 oz
¼ cup	Almonds	40 g / 1½ oz
	Confectioner's (icing) sugar	
	Mint leaves	
1	Orange	1
1	Lemon	1

1. Halve a ripe, sweet watermelon and a honeydew melon. Remove seeds. Scoop out little balls of flesh into a large bowl.
2. Scald the peaches in hot water, skin and cube. Wash the raspberries under running water and combine with the peaches and melons. Cover the bowl and refrigerate for 45 minutes.
3. Drop the almonds into boiling water, skin and flake, add to the well chilled fruit salad. Sprinkle with sugar and garnish with mint leaves.
4. Pour over the juice of the orange and lemon and allow to chill for 15 minutes before serving.

Spuma di fragole

Strawberry Mousse

00:30 | 00:00

American	Ingredients	Metric/Imperial
14 oz	Strawberries	400 g / 14 oz
3 tbsp	Confectioner's (icing) sugar	2 tbsp
1 tbsp	Orange liqueur	1 tbsp
1 cup	Whipping (double) cream	225 ml / 8 fl oz
2	Egg whites	2

1. Hull, wash and dry the strawberries. Reserve some for decoration and blend the rest with the sugar and the orange liqueur in a blender, then pour into a bowl.
2. Whip the cream and carefully fold most of it into the strawberry mixture, retain a little for decoration.
3. Whisk the egg whites until stiff and fold into the mixture carefully. Turn into a serving dish and serve with the cream.

Mattonella di frutta

Fruit Brick

This recipe is suitable for fruit which gives juice when mashed, such as strawberries, raspberries, grapes, bilberries, mulberries, oranges, peaches, morello cherries. Use fruit of one kind only.

00:45 Chilling time 03:00 | 00:10

American	Ingredients	Metric/Imperial
1 quart	Fresh fruit to make fruit juice	1 litre / 1¾ pints
½ cup	Potato flour	8 tbsp
	Sugar to taste	
1	Orange	1
½ cup	Whipping (double) cream	125 ml / 4 fl oz

1. Prepare, wash and mash the fruit using a spoon, sieve, food mill, blender or food processor.
2. Strain the juice, measure the liquid and pour into a large pan. For each 1 quart [1 litre / 1¾ pints] add the measured potato flour.
3. Add sugar to taste depending on the sweetness of the fruit. Cut the orange rind, without pith, into thin strips and add to the pan. Bring slowly to the boil, stirring all the time.
4. Remove from the heat but continue stirring from time to time for a further 20 minutes. Pour into a rectangular loaf pan rinsed in cold water. Chill for 3 hours in the refrigerator.

Bavarese all'amaretto

Mousse with Macaroons

00:45 | 00:15

American	Ingredients	Metric/Imperial
4	Egg yolks	4
2½ cups	Milk	600 ml / 1 pint
½ cup	Sugar	100 g / 4 oz
¼ cup	Flour	25 g / 1 oz
1	Vanilla pod	1
1	Lemon	1
25	Macaroons	25
⅓ cup	Candied fruit	50 g / 2 oz
¼ lb	Plain chocolate	100 g / 4 oz
½ cup	Brandy, rum or maraschino liqueur	125 ml / 4 fl oz
1 cup	Whipped cream	225 ml / 8 fl oz

1. Make a custard by whisking together the eggs, milk, sugar, flour, vanilla and rind of the lemon in a double boiler until thick.
2. Allow to cool. Add 5 crumbled macaroons and the chopped candied fruit.
3. Melt the plain chocolate in a bowl over hot water and mix into the custard.
4. Soak the macaroons in the liqueur diluted with 2 tablespoons water or fruit juice and line the base and sides of a serving dish with the macaroons.
5. Fold the lightly whipped cream into the custard, mixing very delicately. Pour into the dish and refrigerate.

Suprême de la Cote D'Azur

Apple Ring with Candied Fruit

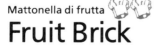

00:30 | 00:30

American	Ingredients	Metric/Imperial
2 lb	Apples	1 kg / 2 lb
1¾ cups	Sugar	400 g / 14 oz
2	Lemons	2
¼ lb	Candied fruit	100 g / 4 oz
2 tsp	Gelatin	2 tsp
1 cup	Whipped cream	225 ml / 8 fl oz
1 tbsp	Rum	1 tbsp

Strawberry mousse

1. Peel, core and slice the apples. Put sugar and about 1/4 cup [50 ml / 2 fl oz] water in a saucepan. Boil until it turns into a thick syrup – but do not burn the sugar.
2. Grate the peel from the lemons and add to the pan with apples, lemon juice and half the candied fruits. Cook until the mixture is transparent and dry, stir in the gelatin which has been dissolved in 2 tablespoons boiling water.
3. Turn the apple mixture into a ring mold and leave in the refrigerator overnight.
4. Turn out and spread over the whipped cream flavored with rum. Decorate with candied fruits.

Cook's tip: for the best result this sweet should be made at least 24 hours before serving.

Frutta brinata

Frosted Fruit

Preparation 00:25 — Cooking 00:25

American	Ingredients	Metric/Imperial
½ lb	*Seedless grapes*	*225 g / 8 oz*
¼ lb	*White currants*	*100 g / 4 oz*
¼ lb	*Red currants*	*100 g / 4 oz*
2	*Egg whites*	*2*
1 cup	*Fine granulated (castor) sugar*	*225 g / 8 oz*

1. Preheat the oven to 350°F / 180°C / Gas Mark 4.
2. Using sharp scissors, cut the bunch of grapes into several small bunches. Put these and the currants in a colander and wash under running cold water. Spread out to dry on a cloth.
3. Whisk the egg whites until stiff. Dip the fruit in the egg whites and sprinkle with sugar. Arrange on a baking tray and cover with buttered wax (greaseproof) paper. Bake for a few minutes in a moderate oven until the frosting hardens. Serve cold, on a dish covered with a colored napkin to provide a bright contrast to the bunches of frosted fruit.

Frutta sciroppata

Fruit in Syrup

Preparation 00:30 — Cooking 00:03

American	Ingredients	Metric/Imperial
2 lb	*Apples, pears, peaches, pineapple or Figs, cherries, plums, apricots*	*1 kg / 2 lb*
2 cups	*Water*	*450 ml / ¾ pint*
1½ cups	*Sugar*	*350 g / 12 oz*
1	*Small piece of lemon rind*	*1*

1. The fruit used for this recipe should be in perfect condition and not very ripe. Peel the apples, pears, peaches, pineapple, etc. Or if using figs, cherries, plums and apricots, do not peel. Cut large fruit into chunks and small fruit in half, leaving figs whole.
2. Prepare the syrup by boiling water with the sugar and lemon rind for 2-3 minutes. Pour onto a serving bowl, allow to cool, then add prepared fruits.
3. Chill in the refrigerator, then serve with whipped cream.

Gelato di crema dell'Ivana

Ivana Cream Ice Cream

Preparation 00:35 (Freezing time 05:00) — Cooking 00:07

American	Ingredients	Metric/Imperial
8	*Eggs*	*8*
½ lb	*Sugar*	*225 g / 8 oz*
1 quart	*Milk*	*1 litre / 1¾ pints*
1	*Vanilla stick*	*1*
1¼ cups	*Whipped cream*	*300 ml / ½ pint*
8	*Cherries in liqueur*	*8*

1. Whisk the egg yolks and sugar together thoroughly, using an electric whisk if possible.
2. Heat the milk and vanilla and remove from the heat as soon as it begins to boil. Remove the vanilla and gradually pour the milk into the egg mixture (as if pouring oil into mayonnaise), stirring vigorously all the time. Lastly fold in the stiffly whipped cream.
3. Pour the mixture into a rectangular mold and freeze, preferably freezing it as rapidly as possible. After 30 minutes, take it out of the freezer and whisk.
4. Pour into a cold round mold. Cover with cling wrap and freeze again at normal freezer temperature.
5. To serve, run the mold under warm water for a second and turn out on to a serving dish. Decorate with the cherries.

Gelato, melone e ribes

Ice Cream, Melon and Red Currants

Preparation 00:30 (Refrigeration time 01:00) — Cooking 00:00

American	Ingredients	Metric/Imperial
2	*Melons*	*2*
½ cup	*Porto or marsala wine*	*125 ml / 4 fl oz*
½ lb	*Red currants*	*225 g / 8 oz*
2 cups	*Strawberry ice cream*	*450 ml / ¾ pint*

1. Using a ball utensil, scoop out the melons making lots of little balls. Put these in a bowl and pour over porto or sweet marsala and refrigerate for about 1 hour.
2. Carefully wash the red currants and remove the stalks. Put the currants on a plate.
3. Take the melon out of the refrigerator and scoop out small ice cream balls with the same scoop, mixing these with the melon. Decorate by scattering the red currants over the top. Serve immediately.

Sorbetto alle fragole

Strawberry Sorbet

Preparation 00:25 (Freezing time 04:00) — Cooking 00:20

American	Ingredients	Metric/Imperial
Scant 2 cups	*Sugar*	*400 g / 14 oz*
1¼ cups	*Water*	*300 ml / ½ pint*
3 lb	*Strawberries*	*1.4 kg / 3 lb*
3 tbsp	*Strega liqueur*	*1 tbsp*

1. Put the sugar in the water in a thick based saucepan, mix round before putting on the heat. Allow to dissolve over a very low heat without stirring. Cook until a thick but colorless syrup is formed. Allow to cool.
2. Hull the strawberries and wash and allow to drain well. Sprinkle on the liqueur.
3. Mash the strawberries to a pulp in a blender or food processor.
4. Pour the strawberry pureé into the cold syrup and tip the whole mixture into a fairly shallow pan. Freeze for 2 hours and stir, freeze again for a further 2 hours.
5. Remove from the freezer at least 15 minutes before serving and spoon into individual glasses. Decorate with strawberries if available.

Strawberry sorbet

__1.__ Add sugar to water in a thick-based saucepan and mix round before putting on the heat. Allow to dissolve over a low heat without stirring. Cook until a thick syrup is formed.

__2.__ Hull the strawberries, wash and drain well. Mash the strawberries.

__3.__ Mix the mashed strawberries with the syrup. Ladle the mixture into the container.

__4.__ Scrape down the sorbet after the first freezing.

__5.__ Whisk to break down the ice particles.

__6.__ Return the whisked mixture to the container for the final freezing.

1

2

3

4

5

6

Making Cakes and Pastries

Equipment

It is difficult to make successful cakes and pastries without some of the tools of the trade. The correct sized cake pan for the recipe will always give a more successful result otherwise you must adjust the recipe to suit the pan. If a mixture should be cooked in 8 in / 20 cm cake pan it will overflow if cooked in a smaller pan. A mixture which is supposed to be cooked in a 6 in / 15 cm pan will give a very thin cake if cooked in a 8 in / 20 cm pan. Therefore it is advisable to select the correct pans for cooking cakes.

Buy the best quality baking pans you can afford and, if carefully treated, they will last for years.

Equipment for pastry making
1 bowl, measuring jug, palette knife or one with a flat blade, rolling pin, baking sheet, flan ring, wire rack. Not essential, but useful is a flour dredger for flouring the table, a rolling pin and a pastry brush for glazing.

Equipment for cake making
1 bowl, wooden spoon or electric mixer, whisk for eggs, measuring jug, plastic spatula, cake pans (especially good, are the ones with loose bottoms). A ring mold can be used for both rice, sponge mixtures and yeast mixtures such as rum babas. A pastry brush is useful for oiling pans and a wire rack is best for cooling cakes.

Nylon piping bags
These are useful for making choux pastry, shaping biscuits,

piping potatoes and cream mixtures both sweet and savory. Piping bags can be made at home from wax (greaseproof) paper and these are especially suitable for icing cakes.

Nozzles
These metal or plastic nozzles come in many different sizes from the small shapes for cake icing to the large nozzles with plain or star shapes which are used for potatoes, choux pastry and cream.

Cake making

According to the ingredients used, cakes can be classified according to the following methods of preparation:

Rubbing-in method
The fat is rubbed into the flour and this method is only suitable for recipes with half or less than half, fat to flour.

Creaming method
The fat and sugar are creamed together and this method is used for recipes with half, or more than half, fat to flour.

Melting method
The fat is melted with treacle, syrup and sugar for ginger-bread which characteristically has a high proportion of sugary ingredients, mostly treacle or syrup.

Whisking or sponge-cake method
The eggs and sugar are whisked together for sponge cakes, genoese sponges and Swiss rolls in which the proportion of these ingredients to flour is high.

Common faults in cake making

Rubbed-in and creamed mixtures
1. Uneven texture with holes
Stirring and uneven mixing of flour.
Spooning the mixture into the tin so that pockets of air become trapped.

2. Dry and crumbly cake
Too much baking powder.
Oven temperature too cool.

3. Cracking and forming a dome
Oven temperature too hot.
Mixture too stiff.
Cake tin too small.
Cake may have been put too near the top of the oven.

4. Sinking fruit
Wet fruit. Dry thoroughly if washing fruit by spreading out on a baking tray and leave in a warm place for 24 hours. Glacé cherries should be washed, dried and lightly floured.
Opening the oven door while cake is still rising.
Too much raising agent.

5. Cakes which sink in the middle
Too much raising agent.
Mixture may have been too soft.
Oven temperature too cool therefore centre of cake does not rise and cook.
Oven temperature too hot so that cake is risen on outside before it is cooked in the middle.

6. Lack of protection
Not lining pan properly will cause burning and dry cakes.

Whisked sponges
1. Heavy texture
Not enough air being enclosed during whisking of eggs and sugar.
Flour being beaten into mixture instead of being lightly folded in.

2. Fatty layer
Where fat is used in a whisked sponge it should be lukewarm not hot and poured round the edge of the mixture, not straight into the middle, and the mixture mixed evenly.

Pastry

Lining a flan ring
Put a flan ring on a baking sheet. If you have trouble with pastry sticking, oil the flan ring lightly first but if there is half fat to flour in the pastry recipe this should not be necessary. Roll out the pastry into a round shape, giving it a half turn to the right after each rolling to keep the shape. Roll out about 2 in / 5 cm larger than the flan ring. Then:
1. Lift the pastry round the rolling pin and ease gently into the flan ring without breaking or stretching.
2. Press down into flan ring with the back of the forefinger, again avoid stretching the pastry or it will shrink in the cooking.
3. Prick the bottom with a fork and neaten the edges of the flan case with a rolling pin to remove excess pastry.
4. Fill with baking beans if you wish to bake blind.

Cook's tip: 6 in / 15 cm flan ring requires 4 oz / 100 g pastry.
7-8 in / 18-20 cm flan ring requires 6 oz / 150 g pastry.
10-12 in / 25-30 cm flan ring requires 8 oz / 250 g pastry.

Baking blind
1. Cut a round of non-stick paper or greased wax (greaseproof) paper about 2 in / 5 cm larger than the flan. Place greased side down in the pastry case and fill with dried baking beans, pasta or crusts. This keeps the pastry flat.
2. Bake the flan case in the second shelf of a pre-heated oven 400°F / 200°C / Gas Mark 6 for 15 minutes.
3. Remove the paper with baking beans from the flan ring and finish for a further 10-15 minutes or until golden brown all over. Continue cooking.

Cook's tip: the baking beans can be stored in a jar and used over and over again.

To make rich shortcrust pastry
(for quantities see page 452)
1. *Sift the flour onto the table, make a well in the centre of the flour.*
2. *Cut the fat into small knots, add to the flour, sprinkle with flour from the outside of the ring. Add the egg yolks, sugar, grated lemon rind and a pinch of salt. Mix together with the hands and knead into a smooth paste. If too firm, add a few drops of cold water. Form into a ball, wrap in wax (greaseproof) paper and allow to rest in a cool place. Use as required for sweet pies and flans.*

Basic Shortcrust Pastry

00:15 Resting time 00:20 — 00:00

American	Ingredients	Metric/Imperial
2 cups	*All purpose (plain) flour*	*225 g / 8 oz*
½ tsp	*Salt*	*½ tsp*
½ cup	*Butter or hard margarine*	*100 g / 4 oz*
½ cup	*Cold water*	*8 tablespoons*

1. Sift the flour and salt into a bowl. Cut the butter into small pieces and add to the flour.
2. Rub the fat into the flour with the tips of the fingers until the mixture becomes like fine bread crumbs.
3. Add half the water and mix with a round bladed knife, add remaining water gradually until a firm but not sticky dough is obtained. The bowl should be quite clean at the end of mixing. Wrap in film and leave to rest in a cool place for 20 minutes. Use as required for savory tarts and pies.

Pasta frolla 

Italian Shortcrust Pastry

00:30 plus time to rest — 00:00

American	Ingredients	Metric/Imperial
3 cups	*All purpose (plain) flour*	*350 g / 12 oz*
¾ cup	*Butter*	*175 g / 6 oz*
¼ cup	*Fine granulated (castor) sugar*	*50 g / 2 oz*
2	*Fresh egg yolks*	*2*
½	*Lemon*	*½*
	Salt	

1. Sift the flour on the worktop and make a well in the centre.
2. Put the butter, cut up and slightly softened, into the well with the sugar, yolks, grated lemon rind and a pinch of salt. Blend the ingredients together, working them just enough to mix well, but not more. If too firm, add a few drops of cold water. Form into a ball, wrap in wax (greaseproof) paper and allow to rest in a cool place. Use this shortcrust pastry as required for sweet pies and flans.

Choux pastry 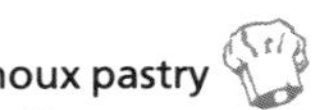

Choux Pastry

00:05 — 00:35

American	Ingredients	Metric/Imperial
3 tbsp	*Butter or margarine*	*40 g / 1½ oz*
⅔ cup	*Water*	*150 ml / ¼ pint*
⅓ cup	*All purpose (plain) flour*	*65 g / 2½ oz*
	Salt	
2	*Eggs*	*2*

1. Preheat the oven to 400°F / 200°C / Gas Mark 6.
2. Put the butter into the water and melt slowly over a low heat, bring to the boil on a high heat.
3. Tip in the sifted flour and a pinch of salt all together into boiling liquid. Beat vigorously until the paste is smooth and forms a ball of dough in the pan (do not over heat at this stage). Allow to cool slightly.
4. Add the beaten eggs a little at a time, beating well to give a smooth glossy mixture.
5. Pipe onto an oiled baking sheet as éclair shaped lengths, rounds or large shapes for cream buns. Smaller shapes for profiteroles can be formed with a tablespoon or teaspoon.
6. Cook in the oven according to size for 25-30 minutes. Remove when golden and puffed, slit and remove doughy centre and return to the oven for 5 minutes to dry.
7. Fill with whipped cream, butter cream (see opposite) and coat with melted chocolate or dredge with confectioner's (icing) sugar.

1

2

3

4

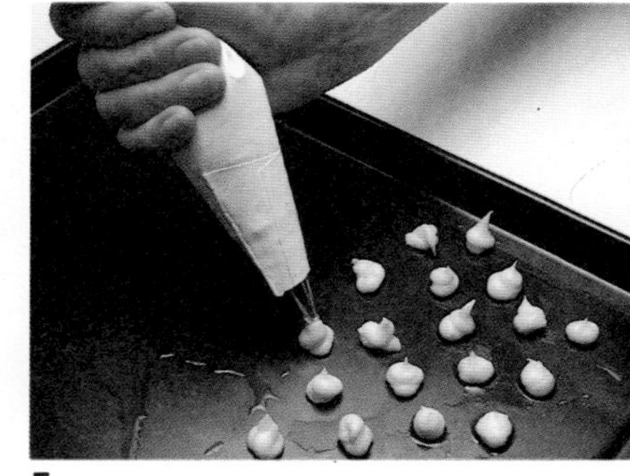
5

Choux pastry
1. *Melt the butter and water in a pan over a low heat. Bring to the boil over a high heat. Off the heat, mix in the sifted flour and a pinch of salt into the melted butter.*
2. *Beat vigorously until the dough is smooth and forms a ball.*
3. *Add the beaten egg a little at a time, beating well after each addition.*
4. *Spoon into a piping bag.*
5. *Pipe onto an oiled baking sheet as éclair shaped lengths or large or small rounds.*

La Gourgère

Burgundian Pastry

00:15 00:40

American	Ingredients	Metric/Imperial
1¼ cups	*Water*	*300 ml / ½ pint*
⅓ cup	*Butter*	*75 g / 3 oz*
	Salt	
1¼ cups	*All purpose (plain) flour*	*150 g / 5 oz*
4	*Eggs*	4
1 cup	*Grated gruyère cheese*	*100 g / 4 oz*

1. Preheat the oven to 400°F / 200°C / Gas Mark 6.
2. Bring the water to boil with butter and salt. Then toss in the sifted flour all at once, stirring vigorously with a wooden spoon. Stop when the dough comes away from the saucepan.
3. Remove from the heat and continue to stir until the mixture has become tepid. Add the beaten eggs, one at a time, still working with a wooden spoon until the dough is again blended. Still mixing, add the gruyère.
4. Butter an 8 in / 20 cm baking pan, pipe with a plain pipe or cover with spoonfuls of this dough, without smoothing it, but gradually covering it with further spoonfuls of mixture. If using a spoon, dip in boiling water before collecting the dough, to make the task easier.
5. Put the baking pan in the oven. Take out of the oven and leave to become lukewarm before serving.

Cook's tip: the secret of success for this recipe is working the eggs one at a time and not adding a new egg until the previous batch is thoroughly blended with the dough.

Creme al burro

Butter Cream

00:25 00:20

American	Ingredients	Metric/Imperial
3	*Egg yolks*	3
Generous ⅓ cup	*Fine granulated (castor) sugar*	*75 g / 3 oz*
1 cup	*Milk*	*225 ml / 8 fl oz*
1	*Lemon*	1
1 cup	*Butter*	*225 g / 8 oz*
½ tsp	*Vanilla essence*	*½ tsp*

1. Whisk the egg yolks and the sugar to obtain a pale creamy mixture.
2. Boil the milk and the finely grated lemon rind and pour this gradually into the egg mixture, stirring carefully.
3. Pour into a saucepan and cook over a very low heat, stirring continuously until the cream thickens. Turn off the heat and allow to cool.
4. Soften the butter and put it in a bowl. Beat with a wooden spoon until it is light and creamy. Combine the cream with the butter, a little at a time, beating constantly with the wooden spoon to ensure that the mixture is smooth.
5. Add the vanilla essence and cream again. This mixture is used for filling cakes.

Cook's tip: this cream can be flavored with 1 tablespoon cocoa blended with 1 tablespoon boiling water or 1 tablespoon strong coffee essence. Rum, brandy or liqueurs can also be used according to taste.

Salame nero

Chocolate Roll

00:30
Chilling time 02:00
00:00

American	Ingredients	Metric/Imperial
¼ lb	*Candied fruit*	*100 g / 4 oz*
1 tbsp	*Pistachio nuts*	*1 tbsp*
10 oz	*Shortbread biscuits*	*275 g / 10 oz*
½ lb	*Mascarpone cheese*	*225 g / 8 oz*
2 cups	*Confectioner's (icing) sugar*	*225 g / 8 oz*
2	*Eggs, separated*	2
5 oz	*Cocoa*	*150 g / 5 oz*
1 tbsp	*Liqueur*	*1 tbsp*
	Oil	
	Whipped cream	

1. Cut up the candied fruit, leaving a little for decoration. Blanch the pistachio nuts in boiling water.
2. Crumble the biscuits in a blender or in a plastic bag, broken down with a rolling pin.
3. Cream together in a bowl the mascarpone and the sugar until the mixture is creamy and fluffy. Add the egg yolks one at a time to the mascarpone. Mix in the candied fruit, cocoa, the crumbled biscuits and nuts. Carefully add the liqueur drop by drop.
4. Whisk the egg whites and carefully fold into the mixture. Turn the mixture onto a sheet of oiled, wax (greaseproof) paper and shape into a roll. Wrap the paper round and refrigerate for at least 2 hours.
5. Remove the paper before serving, lay the roll on a serving dish and decorate with whipped cream and candied fruit.

Pasta sfogliata

Puff Pastry

02:00
including resting time
00:00

American	Ingredients	Metric/Imperial
2½ cups	*Flour*	*275 g / 10 oz*
1 tsp	*Salt*	*1 tsp*
1 cup	*Butter*	*225 g / 8 oz*

1. Sift the flour onto the board, add the salt and ½ cup [125 ml / 4 fl oz] cold water. Knead quickly with the fingertips until a firm dough is formed. Shape into a ball, wrap in wax (greaseproof) paper and allow to rest in the refrigerator for about 20 minutes.
2. Return the dough to the board, beat it with a fist and roll out to form a square of 8 in × 8 in [20 cm × 20 cm]. In the centre put the softened (but not warm) butter. Fold the corners of the dough over the butter, like an envelope.
3. Roll out the dough on the lightly floured board to incorporate the butter and form a rectangle. The dough should not be too firm.
4. Fold the dough in 2, to have a square again, seal the edges with the rolling pin. This is called 'the first turn of the pastry'.
5. Repeat and allow the pastry to rest in the refrigerator for about 20 minutes wrapped in wax (greaseproof) paper.
6. Repeat this step 4 times until 'six turns' have been completed. Seal the edges between turns.
7. Allow to rest in refrigerator every second 'turn'. After the sixth turn the puff pastry is ready for use.

Torta marrons glacés

Glazed Chestnut Cake

Preparation: 01:00 — Cooking: 00:30

American	Ingredients	Metric/Imperial
2 lb	*Chestnuts*	*1 kg / 2 lb*
1 cup	*Milk*	*225 ml / 8 fl oz*
1 tsp	*Vanilla sugar*	*1 tsp*
3	*Eggs, separated*	*3*
1 cup	*Confectioner's (icing) sugar*	*100 g / 4 oz*
1 tbsp	*Rum*	*1 tbsp*
3 drops	*Pink food coloring*	*3 drops*

1. Carefully shell chestnuts, cook in hot water for 30 minutes and mash through a sieve or in a blender.
2. Preheat the oven to 350°F / 180°C / Gas Mark 4.
3. Mix the chestnuts with the milk, vanilla sugar, 3 yolks and lastly fold in 3 stiffly whisked whites. Carefully fold all the ingredients without beating.
4. Butter an 8 in / 20 cm round baking pan, line with wax (greaseproof) paper and fill to half its height with the mixture.
5. Bake in a moderate oven for 30 minutes. Cool and turn onto a serving dish.
6. Combine the confectioner's sugar with the rum and a few drops of pink food coloring to make a coating consistency and spread over top and sides with a warm blade. Serve when the glacé has set.

Torta di ciliegie

Cherry Cake

Preparation: 00:15 — Cooking: 00:30 to 00:40

American	Ingredients	Metric/Imperial
¾ lb	*Ripe cherries*	*350 g / 12 oz*
¾ cup	*Fine granulated (castor) sugar*	*175 g / 6 oz*
1 tbsp	*Brandy*	*1 tbsp*
¾ cup	*Butter*	*175 g / 6 oz*
4	*Eggs*	*4*
1½ cups	*Flour*	*175 g / 6 oz*
	Baking powder	
½ cup	*Ground almonds*	*50 g / 2 oz*

1. Preheat the oven to 350°F / 180°C / Gas Mark 4.
2. Wash and dry the cherries and remove the stalks. Cut in half and pit (stone). Sprinkle with softened sugar and brandy, leave to soak for 15 minutes and then remove and dry on absorbent kitchen towels.
3. Put the butter in little lumps in a bowl and work in the sugar. Cream the mixture until light and fluffy.
4. Add the beaten egg yolks a little at a time with a spoonful of sifted flour between batches of egg. Fold in remaining flour mixed with baking powder.
5. Whisk the whites until stiff, fold in the ground almonds. Fold into the creamed mixture retaining as much air as possible.
6. Oil a 7 in / 17½ cm square cake pan, put a square of parchment (waxed) paper on the bottom of the pan, arrange cherries on the paper, tip in cake mixture and spread evenly.
7. Bake in the oven for 30-40 minutes or until golden brown and mixture springs back when pressed lightly in the middle. Allow to stand for 5 minutes in the pan, then turn upside down on a wire rack and allow to stand for 2 minutes, tap the bottom of the pan and turn out. The cherries should stay on top of the cake if the paper is removed carefully. Cool before serving.

Cook's tip: when fresh cherries are out of season, use washed chopped glacé cherries.

Torta sabbiosa

Madeira Cake

Preparation: 00:20 — Cooking: 00:30

American	Ingredients	Metric/Imperial
1 cup	*Butter*	*225 g / 8 oz*
¾ cup	*Sugar*	*175 g / 6 oz*
1	*Lemon*	*1*
3	*Eggs*	*3*
1 cup	*Flour*	*100 g / 4 oz*
¼ lb	*Potato flour*	*100 g / 4 oz*
2 tsp	*Baking powder*	*2 tsp*
	Butter and flour for the cake pan	

1. Preheat the oven to 375°F / 190°C / Gas Mark 5.
2. Soften the butter and thoroughly cream with the sugar using a wooden spoon. Add finely grated rind of the lemon.
3. When smooth and fluffy, add egg yolks, one at a time. Combine the flour, potato flour and baking powder and mix in.
4. Whisk the egg whites until stiff and gradually fold into the creamed mixture.
5. Turn into a deep 8 in / 20 cm buttered floured cake pan and bake in the oven for about 30 minutes without opening the door. Turn out and allow to cool.

Cook's tip: sometimes thin strips of candied lemon or orange peel is added to the top of the cake before cooking.

Pan di Spagna

Sponge Cake

Preparation: 00:20 — Cooking: 00:30

American	Ingredients	Metric/Imperial
4	*Eggs*	*4*
2 cups	*Confectioner's (icing) sugar*	*225 g / 8 oz*
1	*Lemon*	*1*
1 cup	*All purpose (plain) flour*	*100 g / 4 oz*
	Butter	

1. Preheat the oven to 350°F / 180°C / Gas Mark 4.
2. Separate the eggs. Beat the yolks with the sugar in a bowl over a saucepan of warm water. Begin slowly, then with more energy, until the sugar is well incorporated and the mixture looks almost white.
3. Whisk the whites until quite stiff and fold carefully with a metal spoon into the mixture. Add grated lemon peel and sift in the flour. Mix well folding with a metal spoon and turn into a buttered and lightly floured 8 in / 20 cm baking pan.
4. Bake in a preheated oven for 30 minutes. The cake is cooked when it offers a certain resistance when pressed in the middle. A few minutes after taking it out of the oven, invert the pan onto a rack, remove and leave the cake until cool. This cake can be served with any filling.

Sponge cake

Plumcake

Plum Cake

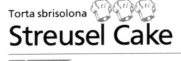

00:45 00:45

American	Ingredients	Metric/Imperial
1 cup	Butter	225 g / 8 oz
1 cup	Fine granulated (castor) sugar	225 g / 8 oz
5	Eggs	5
¼ cup	Milk	50 ml / 2 fl oz
1	Lemon	1
2 cups	All purpose (plain) flour	225 g / 8 oz
1 tsp	Baking powder	1 tsp
⅓ cup	Sultanas	50 g / 2 oz
2 oz	Candied fruit	50 g / 2 oz
1 cup	Confectioner's (icing) sugar	100 g / 4 oz
1 tbsp	Kirsch	1 tbsp
	Morello cherries for decorating	

1. Preheat the oven to 350°F / 180°C / Gas Mark 4. Prepare an 8 in / 20 cm deep cake pan by rubbing well with a buttered paper.
2. Cream the butter and fine granulated sugar thoroughly. When thick and fluffy beat in 3 whole eggs followed by 2 yolks adding a little sifted flour between eggs. Then add milk and grated rind of lemon. Gradually add the sifted flour and baking powder, mixing well. Dip the sultanas and candied fruit in a little flour and fold into the mixture.
3. Turn into the cake pan and cook in the centre of the oven for at least 45 minutes.
4. While the cake is baking, prepare the icing. Mix the confectioner's sugar with 2 teaspoons water and 1 teaspoon kirsch, beat until smooth. When the cake is cooked, remove it from the oven, allow to cool and cover the top with the icing. Decorate with morello or glacé cherries.

Torta di ricotta

Ricotta Cake

00:35 00:45

American	Ingredients	Metric/Imperial
½ lb	Fresh ricotta	225 g / 8 oz
1 cup	Fine granulated (castor) sugar	225 g / 8 oz
2	Eggs, separated	2
2 cups	All purpose (plain) flour	225 g / 8 oz
	Salt	
1 tsp	Baking powder	1 tsp
1	Lemon	1
	Butter and flour for the baking pan	
	Confectioner's (icing) sugar	

1. Beat the ricotta and the sugar in a large bowl either with a wooden spoon or an electric mixer. After 10 minutes add the yolks one by one and continue beating.
2. Preheat the oven to 350°F / 180°C / Gas Mark 4.
3. Sift the flour into a bowl with the salt and baking powder. Mix well with the ricotta mixture and add the finely grated lemon peel.
4. Whisk the egg whites and carefully fold in. Turn into an 8 in / 20 cm buttered and floured baking pan, spread evenly and bake in a preheated moderate oven for 45 minutes. Insert a fine skewer to test whether it is sufficiently cooked. The skewer must come out clean. Turn on to a wire rack and allow to cool. Dust with confectioner's sugar and serve cold.

Torta sbrisolona

Streusel Cake

00:25 01:00

American	Ingredients	Metric/Imperial
2 cups	All purpose (plain) flour	225 g / 8 oz
1⅔ cups	Cornmeal	225 g / 8 oz
2 tsp	Vanilla sugar	2 tsp
1⅔ cups	Ground almonds	225 g / 8 oz
¾ cup	Fine granulated (castor) sugar	175 g / 6 oz
½	Lemon	½
2	Egg yolks	2
¾ cup	Butter	175 g / 6 oz
	Confectioner's (icing) sugar	

1. Preheat the oven to 350°F / 180°C / Gas Mark 4.
2. Sift the flour, cornmeal and vanilla on to a board and form a well in the middle.
3. Add the almonds into the well with the sugar, grated lemon peel, yolks and butter.
4. Work all the ingredients quickly together with the fingertips until it forms a crumbly mixture – not a smooth paste. Transfer into a deep buttered baking pan. This 'streusel' mixture will hold together when cooked. Bake in a preheated oven for about 1 hour.
5. Remove from the oven, shake the pan to detach and turn onto a serving plate. Dust thickly with confectioner's sugar.

Cook's tip: the cake keeps well if wrapped in foil.

Torrone d'Alba

Almond Slices

00:30 00:15

American	Ingredients	Metric/Imperial
6½ cups	Almonds	1 kg / 2 lb
1 scant cup	Sugar	200 g / 7 oz
2 lb	Honey	1 kg / 2 lb
2	Egg whites	2
	Sheets of rice paper	

1. Blanch the almonds and split (or use slivered almonds). Toast under a hot broiler (grill) for a few seconds.
2. Dissolve the sugar in ¼ cup [50 ml / 2 fl oz] water over a low heat, then bring to the boil.
3. Remove from the heat, add the honey and cook until a small quantity dropped on a cold surface top sets and readily cracks.
4. Whisk the egg whites until very stiff and gently fold into the syrup mixture. Add almonds to the mixture.
5. Pour the almond mixture into a flat pan lined with rice paper and cover with more rice paper.
6. Allow to cool, turn onto a plate, slice and serve.

Almond slices

Golden slices

Torta piemontese

Piedmontese Cake

01:00 01:00

American	Ingredients	Metric/Imperial
1¾ cups	Almonds	225 g / 8 oz
1 cup	Confectioner's (icing) sugar	100 g / 4 oz
6	Eggs	6
1 scant cup	Fine granulated (castor) sugar	200 g / 7 oz
⅔ cup	Cornmeal	75 g / 3 oz
⅓ cup	All purpose (plain) flour	40 g / 1½ oz
	Salt	
½ cup	Sultanas	65 g / 2½ oz
¼ cup	Butter	50 g / 2 oz
1 tbsp	Brandy	1 tbsp

1. Blanch and toast the almonds. Pound half with all the confectioner's (icing) sugar less 2 tablespoons [15 g / ½ oz] and grind the other half and put on one side. (This step can be done quickly in a blender or food processor.)
2. Preheat the oven to 400°F / 200°C / Gas Mark 6.
3. Break the eggs into a bowl, add the fine sugar, put on top of a pan of warm water on a low heat and beat until the mixture has warmed up.
4. Remove from the heat and continue beating until the mixture is light and creamy.
5. Sift the cornmeal, plain flour, potato flour and a pinch of salt into a bowl, sift again into the egg mixture folding in carefully. Add the ground almonds and soaked sultanas. Finally add the melted butter and the brandy.
6. Turn into a buttered baking pan and bake in a hot oven for about 1 hour. When the cake is ready, dust with remaining confectioner's sugar and sprinkle with ground almonds.

Chiacchiere

Golden Slices

01:00 00:10

American	Ingredients	Metric/Imperial
2 cups	All purpose (plain) flour	225 g / 8 oz
¼ cup	Fine granulated (castor) sugar	50 g / 2 oz
½ tsp	Vanilla essence	½ tsp
2 tbsp	Butter	25 g / 1 oz
2	Eggs	2
1 tbsp	Marsala	1 tbsp
	Oil for frying	
3 tbsp	Confectioner's (icing) sugar	2 tbsp

1. Mix the sifted flour, sugar and vanilla in a bowl, make a well in the centre. Soften the butter and place with the eggs in the middle of the flour. Mix to a smooth dough adding a little marsala if it is too dry.
2. Roll out the dough on a floured board to a thin sheet and cut out rectangles. A serrated pastry wheel is useful for this. Make 3 cuts in the middle of each rectangle, but do not take them to the edges.
3. Half fill a thick pan with oil and heat. Put in the rectangles and cook until they are golden brown.
4. Spread on absorbent kitchen towels to absorb the excess fat, sprinkle with confectioner's (icing) sugar before serving.

Torta diplomatica 

Diplomat's Cake

02:00 01:00

American	Ingredients	Metric/Imperial
⅓ cup	Butter	75 g / 3 oz
2 cups	Confectioner's (icing) sugar	225 g / 8 oz
	A few drops of vanilla essence	
1	Egg yolk	1
1 tbsp	Rum	1 tbsp
½ lb	Puff pastry (see page 453)	225 g / 8 oz
1	Sponge cake (see page 454)	1
½ cup	Maraschino	125 ml / 4 fl oz
1 lb	Apricot jam	450 g / 1 lb
½ cup	Chopped toasted hazelnuts	50 g / 2 oz

1. Preheat the oven to 425°F / 220°C / Gas Mark 7.
2. Cream together the softened butter, 1½ cups [175 g / 6 oz] sugar and the vanilla essence. Add the egg yolk and the rum, cream until smooth and light.
3. Cut the puff pastry into 2 equal pieces, roll out, prick with a fork and bake on 2 lightly buttered sheets. Allow to cool on a wire tray.
4. With a sharp knife, cut the sponge cake into 4 rounds. Lay a round of sponge cake on the first piece of puff pastry and trim to obtain a match. Repeat with the other piece of puff pastry.
5. Place a round of sponge cake on the serving dish and soak in maraschino. Cover with a third of the butter cream. Cover with a round of sponge cake soaked in maraschino. Spread on a layer of sieved apricot jam. Follow with a layer of puff pastry, more apricot jam, sponge cake, ending with the puff pastry.
6. Press down lightly with a spatula. Spread the remaining cream and crushed hazelnuts on the sides. Dust with confectioner's sugar and keep in a cool place.

Tortei veneti

Venetian Potato Cake

00:30 01:05

American	Ingredients	Metric/Imperial
1 lb	Potatoes	500 g / 1 lb
	Salt	
¼ cup	Butter	50 g / 2 oz
½ cup	Sugar	100 g / 4 oz
1¼ cups	All purpose (plain) flour	150 g / 5 oz
1	Egg	1
	Oil for frying	

1. Cook the unpeeled potatoes with a little salt. Drain, skin and mash, leave to cool.
2. Melt the butter and add to the purée. Stir in the sugar, sifted flour and egg, working all the ingredients well together.
3. Preheat the oven to 350°F / 180°C / Gas Mark 4.
4. Heat the oil until hot. Form the mixture into cakes and fry until golden on each side. When they are golden on one side, carefully turn them over with a palette knife without breaking them. Drain on kitchen towels. Place them 4 at a time on an oiled baking sheet, bake for 15 minutes and serve hot.

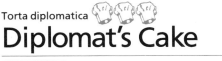

Maritozzi 

Raisin Buns

01:15 | 00:15

American	Ingredients	Metric/Imperial
½ oz	*Dry active yeast*	15 g / ½ oz
1¾ cups	*Flour*	200 g / 7 oz
3 tbsp	*Sugar*	2 tbsp
⅓ cup	*Sultanas*	50 g / 2 oz
1 tbsp	*Pine kernels*	1 tbsp
	Salt	
2 oz	*Candied orange peel*	50 g / 2 oz
	Butter for baking sheet	

1. Combine the reconstituted yeast with a little flour and allow to stand until it has doubled in volume.
2. Knead in the remaining slightly warmed flour, the sugar, sultanas, pine kernels, salt and finely sliced candied orange peel. Add enough hand-hot water (100°F / 43°C) to form a soft dough.
3. Preheat the oven to 425°F / 210°C / Gas Mark 7.
4. Form small balls the size of an egg, place on a buttered and floured baking sheet, cover and leave in a dry place to rise.
5. Then flatten with the palm of the hand and bake in the oven. Serve at once when cooked.

Pampepato

Fruit and Honey Cake

00:25 | 00:45

American	Ingredients	Metric/Imperial
¼ lb	*Honey*	100 g / 4 oz
Generous ⅓ cup	*Sugar*	75 g / 3 oz
½ tsp	*Bicarbonate of soda*	½ tsp
1 tsp	*Aniseed*	1 tsp
1¼ cups	*Flour*	150 g / 5 oz
½ cup	*Raisins soaked in water*	75 g / 3 oz
½ cup	*Blanched almonds*	50 g / 2 oz
¼ cup	*Shelled walnuts*	25 g / 1 oz
¼ cup	*Pine kernels*	25 g / 1 oz
1 oz	*Candied citron*	25 g / 1 oz
2 oz	*Flaked chocolate*	50 g / 2 oz
½ tsp	*Cinnamon*	½ tsp
	Salt and pepper	
¼ tsp	*Nutmeg*	¼ tsp
	Butter and flour for the baking pan	

1. Preheat the oven to 350°F / 180°C / Gas Mark 4.
2. Dissolve most of the honey, sugar, bicarbonate and aniseed in a bowl, adding water 2-3 tablespoons at a time and stirring constantly.
3. Slowly sift in the flour. Work the mixture with a wooden spoon.
4. Dry the raisins and add to the mixture with the almonds, walnuts, pine kernels, citron, chocolate, cinnamon, pinch of salt, pepper and nutmeg. Blend well and turn into a buttered and floured loaf pan or 6 in / 15 cm round cake pan. Level the top and brush all over with remaining melted honey. Bake in the oven for 45 minutes until the cake is a dark, golden color. Allow to cool before serving.

Tarte mousseline

Gâteau Mousseline

00:45 | 00:30

American	Ingredients	Metric/Imperial
3	*Eggs, separated*	3
½ cup	*Sugar*	100 g / 4 oz
½ cup	*Flour*	50 g / 2 oz
1 tsp	*Baking powder*	1 tsp
1 tbsp	*Butter*	15 g / ½ oz
1 cup	*Whipped cream*	200 ml / 7 fl oz
	Confectioner's (icing) sugar	

1. Preheat the oven to 350°F / 180°C / Gas Mark 4.
2. Whisk the egg yolks and sugar in a bowl over hot water for a few minutes, then remove from the heat and beat until light and fluffy.
3. In a clean bowl with a dry whisk, mix the egg whites until the mixture stands in soft peaks.
4. Sift the flour with the baking powder and fold into the egg yolk mixture alternately with the egg whites. Fold carefully to mix ingredients without losing air.
5. Grease an 8 in / 20 cm cake pan with butter and flour lightly, tip in the cake mixture and bake for 30 minutes.
6. Allow to cool for 4 minutes in the pan, turn out onto a new tray and cool.
7. Cut the cake in half to make 2 rounds, sandwich together with the whipped cream and serve sprinkled with a thick layer of confectioner's sugar.

Torta Moka

Gâteau Moka

00:35 | 00:30 for the cake

American	Ingredients	Metric/Imperial
3	*Egg yolks*	3
½ cup	*Sugar*	100 g / 4 oz
1 cup	*Milk*	225 ml / 8 fl oz
1	*Piece of vanilla pod*	1
¼ cup	*Strong coffee*	50 ml / 2 fl oz
⅓ cup	*Butter*	75 g / 3 oz
1	*Sponge cake (see page 454)*	1
¾ cup	*Chopped sweet blanched almonds*	75 g / 3 oz
2 oz	*Flaked chocolate*	50 g / 2 oz

1. Thoroughly whisk the yolks and sugar until white and fluffy.
2. Boil the milk with the vanilla and slowly pour in the mixture, stirring all the time, add the coffee. Turn into a double saucepan and cook on a low heat, stirring until the cream is thick without boiling. Remove from the heat and keep stirring for a few more minutes. Soften and cream the butter and gradually add to the coffee cream. Allow to cool.
3. With a sharp knife cut the sponge cake horizontally in half, giving 2 rounds. Place one on a serving dish, spread part of the cream on top and sprinkle with almonds. Cover with the second round. With a spatula spread the rest of the cream on the top and sides. Sprinkle the cake with the flaked chocolate.

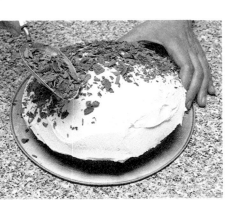

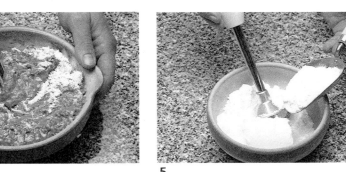

1 2 3

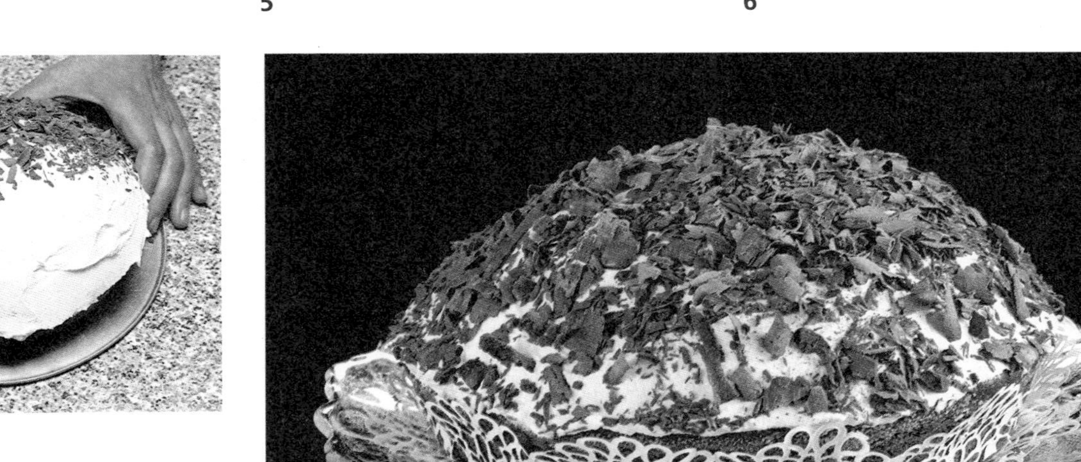

4 5 6

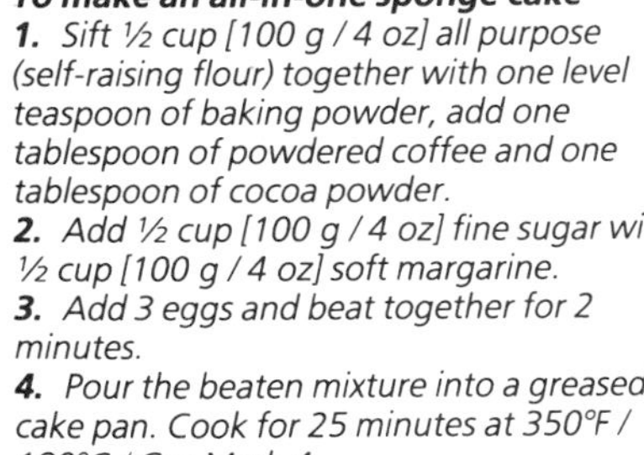

7

To make an all-in-one sponge cake

1. *Sift ½ cup [100 g / 4 oz] all purpose (self-raising flour) together with one level teaspoon of baking powder, add one tablespoon of powdered coffee and one tablespoon of cocoa powder.*

2. *Add ½ cup [100 g / 4 oz] fine sugar with ½ cup [100 g / 4 oz] soft margarine.*

3. *Add 3 eggs and beat together for 2 minutes.*

4. *Pour the beaten mixture into a greased cake pan. Cook for 25 minutes at 350°F / 180°C / Gas Mark 4.*

5. *To make the coffee cream, use the quantities given in Gâteau Moka opposite. Whisk the egg yolks and sugar until white and fluffy. Boil the milk and vanilla and add the beaten yolks and sugar, cook on a low heat stirring until thick, add the coffee. Allow to cool slightly. Soften and cream the butter and add to the coffee cream.*

6. *Whip 1 cup [125 ml / 4 fl oz] thick cream and grate some chocolate for decoration. Sandwich the cake together with the cooled moka cream.*

7. *Pile whipped cream on top and decorate with grated chocolate.*

Pasta di mandorle

Almond Paste

00:00 | 00:00

American	Ingredients	Metric/Imperial
2⅔ cups	*Confectioner's (icing) sugar*	350 g / 12 oz
2¼ cups	*Ground almonds*	350 g / 12 oz
2	*Eggs*	2
1 tsp	*Lemon juice*	1 tsp
3 tbsp	*Cornstarch (cornflour)*	2 tbsp

1. Sift the confectioner's sugar into a bowl, add the ground almonds. Make a well in the centre and add the lightly beaten eggs and a few drops of lemon juice.
2. Form into a stiff dough and lightly knead in a little extra confectioner's (icing) sugar mixed with cornstarch (cornflour).
3. Use for decorating rich fruit cakes or making sweets.

Cook's tip: for extra flavor work in vanilla, rum, brandy, coffee or chocolate with the lemon juice in step 1. Varying the amount according to taste.

Giochini di pasta di mandorle

Marzipan Shapes

00:15 | 00:10

American	Ingredients	Metric/Imperial
2 cups	*Ground almonds*	225 g / 8 oz
2 cups	*Confectioner's (icing) sugar*	225 g / 8 oz
3	*Egg whites*	3
1 tsp	*Port*	1 tsp

1. Preheat the oven to 400°F / 200°C / Gas Mark 6.
2. Tip the almonds into a bowl. Add the sugar and mix thoroughly. Add a drop of port and work the unbeaten egg whites in the mixture a spoonful at a time, stirring well to form a firm paste.
3. Moisten the worktop surface and then spread the paste about ½ in / 1.25 cm thick. Shape as you like, making little animals, cars or stars etc. Cook the shapes in a hot oven on a buttered baking sheet for about 10 minutes.

Pan di Spagna alle lamponi

Sponge Cake with Raspberries

00:30 | 00:30

American	Ingredients	Metric/Imperial
¾ lb	*Raspberries*	350 g / 12 oz
½ cup	*Confectioner's (icing) sugar*	50 g / 2 oz
½ cup	*Spumante, or dry white wine (or lemon juice)*	125 ml / 4 fl oz
1	*Sponge cake (see page 454)*	1
1 cup	*Zabaglione (see page 438)*	225 ml / 8 fl oz
	Whipped cream	

1. Sprinkle the raspberries with sugar, pour over the wine or some lemon juice, mix well and leave to soak for about 1 hour.
2. With a sharp knife cut the sponge cake into three rounds. Place the first round on a serving plate and cover with half the raspberries and all of the juice. Pour over half of the zabaglione. Cover with the second round of sponge cake and repeat the operation. Cover with the last round. Decorate with rosettes of whipped cream and a few whole raspberries.

Salame finto di cioccolata

Chocolate Sausage

00:35 Chilling time 04:00 | 00:00

American	Ingredients	Metric/Imperial
½ lb	*Sweet crackers (digestive biscuits)*	225 g / 8 oz
1 tsp	*Instant coffee*	1 tsp
⅔ cup	*Butter*	150 g / 5 oz
1 tbsp	*Liqueur*	1 tbsp
⅓ cup	*Sugar*	65 g / 2½ oz
¼ lb	*Sweet cocoa*	100 g / 4 oz
2	*Eggs, separated*	2
10	*Walnuts*	10

1. Crumble the crackers (biscuits), pounding them in a blender or food processor or crumb in a plastic bag with a rolling pin.
2. Mix the crumbs with the instant coffee, dissolved in a little boiling water, the butter, liqueur, sugar and sweet cocoa. Add the egg yolks, the stiffly beaten egg whites, mix well and add more cocoa to make a firm mixture.
3. Shape into a sausage, wrap in foil and chill for 1 hour.
4. Chop the walnuts, cover a piece of paper with the nuts, unwrap the sausage and roll over the nuts so that they penetrate the sausage. Return to foil and chill for a further 3 hours.
5. Place on a serving plate and slice at the table.

Sponge cake with raspberries

ITALIAN INDEX

Q

R

S

ENGLISH INDEX

C

D

E

F

G

H

I

J

L

M

N

O

P

S

YOUR RECIPE NOTES

Picture Acknowledgements

The publishers would like to thank the following organizations and individuals for their kind permission to reproduce the pictures in this book:

Archivio IGDA 13, 14, 15, 21, 25, 28-9, 34, 37, 38, 40, 41, 48, 49, 50, 51, 54, 58, 59, 86, 95, 102, 108, 111, 117, 122, 124, 125, 128, 129, 136, 138, 139, 141, 145, 154, 155, 156, 157, 158, 159, 163, 177, 180, 184, 185, 188, 195, 203, 207, 208, 209, 212, 214, 217, 219, 220, 222, 232, 233, 246, 247, 250, 255, 262, 264, 268, 271, 275, 280, 283, 286, 287, 288, 294, 313, 316, 318, 319, 328, 334, 362, 371, 388, 390, 392, 393, 398, 409, 412-3, 418, 419, 421, 432, 434, 440, 443, 445, 449, 450, 451, 452, 461

Badia a Coltibuono 30

Anthony Blake Photo Library 24, 27, 31, 33

Michael Boys 23, 26

BPCC/Aldus Archive 153

Gary Chowitz/EWA 1

Consorzio del Formaggio Parmigiano Reggiano 17

Jan Traylen/Patrick Eagar 20

Editoriale Del Drago Milano 47, 61, 62, 65, 67, 68, 70, 73, 75, 77, 81, 83, 84, 85, 89, 90, 91, 93, 98, 100, 101, 103, 104, 105, 107, 113, 115, 118, 120, 121, 127, 130, 131, 133, 135, 140, 143, 145, 148, 149, 150, 161, 166, 169, 173, 175, 183, 187, 190, 191, 196, 198, 207, 211, 216, 221, 223, 227, 229, 234, 236, 239, 240, 243, 244, 249, 253, 254, 257, 258, 261, 267, 269, 277, 278, 282, 285, 293, 299, 303, 304, 306, 307, 309, 311, 321, 322, 324, 327, 332, 333, 335, 337, 341, 342, 346, 349, 350, 351, 355, 358, 361, 365, 373, 377, 378, 380, 381, 383, 384, 385, 386, 387, 389, 397, 400, 401, 403, 405, 407, 410, 415, 416, 417, 423, 425, 427, 428, 430, 437, 439, 441, 444, 447, 455, 457, 458, 462, 463

Galbani (London) Ltd. 36, 45

Italian Trade Centre, London 9

Maison de Marie-Claire/Bouchet/Le Foll 2-3

Maison de Marie-Claire/Dirand 10

Maison de Marie-Claire/Schoumacher/Duffas 6-7

Masi Agricola S.p.A. 22

Conny van Kasteel 29 right, 42